The Council of State Governments

STATE DIRECTORY

Directory III—
Administrative Officials

The Council of State Governments
2760 Research Park Drive
Lexington, KY 40511

Contact the Publication Sales Department at
1-800-800-1910 or sales@csg.org to order:

Directory I—Elective Officials 2007,

Directory II—Legislative Leadership, Committees and Staff 2007,

Directory III—Administrative Officials 2007

or mailing lists of state government officials.

The Council of State Governments is the nation's only organization serving every elected and appointed official in all three branches of each state and territorial government through its national office, as well as regional offices based in the East, Midwest, South and West. CSG champions excellence in state government by advocating multi-state shared problem solving and states' rights by tracking national conditions, trends, and innovations, and through nonpartisan groundbreaking leadership training and support.

The Council of State Governments

Daniel M. Sprague, Executive Director

2760 Research Park Drive ▪ P.O. Box 11910 ▪ Lexington, KY 40578-1910 ▪ (859) 244-8000 ▪ Fax: (859) 244-8001 ▪ www.csg.org

Eastern Office
Alan V. Sokolow, Director
100 Wall Street, 20th Floor
New York, NY 10005
(212) 482-2320
Fax: (212) 482-2344
www.csgeast.org

Midwestern Office
Michael H. McCabe, Director
701 East 22nd Street, Suite 110
Lombard, IL 60148
(630) 925-1922
Fax: (630) 925-1930
www.csgmidwest.org

Southern Office
Colleen Cousineau, Director
P.O. Box 98129
Atlanta, GA 30359
(404) 633-1866
Fax: (404) 633-4896
www.slcatlanta.org

Western Office
Kent Briggs, Director
1107 9th Street, Suite 650
Sacramento, CA 95814
(916) 553-4423
Fax: (916) 446-5760
www.csgwest.org

Washington Office
Jim Brown, General Counsel and Director
444 N. Capitol Street, NW, Suite 401
Washington, DC 20001
(202) 624-5460
Fax: (202) 624-5452
www.csg.org

Editorial Staff

Kelley Arnold ▪ Jessica Clay ▪ Eric Lancaster ▪ Heather Perkins ▪ Andy Teague

Special thanks to the CSG Regional Offices
and the Clerks and Secretaries of the legislature for each state.

Printed in the United States of America
ISBN #978-0-87292-836-7
Price: $65.00

Table of Contents

How to Use This Directory

This annual directory provides basic information about elected and appointed officials with primary responsibility in more than 110 state government functions. The directory includes names, addresses, telephone, fax and e-mail addresses. The information is organized alphabetically by function (e.g., Labor) and by state and U.S. jurisdiction name. Generally, there is one entry per function for each state or U.S. jurisdiction. State names and jurisdictions are not listed if there is not a corresponding entry for a given section.

CSG collected the information for the 2007 directory between February and April 2007. The data contained in this volume was compiled through one of three methods. First, national associations were given the opportunity to provide a roster for the directory. For those categories that did not have rosters provided, the information was gathered through two other methods. Each state and territory was sent a survey requesting updated information for their administrative officials. If states did not respond to the surveys, CSG staff collected the updated information from state-sponsored Web sites or phone calls to state offices.

Party Abbreviations

D	Democrat
R	Republican
REFORM	Reform
C	Covenant
I	Independent
L	Libertarian
S	Statehood
ICM	Independent Citizen Movement
DFL	Democratic-Farmer-Labor
NP	Nonpartisan
P	Progressive
NPP	New Progressive Party
PDP	Popular Democratic Party
PIP	Puerto Rican Independent Party
RA	Rural Alaskan
TRIBAL	Delegate representing a Native American tribe
U	Unenrolled

Adjutant General

The executive or administrative head of the state's military service.

ALABAMA
Maj. Gen. Mark Bowen
Adjutant General
State Military Department
P.O. Box 3711
Montgomery, AL 36109
P: (334) 271-7200
F: (334) 271-7366

ALASKA
Maj. Gen. Craig Campbell
Adjutant General
Department of Military & Veterans Affairs
P.O. Box 5800
Fort Richardson, AK 99505
P: (907) 428-6003
F: (907) 428-6019
E: craig.campbell2@us.army.mil

AMERICAN SAMOA
Hon. Afa Ripley Jr.
Attorney General
Office of the Attorney General
American Samoa Government
Executive Office Building, Utulei
Pago Pago, AS 96799
P: (684) 633-4163
F: (684) 633-1838

ARIZONA
Maj. Gen. David P. Rataczak
Adjutant General
National Guard
5636 East McDowell Road
Phoenix, AZ 85008
P: (602) 267-2700

ARKANSAS
Maj. Gen. William D. Wofford
Adjutant General
Military Department
Camp Robinson
North Little Rock, AR 72199
P: (510) 212-5001
F: (510) 212-5009
E: william.d.wofford@ar.ngb.army.mil

CALIFORNIA
Maj. Gen. William H. Wade II
Adjutant General
State Military Forces
9800 Goethe Road
Sacramento, CA 95827
P: (916) 854-3500
F: (916) 854-3671

COLORADO
Brig. Gen. H. Michael Edwards
Adjutant General
Department of Military Affairs
6848 South Revere Parkway
Englewood, CO 80112
P: (720) 250-1500

CONNECTICUT
Brig. Gen. Thaddeus Martin
Adjutant General
National Guard Armory
360 Broad Street
Hartford, CT 06105
P: (860) 524-4953
F: (860) 524-4898

DELAWARE
Maj. Gen. Francis D. Vavala
Adjutant General
National Guard
First Regiment Road
Wilmington, DE 19808
P: (302) 326-7001
F: (302) 326-7196
E: frank.vavala@de.ngb.army.mil

DISTRICT OF COLUMBIA
Brig. Gen. Errol R. Schwartz
Adjutant General
National Guard
National Guard Armory
2001 East Capitol Street, SE
Washington, DC 20003
P: (202) 685-9790

FLORIDA
Maj. Gen. Douglas Burnett
Adjutant General
National Guard
St. Francis Barracks
82 Marine Street
St. Augustine, FL 32085
P: (904) 823-0010
E: douglas.burnett@fl.ngb.army.mil

GEORGIA
Maj. Gen. David Poythress
Adjutant General
Department of Defense
P.O. Box 17965
Atlanta, GA 30316
P: (678) 569-6061
E: doc@ga.ngb.army.mil

GUAM
Brig. Gen. Donald Goldhorn
Adjutant General
Office of the Adjutant General
430 Route 16, Building 300, Room 113
Barrigada, GU 96913
P: (671) 735-0406
F: (671) 735-0836

HAWAII
Maj. Gen. Robert G.F. Lee
Adjutant General
Department of Defense
3949 Diamond Head Road
Honolulu, HI 96816
P: (808) 733-4258
F: (808) 733-4236

IDAHO
Maj. Gen. Lawrence LaFrenz
Adjutant General
Military Division
4040 West Guard Building 600
Boise, ID 83705
P: (208) 422-5242
F: (208) 422-6179

ILLINOIS
Brig. Gen. Randal E. Thomas
Adjutant General
National Guard
1301 North MacArthur Boulevard
Springfield, IL 62702
P: (217) 761-3500
F: (217) 761-3736
E: randal.e.thomas@il.ngb.army.mil

INDIANA
Maj. Gen. R. Martin Umbarger
Adjutant General
Adjutant General's Office
2002 South Holt Road
Indianapolis, IN 46241
P: (317) 247-3558
F: (317) 247-3540

IOWA
Maj. Gen. Ron Dardis
Adjutant General
Office of the Adjutant General
Joint Forces HQ
7105 Northwest 70th Avenue
Johnston, IA 50131
P: (515) 252-4211

KANSAS
Maj. Gen. Tod M. Bunting
Adjutant General
Adjutant General's Department
2800 Southwest Topeka Boulevard
Topeka, KS 66611
P: (913) 274-1001
F: (913) 274-1682

KENTUCKY
Maj. Gen. Donald C. Storm
Adjutant General
Department of Military Affairs
Boone National Guard Center
100 Minuteman Parkway
Frankfort, KY 40601
P: (502) 607-1558
F: (502) 607-1240

LOUISIANA
Maj. Gen. Bennett C. Landreneau Jr.
Adjutant General
National Guard
Headquarters Building
Jackson Barracks
New Orleans, LA 70146
P: (504) 278-8211
F: (504) 278-6554

MAINE
Maj. Gen. John W. Libby
Adjutant General
Military Bureau
Camp Keyes
Augusta, ME 04333
P: (207) 626-4205
F: (207) 476-4341

MARYLAND
Maj. Gen. Bruce F. Tuxill
Adjutant General
Military Department
5th Regiment Armory
219 29th Division Street
Baltimore, MD 21201
P: (410) 576-6097
F: (410) 576-6079
E: bruce.tuxill@md.ngb.army.mil

Adjutant General

MASSACHUSETTS
Brig. Gen. Oliver J. Mason Jr.
Adjutant General
Headquarters, Massachusetts National Guard
50 Maple Street
Milford, MA 01757
P: (508) 233-6552
F: (508) 233-6554

MICHIGAN
Maj. Gen. Thomas G. Cutler
Adjutant General
Department of Military & Veterans Affairs
3411 North Martin Luther King
Lansing, MI 48906
P: (517) 481-8083
F: (517) 481-8125
E: cutlert@michigan.gov

MINNESOTA
Maj. Gen. Larry W. Shellito
Adjutant General
Department of Military Affairs
Veterans Services Building
20 West 12th Street, #115
St. Paul, MN 55155
P: (651) 268-8924
F: (651) 282-4541

MISSISSIPPI
Maj. Gen. Harold A. Cross
Adjutant General
National Guard
P.O. Box 5027
Jackson, MS 39296
P: (601) 313-6232
F: (601) 313-6251

MISSOURI
Maj. Gen. King E. Sidwell
Adjutant General
National Guard
2302 Militia Drive
Jefferson City, MO 65101
P: (573) 638-9710
F: (573) 638-9722
E: king.sidwell@us.army.mil

MONTANA
Maj. Gen. Randall Mosley
Adjutant General
Department of Military Affairs
P.O. Box 4789
Fort Harrison, MT 59636
P: (406) 841-3000
F: (406) 841-3011
E: randall.mosley@mt.ngb.army.mil

NEBRASKA
Maj. Gen. Roger Lempke
Adjutant General
National Guard
1300 Military Road
Lincoln, NE 68508
P: (402) 309-7100
F: (402) 309-7147
E: roger.lempke@ne.ngb.army.mil

NEVADA
Brig. Gen. Cynthia Kirkland
Adjutant General
Military Department
2460 Fairview Drive
Carson City, NV 89701
P: (775) 887-7302
F: (775) 887-7315

NEW HAMPSHIRE
Brig. Gen. Kenneth R. Clark
Adjutant General
National Guard
4 Pembroke Road
Concord, NH 03301
P: (603) 225-1200
F: (603) 225-1257
E: k.clark@us.army.mil

NEW JERSEY
Maj. Gen. Glenn K. Rieth
Adjutant General
Department of Military and Veterans Affairs
P.O. Box 340
Trenton, NJ 08625
P: (609) 530-6957
F: (609) 530-7191
E: glenn.rieth@njdmava.state.nj.us

NEW MEXICO
Brig. Gen. Kenny C. Montoya
Adjutant General
Military Affairs Department
47 Bataan Boulevard
East Frontage Road
Santa Fe, NM 87508
P: (505) 474-1200

NEW YORK
Maj. Gen. Joseph J. Taluto
Adjutant General
Division of Military & Naval Affairs
330 Old Niskayuna Road
Latham, NY 12110
P: (518) 786-4500

NORTH CAROLINA
Maj. Gen. William Ingram Jr.
Adjutant General
National Guard
4105 Reedy Creek Road
Raleigh, NC 27607
P: (919) 664-6101
F: (919) 664-6400
E: william.ingram@nc.ngb.army.mil

NORTH DAKOTA
Maj. Gen. David A. Sprynczynatyk
Adjutant General
National Guard
Fraine Barracks
P.O. Box 5511
Bismarck, ND 58506
P: (701) 333-2001
F: (701) 333-2017
E: david.sprynczynatyk@us.army.mil

OHIO
Maj. Gen. Gregory L. Wayt
Adjutant General
National Guard
2825 West Dublin Granville Road
Columbus, OH 43235
P: (614) 336-7070
F: (614) 336-7074

OKLAHOMA
Maj. Gen. Harry M. Wyatt III
Adjutant General and Secretary of the Military
Military Department
3501 Military Circle, Northeast
Oklahoma City, OK 73111
P: (405) 228-5201
F: (405) 228-5524

OREGON
Brig. Gen. Raymond C. Rees
Adjutant General
Military Department
P.O. Box 14350
Salem, OR 97309
P: (503) 584-3991
F: (503) 945-3987

PENNSYLVANIA
Maj. Gen. Jessica L. Wright
Adjutant General
Department of Military Affairs
Building P-0 47 200
Fort Indiantown Gap
Annville, PA 17003
P: (717) 861-8500

PUERTO RICO
Col. David Carrion Baralt
Adjutant General
National Guard
P.O. Box 9023786
San Juan, PR 00901
P: (787) 721-3131
F: (787) 723-6360

RHODE ISLAND
Maj. Gen. Robert T. Bray
Adjutant General
National Guard Headquarters
Command Readiness Center
645 New London Avenue
Cranston, RI 02920
P: (401) 275-4102
F: (401) 275-4338

SOUTH CAROLINA
Maj. Gen. Stan Spears
Adjutant General
Military Department
One National Guard Road
Columbia, SC 29201
P: (803) 806-4217
E: stanhope.spears@sc.ngb.army.mil

SOUTH DAKOTA
Maj. Gen. Mike Gorman
Adjutant General
National Guard
2823 West Main Street
Rapid City, SD 57702
P: (605) 737-6702
F: (605) 737-6677
E: mike.gorman@sd.ngb.army.mil

TENNESSEE
Maj. Gen. Gus L. Hargett Jr.
Adjutant General
Military Department
Houston Barracks
P.O. Box 41502
Nashville, TN 37204
P: (615) 313-3001
F: (615) 313-3100
E: gus.hargett@tn.ngb.army.mil

TEXAS
Maj. Gen. Charles G. Rodriguez
Adjutant General
Adjutant General's Department
2200 West 35th Street
P.O. Box 5218
Austin, TX 78703
P: (512) 782-5006
F: (512) 465-5578

U.S. VIRGIN ISLANDS
Mr. Renaldo Rivera
Adjutant General
National Guard
4031 LaGrande Princess, Lot 1B
Christiansted, VI 00820
P: (340) 712-7710
F: (340) 712-7711
E: renaldo.rivera
@vi.ngb.army.mil

UTAH
Maj. Gen. Brian L. Tarbet
Adjutant General
Army National Guard
12953 South Minuteman Drive
Draper, UT 84020
P: (801) 523-4401
F: (801) 523-4677
E: btarbet@utah.gov

VERMONT
Maj. Gen. Michael D. Dubie
Adjutant General
National Guard
789 Vermont National Guard
Colchester, VT 05446
P: (802) 338-3124
F: (802) 338-3425
E: michael.dubie
@vt.ngb.army.mil

VIRGINIA
Maj. Gen. Robert Newman Jr.
Adjutant General
Virginia National Guard
202 North 9th Street, Fourth Floor
9th Street Office Building
Richmond, VA 23219
P: (804) 786-4406
F: (804) 371-0073
E: robert.newman
@us.army.mil

WASHINGTON
Maj. Gen. Timothy J. Lowenberg
Adjutant General
National Guard
Camp Murray, Building 1
Tacoma, WA 98430
P: (253) 512-8201
F: (253) 512-8497

WEST VIRGINIA
Maj. Gen. Allen E. Tackett
Adjutant General
Army National Guard
1703 Coonskin Drive
Charleston, WV 25311
P: (304) 561-6316
F: (304) 561-6327
E: allen.tackett
@wv.ngb.army.mil

WISCONSIN
Maj. Gen. Al Wilkening
Adjutant General
Department of Military Affairs
P.O. Box 8111
Madison, WI 53708
P: (608) 242-3001
F: (608) 242-3111
E: al.wilkening
@wi.ngb.army.mil

WYOMING
Maj. Gen. Edward L. Wright
Adjutant General
Military Department
5500 Bishop Boulevard
Cheyenne, WY 82009
P: (307) 772-5234
F: (307) 772-5010
E: ed.boenisch
@wy.ngb.army.mil

Administration

Umbrella agency of administration that coordinates administrative services provided to state agencies.

Information provided by:

National Association of State Chief Administrators
Marcia Stone
Association Director
2760 Research Park Drive
P.O. Box 11910
Lexington, KY 40578
P: (859) 244-8181
F: (859) 244-8001
mstone@csg.org
www.nasca.org

ALABAMA
Mr. Jim Main
Director
Department of Finance
600 Dexter Avenue, Suite N-105
Montgomery, AL 36130
P: (334) 242-7160
F: (334) 353-3300
E: jim.main@finance.alabama.gov

ALASKA
Mr. Scott Nordstand
Commissioner
Department of Administration
P.O. Box 110208
Juneau, AK 99811
P: (907) 465-2200
E: scott_nordstand@admin.state.ak.us

ARIZONA
Mr. William Bell
Director
Department of Administration
100 North 15th Avenue, Suite 401
Phoenix, AZ 85007
P: (602) 542-1500
E: bill.bell@azdoa.gov

ARKANSAS
Ms. Janis Harrison
Administrator
Department of Finance & Administration
Office of Administrative Services
P.O. Box 2485
Little Rock, AR 72203
P: (501) 324-9057
F: (501) 324-9070
E: janis.harrison@dfa.state.ar.us

CALIFORNIA
Mr. Ronald Joseph
Acting Director
Department of General Services
P.O. Box 989052
West Sacramento, CA 95798
P: (916) 376-8000
F: (916) 376-5018
E: ronald.joseph@dgs.ca.gov

COLORADO
Mr. Richard Gonzales
Executive Director
Department of Personnel & Administration
1600 Broadway, Suite 1030
Denver, CO 80202
P: (303) 866-6559
E: rich.gonzales@state.co.us

CONNECTICUT
Ms. Anne Gnazzo
Commissioner
Department of Administration
165 Capitol Avenue, Room 491
Hartford, CT 06106
P: (860) 713-5100
F: (860) 713-7481
E: anne.gnazzo@po.state.ct.us

DELAWARE
Ms. Jennifer W. Davis
Director
Office of Management & Budget
122 William Penn Street
Dover, DE 19901
P: (302) 739-4204
F: (302) 739-5661
E: jennifer.davis@state.de.us

FLORIDA
Mr. Tom Lewis Jr.
Secretary
Department of Management Services
4050 Esplanade Way, Suite 280
Tallahassee, FL 32399
P: (850) 488-2786
F: (850) 922-6149
E: tom.lewis@myflorida.com

GEORGIA
Mr. Brad Douglas
Commissioner
Department of Administrative Services
Procurement
200 Piedmont Avenue
Atlanta, GA 30334
P: (404) 656-3002
E: bdouglas@doas.ga.gov

HAWAII
Mr. Russ K. Saito
State Comptroller
Department of Accounting & General Services
1151 Punchbowl Street, Room 412
Honolulu, HI 96813
P: (808) 586-0400
F: (808) 586-0775

IDAHO
Mr. Keith Johnson
Director
Department of Administration
650 West State Street, Room 100
P.O. Box 83720
Boise, ID 83720
P: (208) 332-1824
F: (208) 334-2307
E: keith.johnson@adm.idaho.gov

ILLINOIS
Ms. Maureen O'Donnell
Acting Director
Department of Central Management Services
100 West Randolph Street, Suite 4-400
Chicago, IL 60601
P: (312) 814-2144

INDIANA
Ms. Carrie Henderson
Commissioner
Department of Administration
Room W478
402 West Washington Street
Indianapolis, IN 46204
P: (317) 232-3043
E: chenderson@idoa.in.gov

IOWA
Ms. Mollie K. Anderson
Director
Department of Administrative Services
Hoover Building, 3rd Floor
1305 East Walnut
Des Moines, IA 50319
P: (515) 281-5360
F: (515) 281-6140
E: mollie.anderson@iowa.gov

KANSAS
Mr. Duane Goossen
Secretary
Department of Administration
1000 Southwest Jackson Street
Suite 500
Topeka, KS 66612
P: (785) 296-2822
F: (785) 296-0231
E: duane.goossen@da.state.ks.us

KENTUCKY
Mr. Howard "Burr" Lawson
Executive Director
Department of Administration
200 Fair Oaks Lane
Frankfort, KY 40601
P: (502) 564-7430
F: (502) 564-4279
E: burr.lawson@ky.gov

LOUISIANA
Mr. Jerry Luke LeBlanc
Commissioner of Administration
Office of the Governor
Division of Administration
P.O. Box 94095
Baton Rouge, LA 70804
P: (225) 342-7000
F: (225) 342-1057
E: commissioner@doa.state.la.us

MAINE
Ms. Rebecca Wyke
Commissioner
Department of Administrative & Financial Services
76 State House Station
Augusta, ME 04333
P: (207) 624-7800
F: (207) 624-7804
E: rebeccawyke@maine.gov

MARYLAND
Mr. Alvin Collins
Secretary
Department of General Services
301 West Preston Street, Room 1401
Baltimore, MD 21201
P: (410) 767-4960
E: alvin.collins@dgs.state.md.us

MASSACHUSETTS
Ms. Leslie A. Kirwan
Secretary
Office for Administration & Finance
State House, Room 373
Boston, MA 02133
P: (617) 727-2040
F: (617) 727-2779
E: leslie.a.kirwan@state.ma.us

MICHIGAN
Ms. Lisa Webb Sharpe
Director
Department of Management & Budget
320 South Walnut
Lansing, MI 48909
P: 517-373-1004
E: webbsharpel@michigan.gov

MINNESOTA
Ms. Dana Badgerow
Commissioner
Department of Administration
200 Administration Building
50 Sherburne Avenue
St. Paul, MN 55155
P: (651) 201-2555
F: (651) 297-7909
E: dana.badgerow@state.mn.us

MISSISSIPPI
Mr. J.K. Stringer Jr.
Executive Director/State Fiscal Officer
Department of Finance & Administration
P.O. Box 267
Jackson, MS 39205
P: (601) 359-3402
F: (601) 359-2405
E: stringer@dfa.state.ms.us

MISSOURI
Mr. Michael N. Keathley
Commissioner
Office of Administration
State Capitol, Room 125
Jefferson City, MO 65102
P: (573) 751-1851

MONTANA
Ms. Janet Kelly
Director
Department of Administration
125 North Roberts Street
P.O. Box 200101
Helena, MT 59620
P: (406) 444-3033
F: (406) 444-6194
E: jakelly@mt.gov

NEBRASKA
Mr. Carlos Castillo
Director
Department of Administrative Services
State Capitol, Suite 1315
Lincoln, NE 68509
P: (402) 471-2331
E: carlos.castillo@email.state.ne.us

NEVADA
Mr. John Comeaux
Director
Department of Administration
209 East Musser Street, Room 200
Carson City, NV 89701
P: (775) 684-0222
F: (702) 687-0260
E: pcomeaux@budget.state.nv.us

NEW HAMPSHIRE
Mr. Donald S. Hill
Commissioner
Department of Administrative Services
25 Capitol Street, Room 120
Concord, NH 03301
P: (603) 271-3201
F: (603) 271-6600
E: don.hill@nh.gov

NEW JERSEY
Mr. Jenkins F. Edmund
Director
Division of Property Management & Construction
Department of Treasury
P.O. Box 034
Trenton, NJ 08625
P: (609) 292-4330
F: (609) 984-8495
E: edmund.jenkins@treas.state.nj.us

NEW MEXICO
Mr. Arturo Jaramillo
Secretary
Department of General Administration
P.O. Box 26110
Santa Fe, NM 87502
P: (505) 827-2000
F: (505) 827-2041
E: art.jaramillo@state.nm.us

NEW YORK
Mr. John Egan
Commissioner
Office of General Services
Corning Tower Building, 41st Floor
Empire State Plaza
Albany, NY 12242
P: (518) 474-5991
F: (518) 473-6814

NORTH CAROLINA
Mr. Britt Cobb
Secretary
Department of Administration
1301 Mail Service Center
Raleigh, NC 27699
P: (919) 807-2341
E: britt.cobb@ncmail.net

NORTH DAKOTA
Ms. Pam Sharp
Director
Office of Management & Budget
600 East Boulevard, 4th Floor
Bismarck, ND 58505
P: (701) 328-4904
F: (701) 328-3230
E: psharp@nd.gov

OHIO
Ms. Carol Drake
Director
Department of Administrative Services
30 East Broad Street, Suite 4040
Columbus, OH 43215
P: (614) 466-6511
F: (614) 644-8151
E: carol.drake@das.state.oh.us

Mr. Hugh Quill
Director
Department of Administrative Services
30 East Broad Street, Suite 4040
Columbus, OH 43215
P: (614) 466-6511
F: (614) 644-8151
E: hugh.quill@das.state.oh.us

OKLAHOMA
Mr. John Richard
Director
Department of Central Services
2401 North Lincoln Boulevard, Suite 206
P.O. Box 53218
Oklahoma City, OK 73152
P: (405) 521-4027
F: (405) 521-6403
E: john_richard@dcs.state.ok.us

OREGON
Ms. Laurie A. Warner
Director
Department of Administrative Services
155 Cottage Street, Northeast, U20
Salem, OR 97301
P: (503) 378-3106
F: (503) 373-7643

PENNSYLVANIA
Mr. James Creedon
Secretary
Department of General Services
515 North Office Building
Harrisburg, PA 17125
P: (717) 787-5996
F: (717) 772-2026
E: gs-secretary@state.pa.us

Mr. Joseph S. Martz
Secretary of Administration
Governor's Office of Administration
Office of Governor
207 Finance Building
Harrisburg, PA 17120
P: (717) 787-9945
F: (717) 783-4374
E: joemartz@state.pa.us

RHODE ISLAND
Ms. Beverly Najarian
Director
Department of Administration
1 Capitol Hill
Providence, RI 02908
P: (401) 222-2280
F: (401) 222-6436
E: bnajarian@admin.ri.gov

SOUTH CAROLINA
Mr. Henry J. White
Executive Director
Office of General Services
Budget & Control
P.O. Box 12444
Columbia, SC 29211
P: (803) 734-2320
F: (803) 734-2117

Administration

TENNESSEE
Ms. Gwendolyn Sims Davis
Commissioner
Department of General Services
24th Floor
312 8th Avenue North
Nashville, TN 37243
P: (615) 741-9263
F: (615) 532-8594
E: gwendolyn.s.davis
@state.tn.us

TEXAS
Mr. Edward Johnson
Executive Director
Building & Procurement
Commission
1711 San Jacinto
Austin, TX 78701
P: (512) 463-6363
E: edward.johnson
@tbpc.state.tx.us

UTAH
Ms. Kimberly Hood
Executive Director
Department of Administrative
Services
3120 State Office Building
Salt Lake City, UT 84114
P: (801) 538-3215
F: (801) 538-3844
E: khood@utah.gov

VERMONT
Ms. Tasha Wallis
Commissioner
Department of Buildings &
General Services
Two Governor Aiken Avenue
Montpelier, VT 05633
P: (802) 828-3519
F: (802) 828-3533
E: tasha.wallis@state.vt.us

VIRGINIA
Ms. Viola O. Baskerville
Secretary
Department of Administration
Patrick Henry Building, 3rd
Floor
1111 East Broad Street
Richmond, VA 23219
P: (804) 786-1201
F: (804) 371-0038
E: viola.baskerville
@governor.virginia.gov

Mr. Richard F. Sliwoski
Director
Department of General Services
202 North 9th Street, Room 209
Richmond, VA 23219
P: (804) 786-3263
F: (804) 371-7934
E: richard.sliwoski
@dgs.virginia.gov

WASHINGTON
Ms. Linda Bremer
Director
Department of General
Administration
P.O. Box 41000
Olympia, WA 98504
P: (360) 902-7300
F: (360) 586-5898
E: lbremer@ga.wa.gov

WEST VIRGINIA
Mr. Robert Ferguson
Secretary
Department of Administration
1900 Kanawha Boulevard, East
Charleston, WV 25305
P: (304) 558-4331
F: (304) 558-2999
E: rferguson@wvadmin.gov

WISCONSIN
Mr. Stephen Bablitch
Secretary
Department of Administration
101 East Wilson Street, 10th
Floor
Madison, WI 53703
P: (608) 266-1741
E: stephen.bablitch
@doa.state.wi.us

WYOMING
Mr. Earl Kabeiseman
Director
Department of Administration &
Information
Room 104, 2001 Capitol
Avenue
Cheyenne, WY 82002
P: (307) 777-7201
F: (307) 777-3633

Aging

Develops and strengthens services for the aged and conducts or promotes research into their problems.

ALABAMA
Ms. Irene Collins
Executive Director
Department of Senior Services
P.O. Box 301851
770 Washington Avenue, Suite 470
Montgomery, AL 36130
P: (334) 242-5743
F: (334) 242-5594
E: icollins@adss.state.al.us

ALASKA
Ms. Denise Daniello
Executive Director
Commission on Aging
Department of Health & Social Services
P.O. Box 110693
Juneau, AK 99811
P: (907) 465-4879
F: (907) 465-1398
E: denise_daniello@health.state.ak.us

AMERICAN SAMOA
Mr. Taesaliali'l F. Lutu
Director
Territorial Administration on Aging
American Samoa Government
Pago Pago, AS 96799
P: (684) 633-1251
F: (684) 633-2533

ARIZONA
Mr. Rex Critchfield
Acting Assistant Director
Division of Aging & Adult Services
Department of Economic Security
1789 West Jefferson, #950A
Phoenix, AZ 85007
P: (602) 542-4446
F: (602) 542-6575
E: rcritchfield@azdes.gov

ARKANSAS
Mr. Herb Sanderson
Director
Division of Aging & Adult Services
P.O. Box 1437, Slot S530
Little Rock, AR 72203
P: (501) 682-2441
F: (501) 682-8155
E: Herb.Sanderson@mail.state.ar.us

CALIFORNIA
Ms. Lynn Daucher
Director
Department of Aging
1300 National Drive, #200
Sacramento, CA 95834
P: (916) 419-7500
F: (916) 928-2268

COLORADO
Ms. Jeanette Hensley
Director
Division of Aging & Adult Services
1575 Sherman Street
Ground Floor
Denver, CO 80203
P: (303) 866-2636
F: (303) 866-2696
E: Jeanette.Hensley@state.co.us

CONNECTICUT
Ms. Pamela Giannini
Director
Bureau of Aging, Community, & Social Work Services
Department of Social Services
25 Sigourney Street
Hartford, CT 06106
P: (860) 424-5277
F: (860) 424-5301
E: pamela.giannini@po.state.ct.us

DELAWARE
Mr. Allan Zaback
Director
Division of Services for Aging & Adults with Physical Disabilities
Department of Health & Social Services
1901 North DuPont Highway
New Castle, DE 19720
P: (302) 255-9390
F: (302) 255-4445
E: azaback@state.de.us

DISTRICT OF COLUMBIA
Mr. Sam Gawad
Interim Director
Office on Aging
One Judiciary Square
441 4th Street, Northwest, 9th Floor
Washington, DC 20001
P: (202) 724-5622
F: (202) 724-4979

FLORIDA
Mr. Douglas Beach
Secretary
Department of Elder Affairs
4040 Esplanade Way, Suite 315
Talllahassee, FL 32399
P: (850) 414-2000
F: (850) 414-2004

GEORGIA
Ms. Maria Greene
Director
Division for Aging Services
2 Peachtree Street, Northwest
9th Floor
Atlanta, GA 30303
P: (404) 657-5258
F: (404) 657-5285
E: magreene@dhr.state.ga.us

GUAM
Mr. Arthur U. San Agustin
Director
Division of Senior Citizens
123 Chalan Kareta, Route 10
Mangilao, GU 96923
P: (671) 735-7102
F: (671) 734-5910
E: chiefdsc@dphss.govguam.net

HAWAII
Ms. Pat Sasaki
Director
Executive Office on Aging
No. 1 Capitol District
250 South Hotel Street, Suite 406
Honolulu, HI 96813
P: (808) 586-0100
F: (808) 586-0185
E: pasasaki@mail.health.state.hi.us

IDAHO
Ms. Lois Bauer
Administrator
Commission on Aging
3380 Americana Terrace, #120
P.O. Box 83720
Boise, ID 83720
P: (208) 334-3833
F: (208) 334-3033
E: lbauer@aging.idaho.gov

ILLINOIS
Mr. Charles Johnson
Director
Department on Aging
421 East Capitol Avenue
Springfield, IL 62701
P: (217) 785-2870
F: (217) 785-4477
E: Charles.Johnson@aging.state.il.us

INDIANA
Mr. Stephen Smith
Director
Division of Aging
402 West Washington Street
P.O. Box 7083
Indianapolis, IN 46207
P: (317) 232-7123
F: (317) 232-7867
E: stephen.smith@fssa.in.gov

IOWA
Mr. John McCalley
Director
Department of Elder Affairs
Jessie Parker Building
510 East 12th Street, Suite 2
Des Moines, IA 50319
P: (515) 725-3333
F: (515) 725-3300
E: john.mccalley@iowa.gov

KANSAS
Ms. Kathy Greenlee
Acting Secretary
Department on Aging
New England Building
503 South Kansas Avenue
Topeka, KS 66603
P: (785) 296-5222
F: (785) 296-0256
E: kathygreenlee@aging.state.ks.us

KENTUCKY
Ms. Deborah Anderson
Commissioner
Department for Aging & Independent Living
Cabinet for Health & Family Services
275 East Main Street, 3W-F
Frankfort, KY 40621
P: (502) 564-6930
F: (502) 564-4595

Aging

LOUISIANA
Mr. Godfrey White
Executive Director
Governor's Office of Elderly Affairs
P.O. Box 80374
412 North 4th Street
Baton Rouge, LA 70802
P: (225) 342-7100
F: (225) 342-7133
E: gpwhite@goea.state.la.us

MAINE
Ms. Diana Scully
Director
Bureau of Elder & Adult Services
442 Civic Center Drive
11 State House Station
Augusta, ME 04333
P: (207) 287-9200
F: (207) 287-9229
E: diana.scully@maine.gov

MARYLAND
Ms. Gloria Gary Lawlah
Secretary
Department of Aging
301 West Preston Street, Suite 1007
Baltimore, MD 21201
P: (410) 767-1102
F: (410) 333-7943
E: ggl@ooa.state.md.us

MASSACHUSETTS
Ms. Jennifer Davis Carey
Secretary
Executive Office of Elder Affairs
One Ashburton Place, 5th Floor
Boston, MA 02108
P: (617) 222-7451
F: (617) 727-6944
E: jennifer.d.carey@state.ma.us

MICHIGAN
Ms. Sharon Gire
Executive Director
Office of Services to the Aging
P.O. Box 30676
7109 West Saginaw, First Floor
Lansing, MI 48909
P: (517) 373-8230
F: (517) 373-4092
E: OSADirector@michigan.gov

MINNESOTA
Ms. Jean Woods
Executive Director
Board on Aging
Aging & Adult Services Division
P.O. Box 64976
St. Paul, MN 55164
P: (651) 431-2500
F: (651) 431-7453
E: mba@state.mn.us

MISSISSIPPI
Ms. Marion Dunn Tutor
Director
Council on Aging
Division of Aging & Adult Services
750 North State Street
Jackson, MS 39202
P: (601) 359-4925
F: (601) 359-4370
E: Mdunn-tutor@mdhs.state.ms.us

MISSOURI
Ms. Brenda Campbell
Division Director
Division of Senior & Disability Services
Department of Health & Senior Services
P.O. Box 570
Jefferson City, MO 65102
P: (573) 526-3626
F: (573) 751-8687
E: Brenda.Campbell@dhss.mo.gov

MONTANA
Mr. Charlie Rehbein
Chief
Aging Services Bureau
111 Sanders Street, Room 210
Helena, MT 59620
P: (406) 444-7788
F: (406) 444-7743
E: crehbein@mt.gov

NEBRASKA
Ms. Joann Weis
Director
Division of Aging & Disability Services
P.O. Box 95044
301 Centennial Mall-South
Lincoln, NE 68509
P: (402) 471-2307
F: (402) 471-4619
E: joann.weis@hhss.ne.gov

NEVADA
Ms. Carol Sala
Administrator
Division for Aging Services
Department of Human Resources
3416 Goni Road, Builing D-132
Carson City, NV 89706
P: (775) 687-4210
F: (775) 687-4264
E: csala@aging.state.nv.us

NEW HAMPSHIRE
Ms. Diane Langley
Interim Bureau Administrator
Bureau of Elderly & Adult Services
Brown Building, 129 Pleasant Street
Concord, NH 03301
P: (603) 271-4394
F: (603) 271-4643
E: dlangley@dhhs.state.nh.us

NEW JERSEY
Mr. Matthew D'Oria
Deputy Commissioner
Senior Services & Health Systems
Department of Health & Senior Services
P.O. Box 360
Trenton, NJ 08625
P: (609) 292-7837

NEW MEXICO
Ms. Deborah Armstrong
Department Secretary
Aging & Long Term Care Services Department
Toney Anaya Building
2550 Cerrillos Road
Santa Fe, NM 87505
P: (505) 476-4755
F: (505) 827-7649
E: Debbie.Armstrong@state.nm.us

NEW YORK
Mr. Michael Burgess
Director
Office for the Aging
Two Empire State Plaza, Suite 201
Albany, NY 12223
P: (518) 474-7012
F: (518) 474-1398

NORTH CAROLINA
Mr. Dennis Streets
Division Director
Division of Aging & Adult Services
2101 Mail Service Center
693 Palmer Drive
Raleigh, NC 27699
P: (919) 733-3983
F: (919) 733-0443
E: dennis.streets@ncmail.net

NORTH DAKOTA
Ms. Linda Wright
Director
Aging Services Division
Department of Human Services
600 East Boulevard, Department 325
Bismarck, ND 58505
P: (701) 328-4601
F: (701) 328-2359
E: sowril@state.nd.us

NORTHERN MARIANA ISLANDS
Mr. Howard Macaranas
Director
Department of Community & Cultural Affairs
Office on Aging
P.O. Box 502178
Saipan, MP 96950
P: (670) 233-1320
F: (670) 233-1327
E: Aging@vzpacifica.net

OHIO
Ms. Barbara Riley
Director
Department of Aging
50 West Broad Street, 9th Floor
Columbus, OH 43215
P: (614) 466-7246
F: (614) 995-1049

OKLAHOMA
Mr. Carey Garland
Director
Aging Services Division
P.O. Box 25352
2401 Northwest 23rd Street, Suite 40
Oklahoma City, OK 73107
P: (405) 521-2281
F: (405) 521-2086
E: carey.garland@okdhs.org

OREGON
Mr. James D. Toews
Interim Director
Senior & Disabled Services Division
500 Summer Street, Northeast
1st Floor, E-02
Salem, OR 97301
P: (503) 945-5811
F: (503) 373-7823
E: dhs.info@state.or.us

PENNSYLVANIA
Ms. Nora Dowd Eisenhower
Secretary
Department of Aging
555 Walnut Street, 5th Floor
Harrisburg, PA 17101
P: (717) 783-1550
F: (717) 772-3382
E: ndowd@state.pa.us

PUERTO RICO
Ms. Rossana Lopez Leon
Executive Director
Governor's Office for Elderly Affairs
P.O. Box 191179
San Juan, PR 00919
P: (787) 721-6121
F: (787) 721-6510
E: rlopez@ogave.gobierno.pr

RHODE ISLAND
Ms. Corinne Russo
Director
Department of Elderly Affairs
Benjamin Rush Building, #55
35 Howard Avenue
Cranston, RI 02920
P: (401) 462-0500
F: (401) 462-0503
E: crusso@dea.state.ri.us

SOUTH CAROLINA
Mr. Curtis Loftis
Director
Lieutenant Governor's Office on Aging
1301 Gervais Street, Suite 200
Columbia, SC 29201
P: (803) 734-9900
F: (803) 734-9886

SOUTH DAKOTA
Ms. Marilyn Kinsman
Administrator
Office of Adult Services & Aging
Kneip Building
700 Governors Drive
Pierre, SD 57501
P: (605) 773-4447
F: (605) 773-6834
E: marilyn.kinsman@state.sd.us

TENNESSEE
Ms. Nancy C. Peace
Executive Director
Commission on Aging & Disability
Andrew Jackson Building
500 Deaderick Street, #825
Nashville, TN 37243
P: (615) 741-2056
F: (615) 741-3309
E: nancy.peace@state.tn.us

TEXAS
Ms. Maxcine Thomlinson
Program Director
Department of Aging & Disability Services
701 West 51st
P.O. Box 149030
Austin, TX 78714
P: (512) 438-4505
F: (512) 438-4220

U.S. VIRGIN ISLANDS
Ms. Eva Williams
Administrator
Senior Citizen Affairs Administration
Department of Human Services
19 Estate Diamond, Fredericksted
St. Croix, VI 00840
P: (340) 692-5950
F: (340) 692-2062
E: brodina@viaccess.net

UTAH
Mr. Alan Ormsby
Director
Division of Aging & Adult Services
120 North 200 West, Room 325
P.O. Box 45500
Salt Lake City, UT 84103
P: (801) 538-4641
F: (801) 538-4395
E: akormsby@utah.gov

VERMONT
Mr. Patrick Flood
Commissioner
Department of Aging & Disabilities
103 South Main Street, Osgood #1
Waterbury, VT 05671
P: (802) 241-2400
F: (802) 241-2325
E: patrick.flood@dail.state.vt.us

VIRGINIA
Ms. Julie Christopher
Commissioner
Department for the Aging
1610 Forest Avenue, Suite 100
Richmond, VA 23299
P: (804) 662-9333
F: (804) 662-9354
E: julie.christopher@vda.virginia.gov

WASHINGTON
Ms. Kathy Leitch
Assistant Secretary
Aging & Disability Services
Mail Stop 45050
14th and Jefferson, Office Building 2
Olympia, WA 98504
P: (360) 902-7797
F: (360) 902-7848
E: leitckj@dshs.wa.gov

WEST VIRGINIA
Ms. Sandra Vanin
Commissioner
Bureau of Senior Services
1900 Kanawha Boulevard, East
3003 Town Center Mall
Charleston, WV 25305
P: (304) 558-3317
F: (304) 558-5609
E: svanin@boss.state.wv.us

WISCONSIN
Ms. Donna McDowell
Bureau Director
Bureau of Aging & Disability Resources
One West Wilson Street, Room 450
P.O. Box 7851
Madison, WI 53707
P: (608) 266-2536
F: (608) 267-3203
E: mcdowdb@dhfs.state.wi.us

WYOMING
Ms. Beverly Morrow
Administrator
Aging Division
Department of Health
6101 Yellow Stone Road, Room 259B
Cheyenne, WY 82002
P: (307) 777-7986
F: (307) 777-5340
E: bmorro@state.wy.us

Agriculture

Enforces agriculture laws and administers agricultural programs in the state.

ALABAMA
Mr. Ron Sparks
Commissioner
Department of Agriculture & Industries
Richard Beard Building
P.O. Box 3336
Montgomery, AL 36109
P: (334) 240-7100
F: (334) 240-7190

ALASKA
Mr. Larry DeVilbiss
Director
Division of Agriculture
Department of Natural Resources
1800 Glenn Highway, Suite 12
Palmer, AK 99645
P: (907) 761-3867
F: (907) 745-7112

AMERICAN SAMOA
Mr. Apefa'i Taifane
Director
Department of Agriculture
American Samoa Government
Executive Office Building, Utulei
Pago Pago, AS 96799
P: (684) 699-1497
F: (684) 699-4031

ARIZONA
Mr. Donald Butler
Director
Department of Agriculture
1688 West Adams
Phoenix, AZ 85007
P: (602) 542-0990
F: (602) 542-5420

ARKANSAS
Mr. Richard Bell
Secretary
Department of Agriculture
#1 Natural Resources Drive
Little Rock, AR 72205
P: (501) 663-4851
F: (501) 683-4852

CALIFORNIA
Mr. A.G. Kawamura
Secretary
Department of Food & Agriculture
1220 N Street
Suite 400
Sacramento, CA 95814
P: (916) 654-0433
F: (916) 654-0403

COLORADO
Mr. John Stulp
Commissioner
Department of Agriculture
700 Kipling Street, Suite 4000
Lakewood, CO 80215
P: (303) 239-4100
F: (303) 239-4125

CONNECTICUT
Mr. F. Philip Prelli
Commissioner
Department of Agriculture
165 Capitol Avenue
Hartford, CT 06106
P: (860) 713-2500
F: (860) 713-2514

DELAWARE
Mr. Michael T. Scuse
Secretary
Department of Agriculture
2320 South DuPont Highway
Dover, DE 19901
P: (302) 698-4500
F: (302) 697-4463

FLORIDA
Mr. Charles Bronson
Commissioner
Department of Agriculture & Consumer Services
The Capitol, PL10
Tallahassee, FL 32399
P: (850) 488-3022
F: (850) 922-4936

GEORGIA
Mr. Tommy Irvin
Commissioner
Department of Agriculture
204 Agriculture Building
19 Martin Luther King, Jr. Drive SW
Atlanta, GA 30334
P: (404) 656-3600
F: (404) 651-8206

GUAM
Mr. Paul C. Bassler
Director
Department of Agriculture
192 Dairy Road
Mangilao, GU 96923
P: (671) 734-3942
F: (671) 734-6569

HAWAII
Ms. Sandra Lee Kunimoto
Chairperson
Board of Agriculture
1428 South King Street
Honolulu, HI 96814
P: (808) 973-9560
F: (808) 973-9613

IDAHO
Ms. Celia R. Gould
Director
Department of Agriculture
2270 Old Penitentiary Road
P.O. Box 790
Boise, ID 83701
P: (208) 332-8503
F: (208) 334-2170
E: cgould@idahoag.us

ILLINOIS
Mr. Charles A. Hartke
Director
Department of Agriculture
State Fairgrounds
P.O. Box 19281
Springfield, IL 62794
P: (217) 782-2172
F: (217) 785-4505

INDIANA
Mr. Andy Miller
Director
Department of Agriculture
101 West Ohio Street, Suite 1200
Indianapolis, IN 46204
P: (317) 232-8770
F: (317) 232-1362
E: amiller@isda.in.gov

KANSAS
Mr. Adrian J. Polansky
Secretary
Department of Agriculture
109 Southwest 9th Street, 4th Floor
Topeka, KS 66612
P: (785) 296-3556
F: (785) 296-8389

KENTUCKY
Mr. Richie Farmer
Commissioner
Department of Agriculture
32 Fountain Place
Frankfort, KY 40601
P: (502) 564-5126
F: (502) 564-5016

LOUISIANA
Mr. Bob Odom
Commissioner
Department of Agriculture & Forestry
P.O. Box 631
Baton Rouge, LA 70821
P: (225) 922-1234
F: (225) 922-1253

MAINE
Mr. Seth Bradstreet
Commissioner
Department of Agriculture, Food & Rural Resources
Deering Building, AMHI Complex
28 State House Station
Augusta, ME 04333
P: (207) 287-3419
F: (207) 287-7548

MARYLAND
Mr. Roger L. Richardson
Secretary
Department of Agriculture
50 Harry S. Truman Parkway
Annapolis, MD 21401
P: (410) 841-5880
F: (410) 841-5914

MASSACHUSETTS
Mr. Scott J. Soares
Acting Commissioner
Department of Agricultural Resources
251 Causeway Street, Suite 500
Boston, MA 02114
P: (617) 626-1701
F: (617) 626-1850

MICHIGAN
Mr. Mitch Irwin
Director
Department of Agriculture
P.O. Box 30017
525 West Allegan Street
Lansing, MI 48933
P: (517) 373-1052
F: (517) 335-1423
E: irwinm1@michigan.gov

MINNESOTA
Mr. Gene Hugoson
Commissioner
Department of Agriculture
Freeman Office Building
625 Robert Street, North
St. Paul, MN 55155
P: (651) 201-6219
F: (651) 201-6118
E: gene.hugoson@state.mn.us

MISSISSIPPI
Dr. Lester Spell Jr.
Commissioner
Department of Agriculture & Commerce
121 North Jefferson Street
Jackson, MS 39201
P: (601) 359-1100
F: (601) 354-7710
E: Spell@mdac.state.ms.us

MISSOURI
Mr. Matt Boatright
Interim Director
Department of Agriculture
P.O. Box 630
Jefferson City, MO 65102
P: (573) 751-3359
F: (573) 751-1784
E: matt.boatright@mda.mo.gov

MONTANA
Ms. Nancy K. Peterson
Director
Department of Agriculture
P.O. Box 200201
303 North Roberts Street
Helena, MT 59620
P: (406) 444-3144
F: (406) 444-5409
E: agr@mt.gov

NEBRASKA
Mr. Greg Ibach
Director
Department of Agriculture
P.O. Box 94947
301 Centennial Mall South, 4th Floor
Lincoln, NE 68509
P: (402) 471-2341
F: (402) 471-6876

NEVADA
Ms. Dina Rise
Director
Department of Agriculture
350 Capitol Hill Avenue
Reno, NV 89502
P: (775) 688-1190
F: (775) 688-1178
E: dorise@agri.state.nv.us

NEW HAMPSHIRE
Mr. Stephen H. Taylor
Commissioner
Department of Agriculture, Markets & Food
P.O. Box 2042
Concord, NH 03302
P: (603) 271-3551
F: (603) 271-1109
E: staylor@agr.state.nh.us

NEW JERSEY
Mr. Charles M. Kuperus
Secretary
Department of Agriculture
P.O. Box 330
John Fitch Plaza
Trenton, NJ 08625
P: (609) 292-3976
F: (609) 292-3978

NEW MEXICO
Dr. I. Miley Gonzalez
Director/Secretary
Department of Agriculture
MSC 3189, P.O. Box 30005
3190 South Espina
Las Cruces, NM 88003
P: (505) 646-3007
F: (505) 646-8120
E: nmagsec@nmda.nmsu.edu

NEW YORK
Mr. Patrick Hooker
Commissioner
Department of Agriculture & Markets
10B Airline Drive
Albany, NY 12235
P: (518) 457-8876
F: (518) 457-3087

NORTH CAROLINA
Mr. Steve Troxler
Commissioner
Department of Agriculture & Consumer Services
1001 Mail Service Center
2 West Edenton Street
Raleigh, NC 27699
P: (919) 733-7125
F: (919) 733-1141

NORTH DAKOTA
Mr. Roger Johnson
Commissioner
Department of Agriculture
600 East Boulevard Avenue
Department 602
Bismarck, ND 58505
P: (701) 328-4754
F: (701) 328-4567

NORTHERN MARIANA ISLANDS
Mr. Donald P. Flores
Director
Division of Agriculture
Department of Lands & Natural Resources
Caller Box 10007, Capital Hill
Saipan, MP 96950
P: (670) 256-3318
F: (670) 256-7154

OHIO
Mr. Robert J. Boggs
Director
Department of Agriculture
8995 East Main Street
Reynoldsburg, OH 43068
P: (614) 466-2732
F: (614) 466-6124

OKLAHOMA
Mr. Terry Peach
Commissioner
Department of Agriculture, Food & Forestry
2800 North Lincoln Boulevard
Oklahoma City, OK 73105
P: (405) 522-5719
F: (405) 522-4912

OREGON
Ms. Katy Coba
Director
Department of Agriculture
635 Capitol Street, Northeast
Salem, OR 97301
P: (503) 986-4552
F: (503) 986-4750

PENNSYLVANIA
Mr. Dennis Wolff
Secretary
Department of Agriculture
2301 North Cameron Street
Harrisburg, PA 17110
P: (717) 772-2853
F: (717) 705-8402

PUERTO RICO
Mr. Jose O. Fabre Laboy
Executive Director
Department of Agriculture
Apartado 10163
Santurce, PR 00909
P: (787) 721-2120
F: (787) 723-8512

RHODE ISLAND
Mr. Kenneth Ayars
Chief
Division of Agriculture, DEM
235 Promenade Street, Room 370
Providence, RI 02908
P: (401) 222-2781 Ext. 4500
F: (401) 222-6047

SOUTH CAROLINA
Mr. Hugh E. Weathers
Commissioner
Department of Agriculture
Wade Hampton Office Building
P.O. Box 11280
Columbia, SC 29211
P: (803) 734-2190
F: (803) 734-2192

SOUTH DAKOTA
Mr. William Even
Secretary
Department of Agriculture
Foss Building
523 East Capitol Avenue
Pierre, SD 57501
P: (605) 773-5425
F: (605) 773-5926
E: bill.even@state.sd.us

TENNESSEE
Mr. Ken Givens
Commissioner
Department of Agriculture
Melrose Station
P.O. Box 40627
Nashville, TN 37204
P: (615) 837-5100
F: (615) 837-5333

U.S. VIRGIN ISLANDS
Dr. Lawrence Lewis
Commissioner
Department of Agriculture
#1 Estate Lower Love
St. Croix, VI 00850
P: (340) 778-0997
F: (340) 778-7977

UTAH
Mr. Leonard Blackham
Commissioner
Department of Agriculture & Food
350 North Redwood Road
Salt Lake City, UT 84114
P: (801) 538-7101
F: (801) 538-7126
E: lmblackham@utah.gov

Agriculture

VERMONT
Mr. Roger Allbee
Secretary
Agency of Agriculture, Food & Markets
Drawer 20
116 State Street
Montpelier, VT 05620
P: (802) 828-2430
F: (802) 828-2361

VIRGINIA
Mr. Donald G. Blankenship
Acting Commissioner
Department of Agriculture & Consumer Services
102 Governor Street
Oliver Hill Building
Richmond, VA 23219
P: (804) 786-3501
F: (804) 371-2945
E: don.blankenship@vdacs.virginia.gov

WASHINGTON
Ms. Valoria Loveland
Director
Department of Agriculture
P.O. Box 42560
Olympia, WA 98504
P: (360) 902-1887
F: (360) 902-2092

WEST VIRGINIA
Mr. Gus R. Douglass
Commissioner
Department of Agriculture
1900 Kanawha Boulevard East
Charleston, WV 25305
P: (304) 558-2201
F: (304) 558-2203
E: douglass@ag.state.wv.us

WISCONSIN
Mr. Rod Nilsestuen
Secretary
Department of Agriculture, Trade & Consumer Protection
2811 Agriculture Drive
P.O. Box 8911
Madison, WI 53708
P: (608) 224-5012
F: (608) 224-5045

WYOMING
Mr. John Etchepare
Director
Department of Agriculture
2219 Carey Avenue
Cheyenne, WY 82002
P: (307) 777-6569
F: (307) 777-6593

Alcohol and Substance Abuse

Plans, establishes and administers programs for the prevention, treatment, and rehabilitation of alcohol and/or drug and other abusers.

ALABAMA
Mr. Kent Hunt
Associate Commissioner
Substance Abuse Division
Department of Mental Health/Retardation
P.O. Box 301410
Montgomery, AL 36130
P: (334) 242-3961
F: (334) 242-0759
E: kent.hunt@mh.alabama.gov

ALASKA
Ms. Stacy Toner
Acting Director
Division of Behavioral Health
Department of Health & Social Services
P.O. Box 110620
Juneau, AK 99801
P: (907) 465-3370
F: (907) 465-5864
E: stacy_toner@health.state.ak.us

AMERICAN SAMOA
Mr. Talia Fa'afetai I'aulualo
Director
Department of Human & Social Services
American Samoa Government
Pago Pago, AS 96799
P: (684) 633-1187
F: (684) 633-7449

ARIZONA
Ms. Christina A. Dye
Chief
Bureau of Substance Abuse Treatment & Prevention Services
150 North 18th Avenue
2nd Floor
Phoenix, AZ 85007
P: (602) 364-4558
F: (602) 364-4570

ARKANSAS
Mr. Joe Hill
Director
Office of Alcohol & Drug Prevention
4313 West Markham
Little Rock, AR 72205
P: (501) 686-9871
F: (501) 686-9035
E: Joe.Hill@arkansas.gov

CALIFORNIA
Ms. Renee Zito
Director
Department of Alcohol & Drug Programs
1700 K Street, 5th Floor
Sacramento, CA 95814
P: (916) 445-1943
F: (916) 324-7338

COLORADO
Ms. Janet Wood
Director
Alcohol & Drug Abuse Division
4055 South Lowell Boulevard
Denver, CO 80236
P: (303) 866-7480
F: (303) 866-7481
E: janet.wood@state.co.us

CONNECTICUT
Dr. Thomas A. Kirk Jr.
Commissioner
Department of Mental Health & Addiction Services
410 Capitol Avenue, MS#14COM
Hartford, CT 06106
P: (860) 418-6700
F: (860) 418-6691
E: thomas.kirk@po.state.ct.us

DELAWARE
Ms. Renata J. Henry
Director
Division of Substance Abuse & Mental Health
Department of Health & Social Services
1901 North Dupont Highway
New Castle, DE 19720
P: (302) 255-9398
F: (302) 255-4427
E: Renata.Henry@state.de.us

Mr. Jack Kemp
Director of Alcoholism and Drug Services
Division of Substance Abuse & Mental Health
1901 North DuPont Highway, Main Building
Central Office
New Castle, DE 19720
P: (302) 255-9433
F: (302) 255-4427
E: Jack.Kemp@state.de.us

DISTRICT OF COLUMBIA
Mr. Robert Johnson
Senior Deputy Director
Addiction Prevention & Recovery Administration
825 North Capitol Street, Northeast
Washington, DC 20002
P: (202) 442-9152

FLORIDA
Mr. Kenneth DeCerchio
Acting Deputy Secretary for Substance Abuse & Mental Health
Department of Children & Families
1317 Winewood Boulevard
Building #6
Tallahassee, FL 32399
P: (850) 921-8461
F: (850) 414-9042
E: ken_decerchio@dcf.state.fl.us

GEORGIA
Ms. Gwendolyn B. Skinner
Division Director
Division of Mental Health, Developmental Disabilities & Addictive Disease
Department of Human Resources
2 Peachtree Street, Suite 22.224
Atlanta, GA 30303
P: (404) 657-2260
F: (404) 657-1137
E: gbskinner@dhr.ga.gov

GUAM
Dr. Andrea Leitheiser
Director
Department of Mental Health & Substance Abuse
790 Governor Carlos G. Camacho Road
Tamuning, GU 96913
P: (671) 647-5330
F: (671) 649-6948

HAWAII
Mr. Keith Yamamoto
Division Chief
Alcohol & Drug Abuse Division
601 Kamokila Boulevard
Kapolei, HI 96707
P: (808) 692-7506
F: (808) 692-7521
E: kyamamoto@mail.health.state.hi.us

IDAHO
Mr. Pharis Stanger
Program Manager
FACS Division, Substance Abuse Program
P.O. Box 83720-5th Floor
Boise, ID 83720
P: (208) 334-4944
F: (208) 334-6664
E: stangerp@dhw.idaho.gov

ILLINOIS
Ms. Theodora Binion Taylor
Associate Director
Division of Alcoholism & Substance Abuse
100 W. Randolph Street, Suite 5-600
Chicago, IL 60601
P: (312) 814-2300
F: (312) 814-3838
E: DHSASA4@dhs.state.il.us

INDIANA
Ms. Cathy Boggs
Director
Division of Mental Health & Addiction
402 West Washington St., Room W-353
Indianapolis, IN 46204
P: (317) 232-4319
F: (317) 233-3472
E: cathy.boggs@fssa.in.gov

IOWA
Ms. Julie McMahon
Division Director
Health Promotion & Chronic Disease Prevention
Lucas State Office Building
321 East 12th Street
Des Moines, IA 50319
P: (515) 281-3104
F: (515) 242-6013

Alcohol and Substance Abuse

KANSAS
Ms. Donna Doolin
Acting Director
Addiction & Prevention Services
Docking State Office Building
915 Southwest Harrison Street-10th Floor
Topeka, KS 66612
P: (785) 296-6807
F: (785) 296-7275
E: dxmd@srskansas.org

KENTUCKY
Ms. Donna Hillman
Director
Division of Mental Health & Substance Abuse
100 Fair Oaks Lane, 4E-D
Frankfort, KY 40621
P: (502) 564-4456
F: (502) 564-9010

LOUISIANA
Mr. Michael Duffy
Assistant Secretary
Office for Addictive Disorders
P.O. Box 2790, Bin #18
1201 Capitol Access Road
Baton Rouge, LA 70821
P: (225) 342-6717
F: (225) 342-3875

MAINE
Ms. Kimberly Johnson
Director
Office of Substance Abuse
159 State House Station
Augusta, ME 04333
P: (207) 287-6344
F: (207) 287-4334
E: Kimberly.Johnson@maine.gov

MARYLAND
Dr. Peter F. Luongo
Director
Alcohol & Drug Abuse Administration
Spring Grove Hospital Center
55 Wade Avenue
Catonsville, MD 21228
P: (410) 402-8600
F: (410) 402-8601
E: pluongo@dhmh.state.md.us

MASSACHUSETTS
Mr. Michael Botticelli
Assistant Commissioner for Substance Abuse Services
Department of Public Health
250 Washington Street
Boston, MA 02108
P: (617) 624-5111
F: (617) 624-5261

MICHIGAN
Mr. Patrick Barrie
Deputy Director
Mental Health & Substance Abuse Administration
Department of Community Health
320 South Walnut Street
Lansing, MI 48913
P: (517) 335-0196
F: (517) 335-4798
E: barriep@michigan.gov

MINNESOTA
Mr. Charles M. Heinecke
Acting Director
Chemical Health Division
Department of Human Services
P.O. Box 64977
St. Paul, MN 55164
P: (651) 431-2460
F: (651) 431-7449

MISSISSIPPI
Mr. Herbert Loving
Director
Division of Alcohol & Drug Abuse
Robert E. Lee State Office Building
239 North Lamar Street, 11th Floor
Jackson, MS 39201
P: (601) 359-1288
F: (601) 359-6295
E: hloving@msdmh.org

MISSOURI
Mr. Mark Stringer
Director
Division of Alcohol & Drug Abuse
P.O. Box 687
Jefferson City, MO 65102
P: (573) 751-9499
F: (573) 751-7814
E: mark.stringer@dmh.mo.gov

MONTANA
Ms. Joan Cassidy
Chief
Chemical Dependency Services
555 Fuller Avenue
P.O. Box 202905
Helena, MT 59620
P: (406) 444-6981
F: (406) 444-4435
E: jcassidy@mt.gov

NEBRASKA
Mr. Ron Sorensen
Administrator, Behavioral Health Services
Office of Mental Health, Substance Abuse & Addiction Services
Department of Health & Human Services
P.O. Box 98925
Lincoln, NE 68509
P: (402) 479-5517
F: (402) 479-5162
E: Ron.Sorenson@hhss.ne.gov

NEVADA
Ms. Maria D. Canfield
Chief
Bureau of Alcohol & Drug Abuse
505 East King Street, Room 500
Carson City, NV 89701
P: (775) 684-4190
F: (775) 684-4185
E: mcanfield@nvhd.state.nv.us

NEW HAMPSHIRE
Mr. Joseph Harding
Director
Office of Alcohol and Drug Policy
105 Pleasant Street
Concord, NH 03301
P: (603) 271-6104
F: (603) 271-6116
E: jharding@dhhs.state.nh.us

NEW JERSEY
Ms. Raquel Mazon-Jeffers
Director
Division of Addiction Services
P.O. Box 362
120 South Stockton Street, 3rd Floor
Trenton, NJ 08625
P: (609) 292-5760

NEW MEXICO
Ms. Pamela S. Hyde
Cabinet Secretary
Human Services Department
2009 South Pacheco, Pollon Plaza
P.O. Box 2348
Santa Fe, NM 87504
P: (505) 827-7750
F: (505) 827-3185

NEW YORK
Ms. Karen Carpenter-Palumbo
Commissioner
Office of Alcohol & Substance Abuse Services
1450 Western Avenue
Albany, NY 12203
P: (518) 457-2061
F: (518) 457-5474

NORTH CAROLINA
Mr. Michael Moseley
Director
Developmental Disabilities & Substance Abuse Services
Division of Mental Health
3007 Mail Service Center
Raleigh, NC 27699
P: (919) 733-4670 Ext. 231
F: (919) 733-9455
E: michael.moseley@ncmail.net

NORTH DAKOTA
Mr. Don Wright
Unit Administrator
Division of Mental Health & Substance Abuse Services
600 South 2nd Street, Suite 1E
Bismarck, ND 58504
P: (701) 328-8922
F: (701) 328-8969
E: sowrid@state.nd.us

NORTHERN MARIANA ISLANDS
Mr. Joseph P. Villagomez
Secretary of Public Health
Community Guidance Center
P.O. Box 500409
Saipan, MP 96950
P: (670) 236-8201
F: (670) 234-8930
E: jkvsaipan@aol.com

OHIO
Ms. Angela Cornelius
Director
Department of Alcohol & Drug Addiction Services
280 North High Street, 12th Floor
Columbus, OH 43215
P: (614) 466-3445
F: (614) 728-4936

OKLAHOMA
Mr. Sonny Scott
Interim Deputy Commissioner, Substance Abuse Services
Department of Mental Health & Substance Abuse Services
P.O. Box 53277
Oklahoma City, OK 73152
P: (405) 522-3908
F: (405) 522-3650

OREGON
Mr. Robert E. Nikkel
Administrator
DHS - Mental Health & Addiction Services
500 Summer Street, Northeast
3rd Floor, E86
Salem, OR 97301
P: (503) 945-9704
F: (503) 373-7327
E: dhs.info@state.or.us

PENNSYLVANIA
Mr. Gene R. Boyle
Director
Bureau of Drug & Alcohol Programs
02 Kline Plaza, Suite B
Harrisburg, PA 17104
P: (717) 783-8200
F: (717) 787-6285

RHODE ISLAND
Mr. Craig Stenning
Executive Director
Division of Behavioral Healthcare Services
Division of Developmental Disabilities
14 Harrington Road
Cranston, RI 02920
P: (401) 462-2339
F: (401) 462-6636
E: cstenning@mhrh.ri.gov

SOUTH CAROLINA
Mr. Lee Catoe
Director
Department of Alcohol & Other Drug Abuse Services
101 Executive Center Drive
Suite 215
Columbia, SC 29210
P: (803) 896-5551
F: (803) 896-5557
E: leecatoe@daodas.state.sc.us

SOUTH DAKOTA
Mr. Gib Sudbeck
Director
Division of Alcohol & Drug Abuse
Hillsview Plaza
C/o 500 East Capitol
Pierre, SD 57501
P: (605) 773-3123
F: (605) 773-7076
E: gib.sudbeck@state.sd.us

TENNESSEE
Dr. Stephanie W. Perry
Assistant Commissioner
Bureau of Alcohol & Drug Abuse Services
Cordell Hull Building, 3rd Floor
425 5th Avenue North
Nashville, TN 37247
P: (615) 741-1921
F: (615) 532-2419
E: Stephanie.Perry@state.tn.us

TEXAS
Mr. Joe Vesowate
Assistant Commissioner for Mental Health
Mental Health and Substance Abuse Services
Department of Health Services
1100 West 49th Street
Austin, TX 78456
P: (512) 206-5797

U.S. VIRGIN ISLANDS
Ms. Denese Marshall
Director
Department of Mental Health, Alcoholism & Drug Dependency Services
Barbell Plaza South
St. Thomas, VI 00802
P: (340) 774-4888
F: (340) 774-4701
E: denese.marshall@usvi-doh.org

UTAH
Mr. Mark Payne
Director
Division of Substance Abuse & Mental Health
Department of Human Services
120 North 200 West, #209
Salt Lake City, UT 84103
P: (801) 538-3939
F: (801) 538-4696
E: mpayne@utah.gov

VERMONT
Ms. Barbara Cimaglio
Deputy Commissioner
Office of Alcohol & Drug Abuse Programs
P.O. Box 70
Burlington, VT 05402
P: (802) 651-1550
F: (802) 651-1573
E: bcimagl@vdh.state.vt.us

VIRGINIA
Mr. Kenneth B. Batten
Director
Office of Substance Abuse Services
Department of MHMR&SAS
P.O. Box 1797
Richmond, VA 23218
P: (804) 371-2154
F: (804) 371-6638
E: kenneth.batten@co.dmhmrsas.virginia.gov

WASHINGTON
Mr. Doug Allen
Director
Division of Alcohol & Substance Abuse
P.O. Box 45330
Olympia, WA 98504
P: (360) 438-8200

WEST VIRGINIA
Mr. Steve Mason
Director
Division on Alcoholism & Drug Abuse
350 Capitol Street, Room 350
Charleston, WV 25301
P: (304) 558-4224
F: (304) 558-1008
E: stevemason@wvdhhr.org

WISCONSIN
Ms. Joyce Bohn Allen
Director
Bureau of Mental Health & Substance Abuse Services
1 West Wilson Street, Room 434
P.O. Box 7851
Madison, WI 53707
P: (608) 266-1351
F: (608) 266-1533
E: allenjb@dhfs.state.wi.us

WYOMING
Ms. Korin Schmidt
Administrator
Substance Abuse Division
6101 North Yellowstone, Room 220
Cheyenne, WY 82002
P: (307) 777-3365
F: (307) 777-7006

Alcoholic Beverage Control

Administers and enforces the laws governing the manufacturing, distribution, and dispensing of alcoholic beverages.

Information provided by:

National Alcohol Beverage Control Association
Jim Sgueo
President & CEO
4401 Ford Avenue, Suite 700
Alexandria, VA 22302
P: (703) 578-4200
F: (703) 820-3551
jsgueo@nabca.org
www.nabca.org

ALABAMA
Mr. Randall C. Smith
Administrator
Alcohol Beverage Control Board
2715 Gunter Park Drive, West
P.O. Box 1151
Montgomery, AL 36101
P: (334) 260-5417
F: (334) 277-2150
E: randall.smith@abcboard.alabama.gov

IDAHO
Mr. James M. Nally
Superintendent
State Liquor Dispensary
1349 East Beechcraft Court
P.O. Box 179001
Boise, ID 83717
P: (208) 334-5300
F: (208) 334-2533
E: dyke.nally@liquor.idaho.gov

IOWA
Ms. Lynn M. Walding
Administrator
Alcoholic Beverages Division
1918 Southeast Hulsizer Avenue
Ankeny, IA 50021
P: (515) 281-7402
F: (515) 281-7385
E: walding@Iowabd.com

MAINE
Mr. Dan A. Gwadosky
Director
State Liquor & Lottery Commission
#8 State House Station
Augusta, ME 04333
P: (207) 287-3721
F: (207) 287-6769
E: dgwadosky@maine.gov

MARYLAND
Mr. George F. Griffin
Director
Department of Liquor Control
16650 Crabbs Branch Way
Rockville, MD 20855
P: (240) 777-1922
F: (240) 777-1962
E: george.griffin@montgomerycountymd.gov

MICHIGAN
Ms. Nida R. Samona
Chair
Liquor Control Commission
7150 Harris Drive
P.O. Box 30005
Lansing, MI 48909
P: (517) 322-1353
F: (517) 322-5188
E: nrsamon@michigan.gov

MISSISSIPPI
Ms. Alice Gorman
Deputy Commissioner
State Tax Commission, Alcoholic Beverage Control Division
Alcohol Beverage Control Division
P.O. Box 22828
Jackson, MS 39225
P: (601) 923-7411
F: (601) 923-7423
E: agorman@mstc.state.ms.us

MONTANA
Ms. Shauna Helfert
Sub-Process Lead, Liquor Distribution
Department of Revenue
Mitchell Building, Room 455
Helena, MT 59624
P: (406) 444-2460
F: (406) 444-3696
E: shelfert@state.mt.gov

NEW HAMPSHIRE
Mr. Anthony C. Maiola
Chair
State Liquor Commission
Storrs Street
P.O. Box 503
Concord, NH 03301
P: (603) 271-3132
F: (603) 271-3121
E: amaiola@liquor.state.nh.us

NORTH CAROLINA
Mr. Douglas A. Fox
Chair
Alcoholic Beverage Control Commission
3322 Garner Road
4307 Mail Service Center
Raleigh, NC 27699
P: (919) 779-0700
F: (919) 662-3583
E: herringm@ncabc.com

Mr. Gary Pendleton
Director
North Carolina Association of ABC Boards
2601 Oberlin Road
Raleigh, NC 27608
P: (919) 781-4167
F: (919) 781-3589

OHIO
Mr. Terry Poole
Superintendent
Department of Commerce
Division of Liquor Control
6606 Tussing Road
Reynoldsburg, OH 43068
P: (614) 644-2472
F: (614) 644-2480
E: terry.poole@com.state.oh.us

OREGON
Mr. Philip D. Lang
Chair
Liquor Control Commission
9079 Southeast McLoughlin Boulevard
Portland, OR 97222
P: (503) 872-5242
F: (503) 872-5266
E: pdavidlang@msn.com

PENNSYLVANIA
Mr. Patrick J. Stapleton III
Chair
Liquor Control Board
Room 517
Northwest Office Building
Harrisburg, PA 17124
P: (717) 787-2696
F: (717) 772-3714
E: pstapleton@state.pa.us

UTAH
Mr. Kenneth F. Wynn
Director
Department of Alcoholic Beverage Control
1625 South 900 West
P.O. Box 30408
Salt Lake City, UT 84130
P: (801) 977-6800
F: (801) 977-6889
E: kwynn@utah.gov

VERMONT
Mr. Walter E. Freed
Chair
Department of Liquor Control
13 Green Mountain Drive, Drawer 20
Montpelier, VT 05620
P: (802) 828-2345
F: (802) 828-2803
E: wefreed@aol.com

VIRGINIA
Ms. Susan R. Swecker
Chair
Alcohol Beverage Control Board
2901 Hermitage Road
P.O. Box 27491
Richmond, VA 23261
P: (804) 213-4404
F: (804) 213-4411
E: susan.swecker@abc.virginia.gov

WASHINGTON
Ms. Lorraine Lee
Chair
State Liquor Control Board
3000 Pacific Avenue, Southeast
P.O. Box 43080
Olympia, WA 98504
P: (360) 664-1600
F: (360) 586-3190
E: llee@liq.wa.gov

WEST VIRGINIA
Mr. Dallas Staples
Commissioner
Alcohol Beverage Control Administration
322 70th Street, Southeast
Charleston, WV 25304
P: (304) 558-2481
F: (304) 558-0081
E: dstaples@abcc.state.wv.us

WYOMING
Mr. Edmund J. Schmidt
Director
Department of Revenue, Liquor Division
Herschler Building
122 West 25th Street, 2nd West
Cheyenne, WY 82002
P: (307) 777-5287
F: (307) 777-7722
E: Ed.Schmidt@wyo.gov

Arbitration and Mediation

Promotes the settlement of a variety of labor disputes.

ALABAMA
Mr. Jim Bennett
Commissioner
Department of Labor
P.O. Box 303500
Montgomery, AL 36130
P: (334) 242-3460
F: (334) 240-3417
E: jbennett@alalabor.state.al.us

ALASKA
Mr. Clark "Click" Bishop
Commissioner
Department of Labor & Workforce Development
P.O. Box 21149
Juneau, AK 99802
P: (907) 465-2700
F: (907) 465-2784
E: commissioner_labor@labor.state.ak.us

AMERICAN SAMOA
Mr. Puni Penei Sewell
Director
Department of Human Resources
American Samoa Government
Pago Pago, AS 96799
P: (683) 644-4485
F: (684) 633-1139
E: sewells_l@hotmail.com

ARIZONA
Mr. Larry J. Etchechury
Director
Industrial Commission
800 West Washington Street
P.O. Box 19070
Phoenix, AZ 85007
P: (602) 542-4411
F: (602) 542-7889
E: letchechury@ica.state.az.us

ARKANSAS
Mr. James Salkeld
Director
Department of Labor
10421 West Markham Street
Suite 100
Little Rock, AR 72205
P: (501) 682-4541
F: (501) 682-4535
E: james.salkeld@arkansas.gov

CALIFORNIA
Mr. Curtis Lyon
Presiding Mediator
State Mediation & Conciliation Service
1515 Clay Street, Suite 2206
Oakland, CA 94612
P: (510) 873-6465
F: (510) 873-6475

COLORADO
Mr. Don J. Mares
Executive Director
Department of Labor & Employment
1515 Arapahoe Street, Suite 375
Denver, CO 80202
P: (303) 318-8000
F: (303) 318-8048
E: don.mares@state.co.us

CONNECTICUT
Ms. Patricia Mayfield
Commissioner
Department of Labor
200 Folly Brook Boulevard
Wethersfield, CT 06109
P: (860) 263-6505
F: (860) 263-6529
E: patricia.mayfield@po.state.ct.us

DELAWARE
Mr. Thomas B. Sharp
Secretary of Labor
Department of Labor
4425 North Market Street, 4th Floor
Wilmington, DE 19802
P: (302) 761-8000
F: (302) 761-6621
E: tom.sharp@state.de.us

DISTRICT OF COLUMBIA
Ms. Summer Spencer
Acting Director
Department of Employment Services
609 H Street, NE
Washington, DC 20002
P: (202) 724-7000

FLORIDA
Ms. Donna Maggart Poole
Chair
Public Employees Relations Commission
4050 Esplanade Way, Room 150
Tallahassee, FL 32399
P: (850) 488-8641
F: (850) 488-9704

GEORGIA
Mr. Michael L. Thurmond
Commissioner
Department of Labor
Sussex Place, Room 600
148 International Boulevard, Northeast
Atlanta, GA 30303
P: (404) 232-3001
F: (404) 232-3017
E: commissioner@dol.state.ga.us

GUAM
Ms. Maria Connelley
Director
Department of Labor
414 West Soledad, Suite 400
GCIC Building, P.O. Box 9970
Tamuning, GU 96931
P: (671) 475-7046
F: (671) 475-7045

Mr. Vernon Perez
Executive Director
Civil Service Commission
490 Chalan Palasyo, Hagatna Heights
P.O. Box 3156
Hagatna, GU 96932
P: (671) 475-1300
F: (671) 475-3301

HAWAII
Mr. Nelson B. Befitel
Director
Department of Labor & Industrial Relations
Princess Keelikolani Building
830 Punchbowl Street, Room 321
Honolulu, HI 96813
P: (808) 586-8844
F: (808) 586-9099
E: dlir.director@hawaii.gov

IDAHO
Mr. Roger B. Madsen
Director
Department of Labor
317 West Main Street
Boise, ID 83735
P: (208) 332-3579
F: (208) 334-6430
E: rmadsen@cl.idaho.gov

ILLINOIS
Mr. John F. Broson
Executive Director
Labor Relations Board
160 North LaSalle Street, Suite S-400
Chicago, IL 60601
P: (312) 793-6400
F: (312) 793-6989

INDIANA
Ms. Lori A. Torres
Commissioner
Department of Labor
Indiana Government Center-South
402 West Washington Street, Room W-195
Indianapolis, IN 46204
P: (317) 232-2378
F: (317) 233-5381
E: ltorres@dol.in.gov

IOWA
Mr. Steve Slater
Interim Labor Commissioner
Division of Labor Services
1000 East Grand Avenue
Des Moines, IA 50319
P: (515) 281-3447
F: (515) 281-4698

KANSAS
Mr. George Vega
Director
Division of Personnel Services
Division of Personnel Services
900 Southwest Jackson, Room 951-S
Topeka, KS 66612
P: (785) 296-2541
F: (785) 296-3655
E: george.vega@da.state.ks.us

KENTUCKY
Mr. Tom Cannady
Executive Director
Office of Labor-Management Relations & Mediation
1047 US Highway 127 South
Suite 4
Frankfort, KY 40601
P: (502) 564-3070, ext. 227
F: (502) 696-5794
E: tom.cannady@ky.gov

LOUISIANA
Mr. John Warner Smith
Secretary of Labor
Department of Labor
P.O. Box 94094
1001 North 23rd Street
Baton Rouge, LA 70804
P: (225) 342-3011
F: (225) 342-3778
E: jwsmith@ldol.state.la.us

MAINE
Ms. Laura Fortman
Commissioner of Labor
Department of Labor
P.O. Box 259
Augusta, ME 04332
P: (207) 287-3787
F: (207) 287-5292
E: laura.fortman@maine.gov

MARYLAND
Mr. Thomas E. Perez
Secretary
Department of Labor, Licensing & Regulation
500 North Calvert Street, Room 401
Baltimore, MD 21202
P: (410) 230-6020
F: (410) 333-0853
E: tperez@dllr.state.md.us

MASSACHUSETTS
Ms. Susan Jeghelian
Executive Director
Office of Dispute Resolution
100 Morrissey Boulevard
McCormack Building, Room 627
Boston, MA 02125
P: (617) 287-4047
F: (617) 287-4049
E: susan.jeghelian@umb.edu

MICHIGAN
Mr. R. Thomas Martin
Director
Office of Policy & Legislative Affairs
P.O. Box 30004
Lansing, MI 48909
P: (517) 241-4580
F: (517) 241-9822
E: tmarti@michigan.gov

Ms. Ruthanne Okun
Director
Bureau of Employment Relations
3026 West Grand Blvd, Ste 2-750
P.O. Box 02988
Detroit, MI 48202
P: (313) 456-3519
F: (313) 456-3511
E: rokun@michigan.gov

MINNESOTA
Mr. James Cunningham
Commissioner
Bureau of Mediation Services
1380 Energy Lane, Suite 2
St. Paul, MN 55108
P: (651) 649-5433
F: (651) 643-3013
E: james.cunningham@state.mn.us

MISSOURI
Mr. William Ringer
Chair
Labor & Industrial Relations Commission
3315 West Truman Boulevard, Room 202
P.O. Box 599
Jefferson City, MO 65102
P: (573) 751-2461
F: (573) 751-7806
E: william.ringer@dolir.mo.gov

MONTANA
Ms. Janet Kelly
Director
Department of Administration
125 North Roberts Street
P.O. Box 200101
Helena, MT 59620
P: (406) 444-3033
F: (406) 444-6194
E: jakelly@mt.gov

NEBRASKA
Ms. Annette Hord
Administrator
Commission of Industrial Relations
P.O. Box 94864
Lincoln, NE 68509
P: (402) 471-2934
F: (402) 471-6597

NEVADA
Ms. Julie Contreras
Commissioner
Local Government Employee - Management Relations Board
2501 East Sahara Avenue
Suite 203
Las Vegas, NV 89104
P: (702) 486-4504
F: (702) 486-4355
E: emrb@dbi.state.nv.us

NEW HAMPSHIRE
Mr. George N. Copadis
Commissioner of Labor
Department of Labor
95 Pleasant Street
Concord, NH 03301
P: (603) 271-3171
F: (603) 271-6852
E: gcopadis@labor.state.nh.us

NEW JERSEY
Mr. David J. Socolow
Commissioner
Department of Labor & Workforce Development
P.O. Box 110
Trenton, NJ 08625
P: (609) 292-2975
F: (609) 633-9271
E: janet.sliwinkski@dol.state.nj.us

NEW MEXICO
Ms. Betty Sparrow Davis
Cabinet Secretary
Department of Labor
401 Broadway, Northeast
P.O. Box 1928
Albuquerque, NM 87103
P: (505) 841-8405
F: (505) 841-8491
E: bdoris@state.nm.us

NEW YORK
Ms. Patricia Smith
Commissioner
Department of Labor
345 Hudson Street
Albany, NY 10014
P: (518) 457-2741
F: (518) 457-6908
E: nysdol@labor.state.ny.us

NORTH CAROLINA
Ms. Cherie K. Berry
Commissioner
Department of Labor
1101 Mail Service Center
4 West Edenton Street
Raleigh, NC 27699
P: (919) 733-7166
F: (919) 733-6197
E: cberry@mail.dol.state.nc.us

NORTH DAKOTA
Ms. Lisa Fair McEvers
Commissioner of Labor
Department of Labor
600 East Boulevard Avenue, Department 406
Bismarck, ND 58505
P: (701) 328-2660
F: (701) 328-2031
E: labor@nd.gov

NORTHERN MARIANA ISLANDS
Mr. Gil M. San Nicolas
Secretary
Department of Labor
Caller Box 10007
Saipan, MP 96950
P: (670) 322-9834
F: (670) 322-2633

OHIO
Mr. Hugh Quill
Director
Department of Administrative Services
30 East Broad Street, Suite 4040
Columbus, OH 43215
P: (614) 466-6511
F: (614) 644-8151
E: hugh.quill@das.state.oh.us

OKLAHOMA
Mr. Lloyd L. Fields
Commissioner of Labor
Department of Labor
4001 North Lincoln Boulevard
Oklahoma City, OK 73105
P: (405) 528-1500
F: (405) 528-5751
E: lfields@oklaosf.state.ok.us

OREGON
Mr. Paul Gamson
Chair
Employment Relations Board
528 Cottage Street, Northeast
Suite 400
Salem, OR 97301
P: (503) 378-3807 Ext. 224
F: (503) 373-0021

PENNSYLVANIA
Mr. Stephen Schmerin
Secretary
Department of Labor & Industry
Labor and Industry Building, Room 1700
Harrisburg, PA 17121
P: (717) 787-5279
F: (717) 787-8826
E: sschmerin@state.pa.us

Arbitration and Mediation

PUERTO RICO
Mr. Roman M. Velasco Gonzalez
Secretary
Department of Labor
Prudencio Rivera-Martinez Building
505 Munoz Rivera Avenue, 21st Floor
Hato Rey, PR 00918
P: (787) 754-2119
F: (787) 753-9550

RHODE ISLAND
Ms. Adelita Orefice
Director
Department of Labor & Training
1511 Pontiac Avenue
Cranston, RI 02920
P: (401) 462-8870
F: (401) 462-8872
E: aorefice@dlt.state.ri.us

SOUTH CAROLINA
Ms. Adrienne R. Youmans
Director
Department of Labor, Licensing & Regulation
P.O. Box 11329
Columbia, SC 29211
P: (803) 896-4300
F: (803) 896-4393
E: youmansa@llr.sc.gov

SOUTH DAKOTA
Ms. Pamela Roberts
Secretary of Labor
Department of Labor
700 Governors Drive
Pierre, SD 57501
P: (605) 773-3101
F: (605) 773-4211
E: pamela.roberts@state.sd.us

TENNESSEE
Mr. James G. Neeley
Commissioner
Department of Labor & Workforce Development
Andrew Johnson Tower, 8th Floor
Nashville, TN 37243
P: (615) 741-6642
F: (615) 741-5078
E: james.neeley@state.tn.us

TEXAS
Mr. Larry Temple
Executive Director
Workforce Commission
TWC Building
101 East 15th Street, Room 618
Austin, TX 78778
P: (512) 463-0735
F: (512) 475-2321
E: larry.temple@twc.state.tx.us

U.S. VIRGIN ISLANDS
Mr. Albert Bryant Jr.
Commissioner
Department of Labor
2203 Church Street
Christiansted, VI 00820
P: (340) 773-1994
F: (340) 773-0094

UTAH
Ms. Sherrie Hayashi
Commissioner
Labor Commission
P.O. Box 146600
Salt Lake City, UT 84114
P: (801) 530-6880
F: (801) 530-6804
E: ahayashi@utah.gov

VERMONT
Mr. Tim Noonan
Executive Director
Labor Relations Board
13 Baldwin Street
Monpelier, VT 05633
P: (802) 828-2700
F: (802) 828-2392
E: tnoonan@lbr.state.vt.us

VIRGINIA
Mr. C. Ray Davenport
Commissioner
Department of Labor & Industry
13 South 13th Street
Richmond, VA 23219
P: (804) 786-2377
F: (804) 371-6524
E: ray.davenport@doli.virginia.gov

WASHINGTON
Ms. Judy Schurke
Acting Director
Department of Labor & Industries
P.O. Box 44001
Olympia, WA 98504
P: (360) 902-4200
F: (360) 902-4202

WEST VIRGINIA
Mr. David M. Mullins
Commissioner
Division of Labor
Bureau of Commerce, Room B-749
State Capitol Complex, Building 6
Charleston, WV 25305
P: (304) 558-7890
F: (304) 558-3797
E: dmullins@labor.state.wv.us

WISCONSIN
Ms. Roberta Gassman
Secretary
Department of Workforce Development
P.O. Box 7946
Madison, WI 53707
P: (608) 267-9692
F: (608) 266-1784
E: roberta.gassman@dwd.state.wi.us

Archives

Identifies, acquires, preserves and makes available state government records of continuing historical and research value.

ALABAMA
Dr. Ed C. Bridges
Director
Department of Archives & History
624 Washington Avenue
Montgomery, AL 36130
P: (334) 242-4441
E: ed.bridges@archives.alabama.gov

ALASKA
Ms. Kay Shelton
Director
Division of Libraries, Archives & Museums
Department of Education
P.O. Box 110571
Juneau, AK 99811
P: (907) 465-2912
F: (907) 465-2151
E: kay_shelton@eed.state.ak.us

ARIZONA
Ms. Gladys Ann Wells
Director
State Library, Archives & Public Records
Archives & Public Records
State Capitol, Room 200
Phoenix, AZ 85007
P: (602) 542-4035
F: (602) 542-4972
E: gawells@lib.az.us

ARKANSAS
Ms. Wendy Richter
State Historian
History Commission
#1 Capitol Mall
Little Rock, AR 72201
P: (501) 682-6900
F: (501) 682-6916
E: wendy.richter@arkansas.gov

CALIFORNIA
Ms. Nancy Zimmelman
Director
State Archives
1020 O Street
Sacramento, CA 95814
P: (916) 653-7715
F: (916) 653-7363

COLORADO
Mr. Terry Ketelsen
State Archivist
Information/Archival Services
1313 Sherman Street
Room 1B-20
Denver, CO 80203
P: (303) 866-2055
F: (303) 866-2257

CONNECTICUT
Mr. Mark Jones
State Archivist
State Library & Archives
231 Capitol Avenue
Hartford, CT 06106
P: (860) 757-6511
F: (860) 757-6542
E: mjones@cslib.org

DELAWARE
Mr. Timothy A. Slavin
State Historic Preservation Officer
Division of Historical & Cultural Affairs
21 The Green
Dover, DE 19901
P: (302) 739-5313
F: (302) 739-6711
E: timothy.slavin@state.de.us

DISTRICT OF COLUMBIA
Hon. Stephanie Scott
Secretary of the District
Office of the Secretary
1350 Pennsylvania Avenue, Northwest
Suite 419
Washington, DC 20004
P: (202) 727-6306
F: (202) 727-3582
E: Stephanie.Scott@dc.gov

FLORIDA
Mr. Jim Berberich
Chief
Bureau of Archives & Records Management
R.A. Gray Building
500 South Bronough Street
Tallahassee, FL 32399
P: (850) 245-6701
F: (850) 488-4894
E: jberberich@dos.state.fl.us

GEORGIA
Mr. David W. Carmichael
Director
The Georgia Archives
5800 Jonesboro Road
Morrow, GA 30260
P: (678) 364-3700

GUAM
Ms. Connie Mendiola
Territorial Librarian
Guam Public Library
254 Martyr Street
Hagatna, GU 96910
P: (671) 475-4751
F: (671) 477-9777

Mr. Antonio M. Palomo
Administrator
Department of Chamorro Affairs
Barracks 13-6 Seagull Avenue
Tiyan
212 Aspinall Avenue
Hagatna, GU 96932
P: (671) 475-4279
F: (671) 475-4227

HAWAII
Ms. Susan E. Shaner
State Archivist
Department of Accounting & General Services
Iolani Palace Grounds
Honolulu, HI 96813
P: (808) 586-0310
F: (808) 586-0330
E: susan.e.shaner@hawaii.gov

IDAHO
Ms. Linda Morton-Keithley
Administrator/Librarian
State Historical Society Library & Archives
450 North 4th Street
Boise, ID 83702
P: (208) 334-5335
F: (208) 334-3198
E: linda.morton-keithley@ishs.idaho.gov

ILLINOIS
Mr. David A. Joens
Executive Director
State Archives
Margaret Cross Norton Building
Capitol Complex
Springfield, IL 62756
P: (217) 782-4682
F: (217) 524-3930

INDIANA
Mr. Alan January
Director
State Archives
6440 East 30th Street
Indianapolis, IN 46219
P: (317) 232-3031
F: (317) 591-5222
E: ajanuary@icpr.in.gov

IOWA
Mr. Gordon Hendrickson
State Archivist & Bureau Chief
State Library
600 East Locust
Des Moines, IA 50319
P: (515) 281-8875
F: (515) 282-0502
E: gordon.hendrickson@iowa.gov

KANSAS
Ms. Patricia Michaelis
State Archivist
State Historical Society
6425 Southwest 6th Avenue
Topeka, KS 66615
P: (785) 272-8681 Ext. 270
F: (785) 272-8682

KENTUCKY
Mr. Richard N. Belding
Director
Public Records Division
Department for Libraries & Archives
300 Coffee Tree Road
Frankfort, KY 40602
P: (502) 564-8300
F: (502) 564-5773
E: richard.belding@ky.gov

LOUISIANA
Dr. Florent Hardy Jr.
State Archivist
Archives & Records Management Division
3851 Essen Lane
Baton Rouge, LA 70809
P: (225) 922-1200
F: (225) 922-0433
E: florent.hardy@sos.louisiana.gov

MAINE
Mr. James Henderson
State Archivist
State Archives
84 State House Station
Augusta, ME 04333
P: (207) 287-5793

MARYLAND
Dr. Edward C. Papenfuse
State Archivist
State Archives
350 Rowe Boulevard
Annapolis, MD 21401
P: (410) 260-6401
E: edp@mdsa.net

Archives

MASSACHUSETTS
Dr. John D. Warner Jr.
Archivist
State Archives
220 Morrissey Boulevard
Boston, MA 02125
P: (617) 727-2816
F: (617) 288-8429

MICHIGAN
Mr. David J. Johnson
State Archivist
State Archives
702 West Kalamazoo Street
P.O. Box 30740
Lansing, MI 48909
P: (517) 373-1408

MINNESOTA
Dr. Nina Archabal
State Historic Preservation Officer
Historical Society
345 Kellogg Boulevard West
St. Paul, MN 55102
P: (651) 296-2747
F: (651) 296-1004

MISSISSIPPI
Mr. H.T. Holmes
State Historic Preservation Officer
Department of Archives & History
P.O. Box 571
Jackson, MS 39205
P: (601) 576-6850
E: hholmes@mdah.state.ms.us

MISSOURI
Dr. Kenneth Winn
State Archivist
State Archives
600 West Main Street
P.O. Box 778
Jefferson City, MO 65102
P: (573) 751-4717
F: (573) 526-3867
E: kenneth.winn@sos.mo.gov

MONTANA
Dr. Mark Baumler
State Historic Preservation Officer
Historical Society
225 North Roberts
P.O. Box 201201
Helena, MT 59620
P: (406) 444-7717
F: (406) 444-2696
E: mbaumler@mt.gov

NEBRASKA
Hon. John A. Gale (R)
Secretary of State
Office of the Secretary of State
1445 K Street, Suite 2300
P.O. Box 94608
Lincoln, NE 68509
P: (402) 471-2554
F: (402) 471-3237
E: secretaryofstate@sos.ne.gov

NEVADA
Mr. Guy Rocha
Interim Administrator & State Librarian
State Library & Archives
100 North Stewart Street
Carson City, NV 89701
P: (775) 684-3317
F: (775) 684-3311
E: glrocha@clan.lib.nv.us

NEW HAMPSHIRE
Mr. Frank C. Mevers
Director & State Archivist
Division of Archives & Records Management
71 South Fruit Street
Concord, NH 03301
P: (603) 271-2236
E: fmevers@sos.state.nh.us

NEW JERSEY
Mr. Karl Niederer
Division Director
Division of Archives & Records Management
225 West State Street, Level 2
P.O. Box 307
Trenton, NJ 08625
P: (609) 530-3299
F: (609) 292-9105
E: Karl.Niederer@sos.state.nj.us

NEW MEXICO
Ms. Sandra Jaramillo
State Records Administrator
State Records Center & Archives
1205 Camino Carlos Rey
Santa Fe, NM 87507
P: (505) 476-7911
F: (505) 476-7901
E: sandra.jaramillo@state.nm.us

NEW YORK
Mr. Richard P. Mills
Commissioner
Education Department
State Education Building
Albany, NY 12234
P: (518) 474-5844
E: rmills@mail.nysed.gov

NORTH CAROLINA
Dr. Jeffrey J. Crow
Deputy Secretary & State Historic Preservation Officer
Division of Archives & History
4610 Mail Service Center
109 East Jones Street
Raleigh, NC 27699
P: (919) 807-7280
F: (919) 733-8807
E: jeff.crow@ncmail.net

NORTH DAKOTA
Mr. Merlan E. Paaverud Jr.
State Historical Preservation Officer
State Historical Society
612 East Boulevard Avenue
Bismarck, ND 58505
P: (701) 328-2666
F: (701) 328-3710
E: mpaaverud@nd.gov

NORTHERN MARIANA ISLANDS
Mr. Herbert S. Del Rosario
Director
NMC Archives
P.O. Box 501250
Saipan, MP 96950
P: (670) 234-7394
F: (670) 234-0759
E: herbertr@nmcnet.edu

OHIO
Mr. William K. Laidlaw Jr.
Director
Historical Society
1982 Velma Avenue
Columbus, OH 43211
P: (614) 297-2300

OKLAHOMA
Mr. Gary Harrington
Division Administrator
Office of Archives & Records
200 North East 18th Street
Oklahoma City, OK 73105
P: (405) 522-3577
F: (405) 525-7804

OREGON
Ms. Mary Beth Herkert
State Archivist
State Archives
800 Summer Street, Northeast
Salem, OR 97301
P: (503) 373-0701 Ext. 237
F: (503) 373-0953
E: reference.archives@state.or.us

PENNSYLVANIA
Ms. Barbara Franco
State Historic Preservation Officer
Historical & Museum Commission
300 North Street
Harrisburg, PA 17120
P: (717) 787-3362
F: (717) 787-9924

RHODE ISLAND
Ms. R. Gwenn Stearn
Archives Director
Public Records
337 Westminster Street
Providence, RI 02903
P: (401) 222-2353
F: (401) 222-3199
E: reference@archives.state.ri.us

SOUTH CAROLINA
Dr. Rodger E. Stroup
State Historic Preservation Officer
Department of Archives & History
8301 Parklane Road
Columbia, SC 29223
P: (803) 896-6187
F: (803) 896-6167

SOUTH DAKOTA
Ms. Marvene Riis
Acting State Archivist
State Historical Society
Cultural Heritage Center
900 Governors Drive
Pierre, SD 57501
P: (605) 773-3804
F: (605) 773-6041
E: marvene.riis@state.sd.us

TENNESSEE
Ms. Jeanne D. Sugg
State Librarian & Archivist
State Library & Archives
403 7th Avenue, North
Nashville, TN 37243
P: (615) 741-7996
F: (615) 532-9293
E: jeanne.sugg@state.tn.us

TEXAS
Mr. Chris La Plante
Director
Archives & Information Services
State Library & Archives Commission
P.O. Box 12927
Austin, TX 78711
P: (512) 463-5480
E: cris.laplante@tsl.state.tx.us

U.S. VIRGIN ISLANDS
Mr. Wallace Williams
Territorial Librarian
Division of Libraries, Archives & Museums
1122 Kings Street
St. Croix, VI 00820
P: (304) 773-5715
E: wallacewilliams@msn.com

UTAH
Ms. Patricia Smith-Mansfield
Director
Division of State Archives
Department of Administrative Services
346 South Rio Grande
Salt Lake City, UT 84101
P: (801) 531-3850
F: (801) 531-3854
E: pmansfie@utah.gov

VERMONT
Mr. D. Gregory Sanford
State Archivist
Office of the Secretary of State
Redstone Bulding
26 Terrace Street
Montpelier, VT 05609
P: (802) 828-2369
F: (802) 828-2496
E: gsanford@sec.state.vt.us

VIRGINIA
Mr. Nolan T. Yelich
State Librarian
The Library of Virginia
800 East Broad Street
Richmond, VA 23219
P: (804) 692-3535
F: (804) 692-3594
E: nyelich@lva.lib.va.us

WASHINGTON
Mr. Jerry Handfield
State Archivist
State Library & Archives
P.O. Box 40238
Olympia, WA 98504
P: (360) 586-2664
F: (360) 664-8814
E: jhandfield@secstate.wa.gov

WEST VIRGINIA
Mr. John Bowyer
Director
Division of Culture & History
Capitol Complex, Cultural Center
Charleston, WV 25305
P: (304) 558-0220
F: (304) 558-2779
E: jbowyer@wvculture.org

WISCONSIN
Mr. Peter Gottlieb
Administrator
Library-Archives Division
816 State Street, Room 300
Madison, WI 53706
P: (608) 264-6480
F: (608) 264-6486
E: pgottlieb@whs.wisc.edu

WYOMING
Mr. Tony Adams
State Archivist
Department of State Parks & Cultural Resources
2301 Central Avenue
Barrett Building
Cheyenne, WY 82002
P: (307) 777-7826
F: (307) 777-3543
E: tadams@state.wy.us

Attorney General

The chief legal officer of the state who represents the state or its offices in all litigation.

ALABAMA
Hon. Troy King (R)
Attorney General
Office of the Attorney General
State House
11 South Union Street
Montgomery, AL 36130
P: (334) 242-7300
F: (334) 242-7458

ALASKA
Hon. Talis J. Colberg (R) (appointed)
Attorney General
Office of the Attorney General
P.O. Box 110300
Juneau, AK 99811
P: (907) 465-2133
F: (907) 465-2075
E: Attorney.General@law.state.ak.us

AMERICAN SAMOA
Hon. Afa Ripley Jr. (appointed)
Attorney General
Office of the Attorney General
American Samoa Government
Executive Office Building, Utulei
Pago Pago, AS 96799
P: (684) 633-4163
F: (684) 633-1838

ARIZONA
Hon. Terry Goddard (D)
Attorney General
Office of the Attorney General
1275 West Washington Street
Phoenix, AZ 85007
P: (602) 542-5025
F: (602) 542-4085
E: ag.inquiries@azag.gov

ARKANSAS
Hon. Dustin McDaniel (D)
Attorney General
Office of the Attorney General
200 Tower Building
323 Center Street
Little Rock, AR 72201
P: (800) 482-8982

CALIFORNIA
Hon. Edmund G. Brown Jr. (D)
Attorney General
Office of the Attorney General
1300 I Street, Suite 1740
Sacramento, CA 95814
P: (916) 445-9555
F: (916) 323-5341

COLORADO
Hon. John Suthers (R)
Attorney General
Office of the Attorney General
1525 Sherman Street
Denver, CO 80203
P: (303) 866-4500
F: (303) 866-4745
E: john.suthers@state.co.us

CONNECTICUT
Hon. Richard Blumenthal (D)
Attorney General
Office of the Attorney General
55 Elm Street
Hartford, CT 06141
P: (860) 808-5318
F: (860) 808-5291

DELAWARE
Hon. Joseph Biden III (D)
Attorney General
Office of the Attorney General
Carvel State Office Building
820 North French Street
Wilmington, DE 19801
P: (302) 577-8338

DISTRICT OF COLUMBIA
Hon. Linda Singer (D) (appointed)
Acting Attorney General
Office of the Attorney General
John A. Wilson Building
1350 Pennsylvania Avenue NW, Suite 407
Washington, DC 20004
P: (202) 724-1305
F: (202) 347-8922

FLORIDA
Hon. Bill McCollum (R)
Attorney General
Office of the Attorney General
The Capitol
PL 01
Tallahassee, FL 32399
P: (850) 414-3300

GEORGIA
Hon. Thurbert E. Baker (D)
Attorney General
Office of the Attorney General
40 Capitol Square, SW
Atlanta, GA 30334
P: (404) 656-3300

GUAM
Hon. Alicia Limtiaco
Attorney General
Office of the Attorney General
Suite 2-200E, Judicial Center Building
120 West O'Brien Drive
Hagatna, GU 96910
P: (671) 475-3409

HAWAII
Hon. Mark J. Bennett (R) (appointed)
Attorney General
Office of the Attorney General
425 Queen Street
Honolulu, HI 96813
P: (808) 586-1500
F: (808) 587-1239

IDAHO
Hon. Lawrence Wasden (R)
Attorney General
Office of the Attorney General
P.O. Box 83720
Boise, ID 83720
P: (208) 334-2400
F: (208) 334-3446

ILLINOIS
Hon. Lisa Madigan (D)
Attorney General
Office of the Attorney General
500 South Second Street
Springfield, IL 62706
P: (217) 782-1090

INDIANA
Hon. Steve Carter (R)
Attorney General
Office of the Attorney General
302 West Washington Street
Indianapolis, IN 46204
P: (317) 232-6201
F: (317) 232-7979

IOWA
Hon. Tom Miller (D)
Attorney General
Office of the Attorney General
1305 East Walnut Street
Des Moines, IA 50319
P: (515) 281-5164
F: (515) 281-4209

KANSAS
Hon. Paul Morrison (D)
Attorney General
Office of the Attorney General
120 Southwest 10th Avenue, 2nd Floor
Topeka, KS 66612
P: (785) 296-2215
F: (785) 296-6296

KENTUCKY
Hon. Gregory D. Stumbo (D)
Attorney General
Office of the Attorney General
700 Capitol Avenue
Suite 118
Frankfort, KY 40601
P: (502) 696-5300
F: (502) 564-2894

LOUISIANA
Hon. Charles C. Foti Jr. (D)
Attorney General
Office of the Attorney General
P.O. Box 94095
Baton Rouge, LA 70804
P: (225) 342-7013
F: (225) 342-7335

MAINE
Hon. G. Steven Rowe (D)
Attorney General
Office of the Attorney General
State House Station 6
Augusta, ME 04333
P: (207) 626-8800

MARYLAND
Hon. Douglas F. Gansler (D)
Attorney General
Office of the Attorney General
200 Saint Paul Place
Baltimore, MD 21202
P: (410) 576-6300

MASSACHUSETTS
Hon. Martha Coakley (D)
Attorney General
Office of the Attorney General
One Ashburton Place
Boston, MA 02108
P: (617) 727-2200

MICHIGAN
Hon. Michael Cox (R)
Attorney General
Office of the Attorney General
P.O. Box 30212
525 West Ottawa Street
Lansing, MI 48909
P: (517) 373-1110
F: (517) 335-4213

MINNESOTA
Hon. Lori Swanson (DFL)
Attorney General
Office of the Attorney General
State Capitol, Suite 102
St. Paul, MN 55155
P: (651) 296-3353
F: (651) 297-4193
E: attorney.general@state.mn.us

MISSISSIPPI
Hon. Jim Hood (D)
Attorney General
Office of the Attorney General
Carroll Gastin Justice Building
450 High Street
Jackson, MS 39201
P: (601) 359-3680
E: msag05@ago.state.ms.us

MISSOURI
Hon. Jay Nixon (D)
Attorney General
Office of the Attorney General
207 West High Street
P.O. Box 899
Jefferson City, MO 65102
P: (573) 751-3321
F: (573) 751-0774
E: ag@ago.mo.gov

MONTANA
Hon. Mike McGrath (D)
Attorney General
Office of the Attorney General
Department of Justice
P.O. Box 201401
Helena, MT 59620
P: (406) 444-2026
F: (404) 444-3549
E: contactdoj@mt.gov

NEBRASKA
Hon. Jon C. Bruning (R)
Attorney General
Office of the Attorney General
State Capitol
P.O. Box 98920
Lincoln, NE 68509
P: (402) 471-2682
F: (402) 471-3297

NEVADA
Hon. Catherine Cortez Masto (D)
Attorney General
Office of the Attorney General
100 North Carson Street
Carson City, NV 89701
P: (775) 684-1100
F: (775) 684-1108

NEW HAMPSHIRE
Hon. Kelly Ayotte (R) (appointed)
Attorney General
Office of the Attorney General
State House Annex
33 Capitol Street
Concord, NH 03301
P: (603) 271-3658
F: (603) 271-2110

NEW JERSEY
Hon. Stuart Rabner (D) (appointed)
Attorney General
Office of the Attorney General
Richard J. Hughes Justice Complex
25 Market Street, CN 080
Trenton, NJ 08625
P: (609) 292-8740

NEW MEXICO
Hon. Gary K. King (D)
Attorney General
Office of the Attorney General
P.O. Drawer 1508
408 Galisteo Street, Villagra Building
Santa Fe, NM 87504
P: (505) 827-6000
F: (505) 827-5826

NEW YORK
Hon. Andrew M. Cuomo (D)
Attorney General
Office of the Attorney General
The Capitol
Albany, NY 12224
P: (518) 474-7330

NORTH CAROLINA
Hon. Roy A. Cooper III (D)
Attorney General
Office of the Attorney General
Department of Justice
P.O. Box 629
Raleigh, NC 27602
P: (919) 716-6400
F: (919) 716-6750

NORTH DAKOTA
Hon. Wayne Stenehjem (R)
Attorney General
Office of the Attorney General
State Capitol
600 East Boulevard Avenue, Dept. 125
Bismarck, ND 58505
P: (701) 328-2210
F: (701) 328-2226
E: ndag@nd.gov

NORTHERN MARIANA ISLANDS
Hon. Matthew T. Gregory
Attorney General
Office of the Attorney General
Capitol Hil, Caller Box 10007
Saipan, MP 95960
P: (670) 664-2341
F: (670) 664-2349
E: matt@gregoryfirm.com

OHIO
Hon. Marc Dann (D)
Attorney General
Office of the Attorney General
30 East Broad Street
17th Floor
Columbus, OH 43215
P: (614) 466-4320

OKLAHOMA
Hon. W.A. Drew Edmondson (D)
Attorney General
Office of the Attorney General
State Capitol, Room 112
2300 North Lincoln Boulevard
Oklahoma City, OK 73105
P: (405) 521-3921
F: (405) 521-6246

OREGON
Hon. Hardy Myers (D)
Attorney General
Office of the Attorney General
Justice Building
1162 Court Street, Northeast
Salem, OR 97301
P: (503) 378-4732
F: (503) 378-4017

PENNSYLVANIA
Hon. Tom Corbett (R)
Attorney General
Office of the Attorney General
16th Floor
Strawberry Square
Harrisburg, PA 17120
P: (717) 787-3391
F: (717) 787-8242

PUERTO RICO
Hon. Roberto J. Sanchez-Ramos
Attorney General
Office of the Attorney General
G.P.O. Box 902192
San Juan, PR 00902
P: (787) 721-2900
F: (787) 724-4770

RHODE ISLAND
Hon. Patrick C. Lynch (D)
Attorney General
Office of the Attorney General
150 South Main Street
Providence, RI 02903
P: (401) 274-4400

SOUTH CAROLINA
Hon. Henry D. McMaster (R)
Attorney General
Office of the Attorney General
Rembert C. Dennis Office Building
P.O. Box 11549
Columbia, SC 29211
P: (803) 734-3970
F: (803) 734-4323

SOUTH DAKOTA
Hon. Larry Long (R)
Attorney General
Office of the Attorney General
1302 East Highway 14, Suite 1
Pierre, SD 57501
P: (605) 773-3215
F: (605) 773-4106
E: larry.long@state.sd.us

TENNESSEE
Hon. Robert E. Cooper (appointed)
Attorney General
Office of the Attorney General
500 Charlotte Avenue
Nashville, TN 37243
P: (615) 741-5860

TEXAS
Hon. Greg Abbott (R)
Attorney General
Office of the Attorney General
P.O. Box 12548
Austin, TX 78711
P: (512) 463-2100
F: (512) 475-4433

U.S. VIRGIN ISLANDS
Hon. Vincent Frazer (appointed)
Acting Attorney General
Office of the Attorney General
Department of Justice, G.E.R.S. Complex
488-50C Kronprinsdens Gade
St. Thomas, VI 00802
P: (340) 774-5666
F: (340) 774-9710

UTAH
Hon. Mark L. Shurtleff (R)
Attorney General
Office of the Attorney General
State Capitol Complex, Suite E320
Salt Lake City, UT 84114
P: (801) 538-1191
F: (801) 538-1121
E: MSHURTLEFF@utah.gov

Attorney General

VERMONT
Hon. William H. Sorrell (D)
Attorney General
Office of the Attorney General
109 State Street
Montpelier, VT 05609
P: (802) 828-3173
F: (802) 828-3187

VIRGINIA
Hon. Robert F. McDonnell (R)
Attorney General
Office of the Attorney General
900 East Main Street
Richmond, VA 23219
P: (804) 786-2071
E: mail@oag.state.va.us

WASHINGTON
Hon. Rob McKenna (R)
Attorney General
Office of the Attorney General
1125 Washington Street, Southeast
P.O. Box 40100
Olympia, WA 98504
P: (360) 753-6200
F: (360) 664-0228

WEST VIRGINIA
Hon. Darrell V. McGraw Jr. (D)
Attorney General
Office of the Attorney General
Room 26E, 1900 Kanawha Boulevard, East
Charleston, WV 25305
P: (304) 558-2021
F: (304) 558-0140

WISCONSIN
Hon. J.B. Van Hollen (R)
Attorney General
Office of the Attorney General
State Capitol
P.O. Box 7857
Madison, WI 53707
P: (608) 266-1221

WYOMING
Hon. Patrick J. Crank (D) (appointed)
Attorney General
Office of the Attorney General
State Capitol Building
Cheyenne, WY 82002
P: (307) 777-7841
F: (307) 777-6869

Auditor

Determines that governmental funds are handled appropriately and assesses how effectively government organizations are achieving their purposes.

Information provided by:

National Association of State Auditors, Comptrollers & Treasurers
Kinney Poynter
Executive Director
449 Lewis Hargett Circle
Suite 290
Lexington, KY 40503
P: (859) 276-1147
F: (859) 278-0507
kpoynter@nasact.org
www.nasact.org

ALABAMA
Mr. Ronald L. Jones
Chief Examiner
Office of the Examiner of Public Accounts
50 North Ripley Street, Room 3201
Montgomery, AL 36104
P: (334) 242-9200
F: (334) 242-4570
E: ron.jones@examiners.state.al.us

Hon. S. Samantha Shaw (R)
State Auditor
Office of the State Auditor
State Capitol, Room S-101
600 Dexter Avenue
Montgomery, AL 36130
P: (334) 242-7010
F: (334) 242-7650
E: sam.shaw@auditor.alabama.gov

ALASKA
Ms. Pat Davidson
Legislative Auditor
Division of Legislative Audit
P.O. Box 113300
Juneau, AK 99811
P: (907) 465-3830
F: (907) 465-2347
E: pat_davidson@legis.state.ak.us

Ms. Kristin Kay Dzinich
In Charge Auditor
Division of Legislative Audit
P.O. Box 113300
Juneau, AK 99811
P: (907) 465-3830
E: kristin_dzinich@legis.state.ak.us

ARIZONA
Ms. Debra K. Davenport
Auditor General
Office of the Auditor General
2910 North 44th Street,
Phoenix, AZ 85018
P: (602) 553-0333
F: (602) 553-0051
E: ddavenport@auditorgen.state.az.us

ARKANSAS
Mr. Roger Norman
Office of the Legislative Auditor
172 State Capitol
Little Rock, AR 72201
P: (602) 604-7800
E: rnorman@lapo.state.ar.us

CALIFORNIA
Ms. Elaine M. Howle
State Auditor
Bureau of State Audits
555 Capitol Mall, Suite 300
Sacramento, CA 95814
P: (916) 445-0255
F: (916) 322-7801
E: elaineh@bsa.ca.gov

COLORADO
Ms. Sally Symanski
State Auditor
Office of the State Auditor
Legislative Service Building
200 East 14th Avenue
Denver, CO 80203
P: (303) 869-2800
F: (303) 869-3060
E: sally.symanski@state.co.us

CONNECTICUT
Hon. Robert G. Jaekle
Auditor of Public Accounts
Office of the Auditors of Public Accounts
Room 114, State Capitol Building
Hartford, CT 06106
P: (860) 240-8653
F: (860) 240-8655
E: robert.jaekle@po.state.ct.us

Hon. Kevin P. Johnston
Auditor of Public Accounts
Office of the Auditors of Public Accounts
Room 116, State Capitol Building
Hartford, CT 06106
P: (860) 240-8651
F: (860) 240-8655
E: kevin.johnston@po.state.ct.us

DELAWARE
Hon. R. Thomas Wagner Jr. (R)
Auditor of Accounts
Office of the Auditor of Accounts
Townsend Building, Suite 1
401 Federal Street
Dover, DE 19901
P: (302) 739-4241
F: (302) 739-6707
E: rwagner@state.de.us

DISTRICT OF COLUMBIA
Ms. Deborah Kay Nichols
Auditor
Office of the Auditor
717 14th Street, Northwest, Suite 900
Washington, DC 20005
P: (202) 727-3600
E: Deborah.Nichols@dc.gov

FLORIDA
Mr. Haesun Baek
Lead Senior Auditor
Office of the Auditor General
111 West Madison Street
Tallahassee, FL 32399
P: (850) 487-9183
E: haesunbaek@aud.state.fl.us

Mr. David A. Blanton
Audit Supervisor
Office of the Auditor General
5015 South Florida Avenue, Suite 406
Lakeland, FL 33813
P: (863) 648-3165
E: davidblanton@aud.state.fl.us

Ms. Cheryl Jones
Auditor
Auditor General Office
111 West Madison Street
Tallahassee, FL 32399
P: (850) 487-9108
E: cheryljones@aud.state.fl.us

Mr. William O. Monroe
Auditor General
Office of the Auditor General
G74 Pepper Building
111 West Madison Street
Tallahassee, FL 32399
P: (850) 488-5534
F: (850) 488-6975
E: billmonroe@aud.state.fl.us

Ms. Cheryl B. Pueschel
Audit Supervisor
Office of the Auditor General
111 West Madison Street
Tallahassee, FL 32399
P: (850) 488-7435
E: cherylpueschel@aud.state.fl.us

Mr. David R. Vick
Audit Manager
Office of the Auditor General
111 West Madison Street
Tallahassee, FL 32399
P: (850) 487-9183
E: davidvick@aud.state.fl.us

GEORGIA
Mr. Russell W. Hinton
State Auditor
Department of Audits & Accounts
270 Washington Street, SW
Suite 1-156
Atlanta, GA 30334
P: (404) 656-0493
F: (404) 657-5538
E: hintonrw@audits.ga.gov

GUAM
Ms. Doris Flores Brooks
Public Auditor
Office of the Public Auditor
Suite 401 Pacific News Building
238 Archbishop Flores Street
Hagatna, GU 96910
P: (671) 475-0390
F: (671) 472-7951
E: dfbrooks@guamopa.org

HAWAII
Ms. Marion M. Higa
State Auditor
Office of the Auditor
465 South King Street, Room 500
Honolulu, HI 96813
P: (808) 587-0800
F: (808) 587-0830
E: mmhiga@auditor.state.hi.us

Auditor

IDAHO
Mr. Don Berg
Supervisor, Legislative Audits
Office of Legislative Audits
Legislative Services
P.O. Box 83720
Boise, ID 83720
P: (208) 334-2475
F: (208) 334-2125
E: dberg@lso.idaho.gov

Mr. Rakesh Mohan
Director
Office of Performance Evaluations
700 West State Street, Suite 10
Boise, ID 83720
P: (208) 334-3880
F: (208) 334-3871
E: rmohan@ope.state.id.us

ILLINOIS
Mr. Andrew Gottschalk
Partner
KPMG LLP
303 East Wacker Drive
Chicago, IL 60601
P: (312) 665-2883
E: agottschalk@kpmg.com

Hon. William G. Holland
Auditor General
Office of the Auditor General
Iles Park Plaza
740 East Ash Street
Springfield, IL 62703
P: (217) 782-3536
F: (217) 785-8222
E: oag49@mail.state.il.us

INDIANA
Mr. Bruce Hartman
State Examiner
State Board of Accounts
302 West Washington Street
Room E-418
Indianapolis, IN 46204
P: (317) 232-2524
F: (317) 232-4711
E: bhartman@sboa.in.gov

Mr. James P. Sperlik
Office of Fiscal Management & Analysis
Legislative Services Agency
302 State House
Indianapolis, IN 46204
P: (317) 232-9866
F: (317) 232-2554
E: jsperlik@iga.state.in.us

IOWA
Hon. David A. Vaudt (R)
Auditor of State
Office of the Auditor of State
State Capitol
1007 East Grand Avenue
Des Moines, IA 50319
P: (515) 281-5835
F: (515) 242-6134
E: david.vaudt@auditor.state.ia.us

KANSAS
Ms. Barbara J. Hinton
Legislative Post Auditor
Office of the Legislative Post Auditor
FirStar Building, Suite 1200
801 Southwest Jackson Street
Topeka, KS 66612
P: (785) 296-3792
F: (785) 296-4482
E: barbh@lpa.state.ks.us

KENTUCKY
Mr. Gregory Giesler
Administrative Branch Manager
Auditor of Public Accounts
105 Sea Hero Road, Suite 2
Frankfort, KY 40601
P: (502) 573-0050
E: gregory.giesler@auditor.ky.gov

Ms. Jennifer M. Harper
Audit Manager
Auditor of Public Accounts
105 Sea Hero Road, Suite 2
Frankfort, KY 40601
P: (502) 573-0050
E: jenniferm.harper@auditor.ky.gov

Hon. Crit Luallen
State Auditor
Office of the Auditor of Public Accounts
105 Sea Hero Road, Suite 2
Frankfort, KY 40601
P: (502) 573-0050
F: (502) 573-0067
E: crit.luallen@auditor.ky.gov

LOUISIANA
Ms. Jennifer Rabalais
Office of the Legislative Auditor
P.O. Box 94397
Baton Rouge, LA 70804
P: (225) 339-3800
E: jrabalais@lla.state.la.us

Mr. Steve J. Theriot
Legislative Auditor
Office of the Legislative Auditor
P.O. Box 94397
1600 North 3rd Street
Baton Rouge, LA 70804
P: (225) 339-3839
F: (225) 339-3870
E: stheriot@lla.state.la.us

MAINE
Hon. Neria R. Douglass (D)
State Auditor
Department of Audit
66 State House Station
Augusta, ME 04333
P: (207) 624-6250
F: (207) 624-6273
E: neria.r.douglass@maine.gov

MARYLAND
Mr. Bruce A. Myers
Legislative Auditor
Office of Legislative Audits
301 West Preston Street, Room 1202
Baltimore, MD 21201
P: (410) 946-5900
F: (410) 946-5998
E: bmyers@ola.state.md.us

MASSACHUSETTS
Hon. A. Joseph DeNucci (D)
Auditor of the Commonwealth
Office of the Auditor of the Commonwealth
State House, Room 229
Boston, MA 02133
P: (617) 727-2075
F: (617) 727-2383
E: edward.palladino@sao.state.ma.us

MICHIGAN
Hon. Thomas H. McTavish
Auditor General
Office of the Auditor General
201 North Washington Square
Suite 600, Victor Center
Lansing, MI 48913
P: (517) 334-8050
F: (517) 334-8079
E: mctavist@michigan.gov

MINNESOTA
Mr. James Nobles
Legislative Auditor
Office of the Legislative Auditor
Centennial Office Building, Room 140
658 Cedar Street, 1st Floor South
St. Paul, MN 55155
P: (651) 296-4710
F: (651) 296-4712
E: james.nobles@state.mn.us

Hon. Rebecca Otto (DFL)
State Auditor
Office of the State Auditor
525 Park Street, Suite 500
St. Paul, MN 55103
P: (615) 296-2524
F: (615) 296-4755
E: stateauditor@osa.state.mn.us

MISSISSIPPI
Mr. Max Arinder
Executive Director
Joint Committee on Performance Evaluation & Expenditure Review
P.O. Box 1204
Jackson, MS 39215
P: (601) 359-1226
F: (601) 359-1420
E: arinder@peer.state.ms.us

Hon. Phil Bryant (R)
State Auditor
Office of the State Auditor
P.O. Box 956
Jackson, MS 39201
P: (601) 576-2641
F: (601) 576-2687
E: phil@osa.state.ms.us

MISSOURI
Hon. Susan Montee (D)
State Auditor
Office of the State Auditor
State Capitol, Room 224
P.O. Box 869
Jefferson City, MO 65102
P: (573) 751-4824
F: (573) 751-7984
E: susan.montee@auditor.mo.gov

MONTANA
Mr. Scott A. Seacat
Legislative Auditor
Office of Legislative Audits
Room 160, State Capitol Building
P.O. Box 201705
Helena, MT 59620
P: (406) 444-3200
F: (406) 444-9784
E: sseacat@state.mt.us

NEBRASKA
Hon. Mike Foley (R)
State Auditor
Office of the Auditor of Public Accounts
Room 2303, State Capitol
Lincoln, NE 68509
P: (402) 471-2111
F: (402) 471-3301
E: mike.foley@apa.ne.gov

NEVADA
Mr. Paul Townsend
Legislative Auditor
Legislative Counsel Bureau
Audit Division
401 South Carson Street
Carson City, NV 89701
P: (775) 684-6815
E: townsend@lcb.state.nv.us

NEW HAMPSHIRE
Mr. Michael L. Buckley
Legislative Budget Assistant
Legislative Budget Office
Room 102, State House
107 North Main Street
Concord, NH 03301
P: (603) 271-2389
F: (603) 271-1097
E: mike.buckley@leg.state.nh.us

NEW JERSEY
Hon. Richard L. Fair
State Auditor
Office of the State Auditor
P.O. Box 067
Trenton, NJ 08625
P: (609) 292-1259
F: (609) 633-0834
E: rfair@njleg.org

Mr. Ken George Kramli
Principal Auditor
Office of the State Auditor
125 South Warren Street
Trenton, NJ 08625
P: (609) 292-3700
E: kkramli@njleg.org

NEW MEXICO
Hon. Hector H. Balderas (D)
State Auditor
Office of the State Auditor
2113 Warner Circle
Santa Fe, NM 87505
P: (505) 827-3500
F: (505) 827-3512
E: hector.balderas@osa.state.nm.us

Mr. Manu Patel
Performance Audit Manager
Legislative Finance Committee
325 Don Gaspar
Santa Fe, NM 87501
P: (505) 986-4550
F: (505) 986-4644
E: manu.patel@nmlegis.gov

NEW YORK
Hon. Lynn Canton
Deputy Comptroller
Office of the State Comptroller
110 State Street, 11th Floor, SAB
Albany, NY 12236
P: (518) 474-3271
F: (518) 473-6012
E: lcanton@osc.state.ny.us

Hon. Tom Sanzillo
Acting Comptroller
Office of the State Comptroller
110 State Street
Albany, NY 12236
P: (518) 474-4044

NORTH CAROLINA
Hon. Leslie W. Merritt Jr. (R)
State Auditor
Office of the State Auditor
2 South Salisbury Street
20601 Mail Service Center
Raleigh, NC 27699
P: (919) 807-7526
F: (919) 807-7668
E: Les_Merritt@ncauditor.net

NORTH DAKOTA
Hon. Robert R. Peterson (R)
State Auditor
Office of the State Auditor
State Capitol
600 East Boulevard, 3rd Floor
Bismarck, ND 58505
P: (701) 328-2241
F: (701) 328-1406
E: rpeterso@state.nd.us

Mr. Jim Smith
Legislative Budget Analyst & Auditor
Office of Legislative Budget Analyst & Auditor
State Capitol Building
600 East Boulevard Avenue
Bismarck, ND 58501
P: (701) 328-2916
F: (701) 328-3615
E: jsmith@state.nd.us

OHIO
Hon. Mary Taylor (R)
Auditor of State
Office of the Auditor of State
88 East Broad Street, 5th Floor
P.O. Box 1140
Columbus, OH 43216
P: (614) 466-4514
E: mtaylor@auditor.state.oh.us

OKLAHOMA
Hon. Jeff McMahan (D)
State Auditor & Inspector
Office of the State Auditor & Inspector
State Capitol, Room 100
2300 North Lincoln
Oklahoma City, OK 73105
P: (405) 521-3495
F: (405) 522-3126
E: auditor@sai.state.ok.us

OREGON
Mr. Charles A. Hibner
Director
Division of Audits
255 Capitol Street, Northeast, Suite 500
Salem, OR 97310
P: (503) 986-2283
F: (503) 378-6767
E: charles.a.hibner@state.or.us

PENNSYLVANIA
Mr. Philip R. Durgin
Executive Director
Legislative Budget & Finance Committee
400A Finance Building
P.O. Box 8737
Harrisburg, PA 17105
P: (717) 783-1600
F: (717) 787-5487
E: pdurgin@lbfc.legis.state.pa.us

Hon. Jack Wagner (D)
Auditor General
Department of the Auditor General
229 Finance Building
Harrisburg, PA 17120
P: (717) 787-2543
F: (717) 783-4407
E: auditorgen@auditorgen.state.pa.us

PUERTO RICO
Mr. Manuel Diaz-Saldana
Comptroller
Office of the Comptroller
P.O. Box 366069
San Juan, PR 00936
P: (787) 250-3300
F: (787) 751-6768
E: ocpr@ocpr.gov.pr

RHODE ISLAND
Mr. Ernest A. Almonte
Auditor General
Office of the Auditor General
86 Weybosset Street
Providence, RI 02903
P: (401) 222-2435
F: (401) 222-2111
E: ernest.almonte@oag.ri.gov

SOUTH CAROLINA
Hon. Richard H. Gilbert Jr.
Deputy State Auditor
Office of the State Auditor
1401 Main Street, Suite 1200
Columbia, SC 29201
P: (803) 253-4160
E: rgilbert@osa.state.sc.us

Mr. George L. Schroeder
Director
Legislative Audit Council
133 Elmwood Avenue, Suite 315
Columbia, SC 29201
P: (803) 253-7612
F: (803) 253-7639
E: gschroeder@sclac.state.sc.us

SOUTH DAKOTA
Mr. Martin Guindon
Auditor General
Department of Legislative Audit
427 South Chapelle
C/O 500 East Capitol
Pierre, SD 57501
P: (605) 773-3595
F: (605) 773-6454
E: marty.guindon@state.sd.us

Auditor

TENNESSEE
Mr. John G. Morgan
Comptroller of the Treasury
Office of the Comptroller of the Treasury
State Capitol, First Floor
Nashville, TN 37243
P: (615) 741-2501
F: (615) 741-7328
E: john.morgan@state.tn.us

TEXAS
Mr. John Keel
State Auditor
Office of the State Auditor
1501 North Congress, 4th Floor
P.O. Box 12067
Austin, TX 78701
P: (512) 936-9500
F: (512) 936-9400

UTAH
Hon. Auston G. Johnson (R)
State Auditor
Office of the State Auditor
East Office Building, Suite E310
P.O. Box 142310
Salt Lake City, UT 84114
P: (801) 538-1361
F: (801) 538-1383
E: austonjohnson@utah.gov

Mr. John Schaff
Auditor General
Office of the Legislative Auditor General
W315 State Capitol Complex
P.O. Box 140151
Salt Lake City, UT 84114
P: (801) 538-1033
F: (801) 538-1063
E: jschaff@utah.gov

VERMONT
Hon. Thomas M. Salmon (D)
State Auditor
Office of the Auditor of Accounts
132 State Street
Montpelier, VT 05602
P: (802) 828-2281
F: (802) 828-2198
E: tom.salmon@state.vt.us

VIRGINIA
Hon. Walter J. Kucharski
Auditor of Public Accounts
Office of the Auditor of Public Accounts
P.O. Box 1295
Richmond, VA 23218
P: (804) 225-3350
F: (804) 225-3357
E: walter.kucharski@apa.virginia.gov

Mr. Phil Leone
Director
Joint Legislative Audit & Review Commission
910 Capitol Street, Suite 111
Richmond, VA 23219
P: (804) 786-1258
F: (804) 371-0101
E: phil.leone@leg.virginia.gov

WASHINGTON
Ms. Ruta Fanning
Legislative Auditor
Office of the Legislative Auditor
506 16th Avenue, Southeast
Olympia, WA 98501
P: (360) 786-5171
F: (360) 786-5180
E: fanning.ruta@leg.wa.gov

Hon. Brian Sonntag (D)
State Auditor
Office of the State Auditor
P.O. Box 40021
Olympia, WA 98504
P: (360) 902-0360
F: (360) 753-0646
E: sonntagb@sao.wa.gov

WEST VIRGINIA
Mr. Thedford L. Shanklin
Director
Office of the Legislative Auditor
State Capitol Complex, Building 1
Room 329 West
Charleston, WV 25305
P: (304) 347-4880
F: (304) 347-4889
E: tshankli@mail.wvnet.edu

WISCONSIN
Ms. Janice L. Mueller
State Auditor
Legislative Audit Bureau
22 East Mifflin Street, Suite 500
Madison, WI 53703
P: (608) 266-2818
F: (608) 267-0410
E: janice.mueller@legis.state.wi.us

WYOMING
Mr. Michael Geesey
Director/Administrator
Department of Audit
Herschler Building, 3rd Floor, East Wing
Cheyenne, WY 82002
P: (307) 777-5312
F: (307) 777-5341
E: probinson@wyaudit.state.wy.us

Banking

Administers laws regulating the operation of banking institutions in the state.

ALABAMA
Mr. John Harrison
Director
Banking Department
401 Adams Avenue, Suite 680
Montgomery, AL 36130
P: (334) 242-3585
F: (334) 242-3500
E: john.harrison@banking.alabama.gov

ALASKA
Mr. Mark R. Davis
Director
Department of Commerce, Community & Economic Development
Banking, Securities & Corporations
P.O. Box 110807
Juneau, AK 99811
P: (907) 465-2521
F: (907) 465-2549

AMERICAN SAMOA
Mr. Vaivao Logotaeao Etelagi
President
Development Bank of American Samoa
P.O. Box 9
Pago Pago, AS 96799
P: (684) 633-4031
F: (684) 633-1163

ARIZONA
Mr. Tom Wood
Manager
Banks, Trust Companies & Savings and Loans
Financial Institutions Division
2910 North 44th Street, Suite 310
Phoenix, AZ 85018
P: (602) 255-4421
F: (602) 381-1225

ARKANSAS
Mr. Robert Adcock Jr.
Commissioner
Securities Department
400 Hardin, Suite 100
Little Rock, AR 72211
P: (501) 324-9019
F: (501) 324-9028
E: bunnya@banking.state.ar.us

CALIFORNIA
Mr. Michael A. Kelley
Commissioner
Department of Financial Institutions
111 Pine Street, Suite 1100
San Francisco, CA 94111
P: (415) 263-8507
F: (415) 989-5310

COLORADO
Mr. Richard Fulkerson
Commissioner
Division of Banking
1560 Broadway
Suite 1175
Denver, CO 80202
P: (303) 894-7575
F: (303) 894-7570
E: richard.fulkerson@dora.state.co.us

CONNECTICUT
Mr. Howard Pitkin
Commissioner
Department of Banking
260 Constitution Plaza
Hartford, CT 06103
P: (860) 240-8100
F: (860) 240-8178

DELAWARE
Mr. Robert A. Glen
Commissioner
Office of State Banks
555 East Lockerman Street, Suite 210
Dover, DE 19901
P: (302) 739-4235
F: (302) 739-3609

DISTRICT OF COLUMBIA
Mr. Lawrence H. Mirel
Director
Department of Insurance, Securities & Banking
810 1st Street, Northeast
Suite 701
Washington, DC 20002
P: (202) 442-7773
F: (202) 535-1196

FLORIDA
Hon. Alex Sink (D)
Chief Financial Officer
Department of Financial Services
Fletcher Building, Suite 516
200 East Gaines Street
Tallahassee, FL 32399
P: (850) 413-2850
F: (850) 413-2950
E: alex.sink@fldfs.com

GEORGIA
Mr. Rob Braswell
Commissioner
Department of Banking & Finance
2990 Brandywine Road, Suite 200
Atlanta, GA 30341
P: (770) 986-1621
F: (770) 986-1655
E: robertb@dbf.state.ga.us

GUAM
Mr. Artemio B. Illagan
Acting Director
Department of Revenue & Taxation
13-1 Mariner Drive, Tiyan
P.O. Box 23607
Barrigada, GU 96921
P: (671) 475-1817
F: (671) 472-2643

HAWAII
Mr. Dominic B. Griffin III
Commissioner
Division of Financial Institutions
335 Merchant Street
Room 221
Honolulu, HI 96813
P: (808) 586-2820
F: (808) 586-2818

IDAHO
Mr. Gavin Gee
Director
Department of Finance
700 West State Street, 2nd Floor
Boise, ID 83702
P: (208) 332-8010
F: (208) 332-8097
E: gavin.gee@finance.idaho.gov

ILLINOIS
Mr. D. Lorenzo Padron
Director
Division of Banking
310 South Michigan Avenue, Suite 2130
Chicago, IL 60604
P: (312) 793-1418
F: (312) 793-0756
E: DLPadron@idfpr.com

INDIANA
Ms. Judith Ripley
Director
Department of Financial Institutions
30 South Meridian Street, Suite 300
Indianapolis, IN 46204
P: (317) 232-3955
F: (317) 232-7655
E: jripley@dfi.state.in.us

IOWA
Mr. Thomas B. Gronstal
Superintendent
Division of Banking
200 East Grand Avenue, Suite 300
Des Moines, IA 50309
P: (515) 281-4014
F: (515) 281-4862

KANSAS
Mr. Tom Thull
Commissioner
Office of the State Banking Commissioner
700 Southwest Jackson Street, Suite 300
Topeka, KS 66603
P: (785) 296-2266
F: (785) 296-0168

KENTUCKY
Mr. Cordell Lawrence
Executive Director
Office of Financial Institutions
1025 Capital Center Drive
Frankfort, KY 40601
P: (502) 573-3390
F: (502) 573-0086
E: cordell.lawrence@ky.gov

LOUISIANA
Mr. John P. Ducrest
Commissioner
Office of Financial Institutions
8660 United Plaza Boulevard, 2nd Floor
Baton Rouge, LA 70809
P: (225) 925-4660
F: (225) 925-4548
E: ofila@ofi.state.la.us

MAINE
Mr. Howard Gray
Superintendent
Bureau of Banking
36 State House Station
Augusta, ME 04333
P: (207) 624-8648

MARYLAND
Mr. Charles W. Turnbaugh
Commissioner of Financial Regulation
Department of Labor, Licensing & Regulation
500 North Calvert Street
Room 402
Baltimore, MD 21202
P: (410) 230-6100
F: (410) 333-0475
E: cturnbaugh@dllr.state.md.us

Banking

MASSACHUSETTS
Mr. Steven Antonakes
Commissioner
Division of Banks
1 South Station, 3rd Floor
Boston, MA 02110
P: (617) 956-1500
F: (617) 956-1599

MICHIGAN
Ms. Linda A. Watters
Commissioner
Office of Financial & Insurance Services
Department of Labor & Economic Growth
611 West Ottawa Street, Third Floor
Lansing, MI 48933
P: (877) 999-6442
F: (517) 241-3953
E: ofis-sec-info@michigan.gov

MINNESOTA
Mr. Glenn Wilson
Commissioner
Department of Commerce
85 7th Place East, Suite 500
St. Paul, MN 55101
P: (651) 296-6025
F: (651) 282-2568
E: glenn.wilson@state.mn.us

MISSISSIPPI
Mr. John S. Allison
Commissioner
Department of Banking & Consumer Finance
501 North West Street
901 Woolfolk Building, Suite A
Jackson, MS 39202
P: (601) 359-1031
F: (601) 359-3557
E: jallison@dbcf.state.ms.us

MISSOURI
Mr. Eric McClure
Commissioner
Division of Finance
Truman Building, Room 630
P.O. Box 716
Jefferson City, MO 65102
P: (573) 751-2545
F: (573) 751-9192
E: eric.mcclure@ded.mo.gov

MONTANA
Ms. Annie Goodwin
Commissioner
Division of Banking & Financial Institutions
P.O. Box 200546
301 South Park, Suite 316
Helena, MT 59620
P: (406) 841-2920
F: (406) 841-2930
E: angoodwin@mt.gov

NEBRASKA
Mr. John Munn
Director
Department of Banking
P.O. Box 95006
Lincoln, NE 68509
P: (402) 471-2171
E: john.munn@bkg.state.ne.us

NEVADA
Mr. Steven Kondrup
Acting Commissioner
Financial Institutions Division
2501 East Sahara Avenue
Suite 300
Las Vegas, NV 89104
P: (702) 486-4120
F: (702) 486-4563
E: skondrup@fid.state.nv.us

NEW HAMPSHIRE
Mr. Peter C. Hildreth
Commissioner
Banking Department
64 B Old Suncook Road
Concord, NH 03301
P: (603) 271-3561
F: (603) 271-1090
E: phildreth@banking.state.nh.us

NEW JERSEY
Mr. Steven M. Goldman
Commissioner
Department of Banking & Insurance
P.O. Box 325
Trenton, NJ 08625
P: (609) 292-5360
F: (609) 663-3601
E: commissioner@dobi.state.nj.us

NEW MEXICO
Mr. William J. Verant
Director
Financial Institutions Division
Regulation & Licensing Department
2550 Cerrillos Road
Santa Fe, NM 87505
P: (505) 476-4885
F: (505) 476-4511
E: william.verant@state.nm.us

NEW YORK
Mr. Richard Neiman
Superintendent
Banking Department
1 State Street
New York, NY 10001
P: (212) 827-7099
F: (518) 473-7204

NORTH CAROLINA
Mr. Joseph A. Smith Jr.
Commissioner of Banks
Banking Commission
316 West Edenton Street
4309 Mail Service Center
Raleigh, NC 27699
P: (919) 733-3016
F: (919) 733-6918
E: jsmith@nccob.org

NORTH DAKOTA
Mr. Timothy J. Karsky
Commissioner
Department of Financial Institutions
2000 Schafer Street, Suite G
Bismarck, ND 58501
P: (701) 328-9933
F: (701) 328-9955
E: tkarsky@nd.gov

NORTHERN MARIANA ISLANDS
Mr. James A. Santos
Director
Department of Commerce
Caller Box 10007, Capital Hill
Saipan, MP 96950
P: (670) 664-3000
F: (670) 664-3070
E: commercedept@vzpacifica.net

OHIO
Mr. Michael Roark
Deputy Superintendent
Division of Financial Institutions
77 South High Street, 21st Floor
Columbus, OH 43215
P: (614) 728-8400

OKLAHOMA
Mr. Mick Thompson
Commissioner
State Banking Department
4545 North Lincoln Boulevard, Suite 164
Oklahoma City, OK 73105
P: (405) 521-2782
F: (405) 522-2993

OREGON
Mr. David C. Tatman
Division Administrator
Division of Finance & Corporate Securities
350 Winter Street, Northeast, Room 410
Salem, OR 97301
P: (503) 378-4387
F: (503) 947-7862

PENNSYLVANIA
Ms. Victoria A. Reider
Acting Secretary of Banking
Department of Banking
17 North Second Street, 13th Floor
Harrisburg, PA 17101
P: (717) 214-8343
F: (717) 787-8773

PUERTO RICO
Mr. Alfredo Padilla
Commissioner of Financial Institutions
Office of the Commissioner of Financial Institutions
P.O. Box 11855
San Juan, PR 00910
P: (787) 723-3131
F: (787) 723-4042

RHODE ISLAND
Mr. Dennis F. Ziroli
Associate Director & Superintendent of Banking
Banking Regulations Division
233 Richmond Street
Providence, RI 02903
P: (401) 222-2405
F: (401) 222-5628
E: dziroli@dbr.state.ri.us

SOUTH CAROLINA
Ms. Paige Parsons
Senior Assistant State Treasurer, Banking
Office of the State Treasurer
P.O. Box 11778
Columbia, SC 29211
P: (803) 734-9822
E: paige.parsons@sto.sc.gov

Hon. Thomas Ravenel (R)
State Treasurer
Office of the Treasurer
P.O. Box 11778
Columbia, SC 29211
P: (803) 734-2101
F: (803) 734-2690
E: treasurer@sto.sc.gov

SOUTH DAKOTA
Mr. Roger Novotny
Director
Division of Banking
Department of Revenue & Regulation
217 1/2 West Missouri
Pierre, SD 57501
P: (605) 773-3421
F: (605) 773-5367
E: roger.novotny@state.sd.us

TENNESSEE
Mr. Greg Gonzales
Commissioner
Department of Financial Institutions
511 Union Street, Suite 400
Nashville, TN 37219
P: (615) 741-5603
F: (615) 253-6306

TEXAS
Mr. Randall S. James
Commissioner
Department of Banking
2601 North Lamar Boulevard
Austin, TX 78705
P: (512) 475-1325
F: (512) 475-1313
E: randall.james@banking.state.tx.us

UTAH
Mr. G. Edward Leary
Commissioner
Department of Financial Institutions
324 South State, Suite 201
P.O. Box 146800
Salt Lake City, UT 84114
P: (801) 538-8761
F: (801) 538-8894
E: ELEARY@utah.gov

VERMONT
Ms. Paulette J. Thabault
Commissioner
Department of Banking, Insurance, Securities & Health Care
89 Main Street
Drawer 20
Montpelier, VT 05620
P: (802) 828-3301
F: (802) 828-3306

VIRGINIA
Mr. E. Joseph Face Jr.
Director
Bureau of Financial Institutions
1300 East Main Street, Suite 800
P.O. Box 640
Richmond, VA 23218
P: (804) 371-9657
F: (804) 371-9416
E: joe.face@scc.virginia.gov

WASHINGTON
Mr. Scott Jarvis
Director
Department of Financial Institutions
P.O. Box 41200
Olympia, WA 98504
P: (360) 902-8700
F: (360) 586-5068

WEST VIRGINIA
Mr. Larry A. Stark
Commissioner
Division of Banking
Building 3, Room 311-A
1800 Washington Street, East
Charleston, WV 25305
P: (304) 558-2294
F: (304) 558-0442
E: lstark@wvdob.org

WISCONSIN
Mr. Michael Mach
Administrator
Division of Banking
345 West Washington Avenue
P.O. Box 7876
Madison, WI 53707
P: (608) 261-7578
F: (608) 267-6889

Borders Management

Oversees and regulates the flow of transportation and immigration over state and international borders.

AMERICAN SAMOA
Hon. Afa Ripley Jr.
Attorney General
Office of the Attorney General
American Samoa Government
Executive Office Building, Utulei
Pago Pago, AS 96799
P: (684) 633-4163
F: (684) 633-1838

GEORGIA
Mr. Harold Linnenkohl
Commissioner
Department of Transportation
2 Capitol Square, Southwest
Atlanta, GA 30334
P: (404) 656-5206
F: (404) 463-6336
E: harold.linnenkohl@dot.state.ga.us

GUAM
Mr. Ricardo C. Blas
Department of Customs & Quarantine
Building 13-16, 17 Mariner Drive, Tiyan
Barrigada, GU 96932
P: (671) 475-6202
F: (671) 475-6227

KANSAS
Col. William Seck
Superintendent
Kansas Highway Patrol
122 Southwest 7th Street
Topeka, KS 66603
P: (785) 296-6800
F: (785) 296-3049
E: wseck@mail.khp.state.ks.us

MASSACHUSETTS
Col. Mark F. Delaney
Superintendent
State Police
470 Worcester Road
Framingham, MA 01702
P: (508) 820-2300
F: (617) 727-6874

MINNESOTA
Mr. Michael Campion
Commissioner
Department of Public Safety
Bremer Tower, Suite 1000
445 Minnesota Street
St. Paul, MN 55101
P: (651) 201-7000
F: (651) 297-5728
E: michael.campion@state.mn.us

MISSOURI
Mr. Mark S. James
Director
Department of Public Safety
301 West High Street
Truman Building, Room 870
Jefferson City, MO 65102
P: (573) 751-4905
F: (573) 751-5399
E: Mark.James@dps.mo.gov

MONTANA
Hon. Mike McGrath (D)
Attorney General
Office of the Attorney General
Department of Justice
P.O. Box 201401
Helena, MT 59620
P: (406) 444-2026
F: (404) 444-3549
E: contactdoj@mt.gov

NEW HAMPSHIRE
Mr. John J. Barthelmes
Commissioner
Department of Safety
33 Hazen Drive
Concord, NH 03305
P: (603) 271-2791
F: (603) 271-3903
E: jbarthelmes@safety.state.nh.us

NEW MEXICO
Mr. Rick Homans
Director
Economic Development Department
1100 South St. Francis Drive, Suite 1060
Joseph Montoya Building
Santa Fe, NM 87505
P: (505) 476-3736
F: (505) 827-0328
E: edd.info@state.nm.us

NORTH DAKOTA
Mr. Greg Wilz
Director
Department of Homeland Security
P.O. Box 5511
Bismarck, ND 58506
P: (701) 328-8100
F: (701) 328-8181
E: gwilz@nd.gov

NORTHERN MARIANA ISLANDS
Hon. Matthew T. Gregory
Attorney General
Office of the Attorney General
Capitol Hil, Caller Box 10007
Saipan, MP 95960
P: (670) 664-2341
F: (670) 664-2349
E: matt@gregoryfirm.com

SOUTH CAROLINA
Mr. H.B. Buck Limehouse
Director
Department of Transportation
955 Park Street
Columbia, SC 29201
P: (803) 737-1302

U.S. VIRGIN ISLANDS
Mr. Darlan Brin
Executive Director
Port Authority
P.O. Box 301707
St. Thomas, VI 00803
P: (340) 774-1629
F: (340) 774-0025
E: dbrin@viport.com

UTAH
Mr. Richard Clasby
Director, Motor Carriers
Department of Transportation - Operations - Motor Carriers
4501 South 2700 West
P.O. Box 148240
Salt Lake City, UT 84119
P: (801) 965-4156
F: (801) 965-4847
E: rclasby@utah.gov

VIRGINIA
Mr. Jerry L. Bridges
Executive Director
Port Authority
600 World Trade Center
Norfolk, VA 23510
P: (757) 683-2103
F: (757) 683-8500
E: jbridges@portofvirginia.com

WASHINGTON
Maj. Gen. Timothy J. Lowenberg
Adjutant General
Military Department
Camp Murray, Building 1
Tacoma, WA 98430
P: (253) 512-8201
F: (253) 512-8497

Budget

Collects and analyzes budget requests and supporting materials and prepares the executive budget documents.

ALABAMA
Mr. Jim Main
Director
Department of Finance
600 Dexter Avenue, Suite N-105
Montgomery, AL 36130
P: (334) 242-7160
F: (334) 353-3300
E: jim.main
@finance.alabama.gov

Mr. Bill Newton
Executive Budget Office
11 South Union Street
Room 237
Montgomery, AL 36104
P: (334) 242-7230
F: (334) 242-3776

ALASKA
Ms. Karen Rehfeld
Director
Office of Management & Budget
P.O. Box 110020
Juneau, AK 99811
P: (907) 465-4660
F: (907) 465-3640
E: karen_rehfeld
@gov.state.ak.us

ARIZONA
Mr. James Apperson
Director
Office of Strategic Planning & Budgeting
1700 West Washington
Phoenix, AZ 85007
P: (602) 542-5381
F: (602) 542-0868
E: ospbadmin@az.gov

ARKANSAS
Mr. Richard Weiss
Director
Department of Finance & Administration
1509 West 7th Street, Room 401
DFA Building
Little Rock, AR 72201
P: (501) 682-2242
F: (501) 682-1029
E: richard.weiss
@dfa.state.ar.us

CALIFORNIA
Mr. Mike Genest
Director
Department of Finance
State Capitol, 1st Floor
Sacramento, CA 95814
P: (916) 445-4141

COLORADO
Mr. Todd Saliman
Director
Office of State Planning & Budgeting
200 East Colfax, Room 111
Denver, CO 80203
P: (303) 866-3317
F: (303) 866-3044

CONNECTICUT
Mr. Robert Genuario
Secretary
Office of Policy & Management
450 Capitol Avenue
Hartford, CT 06106
P: (860) 418-6500
E: robert.genuario
@po.state.ct.us

DELAWARE
Ms. Jennifer W. Davis
Director
Office of Management & Budget
122 William Penn Street
Dover, DE 19901
P: (302) 739-4204
F: (302) 739-5661
E: jennifer.davis
@state.de.us

DISTRICT OF COLUMBIA
Dr. Natwar M. Gandhi
Chief Financial Officer
Office of the Chief Financial Officer
1350 Pennsylvania Avenue, Northwest
Suite 203
Washington, DC 20004
P: (202) 727-2476
F: (202) 727-1643
E: ocfo@dc.gov

FLORIDA
Mr. Jerry McDaniel
Director
Office of Policy & Budget
The Capitol
Tallahassee, FL 32399
P: (850) 488-7810
F: (850) 488-9005

GEORGIA
Ms. Shelley Nickel
Director
Office of Planning & Budget
270 Washington Street, Southwest
Atlanta, GA 30334
P: (404) 656-3820
F: (404) 656-3828
E: shelley.nickel
@opb.state.ga.us

GUAM
Mr. Carlos Bordallo
Director
Bureau of Budget & Management Research
P.O. Box 2950
Hagatna, GU 96932
P: (671) 475-9412
F: (671) 472-2825

HAWAII
Hon. Georgina K. Kawamura
Director of Finance
Department of Budget & Finance
P.O. Box 150
Honolulu, HI 96810
P: (808) 586-1518
F: (808) 586-1976
E: Hi.BudgetandFinance
@hawaii.gov

IDAHO
Mr. Brad Foltman
Administrator
Division of Financial Management
Statehouse
P.O. Box 83720
Boise, ID 83720
P: (208) 334-3900
F: (208) 334-2438
E: bfoltman@dfm.idaho.gov

ILLINOIS
Ms. Ginger Ostro
Director
Governor's Office of Management & Budget
108 State House
Springfield, IL 60706
P: (217) 782-4520
F: (217) 524-1514

INDIANA
Mr. Charles E. Schalliol
Director
State Budget Agency
200 West Washington Street
Room 212
Indianapolis, IN 46204
P: (317) 232-0696

IOWA
Mr. Charles Krogmeier
Director
Department of Management
State Capitol Building
Des Moines, IA 50319
P: (515) 242-5192
E: charles.krogmeier
@iowa.gov

KANSAS
Mr. Duane Goossen
Secretary
Division of the Budget
1000 Southwest Jackson Street
Suite 500
Topeka, KS 66612
P: (785) 296-2822
F: (785) 296-0231
E: duane.goossen
@da.state.ks.us

KENTUCKY
Mr. Bradford L. Cowgill
State Budget Director
Office of State Budget Director
702 Capital Avenue, Room 284
Frankfort, KY 40601
P: (502) 564-7300
F: (502) 564-6684
E: Brad.Cowgill@ky.gov

LOUISIANA
Mr. Ray Stockstill
Budget Director
Office of Planning & Budget
P.O. Box 94095
Baton Rouge, LA 70804
P: (225) 342-7005
F: (225) 342-7220
E: ofila@ofi.louisiana.gov

MAINE
Ms. Ellen Schneiter
State Budget Office
Department of Administration & Financial Services
Burton M. Cross State Office Building
109 Sewall Street, 3rd Floor
Augusta, ME 04333
P: (207) 624-8678
F: (207) 624-8637
E: robert.v.leclair
@maine.gov

MARYLAND
Ms. T. Eloise Foster
Secretary
Department of Budget & Management
45 Calvert Street, 1st Floor
Annapolis, MD 21401
P: (410) 260-7041
F: (410) 974-2585
E: efoster@dbm.state.md.us

Budget

MASSACHUSETTS
Mr. Matthew J. Gorzkowicz
Assistant Secretary for Budget
Fiscal Affairs Division
Room 272, State House
Boston, MA 02133
P: (617) 727-2081
F: (617) 727-2050

MICHIGAN
Mr. Robert L. Emerson
Budget Director
Office of the State Budget
111 South Capitol
Lansing, MI 48913
P: (517) 373-7560
F: (517) 241-5428

MINNESOTA
Mr. Tom J. Hanson
Commissioner
Department of Finance
Centennial Office Building, Suite 400
658 Cedar Street
St. Paul, MN 55155
P: (651) 201-8010
F: (651) 296-7714
E: Tom.J.Hanson@state.mn.us

MISSISSIPPI
Mr. J.K. Stringer Jr.
Executive Director/State Fiscal Officer
Department of Finance & Administration
P.O. Box 267
Jackson, MS 39205
P: (601) 359-3402
F: (601) 359-2405
E: stringer@dfa.state.ms.us

MISSOURI
Mr. Larry W. Schepker
Director
Division of Budget & Planning
P.O. Box 809
Capitol Building, Room 124
Jefferson City, MO 65102
P: (573) 751-3925
F: (573) 526-4811
E: larry.schepker@oa.mo.gov

MONTANA
Mr. David Ewer
Director
Office of Budget & Program Planning
State Capitol, Room 277
P.O. Box 200802
Helena, MT 59620
P: (406) 444-3616
F: (406) 444-4670
E: dewer@mt.gov

NEBRASKA
Mr. Gerry A. Oligmueller
Acting Director
Budget Division
P.O. Box 94664
Lincoln, NE 68509
P: (402) 471-2331
F: (402) 471-4157
E: gerry.oligmueller@budget.ne.gov

NEVADA
Mr. Andrew K. Clinger
Director
Department of Administration
209 East Musser Street, Room 200
Carson City, NV 89701
P: (775) 684-0222
F: (775) 684-0260
E: aclinger@budget.state.nv.us

NEW HAMPSHIRE
Mr. Donald S. Hill
Commissioner
Department of Administrative Services
25 Capitol Street, Room 120
Concord, NH 03301
P: (603) 271-3201
F: (603) 271-6600
E: don.hill@nh.gov

NEW JERSEY
Ms. Charlene Holzbaur
Director
Office of Management & Budget
Department of Treasury
P.O. Box 221
Trenton, NJ 08625
P: (609) 292-6746
F: (609) 633-8179
E: charlene.holzbaur@treas.state.nj.us

NEW MEXICO
Ms. Dannette Burch
Deputy Secretary for Budget & Policy
State Budget Division
Bataan Memorial Building, Suite 190
407 Galisteo Street
Santa Fe, NM 87501
P: (505) 827-4987
F: (505) 827-3861

NEW YORK
Mr. Paul Francis
Director
Division of Budget
State Capitol
Albany, NY 12224
P: (518) 474-2300
F: (518) 474-6572

NORTH CAROLINA
Mr. David McCoy
State Budget Officer
Office of State Budget & Management
116 West Jones Street
20320 Mail Service Center
Raleigh, NC 27699
P: (919) 807-4700
F: (919) 733-0640
E: david.mccoy@ncmail.net

NORTH DAKOTA
Ms. Sheila Peterson
Director
Fiscal Management Division
600 East Boulevard Avenue
Department 110
Bismarck, ND 58505
P: (701) 328-4904
F: (701) 328-3230

NORTHERN MARIANA ISLANDS
Mr. Antonio S. Muna
Special Assistant
Office of Management & Budget
Caller Box 10007, Capitol Hill
Saipan, MP 96950
P: (670) 664-2265
F: (670) 664-2272

OHIO
Ms. J. Pari Sabety
Director
Office of Budget & Management
30 East Broad Street, 34th Floor
Columbus, OH 43215
P: (614) 466-4034
F: (614) 644-3147
E: pari.sabety@obm.state.oh.us

OKLAHOMA
Mr. Tony Hutchinson
Director
Office of State Finance
2300 North Lincoln Boulevard, Suite 122
Oklahoma City, OK 73105
P: (405) 521-2141
F: (405) 522-3902

OREGON
Mr. George Naughton
Administrator
Department of Administrative Services
155 Cottage Street, Northeast
Salem, OR 97301
P: (503) 378-3106
F: (503) 378-2322
E: george.naughton@state.or.us

PENNSYLVANIA
Mr. Michael Masch
Secretary
Office of the Budget
Office of the Governor
207 Finance Building
Harrisburg, PA 17101
P: (717) 787-9945
F: (717) 787-4523
E: mmasch@state.pa.us

PUERTO RICO
Mr. Jose Guillermo Davila
Director
Office of Budget & Management
254 Cruz Street
P.O. Box 9023228
San Juan, PR 00902
P: (787) 725-9420
F: (787) 721-8329

RHODE ISLAND
Ms. Rosemary Booth Gallogly
Executive Director/State Budget Officer
Budget Office
One Capitol Hill
Providence, RI 02908
P: (401) 222-6300
E: roseb@budget.state.ri.us

SOUTH CAROLINA
Mr. Les Boles
Director
Office of State Budget
1201 Main Street, Suite 870
Columbia, SC 29201
P: (803) 734-2280
F: (803) 734-0645

SOUTH DAKOTA
Mr. Jason Dilges
Commissioner
Bureau of Finance & Management
State Capitol
500 East Capitol Avenue
Pierre, SD 57501
P: (605) 773-3411
F: (605) 773-4711
E: jason.dilges@state.sd.us

TENNESSEE
Mr. Dave Goetz Jr.
Commissioner
Department of Finance & Administration
State Capitol, 1st Floor
600 Charlotte Avenue
Nashville, TN 37243
P: (615) 741-2401
F: (615) 741-9872

TEXAS
Mr. Mike Morrissey
Director
Budget, Planning & Policy
Office of the Governor
P.O. Box 12428
Austin, TX 78711
P: (512) 463-1778
F: (512) 463-1975

U.S. VIRGIN ISLANDS
Ms. Debra Gottlieb
Director
Office of Management & Budget
#41 Norre Gade
Emancipation Garden Station, 2nd Floor
St. Thomas, VI 00802
P: (340) 774-0069

UTAH
Mr. Richard Ellis
Director
Governor's Office of Planning & Budget
State Capitol Complex, Suite E210
P.O. Box 142210
Salt Lake City, UT 84114
P: (801) 538-1562
F: (801) 538-1547
E: RELLIS@utah.gov

Mr. John Nixon
Director
Governor's Office of Planning & Budget
State Capitol Complex, Suite E210
P.O. Box 142210
Salt Lake City, UT 84114
P: (801) 538-1562
F: (801) 538-1547
E: jnixon@utah.gov

VERMONT
Mr. Jim Reardon
Commissioner
Department of Finance & Management
109 State Street
Montpelier, VT 05602
P: (802) 828-2376
F: (802) 828-2428
E: jim.reardon@state.vt.us

VIRGINIA
Mr. Richard D. Brown
Director
Department of Planning & Budget
1111 East Broad Street
Patrick Henry Building
Richmond, VA 23219
P: (804) 786-2269
F: (804) 225-3291
E: ric.brown@dpb.virginia.gov

WASHINGTON
Mr. Victor Moore
Director
Office of Financial Management
P.O. Box 43113
Olympia, WA 98504
P: (360) 902-0530
F: (360) 664-2832
E: victor.moore@ofm.wa.gov

WEST VIRGINIA
Mr. Mike McKown
Director
State Budget Office
Building 1, Room 310-W
1900 Kanawha Boulevard, East
Charleston, WV 25305
P: (304) 558-0040
F: (304) 558-1588
E: mmckown@wvbudget.gov

WISCONSIN
Mr. David Schmiedicke
State Budget Director
Division of Executive Budget & Finance
101 East Wilson Street, 10th Floor
P.O. Box 7864
Madison, WI 53707
P: (608) 266-1035
F: (608) 267-0626

WYOMING
Mr. Mike McVay
Administrator
Department of Administration & Information
2001 Capitol Avenue
Emerson Building, Room 105
Cheyenne, WY 82002
P: (307) 777-7203
F: (307) 777-3688

Building Codes

Establishes and enforces standards of construction, materials and occupancy for all buildings.

ALABAMA
Mr. Kippy Tate
Director
Building Commission
770 Washington Avenue
4th Floor, Suite 444
Montgomery, AL 36130
P: (334) 242-4082
F: (334) 242-4182
E: phyllis.thomas@bc.alabama.gov

ALASKA
Mr. Steven Belanger
Acting Director
Division of Fire Prevention
Department of Public Safety
5700 East Tudor Road
Anchorage, AK 99507
P: (907) 269-5491
F: (907) 276-7018
E: steven_belanger@dps.state.ak.us

ARIZONA
Mr. Robert Barger
Director
Department of Fire, Building & Life Safety
1110 West Washington, Suite 100
Phoenix, AZ 85007
P: (602) 364-1003
F: (602) 364-1052

ARKANSAS
Mr. Whit Waller
Director
Manufactured Home Commission
101 East Capitol Avenue, Suite 210
Little Rock, AR 72201
P: (501) 324-9032
F: (501) 683-3538
E: Whit.Waller@arkansas.gov

CALIFORNIA
Mr. Richard Conrad
Executive Director
Division of the State Architect
1102 Q Street, Suite 5100
Sacramento, CA 95814
P: (916) 445-8100
F: (916) 445-3521
E: Richard.Conrad@dgs.ca.gov

Mr. David F. Thorman
State Architect
Division of the State Architect
1102 Q Street, Suite 5100
Sacramento, CA 95814
P: (916) 445-8100
F: (916) 324-0207

COLORADO
Ms. Kathi Williams
Director
Division of Housing
Department of Local Affairs
1313 Sherman, Room 518
Denver, CO 80203
P: (303) 866-2033
F: (303) 866-4077

CONNECTICUT
Mr. Christopher Laux
State Building Inspector
Division of Fire, Emergency & Building Services
Department of Public Safety
1111 Country Club Road
Middletown, CT 06457
P: (860) 685-8310
F: (860) 685-8365
E: christopher.laux@po.state.ct.us

DELAWARE
Mr. Grover P. Ingle
Acting State Fire Marshal
Office of the State Fire Marshal
1537 Chestnut Grove Road
Dover, DE 19904
P: (302) 739-5665
F: (302) 739-6794

FLORIDA
Ms. Ila Jones
Community Program Administrator
Department of Community Affairs
Codes & Standards
2555 Shumard Oak Boulevard
Tallahassee, FL 32399
P: (850) 487-1824
F: (850) 414-8436
E: ila.jones@dca.state.fl.us

GEORGIA
Mr. Ted Miltiades
Manager, Construction Codes Program
Department of Community Affairs
60 Executive Park South, Northeast
Atlanta, GA 30329
P: (404) 679-3106
F: (404) 679-0646
E: tmiltiad@dca.state.ga.us

HAWAII
Mr. Ken Silva
Chair
State Fire Council
Dept. of Labor & Industrial Relations
3375 Koapaka Street, H-425
Honolulu, HI 96819
P: (808) 831-7778
F: (808) 831-7750

IDAHO
Mr. Jack Rayne
Building Bureau Chief
Division of Building Safety
1090 East Watertower Street
Meridian, ID 83642
P: (208) 332-7151
F: (208) 855-9399
E: jrayne@dbs.idaho.gov

ILLINOIS
Ms. Laura Kozemczak
Division Staff
Division of Building Codes & Regulations
Stratton Office Building, 3rd Floor
401 South Spring Street
Springfield, IL 62706
P: (217) 557-7500
F: (217) 557-7913
E: laura.kozemczak@illinois.gov

INDIANA
Mr. Don Bradley
Director
Code Enforcement & Plan Review Branch
Division of Fire & Building Services
402 West Washington Street, Room W246
Indianapolis, IN 46204
P: (317) 232-2222
F: (317) 232-0307
E: dbradley@dhs.in.gov

IOWA
Mr. W. Stuart Crine
Building Code Commissioner
Department of Public Safety
State Building Code Bureau
401 Southwest 7th Street, Suite N
Des Moines, IA 50309
P: (515) 281-5821
F: (515) 242-6299
E: crine@dps.state.ia.us

KANSAS
Mr. Jack Alexander
State Fire Marshal
Fire Marshal Department
700 Southwest Jackson Street, Suite 600
Topeka, KS 66603
P: (785) 296-3401
F: (785) 296-0151

KENTUCKY
Mr. Van Cook
Executive Director
Office of Housing, Buildings & Construction
101 Sea Hero Road, Suite 100
Frankfort, KY 40601
P: (502) 573-0364
F: (502) 573-1057
E: Van.Cook@ky.gov

LOUISIANA
Mr. Jerry Jones
Director of Facility Planning
Department of Facility Planning
P.O. Box 94095
Baton Rouge, LA 70804
P: (225) 342-0849
F: (225) 342-7624
E: jerry.jones@la.gov

MAINE
Mr. Robert LeClair
Executive Director
Manufactured Housing Board
35 State House Station
Augusta, ME 04333
P: (207) 624-8678
F: (207) 624-8637
E: robert.v.leclair@maine.gov

MARYLAND
Mr. Ed Landon
Department of Housing & Community Development
Codes Administration
100 Community Place
Crownsville, MD 21032
P: (410) 514-7444
F: (410) 987-8902
E: landon@mdhousing.org

MASSACHUSETTS
Mr. Thomas G. Gatzunis
Commissioner
Department of Public Safety
One Ashburton Place, Room 1301
Boston, MA 02108
P: (617) 727-3200
F: (617) 227-1754
E: thomas.gatzunis@state.ma.us

MICHIGAN
Mr. Henry Green
Executive Director
Bureau of Construction Codes & Fire Safety
P.O. Box 30254
Lansing, MI 48909
P: (517) 241-9302
F: (517) 241-9570
E: HLGreen@michigan.gov

MINNESOTA
Mr. Thomas Anderson
State Building Official
Department of Labor & Industry
Building Codes & Standards
443 Lafayette Road, North
St. Paul, MN 55155
P: (651) 284-5068
F: (651) 284-5749
E: tom.c.anderson@state.mn.us

MISSISSIPPI
Mr. Millard D. Mackey
Chief Deputy Fire Marshal
State Fire Marshal's Office
P.O. Box 79
Jackson, MS 39205
P: (601) 359-1076
E: firemarshal@mid.state.ms.us

MISSOURI
Mr. Ronald Pleus
Manager
Department of Manufactured Housing & Modular Units
P.O. Box 360
Jefferson City, MO 65102
P: (800) 819-3180
F: (583) 522-2509
E: ron.pleus@psc.mo.gov

MONTANA
Mr. Tim Lloyd
Program Manager
Bureau of Building & Measurement Standards
301 South Park Avenue, Room 430
P.O. Box 200516
Helena, MT 59620
P: (406) 841-2058
F: (406) 841-2050
E: tlloyd@mt.gov

NEBRASKA
Mr. Mark Luttich
Department Director
Public Service Commission
P.O. Box 94927
Lincoln, NE 68509
P: (402) 471-0518
F: (402) 471-7709
E: mark.luttich@psc.ne.gov

NEVADA
Ms. Renee Diamond
Administrator
Department of Business & Industry
Manufactured Housing Division
2501 East Sahara, Suite 204
Las Vegas, NV 89104
P: (702) 486-4135
F: (702) 486-4309
E: rdiamond@mhd.state.nv.us

NEW HAMPSHIRE
Mr. J. William Degnan
State Fire Marshal
Department of Safety
Division of Fire Safety
33 Hazen Drive
Concord, NH 03305
P: (603) 271-3294
F: (603) 271-1091
E: bdegnan@safety.state.nh.us

NEW JERSEY
Mr. William Connolly
Director
Division of Codes & Standards
101 South Broad Street
P.O. Box 800
Trenton, NJ 08625
P: (609) 292-6055
F: (609) 984-6696

NEW MEXICO
Ms. Lisa Martinez
Director
Construction Industries Division
Regulation & Licensing Department
2550 Cerrillos Road
Santa Fe, NM 87505
P: (505) 476-4700
F: (505) 476-4511
E: lisa.martinez@state.nm.us

NEW YORK
Mr. Ronald Piester
Deputy Secretary of State
Department of State
41 State Street
Albany, NY 12231
P: (518) 473-3366
F: (518) 486-4068

NORTH CAROLINA
Mr. Chris Noles
Deputy Commissioner
Department of Insurance-OSFM
Engineering & Codes
322 Chapanoke Road, Suite 200
Raleigh, NC 27603
P: (919) 661-5880
F: (919) 662-4414
E: cnoles@ncdoi.net

NORTHERN MARIANA ISLANDS
Mr. Francisco Q. Guerrero
Officer in Charge
Building Safety Code
Caller Box 10007, Capital Hill
Saipan, MP 96950
P: (670) 235-5828
F: (670) 235-6346

OHIO
Mr. Billy Phillips
Executive Secretary
Department of Commerce
Board of Building Standards
P.O. Box 4009
Reynoldsburg, OH 43068
P: (614) 644-2613
F: (614) 752-9760
E: billy.phillips@com.state.oh.us

OKLAHOMA
Mr. Winston Neal
Operations Chief
Office of the State Fire Marshal
2401 Northwest 23rd, Suite 4
Oklahoma City, OK 73107
P: (405) 522-5014
F: (405) 522-5028

OREGON
Mr. Mark S. Long
Administrator
Building Codes Division
P.O. Box 14470
Salem, OR 97309
P: (503) 378-3176
F: (503) 378-2322
E: mark.long@state.or.us

PENNSYLVANIA
Mr. Mark Conte
Chief, Housing Standards Division
Department of Community & Economic Development
400 North Street, 4th Floor
Harrisburg, PA 17120
P: (717) 720-7413
F: (717) 783-4663
E: mconte@state.pa.us

RHODE ISLAND
Mr. Daniel R. De Dentro
Deputy Commissioner
State Building Commission
One Capitol Hill, 2nd Floor
Providence, RI 02908
P: (401) 222-3032
F: (401) 222-2599
E: dand@gw.doa.state.ri.us

SOUTH CAROLINA
Mr. Gary Wiggins
Administrator
Building Codes Council
110 Centerview Drive, Suite 102
Kingstree Building
Columbia, SC 29210
P: (803) 896-4688
F: (803) 896-4814
E: wigginsg@llr.sc.gov

SOUTH DAKOTA
Mr. Allen Christie
State Fire Marshal
Department of Public Safety
118 West Capitol Avenue
Pierre, SD 57501
P: (605) 773-3562
F: (605) 773-6631
E: fireinfo@state.sd.us

TENNESSEE
Mr. Emmett H. Turner
Assistant Commissioner
Division of Fire Prevention
State Fire Marshal
500 James Robertson Parkway, 3rd Floor
Nashville, TN 37243
P: (615) 741-2981
F: (615) 741-1583
E: emmett.turner@state.tn.us

Building Codes

TEXAS
Mr. Duane Waddill
Executive Director
Residential Construction Commission
P.O. Box 13144
Austin, TX 78711
P: (512) 463-9534
F: (512) 463-9507
E: duane.waddill@trcc.state.tx.us

UTAH
Mr. Dan S. Jones
Bureau Manager
Division of Occupational & Professional Licensing
160 East 300 South
P.O. Box 146741
Salt Lake City, UT 84114
P: (801) 530-6720
F: (801) 530-6511
E: dansjones@utah.gov

VERMONT
Mr. John Woods Jr.
Director
Division of Fire Safety
Department of Public Safety
1311 U.S. Route 302-Berlin
Barre, VT 05641
P: (802) 479-7561
F: (802) 479-7562
E: jwood@dps.state.vt.us

VIRGINIA
Mr. Emory Rodgers
Deputy Director
Department of Housing & Community Development
Division of Building & Fire
501 North Second Street
Richmond, VA 23219
P: (804) 371-7150
F: (804) 371-7092
E: emory.rodgers@dhcd.virginia.gov

WASHINGTON
Mr. Tim Nogler
Managing Director
State Building Code Council
P.O. Box 48300
Olympia, WA 98504
P: (360) 725-2969
F: (360) 586-5880
E: timn@cted.wa.gov

WEST VIRGINIA
Mr. Sterling Lewis Jr.
State Fire Marshal
State Fire Commission
1207 Quarrier Street, 2nd Floor
Charleston, WV 25301
P: (304) 558-2191
F: (304) 558-2537
E: slewis@wvfiremarshal.org

WISCONSIN
Mr. Ronald L. Buchholz
Deputy Administrator
Safety & Building Division
Safety & Building Division
P.O. Box 2599
Madison, WI 53701
P: (608) 266-1817
F: (608) 266-9946
E: rbuchholz@commerce.state.wi.us

WYOMING
Mr. Jim Narva
State Fire Marshal
Department of Fire Prevention & Electrical Safety
Herschler 1 West
Cheyenne, WY 82002
P: (307) 777-7288
F: (307) 777-7119
E: jnarva@state.wy.us

Campaign Finance Administration

Administers and enforces campaign finance laws.

ALABAMA
Hon. Beth Chapman (R)
Secretary of State
Office of the Secretary of State
State House
600 Dexter Avenue
Montgomery, AL 36104
P: (334) 242-7205
F: (334) 242-4993
E: beth.chapman
@sos.alabama.gov

ALASKA
Ms. Brooke Miles
Director
Public Offices Commission
2221 East Northern Lights Boulevard
Room 128
Anchorage, AK 99508
P: (907) 276-4176
F: (907) 276-7018
E: brooke_miles
@admin.state.ak.us

AMERICAN SAMOA
Mr. Soliai T. Fuimaono
Chief Election Officer
Territorial Election Office
P.O. Box 3790
Pago Pago, AS 96799
P: (684) 633-2522
F: (684) 633-7116

ARIZONA
Hon. Jan Brewer (R)
Secretary of State
Office of the Secretary of State
7th Floor, State Capitol
1700 West Washington Street
Phoenix, AZ 85007
P: (520) 628-6583
F: (520) 628-6938
E: lglenn@azsos.gov

ARKANSAS
Hon. Charlie Daniels (D)
Secretary of State
Office of the Secretary of State
256 State Capitol Building
Little Rock, AR 72201
P: (501) 682-1010
F: (501) 682-3510
E: larowland
@sosmail.state.ar.us

CALIFORNIA
Ms. Caren Daniels-Meade
Chief
Political Reform Division
1500 11th Street, 5th Floor
Sacramento, CA 95814
P: (916) 657-2166
F: (916) 653-3214

COLORADO
Ms. Holly Lowder
Director of Elections
Elections Division
Department of State
1700 Broadway, Suite 200
Denver, CO 80290
P: (303) 894-2200 Ext. 6301
F: (303) 869-4861
E: holly.lowder
@sos.state.co.us

CONNECTICUT
Hon. Susan Bysiewicz (D)
Secretary of State
Office of the Secretary of State
State Capitol, Room 104
Hartford, CT 06105
P: (860) 509-6200
F: (860) 509-6209
E: Susan.Bysiewicz
@po.state.ct.us

DELAWARE
Mr. Frank Calio
State Election Commissioner
Department of Elections
111 South West Street, Suite 10
Dover, DE 19904
P: (302) 739-4277
F: (302) 739-6794

DISTRICT OF COLUMBIA
Ms. Cecily Collier-Montgomery
Director
Office of Campaign Finance
2000 14th Street, Northwest
Suite 433
Washington, DC 20009
P: (202) 671-0547
F: (202) 671-0658

FLORIDA
Ms. Amy K. Tuck
Director
Division of Elections
Room 316, R.A. Gray Building
500 South Bronough Street
Tallahassee, FL 32399
P: (850) 245-6200
F: (850) 245-6217
E: DivElections
@dos.state.fl.us

GEORGIA
Mr. C. Theodore Lee
Executive Secretary
State Ethics Commission
205 Jesse Hill Jr. Drive, South East
Suite 478, East Tower
Atlanta, GA 30334
P: (404) 463-1980
F: (404) 463-1988
E: ethics
@ethics.state.ga.us

GUAM
Mr. Gerald A. Taitano
Executive Director
Elections Commission
GCIC Building, Suite 200
414 West Soledad Avenue
Hagatna, GU 96910
P: (671) 477-9791
F: (671) 477-1895

HAWAII
Ms. Barbara Wong
Executive Director
Campaign Spending Commission
235 South Beretania Street, Room 300
Honolulu, HI 96813
P: (808) 586-0285
F: (808) 586-0288

IDAHO
Hon. Ben T. Ysursa (R)
Secretary of State
Office of the Secretary of State
State Capitol, Room 203
Boise, ID 83720
P: (208) 334-2300
F: (208) 334-2282
E: bysursa@sos.idaho.gov

ILLINOIS
Mr. Daniel W. White
Executive Director
State Board of Elections
1020 South Spring Street
P.O. Box 4187
Springfield, IL 62708
P: (217) 782-4141
F: (217) 782-5959

INDIANA
Mr. Brad King
Co-Director
Elections Division
302 West Washington, Room E204
Indianapolis, IN 46204
P: (317) 233-3939
F: (317) 233-6793
E: bking@iec.state.in.us

Ms. Pamela Potesta
Co-Director
Elections Division
302 West Washington, Room E204
Indianapolis, IN 46204
P: (317) 232-3939
F: (317) 233-6793
E: ppotesta@iec.state.in.us

IOWA
Mr. W. Charles Smithson
Executive Director & Legal Counsel
Ethics & Campaign Disclosure Board
510 East 12th Street, Suite 1A
Des Moines, IA 50319
P: (515) 281-3489
F: (515) 281-3701
E: charlie.smithson
@iowa.gov

KANSAS
Ms. Carol Williams
Executive Director
Governmental Ethics Commission
109 Southwest 9th Street, 5th Floor
Topeka, KS 66612
P: (785) 296-4219
F: (785) 296-2548

KENTUCKY
Ms. Sarah M. Jackson
Executive Director
Registry of Election Finance
140 Walnut Street
Frankfort, KY 40601
P: (502) 573-2226
F: (502) 573-5622
E: sarahm.jackson@ky.gov

LOUISIANA
Mr. R. Gray Sexton
Executive Director
Ethics Administration
2415 Quail Drive, Third Floor
Baton Rouge, LA 70808
P: (225) 763-8777
F: (225) 763-8780

MAINE
Mr. Jonathan Wayne
Executive Director
Commission on Governmental Ethics & Election Practices
125 State House Station
Augusta, ME 04333
P: (207) 287-4179
F: (207) 287-6775

Campaign Finance Administration

MARYLAND
Mr. Jared DeMarinis
Director
Division of Candidacy & Campaign Finance
P.O. Box 6486
Annapolis, MD 21404
P: (410) 269-2840
F: (410) 974-5415

MASSACHUSETTS
Mr. Michael J. Sullivan
Director
Office of Campaign & Political Finance
One Ashburton Place, Room 411
Boston, MA 02108
P: (617) 727-8352
F: (617) 727-6549

MICHIGAN
Mr. Christopher M. Thomas
Director
Bureau of Elections
Mutual Building, 4th Floor
208 North Capitol Avenue
Lansing, MI 48918
P: (517) 373-2540
F: (517) 241-2784

MINNESOTA
Ms. Jeanne Olson
Executive Director
Campaign Finance & Public Disclosure Board
Centennial Office Building, Suite 190
658 Cedar Street
St. Paul, MN 55155
P: (651) 296-1721
F: (651) 296-1722
E: jeanne.olson@state.mn.us

MISSISSIPPI
Mr. Jay Eads
Assistant Secretary of State for Elections
Elections Division
P.O. Box 136
401 Mississippi Street
Jackson, MS 39205
P: (601) 359-6368
F: (601) 359-5019

MISSOURI
Mr. Joseph Carroll
Director
Ethics Commission
P.O. Box 1254
Jefferson City, MO 65102
P: (573) 751-2020
F: (573) 526-4506
E: joe.carroll@mec.mo.gov

MONTANA
Mr. Dennis Unsworth
Commissioner
Office of the Commissioner of Political Practices
1205 Eighth Avenue
P.O. Box 202401
Helena, MT 59620
P: (406) 444-2942
F: (406) 444-1643
E: dunsworth@mt.gov

NEBRASKA
Mr. Frank Daley
Executive Director
Accountability & Disclosure Commission
P.O. Box 95086
Lincoln, NE 68509
P: (402) 471-2522
F: (402) 471-6599

NEW HAMPSHIRE
Hon. William M. Gardner (D)
Secretary of State
Office of the Secretary of State
State House, Room 204
Concord, NH 03301
P: (603) 271-3242
F: (603) 271-6316
E: kladd@sos.state.nh.us

NEW JERSEY
Dr. Frederick M. Herrmann
Executive Director
Election Law Enforcement Commission
P.O. Box 185
Trenton, NJ 08625
P: (609) 292-8700
F: (609) 777-1457

NEW MEXICO
Hon. Mary Herrera (D)
Secretary of State
Office of the Secretary of State
325 Don Gaspar, Suite 300
State Capitol Annex, North
Santa Fe, NM 87503
P: (505) 827-3600
F: (505) 827-3634
E: MaryE.Herrera@state.nm.us

Mr. Daniel A. Ivey-Soto
Director of Elections/Legal Counsel
Bureau of Elections
State Capitol Annex North
325 Don Gaspar, Suite 300
Santa Fe, NM 87503
P: (505) 827-3600
F: (505) 827-8403
E: Elections@state.nm.us

NEW YORK
Mr. Peter Kosinski
Co-Executive Director
State Board of Elections
40 Steuben Street
Albany, NY 12207
P: (518) 474-8100
F: (518) 486-4068
E: pkosinski@elections.state.ny.us

Mr. Stanley Zalen
Co-Executive Director
State Board of Elections
40 Steuben Street
Albany, NY 12207
P: (518) 474-8100
F: (518) 486-4068
E: szalen@elections.state.ny.us

NORTH CAROLINA
Ms. Kim W. Strach
Executive Director
State Board of Elections
P.O. Box 27255
Raleigh, NC 27611
P: (919) 715-2334
F: (919) 715-8047
E: kim.strach@ncmail.net

NORTH DAKOTA
Ms. LeeAnn Oliver
Elections Specialist
Office of the Secretary of State
600 East Boulevard Avenue, 1st Floor
Bismarck, ND 58505
P: (701) 328-4146
F: (701) 328-2992
E: loliver@nd.gov

NORTHERN MARIANA ISLANDS
Mr. Michael S. Sablan
Auditor
Office of the Public Auditor
P.O. Box 501399
1236 Yap Drive, Capitol Hill
Saipan, MP 96950
P: (670) 322-6481
F: (670) 322-7812
E: mssablan@opacnmi.com

OKLAHOMA
Ms. Marilyn Hughes
Executive Director
Ethics Commission
State Capitol Building, Room B-5
2300 North Lincoln Boulevard
Oklahoma City, OK 73105
P: (405) 521-3451
F: (405) 521-4905

OREGON
Mr. John Lindback
Director
Secretary of State, Elections Division
141 State Capitol
Salem, OR 97310
P: (503) 986-1518
F: (503) 373-7414
E: elections-division@sosinet.sos.state.or.

PUERTO RICO
Mr. Ramon Gonzalez
President
State Election Commission
P.O. Box 19555
Hato Rey, PR 00919
P: (787) 777-8682
F: (787) 296-0173

RHODE ISLAND
Mr. Ernest A. Almonte
Auditor General
Office of the Auditor General
86 Weybosset Street
Providence, RI 02903
P: (401) 222-2435
F: (401) 222-2111
E: ernest.almonte@oag.ri.gov

SOUTH CAROLINA
Mr. Herbert Hayden Jr.
Executive Director
State Ethics Commission
5000 Thurmond Mall, Suite 250
Columbia, SC 29201
P: (803) 253-4192
F: (803) 253-7539
E: herb@ethics.state.sc.us

SOUTH DAKOTA
Hon. Chris Nelson (R)
Secretary of State
Office of the Secretary of State
State Capitol
500 East Capitol Avenue
Pierre, SD 57501
P: (605) 773-3537
F: (605) 773-6580
E: sdsos@state.sd.us

TENNESSEE
Mr. William F. Long Jr.
Chair
Registry of Election Finance
404 James Robertson Parkway
Suite 1614
Nashville, TN 37243
P: (615) 741-7959
F: (615) 532-8905

Ms. Lee Anne Murray
Chair
Registry of Election Finance
404 James Robertson Parkway
Suite 1614
Nashville, TN 37243
P: (615) 741-7959
F: (615) 532-8905

TEXAS
Mr. David A. Reisman
Executive Director
Ethics Commission
201 East 14th Street, 10th Floor
P.O. Box 12070
Austin, TX 78711
P: (512) 463-5800
F: (512) 463-5777

U.S. VIRGIN ISLANDS
Mr. John Abramson
Supervisor of Elections
Election System
P.O. Box 1499, Kingshill
St. Croix, VI 00851
P: (340) 773-1021
F: (340) 773-4523

UTAH
Hon. Gary R. Herbert (R)
Lieutenant Governor
Office of the Lieutenant Governor
203 State Capitol
Salt Lake City, UT 84114
P: (801) 538-1520
F: (801) 538-1557
E: GHERBERT@utah.gov

VERMONT
Hon. Deborah L. Markowitz (D)
Secretary of State
Office of the Secretary of State
26 Terrace Street
Montpelier, VT 05609
P: (802) 828-2148
F: (802) 828-2496
E: dmarkowitz@sec.state.vt.us

VIRGINIA
Ms. Jean Jensen
Secretary
State Board of Elections
200 North 9th Street, Room 101
Richmond, VA 23219
P: (800) 864-8903
F: (804) 371-0194
E: jean.jensen@sbe.virginia.gov

WASHINGTON
Ms. Vicki Rippie
Executive Director
Public Disclosure Commission
711 Capitol Way, Room 206
P.O. Box 40908
Olympia, WA 98504
P: (360) 586-4838
F: (360) 753-1112
E: vrippie@pdc.wa.gov

WEST VIRGINIA
Hon. Betty S. Ireland (R)
Secretary of State
Office of the Secretary of State
Building 1, Suite 157K
1900 Kanawha Boulevard, East
Charleston, WV 25305
P: (304) 558-6000
F: (304) 558-0900
E: wvsos@wvsos.com

WISCONSIN
Mr. Kevin J. Kennedy
Executive Director
State Elections Board
17 West Main Street, Suite 310
Madison, WI 53703
P: (608) 266-8087
F: (608) 267-0500
E: kevin.kennedy@seb.state.wi.us

WYOMING
Hon. Max Maxfield (R)
Secretary of State
Office of the Secretary of State
State Capitol
Cheyenne, WY 82002
P: (307) 777-5333
F: (307) 777-6217
E: Secofstate@state.wy.us

Chief Information Officer

Oversees state information technology operations and develops, implements, and monitors state IT initiatives.

Information provided by:

National Association of State Chief Information Officers
Doug Robinson
Executive Director
201 East Main Street
Suite 1405
Lexington, KY 40507
P: (859) 514-9153
F: (859) 514-9166
drobinson@amrms.com
www.nacio.org

ALABAMA
Mr. Jim Burns
Chief Information Officer
Information Services Division
Department of Finance
64 North Union Street, Suite 200
Montgomery, AL 36104
P: (334) 242-3433
F: (334) 242-3999
E: jim.burns
@isd.alabama.gov

ALASKA
Mr. Mike Callahan
Director
Enterprise Technology Services Division
Department of Administration
5900 East Tudor Road
Anchorage, AK 99507
P: (907) 269-5749
E: mike_callahan
@admin.state.ak.us

ARIZONA
Mr. Chris Cummiskey
Chief Information Officer
Government Information Technology Agency
100 North 15th Avenue, Suite 440
Phoenix, AZ 85007
P: (602) 364-4770
F: (602) 364-4799
E: ccummiskey@azgita.gov

ARKANSAS
Ms. Claire Bailey
Interim Executive Chief Information Officer
Department of Information Systems
#1 Capitol Mall, 3rd Floor
Little Rock, AR 72203
P: (501) 682-9990
F: (501) 682-9465
E: claire.bailey
@arkansas.gov

CALIFORNIA
Mr. J. Clark Kelso
Chief Information Officer
Office of the Governor
3455 5th Avenue
Sacramento, CA 95817
P: (916) 739-7302
F: (916) 739-7072
E: ckelso@pacific.edu

COLORADO
Mr. Michael W. Locatis
Chief Information Officer
Technology Agency
225 East 16th Avenue, Suite 260
Denver, CO 80203
P: (303) 866-6160
F: (303) 866-6454
E: mike.locatis@state.co.us

DELAWARE
Mr. Thomas M. Jarrett
Chief Information Officer
Department of Technology & Information
801 Silver Lake Boulevard
Dover, DE 19904
P: (302) 739-9629
F: (302) 739-1442
E: thomas.jarrett
@state.de.us

FLORIDA
Mr. David Taylor
Chief Information Officer
Department of Health
4052 Bald Cyprus Way, B05
Tallahassee, FL 32399
P: (850) 245-4471
F: (850) 922-5149
E: david_taylor
@doh.state.fl.us

GEORGIA
Mr. Patrick Moore
Executive Director & State Chief Information Officer
Georgia Technology Authority
100 Peachtree Street, Suite 2300
Atlanta, GA 30303
P: (404) 463-3550
F: (404) 463-2380
E: pmoore@gta.ga.gov

HAWAII
Mr. Russ K. Saito
State Comptroller
Department of Accounting & General Services
1151 Punchbowl Street, Room 412
Honolulu, HI 96813
P: (808) 586-0400
F: (808) 586-0775

IDAHO
Mr. Kevin Iwersen
Statewide Technology Coordinator
Department of Administration
650 West State Street, Room 100
Boise, ID 83720
P: (208) 332-1875
F: (208) 334-2307
E: kevin.iwersen
@adm.idaho.gov

ILLINOIS
Mr. Rafael C. Diaz
Chief Information Officer
Department of Central Management Services
120 West Jefferson, Floor 2
Springfield, IL 62702
P: (217) 782-9798
F: (217) 557-7675

INDIANA
Mr. Gerry Weaver
Chief Information Officer
Office of Technology
100 North Senate Avenue, Room N551
Indianapolis, IN 46204
P: (317) 232-3172
F: (317) 232-0748
E: gweaver@iot.in.gov

IOWA
Mr. John P. Gillispie
Chief Operating Officer
Information Technology Enterprise
Department of Administrative Services
Hoover Building, Level B
Des Moines, IA 50319
P: (515) 281-3462
F: (515) 281-6137
E: john.gillispie@iowa.gov

KANSAS
Ms. Denise Moore
Chief Information Technology Officer
Division of Communications
Department of Administration
900 Southwest Jackson Street, Room 751-S
Topeka, KS 66612
P: (785) 296-3463
F: (785) 296-1168
E: denise.moore
@da.state.ks.us

KENTUCKY
Mr. Mark Rutledge
Chief Information Officer
Commonwealth Office of Technology
Finance & Administration Cabinet
702 Capitol Avenue, Suite 258
Frankfort, KY 40601
P: (502) 564-1201
F: (502) 564-0421
E: mark.rutledge@ky.gov

LOUISIANA
Mr. Rizwan Ahmed
Chief Information Officer
Office of Information Technology
Division of Administration
P.O. Box 94095
Baton Rouge, LA 70804
P: (225) 342-7105
F: (225) 219-4994
E: rizwan.ahmed@la.gov

MAINE
Mr. Dick Thompson Jr.
Chief Information Officer
Department of Administration & Financial Services
Office of Information Technology
26 Edison Drive
Augusta, ME 04333
P: (207) 624-7568
F: (207) 287-5623
E: richard.b.thompson
@maine.gov

MARYLAND
Mr. Ellis L. Kitchen
Chief Information Officer
Office of Information Technology
Department of Budget & Management
45 Calvert Street
Annapolis, MD 21401
P: (410) 260-2994
F: (410) 974-5615
E: ekitchen@dbm.state.md.us

MASSACHUSETTS
Ms. Bethann Pepoli
Acting Chief Information Officer
Information Technology Division
1 Ashburton Place, Floor 8
Boston, MA 02108
P: (617) 626-4529
F: (617) 727-3766
E: bethann.pepoli@state.ma.us

MICHIGAN
Ms. Teri M. Takai
Director and Chief Information Officer
Department of Information Technology
111 South Capitol Avenue, Floor 8
Romney Building
Lansing, MI 48913
P: (517) 373-1006
F: (517) 373-8213
E: takait@michigan.gov

MINNESOTA
Mr. Gopal Khanna
Chief Information Officer
Office of Enterprise Technology
658 Cedar Street, Floor4
St. Paul, MN 55155
P: (651) 556-8007
F: (651) 215-3877
E: gopal.khanna@state.mn.us

MISSISSIPPI
Mr. David L. Litchliter
Executive Director
Department of Information Technology Services
301 North Lamar Street, Suite 508
Jackson, MS 39201
P: (601) 359-1395
F: (601) 354-6016
E: david.litchliter@its.state.ms.us

MISSOURI
Mr. Dan Ross
Chief Information Officer
Information Technology Services Division
301 West High Street, Room 280
Jefferson City, MO 65102
P: (573) 526-7746
F: (573) 526-0132
E: dan.ross@oa.mo.gov

MONTANA
Mr. Dick Clark
Chief Information Officer
Information Technology Services Division
Department of Administration
P.O. Box 200113
Helena, MT 59620
P: (406) 444-2700
F: (406) 444-2701
E: dclark@mt.gov

NEBRASKA
Ms. Brenda L. Decker
Chief Information Officer
Department of Administrative Services
Office of the CIO
521 South 14th Street, Suite 300
Lincoln, NE 68508
P: (402) 471-3717
F: (402) 471-4864
E: bdecker@notes.state.ne.us

NEVADA
Mr. Dan Stockwell
Chief Information Officer
Department of Information Technology
505 East King Street, Room 403
Carson City, NV 89701
P: (775) 687-1294
F: (775) 684-5846
E: stockwell@doit.state.nv.us

NEW HAMPSHIRE
Mr. Richard C. Bailey Jr.
Chief Information Officer
Office of Information Technology
Department of Administrative Services
27 Hazen Drive
Concord, NH 03301
P: (603) 271-1538
E: rbailey@nh.gov

NEW JERSEY
Mr. Adel W. Ebeid
Chief Information Officer
Office of Information Technology
200/300 Riverview Plaza
P.O. Box 212
Trenton, NJ 08625
P: (609) 984-4082
F: (609) 633-9100
E: abel.ebeid@oit.state.nj.us

NEW MEXICO
Mr. Roy Soto
Chief Information Officer
Office of the Chief Information Officer
5301 Central Avenue, Northeast
Suite 1500
Albuquerque, NM 87108
P: (505) 841-6605
F: (505) 841-4780
E: Roy.Soto@state.nm.us

NEW YORK
Dr. Michael Mittleman
Chief Information Officer
Office of the Chief Information Officer
P.O. Box 2062
Albany, NY 12220
P: (518) 408-2140
F: (518) 408-2223
E: michael.mittleman@cio.state.ny.us

NORTH CAROLINA
Mr. George Bakolia
Chief Information Officer
Office of Information Technology Services
P.O. Box 17209
Raleigh, NC 27619
P: (919) 981-2680
F: (919) 981-2548
E: george.bakolia@ncmail.net

NORTH DAKOTA
Ms. Lisa Feldner
Chief Information Officer
Information Technology Department
600 East Boulevard Avenue, Room 103
Bismarck, ND 58505
P: (701) 328-1000
F: (701) 328-0301
E: lfeldner@nd.gov

OHIO
Mr. R. Steve Edmonson
Chief Information Officer
Office of Information Technology
30 East Broad Street, Floor 39
Columbus, OH 43215
P: (614) 644-6446
F: (614) 644-9382
E: steve.edmonson@oit.ohio.gov

OKLAHOMA
Mr. Joe Fleckinger
Director
Information Services Division
Office of State Finance
2209 North Central Avenue
Oklahoma City, OK 73105
P: (405) 522-4026
F: (405) 522-3042
E: joe.fleckinger@osf.ok.gov

PENNSYLVANIA
Ms. Kristen Miller
Chief Information Officer
Office of Administration
Office of Information Technology
209 Finance Building
Harrisburg, PA 17120
P: (717) 214-1915
F: (717) 783-4374
E: krismiller@state.pa.us

RHODE ISLAND
Mr. James Berard
Director of Information Technology Operations
Division of Information Technology
Department of Administration
One Capitol Hill, Floor 2
Providence, RI 02908
P: (401) 222-4583
F: (401) 222-3191
E: jberard@doit.ri.gov

SOUTH CAROLINA
Dr. Jim Bryant
Chief Information Officer
Office of the Chief Information Officer
Budget & Control Board
4430 Broad River Road
Columbia, SC 29210
P: (803) 896-0520
F: (803) 896-0789
E: jabryant@cio.sc.gov

SOUTH DAKOTA
Mr. Otto Doll
Commissioner
Bureau of Information & Telecommunications
Kneip Building
700 Governors Drive
Pierre, SD 57501
P: (605) 773-4165
F: (605) 773-6040
E: otto.doll@state.sd.us

Chief Information Officer

TENNESSEE
Mr. Bill Ezell
Chief Information Officer
Office for Information Resources
William R. Snodgrass Tennessee Towers
16th Floor, 312 8th Avenue, North
Nashville, TN 37243
P: (615) 741-3700
F: (615) 532-0471
E: bill.ezell@state.tn.us

TEXAS
Mr. Brian Rawson
Director
Department of Information Resources
300 West 15th Street, Suite 1300
P.O. Box 13564
Austin, TX 78701
P: (512) 463-9909
F: (512) 475-4759
E: brian.rawson@dir.state.tx.us

UTAH
Mr. Stephen Fletcher
Chief Information Officer & Executive Director
Office of the Governor
1 State Office Building, Floor 6
P.O. Box 141172
Salt Lake City, UT 84114
P: (801) 538-3298
F: (801) 538-3622
E: sfletcher@utah.gov

VERMONT
Mr. Thomas Murray
Commissioner & Chief Information Officer
Department of Information & Innovation
133 State Street, Floor 5
Montpelier, VT 05633
P: (802) 828-4141
F: (802) 828-3398
E: thomas.murray@state.vt.us

VIRGINIA
Mr. Lemuel C. Stewart Jr.
Chief Information Officer
Information Technologies Agency
110 South 7th Street
Richmond, VA 23219
P: (804) 343-9002
F: (804) 343-9048
E: lem.stewart@vita.virginia.gov

WASHINGTON
Mr. Gary Robinson
Chief Information Officer
Department of Information Services
1110 Jefferson Street, Southeast
P.O. Box 42445
Olympia, WA 98504
P: (360) 902-3500
F: (360) 664-0733
E: garyr@dis.wa.gov

WEST VIRGINIA
Mr. Kyle Schafer
Chief Technology Officer
Governor's Office of Technology
One Davis Square
321 Capitol Street
Charleston, WV 25301
P: (304) 558-3784
F: (304) 558-0136
E: kschafer@wvgot.org

WISCONSIN
Mr. Oskar Anderson
Chief Information Officer
Office of the Secretary
Department of Administration
P.O. Box 7844
Madison, WI 53707
P: (608) 264-9502
F: (608) 267-0626
E: oskar.anderson@wisconsin.gov

Chief Justice

The chief justice or judge of the state court of last resort.

ALABAMA
Hon. Sue Bell Cobb
Chief Justice
Supreme Court
300 Dexter Avenue
Montgomery, AL 36104
P: (334) 242-4609

ALASKA
Hon. Dana Fabe
Chief Justice
Supreme Court
303 K Street
Anchorage, AK 99501
P: (907) 264-0622
F: (907) 264-0768

AMERICAN SAMOA
Hon. F. Michael Kruse
Chief Justice
High Court
Courthouse, P.O. Box 309
Pago Pago, AS 96799
P: (684) 633-1410
F: (684) 633-1318

ARIZONA
Hon. Ruth V. McGregor
Chief Justice
Supreme Court
1501 West Washington Street
Phoenix, AZ 85007
P: (602) 542-9300

ARKANSAS
Hon. Jim Hannah
Chief Justice
Supreme Court
625 Marshall Street
Justice Building
Little Rock, AR 72201
P: (501) 682-6873
F: (501) 683-4006

CALIFORNIA
Hon. Ronald M. George
Chief Justice
Supreme Court
350 McAllister Street
San Francisco, CA 94102
P: (415) 865-7000

COLORADO
Hon. Mary J. Mullarkey
Chief Justice
Supreme Court
2 East 14th Avenue, Fourth Floor
Denver, CO 80203
P: (303) 861-1111 Ext. 271

CONNECTICUT
Hon. William J. Sullivan
Chief Justice
Supreme Court
Supreme Court Building
231 Capitol Avenue
Hartford, CT 06106
P: (860) 757-2200
F: (860) 757-2217

DELAWARE
Hon. Myron T. Steele
Chief Justice
Supreme Court
57 The Green
Dover, DE 19901
P: (302) 739-4214
F: (302) 739-2004

DISTRICT OF COLUMBIA
Hon. Eric Washington
Chief Judge
Supreme Court
Moultrie Courthouse
500 Indiana Avenue, Northwest, 6th Floor
Washington, DC 20001
P: (202) 879-2771

FLORIDA
Hon. R. Fred Lewis
Chief Justice
Supreme Court
Florida Supreme Court
500 South Duval Street
Tallahassee, FL 32399
P: (850) 488-0007

GEORGIA
Hon. Leah Ward Sears
Chief Justice
Supreme Court
244 Washington Street, Southwest
Room 572, State Office Annex
Atlanta, GA 30334
P: (404) 656-3470
F: (404) 656-2253

GUAM
Hon. F. Phillip Carbullido
Chief Justice
Supreme Court
Suite 300, Guam Judicial Center
120 West O'Brien Drive
Hagatna, GU 96910
P: (671) 475-3162
F: (671) 475-3140

HAWAII
Hon. Ronald T.Y. Moon
Chief Justice
Supreme Court
417 South King Street
Honolulu, HI 96813
P: (808) 539-4919
F: (808) 539-4928

IDAHO
Hon. Gerald F. Schroeder
Chief Justice
Supreme Court
P.O. Box 83720
451 West State Street
Boise, ID 83720
P: (208) 334-3324
F: (208) 947-7590

ILLINOIS
Hon. Robert R. Thomas
Chief Justice
Supreme Court
Supreme Court Building
200 East Capitol Avenue
Springfield, IL 62701
P: (217) 782-2035

INDIANA
Hon. Randall T. Shepard
Chief Justice
Supreme Court
315 Indiana State House
Indianapolis, IN 46204
P: 317.232.1930

IOWA
Hon. Marsha K. Ternus
Chief Justice
Supreme Court
Iowa Judicial Branch Building
111 East Court Avenue
Des Moines, IA 50319
P: (515) 281-5174

KANSAS
Hon. Kay McFarland
Chief Justice
Supreme Court
Judicial Center
301 West 10th Street
Topeka, KS 66612
P: (785) 296-5322
F: (785) 291-3274

KENTUCKY
Hon. Joseph E. Lambert
Chief Justice
Supreme Court
Capitol Building, Room 231
700 Capital Avenue
Frankfort, KY 40601
P: (502) 564-4162

LOUISIANA
Hon. Pascal F. Calogero Jr.
Chief Justice
Supreme Court
400 Royal Street
New Orleans, LA 70130
P: (504) 310-2300

MAINE
Hon. Leigh I. Saufley
Chief Justice
Supreme Judicial Court
142 Federal Street
P.O. Box 368
Portland, ME 04112
P: (207) 822-4286

MARYLAND
Hon. Robert M. Bell
Chief Judge
Court of Appeals
634 Courthouse East
111 North Calvert Street
Baltimore, MD 21202
P: (410) 333-6396

MASSACHUSETTS
Hon. Margaret H. Marshall
Chief Justice
Supreme Judicial Court
One Pemberton Square
Boston, MA 02108
P: (617) 557-1000

MICHIGAN
Hon. Clifford W. Taylor
Chief Justice
Supreme Court
Hall of Justice
925 W. Ottawa Street
Lansing, MI 48915
P: (517) 373-8635
F: (517) 373-8980

MINNESOTA
Hon. Russell A. Anderson
Chief Justice
Supreme Court
Supreme Court
25 Constitution Avenue
St. Paul, MN 55155
P: (651) 297-5529
F: (651) 297-4149

MISSISSIPPI
Hon. James W. Smith Jr.
Chief Justice
Supreme Court
450 High Street
P.O. Box 117
Jackson, MS 39205
P: (601) 359-2094
F: (601) 359-2443

Chief Justice

MISSOURI
Hon. Michael A. Wolff
Chief Justice
Supreme Court
P.O. Box 150
Jefferson City, MO 65102
P: (573) 751-4144
F: (573) 751-7514

MONTANA
Hon. Karla M. Gray
Chief Justice
Supreme Court
215 North Sanders
P.O. Box 203001
Helena, MT 59620
P: (406) 444-5490
F: (406) 444-3274

NEBRASKA
Hon. Michael G. Heavican
Chief Justice
Supreme Court
State Capitol, Room 2214
Lincoln, NE 68509
P: (402) 471-3738
F: (402) 471-2197

NEVADA
Hon. A. William Maupin
Chief Justice
Supreme Court
201 South Carson Street
Carson City, NV 89701
P: (775) 684-1600

NEW HAMPSHIRE
Hon. John T. Broderick Jr.
Chief Justice
Supreme Court
One Noble Drive
Concord, NH 03301
P: (603) 271-3751
F: (603) 271-6630

NEW JERSEY
Hon. James Zazzali
Chief Justice
Supreme Court
Hughes Justice Complex
P.O. Box 970
Trenton, NJ 08625
P: (609) 292-4837

NEW MEXICO
Hon. Richard C. Bosson
Chief Justice
Supreme Court
P.O. Box 848
Santa Fe, NM 87504
P: (505) 827-4860

NEW YORK
Hon. Judith S. Kaye
Chief Judge
New York State Unified Court System
230 Park Avenue
Suite 826
New York, NY 10169
P: (212) 661-6787
F: (212) 682-2778

NORTH CAROLINA
Hon. Sarah Parker
Chief Justice
Supreme Court
P.O. Box 2170
Raleigh, NC 27602
P: (919) 733-3723

NORTH DAKOTA
Hon. Gerald W. VandeWalle
Chief Justice
Supreme Court
State Capitol Building
600 East Boulevard Avenue, Dept. 180
Bismark, ND 58505
P: (701) 328-2221
F: (701) 328-4480
E: GVandeWalle@ndcourts.gov

NORTHERN MARIANA ISLANDS
Hon. Miguel S. Demapan
Chief Justice
Supreme Court
P.O. Box 502165
Saipan, MP 96950
P: (670) 236-9700
F: (670) 236-9702

OHIO
Hon. Thomas J. Moyer
Chief Justice
Supreme Court
65 South Front Street
Columbus, OH 43215
P: (614) 387-9010
F: (614) 387-9019

OKLAHOMA
Hon. James Winchester
Chief Justice
Supreme Court
State Capitol, Room B-2
2300 North Lincoln Boulevard
Oklahoma City, OK 73105
P: (405) 521-2163

OREGON
Hon. Paul J. De Muniz
Chief Justice
Supreme Court
1163 State Street
Salem, OR 97301
P: (503) 986-5709
F: (503) 986-5730

PENNSYLVANIA
Hon. Ralph J. Cappy
Chief Justice
Supreme Court
3130 One Oxford Center
Pittsburgh, PA 15219
P: (412) 565-2700
F: (412) 565-7637

PUERTO RICO
Hon. Federico Hernandez-Denton
Chief Justice
Supreme Court
P.O. Box 9022392
San Juan, PR 00902
P: (787) 724-3535
F: (787) 724-3551

RHODE ISLAND
Hon. Frank J. Williams
Chief Justice
Supreme Court
Licht Judicial Complex
250 Benefit Street
Providence, RI 02903
P: (401) 222-3290
F: (401) 222-1351

SOUTH CAROLINA
Hon. Jean Hoefer Toal
Chief Justice
Supreme Court
P.O. Box 11330
Columbia, SC 29211
P: (803) 734-1080
F: (803) 734-1499

SOUTH DAKOTA
Hon. David Gilbertson
Chief Justice
Supreme Court
500 East Capitol Avenue
Pierre, SD 57501
P: (605) 773-3511
F: (605) 773-6128

TENNESSEE
Hon. William M. Barker
Chief Justice
Supreme Court
540 McCallie Avenue, Suite 410
Chattanooga, TN 37402
P: (615) 741-2681

TEXAS
Hon. Wallace B. Jefferson
Chief Justice
Supreme Court
201 West Fourteenth Street
P.O. Box 12248, Capitol Station
Austin, TX 78711
P: (512) 463-7899
F: (512) 708-8191

U.S. VIRGIN ISLANDS
Hon. Darryl Dean Donohue
Presiding Judge
Territorial Court
R.H. Amphlett Leader Justice Complex
P.O. Box 929
Christiansted, VI 00821

UTAH
Hon. Christine M. Durham
Chief Justice
Supreme Court
450 South State Street
P.O. Box 140210
Salt Lake City, UT 84114
P: (801) 238-7945
F: (801) 238-7980

VERMONT
Hon. Paul L. Reiber
Chief Justice
Supreme Court
109 State Street
Montpelier, VT 05609
P: (802) 828-3278
F: (802) 828-4750

VIRGINIA
Hon. Leroy Roundtree Hassell Sr.
Chief Justice
Supreme Court
100 North Ninth Street
P.O. Box 1315
Richmond, VA 23219
P: (804) 786-6404
F: (804) 225-2406

WASHINGTON
Hon. Gerry L. Alexander
Chief Justice
Supreme Court
415 12th Avenue, Southwest
P.O. Box 40929
Olympia, WA 98504
P: (360) 357-2029
F: (360) 357-2102

WEST VIRGINIA
Hon. Robin Davis
Chief Justice
Supreme Court of Appeals
Capitol Complex
Building 1, Room E-301
Charleston, WV 25305
P: (304) 558-4811
F: (304) 558-3815
E: robindavis@courtswv.org

WISCONSIN
Hon. Shirley S. Abrahamson
Chief Justice
Supreme Court
16 East State Capitol
P.O. Box 1688
Madison, WI 53701
P: (608) 266-1885
F: (608) 261-8299

WYOMING
Hon. Barton R. Voigt
Chief Justice
Supreme Court
Supreme Court Building
2301 Capitol Avenue
Cheyenne, WY 82001
P: (307) 777-7316
F: (307) 777-6129

Child Support Enforcement

Processes child support cases and implements required provisions of child support enforcement program.

ALABAMA
Mr. Tom Bernier
Director
Child Support Enforcement Division
50 North Ripley Street
Mongtomery, AL 36130
P: (334) 242-9321
F: (334) 242-0606
E: tbernier@dhr.state.al.us

ALASKA
Mr. John Mallonee
Director
Child Support Enforcement
Department of Revenue
550 West 7th Avenue, Suite 310
Anchorage, AK 99501
P: (907) 269-6800
F: (907) 269-6868

AMERICAN SAMOA
Mr. Talia Fa'afetai I'aulualo
Director
Department of Human & Social Services
American Samoa Government
Pago Pago, AS 96799
P: (684) 633-1187
F: (684) 633-7449

ARIZONA
Ms. Annmarie Mena
Acting Assistant Director
Division of Child Support Enforcement
3443 North Central
Phoenix, AZ 85012
P: (602) 274-7646

ARKANSAS
Mr. Dan McDonald
Administrator
Office of Child Support Enforcement
400 East Capitol Avenue
Little Rock, AR 72201
P: (501) 682-6169
F: (501) 682-6002
E: dan.mcdonald@ocse.state.ar.us

CALIFORNIA
Ms. Greta J. Wallace
Director
Department of Child Support Services
1120 International Drive
Rancho Cordova, CA 95742
P: (916) 464-5300
F: (916) 464-5211

COLORADO
Mr. John Bernhart
Director
Division of Child Support Enforcement
Department of Human Services
1575 Sherman Street, 5th Floor
Denver, CO 80203
P: (303) 866-3985
F: (303) 866-4360

CONNECTICUT
Ms. Diane Fray
Chief
Bureau of Child Support Enforcement
25 Sigourney Street
Hartford, CT 06106
P: (860) 424-5253
F: (860) 951-2996
E: diane.fray@po.state.ct.us

DELAWARE
Mr. Charles E. Hayward
Division Director
Delaware Health & Social Services, Child Support Enforcement
P.O. Box 904
New Castle, DE 19720
P: (302) 577-4807
F: (302) 577-4811
E: chayward@state.de.us

DISTRICT OF COLUMBIA
Ms. Benidia Rice
Deputy Attorney General
Child Support Enforcement Division
441 4th Street, Northwest
Suite 550N
Washington, DC 20001
P: (202) 442-9900

FLORIDA
Ms. Ann Mims
Director
Child Support Enforcement Program
P.O. Box 8030
Tallahassee, FL 32314

GEORGIA
Ms. Cindy Moss
Director
Office of Child Support Enforcement
Two Peachtree Street, Northwest
Atlanta, GA 30303
P: (404) 463-8800

GUAM
Hon. Alicia Limtiaco
Attorney General
Office of the Attorney General
Suite 2-200E, Judicial Center Building
120 West O'Brien Drive
Hagatna, GU 96910
P: (671) 475-3409

HAWAII
Mr. Gary Kemp
Administrator
Child Support Enforcement Agency
601 Kamokila Boulevard, Suite 251
Kapolei, HI 96707
P: (808) 692-8265

IDAHO
Ms. Terri Meyer
Bureau Chief
Bureau of Child Support Operations
P.O. Box 83720-0036
Boise, ID 83720
P: (208) 334-6673
F: (208) 334-5817
E: meyert@dhw.idaho.gov

ILLINOIS
Ms. Pam Compton Lowry
Administrator
Child Support Enforcement
509 South 6th Street
Springfield, IL 62701
P: (217) 782-2624
F: (217) 524-4608

INDIANA
Ms. Wendy Yerkes
Deputy Director
Division of Child Support
402 West Washington Street, Room 360
Indianapolis, IN 46207
P: (317) 232-2892

IOWA
Ms. Carol Eaton
Chief
Bureau of Collections
1305 East Walnut Street
Des Moines, IA 50319
P: (515) 281-5647

Ms. Jeanne Nesbit
Division Administrator
Division of Child Support Recovery, Case Management & Refugee Services
1305 East Walnut Street
Des Moines, IA 50319
P: (515) 281-8580

KANSAS
Mr. James A. Robertson
Director
Child Support Enforcement
P.O. Box 0497
Topeka, KS 66601
P: (785) 296-3237
F: (785) 296-5206

KENTUCKY
Mr. Monte D. Gross
Director
Division of Child Support
P.O. Box 2150
Frankfort, KY 40602
P: (502) 564-2285
F: (502) 564-5988

LOUISIANA
Ms. Robbie Endris
Executive Director
Support Enforcement Services Division
P.O. Box 94065
Baton Rouge, LA 70804
P: (225) 342-4780
F: (225) 342-7397
E: rendris@dss.state.la.us

Mr. Adren O. Wilson
Assistant Secretary
Office of Family Support
627 North 4th Street
P.O. Box 94065
Baton Rouge, LA 70804
P: (225) 342-3950
F: (225) 219-9399
E: Adren.Wilson@dss.state.la.us

MAINE
Mr. Steve Hussey
Director
Child Support Enforcement
11 State House Station
Augusta, ME 04333
P: (207) 287-2887
F: (207) 287-6883

MARYLAND
Mr. Joseph Jackins
Acting Executive Director
Child Support Enforcement Division
Saratoga State Center
311 West Saratoga Street
Baltimore, MD 21201
P: (410) 767-7573
E: jjackins@dhr.state.md.us

MASSACHUSETTS
Mr. Alan L. LeBovidge
Commissioner
Department of Revenue
100 Cambridge Street, 8th Floor
Boston, MA 02114
P: (617) 626-2201
F: (617) 626-2299

MICHIGAN
Ms. Marilyn Stephen
Director
Office of Child Support
P.O. Box 30478
Lansing, MI 48909
P: (517) 241-7460
F: (517) 373-4980

MINNESOTA
Mr. Wayland Campbell
Director
Child Support Enforcement Division
444 Lafayette Road
St. Paul, MN 55155
P: (651) 431-4400
F: (651) 431-7517

MISSISSIPPI
Mr. Wally Naylor
Director
Division of Child Support Enforcement
75 North State Street
P.O. Box 352
Jackson, MS 39205
P: (601) 359-4861
F: (601) 359-4415
E: wnaylor@mdhs.state.ms.us

MISSOURI
Ms. Janel Luck
Interim Division Director
Family Support Division
P.O. Box 2320
615 Howerton Court
Jefferson City, MO 65102
P: (573) 751-4247
F: (573) 751-0507

MONTANA
Mr. Lonnie J. Olson
Administrator
Child Support Enforcement Division
3075 North Montana, Suite 112
P.O. Box 202943
Helena, MT 59620
P: (406) 444-3338
F: (406) 444-1370

NEBRASKA
Mr. Daryl D. Wusk
Administrator
Office of Economic & Family Support
Department of Health & Human Services
P.O. Box 94728
Lincoln, NE 68509
P: (402) 479-5555
F: (402) 479-5543

NEVADA
Ms. Louise Bush
Welfare Division, Child Support Enforcement
1470 College Parkway
Carson City, NV 89706
P: (775) 684-0500
F: (775) 684-0646
E: lbush@welfare.state.nv.us

NEW HAMPSHIRE
Ms. Mary S. Weatherill
Director
Division of Child Support Services
129 Pleasant Street
Concord, NH 03301
P: (603) 271-4221
F: (603) 271-4787

NEW JERSEY
Ms. Alisha A. Griffin
Assistant Director
Department of Human Services, Child Support
P.O. Box 716
Trenton, NJ 08625
P: (609) 584-5093
F: (609) 588-2064

NEW MEXICO
Ms. Kathleen B. Valdes
Acting Director
Child Support Enforcement Division
1120 Paseo De Perelta
PERA Building
Santa Fe, NM 87505
P: (505) 476-7207
F: (505) 476-7045

NEW YORK
Mr. Scott E. Cade
Deputy Commissioner
Division of Child Support Enforcement
40 North Pearl Street, 13th Floor
Albany, NY 12243
P: (518) 474-1078
F: (518) 486-3127

NORTH CAROLINA
Mr. Barry Miller
Director
Child Support Enforcement
P.O. Box 20800
Raleigh, NC 27609
P: (919) 255-3800
F: (919) 212-3840
E: barry.miller@ncmail.net

NORTH DAKOTA
Mr. Mike Schwindt
Director
Department of Human Services, Child Support Enforcement
1929 North Washington Street
P.O. Box 7190
Bismarck, ND 58507
P: (701) 328-3582
F: (701) 328-6575

OHIO
Ms. Helen Jones-Kelley
Director
Department of Job & Family Services
30 East Broad Street, 31st Floor
Columbus, OH 43215
P: (614) 466-6282
F: (614) 466-2815
E: jonesh@odjfs.state.oh.us

OKLAHOMA
Mr. Gary Dart
Director
Child Support Enforcement Division
P.O. Box 25352
Oklahoma City, OK 73125
P: (405) 522-5871
F: (405) 522-2753
E: gary.dart@okdhs.org

OREGON
Ms. Cindy Chinnock
Director
Division of Child Support
494 State Street, Northeast
Suite 300
Salem, OR 97304
P: (503) 945-5600
F: (503) 986-6158
E: doj.info@state.or.us

PENNSYLVANIA
Mr. Daniel Richard
Director
Bureau of Child Support Enforcement
1303 North 7th Street
P.O. Box 8018
Harrisburg, PA 17105
P: (717) 783-9659
F: (717) 772-4936

RHODE ISLAND
Ms. Sharon A. Santilli
Director
Office of Child Support Services
77 Dorrance Street
Providence, RI 02903
P: (401) 222-2847

SOUTH CAROLINA
Ms. Kathleen M. Hayes
Director
Department of Social Services
P.O. Box 1520
Columbia, SC 29202
P: (803) 898-7360
F: (803) 898-7277

SOUTH DAKOTA
Mr. Terry Walter
Administrator
Office of Child Support Enforcement
Kneip Building
700 Governors Drive
Pierre, SD 57501
P: (605) 773-3641
F: (605) 773-7295
E: terry.walter@state.sd.us

TENNESSEE
Mr. Michael L. Adams
Assistant Commissioner
Office of Child Support
400 Deaderick Street
Nashville, TN 37248
P: (615) 313-4712
F: (615) 532-2791

TEXAS
Ms. Alicia Key
Deputy Attorney General for Child Support
Office of the Attorney General
P.O. Box 12548
Austin, TX 78711
P: (512) 460-6000

Child Support Enforcement

U.S. VIRGIN ISLANDS
Ms. Regina De Chabert
Director
Paternity & Child Support Division
2 Nisky Center, Second Floor
Suite 500
St. Thomas, VI 00802
P: (340) 775-3070
F: (340) 775-3248

UTAH
Mr. Mark Brasher
Director
Office of Recovery Services
Department of Human Services
515 East 100 South
Salt Lake City, UT 84102
P: (801) 536-8901
F: (801) 536-8509
E: mbrasher@utah.gov

VERMONT
Mr. Jeffrey Cohen
Director
Office of Child Support
103 South Main Street, A Building
Waterbury, VT 05676
P: (802) 241-2319
F: (802) 244-1483

VIRGINIA
Mr. Nathaniel L. Young
Deputy Commissioner & Director
Division of Child Support Enforcement
7 North 8th Street
Richmond, VA 23219
P: (804) 692-1501
F: (804) 692-2353
E: nick.young@dss.virginia.gov

WASHINGTON
Mr. Adolfo Capestany
Director
Division of Child Support Enforcement
P.O. Box 11520
Tacoma, WA 98411
P: (360) 664-5445

WEST VIRGINIA
Ms. Susan Shelton Perry
Commissioner
Bureau for Child Support Enforcement
Building 6, Room 817
1900 Kanawha Boulevard, East
Charleston, WV 25305
P: (304) 558-0909
F: (304) 558-4092
E: susanperry@wvdhhr.org

WISCONSIN
Ms. Susan Pfeiffer
Director
Child Support Bureau
Division of Economic Support
P.O. Box 7935
Madison, WI 53707
P: (608) 266-9909
F: (608) 267-2824

WYOMING
Ms. Brenda Lyttle
Director
Child Support Enforcement Program
2300 Capitol Avenue
Hathaway Building, 3rd Floor
Cheyenne, WY 82002
P: (307) 777-6948
F: (307) 777-3693

Children and Youth Services

Implements programs designed to protect children and youth against abuse, neglect and exploitation.

ALABAMA
Mr. Richard Dorrough
Director
Department of Children's Affairs
RSA Tower, Suite 1670
201 Monroe Street
Montgomery, AL 36130
P: (334) 223-0502
F: (334) 240-3054

ALASKA
Ms. Tammy Sandoval
Deputy Commissioner
Office of Children's Services
Department of Health & Social Services
P.O. Box 110630
Juneau, AK 99811
P: (907) 465-3191
F: (907) 465-3397

AMERICAN SAMOA
Mr. Talia Fa'afetai I'aulualo
Director
Department of Human & Social Services
American Samoa Government
Pago Pago, AS 96799
P: (684) 633-1187
F: (684) 633-7449

ARIZONA
Mr. Ken Deibert
Deputy Director
Division of Children, Youth & Families
1717 West Jefferson
Phoenix, AZ 85007
P: (602) 542-3598

ARKANSAS
Ms. Pat Page
Director
Division of Children & Family Services
P.O. Box 1437, Slot S560
Little Rock, AR 72203
P: (501) 682-8008
F: (501) 682-6968
E: pat.page@arkansas.gov

CALIFORNIA
Mr. Cliff Allenby
Interim Director
Department of Social Services
744 P Street
Sacramento, CA 95814
P: (916) 657-2598
F: (916) 654-6012
E: cliff.allenby@dss.ca.gov

COLORADO
Ms. Rosemarie Allen
Office Manager
Division of Child Care Services
Department of Human Services
1575 Sherman Street, 1st Floor
Denver, CO 80203
P: (303) 866-5493
F: (303) 866-4453
E: rosemarie.allen@state.co.us

CONNECTICUT
Ms. Darlene Dunbar
Commissioner
Department of Children & Families
505 Hudson Street
Hartford, CT 06106
P: (860) 550-6300
E: darlene.dunbar@po.state.ct.us

DELAWARE
Ms. Cari DeSantis
Secretary
Department of Services for Children, Youth & Their Families
1825 Faulkland Road
Wilmington, DE 19805
P: (302) 633-2503
F: (302) 995-8290

DISTRICT OF COLUMBIA
Ms. Sharlynn Bobo
Interim Director
Child & Family Services Agency
400 6th Street, Southwest
5th Floor
Washington, DC 20024
P: (202) 442-6000
F: (202) 727-6505

FLORIDA
Mr. Bob Butterworth
Secretary
Department of Children & Families
1317 Winewood Boulevard
Building 1, Room 202
Tallahassee, FL 32399
P: (850) 487-1111
F: (850) 922-2993

GEORGIA
Ms. Mary Dean Harvey
Director
Division of Family & Children Services
Two Peachtree Street, Suite 18-486
Atlanta, GA 30303
P: (404) 657-7660
F: (404) 508-7289

GUAM
Mr. Arthur U. San Agustin
Director
Department of Health & Social Services
123 Chalan Kareta, Route 10
Mangilao, GU 96923
P: (671) 735-7102
F: (671) 734-5910
E: chiefdsc@dphss.govguam.net

HAWAII
Mr. Gary Kemp
Administrator
Child Support Enforcement Agency
601 Kamokila Boulevard, Suite 251
Kapolei, HI 96707
P: (808) 692-8265

IDAHO
Ms. Michelle Britton
Administrator
Division of Family & Community Services
450 West State Street
5th Floor, Pete T. Cenarrusa Building
Boise, ID 83720
P: (208) 334-0461
F: (208) 334-6699

ILLINOIS
Mr. Erwin McEwen
Acting Director
Department of Children & Family Services
406 East Monroe Street
Springfield, IL 62701
P: (217) 785-2509
F: (217) 785-1052

INDIANA
Mr. James F. Robertson IV
Director, Division of Family Resources
Family & Social Services Administration
402 West Washington Street, Room W392
P.O. Box 7083
Indianapolis, IN 46207
P: (317) 232-4704
F: (317) 233-4693

IOWA
Ms. Mary Nelson
Division Administrator
Department of Behavioral, Developmental & Protective Services
Hoover Building, 5th Floor
1305 East Walnut Street
Des Moines, IA 50319
P: (515) 281-5521
F: (515) 242-6036
E: mnelson1@dhs.state.ia.us

KANSAS
Ms. Sandra Hazlett
Director
Children & Family Policy
915 Southwest Harrison Street, 5th Floor
Topeka, KS 66612
P: (785) 368-8143
F: (785) 368-8159

KENTUCKY
Mr. Mark Washington
Commissioner
Department for Community Based Services
275 East Main Street, 3W-A
Frankfort, KY 40621
P: (502) 564-3703
F: (502) 564-6907

LOUISIANA
Mr. Adren O. Wilson
Assistant Secretary
Office of Family Support
627 North 4th Street
P.O. Box 94065
Baton Rouge, LA 70804
P: (225) 342-3950
F: (225) 219-9399
E: Adren.Wilson@dss.state.la.us

MAINE
Mr. James Beougher
Director
Bureau of Child & Family Services
11 State House Station
Augusta, ME 04333
P: (207) 287-5060
F: (207) 287-5282

MARYLAND
Ms. Arlene Lee
Executive Director
Governor's Office for Children
301 West Preston Street, Suite 1502
Baltimore, MD 21201
P: (410) 767-4160
F: (410) 333-5248

Children and Youth Services

MASSACHUSETTS
Ms. Jane E. Tewksbury
Commissioner
Department of Youth Services
27 Wormwood Street, Suite 400
Boston, MA 02110
P: (617) 727-7575
F: (617) 727-0696

MICHIGAN
Ms. Wanda Stokes
Bureau Chief
Child & Family Services Bureau
525 West Ottawa
Lansing, MI 48913
P: (517) 373-1114
F: (517) 241-1850

MINNESOTA
Mr. Cal Ludeman
Commissioner
Department of Human Services
Human Services Building
540 Cedar Street
St. Paul, MN 55155
P: (651) 431-2907
F: (651) 431-7443
E: cal.ludeman@state.mn.us

MISSISSIPPI
Ms. Julia Todd
Director
Office of Children & Youth
750 North State Street
P.O. Box 352
Jackson, MS 39205
P: (601) 359-4544
F: (601) 359-4422

MISSOURI
Mr. Tim Decker
Director
Division of Youth Services
221 West High Street
P.O. Box 447
Jefferson City, MO 65102
P: (573) 751-3324
F: (573) 526-4494
E: tim.decker@dss.mo.gov

MONTANA
Ms. Joan Miles
Director
Department of Public Health & Human Services
111 North Sanders, Room 301/308
P.O. Box 4210
Helena, MT 59604
P: (406) 444-5622
F: (406) 444-1970

NEBRASKA
Mr. Scott Adams
Director
Department of Health & Human Services
P.O. Box 95044
Lincoln, NE 68509
P: (402) 471-3121
E: roger.lempke@ne.ngb.army.mil

NEVADA
Mr. Fernando Serrano
Administrator
Division of Child & Family Services
711 East Fifth Street
Carson City, NV 89701
P: (775) 684-4400
F: (775) 684-4455
E: fserrano@dcfs.state.nv.us

NEW HAMPSHIRE
Ms. Nancy Rollins
Director, Division of Community Based Services
Division of Children, Youth & Families
Department of Health & Human Services
105 Pleasant Street, Main Building
Concord, NH 03301
P: (603) 271-8560
F: (603) 271-5058
E: nrollins@dhhs.state.nh.us

NEW JERSEY
Ms. Eileen Crummy
Director
Division of Youth & Family Services
222 South Warren Street
P.O. Box 729, 3rd Floor
Trenton, NJ 08625
P: (609) 292-6920
E: dcf-dyfsdirectorsoffice@dcf.state.nj.us

NEW MEXICO
Ms. Mary-Dale Bolson
Cabinet Secretary
Department of Children, Youth & Families
1120 Paseo De Perelta
PERA Building
Santa Fe, NM 87501
P: (505) 827-7602

NEW YORK
Ms. Gladys Carrion
Commissioner
Office of Children & Youth Services
Capitol View Office Park
52 Washington Street
Rensselaer, NY 12144
P: (518) 474-5522

NORTH CAROLINA
Ms. Pheon Beal
Director
Division of Social Services
325 North Salisbury Street
2401 Mail Service Center
Raleigh, NC 27699
P: (919) 733-4534
F: (919) 733-9386
E: pheon.beal@ncmail.net

NORTH DAKOTA
Mr. Paul Ronningen
Director
Children & Family Services
600 East Boulevard Avenue, 3rd Floor
Judicial Wing
Bismarck, ND 58505
P: (701) 328-3538
F: (701) 328-2359
E: soronp@nd.gov

NORTHERN MARIANA ISLANDS
Ms. Daisy C. Villagomez-Bier
Secretary
Department of Community & Cultural Affairs
Caller Box 10007, Capitol Hill
Saipan, MP 96950
P: (670) 664-2550
F: (670) 664-2560
E: dysdir@saipan.com

OHIO
Mr. Rick Smith
Deputy Director
Office for Children & Families
Department of Job & Family Services
225 East Main Street, 3rd Floor
Columbus, OH 43215
P: (614) 466-1213
F: (614) 466-4359

OKLAHOMA
Ms. Linda S. Smith
Division Administrator
Children & Family Services Division
P.O. Box 25352
Oklahoma City, OK 73125
P: (405) 522-1487
F: (405) 521-4373
E: linda.smith@okdhs.org

OREGON
Ms. Ramona L. Foley
Assistant Director
Children, Adults & Families
500 Summer Street, Northeast
2nd Floor, E-62
Salem, OR 97301
P: (503) 945-5600
F: (503) 581-6198
E: dhs.info@state.or.us

PENNSYLVANIA
Mr. Richard Gold
Deputy Secretary
Office of Children, Youth & Families
P.O. Box 2675
Harrisburg, PA 17105
P: (717) 787-4756
F: (717) 787-0414

PUERTO RICO
Mr. Felix Matos Rodriguez
Secretary
Department of the Family
P.O. Box 11398
San Juan, PR 00910
P: (787) 294-4900
F: (787) 294-0732

RHODE ISLAND
Ms. Patricia Martinez
Executive Director
Department of Children, Youth & Families
101 Friendship Street
Providence, RI 02903
P: (401) 528-3502

SOUTH CAROLINA
Ms. Kathleen M. Hayes
Director
Department of Social Services
P.O. Box 1520
Columbia, SC 29202
P: (803) 898-7360
F: (803) 898-7277

SOUTH DAKOTA
Ms. Virgena Wieseler
Administrator
Office of Child Protection Services
Kneip Building
700 Governors Drive
Pierre, SD 57505
P: (605) 773-3227
F: (605) 773-6834
E: virgena.wieseler@state.sd.us

TENNESSEE
Dr. Viola Miller
Commissioner
Department of Children's Services
Cordell Hull Building, 7th Floor
710 James Robertson Parkway
Nashville, TN 37243
P: (615) 741-9699
F: (615) 532-8079

TEXAS
Mr. Carey Cockerell
Commissioner
Department of Family & Protective Services
P.O. Box 149030
Austin, TX 78714
P: (512) 438-4870

U.S. VIRGIN ISLANDS
Ms. Sedonie Halbert
Commissioner
Department of Human Services
Knud Hansen Complex, Building A
1303 Hospital Grounds
St. Thomas, VI 00802
P: (340) 774-0930
F: (340) 774-3466

UTAH
Mr. Duane Betournay
Director
Division of Child & Family Services
Department of Human Services
120 North 200 West, Room 225
Salt Lake City, UT 84103
P: (801) 538-4089
F: (801) 538-3993
E: dbetournay@utah.gov

VERMONT
Mr. James Morse
Commissioner
Department for Children & Families
103 South Main Street
Waterbury, VT 05671
P: (802) 241-2100
F: (802) 241-2979

VIRGINIA
Mr. Anthony Conyers Jr.
Commissioner
Department of Social Services
7 North 8th Street
Richmond, VA 23219
P: (804) 692-1903
F: (804) 692-1949
E: anthony.conyers@dss.virginia.gov

WASHINGTON
Ms. Cheryl Stephani
Assistant Secretary
Children's Administration
P.O. Box 45710
Olympia, WA 98504
P: (360) 902-7820

WEST VIRGINIA
Ms. Patricia Moore-Moss
Director
Office of Maternal, Child & Family Health
350 Capitol Street, Room 427
Charleston, WV 25301
P: (304) 558-5388
F: (304) 558-2183
E: patmoss@wvdhhr.org

WISCONSIN
Mr. William R. Fiss
Interim Administrator
Division of Children & Family Services
P.O. Box 8916
Madison, WI 53224
P: (608) 267-3728

WYOMING
Mr. Tony Lewis
Interim Director of Family Services
Department of Family Services
Hathaway Building, 3rd Floor
2300 Capitol Avenue
Cheyenne, WY 82002
P: (307) 777-7561
F: (307) 777-7747

Civil Rights

Overall responsibility for preventing and redressing discrimination in employment, education, housing, public accommodations and credit (because of race, color, sex, age, national origin, religion or disability.)

ALASKA
Ms. Paula Haley
Executive Director
Human Rights Commission
800 A Street, Suite 204
Anchorage, AK 99501
P: (907) 276-7474
F: (907) 278-8588

AMERICAN SAMOA
Hon. Afa Ripley Jr.
Attorney General
Office of the Attorney General
American Samoa Government
Executive Office Building, Utulei
Pago Pago, AS 96799
P: (684) 633-4163
F: (684) 633-1838

ARIZONA
Ms. Virginia Herrera-Gonzales
Division Chief Counsel
Office of the Attorney General
1275 West Washington
Phoenix, AZ 85007
P: (602) 542-5263

CALIFORNIA
Mr. Ramon S. Lopez
Bureau Chief
Civil Rights Bureau
744 P Street
Sacramento, CA 95814
P: (916) 654-2107

COLORADO
Mr. Wendell Pryor
Director
Civil Rights Division
1560 Broadway
Suite 1050
Denver, CO 80202
P: (303) 894-2997
F: (303) 894-7830
E: wendell.pryor@dora.state.co.us

CONNECTICUT
Mr. Hamisi Ingram
Executive Director
Commission on Human Rights & Opportunities
21 Grand Street
Hartford, CT 06106
P: (303) 541-3400
F: (860) 246-5068

DELAWARE
Ms. Juana Fuentes-Bowles
Director
Office of Human Relations
820 North French Street, 4th Floor
Wilmington, DE 19801
P: (302) 577-5053
F: (302) 577-3486

DISTRICT OF COLUMBIA
Mr. Gustavo F. Velasquez
Director
Office of Human Rights
441 4th Street, Northwest
Suite 570N
Washington, DC 20001
P: (202) 727-4559
F: (202) 727-9589

FLORIDA
Mr. Derrick Daniel
Executive Director
Commission on Human Relations
2009 Appalache Parkway
Suite 100
Tallahassee, FL 32301
P: (850) 488-7082
F: (850) 488-5291
E: fchrinfo@fchr.myflorida.com

GEORGIA
Mr. Gordon Joyner
Administrator
Commission on Equal Opportunity
Suite 710, International Tower
229 Peachtree Street, North East
Atlanta, GA 30303
P: (404) 656-1736
F: (404) 656-4399

GUAM
Ms. Maria Connelley
Director
Department of Labor
414 West Soledad, Suite 400
GCIC Building, P.O. Box 9970
Tamuning, GU 96931
P: (671) 475-7046
F: (671) 475-7045

Mr. Vernon Perez
Executive Director
Civil Service Commission
490 Chalan Palasyo, Hagatna Heights
P.O. Box 3156
Hagatna, GU 96932
P: (671) 475-1300
F: (671) 475-3301

HAWAII
Mr. William D. Hoshijo
Executive Director
Civil Rights Commission
830 Punchbowl Street
Suite 411
Honolulu, HI 96813
P: (808) 586-8636
F: (808) 586-8655
E: info@hicrc.org

IDAHO
Ms. Leslie Goddard
Director
Human Rights Commission
1109 Main Street
Owyhee Plaza, Suite 400
Boise, ID 83720
P: (208) 334-2873
F: (208) 334-2664
E: lgoddard@ihrc.idaho.gov

ILLINOIS
Mr. Rocco Claps
Director
Department of Human Rights
100 West Randolph
Suite 10-100
Chicago, IL 60601
P: (312) 814-6200
F: (312) 814-1436

INDIANA
Mr. Gregory K. Scott
Executive Director
Civil Rights Commission
100 North Senate, Room N103
Indianapolis, IN 46204
P: (317) 232-2600
F: (317) 232-6580

IOWA
Mr. Ralph Rosenberg
Executive Director
Civil Rights Commission
Grimes State Office Building
400 East 14th Street
Des Moines, IA 50319
P: (515) 281-4121
F: (515) 242-5840
E: ralph.rosenberg@icrc.state.ia.us

KANSAS
Mr. William V. Minner
Executive Director
Human Rights Commission
900 Southwest Jackson Street
Suite 851-S
Topeka, KS 66612
P: (785) 296-3206
F: (785) 296-0589

KENTUCKY
Ms. Linda Strite Murnane
Executive Director
Commission on Human Rights
Heyburn Building, Suite 700
322 West Broadway
Louisville, KY 40202
P: (502) 595-4024
F: (502) 595-4801

LOUISIANA
Hon. Charles C. Foti Jr. (D)
Attorney General
Office of the Attorney General
P.O. Box 94095
Baton Rouge, LA 70804
P: (225) 342-7013
F: (225) 342-7335

MAINE
Ms. Patricia Ryan
Executive Director
Human Rights Commission
51 State House Station
Augusta, ME 04333
P: (207) 624-6050

MARYLAND
Mr. Henry B. Ford
Executive Director
Commission on Human Relations
6 Saint Paul Street, 9th Floor
Baltimore, MD 21202
P: (410) 767-8563
F: (410) 333-1841
E: hford@mail.mchr.state.md.us

MASSACHUSETTS
Ms. Dorca I. Gomez
Commissioner
Commission Against Discrimination
One Ashburton Place, Room 601
Boston, MA 02108
P: (617) 994-6000
F: (617) 994-6024

MICHIGAN
Ms. Linda V. Parker
Director
Department of Civil Rights
Capitol Tower Building
Suite 800
Lansing, MI 48933
P: (517) 335-3165
F: (517) 241-0546
E: parkerlv@michigan.gov

MINNESOTA
Ms. Velma Korbel
Commissioner
Department of Human Rights
190 East 5th Street
Suite 700
St. Paul, MN 55101
P: (651) 296-9038
F: (651) 296-1736
E: velma.korbel@state.mn.us

MISSOURI
Ms. Donna Cavitte
Director
Commission on Human Rights
3315 West Truman Boulevard
P.O. Box 1129
Jefferson City, MO 65102
P: (573) 751-3325
F: (573) 751-2905
E: donna.cavitte
@dolir.mo.gov

MONTANA
Ms. Katherine Kountz
Bureau Chief
Human Rights Bureau
1625 11th Avenue
P.O. Box 1728
Helena, MT 59624
P: (406) 444-2884
F: (406) 444-2798
E: kkountz@state.mt.us

NEBRASKA
Ms. Anne Hobbs
Executive Director
Equal Opportunity Commission
301 Centennial Mall Sourth, 5th Floor
P.O. Box 94934
Lincoln, NE 68509
P: (402) 471-2024
F: (402) 471-4059

NEVADA
Ms. Deborah Madison
Executive Director
Equal Rights Commission
1515 East Tropicana, Suite 590
Las Vegas, NV 89119
P: (702) 486-7616
F: (702) 486-7054
E: demadison@nvdetr.org

NEW HAMPSHIRE
Ms. Katharine Daly
Executive Director
Commission for Human Rights
2 Chennell Drive
Concord, NH 03301
P: (603) 271-6838
F: (603) 271-6339
E: katharine.daly@nh.gov

NEW JERSEY
Mr. J. Frank Vespa-Papaleo
Director
Division on Civil Rights
140 East Front Street
P.O. Box 090
Trenton, NJ 08625
P: (609) 292-4605
F: (609) 984-3812

NEW MEXICO
Ms. Francie Cordova
Director
Human Rights Division
Department of Labor
1596 Pacheco Street
Santa Fe, NM 87505
P: (505) 827-6838
F: (505) 827-6878

NEW YORK
Kumiki Gibson
Commissioner
Division of Human Rights
One Fordham Plaza, 4th Floor
Bronx, NY 10458
P: (718) 741-8326
F: (212) 803-3715

NORTH CAROLINA
Mr. George Allison
Director
Human Relations Commission
217 West Jones Street
1318 Mail Service Center
Raleigh, NC 27699
P: (919) 733-7996
F: (919) 733-3856
E: george.allison
@ncmail.net

NORTH DAKOTA
Ms. Lisa Fair McEvers
Commissioner of Labor
Department of Labor
600 East Boulevard Avenue, Department 406
Bismarck, ND 58505
P: (701) 328-2660
F: (701) 328-2031
E: labor@nd.gov

NORTHERN MARIANA ISLANDS
Hon. Matthew T. Gregory
Attorney General
Office of the Attorney General
Capitol Hil, Caller Box 10007
Saipan, MP 95960
P: (670) 664-2341
F: (670) 664-2349
E: matt@gregoryfirm.com

OHIO
Mr. Aaron Wheeler Sr.
Chair
Civil Rights Commission
1111 East Broad Street, Suite 301
Columbus, OH 43205
P: (614) 466-6715
F: (614) 644-8776

OKLAHOMA
Mr. Kenneth Kendricks
Director
Human Rights Commission
2101 North Lincoln Boulevard, Room 480
Oklahoma City, OK 73105
P: (405) 522-1489
F: (405) 522-3635

OREGON
Ms. Amy Klare
Administrator
Bureau of Labor & Industries
800 North East Oregon Street, #32
Portland, OR 97232
P: (503) 731-4075
F: (503) 731-4606
E: Amy.K.Klare@state.or.us

PENNSYLVANIA
Mr. Homer C. Floyd
Executive Director
Human Relations Commission
301 Chestnut Street, Suite 300
Harrisburg, PA 17101
P: (717) 787-4412

PUERTO RICO
Mr. Osvaldo Burgos Perez
Executive Director
Civil Rights Commission
P.O. Box 192338
San Juan, PR 00919
P: (787) 764-8686
F: (787) 250-1756

RHODE ISLAND
Mr. Michael D. Evora
Executive Director
Commission for Human Rights
180 Westminster Street, 3rd Floor
Providence, RI 02903
P: (401) 222-2661
F: (401) 222-2616

SOUTH CAROLINA
Mr. Jesse Washington Jr.
Commissioner
Human Affairs Commission
P.O. Box 4490
Columbia, SC 29204
P: (803) 737-7800
E: jesse@schac.state.sc.us

SOUTH DAKOTA
Mr. Ray Falk
Director
Division of Human Rights
Kneip Building
700 Governors Drive
Pierre, SD 57501
P: (605) 773-4493
F: (605) 773-4211
E: ray.falk@state.sd.us

Ms. Pamela Roberts
Secretary of Labor
Department of Labor
700 Governors Drive
Pierre, SD 57501
P: (605) 773-3101
F: (605) 773-4211
E: pamela.roberts
@state.sd.us

TENNESSEE
Ms. Shalini Rose
Acting Executive Director
Human Rights Commission
530 Church Street, Suite 305
Nashville, TN 37243
P: (615) 741-5825
F: (615) 253-1886

Civil Rights

TEXAS
Mr. Timothy Braaten
Executive Director
Commission on Law Enforcement Officer Standards & Education
6330 U.S. Highway 290 East, Suite 200
Austin, TX 78723
P: (512) 936-7711
F: (512) 936-7766

U.S. VIRGIN ISLANDS
Mr. Lunsford Williams
Executive Director
Department of Justice
P.O. Box 6645
St. Thomas, VI 00804
P: (340) 776-2485
F: (340) 774-9710

UTAH
Ms. Heather Morrison
Director
Anti-Discrimination & Labor Division
160 East 300 South, 3rd Floor
P.O. Box 146630
Salt Lake City, UT 84114
P: (801) 530-6921
F: (801) 530-7609
E: hmorrison@utah.gov

VERMONT
Mr. Robert Appel
Executive Director
Human Rights Commission
135 State Street
Drawer 33
Montpelier, VT 05633
P: (802) 828-2480
F: (802) 828-2481

VIRGINIA
Ms. Sandra D. Norman
Director
Council on Human Rights
900 East Main Street
Pocahontas Building, 4th Floor
Richmond, VA 23219
P: (804) 225-2292
F: (804) 225-3294
E: sandra.norman@chr.virginia.gov

WASHINGTON
Mr. Marc Brenman
Executive Director
Human Rights Commission
711 South Capitol Way, Suite 402
P.O. Box 42490
Olympia, WA 98504
P: (360) 753-2558
F: (360) 586-2282
E: mbrenman@hum.wa.gov

WEST VIRGINIA
Ms. Ivin Lee
Executive Director
Human Rights Commission
1321 Plaza East
Room 104-106
Charleston, WV 25301
P: (304) 558-2616
F: (304) 558-2248
E: ivinlee@wvdhhr.org

WISCONSIN
Mr. Demetri Fisher
Administrator
Division of Affirmative Action
P.O. Box 7855
Madison, WI 53707
P: (608) 266-3017
F: (608) 267-4592

WYOMING
Hon. Patrick J. Crank (D)
Attorney General
Office of the Attorney General
State Capitol Building
Cheyenne, WY 82002
P: (307) 777-7841
F: (307) 777-6869

Clerk of the State's Highest Court

Individual who keeps records of the state's highest court.

ALABAMA
Mr. Robert G. Esdale
Clerk
Supreme Court
300 Dexter Avenue
Montgomery, AL 36104
P: (334) 242-4609

ALASKA
Ms. Marilyn May
Clerk of the Appellate Courts
Appellate Courts
303 K Street
Anchorage, AK 99501
P: (907) 264-0612

AMERICAN SAMOA
Mr. Robert Gorniak
Chief Clerk
High Court of American Samoa
American Samoa Government
Pago Pago, AS 96799
P: (684) 633-4131
F: (684) 633-1318

ARIZONA
Mr. Noel Dessaint
Clerk of the Court
Supreme Court
1501 West Washington Street
Suite 402
Phoenix, AZ 85007
P: (602) 452-3396

ARKANSAS
Mr. Leslie W. Steen
Clerk of the Courts
Supreme Court
1320 Justice Building
625 Marshall Street
Little Rock, AR 72201
P: (501) 682-6849

CALIFORNIA
Mr. Frederick K. Ohlrich
Clerk/Administrator
Supreme Court
350 McAllister Street
San Francisco, CA 94102
P: (415) 865-7000

COLORADO
Ms. Susan J. Festag
Clerk of the Court
Supreme Court
2 East 14th Avenue, 4th Floor
Denver, CO 80203
P: (303) 861-1111 x277

CONNECTICUT
Ms. Michele T. Angers
Chief Clerk
Supreme Court
231 Capitol Avenue
Hartford, CT 06106
P: (860) 757-2200
F: (860) 757-2217

DELAWARE
Ms. Cathy L. Howard
Supreme Court Clerk
Supreme Court
57 The Green
Dover, DE 19901
P: (302) 739-4187

DISTRICT OF COLUMBIA
Mr. Garland Pinkston Jr.
Clerk
Court of Appeals
Moultrie Courthouse
500 Indiana Avenue, Northwest, 6th Floor
Washington, DC 20001
P: (202) 879-2725

FLORIDA
Mr. Thomas D. Hall
Clerk
Supreme Court
500 South Duval Street
Tallahassee, FL 32399
P: (850) 488-0125
E: supremecourt@flcourts.org

GEORGIA
Ms. Therese S. Barnes
Clerk
Supreme Court
244 Washington Street
Room 572, State Office Annex Building
Atlanta, GA 30334
P: (404) 656-3470
F: (404) 656-2253

GUAM
Ms. Jeanne G. Quinata
Clerk of Court
Supreme Court
Guam Judicial Center, Suite 300
120 West O'Brien Drive
Hagatna, GU 96910
P: (671) 475-3162
F: (671) 475-3140
E: jquinata@guamsupremecourt.com

HAWAII
Mr. Darrell N. Phillips
Chief Clerk
Supreme Court
417 South King Street
Honolulu, HI 96813
P: (808) 539-4919
F: (808) 539-4928

IDAHO
Mr. Stephen Kenyon
Clerk of the Supreme Court
Supreme Court
P.O. Box 83720
451 West State Street
Boise, ID 83720
P: (208) 334-2210
F: (208) 947-7590

ILLINOIS
Ms. Juleann Hornyak
Clerk of the Supreme Court
Supreme Court
Supreme Court Building
200 East Capitol
Springfield, IL 62701
P: (217) 782-2035

INDIANA
Mr. Kevin Smith
Clerk of Supreme Court, Court of Appeals & Tax Court
State Courts
217 State House
200 West Washington Street
Indianapolis, IN 46204
P: (317) 232-1930
F: (317) 232-8365

IOWA
Mr. Keith Richardson
Clerk
Supreme Court
Iowa Judicial Branch Building
1111 East Court Avenue
Des Moines, IA 50319
P: (515) 281-5911

KANSAS
Ms. Carol G. Green
Clerk of the Appellate Courts
Office of the Clerk of the Appellate Courts
Judicial Center, Room 374
301 Southwest 10th Avenue
Topeka, KS 66612
P: (785) 296-3229
F: (785) 296-1028

KENTUCKY
Ms. Susan Stokley Clary
Clerk of the Supreme Court
Supreme Court
700 Capitol Avenue
Room 235, Capitol Building
Frankfort, KY 40601
P: (502) 564-5444

LOUISIANA
Mr. John Tarlton Olivier
Clerk of Court
Supreme Court
Louisiana Supreme Court
400 Royal Street, Suite 4200
New Orleans, LA 70130
P: (504) 310-2300

MAINE
Mr. James C. Chute
Clerk
Supreme Court
142 Federal Street
P.O. Box 368
Portland, ME 04112
P: (207) 822-4146

MARYLAND
Mr. Alexander L. Cummings
Clerk of Court of Appeals
Court of Appeals
Court of Appeals Building
361 Rowe Boulevard
Annapolis, MD 21401
P: (410) 260-1500

MASSACHUSETTS
Ms. Maura Doyle
Clerk
Supreme Judicial Court of Suffolk County
John Adams Courthouse
One Pemberton Square
Boston, MA 02108
P: (617) 557-1100
F: (617) 523-1540

Ms. Susan Mellen
Clerk
Supreme Judicial Court of Commonwealth
John Adams Courthouse
One Pemberton Square
Boston, MA 02108
P: (617) 557-1020
F: (617) 557-1145

Clerk of the State's Highest Court

MICHIGAN
Mr. Corbin Davis
Clerk
Supreme Court
P.O. Box 30052
Lansing, MI 48909
P: (517) 373-0120
E: MSC_Clerk@courts.mi.gov

MINNESOTA
Mr. Frederick K. Grittner
Clerk of Court
Supreme Court
305 Minnesota Judicial Center
25 Rev. Martin Luther King Jr. Boulevard
St. Paul, MN 55155
P: (651) 296-2581

MISSISSIPPI
Ms. Betty Sephton
Clerk
Supreme Court
P.O. Box 249
Jackson, MS 39205
P: (601) 359-3694
F: (601) 359-2407
E: sctclerk@mssc.state.ms.us

MISSOURI
Mr. Thomas F. Simon
Supreme Court Clerk
Supreme Court
P.O. Box 150
Jefferson City, MO 65102
P: (573) 751-4144
F: (573) 751-7514

MONTANA
Mr. Ed Smith
Clerk
Supreme Court
215 North Sanders, Room 323
P.O. Box 203003
Helena, MT 59620
P: (406) 444-3858
F: (406) 444-5705

NEBRASKA
Ms. Lanet S. Asmussen
Clerk
Supreme Court
State Capitol, Room 2413
P.O. Box 98910
Lincoln, NE 68509
P: (402) 471-3731
F: (402) 471-3480

NEVADA
Ms. Janette M. Bloom
Clerk
Supreme Court
201 South Carson Street
Carson City, NV 89701
P: (775) 684-1600
F: (775) 684-1601
E: nvscclerk@nvcourts.nv.gov

NEW HAMPSHIRE
Ms. Eileen Fox
Clerk of Court
Supreme Court
Supreme Court Building
1 Noble Drive
Concord, NH 03301
P: (603) 271-2646

NEW JERSEY
Mr. Stephen W. Townsend
Clerk
Supreme Court Clerk's Office
Hughes Justice Complex
P.O. Box 970
Trenton, NJ 08625
P: (609) 292-4837

NEW MEXICO
Ms. Kathleen Jo Gibson
Chief Clerk
Supreme Court
P.O. Box 848
Santa Fe, NM 87504
P: (505) 827-4860

NEW YORK
Mr. Stuart M. Cohen
Clerk
Court of Appeals
20 Eagle Street
Albany, NY 12207
P: (518) 455-7700
F: (518) 463-6869

NORTH CAROLINA
Ms. Christie Speir Cameron
Clerk
Supreme Court
Clerk's Office
P.O. Box 2170
Raleigh, NC 27602
P: (919) 733-3723

NORTH DAKOTA
Ms. Penny Miller
Clerk of Supreme Court
Supreme Court
State Capitol
600 East Boulevard Avenue, Dept. 180
Bismarck, ND 58505
P: (701) 328-2221
E: PMiller@NDCourts.com

NORTHERN MARIANA ISLANDS
Mr. Chris Kaipat
Clerk
Supreme Court
P.O. Box 502165
Saipan, MP 96950
P: (670) 236-9700
F: (670) 236-9702
E: supreme.court@saipan.com

OHIO
Ms. Marcia Mengel
Clerk
Supreme Court
65 South Front Street, 8th Floor
Columbus, OH 43215
P: (614) 387-9530

OKLAHOMA
Mr. Michael S. Richie
Supreme Court Clerk
Supreme Court
State Capitol, Room B
2300 North Lincoln Boulevard
Oklahoma City, OK 73105
P: (405) 521-2163

OREGON
Mr. Kingsley W. Click
State Court Administrator
Supreme Court
Supreme Court Building
1163 State Street
Salem, OR 97301
P: (503) 986-5500
F: (503) 986-5503
E: ojd.info@ojd.state.or.us

PENNSYLVANIA
Ms. Norina Blynn
Chief Clerk
Supreme Court
434 Main Capitol
P.O. Box 624
Harrisburg, PA 17108
P: (717) 787-6181

Ms. Patricia Johnson
Chief Clerk
Supreme Court
468 City Hall
Philadelphia, PA 19107
P: (215) 560-6370

Ms. Patty Niccola
Chief Clerk
Supreme Court
801 City-County Building
Pittsburgh, PA 15219
P: (412) 565-2816

PUERTO RICO
Ms. Patricia Oton Oliveri
Secretary of Supreme Court
Supreme Court
P.O. Box 9022392
San Juan, PR 00902
P: (787) 723-6033
F: (787) 722-9177

RHODE ISLAND
Ms. Pamela Woodcock-Pfeiffer
Supreme Court Clerk
Supreme Court
250 Benefit Street
Providence, RI 02903
P: (401) 222-3272
F: (401) 222-3599

SOUTH CAROLINA
Mr. Daniel E. Shearouse
Clerk
Supreme Court
P.O. Box 11330
Columbia, SC 29211
P: (803) 734-1080
F: (803) 734-1499

SOUTH DAKOTA
Ms. Shirley A. Jameson-Fergel
Clerk
Supreme Court
State Capitol
500 East Capitol Avenue
Pierre, SD 57501
P: (605) 773-3511
F: (605) 773-6128

TENNESSEE
Mr. Mike Catalano
Clerk of the Appellate Courts
Appellate Courts
401 7th Avenue, North
Nashville, TN 37219
P: (615) 741-2681
F: (615) 532-8757

TEXAS
Mr. Blake Hawthorne
Clerk of the Court
Supreme Court
P.O. Box 12248
Austin, TX 78711
P: (512) 463-1312
F: (512) 463-1365

U.S. VIRGIN ISLANDS
Ms. Denise Abramsen
Clerk
Territorial Court
U.S. Virgin Islands
P.O. Box 70
St. Thomas, VI 00804

UTAH
Ms. Pat H. Bartholomew
Clerk of Court
Supreme Court
450 South State Street
P.O. Box 140210
Salt Lake City, UT 84114
P: (801) 238-7974
F: (801) 578-3999
E: pathb@email.utcourts.gov

VERMONT
Mr. Lee Suskin
Court Administrator and Clerk
Supreme Court
109 State Street
Montpelier, VT 05609
P: (802) 828-3278
F: (802) 828-4750

VIRGINIA
Ms. Patricia Harrington
Clerk
Supreme Court
100 North Ninth Street, 5th Floor
Richmond, VA 23219
P: (804) 786-2251

WASHINGTON
Mr. Ronald R. Carpenter
Clerk
Supreme Court
415 12th Avenue, Southwest
P.O. Box 40929
Olympia, WA 98504
P: (360) 357-2077
F: (360) 357-2102
E: supreme@courts.wa.gov

WEST VIRGINIA
Mr. Rory L. Perry II
Clerk of Court
Supreme Court of Appeals
State Capitol, Room E-317
Charleston, WV 25305
P: (304) 558-2601
F: (304) 558-3815

WISCONSIN
Ms. Cornelia G. Clark
Supreme Court Clerk
Supreme Court
110 East Main Street, Suite 215
P.O. Box 1688
Madison, WI 53701
P: (608) 261-4300
F: (608) 267-0640
E: cornelia.clark@wicourts.gov

WYOMING
Ms. Judy Pacheco
Clerk of Court
Supreme Court
Supreme Court Building
2301 Capitol Avenue, Room 121
Cheyenne, WY 82001
P: (307) 777-7316
F: (307) 777-6129
E: jpacheco@courts.state.wy.us

Commerce

Umbrella agency of commerce responsible for the overall regulation and growth of the state's economy.

ALABAMA
Mr. Neal Wade
Director
Development Office
401 Adams Avenue, 6th Floor
Suite 670
Montgomery, AL 36130
P: (334) 353-1717
F: (334) 242-5669
E: waden@ado.state.al.us

ALASKA
Mr. Emil Notti
Commissioner
Department of Commerce, Community & Economic Development
P.O. Box 110800
Juneau, AK 99981
P: (907) 465-2500
F: (907) 465-5442

AMERICAN SAMOA
Mr. Faleseu Eliu Paopao
Director
Department of Commerce
American Samoa Government
Executive Office Building, Utulei
Pago Pago, AS 96799
P: (684) 633-5155
F: (684) 633-4195

ARIZONA
Ms. Jan Lesher
Director
Department of Commerce
1700 West Washington, Suite 600
Phoenix, AZ 85007
P: (602) 771-1160

ARKANSAS
Ms. Maria Haley
Executive Director
Department of Economic Development
#1 Capitol Mall, 4C-300
Little Rock, AR 72201
P: (501) 682-2052
F: (501) 682-7394
E: mhaley@1800Arkansas.gov

CALIFORNIA
Ms. Yolanda Benson
Deputy Secretary for Jobs & Economic Development
Business, Transportation & Housing Agency
981 9th Street, Suite 2450
Sacramento, CA 95815
P: (916) 323-5408

Mr. Barry Sedlick
Undersecretary & Senior Advisor for Economic Development
Business, Transportation & Housing Agency
980 9th Street, Suite 2450
Sacramento, CA 95814
P: (916) 327-3368
F: (916) 323-5440

COLORADO
Mr. Don Elliman
Director
Office of Economic Development & International Trade
1625 Broadway, Suite 1710
Denver, CO 80202
P: (303) 898-3840
F: (303) 898-3848

CONNECTICUT
Ms. Marie C. O'Brien
President
Connecticut Development Authority
999 West Street
Rocky Hill, CT 06067
P: (860) 258-4200
F: (860) 257-7582
E: cdainfo@po.state.ct.us

DELAWARE
Hon. Harriet Smith Windsor (D)
Secretary of State
Office of the Secretary of State
Townsend Building
P.O. Box 898
Dover, DE 19903
P: (302) 739-4111
F: (302) 739-3811
E: hnsmith@state.de.us

DISTRICT OF COLUMBIA
Mr. Neil O. Albert
Deputy Mayor
Office of the Deputy Mayor for Planning & Economic Development
1350 Pennsylvania Avenue, Northwest
Suite 317
Washington, DC 20004
P: (202) 727-6365
F: (202) 727-6703

FLORIDA
Ms. Keisha Rice
Deputy Director
Office of Tourism, Trade & Economic Development
The Capitol, Room 2001
Tallahassee, FL 32399
P: (850) 487-2568
F: (850) 487-3014

GEORGIA
Mr. Kenneth C. Stewart
Commissioner
Department of Economic Development
75 Fifth Street, Northwest, Suite 1200
Atlanta, GA 30308
P: (404) 962-4000
F: (404) 962-4001

GUAM
Mr. Anthony Blaz
Administrator
Economic Development & Commerce Authority
ITC Building, Suite 226
590 South Marine Drive
Tamuning, GU 96913
P: (671) 647-4375
F: (671) 472-5003

HAWAII
Mr. Lawrence M. Reifurth
Director
Department of Commerce & Consumer Affairs
335 Merchant Street
Honolulu, HI 96813
P: (808) 586-2850
F: (808) 586-2856

IDAHO
Mr. Karl T. Tueller
Deputy Director
Department of Commerce & Labor
P.O. Box 83720
Boise, ID 83720
P: (208) 334-3570
F: (208) 334-2631
E: karl.tueller@cl.idaho.gov

ILLINOIS
Mr. Jack Lavin
Director
Department of Commerce & Economic Opportunity
100 West Randolph, Suite 32-400
Chicago, IL 60601
P: (312) 814-7179
F: (312) 814-1843
E: jlavin@ildceo.net

INDIANA
Mr. Nathan J. Feltman
Secretary of Commerce
Economic Development Corporation
One North Capitol Avenue, Suite 700
Indianapolis, IN 46204
P: (317) 232-8992
F: (317) 233-5123
E: nfeltman@iedc.in.gov

IOWA
Mr. Thomas B. Gronstal
Superintendent
Division of Banking
200 East Grand Avenue, Suite 300
Des Moines, IA 50309
P: (515) 281-4014
F: (515) 281-4862

KANSAS
Mr. David Kerr
Secretary
Department of Commerce
1000 Southwest Jackson Street, Suite 100
Topeka, KS 66612
P: (785) 296-2741
F: (785) 296-3665

KENTUCKY
Mr. George Ward
Secretary
Commerce Cabinet
Capitol Plaza Tower, 24th Floor
500 Mero Street
Frankfort, KY 40601
P: (502) 564-4270
F: (502) 564-1512

LOUISIANA
Mr. Michael Olivier
Secretary
Department of Economic Development
Capitol Annex, 1050 North Third Street
P.O. Box 94185
Baton Rouge, LA 70804
P: (225) 342-5388
F: (225) 342-5389
E: olivier@la.gov

MAINE
Mr. Jack Cashman
Commissioner
Department of Economic & Community Development
59 State House Station
Augusta, ME 04333
P: (207) 624-9805
E: jack.cashman@maine.gov

MARYLAND
Mr. David W. Edgerley
Secretary
Department of Business & Economic Development
217 East Redwood Street, 23rd Floor
Baltimore, MD 21202
P: (410) 767-6301
F: (410) 767-8628
E: dedgerley@choosemaryland.org

MICHIGAN
Mr. Keith W. Cooley
Director
Department of Labor & Economic Growth
611 West Ottawa
P.O. Box 30004
Lansing, MI 48909
P: (517) 373-1820
F: (517) 373-2129

MINNESOTA
Mr. Glenn Wilson
Commissioner
Department of Commerce
85 7th Place East, Suite 500
St. Paul, MN 55101
P: (651) 296-6025
F: (651) 282-2568
E: glenn.wilson@state.mn.us

MISSISSIPPI
Dr. Lester Spell Jr.
Commissioner
Department of Agriculture & Commerce
121 North Jefferson Street
Jackson, MS 39201
P: (601) 359-1100
F: (601) 354-7710
E: Spell@mdac.state.ms.us

MISSOURI
Mr. Greg Steinhoff
Director
Department of Economic Development
301 West High Street
Truman Building, Room 680
Jefferson City, MO 65102
P: (573) 751-4770
F: (573) 751-7258
E: greg.steinhoff@ded.mo.gov

MONTANA
Mr. Anthony Preite
Director
Department of Commerce
301 South Park
P.O. Box 200501
Helena, MT 59620
P: (406) 841-2704
F: (406) 841-2701
E: tpreite@mt.gov

NEBRASKA
Mr. Richard Baier
Director
Department of Economic Development
P.O. Box 94666
Lincoln, NE 68509
P: (402) 471-3111
F: (402) 471-3778

NEVADA
Ms. Mendy K. Elliott
Director
Department of Business & Industry
555 East Washington Avenue
Suite 4900
Las Vegas, NV 89101
P: (802) 486-2750
F: (802) 487-2758
E: director@dbi.state.nv.us

NEW HAMPSHIRE
Mr. George Bald
Commissioner
Department of Resources & Economic Development
P.O. Box 1856
Concord, NH 03302
P: (603) 271-2411
F: (603) 271-2629
E: gbald@dred.state.nh.us

NEW JERSEY
Ms. Virginia S. Bauer
CEO & Secretary
Commerce, Economic Growth & Tourism Commission
20 West State Street
Trenton, NJ 08625
P: (609) 292-2444
F: (609) 292-0082
E: Virginia.Bauer@commerce.state.nj.us

NEW MEXICO
Mr. Rick Homans
Director
Economic Development Department
1100 South St. Francis Drive, Suite 1060
Joseph Montoya Building
Santa Fe, NM 87505
P: (505) 476-3736
F: (505) 827-0328
E: edd.info@state.nm.us

NEW YORK
Mr. Patrick Foye
Commissioner
Empire State Development
633 Third Avenue
New York, NY 10017
P: (212) 803-3700
F: (518) 474-2474

NORTH CAROLINA
Mr. James T. Fain III
Secretary
Department of Commerce
301 North Wilmington Street
4301 Mail Service Center
Raleigh, NC 27699
P: (919) 733-3449
F: (919) 715-9593
E: jfain@nccommerce.com

NORTH DAKOTA
Mr. Shane Goettle
Director
Commerce Department
1600 East Century Avenue, Suite 2
P.O. Box 2057
Bismarck, ND 58502
P: (701) 328-5300
F: (701) 328-5320

NORTHERN MARIANA ISLANDS
Mr. James A. Santos
Director
Department of Commerce
Caller Box 10007, Capital Hill
Saipan, MP 96950
P: (670) 664-3000
F: (670) 664-3070
E: commercedept@vzpacifica.net

OHIO
Ms. Kimberly A. Zurz
Director of Commerce
Department of Commerce
77 South High Street, 23rd Floor
Columbus, OH 43215
P: (614) 466-3636
F: (614) 752-5078
E: kim.zurz@com.state.oh.us

OKLAHOMA
Ms. Natalie Shirley
Secretary of Commerce & Tourism
Department of Commerce
900 North Stiles Avenue
P.O. Box 26980
Oklahoma City, OK 73105
P: (405) 815-5147

OREGON
Mr. Bob Repine
Director
Economic & Community Development Department
775 Summer Street, Northeast, Suite 200
Salem, OR 97301
P: (503) 986-0110
F: (503) 378-5156
E: ODE.Webmaster@state.or.us

PENNSYLVANIA
Mr. Dennis Yablonsky
Secretary
Department of Community & Economic Development
Keystone Building, 4th Floor
Harrisburg, PA 17120
P: (717) 787-3003
F: (717) 787-6866

PUERTO RICO
Mr. Ricardo Rivera
Interim Secretary
Department of Economic Development & Commerce
P.O. Box 362350
Hato Rey, PR 00918
P: (787) 758-4747
F: (787) 753-6874

RHODE ISLAND
Mr. A. Michael Marques
Director
Department of Business Regulation
233 Richmond Street
Providence, RI 02903
P: (401) 222-2246
F: (401) 222-6098

Commerce

SOUTH CAROLINA
Mr. Joseph E. Taylor Jr.
Secretary
Department of Commerce
1200 Main Street, Suite 1600
Columbia, SC 29201
P: (803) 737-0400
F: (803) 737-0418

TENNESSEE
Ms. Leslie A. Newman
Commissioner
Department of Commerce & Insurance
500 James Robertson Parkway
Nashville, TN 37243
P: (615) 741-2241
F: (615) 532-5934

TEXAS
Mr. Mike Chrobak
Director of Bank
Office of the Governor
P.O. Box 12428
Austin, TX 78711
P: (512) 936-0101
F: (512) 936-0303

U.S. VIRGIN ISLANDS
Ms. Beverly Nicholson Doty
Commissioner
Department of Tourism
Elainco Building
78 Contant 1-2-3
St. Thomas, VI 00802
P: (340) 774-8784
F: (340) 774-4390

UTAH
Ms. Francine Giani
Executive Director
Department of Commerce
160 East 300 South
Salt Lake City, UT 84111
P: (801) 530-6431
F: (801) 530-6446
E: fgiani@utah.gov

VERMONT
Mr. Kevin Dorn
Secretary
Agency of Commerce & Community Development
National Life Building
Drawer 20
Montpelier, VT 05620
P: (802) 828-3211
F: (802) 828-3258
E: kevin.dorn@state.vt.us

VIRGINIA
Mr. Patrick O. Gottschalk
Secretary
Office of Commerce & Trade
1111 East Broad Street
Patrick Henry Building
Richmond, VA 23219
P: (804) 786-7831
F: (804) 371-0250
E: patrick.gottschalk@governor.virginia.gov

WASHINGTON
Ms. Juli Wilkerson
Director
Office of Community, Trade & Economic Development
906 Columbia Street, Southwest
P.O. Box 42525
Olympia, WA 98501
P: (360) 725-4011
F: (360) 586-8440
E: juliw@cted.wa.gov

WEST VIRGINIA
Ms. Kelley Goes
Commissioner
Department of Commerce
State Capitol Complex
Building 6, Room 525
Charleston, WV 25303
P: (304) 558-2234
F: (304) 558-2956
E: kgoes@wvdo.org

WISCONSIN
Ms. Mary Burke
Secretary
Department of Commerce
123 West Washington
P.O. Box 7970
Madison, WI 53707
P: (608) 266-7088
F: (608) 266-3447

WYOMING
Mr. Tucker Fagan
Chief Executive Officer
Wyoming Business Council
214 West 15th Street
Cheyenne, WY 82002
P: (307) 777-2800
F: (307) 777-2837

Comptroller

The principal accounting and dispersing officer of the state.

Information provided by:

National Association of State Auditors, Comptrollers & Treasurers
Kinney Poynter
Executive Director
449 Lewis Hargett Circle
Suite 290
Lexington, KY 40503
P: (859) 276-1147
F: (859) 278-0507
kpoynter@nasact.org
www.nasact.org

ALABAMA
Mr. Robert L. Childree
State Comptroller
Office of the State Comptroller
Division of Control & Accounts
100 North Union Street, Suite 220
Montgomery, AL 36130
P: (334) 242-7063
F: (334) 242-7466
E: bob.childree@comptroller.alabama.gov

ALASKA
Ms. Kim Garnero
Division Director
Division of Finance
333 Willoughby Avenue, 10th Floor
Juneau, AK 99811
P: (907) 465-3435
F: (907) 465-2169
E: kim_garnero@admin.state.ak.us

ARIZONA
Mr. D. Clark Partridge
State Comptroller
Department of Administration
100 North 15th Avenue, Suite 302
Phoenix, AZ 85007
P: (602) 542-5405
F: (602) 542-5749
E: clark.partridge@azdoa.gov

ARKANSAS
Mr. Richard Weiss
Director
Department of Finance & Administration
1509 West 7th Street, Room 401
DFA Building
Little Rock, AR 72201
P: (501) 682-2242
F: (501) 682-1029
E: richard.weiss@dfa.state.ar.us

Hon. Jim Wood
State Auditor
Office of the State Auditor
230 State Capitol
Little Rock, AR 72225
P: (501) 682-6030
F: (501) 682-6005
E: auditorstateofar@comcast.net

CALIFORNIA
Hon. John Chiang
State Controller
Office of the State Controller
300 Capitol Mall, Suite 1850
P.O. Box 942850
Sacramento, CA 94250
P: (916) 445-2636
E: jchiang@sco.ca.gov

COLORADO
Ms. Leslie M. Shenefelt
State Controller
Office of the State Controller
633 17th Street, Suite 1500
Denver, CO 80203
P: (303) 866-6200
F: (303) 866-4233
E: leslie.shenefelt@state.co.us

CONNECTICUT
Ms. Nancy Wyman
Comptroller
Office of the Comptroller
55 Elm Street, Suite 307
Hartford, CT 06106
P: (860) 702-3301
F: (860) 702-3319
E: nancy.wyman@po.state.ct.us

DELAWARE
Mr. Richard S. Cordrey
Secretary of Finance
Department of Finance
Carvel State Building, 8th Floor
820 North French Street
Wilmington, DE 19801
P: (302) 577-8984
F: (302) 577-8982
E: marybeth.wilson@state.de.us

DISTRICT OF COLUMBIA
Mr. Anthony Pompa (appointed)
Deputy Chief Financial Officer
Office of the Chief Financial Officer
Office of Financial Operations & Systems
810 First Street Northeast, Suite 200
Washington, DC 20002
P: (202) 442-8200
F: (202) 442-8201
E: anthony.pompa@dc.gov

FLORIDA
Hon. Alex Sink (D)
Chief Financial Officer
Department of Financial Services
Fletcher Building, Suite 516
200 East Gaines Street
Tallahassee, FL 32399
P: (850) 413-2850
F: (850) 413-2950
E: alex.sink@fldfs.com

GEORGIA
Ms. Lynn Vellinga
State Accounting Officer
State Accounting Office
200 Piedmont Avenue, Suite 1604 West
Atlanta, GA 30334
P: (404) 651-7392
F: (404) 463-5089
E: lvellinga@gta.ga.gov

HAWAII
Mr. Russ K. Saito
State Comptroller
Department of Accounting & General Services
1151 Punchbowl Street, Room 412
Honolulu, HI 96813
P: (808) 586-0400
F: (808) 586-0775

IDAHO
Ms. Donna Jones
State Controller
Office of the State Controller
700 West State Street
P.O. Box 83720
Boise, ID 83720
P: (208) 334-3100
E: djones@sco.idaho.gov

ILLINOIS
Hon. Daniel W. Hynes (D)
State Comptroller
Office of the State Comptroller
201 State Capitol Building
Springfield, IL 62706
P: (217) 782-6000
F: (217) 782-7561
E: mandecj@mail.ioc.state.il.us

INDIANA
Hon. Tim Berry (R)
Auditor of State
Office of the State Auditor
Room 240, State House
200 West Washington Street
Indianapolis, IN 46204
P: (317) 232-3300
F: (317) 233-2794
E: tberry@auditor.in.gov

IOWA
Mr. Calvin McKelvogue
Chief Operating Officer
Department of Administrative Services
Hoover State Office Building, 3rd Floor
1305 East Walnut
Des Moines, IA 50319
P: (515) 281-4877
F: (515) 281-5277
E: calvin.mckelvogue@iowa.gov

KANSAS
Mr. Robert Mackey
Director
Division of Accounts & Reports
900 Southwest Jackson Street, Room 351-S
Topeka, KS 66612
P: (785) 296-2314
F: (785) 296-6841
E: bob.mackey@da.state.ks.us

KENTUCKY
Mr. Edgar C. Ross
Controller
Office of the Controller
Room 484, Capitol Annex
702 Capitol Avenue
Frankfort, KY 40601
P: (502) 564-2210
F: (502) 564-6597
E: edc.ross@ky.gov

Comptroller

LOUISIANA
Mr. Jerry Luke LeBlanc
Commissioner of Administration
Department of Administration
Division of Administration
P.O. Box 94095
Baton Rouge, LA 70804
P: (225) 342-7000
F: (225) 342-1057
E: commissioner
@doa.state.la.us

MAINE
Mr. Edward A. Karass
State Controller
Department of Administrative & Financial Services
14 State House Station
111 Sewall Street, 4th Floor
Augusta, ME 04333
P: (207) 626-8420
F: (207) 626-8422
E: edward.a.karass
@maine.gov

MARYLAND
Mr. Peter Franchot
Comptroller of the Treasury
Office ofthe Comptroller
P.O. Box 466
Goldstein Treasury Building
Annapolis, MD 21404
P: (410) 260-4801
E: pfrachot
@comp.state.md.us

MASSACHUSETTS
Mr. Martin J. Benison
Comptroller
Office of the Comptroller
One Ashburton Place, 9th Floor
Boston, MA 02108
P: (617) 973-2315
F: (617) 973-2555
E: martin.benison
@state.ma.us

MICHIGAN
Mr. Michael J. Moody
Director
Office of Financial Management
111 South Capitol Avenue
Romney Building, 7th Floor
Lansing, MI 48913
P: (517) 335-1942
F: (517) 373-6458
E: moodym1@michigan.gov

MINNESOTA
Mr. Tom J. Hanson
Commissioner
Department of Finance
Centennial Office Building, Suite 400
658 Cedar Street
St. Paul, MN 55155
P: (651) 201-8010
F: (651) 296-7714
E: Tom.J.Hanson@state.mn.us

MISSISSIPPI
Mr. J.K. Stringer Jr.
Executive Director/State Fiscal Officer
Department of Finance & Administration
P.O. Box 267
Jackson, MS 39205
P: (601) 359-3402
F: (601) 359-2405
E: stringer@dfa.state.ms.us

MISSOURI
Mr. Thomas J. Sadowski
Director
Division of Accounting
301 West High Street
Truman Building, Room 570,
P.O. Box 809
Jefferson, MO 65102
P: (573) 751-4013
F: (573) 526-9810
E: tom.sadowski@oa.mo.gov

MONTANA
Mr. Paul Christofferson
(appointed)
Administrator
Department of Administration
P.O. Box 200102
Helena, MT 59620
P: (406) 444-4609
F: (406) 444-2812
E: pachristofferson@mt.gov

NEBRASKA
Mr. Paul Carlson
State Accounting Administrator
Department of Administrative Services
Room 1309, State Capitol
Lincoln, NE 68509
P: (402) 471-0600
F: (402) 471-2583
E: pcarlson
@notes.state.ne.us

NEVADA
Hon. Kim R. Wallin
State Controller
Office of the State Controller
Capitol Building
101 N. Carson Street, Suite 5
Carson City, NV 89701
P: (775) 684-5777
F: (775) 684-5696
E: kwallin
@govmail.state.nv.us

NEW JERSEY
Ms. Charlene Holzbaur
Director
Office of Management & Budget
Department of Treasury
P.O. Box 221
Trenton, NJ 08625
P: (609) 292-6746
F: (609) 633-8179
E: charlene.holzbaur
@treas.state.nj.us

NEW MEXICO
Mr. Anthony Armijo
State Controller & Director
NM DOFA, Financial Control Division
Bataan Memorial Building, Suite 166
407 Galisteo Street
Santa Fe, NM 87501
P: (505) 827-3681
F: (505) 827-3692
E: aiacpa@state.nm.us

NORTH CAROLINA
Mr. Robert L. Powell
State Controller
Office of the State Controller
3512 Bush Street
Raleigh, NC 27609
P: (919) 981-5406
F: (919) 981-5567
E: Robert.Powell@ncosc.net

NORTH DAKOTA
Ms. Pam Sharp
Director
Office of Management & Budget
600 East Boulevard, 4th Floor
Bismarck, ND 58505
P: (701) 328-4904
F: (701) 328-3230
E: psharp@nd.gov

OHIO
Ms. J. Pari Sabety
Director
Office of Budget & Management
30 East Broad Street, 34th Floor
Columbus, OH 43215
P: (614) 466-4034
F: (614) 644-3147
E: pari.sabety
@obm.state.oh.us

OKLAHOMA
Ms. Brenda Bolander
State Comptroller
Office of State Finance
2300 North Lincoln Boulevard, Room 122
State Capitol Building
Oklahoma City, OK 73105
P: (405) 521-6162
F: (405) 521-3902
E: brenda.bolander
@osf.ok.gov

OREGON
Mr. John J. Radford
State Controller
Department of Administrative Services
State Controller's Division
155 Cottage Street, Northeast
Salem, OR 97301
P: (503) 378-3156
F: (503) 378-3518
E: john.j.radford
@state.or.us

PENNSYLVANIA
Mr. Harvey C. Eckert
Commonwealth Comptroller
Office of Budget
207 Finance Building
Harrisburg, PA 17120
P: (717) 787-6496
F: (717) 787-3376
E: heckert@state.pa.us

RHODE ISLAND
Mr. Lawrence C. Franklin Jr.
State Controller
Office of Accounts & Control
Department of Administration
One Capitol Hill
Providence, RI 02908
P: (401) 222-6731
F: (401) 222-6437
E: larryf
@gw.doa.state.ri.us

SOUTH CAROLINA
Hon. Richard Eckstrom
Comptroller General
Office of the Comptroller General
305 Wade Hampton Office Building
1200 Senate Street
Columbia, SC 29201
P: (803) 734-2121
F: (803) 734-2064
E: reckstrom@cg.state.sc.us

SOUTH DAKOTA
Hon. Rich Sattgast (R)
State Auditor
Office of the State Auditor
State Capitol Building, 2nd Floor
500 East Capitol
Pierre, SD 57501
P: (605) 773-3341
F: (605) 773-5929
E: rich.sattgast@state.sd.us

TENNESSEE
Ms. Jan Sylvis
Chief of Accounts
Department of Finance & Administration
312 8th Avenue, North, Suite 2100
Nashville, TN 37243
P: (615) 741-2382
F: (615) 532-8532
E: jan.sylvis@state.tn.us

TEXAS
Ms. Susan Combs
Comptroller of Public Accounts
Office of the Comptroller of Public Accounts
P.O. Box 13528, Capitol Station
Austin, TX 78711
P: (512) 463-4444
F: (512) 475-0450
E: scombs@cpa.state.tx.us

UTAH
Mr. John Reidhead
Director
Division of Finance
2110 State Office Building
Salt Lake City, UT 84114
P: (801) 538-3095
F: (801) 538-3244
E: jreidhead@utah.gov

VERMONT
Mr. Jim Reardon
Commissioner
Department of Finance & Management
109 State Street
Montpelier, VT 05602
P: (802) 828-2376
F: (802) 828-2428
E: jim.reardon@state.vt.us

VIRGINIA
Mr. David Von Moll
Comptroller
Department of Accounts
101 North 14th Street, 2nd Floor
James Monroe Building
Richmond, VA 23219
P: (804) 225-2109
F: (804) 786-3356
E: david.vonmoll@doa.virginia.gov

WASHINGTON
Mr. Victor Moore
Director
Office of Financial Management
P.O. Box 43113
Olympia, WA 98504
P: (360) 902-0530
F: (360) 664-2832
E: victor.moore@ofm.wa.gov

WEST VIRGINIA
Hon. Glen B. Gainer III (D)
State Auditor
Office of the State Auditor
Building 1, Room W-100
1900 Kanawha Boulevard
Charleston, WV 25305
P: (304) 558-2251
F: (304) 558-5200
E: glen.gainer@wvsao.gov

Mr. Ross Taylor
State Comptroller
Department of Administration
2101 Washington Street East
P.O. Box 50121
Charleston, WV 25305
P: (304) 558-6181
F: (304) 558-1950
E: rtaylor@wvadmin.gov

WISCONSIN
Mr. Steve Censky
Interim State Controller
State Controller's Office
101 East Wilson Street, 5th Floor
P.O. Box 7932
Madison, WI 53707
P: (608) 266-8158
E: steve.censky@doa.state.wi.us

WYOMING
Hon. Rita Meyer (R)
State Auditor
Office of the State Auditor
Room 114, Capitol Building
Cheyenne, WY 82002
P: (307) 777-7831
F: (307) 777-6983
E: rita.meyer@state.wy.us

Consumer Protection

Investigates consumer complaints, develops consumer education programs and alerts citizens to current consumer concerns within the state.

ALABAMA
Hon. Troy King (R)
Attorney General
Office of the Attorney General
State House
11 South Union Street
Montgomery, AL 36130
P: (334) 242-7300
F: (334) 242-7458

ALASKA
Ms. Signe Andersen
Chief Assistant Attorney General
Fair Business Practices
Department of Law
1031 West 4th Avenue, Suite 200
Anchorage, AK 99501
P: (907) 269-5100
F: (907) 276-8554

AMERICAN SAMOA
Mr. Faleseu Eliu Paopao
Director
Department of Commerce
American Samoa Government
Executive Office Building, Utulei
Pago Pago, AS 96799
P: (684) 633-5155
F: (684) 633-4195

Hon. Afa Ripley Jr.
Attorney General
Office of the Attorney General
American Samoa Government
Executive Office Building, Utulei
Pago Pago, AS 96799
P: (684) 633-4163
F: (684) 633-1838

ARIZONA
Ms. Rene Rebillot
Chief Counsel
Office of the Attorney General
1275 West Washington
Phoenix, AZ 85007
P: (602) 542-3702

ARKANSAS
Ms. Teresa Marks
Deputy Attorney General
Public Protection Department
Office of the Attorney General
323 Center Street, Suite 1100
Little Rock, AR 72201
P: (501) 682-2341
F: (501) 682-8118
E: teresa.marks@arkansasag.gov

CALIFORNIA
Ms. Arwin Flint
Manager
Public Inquiry Unit
Department of Justice
1300 I Street
Sacramento, CA 95814
P: (916) 324-5765

Ms. Karen McGagin
Executive Officer
Office of Victim Services & Restitution
630 K Street
Sacramento, CA 95814
P: (916) 323-3432

COLORADO
Ms. Janet Zavislan
Director
Consumer Protection Division
Department of Law
1525 Sherman Street, 5th Floor
Denver, CO 80203
P: (303) 866-5076
F: (303) 866-5443
E: jan.zavislan@state.co.us

CONNECTICUT
Mr. Jerry Farrell Jr.
Commissioner
Department of Consumer Protection
165 Capitol Avenue
Hartford, CT 06106
P: (860) 713-6050
F: (860) 713-7239

DELAWARE
Ms. Ohla Rybakoff
Director
Consumer Protection Unit
820 North French Street, 4th Floor
Wilmington, DE 19801
P: (302) 577-8600

DISTRICT OF COLUMBIA
Ms. Linda Argo
Interim Director
Department of Consumer & Regulatory Affairs
941 North Capitol Street, Northeast
Suite 9500
Washington, DC 20002
P: (202) 442-8947
F: (202) 442-9445

FLORIDA
Ms. Luann Stiles
Director
Division of Consumer Services
2005 Apalachee Parkway
Rhodes Building
Tallahassee, FL 32399
P: (850) 922-2966

GEORGIA
Mr. Joseph B. Doyle
Administrator
Governor's Office of Consumer Affairs
2 Martin Luther King, Jr. Drive
Suite 356
Atlanta, GA 30334
P: (404) 651-8600
F: (404) 657-9018

GUAM
Hon. Alicia Limtiaco
Attorney General
Office of the Attorney General
Suite 2-200E, Judicial Center Building
120 West O'Brien Drive
Hagatna, GU 96910
P: (671) 475-3409

HAWAII
Mr. Stephen Levins
Executive Director
Office of Consumer Protection
235 South Beretania Street, Suite 801
Honolulu, HI 96813
P: (808) 586-2630
F: (808) 586-2640

IDAHO
Hon. Lawrence Wasden (R)
Attorney General
Office of the Attorney General
P.O. Box 83720
Boise, ID 83720
P: (208) 334-2400
F: (208) 334-3446

ILLINOIS
Ms. Deborah Hagan
Chief
Division of Consumer Protection
500 South Second Street
Springfield, IL 62706
P: (207) 782-1090

INDIANA
Ms. Sheila O'Bryan-McGrath
Director & Chief Counsel
Consumer Protection Division
302 West Washington
Room C525
Indianapolis, IN 46204
P: (317) 232-6217
F: (317) 233-4393
E: sobryan@atg.state.in.us

IOWA
Mr. William Brauch
Director
Consumer Protection Division
Hoover Building
1305 East Walnut
Des Moines, IA 50319
P: (515) 281-5926
F: (515) 281-6771
E: consumer@ag.state.ia.us

KANSAS
Ms. Linda Sheppard
Deputy Attorney General
Consumer Protection Division
Memorial Hall, 2nd Floor
Topeka, KS 66612
P: (785) 296-2215
F: (785) 296-6296

KENTUCKY
Mr. Todd Leatherman
Director
Division of Consumer Protection
1024 Capital Center Drive
Suite 200
Frankfort, KY 40601
P: (502) 696-5387
F: (502) 573-8317
E: TLEATHERMAN@ky.gov

LOUISIANA
Hon. Charles C. Foti Jr. (D)
Attorney General
Department of Justice
P.O. Box 94095
Baton Rouge, LA 70804
P: (225) 342-7013
F: (225) 342-7335

MAINE
Mr. William N. Lund
Director
Office of Consumer Credit Regulation
35 State House Station
Augusta, ME 04333
P: (207) 624-8527

MARYLAND
Mr. William Leibovici
Counsel
Consumer Protection Division
Office of the Attorney General
200 Saint Paul Place
Baltimore, MD 21202
P: (410) 576-6557
F: (410) 576-6566
E: bleibovici@oag.state.md.us

MASSACHUSETTS
Mr. Daniel Crane
Director
Office of Consumer Affairs & Business Regulation
Ten Park Plaza, Suite 5170
Boston, MA 02116
P: (617) 973-8700
F: (617) 973-8798

MICHIGAN
Mr. A. Michael Leffler
Acting Bureau Chief
Consumer Protection & Criminal Prosecution Bureau
G. Mennen Williams Building, 6th Floor
525 West Ottawa Street
Lansing, MI 48909
P: (517) 335-0855

MINNESOTA
Hon. Lori Swanson (DFL)
Attorney General
Office of the Attorney General
State Capitol, Suite 102
St. Paul, MN 55155
P: (651) 296-3353
F: (651) 297-4193
E: attorney.general@state.mn.us

MISSISSIPPI
Mr. Grant Hedgepeth
Director
Consumer Protection Division
P.O. Box 22947
Jackson, MS 39225
P: (601) 359-4230
F: (601) 359-4231
E: ghedg@ago.state.ms.us

MISSOURI
Hon. Jay Nixon (D)
Attorney General
Office of the Attorney General
207 West High Street
P.O. Box 899
Jefferson City, MO 65102
P: (573) 751-3321
F: (573) 751-0774
E: ag@ago.mo.gov

MONTANA
Mr. Matthew Dale
Director
Office of Consumer Protection
1219 8th Avenue
P.O. Box 200151
Helena, MT 59620
P: (406) 444-1907

NEBRASKA
Hon. Jon C. Bruning (R)
Attorney General
Office of the Attorney General
State Capitol
P.O. Box 98920
Lincoln, NE 68509
P: (402) 471-2682
F: (402) 471-3297

NEVADA
Mr. Eric Witkoski
Consumer Advocate
Bureau of Consumer Protection
1000 East William Street
Suite 200
Carson City, NV 89701
P: (775) 684-1180
F: (775) 684-1179
E: comishnr@fyiconsumer.org

NEW HAMPSHIRE
Mr. Richard W. Head
Senior Assistant Attorney General
Office of the Attorney General
33 Capitol Street
Concord, NH 03301
P: (603) 271-3643
F: (603) 271-2110
E: richard.head@doj.nh.gov

NEW JERSEY
Mr. Stephen B. Nolan
Acting Director
Division of Consumer Affairs
124 Halsey Street
Newark, NJ 07102
P: (973) 504-6200
F: (973) 273-8035
E: askconsumeraffairs@lps.state.nj.us

Ms. Kimberly S. Ricketts
Director
Division of Consumer Affairs
Office of Attorney General
P.O. Box 45027
Newark, NJ 07101
P: (973) 504-6200
F: (973) 273-8035
E: askconsumeraffairs@lps.state.nj.us

NEW MEXICO
Hon. Gary K. King (D)
Attorney General
Office of the Attorney General
P.O. Drawer 1508
408 Galisteo Street, Villagra Building
Santa Fe, NM 87504
P: (505) 827-6000
F: (505) 827-5826

NEW YORK
Ms. Mindy Bockstein
Chairperson & Executive Director
State Consumer Protection Board
Corning Tower
Empire State Plaza
Albany, NY 12223
P: (518) 474-3514
F: (518) 474-1418

NORTH CAROLINA
Mr. Josh Stein
Special Deputy
Attorney General's Office
114 West Edenton Street
Raleigh, NC 27602
P: (919) 716-6000
F: (919) 716-6750
E: jstein@ncdoj.gov

NORTH DAKOTA
Mr. Parrell Grossman
Director
Consumer Protection & Antitrust Division
Office of Attorney General
600 East Boulevard Avenue, 17th Floor
Bismarck, ND 58505
P: (701) 328-3404
F: (701) 328-3535
E: pgrossma@nd.gov

NORTHERN MARIANA ISLANDS
Hon. Matthew T. Gregory
Attorney General
Office of the Attorney General
Capitol Hil, Caller Box 10007
Saipan, MP 95960
P: (670) 664-2341
F: (670) 664-2349
E: matt@gregoryfirm.com

OHIO
Hon. Marc Dann (D)
Attorney General
Office of the Attorney General
30 East Broad Street
17th Floor
Columbus, OH 43215
P: (614) 466-4320

OKLAHOMA
Mr. Donald K. Hardin
Administrator
Department of Consumer Credit
4545 North Lincoln Boulevard, #104
Oklahoma City, OK 73105
P: (405) 521-3907
F: (405) 521-6740
E: dhardin@okdocc.state.ok.us

OREGON
Mr. Joel Ario
Insurance Administrator
Insurance Division
350 Winter Street, Northeast
Room 430
Salem, OR 97301
P: (503) 947-7980
F: (503) 378-4351
E: dcbs.insmail@state.or.us

Mr. Ronald Fredrickson
Manager of Consumer Protection
Insurance Division
350 Winter Street, Northeast, Room 440
Salem, OR 97301
P: (503) 947-7277
F: (503) 378-4351
E: dcbs.insmail@state.or.us

Ms. Jan Margosian
Consumer Information Officer
Department of Justice
1162 Court Street, Northeast
Salem, OR 97301
P: (503) 378-4732
F: (503) 378-5017
E: consumer.hotline@doj.state.or.us

Consumer Protection

PENNSYLVANIA
Ms. Linda J. Williams
Director & Chief Deputy Attorney General
Bureau of Consumer Protection
Strawberry Square
Harrisburg, PA 17120
P: (717) 787-9707
F: (717) 787-1190

PUERTO RICO
Mr. Alejandro Garcia Padilla
Secretary
Department of Consumer Affairs
P.O. Box 41059
San Juan, PR 00940
P: (787) 722-7555
F: (787) 726-0077

RHODE ISLAND
Hon. Patrick C. Lynch (D)
Attorney General
Office of the Attorney General
150 South Main Street
Providence, RI 02903
P: (401) 274-4400

SOUTH CAROLINA
Ms. Brandolyn Thomas Pinkston
Administrator
Department of Consumer Affairs
3600 Forest Drive, 3rd Floor
P.O. Box 5757
Columbia, SC 29250
P: (803) 734-4200
F: (803) 734-4286

SOUTH DAKOTA
Ms. Delane Smith
Director
Division of Consumer Protection
Attorney General's Office
1302 East Highway 14, Suite 1
Pierre, SD 57501
P: (605) 773-4400
F: (605) 773-7163
E: consumerhelp@state.sd.us

TENNESSEE
Ms. Mary Clement
Director
Division of Consumer Affairs
500 James Robertson Parkway, 5th Floor
Nashville, TN 37243
P: (615) 741-4737
F: (615) 532-4994

TEXAS
Mr. Rudy Aguilar
Consumer Protection Director
Office of Consumer Credit Commissioner
2601 North Lamar
Austin, TX 78705
P: (512) 936-7627
F: (512) 936-7610
E: rudy.aguilar@occc.state.tx.us

U.S. VIRGIN ISLANDS
Mr. Kenrick Robertson
Commissioner
Department of Licensing & Consumer Affairs
Property & Procurement Building
Sub Base Building 1, Room 205
St. Thomas, VI 00802
P: (340) 774-3130
F: (340) 776-0675
E: dlcacommissioner@dlca.gov.vi

UTAH
Mr. Kevin Olsen
Director
Division of Consumer Protection
160 East 300 South
P.O. Box 146704
Salt Lake City, UT 84114
P: (801) 530-6601
F: (801) 530-6001
E: kvolsen@utah.gov

VERMONT
Ms. Deena Frankel
Director for Consumer Affairs
Department of Public Service
112 State Street
Montpelier, VT 05620
P: (802) 828-2811

WASHINGTON
Hon. Rob McKenna (R)
Attorney General
Office of the Attorney General
1125 Washington Street, Southeast
P.O. Box 40100
Olympia, WA 98504
P: (360) 753-6200
F: (360) 664-0228

WEST VIRGINIA
Ms. Jill Miles
Deputy Attorney General
Consumer Protection & Antitrusts Division
Office of the Attorney General
P.O. Box 1789
Charleston, WV 25326
P: (304) 558-8986
F: (304) 558-5200
E: jim@wvago.gov

WISCONSIN
Ms. Janet Jenkins
Administrator, Trade & Consumer Protection
Department of Agriculture, Trade & Consumer Protection
2811 Agriculture Drive
P.O. Box 8911
Madison, WI 53708
P: (608) 224-4929
F: (608) 224-4939

WYOMING
Hon. Patrick J. Crank (D)
Attorney General
Office of the Attorney General
State Capitol Building
Cheyenne, WY 82002
P: (307) 777-7841
F: (307) 777-6869

Corporate Records

Maintains a variety of corporate filings, records and documents.

ALABAMA
Ms. Jean Jordan
Corporation Records Supervisor
Corporations Division
11 South Union, Room 207
Montgomery, AL 36130
P: (334) 242-5324
F: (334) 240-3138

ALASKA
Mr. Mark R. Davis
Director
Department of Commerce, Community & Economic Development
Banking, Securities & Corporations
P.O. Box 110807
Juneau, AK 99811
P: (907) 465-2521
F: (907) 465-2549

AMERICAN SAMOA
Mr. Faleseu Eliu Paopao
Director
Department of Commerce
American Samoa Government
Executive Office Building, Utulei
Pago Pago, AS 96799
P: (684) 633-5155
F: (684) 633-4195

ARIZONA
Ms. Linda Fisher
Director
Corporations Division
Corporation Commission
1300 West Washington
Phoenix, AZ 85007
P: (602) 542-3521
F: (602) 542-0900
E: director.corp@azcc.gov

ARKANSAS
Hon. Charlie Daniels (D)
Secretary of State
Office of the Secretary of State
256 State Capitol Building
Little Rock, AR 72201
P: (501) 682-1010
F: (501) 682-3510
E: larowland@sosmail.state.ar.us

CALIFORNIA
Ms. Cathy Mitchell
Chief
Business Programs Division
1500 11th Street
Sacramento, CA 95814
P: (916) 653-0721

COLORADO
Mr. Keith Whitelaw
Business Director
Department of State, Business Division
1560 Broadway
Suite 200
Denver, CO 80202
P: (303) 894-2200
F: (303) 869-4864
E: keith.whitelaw@sos.state.co.us

CONNECTICUT
Hon. Susan Bysiewicz (D)
Secretary of State
Office of the Secretary of State
State Capitol, Room 104
Hartford, CT 06105
P: (860) 509-6200
F: (860) 509-6209
E: Susan.Bysiewicz@po.state.ct.us

DELAWARE
Mr. Robert Mathers
Administrator
Division of Corporations
Townsend Building
401 Federal Street, Suite 4
Dover, DE 19901
P: (302) 739-3077
F: (302) 739-2238

DISTRICT OF COLUMBIA
Ms. Linda Argo
Interim Director
Department of Consumer & Regulatory Affairs
941 North Capitol Street, Northeast
Suite 9500
Washington, DC 20002
P: (202) 442-8947
F: (202) 442-9445

FLORIDA
Mr. Jay Kassees
Director
Division of Corporations
409 East Gaines Street
Tallahassee, FL 32399
P: (850) 245-6004
E: jkassees@dos.state.fl.us

GEORGIA
Mr. Chauncey Newsome
Director
Corporations Division
2 Martin Luther King, Jr. Drive, SE
315 West Tower
Atlanta, GA 30334
P: (404) 656-6478
F: (404) 657-2488

GUAM
Mr. Artemio B. Illagan
Acting Director
Department of Revenue & Taxation
13-1 Mariner Drive, Tiyan
P.O. Box 23607
Barrigada, GU 96921
P: (671) 475-1817
F: (671) 472-2643

HAWAII
Mr. Lawrence M. Reifurth
Director
Department of Commerce & Consumer Affairs
335 Merchant Street
Honolulu, HI 96813
P: (808) 586-2850
F: (808) 586-2856

IDAHO
Mr. Mark Stephensen
Supervisor
Business Entity Division
Statehouse, Westwing Basement
700 West Jefferson
Boise, ID 83720
P: (208) 332-2840
F: (208) 334-2847
E: mstephensen@sos.idaho.gov

ILLINOIS
Mr. Robert Durchholz
Administrator
Corporation Division
Howlett Building, Room 328
502 South 2nd Street
Springfield, IL 62756
P: (217) 782-4909

INDIANA
Hon. Todd Rokita (R)
Secretary of State
Office of the Secretary of State
201 State House
Indianapolis, IN 46204
P: (317) 232-6532
F: (317) 233-3283
E: assistant@sos.state.in.us

IOWA
Hon. Michael A. Mauro (D)
Secretary of State
Business Services Division
State House, Room 105
Des Moines, IA 50319
P: (515) 281-8993
F: (515) 242-5952
E: sos@sos.state.ia.us

KANSAS
Ms. Stephanie Mickelson
Deputy Assistant Secretary of State for Business Services
Office of the Secretary of State - Business Services
Memorial Hall, 2nd Floor
Topeka, KS 66612
P: (785) 296-4564
F: (785) 296-4570

KENTUCKY
Ms. Tracy Herman
Corporate Division Director
Office of the Secretary of State
The Capitol
Room 152
Frankfort, KY 40601
P: (502) 564-3490
F: (502) 564-5687
E: therman@kysos.com

LOUISIANA
Ms. Helen J. Cumbo
Administrator
Commercial Division
8549 United Plaza
Baton Rouge, LA 70809
P: (225) 925-4716
F: (225) 925-4410
E: hcumbo@sos.louisiana.gov

MAINE
Ms. Julie L. Flynn
Deputy Secretary of State
Office of the Secretary of State
101 State House Station
Augusta, ME 04333
P: (207) 624-7736
F: (207) 287-5874

MARYLAND
Mr. C. John Sullivan
Director
Department of Assessments & Taxation
301 West Preston Street, Room 605
Baltimore, MD 21201
P: (410) 767-1184
F: (410) 333-5873

Corporate Records

MASSACHUSETTS
Hon. William Francis Galvin (D)
Secretary of the Commonwealth
Office of the Secretary of the Commonwealth
220 Morrissey Blvd.
Boston, MA 02125
P: (617) 727-2816
F: (617) 288-8429
E: cis@sec.state.ma.us

MICHIGAN
Ms. G. Ann Baker
Director
Corporation Division
P.O. Box 30054
Lansing, MI 48909
P: (517) 241-6470
F: (517) 241-0537

MINNESOTA
Hon. Mark Ritchie (DFL)
Secretary of State
Office of the Secretary of State
180 State Office Building
100 Constitution Avenue
St. Paul, MN 55155
P: (651) 296-2803
F: (651) 297-5844
E: secretary.state@state.mn.us

MISSISSIPPI
Mr. Bill Thompson
Assistant Secretary of State
Business Services Division
P.O. Box 136
Jackson, MS 39205
P: (601) 359-1350
F: (601) 359-1499
E: bthompson@sos.state.ms.us

MISSOURI
Mr. Matthew Kitzi
Securities Commissioner
Corporations Division
600 West Main Street
Jefferson City, MO 65101
P: (573) 751-4704
F: (573) 526-3124
E: matt.kitzi@sos.mo.gov

MONTANA
Hon. Brad Johnson (R)
Secretary of State
Office of the Secretary of State
P.O. Box 202801
Helena, MT 59620
P: (406) 444-2034
F: (406) 444-3976
E: sosinfo@mt.gov

NEBRASKA
Hon. John A. Gale (R)
Secretary of State
Office of the Secretary of State
1445 K Street, Suite 2300
P.O. Box 94608
Lincoln, NE 68509
P: (402) 471-2554
F: (402) 471-3237
E: secretaryofstate@sos.ne.gov

NEW HAMPSHIRE
Hon. William M. Gardner (D)
Secretary of State
Office of the Secretary of State
State House, Room 204
Concord, NH 03301
P: (603) 271-3242
F: (603) 271-6316
E: kladd@sos.state.nh.us

NEW JERSEY
Mr. James J. Fruscione
Director
Division of Revenue
P.O. Box 628
Trenton, NJ 08646
P: (609) 292-9292

NEW MEXICO
Ms. Ann Echols
Bureau Chief
Corporations Bureau
P.O. Box 1269
Santa Fe, NM 87504
P: (505) 827-4559
F: (505) 827-6912

Hon. Mary Herrera (D)
Secretary of State
Office of the Secretary of State
325 Don Gaspar, Suite 300
State Capitol Annex, North
Santa Fe, NM 87503
P: (505) 827-3600
F: (505) 827-3634
E: MaryE.Herrera@state.nm.us

NEW YORK
Mr. Daniel E. Shapiro
Director
Division of Corporations
41 State Street
Albany, NY 12231
P: (518) 473-2492
F: (518) 474-1418

NORTH CAROLINA
Ms. Cheri Myers
Director
Office of the Secretary of State
300 North Salisbury Street
Raleigh, NC 27603
P: (919) 807-2050
F: (919) 807-2294
E: cmyers@sosnc.org

NORTH DAKOTA
Ms. Clara Jenkins
Director, Central Indexing
Office of the Secretary of State
600 East Boulevard Avenue, 1st Floor
Bismarck, ND 58505
P: (701) 328-4286
F: (701) 328-2992
E: cjenkins@nd.gov

NORTHERN MARIANA ISLANDS
Hon. Matthew T. Gregory
Attorney General
Office of the Attorney General
Capitol Hil, Caller Box 10007
Saipan, MP 95960
P: (670) 664-2341
F: (670) 664-2349
E: matt@gregoryfirm.com

OKLAHOMA
Hon. M. Susan Savage (D)
Secretary of State
Office of the Secretary of State
State Capitol, Room 101
Oklahoma City, OK 73105
P: (405) 521-3911
F: (405) 521-3771
E: Susan.savage@sos.state.ok.us

OREGON
Mr. Peter Threlkel
Director
Secretary of State, Corporation Division
Public Service Building
255 Capitol Street, Northeast, Suite 151
Salem, OR 97310
P: (503) 986-2205
F: (503) 378-4381
E: Corporation.division@state.or.us

PENNSYLVANIA
Mr. Richard K. House
Director
Corporation Bureau
206 North Office Building
Harrisburg, PA 17120
P: (717) 783-9210
F: (717) 783-2244

RHODE ISLAND
Ms. Maureen Ewing
Director
Corporations Division
100 North Main Street, 1st Floor
Providence, RI 02903
P: (401) 222-3040
E: mewing@sec.state.ri.us

SOUTH CAROLINA
Hon. Mark Hammond (R)
Secretary of State
Office of the Secretary of State
P.O. Box 11350
Columbia, SC 29211
P: (803) 734-2170
F: (803) 734-1661
E: rdaggerhart@sos.sc.gov

SOUTH DAKOTA
Hon. Chris Nelson (R)
Secretary of State
Office of the Secretary of State
State Capitol
500 East Capitol Avenue
Pierre, SD 57501
P: (605) 773-3537
F: (605) 773-6580
E: sdsos@state.sd.us

TENNESSEE
Mr. Robert Grunow
Director of Services
Division of Business Services
William Snodgrass TN Tower, 6th Floor
312 8th Avenue, North
Nashville, TN 37243
P: (615) 741-2286
F: (615) 741-7310

TEXAS
Ms. Lorna Wassdorf
Director
Business & Public Fillings Division
1100 Congress Capitol Building, Rm. 1E.8
P.O. Box 12697
Austin, TX 78711
P: (512) 463-5591
F: (512) 463-5709
E: lwassdorf@sos.state.tx.us

U.S. VIRGIN ISLANDS
Mr. John McDonald
Director
Division of Banking &
Insurance
#18 Kongens Gade
St. Thomas, VI 00802
P: (340) 774-7166
F: (340) 774-9458

UTAH
Ms. Kathy Berg
Director
Division of Corporations &
Commericial Code
Department of Commerce
160 East 300 South
Salt Lake City, UT 84111
P: (801) 530-6216
F: (801) 530-6438
E: kberg@utah.gov

VERMONT
Ms. Betty Poulin
Director
Corporations Division
81 River Street
Heritage Building
Montpelier, VT 05609
P: (802) 828-2386
F: (802) 828-2853
E: bpoulin@sec.state.vt.us

VIRGINIA
Mr. Joel Peck
Clerk
State Corporation Commission
State Corporation Commission
Tyler Building, 1300 East Main
Street
Richmond, VA 23219
P: (804) 371-9733
F: (804) 371-9521
E: joel.peck
@scc.virginia.gov

WASHINGTON
Mr. Mike Ricchio
Director
Corporations, Trademarks &
Limited Partnerships
P.O. Box 40234
Olympia, WA 98504
P: (360) 753-7115
E: mricchio@secstate.wa.gov

WEST VIRGINIA
Hon. Betty S. Ireland (R)
Secretary of State
Office of the Secretary of State
Building 1, Suite 157K
1900 Kanawha Boulevard, East
Charleston, WV 25305
P: (304) 558-6000
F: (304) 558-0900
E: wvsos@wvsos.com

WISCONSIN
Mr. Ray Allen
Administrator
Corporations Bureau
P.O. Box 7846
Madison, WI 53707
P: (608) 261-7577
F: (608) 267-6813

WYOMING
Hon. Max Maxfield (R)
Secretary of State
Office of the Secretary of State
State Capitol
Cheyenne, WY 82002
P: (307) 777-5333
F: (307) 777-6217
E: Secofstate@state.wy.us

Corrections

Manages the state's corrections systems.

Information provided by:

Association of State Correctional Administrators
George and Camille Camp
Executive Directors
213 Court Street
Suite 606
Middleton, CT 06457
P: (860) 704-6410
F: (860) 704-6420
exec@asca.net
www.asca.net

ALABAMA
Mr. Richard Allen
Commissioner
Department of Corrections
P.O. Box 301501
101 South Union Street
Montgomery, AL 36130
P: (334) 353-3870
F: (334) 353-3967
E: rallen@asca.net

ALASKA
Mr. Joe Schmidt
Commissioner
Department of Corrections
802 3rd Street
Douglas, AK 99824
P: (907) 465-4652
F: (907) 465-3390
E: jschmidt@asca.net

ARIZONA
Ms. Dora Schriro
Director
Department of Corrections
1601 West Jefferson Street, MC 445
Phoenix, AZ 85007
P: (602) 542-5225
F: (602) 364-0159
E: dschriro2@asca.net

ARKANSAS
Mr. Larry Norris
Director
Department of Corrections
P.O. Box 8707
Pine Bluff, AR 71611
P: (870) 267-6200
F: (870) 267-6244
E: lnorris@asca.net

CALIFORNIA
Mr. James Tilton
Secretary
Department of Corrections & Rehabilitation
P.O. Box 942883
Sacramento, CA 95815
P: (916) 323-6001
F: (916) 442-2637
E: jtilton@asca.net

COLORADO
Mr. Aristedes Zavaras
Executive Director
Department of Corrections
2862 South Circle Drive, Suite 400
Colorado Springs, CO 80906
P: (719) 226-4701
F: (719) 226-4728
E: azavaras@asca.net

CONNECTICUT
Ms. Theresa Lantz
Commissioner
Department of Correction
24 Wolcott Hill Road
Wethersfield, CT 06109
P: (860) 692-7482
F: (860) 692-7483
E: tlantz@asca.net

DELAWARE
Mr. Carl C. Danberg
Commissioner
Department of Corrections
245 McKee Road
Dover, DE 19904
P: (302) 739-5601
F: (302) 739-8221

DISTRICT OF COLUMBIA
Mr. Devon Brown
Director
Department of Corrections
1923 Vermont Avenue, Northwest
#N-203
Washington, DC 20001
P: (202) 671-2128
F: (202) 332-1470
E: dbrown@asca.net

Mr. Harley Lappin
Director
Federal Bureau of Prisons
320 First Street, Northwest
Suite 654
Washington, DC 20534
P: (202) 307-3250
F: (202) 307-1072
E: hlappin@asca.net

FLORIDA
Mr. James McDonough
Secretary
Department of Corrections
2601 Blair Stone Road
Tallahassee, FL 32399
P: (850) 488-7480
F: (850) 922-2848
E: jmcdonough@asca.net

GEORGIA
Mr. James Donald
Commissioner
Department of Corrections
Twin Towers East, Suite 866
2 Martin Luther King Jr. Drive, SE
Atlanta, GA 30334
P: (404) 656-6002
F: (404) 651-6818
E: jdonald@asca.net

GUAM
Mr. Robert Camacho
Director
Department of Corrections
P.O. Box 3236
Agana, GU 96932
P: (671) 473-7021
F: (671) 473-7024
E: rcamacho@asca.net

HAWAII
Mrs. Iwalani White
Interim Director
Department of Public Safety
919 Ala Moana Boulevard, Room 400
Honolulu, HI 96814
P: (808) 587-1350
F: (808) 587-1421
E: iwhite@asca.net

IDAHO
Mr. Brent Reinke
Director
Department of Corrections
1299 North Orchard Street, Suite 110
Boise, ID 83706
P: (208) 658-2000
F: (208) 327-7404
E: breinke@asca.net

ILLINOIS
Mr. Tony Godinez
Executive Director
Department of Corrections
2700 South California
Chicago, IL 60608
P: (773) 869-2859
F: (773) 869-2562
E: tgodinez@asca.net

Mr. Roger E. Walker Jr.
Director
Department of Corrections
1301 Concordia Court
P.O. Box 19277
Springfield, IL 62794
P: (217) 522-2666
F: (217) 522-8719
E: rwalker@asca.net

INDIANA
Mr. David Donahue
Commissioner
Department of Correction
Government Center South
302 West Washington Street
Indianapolis, IN 46204
P: (317) 232-5711
F: (317) 232-6798
E: ddonahue@asca.net

IOWA
Mr. John Baldwin
Interim Director
Department of Corrections
510 East 12th Street
Des Moines, IA 50319
P: (515) 725-5708
F: (515) 725-5799
E: jbaldwin@asca.net

KANSAS
Mr. Roger Werholtz
Secretary
Department of Corrections
900 Southwest Jackson, 4th Floor
Landon State Office Building
Topeka, KS 66612
P: (785) 296-3317
F: (785) 296-0014
E: rwerholtz@asca.net

KENTUCKY
Mr. John D. Rees
Commissioner
Department of Corrections
P.O. Box 2400
Frankfort, KY 40602
P: (502) 564-4726
F: (502) 564-5037
E: jrees@asca.net

LOUISIANA
Mr. Richard L. Stalder
Secretary
Department of Public Safety & Corrections
P.O. Box 94304, Capitol Station
Baton Rouge, LA 70804
P: (225) 342-6956
F: (225) 342-2486
E: rstalder@asca.net

MAINE
Mr. Martin Magnusson
Commissioner
Department of Corrections
State House Station 111
Augusta, ME 04333
P: (207) 287-4360
F: (207) 287-4370
E: marty.magnusson@state.me.us

MARYLAND
Mr. Gary Maynard
Acting Secretary
Department of Public Safety & Correctional Services
300 East Joppa Road, Suite 1000
Towson, MD 21286
P: (410) 339-5005
F: (410) 339-4243
E: gmaynard@asca.net

MASSACHUSETTS
Ms. Kathleen Dennehy
Commissioner
Department of Correction
50 Maple Street, Suite 3
Milford, MA 01757
P: (508) 422-3330
F: (508) 422-3385
E: kdennehy@asca.net

MICHIGAN
Ms. Patricia Caruso
Director
Department of Corrections
P.O. Box 30003
Lansing, MI 48909
P: (517) 373-1944
F: (517) 373-6883
E: pcaruso@asca.net

MINNESOTA
Ms. Joan Fabian
Commissioner
Department of Corrections
1450 Energy Park Drive, Suite 200
St. Paul, MN 55108
P: (651) 361-7226
F: (651) 642-0414
E: Joan.Fabian@state.mn.us

MISSISSIPPI
Mr. Christopher Epps
Commissioner
Department of Corrections
723 North President Street
Jackson, MS 39202
P: (601) 359-5621
F: (601) 359-5680
E: cepps@asca.net

MISSOURI
Mr. Larry Crawford
Director
Department of Corrections
2729 Plaza Drive
Jefferson City, MO 65109
P: (573) 526-6607
F: (573) 751-4099
E: lcrawford@asca.net

MONTANA
Mr. Mike Ferriter
Director
Department of Corrections
1539 11th Avenue
P.O. Box 201301
Helena, MT 59620
P: (406) 444-4913
F: (406) 444-4920
E: mferriter@asca.net

NEBRASKA
Mr. Bob Houston
Director
Department of Correctional Services
P.O. Box 94661
Folsom & Prospector Place, Building 1
Lincoln, NE 68509
P: (402) 479-5710
F: (402) 479-5623
E: bhouston@asca.net

NEVADA
Mr. Howard Skolnik
Director
Department of Corrections
5500 Snyder Avenue
P.O. Box 7011
Carson City, NV 89702
P: (775) 887-3216
F: (775) 887-3381
E: hskolnik@asca.net

NEW HAMPSHIRE
Mr. William Wrenn
Commissioner
Department of Corrections
P.O. Box 1806
Concord, NH 03302
P: (603) 271-5600
F: (603) 271-5643
E: wwrenn@asca.net

NEW JERSEY
Mr. George Hayman
Commissioner
Department of Corrections
Whittlesey Road
P.O. Box 863
Trenton, NJ 08625
P: (609) 633-2335
F: (609) 777-0445
E: ghayman@asca.net

NEW MEXICO
Mr. Joe Williams
Secretary
Corrections Department
P.O. Box 27116
Santa Fe, NM 87502
P: (505) 827-8885
F: (505) 827-8220
E: jwilliams@asca.net

NEW YORK
Mr. Brian Fischer
Acting Commissioner
Department of Correctional Services
1220 Washington Avenue, Building #2
Albany, NY 12226
P: (518) 457-8134
F: (518) 457-7252
E: bfischer@asca.net

Mr. Martin Horn
Commissioner
Department of Correction
60 Hudson Street, 6th Floor
New York, NY 10013
P: (212) 266-1212
F: (212) 266-1219
E: mhorn@asca.net

NORTH CAROLINA
Mr. Theodis Beck
Secretary
Department of Correction
214 West Jones Street, MSC 4201
Shore Building
Raleigh, NC 27603
P: (919) 716-3700
F: (919) 716-3794
E: tbeck@doc.state.nc.us

NORTH DAKOTA
Ms. Leann Bertsch
Director
Department of Corrections & Rehabilitation
3100 Railroad Avenue
P.O. Box 1898
Bismarck, ND 58502
P: (701) 328-6390
F: (701) 328-6651
E: lbertsch@asca.net

NORTHERN MARIANA ISLANDS
Mr. Lino Tenorio
Acting Secretary
Department of Corrections
Commonwealth of Northern Mariana Islands
P.O. Box 506506 CK
Saipan, MP 96950
P: (670) 664-9061
F: (670) 664-9065

OHIO
Mr. Terry J. Collins
Director
Department of Rehabilitation & Correction
1050 Freeway Drive North
Columbus, OH 43229
P: (614) 752-1164
F: (614) 752-1171
E: tcollins@asca.net

OKLAHOMA
Mr. Justin Jones
Director
Department of Corrections
3400 North Martin Luther King Avenue
P.O. Box 11400
Oklahoma City, OK 73136
P: (405) 425-2505
F: (405) 425-2578
E: jjones@asca.net

OREGON
Mr. Max Williams
Director
Department of Corrections
2575 Center Street, Northeast
Salem, OR 97310
P: (503) 945-0927
F: (503) 373-1173
E: mwilliams@asca.net

PENNSYLVANIA
Mr. Jeffrey Beard
Secretary
Department of Corrections
Box 598
Camp Hill, PA 17011
P: (717) 975-4918
F: (717) 731-0486
E: jbeard@asca.net

Mr. Leon King
Commissioner
Philadelphia Prison System
7901 State Road
Philadelphia, PA 19136
P: (215) 685-8201
F: (215) 685-8577
E: lking@asca.net

Corrections

PUERTO RICO
Mr. Miguel Pereira
Secretary
Department of Correction
P.O. Box 71308
San Juan, PR 00936
P: (787) 775-0020
F: (787) 792-7677
E: mpereira@asca.net

RHODE ISLAND
Mr. A. T. Wall
Director
Department of Corrections
40 Howard Avenue
Cranston, RI 02920
P: (401) 462-2611
F: (401) 462-2630
E: atwall@asca.net

SOUTH CAROLINA
Mr. Jon Ozmint
Director
Department of Corrections
P.O. Box 21787
4444 Broad River Road, Room 300
Columbia, SC 29221
P: (803) 896-8555
F: (803) 896-3972
E: jozmint@asca.net

SOUTH DAKOTA
Mr. Tim Reisch
Secretary
Department of Corrections
3200 East Highway #34
Pierre, SD 57501
P: (605) 773-3478
F: (605) 773-3194
E: treisch@asca.net

TENNESSEE
Mr. George Little
Commissioner
Department of Correction
Rachel Jackson State Office Building
320 6th Avenue North, 4th Floor
Nashville, TN 37243
P: (615) 253-8139
F: (615) 532-8281
E: glittle@asca.net

TEXAS
Mr. Brad Livingston
Executive Director
Department of Criminal Justice
P.O. Box 99
Huntsville, TX 77342
P: (936) 437-2101
F: (936) 437-2123
E: blivingston@asca.net

U.S. VIRGIN ISLANDS
Mr. Rosaldo Horsford
Acting Director
Bureau of Corrections
Department of Justice
RR 1, Box 9955
Kinshill, St. Croix, VI 00850
P: (340) 778-0400
F: (340) 778-2929

UTAH
Mr. Tom Patterson
Executive Director
Department of Corrections
14717 South Minuteman Drive
Draper, UT 84020
P: (801) 545-5513
F: (801) 545-5726
E: tpatterson@asca.net

VERMONT
Mr. Robert Hofmann
Commissioner
Department of Corrections
103 South Main Street
Waterbury, VT 05671
P: (802) 241-2442
F: (802) 241-2565
E: rhofmann@asca.net

VIRGINIA
Mr. Gene Johnson
Director
Department of Corrections
6900 Atmore Drive
Richmond, VA 23225
P: (804) 674-3119
F: (804) 674-3509
E: genejohnson@asca.net

WASHINGTON
Mr. Harold Clarke
Secretary
Department of Corrections
P.O. Box 41101
Olympia, WA 98504
P: (360) 725-8810
F: (360) 664-4056
E: hclarke@asca.net

WEST VIRGINIA
Mr. Jim Rubenstein
Commissioner
Division of Corrections
112 California Avenue, Room 302
Charleston, WV 25305
P: (304) 558-2036 Ext. 35
F: (304) 558-5367
E: jrubenstein@asca.net

WISCONSIN
Mr. Matthew Frank
Secretary
Department of Corrections
P.O. Box 7925
East Washington Avenue
Madison, WI 53707
P: (608) 240-5055
F: (608) 240-3305
E: mfrank@asca.net

WYOMING
Mr. Robert Lampert
Director
Department of Corrections
700 West 21st Street
Cheyenne, WY 82002
P: (307) 777-7405
F: (307) 777-7479
E: rlampert@asca.net

Crime Victims Compensation

Provides compensation to victims of crime.

ALABAMA
Mr. Martin Ramsay
Director
Crime Victims Compensation Commission
100 North Union Street, Suite 778
P.O. Box 1548
Montgomery, AL 36102
P: (334) 242-2086
F: (334) 353-1401
E: marty.ramsay@acvcc.alabama.gov

ALASKA
Ms. Susan Browne
Administrator
Violent Crimes Compensation Board
P.O. Box 110230
Juneau, AK 99811
P: (907) 465-3040
F: (907) 465-2379

AMERICAN SAMOA
Hon. Afa Ripley Jr.
Attorney General
Office of the Attorney General
American Samoa Government
Executive Office Building, Utulei
Pago Pago, AS 96799
P: (684) 633-4163
F: (684) 633-1838

ARIZONA
Hon. Terry Goddard (D)
Attorney General
Office of the Attorney General
1275 West Washington Street
Phoenix, AZ 85007
P: (602) 542-5025
F: (602) 542-4085
E: ag.inquiries@azag.gov

ARKANSAS
Ms. Avis Lane
Director
Community Relations Division
Office of the Attorney General
323 Center Street, Suite 200
Little Rock, AR 72201
P: (501) 682-3659
F: (501) 682-5313
E: avis.lane@arkansasag.gov

CALIFORNIA
Mr. Jonathan Raven
Director
Office of Victims' Services
P.O. Box 944255
Sacramento, CA 94244
P: (916) 324-6289

COLORADO
Ms. Alison Morgan
Acting Director
Division of Public Information & Victim Assistance
Department of Corrections
2862 South Circle Drive
Colorado Springs, CO 80906
P: (719) 226-4773
F: (719) 226-4485
E: alison.morgan@doc.state.co.us

CONNECTICUT
Ms. Karen Chorney
Acting Director
Office of Victims Services
31 Cooke Street
Plainville, CT 06062
P: (860) 566-3015
E: karen.chorney@jud.state.ct.us

DELAWARE
Ms. Gertrude Burke
Executive Secretary/Director
Violent Crimes Compensation Board
240 North James Street
Suite 203
Wilmington, DE 19804
P: (302) 995-8383
F: (302) 995-8387
E: gertrude.burke@state.de.us

DISTRICT OF COLUMBIA
Ms. Laura Reed
Program Director
Crime Victims Compensation Program
515 5th Street, Northwest
Room 104
Washington, DC 20001
P: (202) 879-4216
F: (202) 879-4230

FLORIDA
Ms. Gwen Roache
Chief
Division of Victims Services
The Capitol, PL01
Tallahassee, FL 32399
P: (850) 414-3300
F: (850) 487-1595

GEORGIA
Ms. Schwanda Reynolds Cobb
Division Director
Crime Victims Compensation Program
503 Oak Place, Suite 540
Atlanta, GA 30349
P: (404) 559-4949
F: (404) 559-4960
E: sreynold@cjcc.state.ga.us

GUAM
Hon. Alicia Limtiaco
Attorney General
Office of the Attorney General
Suite 2-200E, Judicial Center Building
120 West O'Brien Drive
Hagatna, GU 96910
P: (671) 475-3409

HAWAII
Ms. Pamela Ferguson-Brey
Executive Director
Crime Victims Compensation Commission
1136 Union Mall
Room 600
Honolulu, HI 96813
P: (808) 587-1143
F: (808) 587-1146

IDAHO
Mr. Bill Von Tagen
Division Chief
Intergovernmental & Fiscal Law Division
Room 210, State House
Boise, ID 83720
P: (208) 334-4155
F: (208) 334-3446
E: bill.vontagen@ag.idaho.gov

ILLINOIS
Ms. Delores J. Martin
Director & Deputy Clerk
Court of Claims
630 South College
Springfield, IL 62756
P: (217) 782-7102

INDIANA
Ms. Sarah Davis
Program Coordinator
Victim Services Division
One North Capitol Avenue, Suite 100
Indianapolis, IN 46204
P: (317) 232-3482
F: (317) 233-3912
E: sdavis@cji.IN.gov

Ms. Sandy Warren
Investigator
Victim Services Compensation Division
One North Capitol, Suite 1000
Indianapolis, IN 46204
P: (317) 234-3523
F: (317) 233-3912
E: swarren@cji.IN.gov

IOWA
Ms. Marti Anderson
Division Director
Crime Victim Assistance Division
Lucas Building, Ground Floor
Des Moines, IA 50319
P: (515) 281-5044
F: (515) 281-8199
E: Marti.Anderson@ag.state.ia.us

KANSAS
Mr. Frank Henderson Jr.
Executive Director
Crime Victims Compensation Board
Memorial Hall, 2nd Floor
Topeka, KS 66612
P: (785) 296-2359
F: (785) 296-0652

KENTUCKY
Mr. Richard Dinkins
Executive Director
Crime Victims Compensation Board
130 Brighton Park Boulevard
Frankfort, KY 40601
P: (502) 573-7986, ext. 228
F: (502) 573-4817
E: richard.dinkins@ky.gov

LOUISIANA
Mr. Michael A. Ranatza
Executive Director
Commission on Law Enforcement
1885 Wooddale Boulevard, Room 1230
Baton Rouge, LA 70806
P: (225) 925-1997
F: (225) 925-1998
E: michael@cole.state.la.us

MAINE
Ms. Denise Giles
Victim Service Coordinator
Department of Corrections
111 State House Station
Augusta, ME 04333
P: (207) 287-2711

Crime Victims Compensation

MARYLAND
Mr. Robin Woolford
Executive Director
Criminal Injuries Compensation Board
6776 Reisterstown Road, Suite 200
Baltimore, MD 21215
P: (410) 585-3010
F: (410) 764-3815
E: rwoolford@dpscs.state.md.us

MASSACHUSETTS
Ms. Deborah Fogarty
Executive Director
Office for Victim Assistance
One Ashburton Place, Room 1101
Boston, MA 02108
P: (617) 727-5200
F: (617) 727-6552

MICHIGAN
Mr. Michael Fullwood
Director
Crime Victim Services Commission
320 South Walnut
Lansing, MI 48913
P: (517) 373-7373
F: (517) 334-9942
E: fullwoodm@michigan.gov

MINNESOTA
Ms. Jeri Boisvert
Executive Director
Department of Public Safety
Suite 2300, 445 Minnesota Street
444 Cedar Street
St. Paul, MN 55101
P: (651) 201-7305
F: (651) 284-3317
E: jeri.boisvert@state.mn.us

MISSISSIPPI
Ms. Sandra Morrison
Director
Crime Victim Compensation Program
P.O. Box 267
Jackson, MS 39205
P: (601) 359-6766
F: (601) 359-3262

MISSOURI
Ms. Susan Sudduth
Program Manager
Crime Victims Compensation Unit
P.O. Box 58
Jefferson City, MO 65102
P: (573) 526-3510
F: (573) 526-4940
E: susan.sudduth@dolir.mo.gov

MONTANA
Mr. Mike Ferriter
Director
Department of Corrections
1539 11th Avenue
P.O. Box 201301
Helena, MT 59620
P: (406) 444-4913
F: (406) 444-4920
E: mferriter@asca.net

NEVADA
Mr. Bryan Nix
Coordinator
Victims of Crime Program
555 East Washington Avenue
Suite 3300
Las Vegas, NV 89101
P: (702) 486-2525
F: (702) 486-1879
E: bnix@hearings.state.nv.us

NEW HAMPSHIRE
Ms. Sandra Matheson
Director
Victim Witness Unit
33 Capitol Street
Concord, NH 03301
P: (603) 271-1237
F: (603) 271-2110
E: sandi.matheson@doj.nh.gov

NEW JERSEY
Mr. Edward Werner
Chair
Violent Crimes Compensation Board
50 Park Place
Newark, NJ 07102
P: (973) 648-2107
F: (976) 648-3937

NEW MEXICO
Mr. Larry Tackman
Director
Crime Victims Reparation Commission
8100 Mountain Road Northeast, Suite 106
Albuquerque, NM 87110
P: (505) 841-9432
F: (505) 841-9437
E: Larry.Tackman@state.nm.us

NEW YORK
Ms. Joan Cusack
Chairperson
Crime Victims Board
55 Hanson Place
Brooklyn, NY 11217
P: (718) 923-4331

NORTH CAROLINA
Ms. Janice W. Carmichael
Director
Victim & Justice Services
512 North Salisbury Street
4703 Mail Service Center
Raleigh, NC 27699
P: (919) 733-7974
F: (919) 715-4209
E: jcarmichael@nccrimecontrol.org

NORTH DAKOTA
Mr. Paul Coughlin
Crime Victim Administrator
Parole & Probation, Department of Corrections and Rehabilitation
P.O. Box 5521
Bismarck, ND 58506
P: (701) 328-6195
F: (701) 328-6651
E: pcoughli@nd.gov

NORTHERN MARIANA ISLANDS
Ms. Rebecca Warfield
Commissioner
Department of Public Safety
Caller Box 10007, Capital Hill
Saipan, MP 96950
P: (670) 664-9022
F: (670) 664-9027
E: doris@cjpa.gov.mp

OHIO
Hon. Marc Dann (D)
Attorney General
Office of the Attorney General
30 East Broad Street
17th Floor
Columbus, OH 43215
P: (614) 466-4320

OKLAHOMA
Ms. Suzanne Breedlove
Administrator
Crime Victims' Compensation Board
2200 Classen Boulevard, Suite 1800
Oklahoma City, OK 73106
P: (405) 557-6704

OREGON
Ms. Connie Gallagher
Director
Crime Victims Assistance
1162 Court Street, Northeast
Salem, OR 97310
P: (503) 378-5348
F: (503) 378-5738
E: doj.info@state.or.us

PENNSYLVANIA
Mr. Michael J. Kane
Executive Director
Commission on Crime & Delinquency
P.O. Box 1167
Harrisburg, PA 17108
P: (717) 705-0888 Ext. 3088
F: (717) 705-0891

PUERTO RICO
Ms. Lidice A. Cardelario Matos
Director
Office of Crime Victims Compensation
Department of Justice
P.O. Box 9020192
San Juan, PR 00902
P: (787) 641-7480
F: (787) 641-7477

RHODE ISLAND
Ms. Ana Giron
Team Leader
Victim Services
150 South Main Street
Providence, RI 02903
P: (401) 274-4400
F: (401) 222-1302

SOUTH CAROLINA
Ms. Ashlie Lancaster
Director
State Office of Victim Assistance
Edgar A. Brown Building
1205 Pendleton Street, Room 401
Columbia, SC 29202
P: (803) 734-1900
F: (803) 734-1708

SOUTH DAKOTA
Ms. Susan Sheppick
Administrator
Crime Victims' Compensation
Kneip Building
700 Governors Drive
Pierre, SD 57501
P: (605) 773-6317
F: (605) 773-6834
E: susan.sheppick@state.sd.us

TENNESSEE
Hon. Dale Sims
State Treasurer
Treasury Department
State Capitol, First Floor
Nashville, TN 37243
P: (615) 741-2956
F: (615) 253-1591
E: dale.sims@state.tn.us

TEXAS
Mr. Herman Millholland
Director
Crime Victim Services
Office of the Attorney General
P.O. Box 12548
Austin, TX 78711
P: (512) 406-5411
F: (512) 671-2579

U.S. VIRGIN ISLANDS
Ms. Sedonie Halbert
Commissioner
Department of Human Services
Knud Hansen Complex, Building A
1303 Hospital Grounds
St. Thomas, VI 00802
P: (340) 774-0930
F: (340) 774-3466

UTAH
Mr. Ron Gordon
Director
Office of Crime Victims Reparations
350 East 500 South, Suite 200
Salt Lake City, UT 84111
P: (801) 238-2367
F: (801) 533-4127
E: rgordon@utah.gov

VERMONT
Ms. Judy Rex
Executive Director
Center for Crime Victim Services
58 South Main Street, Suite 1
Waterbury, VT 05676
P: (802) 241-1250

VIRGINIA
Mr. Leonard G. Cooke
Director
Department of Criminal Justice Services
202 North Ninth Street, 10th Floor
Richmond, VA 23219
P: (804) 786-8718
F: (804) 371-8981
E: leonard.cooke@dcjs.virginia.gov

WASHINGTON
Mr. Cletus Nnanabu
Program Manager
Crime Victims, Department of Labor & Industries
P.O. Box 44520
Olympia, WA 98504
P: (360) 902-5340
F: (360) 902-5333

WEST VIRGINIA
Hon. Darrell V. McGraw Jr. (D)
Attorney General
Office of the Attorney General
Room 26E, 1900 Kanawha Boulevard, East
Charleston, WV 25305
P: (304) 558-2021
F: (304) 558-0140

WISCONSIN
Ms. Cindy O'Donnell
Acting Executive Director
Office of Crime Victims Services
17 West Main Street, 8th Floor
P.O. Box 7851
Madison, WI 53707
P: (608) 266-1300
F: (608) 264-6368

WYOMING
Hon. Patrick J. Crank (D)
Attorney General
Office of the Attorney General
State Capitol Building
Cheyenne, WY 82002
P: (307) 777-7841
F: (307) 777-6869

Criminal Justice

Oversees the administration of justice by providing public safety, assisting victims of crime, analyzing criminal data, administering funds, and providing training and guidance to law enforcement officials.

ALABAMA
Mr. Jim Quinn
Assistant Director
Law Enforcement & Traffic Safety Division
401 Adams Avenue
P.O. Box 5690
Montgomery, AL 36103
P: (334) 242-5811
F: (334) 242-0712
E: jimq@adeca.state.al.us

AMERICAN SAMOA
Mr. Alaalamua L. Filoiali'i
Director
Criminal Justice Planning Agency
Executive Office Building, Utulei
Territory of American Samoa
Pago Pago, AS 96799
P: (684) 633-5221
F: (684) 633-7552
E: faaulena@hotmail.com

ARIZONA
Mr. John Blackburn Jr.
Executive Director
Criminal Justice Commission
1110 West Washington, Suite 230
Phoenix, AZ 85007
P: (602) 364-1146
F: (602) 364-1175
E: JRBlackburn@azcjc.gov

ARKANSAS
Col. Steve Dozier
Director
State Police
#1 State Police Plaza Drive
Little Rock, AR 72209
P: (501) 618-8200
F: (501) 618-8222
E: steve.dozier@asp.arkansas.gov

CALIFORNIA
Mr. Matt Bettenhausen
Director
Office of Homeland Security
Governor's Office
State Capitol, First Floor
Sacramento, CA 95814
P: (916) 324-8908

COLORADO
Ms. Jeanne Smith
Director
Division of Criminal Justice
Department of Public Safety
700 Kipling Street, Suite 3000
Denver, CO 80203
P: (303) 239-4446
F: (303) 239-4491
E: jeanne.smith@cdps.state.co.us

DELAWARE
Mr. James Kane
Executive Director
Criminal Justice Council
Carvel State Office Building
820 North French Street, 10th Floor
Wilmington, DE 19801
P: (302) 577-8693
F: (302) 577-7056
E: jkane@state.de.us

DISTRICT OF COLUMBIA
Ms. Cathy L. Lanier
Chief of Police
Metropolitan Police Department
300 Indiana Avenue, NW
Room 5080
Washington, DC 20001
P: (202) 727-4218
F: (202) 727-9524

FLORIDA
Mr. Gerald Bailey
Commissioner
Department of Law Enforcement
P.O. Box 1489
Tallahassee, FL 32302
P: (850) 410-7001

GEORGIA
Ms. Gale Buckner
Executive Director
Criminal Justice Coordinating Council
503 Oak Place, Suite 540
Atlanta, GA 30349
P: (404) 559-4949
F: (404) 559-4960

GUAM
Mr. Paul Suba
Commander
Police Department
233 Central Avenue
Tiyan, GU 96913
P: (671) 475-8512
F: (671) 472-2825

HAWAII
Hon. Mark J. Bennett (R)
Attorney General
Department of the Attorney General
425 Queen Street
Honolulu, HI 96813
P: (808) 586-1500
F: (808) 587-1239

IDAHO
Col. Jerry Russell
Director
State Police
P.O. Box 700
Meridian, ID 83680
P: (208) 884-7003
F: (208) 884-7090

ILLINOIS
Ms. Lori G. Levin
Executive Director
Criminal Justice Information Authority
120 South Riverside Plaza, Suite 1016
Chicago, IL 60606
P: (312) 793-8550
F: (312) 793-8422
E: llevin@icjia.state.il.us

INDIANA
Mr. Mike Cunegin
Executive Director
Criminal Justice Institute
One North Capitol Avenue, Suite 1000
Indianapolis, IN 46204
P: (317) 232-1233
F: (317) 233-5150
E: cunegin@cji.in.gov

IOWA
Mr. Gary Kendell
Director
Governor's Office of Drug Control Policy
Lucas State Office Building
321 East 12th Street
Des Moines, IA 50319
P: (515) 281-3784
F: (515) 242-6390
E: gary.kendell@iowa.gov

KANSAS
Ms. Juliene Maska
Federal Grants Program Administrator
Office of the Governor
Capitol Building, Room 212S
300 Southwest 10th Avenue
Topeka, KS 66612
P: (785) 291-3205
F: (785) 291-3204
E: juliene.maska@gov.state.ks.us

KENTUCKY
Brig. Gen. Norman E. Arflack
Secretary
Justice & Public Safety Cabinet
125 Holmes Street
Frankfort, KY 40601
P: (502) 564-7554
F: (502) 564-4840

LOUISIANA
Mr. Michael A. Ranatza
Executive Director
Commission on Law Enforcement
1885 Wooddale Boulevard, Room 1230
Baton Rouge, LA 70806
P: (225) 925-1997
F: (225) 925-1998
E: michael@cole.state.la.us

MARYLAND
Ms. Kristen Mahoney
Executive Director
Governor's Office on Crime Control & Prevention
300 E. Joppa Road
Suite 1105
Baltimore, MD 21286
P: (410) 821-2828
F: (410) 321-3116

MASSACHUSETTS
Mr. Kevin Burke
Secretary
Executive Office of Public Safety
One Ashburton Place, Suite 2133
Boston, MA 02108
P: (617) 727-7775
F: (617) 727-4764

MINNESOTA
Mr. Michael Campion
Commissioner
Department of Public Safety
Bremer Tower, Suite 1000
445 Minnesota Street
St. Paul, MN 55101
P: (651) 201-7000
F: (651) 297-5728
E: michael.campion
@state.mn.us

MISSISSIPPI
Mr. Billy V. White Jr.
Executive Director
Division of Public Safety
Planning
Department of Public Safety
3750 I-55 North Frontage Road
Jackson, MS 39211
P: (601) 987-4155
F: (601) 987-4154
E: bwhite@mdps.state.ms.us

MISSOURI
Mr. Mark S. James
Director
Department of Public Safety
301 West High Street
Truman Building, Room 870
Jefferson City, MO 65102
P: (573) 751-4905
F: (573) 751-5399
E: Mark.James@dps.mo.gov

MONTANA
Mr. Roland Mena
Executive Director
Board of Crime Control
3075 North Montana Avenue
P.O. Box 201408
Helena, MT 59620
P: (406) 444-3615
F: (406) 444-4722
E: rmena@mt.gov

NEBRASKA
Mr. Mike Behm
Executive Director
Commission on Law
Enforcement & Criminal Justice
P.O. Box 94946
Lincoln, NE 68509
P: (402) 471-2194
F: (402) 471-2837

NEVADA
Mr. Phillip A. Galeoto
Director
Department of Public Safety
555 Wright Way
Carson City, NV 89711
P: (775) 684-4808
F: (775) 684-4809

NEW HAMPSHIRE
Ms. Rosemary Faretra
Director of Administration
Office of the Attorney General
Department of Justice
33 Capitol Street
Concord, NH 03301
P: (603) 271-1234
F: (603) 271-2110
E: rosemary.faretra
@doj.nh.gov

Ms. Valerie A. Hall
Director of Administration
Office of the Attorney General
Department of Justice
33 Capitol Street
Concord, NH 03301
P: (603) 271-1234
F: (603) 271-2110
E: valerie.hall@doj.nh.gov

NEW YORK
Ms. Denise O'Donnell
Commissioner
Division of Criminal Justice
Services
4 Tower Place
Stuyvesant Plaza
Albany, NY 12203
P: (518) 457-1260
F: (518) 473-1271

NORTH CAROLINA
Mr. David Jones
Executive Director
Governor's Crime Commission
1201 Front Street, Suite 200
4708 Mail Service Center
Raleigh, NC 27699
P: (919) 733-4605
F: (919) 733-4625
E: djones@ncgccd.org

NORTHERN MARIANA ISLANDS
Mr. Jerome Ierome
Executive Director
Criminal Justice Planning
Agency
P.O. Box 5602, CHRB
Saipan, MP 96950
P: (670) 664-4550
F: (670) 664-4560
E: administration
@cda.gov.mp

OHIO
Mr. Karhlton F. Moore
Director
Office of Criminal Justice
Services
140 East Town Street, 14th
Floor
Columbus, OH 43215
P: (614) 466-0286
F: (614) 466-5061

OKLAHOMA
Ms. Suzanne McClain Atwood
Executive Coordinator
District Attorneys Council
421 Northwest 13th, Suite 290
Oklahoma City, OK 73103
P: (405) 264-5000
F: (405) 264-5099
E: Trent.Baggett
@dac.state.ok.us

OREGON
Mr. Craig Prins
Executive Director
Criminal Justice Commission
635 Capitol Street Northeast,
Suite 350
Salem, OR 97301
P: (503) 986-6495
F: (503) 986-4574
E: craig.prins@state.or.us

PENNSYLVANIA
Mr. Michael J. Kane
Executive Director
Commission on Crime &
Delinquency
P.O. Box 1167
Harrisburg, PA 17108
P: (717) 705-0888 Ext. 3088
F: (717) 705-0891

PUERTO RICO
Mr. Luis M. Gonzalez-Javier
Director
Federal Funds Division
Calle Lindberg #6, Miramar
P.O. Box 9020192
San Juan, PR 00902
P: (787) 725-0335
F: (787) 721-7280
E: lgonzalez
@justicia.prstar.net

RHODE ISLAND
Mr. Thomas H. Mongeau
Executive Director
Justice Commission
One Capitol Hill, 4th Floor
Administration Building
Providence, RI 02908
P: (401) 222-4493
F: (401) 222-1294
E: TMongeau
@gw.doa.state.ri.us

SOUTH CAROLINA
Mr. William R. Neill
Deputy Director
Criminal Justice Academy
Department of Public Safety
5400 Broad River Road
Columbia, SC 29212
P: (803) 896-7779
F: (803) 896-7776

TENNESSEE
Ms. Patricia B. Dishman
Director
Office of Criminal Justice
Programs
312 8th Avenue North
Wm. R. Snodgrass Tenn. Tower,
12th Floor
Nashville, TN 37243
P: (615) 741-8277
F: (615) 532-2989
E: patricia.dishman
@state.tn.us

TEXAS
Mr. Brad Livingston
Executive Director
Department of criminal Justice
P.O. Box 99
Huntsville, TX 77342
P: (936) 437-2101
F: (936) 437-2123
E: blivingston@asca.net

U.S. VIRGIN ISLANDS
Mr. Renaldo Rivera
Adjutant General
National Guard
4031 LaGrande Princess, Lot 1B
Christiansted, VI 00820
P: (340) 712-7710
F: (340) 712-7711
E: renaldo.rivera
@vi.ngb.army.mil

Criminal Justice

UTAH
Mr. Robert Yeates
Executive Director
Commission on Criminal & Juvenile Justice
State Capitol Complex, Suite E330
P.O. Box 142330
Salt Lake City, UT 84114
P: (801) 538-1031
F: (801) 538-1024
E: byeates@utah.gov

VERMONT
Maj. Kerry L. Sleeper
Commissioner of Public Safety
Department of Public Safety
103 South Main Street
Waterbury, VT 05671
P: (802) 244-8718
F: (802) 244-5551
E: ksleeper@dps.state.vt.us

VIRGINIA
Mr. Leonard G. Cooke
Director
Department of Criminal Justice Services
202 North Ninth Street, 10th Floor
Richmond, VA 23219
P: (804) 786-8718
F: (804) 371-8981
E: leonard.cooke@dcjs.virginia.gov

WASHINGTON
Ms. Nancy K. Ousley
Assistant Director
Local Government Division
906 Columbia Street Southwest, 3rd Floor
P.O. Box 48350
Olympia, WA 98504
P: (360) 725-3003
F: (360) 753-2950
E: nancyo@cted.wa.gov

WEST VIRGINIA
Mr. J. Norbert Federspiel
Director
Division of Criminal Justice Services
1204 Kanawha Boulevard, East
Charleston, WV 25301
P: (304) 558-8814 Ext. 202
F: (304) 558-0391
E: nfederspiel@wvdcjs.org

WISCONSIN
Mr. David O. Steingraber
Executive Director
Office of Justice Assistance
131 West Wilson Street, Suite 202
Madison, WI 53702
P: (608) 266-3323
F: (608) 266-6676
E: david.steingraber@oja.state.wi.us

WYOMING
Hon. Patrick J. Crank (D)
Attorney General
Office of the Attorney General
State Capitol Building
Cheyenne, WY 82002
P: (307) 777-7841
F: (307) 777-6869

Debt Management

Responsible for structuring debt issues.

ALABAMA
Mr. Jim Main
Director
Department of Finance
600 Dexter Avenue, Suite N-105
Montgomery, AL 36130
P: (334) 242-7160
F: (334) 353-3300
E: jim.main@finance.alabama.gov

ALASKA
Mr. Deven Mitchell
Debt Manager
Treasury Division
Department of Revenue
P.O. Box 110405
Juneau, AK 99811
P: (907) 465-3750
F: (907) 465-2902

AMERICAN SAMOA
Hon. Velega Savali
Treasurer
Department of Treasury
American Samoa Government
Pago Pago, AS 96799
P: (684) 633-4155
F: (684) 633-4100

ARKANSAS
Mr. Mac Dodson
Director
Development Finance Authority
423 Main Street, Suite 500
Little Rock, AR 72201
P: (501) 682-5900
F: (501) 682-5939
E: mdodson@adfa.state.ar.us

CONNECTICUT
Hon. Denise L. Nappier (D)
State Treasurer
Office of State Treasurer
55 Elm Street
Hartford, CT 06106
P: (860) 702-3010
F: (860) 702-3043
E: denise.nappier@po.state.ct.us

DELAWARE
Hon. Jack Markell (D)
State Treasurer
State Treasurer's Office
540 South DuPont Highway, Suite 4
Dover, DE 19901
P: (302) 744-1000
F: (302) 739-5635
E: statetreasurer@state.de.us

FLORIDA
Mr. J. Ben Watkins III
Director
Division of State Bond Finance
P.O. Box 13300
Tallahassee, FL 32317
P: (850) 488-4782
F: (850) 413-1315
E: watkins_ben@fsba.state.fl.us

GEORGIA
Hon. W. Daniel Ebersole
Director, Office of Treasury & Fiscal Services
Office of Treasury & Fiscal Services
200 Piedmont Avenue
Suite 1202, West Tower
Atlanta, GA 30334
P: (404) 656-2168
F: (404) 656-9048
E: OTFSweb@otfs.ga.gov

GUAM
Mr. Carlos Bordallo
Director
Bureau of Budget & Management Research
P.O. Box 2950
Hagatna, GU 96932
P: (671) 475-9412
F: (671) 472-2825

HAWAII
Hon. Georgina K. Kawamura
Director of Finance
Department of Budget Finance
P.O. Box 150
Honolulu, HI 96810
P: (808) 586-1518
F: (808) 586-1976
E: Hi.BudgetandFinance@hawaii.gov

IDAHO
Hon. Ron G. Crane (R)
State Treasurer
State Treasurer's Office
P.O. Box 83720
Boise, ID 83720
P: (208) 334-3200
F: (208) 332-2960

ILLINOIS
Ms. Ginger Ostro
Director
Governor's Office of Management & Budget
108 State House
Springfield, IL 60706
P: (217) 782-4520
F: (217) 524-1514

Mr. Brad Scott
Department of Debt Management
108 State House
Springfield, IL 60706
P: (217) 782-8821

INDIANA
Mr. Ryan C. Kitchell
Executive Director
Finance Authority
One North Capitol Avenue
Suite 900
Indianapolis, IN 46204
P: (317) 233-4334
F: (317) 232-6786

IOWA
Hon. Michael L. Fitzgerald (D)
State Treasurer
State Treasurer's Office
Room 114, Capitol Building
State Capitol
Des Moines, IA 50319
P: (515) 281-5368
F: (515) 281-7562
E: mike.fitzgerald@iowa.gov

KANSAS
Hon. Lynn Jenkins (R)
State Treasurer
Office of the Treasurer
900 Southwest Jackson, Suite 201
Topeka, KS 66612
P: (785) 296-0628
F: (785) 296-7950
E: lynn@treasurer.state.ks.us

KENTUCKY
Mr. T. Thomas Howard
Executive Director
Office of Financial Management
702 Capitol Avenue
Frankfort, KY 40601
P: (502) 564-2924
F: (502) 564-7416

LOUISIANA
Mr. Whitman J. Kling Jr.
Executive Director
State Bond Commission
900 North 3rd Street, 3rd Floor
State Capitol
Baton Rouge, LA 70802
P: (225) 342-0040
F: (225) 342-0064

MAINE
Hon. Matthew Dunlap (D)
Secretary of State
Office of the Secretary of State
148 State House Station
Augusta, ME 04333
P: (207) 626-8400
F: (207) 287-8598
E: sos.office@maine.gov

MARYLAND
Hon. Nancy K. Kopp (D)
State Treasurer
State Treasurer's Office
Goldstein Treasury Building
80 Calvert Street
Annapolis, MD 21404
P: (410) 260-7533

MASSACHUSETTS
Mr. Patrick Landers
Deputy Treasurer for Debt Management
Department of State Treasury
One Ashburton Place, 12th Floor
Boston, MA 02108
P: (617) 367-9333 Ext. 564

MINNESOTA
Mr. Tom J. Hanson
Commissioner
Department of Finance
Centennial Office Building, Suite 400
658 Cedar Street
St. Paul, MN 55155
P: (651) 201-8010
F: (651) 296-7714
E: Tom.J.Hanson@state.mn.us

MISSISSIPPI
Ms. Betsy McLean
Director
Investment & Cash Management Division
P.O. Box 138
Jackson, MS 39205
P: (601) 359-3536
F: (601) 359-2001

Debt Management

MISSOURI
Hon. Sarah Steelman (R)
State Treasurer
Office of the State Treasurer
P.O. Box 210
Jefferson City, MO 65102
P: (573) 751-4123
F: (573) 751-9443
E: sarah.steelman@treasurer.mo.gov

MONTANA
Mr. Paul Christofferson
Administrator
Administrative Financial Services Division
P.O. Box 200102
Helena, MT 59620
P: (406) 444-4609
F: (406) 444-2812
E: pachristofferson@mt.gov

NEBRASKA
Mr. Carlos Castillo
Director
Department of Administrative Services
State Capitol, Suite 1315
Lincoln, NE 68509
P: (402) 471-2331
E: carlos.castillo@email.state.ne.us

NEW HAMPSHIRE
Hon. Catherine Provencher
State Treasurer
State Treasury
25 Capitol Street, Room 121
Concord, NH 03301
P: (603) 271-2621
F: (603) 271-3922
E: cprovencher@treasury.state.nh.us

NEW JERSEY
Ms. Nancy B. Feldman
Director
Office of Public Finance
50 West State Street, 5th Floor
P.O. Box 005
Trenton, NJ 08625
P: (609) 984-8229
E: Nancy.Feldman@treas.state.nj.us

NORTH CAROLINA
Hon. Richard H. Moore (D)
State Treasurer
Department of State Treasurer
325 North Salisbury Street
Raleigh, NC 27603
P: (919) 508-5176
F: (919) 508-5167
E: richard.moore@nctreasurer.com

NORTH DAKOTA
Ms. Pam Sharp
Director
Office of Management & Budget
600 East Boulevard, 4th Floor
Bismarck, ND 58505
P: (701) 328-4904
F: (701) 328-3230
E: psharp@nd.gov

OHIO
Mr. Kurt Kauffman
State Debt Coordinator
Office of Budget & Management
30 East Broad Street, 34th Floor
Columbus, OH 43215
P: (614) 466-0691
F: (614) 728-9295

OKLAHOMA
Mr. James Joseph
State Bond Advisor
State Bond Advisor's Office
5900 North Classen Boulevard
Oklahoma City, OK 73118
P: (405) 602-3100
F: (405) 848-3314
E: jjoseph@oksba.org

OREGON
Mr. Chuck Smith
Director
Debt Management Division
1001 L & I Building
350 Winter Street, Northeast, Suite 100
Salem, OR 97301
P: (503) 378-4930
F: (503) 378-2870
E: ost.webmaster@state.or.us

PENNSYLVANIA
Mr. Thomas Wolf
Secretary
Department of Revenue
1133 Stawberry Sqaure
Harrisburg, PA 17128
P: (717) 783-3680
F: (717) 787-3990

PUERTO RICO
Mr. Alfredo Salazar Conde
President
Government Development Bank for Puerto Rico
P.O. Box 42001
San Juan, PR 00940
P: (787) 722-2525
F: (787) 721-1443

RHODE ISLAND
Hon. Frank T. Caprio (D)
General Treasurer
Office of the General Treasurer
State House, Room 102
Providence, RI 02903
P: (401) 222-2397
F: (401) 222-6140
E: treasurer@treasury.state.ri.us

SOUTH CAROLINA
Mr. Rick Harmon
Senior Assistant State Treasurer, Debt
Office of the State Treasurer
P.O. Box 11778
Columbia, SC 29211
P: (803) 734-2114
F: (803) 734-2039
E: rick.harmon@sto.sc.gov

SOUTH DAKOTA
Hon. Vernon L. Larson (R)
State Treasurer
Office of the State Treasurer
State Capitol
500 East Capitol Avenue
Pierre, SD 57501
P: (605) 773-3378
F: (605) 773-3115
E: vern.larson@state.sd.us

TEXAS
Ms. Kimberly K. Edwards
Executive Director
Public Finance Authority
300 West 15th Street, Suite 411
Austin, TX 78701
P: (512) 463-5544

U.S. VIRGIN ISLANDS
Ms. Debra Gottlieb
Director
Office of Management & Budget
#41 Norre Gade
Emancipation Garden Station, 2nd Floor
St. Thomas, VI 00802
P: (340) 774-0069

UTAH
Hon. Edward T. Alter (R)
State Treasurer
State Treasurer's Office
215 State Capitol
Salt Lake City, UT 84114
P: (801) 538-1042
F: (801) 538-1465
E: ealter@utah.gov

VERMONT
Hon. Jeb Spaulding (D)
State Treasurer
Office of the State Treasurer
109 State Street, 4th Floor
Montpelier, VT 05609
P: (802) 828-1452
F: (802) 828-2772
E: jeb.spaulding@state.vt.us

VIRGINIA
Ms. Evelyn R. Whitley
Director of Debt Management
Debt Management Division
Department of Treasury
101 North 14th Street
Richmond, VA 23219
P: (804) 371-6006
F: (804) 225-3187
E: evie.whitley@trs.virginia.gov

WASHINGTON
Hon. Michael J. Murphy (D)
State Treasurer
Office of the State Treasurer
Legislative Building
P.O. Box 40200
Olympia, WA 98504
P: (360) 902-9000
F: (360) 902-9044
E: michaelj@tre.wa.gov

WEST VIRGINIA
Mr. Craig Slaughter
Executive Director
Investment Management Board
500 Virginia Street, East, Suite 200
Charleston, WV 25314
P: (304) 347-2672
F: (304) 345-5939
E: craigs@wvimb.org

WISCONSIN
Hon. Dawn Marie Sass (D)
State Treasurer
Office of the State Treasurer
1 South Pinckney Street, Suite 550
Madison, WI 53703
P: (608) 266-1714
F: (608) 266-2647
E: dawn.sass@ost.state.wi.us

Develop-mentally Disabled

Oversees the care, treatment and future service needs of the developmentally disabled.

ALABAMA
Ms. Eranell McIntosh-Wilson
Associate Commissioner
Mental Retardation Services/DMH/MR
100 North Union Street
P.O. Box 301410
Montgomery, AL 36130
P: (334) 242-3701
F: (334) 242-0542
E: eranell.mcintosh-wilson@mh.alabama.gov

ALASKA
Mr. Rod Moline
Director
Senior & Disabilities Services
Department of Health & Social Services
P.O. Box 110680
Juneau, AK 99811
P: (907) 465-3372
F: (907) 465-1170

ARIZONA
Ms. Barbara Brent
Assistant Director
Division of Developmental Disabilities
Department of Economic Security
P.O. Box 6123
Phoenix, AZ 85005
P: (602) 542-6853
F: (602) 542-6870

ARKANSAS
Dr. James "Charlie" Green
Director
Division of Developmental Disabilities Services
P.O. Box 1437, Slot N501
Little Rock, AR 72203
P: (501) 682-8665
F: (501) 682-8380
E: charlie.green@arkansas.gov

CALIFORNIA
Ms. Terri Delgadillo
Director
Department of Developmental Services
P.O. Box 944202
Sacramento, CA 94244
P: (916) 654-1897
E: terri.delgadillo@dds.ca.gov

COLORADO
Mr. Fred L. DeCrescentis
Director
Division for Developmental Disabilities
Department of Human Services
3824 West Princeton Circle
Denver, CO 80236
P: (303) 866-7454
F: (303) 866-7470
E: fred.decrescentis@state.co.us

CONNECTICUT
Mr. Peter O'Meara
Commissioner
Department of Mental Retardation
460 Capitol Avenue
Hartford, CT 06106
P: (860) 418-6011
F: (860) 418-6009
E: peter.omeara@po.state.ct.us

DELAWARE
Ms. Marianne Smith
Director
Developmental Disabilities Services/DHSS
Woodbrook Professional Center
1056 South Governor's Ave., Suite 101
Dover, DE 19904
P: (302) 744-9600
F: (302) 744-9632
E: marianne.smith@state.de.us

DISTRICT OF COLUMBIA
Ms. Kate Jesberg
Interim Director
Department of Human Services
64 New York Avenue, NE
6th Floor
Washington, DC 20001
P: (202) 671-4200
F: (202) 671-4381

FLORIDA
Mr. Barney Ray
Director
Agency for Persons with Disabilities
4030 Esplanade Way, Suite 380
Tallahassee, FL 32399
P: (850) 488-1558
F: (850) 922-6456

GEORGIA
Dr. Stephen Hall
Director
Office of Developmental Disabilities
2 Peachtree Street, Northwest
Suite 22.108
Atlanta, GA 30303
P: (404) 657-2260
F: (404) 657-1137
E: srhall1@dhr.state.ga.us

HAWAII
Dr. David F. Fray
Chief
Developmental Disabilities Division
Department of Health
P.O. Box 3378
Honolulu, HI 96801
P: (808) 586-5842
F: (808) 586-5844
E: dffray@mail.health.state.hi.us

IDAHO
Mr. Cameron Gilliland
Adult Developmental Disabilities Program Manager
Division of Family & Community Services
Department of Health & Welfare
450 West State Street, 5th Floor
Boise, ID 83702
P: (208) 334-5536
F: (208) 334-6664
E: gillilac@dhw.idaho.gov

INDIANA
Mr. Peter Bisbecos
Director
Division of Disability & Rehabilitative Services
402 West Washington Street
P.O. Box 7083, MS-18
Indianapolis, IN 46207
P: (317) 232-1147
F: (317) 234-2099
E: peter.bisbecos@fssa.in.gov

IOWA
Ms. Mary Nelson
Division Administrator
Adult, Children & Family Services
Hoover Building, 5th Floor
1305 East Walnut Street
Des Moines, IA 50319
P: (515) 281-5521
F: (515) 242-6036
E: mnelson1@dhs.state.ia.us

KANSAS
Ms. Margaret Zillinger
Director
Community Supports & Services
DSOB, 10 East
915 Southwest Harrison
Topeka, KS 66612
P: (785) 296-3561
F: (785) 296-0557
E: mmz@srskansas.org

KENTUCKY
Ms. Betsy Dunnigan
Interim Director
Division of Mental Retardation
100 Fair Oaks Lane, 4W-C
Frankfort, KY 40621
P: (502) 564-7702
F: (502) 564-0438
E: betsy.dunnigan@ky.gov

LOUISIANA
Ms. Kathy Kliebert
Assistant Secretary
Office for Citizens with Developmental Disabilities
Department of Health & Hospitals
P.O. Box 3117, Bin 21
Baton Rouge, LA 70821
P: (225) 342-0095
F: (225) 342-8823
E: kklieber@dhh.la.gov

MAINE
Ms. Jane J. Gallivan
Program Director
Office of Adults with Cognitive & Physical Disability Services
Department of Health & Human Services
SHS #11, Marquardt Building, 2nd Floor
Augusta, ME 04333
P: (207) 287-4212
F: (207) 287-9915
E: jane.gallivan@maine.gov

MARYLAND
Ms. Nancy Kirchner
Acting Director
Developmental Disabilities Administration
201 West Preston Street, 4th Floor
Room 422C
Baltimore, MD 21201
P: (410) 767-5600
F: (410) 767-5850

MASSACHUSETTS
Mr. Gerry Morrissey
Assistant Secretary-Commissioner
Executive Office of Health & Human Services/ Department of Mental Retardation
500 Harrison Avenue
Boston, MA 02118
P: (617) 624-7723
F: (617) 624-7577
E: Gerry_Morrissey@dmr.state.ma.us

MICHIGAN
Mr. Patrick Barrie
Deputy Director
Mental Health & Substance Abuse Administration
Department of Community Health
320 South Walnut Street
Lansing, MI 48913
P: (517) 335-0196
F: (517) 335-4798
E: barriep@michigan.gov

Ms. Judy Webb
Division Director
Mental Health & Substance Abuse Administration
Lewis Cass Building, 6th Floor
320 South Walnut Street
Lansing, MI 48913
P: (517) 335-4419
F: (517) 241-2969
E: webb@michigan.gov

MINNESOTA
Ms. Laura Doyle
Acting Director
Disability Services & HIV/AIDS Divisions
Department of Human Services
444 Layfayette Road
St. Paul, MN 55155
P: (651) 431-2388
F: (651) 582-1808
E: laura.doyle@state.mn.us

MISSISSIPPI
Mr. Ed Butler
Council on Developmental Disabilities
1101 Robert E. Lee Building
239 North Lamar Street
Jackson, MS 39201
P: (601) 359-6243
F: (601) 359-5330

MISSOURI
Mr. Bernard Simmons
Director
Mental Retardation & Developmental Disabilities
Department of Mental Health
P.O. Box 687
Jefferson City, MO 65102
P: (573) 751-8676
F: (573) 751-9207
E: bernard.simmons@dmh.mo.gov

MONTANA
Mr. Jeff Sturm
Program Director
Developmental Disabilities Program
111 Sanders, Suite 305
Helena, MT 59604
P: (406) 444-2695
F: (406) 444-0230
E: jesturm@state.mt.us

NEBRASKA
Mr. René Ferdinand
Adminstrator
Developmental Disabilities
Health & Human Services System
P.O. Box 98925, W. Campus, Bldg. #14
Lincoln, NE 68509
P: (402) 479-5100
F: (402) 479-5094
E: rene.ferdinand@hhss.ne.gov

NEVADA
Dr. Carlos Brandenburg
Administrator
Division of Mental Health & Developmental Services
Department of Human Resources
505 East King Street, Room 602
Carson City, NV 89701
P: (775) 684-5943
F: (775) 684-5966
E: cbrandenburg@dhr.state.nv.us

NEW HAMPSHIRE
Mr. Matthew Ertas
Director
Division of Developmental Services
State Office Park South
105 Pleasant Street
Concord, NH 03301
P: (603) 271-5026
F: (603) 271-5166
E: mertas@dhhs.state.nh.us

NEW JERSEY
Ms. Jennifer Velez
Acting Commissioner
Department of Human Services
P.O. Box 726
Trenton, NJ 08625
P: (609) 292-0901

NEW MEXICO
Mr. Steve Dossey
Developmental Disabilities Support Services Division
Department of Health
1190 South St. Francis Drive
Santa Fe, NM 87502
P: (505) 827-2574
F: (505) 827-2530

NEW YORK
Ms. Diana Jones Ritter
Acting Commissioner
Office of Mental Retardation & Developmental Disabilities
44 Holland Avenue
Albany, NY 12229
P: (518) 473-1997
F: (212) 803-3715

NORTH DAKOTA
Mr. Mark Kolling
Assistant Director
Developmental Disabilities Services
1237 West Divide, Suite 1A
Bismarck, ND 58501
P: (701) 328-8937
F: (701) 328-8969
E: sokolm@nd.gov

NORTHERN MARIANA ISLANDS
Mr. Antonio Chong
Executive Director
Developmental Disabilities Council
P.O. Box 502565
1312 Anatahan Drive, Capital Hill
Saipan, MP 96950
P: (670) 664-7001
F: (670) 664-7030
E: gddc@cnmiddcouncil.org

OHIO
Mr. John Martin
Director
Department of Mental Retardation & Developmental Disabilities
1810 Sullivant Avenue
Columbus, OH 43223
P: (614) 466-0129
F: (614) 387-0964
E: john.martin@dmr.state.oh.us

OKLAHOMA
Mr. James Nicholson
Division Administrator
Developmental Disabilities Services Division
Department of Human Services
P.O. Box 25352
Oklahoma City, OK 73125
P: (405) 521-6267
F: (405) 522-3037
E: james.nicholson@okdhs.org

OREGON
Ms. Mary Lee Fay
Administrator
Office of Home & Community Supports
Department of Human Services
500 Summer Street, Northeast, E10
Salem, OR 97301
P: (503) 945-9787
F: (503) 373-7902
E: marylee.fay@state.or.us

PENNSYLVANIA
Mr. Kevin Casey
Deputy Secretary
Office of Mental Retardation
Health and Welfare Building, Room 512
P.O. Box 2675
Harrisburg, PA 17105
P: (717) 787-3700
F: (717) 787-6583
E: kecasey@state.pa.us

RHODE ISLAND
Mr. Craig Stenning
Executive Director
Division of Behavioral Healthcare Services
Division of Developmental Disabilities
14 Harrington Road
Cranston, RI 02920
P: (401) 462-2339
F: (401) 462-6636
E: cstenning@mhrh.ri.gov

Developmentally Disabled

SOUTH CAROLINA
Dr. Stan Butkus
Director
Department of Disabilities & Special Needs
P.O. Box 4706
Columbia, SC 29240
P: (803) 898-9769
F: (803) 898-9656
E: sbutkus@ddsn.state.sc.us

SOUTH DAKOTA
Ms. Wanda Seiler
Director
Division of Developmental Disabilities
Hillsview Plaza
C/o 500 East Capitol Avenue
Pierre, SD 57501
P: (605) 773-3438
F: (605) 773-7562
E: wanda.seiler@state.sd.us

TENNESSEE
Mr. Stephen H. Norris
Deputy Commissioner
Division of Mental Retardation Services
Andrew Jackson Office Bldg., 15th Floor
500 Deadrick Street
Nashville, TN 37243
P: (615) 532-6538
E: steve.norris@state.tn.us

TEXAS
Mr. Barry C. Waller
Assistant Commissioner
Provider Service
Department of Aging & Disability Services
Mail Code W-511
P.O. Box 149030
Austin, TX 78714
P: (512) 438-4165
F: (512) 438-5504
E: barry.waller@dads.state.tx.us

UTAH
Dr. George Kelner
Director
Division of Services for People with Disabilities
Department of Human Services
120 North 200 West, Room 411
Salt Lake City, UT 84103
P: (801) 538-4208
F: (801) 538-4279
E: gkelner@utah.gov

VERMONT
Mr. Patrick Flood
Commissioner
Department of Aging & Disabilities
103 South Main Street, Osgood #1
Waterbury, VT 05671
P: (802) 241-2400
F: (802) 241-2325
E: patrick.flood@dail.state.vt.us

VIRGINIA
Mr. Clarence Lee Price
Director
Department of Mental Health, Mental Retardation & Substance Abuse Services
Office of Mental Retardation
P.O. Box 1797
Richmond, VA 23218
P: (804) 786-5850
F: (804) 692-0077
E: c.price@co.dmhmrsas.virginia.gov

WASHINGTON
Ms. Linda Rolfe
Director
Division of Developmental Disabilities
Aging & Disabilities Services Admin.
P.O. Box 45310
Olympia, WA 98504
P: (360) 725-3461
F: (360) 407-0955
E: rolfela@dshs.wa.gov

WEST VIRGINIA
Mr. John Bianconi
Commissioner
Bureau for Behavioral Health & Health Facilities
Department of Health & Human Resources
350 Capitol Street, Room 350
Charleston, WV 25301
P: (304) 558-0298
F: (304) 558-2230
E: jbianconi@wvdhhr.org

WISCONSIN
Mr. Michael Linak
Director
Bureau of Developmental Disabilities Services
1 West Wilson Street, Room 418
P.O. Box 7851
Madison, WI 53707
P: (608) 266-1140
F: (608) 261-6752
E: linakmj@dhfs.state.wi.us

WYOMING
Mr. Cliff Mikesell
Administrator
Developmental Disabilities Division
186E Qwest Building
6101 Yellowstone Road
Cheyenne, WY 82002
P: (307) 777-7115
F: (307) 777-6047
E: cmikes@state.wy.us

Economic Development

Responsible for efforts designed to encourage industry to locate, develop and expand in the state.

ALABAMA
Mr. Neal Wade
Director
Development Office
401 Adams Avenue, 6th Floor
Suite 670
Montgomery, AL 36130
P: (334) 353-1717
F: (334) 242-5669
E: waden@ado.state.al.us

ALASKA
Mr. Emil Notti
Commissioner
Department of Commerce, Community & Economic Development
P.O. Box 110800
Juneau, AK 99981
P: (907) 465-2500
F: (907) 465-5442

AMERICAN SAMOA
Mr. Faleseu Eliu Paopao
Director
Department of Commerce
American Samoa Government
Executive Office Building, Utulei
Pago Pago, AS 96799
P: (684) 633-5155
F: (684) 633-4195

ARIZONA
Ms. Jan Lesher
Director
Department of Commerce
1700 West Washington, Suite 600
Phoenix, AZ 85007
P: (602) 771-1160

ARKANSAS
Ms. Maria Haley
Executive Director
Department of Economic Development
#1 Capitol Mall, 4C-300
Little Rock, AR 72201
P: (501) 682-2052
F: (501) 682-7394
E: mhaley@1800Arkansas.gov

CALIFORNIA
Mr. Dale E. Bonner
Secretary
Business, Transportation & Housing Agency
980 9th Street, Suite 2450
Sacramento, CA 95814
P: (916) 323-5400
F: (916) 343-5440

COLORADO
Mr. Don Elliman
Director
Office of Economic Development & International Trade
1625 Broadway, Suite 1710
Denver, CO 80202
P: (303) 898-3840
F: (303) 898-3848

CONNECTICUT
Mr. James Abromaitis
Commissioner
Department of Community & Economic Development
505 Hudson Street
Hartford, CT 06106
P: (860) 270-8009
F: (860) 270-8008
E: james.abromaitis@po.state.ct.us

DELAWARE
Ms. Judy McKinney-Cherry
Director
Economic Development Office
Carvel State Office Building, 10th Floor
820 North French Street
Wilimington, DE 19801
P: (302) 577-8497
F: (302) 739-2535
E: judy.cherry@state.de.us

DISTRICT OF COLUMBIA
Mr. Neil O. Albert
Deputy Mayor
Office of the Mayor for Planning & Economic Development
1350 Pennsylvania Avenue, Northwest
Suite 317
Washington, DC 20004
P: (202) 727-6365
F: (202) 727-6703

FLORIDA
Ms. Keisha Rice
Deputy Director
Office of Tourism, Trade & Economic Development
The Capitol, Room 2001
Tallahassee, FL 32399
P: (850) 487-2568
F: (850) 487-3014

GEORGIA
Mr. Kenneth C. Stewart
Commissioner
Department of Economic Development
75 Fifth Street, Northwest, Suite 1200
Atlanta, GA 30308
P: (404) 962-4000
F: (404) 962-4001

GUAM
Mr. Anthony Blaz
Administrator
Economic Development & Commerce Authority
ITC Building, Suite 226
590 South Marine Drive
Tamuning, GU 96913
P: (671) 647-4375
F: (671) 472-5003

HAWAII
Mr. Theodore E. Liu
Director
Department of Business, Economic Development & Tourism
P.O. Box 2359
Honolulu, HI 96804
P: (808) 586-2355
F: (808) 586-2377

IDAHO
Mr. Jay E. Engstrom
Administrator, Economic Development
Department of Commerce & Labor
P.O. Box 83720
Boise, ID 83720
P: (208) 334-3570
F: (208) 334-6430
E: jay.engstrom@cl.idaho.gov

ILLINOIS
Mr. Jack Lavin
Director
Department of Commerce & Economic Opportunity
100 West Randolph, Suite 32-400
Chicago, IL 60601
P: (312) 814-7179
F: (312) 814-1843
E: jlavin@ildceo.net

INDIANA
Mr. Nathan J. Feltman
Secretary of Commerce
Economic Development Corporation
One North Capitol Avenue, Suite 700
Indianapolis, IN 46204
P: (317) 232-8992
F: (317) 233-5123
E: nfeltman@iedc.in.gov

IOWA
Mr. Michael L. Tramontina
Director
Department of Economic Development
200 East Grand Avenue
Des Moines, IA 50309
P: (515) 242-4720
F: (515) 242-4809
E: director@iowalifechanging.com

KANSAS
Mr. David Kerr
Secretary
Department of Commerce
1000 Southwest Jackson Street, Suite 100
Topeka, KS 66612
P: (785) 296-2741
F: (785) 296-3665

KENTUCKY
Mr. Gene Fuqua
Acting Secretary
Cabinet for Economic Development
Capital Plaza Tower, 21st Floor
500 Mero Street
Frankfort, KY 40601
P: (502) 564-7670
F: (502) 564-1535

LOUISIANA
Mr. Michael Olivier
Secretary
Department of Economic Development
Capitol Annex, 1050 North Third Street
P.O. Box 94185
Baton Rouge, LA 70804
P: (225) 342-5388
F: (225) 342-5389
E: olivier@la.gov

MAINE
Mr. Jack Cashman
Commissioner
Department of Economic & Community Development
59 State House Station
Augusta, ME 04333
P: (207) 624-9805
E: jack.cashman@maine.gov

Economic Development

MARYLAND
Mr. David W. Edgerley
Secretary
Department of Business & Economic Development
217 East Redwood Street, 23rd Floor
Baltimore, MD 21202
P: (410) 767-6301
F: (410) 767-8628
E: dedgerley@choosemaryland.org

MICHIGAN
Mr. James C. Epolito
President & CEO
Economic Development Corporation
300 North Washington Square
Lansing, MI 48913
P: (517) 241-1273
F: (517) 241-3683
E: jcepolito@michigan.gov

MINNESOTA
Hon. Dan McElroy
Commissioner
Department of Employment & Economic Development
1st National Bank Building
332 Minnesota Street, Suite E200
St. Paul, MN 55101
P: (651) 259-7119
F: (651) 296-4772
E: dan.mcelroy@state.mn.us

MISSISSIPPI
Mr. Gray R. Swoope
Executive Director
Development Authority
P.O. Box 849
Jackson, MS 39205
P: (601) 359-3449
F: (601) 359-3613

MISSOURI
Mr. Greg Steinhoff
Director
Department of Economic Development
301 West High Street
Truman Building, Room 680
Jefferson City, MO 65102
P: (573) 751-4770
F: (573) 751-7258
E: greg.steinhoff@ded.mo.gov

MONTANA
Mr. Evan Barrett
Chief Business Officer
Governor's Office of Economic Development
State Capitol
Helena, MT 59620
P: (406) 444-5470
F: (406) 444-3674
E: ebarrett@mt.gov

NEBRASKA
Mr. Richard Baier
Director
Department of Economic Development
P.O. Box 94666
Lincoln, NE 68509
P: (402) 471-3111
F: (402) 471-3778

NEVADA
Mr. Tim Rubald
Executive Director
Commission on Economic Development
108 Proctor Street
Carson City, NV 89701
P: (775) 687-4325
F: (775) 687-4450
E: dedadmin@bizopp.state.nv.us

NEW HAMPSHIRE
Mr. Michael Vlacich
Director of Economic Development
Department of Resources & Economic Development
P.O. Box 1856
Concord, NH 03302
P: (603) 271-2341
F: (603) 271-6784
E: mvlacich@dred.state.nh.us

NEW JERSEY
Ms. Caren S. Franzini
Chief Executive Officer
Economic Development Authority
36 West State Street
P.O. Box 990
Trenton, NJ 08625
P: (609) 292-1800
F: (609) 292-0885
E: njeda@njeda.com

NEW MEXICO
Mr. Rick Homans
Director
Economic Development Department
1100 South St. Francis Drive, Suite 1060
Joseph Montoya Building
Santa Fe, NM 87505
P: (505) 476-3736
F: (505) 827-0328
E: edd.info@state.nm.us

NEW YORK
Mr. Patrick Foye
Commissioner
Empire State Development
633 Third Avenue
New York, NY 10017
P: (212) 803-3700
F: (518) 474-2474

NORTH DAKOTA
Mr. Paul Lucy
Director
Economic Development & Finance Division
1600 East Century Avenue, Suite 2
P.O. Box 2057
Bismark, ND 58503
P: (701) 328-5388
F: (701) 328-5320
E: plucy@nd.gov

NORTHERN MARIANA ISLANDS
Mr. Oscar C. Camacho
Director
Commonwealth Development Authority
P.O. Box 502149
Saipan, MP 96950
P: (670) 234-6245
F: (670) 234-7144
E: administration@cda.gov.mp

OKLAHOMA
Ms. Natalie Shirley
Secretary of Commerce & Tourism
Department of Commerce
900 North Stiles Avenue
P.O. Box 26980
Oklahoma City, OK 73105
P: (405) 815-5147

OREGON
Mr. Bob Repine
Director
Economic & Community Development Department
775 Summer Street, Northeast, Suite 200
Salem, OR 97301
P: (503) 986-0110
F: (503) 378-5156
E: ODE.Webmaster@state.or.us

PENNSYLVANIA
Mr. Dennis Yablonsky
Secretary
Department of Community & Economic Development
Keystone Building, 4th Floor
Harrisburg, PA 17120
P: (717) 787-3003
F: (717) 787-6866

PUERTO RICO
Mr. Ricardo Rivera
Interim Secretary
Department of Economic Development & Commerce
P.O. Box 362350
Hato Rey, PR 00918
P: (787) 758-4747
F: (787) 753-6874

RHODE ISLAND
Mr. A. Michael Marques
Director
Department of Business Regulation
233 Richmond Street
Providence, RI 02903
P: (401) 222-2246
F: (401) 222-6098

SOUTH CAROLINA
Mr. Joseph E. Taylor Jr.
Secretary
Department of Commerce
1200 Main Street, Suite 1600
Columbia, SC 29201
P: (803) 737-0400
F: (803) 737-0418

SOUTH DAKOTA
Mr. Richard Benda
Secretary
Department of Tourism & Economic Development
Capitol Lake Plaza
711 East Wells Avenue
Pierre, SD 57501
P: (605) 773-3301
F: (605) 773-3256
E: richard.benda@state.sd.us

TENNESSEE
Mr. Matthew Kisber
Commissioner
Department of Economic &
Community Development
312 Eigth Avenue North
11th Floor
Nashville, TN 37243
P: (615) 741-1888

TEXAS
Mr. Aaron Demerson
Executive Director
Office of the Governor
P.O. Box 12428
Austin, TX 78711
P: (512) 936-0101
F: (512) 936-0303

U.S. VIRGIN ISLANDS
Mr. Frank Schulterbrandt
Chief Executive Officer
Economic Development
Authority
1050 Norre Gade
P.O. Box 305038
St. Thomas, VI 00803
P: (340) 774-0100
F: (340) 779-7153

UTAH
Mr. Jason Perry
Executive Director
Governor's Office of Economic
Development
324 South State Street, Suite
500
Salt Lake City, UT 84111
P: (801) 538-8700
F: (801) 538-8888
E: jpperry@utah.gov

VERMONT
Mr. Michael Quinn
Commissioner
Department of Economic
Development
National Life Building
Drawer 20
Montpelier, VT 05620
P: (802) 828-3211
F: (802) 828-3258
E: mike.quinn@state.vt.us

VIRGINIA
Mr. Jeffrey R. Anderson
Executive Director
Economic Development
Partnership
901 East Byrd Street
P.O. Box 798
Richmond, VA 23218
P: (804) 371-8109
F: (804) 371-6524
E: janderson
@yesvirginia.org

WASHINGTON
Ms. Juli Wilkerson
Director
Office of Community, Trade &
Economic Development
906 Columbia Street, Southwest
P.O. Box 42525
Olympia, WA 98501
P: (360) 725-4011
F: (360) 586-8440
E: juliw@cted.wa.gov

WEST VIRGINIA
Mr. Stephen Spence
Executive Director
Development Office
Capitol Complex Building 6,
Room 553
1900 Kanawha Boulevard East
Charleston, WV 25305
P: (304) 558-2234
F: (304) 558-0449
E: sspence@wvdo.org

WISCONSIN
Ms. Pam Christenson
Acting Administrator
Business Development Division
201 West Washington Avenue,
5th Floor
Madison, WI 53703
P: (608) 267-9384

WYOMING
Mr. Tucker Fagan
Chief Executive Officer
Business Council
214 West 15th Street
Cheyenne, WY 82002
P: (307) 777-2800
F: (307) 777-2837

Education (Chief State School Officer)

Overall responsibility for public elementary and secondary school systems.

ALABAMA
Dr. Joseph Morton
Superintendent
Department of Education
50 North Ripley Street
P.O. Box 302101
Montgomery, AL 36104
P: (334) 242-9700
E: jmorton@alsde.edu

ALASKA
Mr. Roger Sampson
Commissioner
Department of Education & Early Development
801 West 10th Street, Suite 200
Juneau, AK 99801
P: (907) 465-2802
F: (907) 465-4156

AMERICAN SAMOA
Dr. Clarie Poumele
Director of Education
Department of Education
American Samoa Government
Pago Pago, AS 96799
P: (684) 633-5237
F: (684) 633-4240

ARIZONA
Mr. Tom Horne
Superintendent of Public Instruction
Department of Education
1535 West Jefferson
Phoenix, AZ 85007
P: (602) 542-5460

ARKANSAS
Mr. Ken James
Director
Department of Education
Arch Ford Education Building
#4 Capitol Mall
Little Rock, AR 72201
P: (501) 682-4205
F: (501) 682-1079
E: kjames@arkedu.k12.ar.us

CALIFORNIA
Mr. Jack O'Connell
State Superintendent of Public Instruction
Department of Education
1430 N Street
Sacramento, CA 95814
P: (916) 319-0800

COLORADO
Dr. William Moloney
Commissioner
Department of Education
201 East Colfax Avenue
Denver, CO 80203
P: (303) 866-6600

CONNECTICUT
Mr. Mark McQuillan
Commissioner
Department of Education
Office of Commissioner
165 Capitol Avenue
Hartford, CT 06145
P: (860) 713-6500

DELAWARE
Ms. Valerie Woodruff
Secretary of Education
Department of Education
Townsend Building, 401 Federal Street
P.O. Box 1402
Dover, DE 19903
P: (302) 739-4601
F: (302) 739-4653

DISTRICT OF COLUMBIA
Dr. Deborah Gist
Director
State Office of Education
441 4th Street, NW
Suite 350-N
Washington, DC 20001
P: (202) 727-6436
F: (202) 727-2834

FLORIDA
Ms. Jeanine Blomberg
Commissioner
Department of Education
Turlington Building, Suite 1614
325 West Gaines Street
Tallahassee, FL 32399
P: (850) 245-0505
F: (850) 245-9667

GEORGIA
Ms. Kathy Cox
State Superintendent of Schools
Department of Education
2054 Twin Towers, East
Atlanta, GA 30334
P: (404) 656-2800
F: (404) 651-6867

GUAM
Mr. Louis Reyes
Superintendent
Department of Education
P.O. Box DE
Hagatna, GU 96932
P: (671) 475-0462
F: (671) 477-1895

HAWAII
Ms. Patricia Hamamoto
Superintendent
Department of Education
P.O. Box 2360
Honolulu, HI 96804
P: (808) 586-3310

IDAHO
Mr. Tom Luna
Superintendent of Public Instruction
State Department of Education
650 West State Street
P.O. Box 83720
Boise, ID 83720
P: (208) 332-6815
E: trluna@sde.idaho.gov

ILLINOIS
Mr. Christopher Koch
Superintendent of Education
Board of Education
100 North First Street
Springfield, IL 62777
P: (217) 782-2221
F: (217) 785-3972

INDIANA
Dr. Suellen Reed
Superintendent of Public Instruction
Department of Education
151 West Ohio Street
Room 229
Indianapolis, IN 46204
P: (317) 232-6665
F: (317) 232-8004
E: sureed@doe.state.in.us

IOWA
Ms. Judy Jeffrey
Director
Department of Education
Grimes State Office Bldg.
400 East 14th Street
Des Moines, IA 50319
P: (515) 281-3436
F: (515) 281-5988

KANSAS
Mr. Dale Dennis
Acting Commissioner of Education
Department of Education
120 Southeast 10th Avenue
Topeka, KS 66612
P: (785) 296-3871
F: (785) 291-3791

KENTUCKY
Mr. Kevin Noland
Commissioner of Education
Department of Education
Capitol Plaza Tower
500 Mero Street
Frankfort, KY 40601
P: (502) 564-3141
F: (502) 564-5680

LOUISIANA
Mr. Cecil Picard
State Superintendent of Education
Department of Education
P.O. Box 94064
Baton Rouge, LA 70804
P: (225) 342-3602
F: (225) 342-7316
E: SuperintendentPicard@la.gov

MAINE
Ms. Susan Gendron
Commissioner
State Department of Education
23 State House Station
Augusta, ME 04333
P: (207) 624-6600

MARYLAND
Dr. Nancy S. Grasmick
State Superintendent
State Department of Education
200 West Baltimore Street
Baltimore, MD 21201
P: (410) 767-0462
F: (410) 333-6033
E: ngrasmick@msde.state.md.us

MASSACHUSETTS
Mr. David P. Driscoll
Commissioner
Department of Education
350 Main Street
Malden, MA 02148
P: (781) 388-3300
F: (781) 338-3370

MICHIGAN
Mr. Mike P. Flanagan
Superindendent of Public Instruction
Department of Education
608 West Allegan Street
P.O. Box 30008
Lansing, MI 48909
P: (517) 373-9235

MINNESOTA
Ms. Alice Seagren
Commissioner
Department of Education
1500 Highway 36 West
Roseville, MN 55113
P: (651) 582-8204
F: (651) 582-8724
E: Alice.Seagren@state.mn.us

MISSISSIPPI
Dr. Hank Bounds
State Superintendent of Education
Department of Education
P.O. Box 771
Jackson, MS 39205
P: (601) 359-3512
F: (601) 359-3242
E: hmbounds@mde.k12.ms.us

MISSOURI
Dr. Kent King
Commissioner
Department of Elementary & Secondary Education
Jefferson Building, 6th Floor
P.O. Box 480
Jefferson City, MO 65102
P: (573) 751-4446
F: (573) 751-1179
E: kent.king@dese.mo.gov

MONTANA
Ms. Linda McCulloch
Superintendent
Office of Public Instruction
P.O. Box 202501
Helena, MT 59620
P: (406) 444-5658
F: (406) 444-2893
E: OPISupt@mt.gov

NEBRASKA
Mr. Doug D. Christensen
Commissioner
Department of Education
P.O. Box 94987
Lincoln, NE 68509
P: (402) 471-2295
F: (402) 471-0117

NEVADA
Mr. Keith Rheault
Superintendent
Department of Education
700 East Fifth Street
Carson City, NV 89701
P: (775) 687-9217
F: (775) 687-9101
E: krheault@doe.nv.gov

NEW HAMPSHIRE
Dr. Lyonel B. Tracy
Commissioner
Department of Education
101 Pleasant Street
Concord, NH 03301
P: (603) 271-3144
F: (603) 271-1953
E: ltracy@ed.state.nh.us

NEW JERSEY
Ms. Lucille E. Davy
Commissioner
Department of Education
100 Riverview Plaza
P.O. Box 500
Trenton, NJ 08625
P: (609) 292-4450
F: (609) 777-4099

NEW MEXICO
Dr. Veronica Garcia
Secretary of Education
Public Education Department
300 Don Gaspar
Santa Fe, NM 87501
P: (505) 827-5800

NEW YORK
Mr. Richard P. Mills
Commissioner
Education Department
State Education Building
Albany, NY 12234
P: (518) 474-5844
E: rmills@mail.nysed.gov

NORTH CAROLINA
Dr. June Atkinson
Superintendent of Public Instruction
Department of Public Instruction
6301 Mail Service Center
Raleigh, NC 27699
P: (919) 807-3430
F: (919) 807-3445
E: jatkinson@dpi.state.nc.us

NORTH DAKOTA
Dr. Wayne G. Sanstead
State Superintendent
Department of Public Instruction
600 East Boulevard Avenue, 11th Floor
Bismarck, ND 58505
P: (701) 328-2260
F: (701) 328-2461
E: wsanstead@nd.gov

NORTHERN MARIANA ISLANDS
Dr. David M. Borja
Commissioner of Education
Public School System
P.O. Box 501370CK
Saipan, MP 96950
P: (670) 664-3700
F: (670) 664-3798

OHIO
Ms. Susan Tave Zelman
Superintendent of Public Instruction
Department of Education
25 South Front Street
Columbus, OH 43215
P: (614) 466-7578
F: (614) 387-0964

OKLAHOMA
Ms. Sandy Garrett
Superintendent of Public Instruction
State Department of Education
2500 North Lincoln Boulevard
Oklahoma City, OK 73105
P: (405) 521-3301
F: (405) 521-6205

OREGON
Ms. Susan Castillo
Superintendent of Public Instruction
Department of Education
255 Capitol Street, Northeast
Salem, OR 97310
P: (503) 378-3569
F: (503) 378-5156
E: ODE.Webmaster@state.or.us

PENNSYLVANIA
Dr. Gerald L. Zahorchak
Secretary
Department of Education
333 Market Street
Harrisburg, PA 17126
P: (717) 787-6788

PUERTO RICO
Mr. Rafael Aragunde Torres
Secretary
Department of Education
P.O. Box 190759
San Juan, PR 00919
P: (787) 759-2000
F: (787) 250-0275

RHODE ISLAND
Mr. Peter McWalters
Commissioner
Department of Elementary & Secondary Education
255 Westminster Street
Providence, RI 02903
P: (401) 222-4600 Ext. 2001
E: peter.mcwalters@ride.ri.gov

SOUTH CAROLINA
Mr. Jim Rex
Superintendent of Education
Department of Education
1006 Rutledge Building
1429 Senate Street
Columbia, SC 29201
P: (803) 734-8492
F: (803) 734-4426

SOUTH DAKOTA
Dr. Rick Melmer
Secretary
Department of Education
Kneip Building
700 Governors Drive
Pierre, SD 57501
P: (605) 773-5669
F: (605) 773-6139
E: rick.melmer@state.sd.us

TENNESSEE
Ms. Lana Seivers
Commissioner
Department of Education
710 James Robertson Parkway
Nashville, TN 37243
P: (615) 741-2731
F: (615) 532-4791

TEXAS
Ms. Shirley Neeley
Commissioner
Education Agency
1701 Congress Avenue
Austin, TX 78701
P: (512) 463-8985

Education (Chief State School Officer)

U.S. VIRGIN ISLANDS
Ms. Lauren Larsen
Acting Commissioner
Department of Education
44-46 Kongens Gade
St. Thomas, VI 00802
P: (340) 774-0100
F: (340) 774-7153

UTAH
Dr. Patti Harrington
State Superintendent
State Board of Education
250 East 500 South
P.O. Box 144200
Salt Lake City, UT 84114
P: (801) 538-7510
F: (801) 538-7521
E: patti.harrington
@schools.utah.gov

VERMONT
Mr. Richard Cate
Commissioner
Department of Education
120 State Street
Montpelier, VT 05620
P: (802) 828-3135
F: (802) 828-3140
E: richardcate
@education.state.vt.us

VIRGINIA
Mr. Billy K. Cannaday Jr.
Superintendent of Public Instruction
Department of Education
101 North 14th Street, 25th Floor
James Monroe Building
Richmond, VA 23219
P: (804) 225-2023
F: (804) 371-2099
E: billy.cannaday
@doe.virginia.gov

WASHINGTON
Ms. Terry Bergeson
Superintendent of Public Instruction
Office of Superintendent of Public Instruction
Old Capitol Building
P.O. Box 47200
Olympia, WA 98504
P: (360) 725-6000
F: (360) 753-6712
E: bergeson@ospi.wednet.edu

WEST VIRGINIA
Dr. Steve Paine
Superintendent of Schools
Department of Education
1900 Kanawha Boulevard, East
Building 6, Room 358-B
Charleston, WV 25305
P: (304) 558-2681
F: (304) 558-0048

WISCONSIN
Ms. Elizabeth Burmaster
Superintendent
Department of Public Instruction
125 South Webster Street
P.O. Box 7841
Madison, WI 53707
P: (608) 266-1771
F: (608) 267-1052

WYOMING
Dr. Jim McBride
Superintendent of Public Instruction
Department of Education
Hathaway Building, 2nd Floor
Cheyenne, WY 82002
P: (307) 777-7675
F: (307) 777-6234

Elections Administration

Administers state election laws and supervises the printing and distribution of ballots.

ALABAMA
Ms. Janice McDonald
Elections Director
Elections Division
P.O. Box 5616
Montgomery, AL 36106
P: (334) 242-7559
F: (334) 242-2444

ALASKA
Ms. Whitney Brewster
Director
Division of Elections
P.O. Box 110017
Juneau, AK 99811
P: (907) 465-4611
F: (907) 465-3203
E: whitney_brewster
@gov.state.ak.us

AMERICAN SAMOA
Mr. Soliai T. Fuimaono
Chief Election Officer
American Samoa Government
P.O. Box 3790
Pago Pago, AS 96799
P: (684) 633-2522
F: (684) 633-7116

ARIZONA
Mr. Joe Kanefield
Election Director
Secretary of State's Office
1700 West Washington, 7th Floor
Phoenix, AZ 85007
P: (602) 542-8683
F: (602) 542-6172

ARKANSAS
Ms. Jill E. Belin
Director of Elections
Secretary of State
State Capitol, Room 026
Little Rock, AR 72201
P: (501) 682-3419
F: (501) 682-3408

Ms. Susie Stormes
Director
State Board of Election Commissioners
501 Woodlane Drive, Suite 122
Little Rock, AR 72201
P: (501) 682-1834
F: (501) 682-1782
E: susie.stormes
@sos.arkansas.gov

CALIFORNIA
Ms. Caren Daniels-Meade
Chief
Election Division
1500 11th Street, 5th Floor
Sacramento, CA 95814
P: (916) 657-2166
F: (916) 653-3214

COLORADO
Ms. Holly Lowder
Director of Elections
Elections Division
Department of State
1700 Broadway, Suite 200
Denver, CO 80290
P: (303) 894-2200 Ext. 6301
F: (303) 869-4861
E: holly.lowder
@sos.state.co.us

CONNECTICUT
Mr. Michael Kozik
Managing Attorney
Legislation & Elections Administration Division
30 Trinity Street
Hartford, CT 06106
P: (860) 509-6100
F: (860) 509-6127

DELAWARE
Mr. Frank Calio
State Election Commissioner
Department of Elections
111 South West Street, Suite 10
Dover, DE 19904
P: (302) 739-4277
F: (302) 739-6794

DISTRICT OF COLUMBIA
Mr. Charles Lowery
Executive Director
Board of Elections & Ethics
441 Fourth Street, Northwest
Suite 250N
Washington, DC 20001
P: (202) 727-2525

FLORIDA
Ms. Amy K. Tuck
Director
Division of Elections
Room 316, R.A. Gray Building
500 South Bronough Street
Tallahassee, FL 32399
P: (850) 245-6200
F: (850) 245-6217
E: DivElections
@dos.state.fl.us

GEORGIA
Ms. Kathy Rogers
Director of Elections
Elections Division
Suite 1104, West Tower
2 Martin Luther King, Jr. Drive, SE
Atlanta, GA 30334
P: (404) 656-2871
F: (404) 651-9531

GUAM
Mr. Gerald A. Taitano
Executive Director
Election Commission
GCIC Building, Suite 200
414 West Soledad Avenue
Hagatna, GU 96910
P: (671) 477-9791
F: (671) 477-1895

HAWAII
Mr. Rex Quidilla
Interim Chief Election Official
Office of Elections
802 Lehua Avenue
Pearl City, HI 96782
P: (808) 453-8683
F: (808) 453-6006

IDAHO
Mr. Tim Hurst
Chief Deputy
Secretary of State
700 West Jefferson, Room 203
Boise, ID 83720
P: (208) 334-2300
F: (208) 334-2282
E: thurst@sos.idaho.gov

ILLINOIS
Mr. Daniel W. White
Executive Director
State Board of Elections
1020 South Spring Street
P.O. Box 4187
Springfield, IL 62708
P: (217) 782-4141
F: (217) 782-5959

INDIANA
Mr. Brad King
Co-Director
Election Division
302 West Washington, Room E204
Indianapolis, IN 46204
P: (317) 233-3939
F: (317) 233-6793
E: bking@iec.state.in.us

Ms. Pamela Potesta
Co-Director
Elections Division
302 West Washington, Room E204
Indianapolis, IN 46204
P: (317) 232-3939
F: (317) 233-6793
E: ppotesta@iec.state.in.us

IOWA
Ms. Sandy Steinbach
Director of Elections
Secretary of State Office
1305 East Walnut Street
Des Moines, IA 50319
P: (515) 281-5823
F: (515) 281-7142

KANSAS
Mr. Brad Bryant
Deputy Assistant for Elections
Office of the Secretary of State
120 Southwest 10th Avenue
Memorial Hall
Topeka, KS 66612
P: (785) 296-4575
F: (785) 368-8033

KENTUCKY
Ms. Sarah Ball Johnson
Executive Director
State Board of Elections
140 Walnut Street
Frankfort, KY 40601
P: (502) 573-7100
F: (502) 573-4369

LOUISIANA
Ms. Angie Laplace
Commissioner of Elections
Elections Division
8549 United Plaza Boulevard
P.O. Box 94125
Baton Rouge, LA 70802
P: (225) 922-0900
F: (225) 922-0945
E: angie.laplace
@sos.louisiana.gov

MAINE
Ms. Julie L. Flynn
Deputy Secretary of State
Bureau of Corporation, Elections & Commissions
101 State House Station
Augusta, ME 04333
P: (207) 624-7736
F: (207) 287-5874

Elections Administration

MARYLAND
Ms. Linda Lamone
State Administrator
State Board of Elections
P.O. Box 6486
Annapolis, MD 21401
P: (410) 269-2840
F: (410) 974-2019

MASSACHUSETTS
Ms. Michelle Tassinari
Legal Counsel
Election Division
One Ashburton Place, Room 1705
Boston, MA 02108
P: (617) 727-2828
F: (617) 742-3238

MICHIGAN
Mr. Christopher M. Thomas
Director
Bureau of Elections
Mutual Building, 4th Floor
208 North Capitol Avenue
Lansing, MI 48918
P: (517) 373-2540
F: (517) 241-2784

MINNESOTA
Mr. Michael E. McCarthy
Election Division Supervisor
Office of the Secretary of State
180 State Office Building
100 Martin Luther King Jr. Boulevard
St. Paul, MN 55155
P: (651) 215-1440
F: (651) 296-9073
E: mike.mccarthy@state.mn.us

MISSISSIPPI
Mr. Jay Eads
Assistant Secretary of State for Elections
Elections Division
P.O. Box 136
401 Mississippi Street
Jackson, MS 39205
P: (601) 359-6368
F: (601) 359-5019

MISSOURI
Mr. Rich Lamb
Executive Deputy Secretary of State
Secretary of State's Office
P.O. Box 1767
Jefferson City, MO 65102
P: (573) 751-2301
F: (573) 526-3242
E: rich.lamb@sos.mo.gov

MONTANA
Ms. Elaine Graveley
Division Deputy
Elections & Government Services Division
P.O. Box 202801
Helena, MT 59620
P: (406) 444-5346
F: (406) 444-2023
E: egraveley@mt.gov

NEBRASKA
Mr. Neal Erickson
Assistant Secretary of State
Election Administration
State Capitol, Suite 2300
Lincoln, NE 68502
P: (402) 471-3229
F: (402) 471-3237
E: neal.erickson@sos.ne.gov

NEVADA
Mr. Matt Griffin
Deputy Secretary of State
Office of the Secretary of State
101 North Carson Street
Suite 3
Carson City, NV 89701
P: (775) 684-5793
F: (775) 684-5718

NEW HAMPSHIRE
Mr. Anthony Stevens
Assistant Secretary of State
Election Division
State House, Room 204
Concord, NH 03301
P: (603) 271-5335
F: (603) 271-7933
E: astevens@sos.state.nh.us

NEW JERSEY
Ms. Maria Del Valle Koch
Acting Director
Division of Elections
44 South Clinton Avenue, 7th Floor
P.O. Box 304
Trenton, NJ 08625
P: (609) 292-3760
F: (609) 777-1280
E: njelections@lps.state.nj.us

NEW MEXICO
Mr. Daniel A. Ivey-Soto
Director of Elections/Legal Counsel
Bureau of Elections
State Capitol Annex North
325 Don Gaspar, Suite 300
Santa Fe, NM 87503
P: (505) 827-3600
F: (505) 827-8403
E: Elections@state.nm.us

NEW YORK
Mr. Peter Kosinski
Co-Executive Director
State Board of Elections
40 Steuben Street
Albany, NY 12207
P: (518) 474-8100
F: (518) 486-4068
E: pkosinski@elections.state.ny.us

Mr. Stanley Zalen
Co-Executive Director
State Board of Elections
40 Steuben Street
Albany, NY 12207
P: (518) 474-8100
F: (518) 486-4068
E: szalen@elections.state.ny.us

NORTH CAROLINA
Mr. Gary Bartlett
Executive Director
State Board of Elections
P.O. Box 27255
Raleigh, NC 27611
P: (919) 733-7173
F: (919) 715-0135
E: gary.bartlett@ncmail.net

NORTH DAKOTA
Mr. Jim Silrum
Deputy Secretary of State
Office of the Secretary of State
600 East Boulevard Avenue
Department 108
Bismarck, ND 58505
P: (701) 328-3660
F: (701) 328-2992

NORTHERN MARIANA ISLANDS
Mr. Gregorio C. Sablan
Executive Director
Commonwealth Election Commission
P.O. Box 470 CHRB
Saipan, MP 96950
P: (670) 664-8683
F: (670) 664-8689

OHIO
Ms. Patricia Wolfe
Director of Elections
Secretary of State
180 East Broad Street, 15th Floor
Columbus, OH 43215
P: (614) 466-2585
F: (614) 752-4360

OKLAHOMA
Mr. Michael Clingman
Secretary of the Senate/Secretary
State Election Board
Room 6, State Capitol
Oklahoma City, OK 73105
P: (405) 521-2391
F: (405) 521-6457

OREGON
Mr. John Lindback
Director
Elections Division
141 State Capitol
Salem, OR 97310
P: (503) 986-1518
F: (503) 373-7414
E: elections-division@sosinet.sos.state.or.

PENNSYLVANIA
Mr. Harry A. VanSickle
Commissioner
Bureau of Commissions, Elections & Legislation
210 North Office Building
Harrisburg, PA 17120
P: (717) 787-5280
F: (717) 705-0721

PUERTO RICO
Mr. Ramon Gonzalez
President
State Election Commission
P.O. Box 19555
Hato Rey, PR 00919
P: (787) 777-8682
F: (787) 296-0173

RHODE ISLAND
Mr. Robert Kando
Executive Director
State Board of Elections
50 Branch Avenue
Providence, RI 02904
P: (401) 222-2345
F: (401) 222-3135

SOUTH CAROLINA
Ms. Marci Andino
Executive Director
State Election Commission
P.O. Box 5987
Columbia, SC 29250
P: (803) 734-9060
F: (803) 734-9366

SOUTH DAKOTA
Ms. Kea Warne
Election Supervisor
Office of the Secretary of State
State Capitol
500 East Capitol Avenue
Pierre, SD 57501
P: (605) 773-3537
F: (605) 773-6580
E: kea.warne@state.sd.us

TENNESSEE
Mr. Brook Thompson
Coordinator of Elections
Secretary of State's Office
312 Eighth Avenue, North
9th Floor
Nashville, TN 37243
P: (615) 741-7956
F: (615) 741-1278

TEXAS
Ms. Ann McGeehan
Division Director
Elections Division
Office of the Secretary of State
P.O. Box 12697
Austin, TX 78711
P: (512) 463-9871
F: (512) 475-2811

U.S. VIRGIN ISLANDS
Mr. John Abramson
Supervisor of Elections
Election System of the Virgin Islands
P.O. Box 1499, Kingshill
St. Croix, VI 00851
P: (340) 773-1021
F: (340) 773-4523

UTAH
Mr. Michael Cragun
Director
Elections Office
State Capitol Complex, Suite 325
P.O. Box 142220
Salt Lake City, UT 84114
P: (801) 538-1041
F: (801) 538-1133
E: mcragun@utah.gov

VERMONT
Ms. Kathy DeWolfe
Director
Elections & Campaign Finance Division
26 Terrace Street, Drawer 09
Montpelier, VT 05609
P: (802) 828-2304
F: (802) 828-5171
E: kdewolfe@sec.state.vt.us

VIRGINIA
Ms. Jean Jensen
Secretary
State Board of Elections
200 North 9th Street, Room 101
Richmond, VA 23219
P: (800) 864-8903
F: (804) 371-0194
E: jean.jensen@sbe.virginia.gov

WASHINGTON
Mr. Nick Handy
Director
Office of Secretary of State, Elections Division
Legislative Building
P.O. Box 40229
Olympia, WA 98504
P: (360) 902-4156
F: (360) 586-5629
E: nhandy@secstate.wa.gov

WEST VIRGINIA
Mr. Jason Williams
Manager, Elections
Office of the Secretary of State
1900 Kanawha Boulevard East
State Capitol, Room 157-K
Charleston, WV 25305
P: (304) 558-6000
F: (304) 558-0900
E: jwilliams@wvsos.com

WISCONSIN
Mr. Kevin J. Kennedy
Executive Director
State Elections Board
17 West Main Street, Suite 310
Madison, WI 53703
P: (608) 266-8087
F: (608) 267-0500
E: kevin.kennedy@seb.state.wi.us

WYOMING
Ms. Peggy Nighswonger
State Elections Director
Secretary of State's Office
Capitol Building, Room B-38
Cheyenne, WY 82002
P: (307) 777-3573
F: (307) 777-7640

Emergency Management

Prepares, maintains and/or implements state disasters plans and coordinates emergency activities.

Information provided by:

National Emergency Management Association
Trina Sheets
Executive Director
P.O. Box 11910
Lexington, KY 40578
P: (859) 244-8000
F: (859) 244-8239
tsheets@csg.org
www.nemaweb.org

ALABAMA
Mr. Bruce Baughman
Director
State Emergency Management Agency
5898 County Road 41
P.O. Drawer 2160
Clanton, AL 35046
P: (205) 280-2201
F: (205) 280-2410
E: bruceb@ema.alabama.gov

ALASKA
Mr. John Madden
Director
Division of Homeland Security & Emergency Management
P.O. Box 5750
Fort Richardson, AK 99505
P: (907) 428-7062
F: (907) 428-7009
E: john_madden@ak-prepared.com

AMERICAN SAMOA
Mr. Leiataua Birdsall Alailima
Homeland Security Advisor
Office of the Governor
EOB 3rd Floor
Pago Pago, AS 96799
P: (684) 699-3800
F: (684) 699-5329
E: bvalailima@yahoo.com

ARIZONA
Mr. Lou Trammell
Director
Division of Emergency Management
5636 East McDowell Road
Phoenix, AZ 85008
P: (602) 231-6245
F: (602) 231-6356
E: Lou.Trammell@azdema.gov

ARKANSAS
Mr. David Maxwell
Director & Homeland Security Adviser
State Department of Emergency Management
P.O. Box 758
Conway, AR 72033
P: (501) 730-9750
F: (501) 730-9778
E: david.maxwell@adem.state.ar.us

CALIFORNIA
Mr. Henry R. Renteria
Director
Governor's Office of Emergency Services
3650 Schriever Avenue
Mather, CA 95655
P: (916) 845-8510
F: (916) 845-8511
E: henry_renteria@oes.ca.gov

COLORADO
Mr. George Epp
Director
Division of Emergency Management
9195 East Mineral Avenue, Suite 200
Centennial, CO 80112
P: (303) 866-4988
F: (720) 852-6750
E: george.epp@state.co.us

CONNECTICUT
Mr. William Hackett
Director
Emergency Management & Homeland Security
360 Broad Street
Hartford, CT 06105
P: (860) 566-3180
F: (860) 256-0855
E: william.j.hackett@po.state.ct.us

DELAWARE
Mr. James Turner
Director
State Emergency Management Agency
165 Brick Store Landing Road
Smyrna, DE 19977
P: (302) 659-2240
F: (302) 659-6855
E: jamie.turner@state.de.us

DISTRICT OF COLUMBIA
Mr. Darrell Darnell
Director
Emergency Management Agency
2720 Martin Luther King Jr. Avenue, SE
2nd Floor
Washington, DC 20032
P: (202) 727-3150
F: (202) 715-7288
E: darrell.darnell@dc.gov

FLORIDA
Mr. Craig Fugate
Director
Division of Emergency Management
2555 Shumard Oak Boulevard
Tallahassee, FL 32399
P: (850) 413-9969
F: (850) 488-1016
E: craig.fugate@dca.state.fl.us

GEORGIA
Mr. Charley English
Director
State Emergency Management Agency
935 East Confederate Ave., SE, Bldg. #2
Atlanta, GA 30316
P: (404) 635-7001
F: (404) 635-7009
E: cenglish@gema.state.ga.us

GUAM
Hon. Michael Cruz (R)
Lieutenant Governor
Office of Homeland Security & Civil Defense
R.J. Bordallo Governor's Complex
P.O. Box 2950
Hagatna, GU 96932
P: (671) 475-9380
F: (671) 477-2007
E: mcruz@guamocd.org

HAWAII
Mr. Edward T. Teixeira
Vice Director
Civil Defense Division
State Department of Defense
3949 Diamond Head Road
Honolulu, HI 96816
P: (808) 733-4300
F: (808) 733-4287
E: eteixeira@scd.hawaii.gov

IDAHO
Mr. William Bishop
Director
Bureau of Homeland Security
4040 West Guard Street, Building 600
Boise, ID 83705
P: (208) 442-3040
F: (208) 442-3044
E: bbishop@bhs.idaho.gov

ILLINOIS
Mr. Andrew Velasquez
Director
State Emergency Management Agency
2200 South Dirksen Parkway
Springfield, IL 62701
P: (217) 782-2800
F: (217) 524-7967
E: andrew.velasquez@illinois.gov

INDIANA
Mr. J. Eric Dietz
Executive Director
Department of Homeland Security
302 West Washington Street, Room E-208
Indianapolis, IN 46235
P: (317) 232-3986
F: (317) 232-3895
E: jedietz@dhs.in.gov

IOWA
Mr. David Miller
Administrator
State Homeland Security & Emergency Management Division
7105 Northwest 70th Avenue
Camp Dodge - W4
Johnston, IA 50131
P: (515) 281-3231
F: (515) 725-3290
E: David.Miller@Iowa.gov

KANSAS
Mr. Bill Chornyak
Deputy Director
Division of Emergency Management
2800 Southwest Topeka Boulevard
Topeka, KS 66611
P: (785) 274-1401
F: (785) 274-1426
E: wmchornyak@agtop.state.ks.us

KENTUCKY
Mr. Clay Bailey
Director
Division of Emergency Management
Boone Center
100 Minuteman Parkway
Frankfort, KY 40601
P: (502) 607-1682
F: (502) 607-1251
E: maxwell.bailey@ky.ngb.army.mil

LOUISIANA
Col. Jeff Smith
Acting Director
Governor's Office of Homeland Security & Emergency Preparedness
7667 Independence Boulevard
Baton Rouge, LA 70806
P: (225) 925-7345
F: (225) 925-7348
E: jsmith@ohsep.louisiana.gov

MAINE
Mr. Charles Jacobs
Acting Director
State Emergency Management Agency
72 State House Station
Augusta, ME 04333
P: (207) 626-4401
F: (207) 287-3180
E: charles.jacobs@maine.gov

Mr. Robert McAleer
Director
State Emergency Management Agency
#72 SHS
45 Commercial Drive, Suite #2
Augusta, ME 04333
P: (207) 624-4401
F: (207) 287-3180
E: Robert.Mcaleer@maine.gov

MARYLAND
Mr. John Droneburg
Director
State Emergency Management Agency
State EOC, Camp Fretterd Military Res.
5401 Rue St. Lo Avenue
Reisterstown, MD 21136
P: (410) 517-3600
F: (410) 517-3610
E: jdroneburg@mema.state.md.us

MASSACHUSETTS
Mr. Ken McBride
Acting Director
State Emergency Management Agency
400 Worcester Road
Framingham, MA 01702
P: (508) 820-2010
F: (508) 820-2015
E: Ken.McBride@state.ma.us

MICHIGAN
Capt. Eddie L. Washington Jr.
Deputy State Director
Emergency Management & Homeland Security Division
Michigan State Police
4000 Collins Road
Lansing, MI 48910
P: (517) 336-2686
F: (517) 333-4987
E: washine@michigan.gov

MINNESOTA
Ms. Kris Eide
Director
Division of Homeland Security & Emergency Management
444 Cedar Street, Suite 223
St. Paul, MN 55101
P: (651) 201-7404
F: (651) 296-0459
E: kris.eide@state.mn.us

MISSISSIPPI
Mr. Mike Womack
Executive Director
Emergency Management Agency
#1 MEMA Drive
P.O. Box 5644
Pearl, MS 39288
P: (601) 933-6362
F: (601) 933-6800
E: mwomack@mema.ms.gov

MISSOURI
Mr. Ronald Reynolds
Director
State Emergency Management Agency
P.O. Box 116
2302 Militia Drive
Jefferson City, MO 65102
P: (573) 526-9101
F: (573) 634-7966
E: ron.reynolds@sema.dps.mo.gov

MONTANA
Mr. Dan McGowan
Administrator
Disaster & Emergency Services Division
Department of Military Affairs
P.O. Box 4789
Ft. Harrison, MT 59636
P: (406) 841-3911
F: (406) 841-3965
E: dmcgowan@mt.gov

NEBRASKA
Mr. Alan Berndt
Assistant Director
State Emergency Management Agency
1300 Military Road
Lincoln, NE 68508
P: (402) 471-7410
F: (402) 471-7433
E: al.berndt@nema.ne.gov

NEVADA
Mr. Frank Siracusa
Director
Division of Emergency Management
2525 South Carson Street
Capitol Complex
Carson City, NV 89711
P: (775) 687-4240
F: (775) 687-6788
E: fsiracusa@dps.state.nv.us

NEW HAMPSHIRE
Mr. Christopher Pope
Director, Department of Safety
Division of Emergency Services
Bureau of Emergency Management
33 Hazen Drive
Concord, NH 03305
P: (603) 271-2231
F: (603) 225-7341
E: cpope@nhoem.state.nh.us

NEW JERSEY
Mr. Richard Arroyo
Commanding Officer
New Jersey State Police
P.O. Box 7068
Old River Road
West Trenton, NJ 08628
P: (609) 963-6932
F: (609) 530-4593
E: LPP3756@gw.njsp.org

NEW MEXICO
Mr. Tim Manning
Director
Office of Emergency Management
Department of Public Safety
130 South Capitol
Santa Fe, NM 85504
P: (505) 476-1050
F: (505) 476-1057
E: Tim.Manning@state.nm.us

NEW YORK
Mr. John Gibb
Director
State Emergency Management Office
1220 Washington Avenue
Building 22
Albany, NY 12226
P: (518) 292-2301
F: (518) 322-4978
E: john.gibb@semo.state.ny.us

NORTH CAROLINA
Mr. Doug Hoell
Director
Division of Emergency Management
4713 Mail Service Center
Raleigh, NC 27699
P: (919) 733-3825
F: (919) 733-5406
E: dhoell@ncem.org

NORTH DAKOTA
Mr. Greg Wilz
Director
State Department of Emergency Services
P.O. Box 5511
Bismarck, ND 58506
P: (701) 328-8100
F: (701) 328-8181
E: gwilz@nd.gov

Emergency Management

NORTHERN MARIANA ISLANDS
Mr. Gregorio Guerrero
Director
Emergency Management Office
Office of the Governor
P.O. Box 10007
Saipan, MP 96950
P: (670) 322-8002
F: (670) 322-7743
E: gguerrero@cnmiemo.gov.mp

OHIO
Ms. Nancy Dragani
Executive Director
State Emergency Management Agency
2855 West Dublin Granville Road
Columbus, OH 43235
P: (614) 889-7152
F: (614) 889-7183
E: ndragani@dps.state.oh.us

OKLAHOMA
Mr. Albert Ashwood
Director
Department of Emergency Management
P.O. Box 53365
Oklahoma City, OK 73152
P: (405) 521-2481
F: (405) 521-4053
E: albert.ashwood@oem.ok.gov

OREGON
Mr. Ken Murphy
Director
Office of Emergency Management
3225 State Street
P.O. Box 14370
Salem, OR 97309
P: (503) 378-2911
F: (503) 373-7833
E: kmurphy@oem.state.or.us

PENNSYLVANIA
Brig. Gen. James Joseph
Director
State Emergency Management Agency
2605 Interstate Drive
Harrisburg, PA 17110
P: (717) 651-2007
F: (717) 651-2040
E: jajoseph@state.pa.us

PUERTO RICO
Nazario Lugo
Executive Director
Emergency Management Agency
P.O. Box 9066597
San Juan, PR 00906
P: (787) 721-3596
F: (787) 725-4244
E: nlugo@aemead.gobierno.pr

RHODE ISLAND
Mr. Robert Warren
Executive Director
State Emergency Management Agency
645 New London Avenue
Cranston, RI 02920
P: (401) 946-9996
F: (401) 944-1891
E: robert.joseph.warren@us.army.mil

SOUTH CAROLINA
Mr. Ron Osborne
Director
State Emergency Management Division
Office of the Adjutant General
2779 Fish Hatchery Road
West Columbia, SC 29172
P: (803) 737-8500
F: (803) 737-8570
E: rosborne@emd.state.sc.us

SOUTH DAKOTA
Ms. Kristi Turman
Director
Division of Emergency Management
118 West Capitol Avenue
Pierre, SD 57501
P: (605) 773-3231
F: (605) 773-3580
E: kristi.turman@state.sd.us

TENNESSEE
Mr. Jim Bassham
Director
State Emergency Management Agency
3041 Sidco Drive
Nashville, TN 37204
P: (615) 741-4332
F: (615) 741-0006
E: jbassham@tnema.org

TEXAS
Mr. Jack Colley
Chief
Governor's Division of Emergency Management
5805 North Lamar Boulevard
P.O. Box 4087
Austin, TX 78773
P: (512) 424-2443
F: (512) 424-2444
E: jack.colley@txdps.state.tx.us

U.S. VIRGIN ISLANDS
Mr. Renaldo Rivera
Adjutant General
Territorial Emergency Management Agency
4031 LaGrande Princess, Lot 1B
Christiansted, VI 00820
P: (340) 712-7710
F: (340) 712-7711
E: renaldo.rivera@vi.ngb.army.mil

UTAH
Mr. Michael Kuehn
Director
Division of Homeland Security
4501 South 2700 West
P.O. Box 141775
Salt Lake City, UT 84114
P: (801) 965-4498
F: (801) 965-4608
E: mkuehn@utah.gov

VERMONT
Ms. Barbara Farr
Director
State Emergency Management Agency
103 South Main Street
Waterbury, VT 05671
P: (800) 347-0488
F: (802) 244-5556
E: bfarr@dps.state.vt.us

VIRGINIA
Mr. Michael Cline
State Coordinator
Department of Emergency Management
10501 Trade Court
Richmond, VA 23236
P: (804) 897-6501
F: (804) 897-6506
E: michael.cline@vdem.virginia.gov

WASHINGTON
Mr. James Mullen
Director
State Emergency Management Division
Building 20, MS: TA-20
Camp Murray, WA 98430
P: (253) 512-7001
F: (253) 512-7207
E: j.mullen@emd.wa.gov

WEST VIRGINIA
Mr. Jimmy Gianato
Director
Division of Homeland Security & Emergency Management
1900 Kanawha Boulevard, East
Building 1, Room EB-80
Charleston, WV 25305
P: (304) 558-5380
F: (304) 344-4538
E: jgianato@wvdmaps.gov

WISCONSIN
Mr. Johnnie Smith
Administrator
State Office of Emergency Management
P.O. Box 7865
Madison, WI 53707
P: (608) 242-3251
F: (608) 242-3247
E: johnnie.smith@dma.state.wi.us

Employment Services

Provides job counseling, testing and placement services in the state.

ALABAMA
Ms. Sylvia Williams
Chief
Employment Services Division
649 Monroe Street
Montgomery, AL 36131
P: (334) 242-8003
F: (334) 242-8012

ALASKA
Mr. Thomas W. Nelson
Director
Division of Employment Security
Dept. of Labor & Workforce Development
P.O. Box 25509
Juneau, AK 99802
P: (907) 465-5933
F: (907) 269-4738
E: thomas_nelson@labor.state.ak.us

AMERICAN SAMOA
Mr. Puni Penei Sewell
Director
Department of Human Resources
American Samoa Government
Pago Pago, AS 96799
P: (683) 644-4485
F: (684) 633-1139
E: sewells_l@hotmail.com

ARIZONA
Mr. Patrick F. Harrington
Assistant Director
Division of Employment & Rehabilitation Services
Department of Economic Security
1789 West Jefferson, Site Code 901A
Phoenix, AZ 85007
P: (602) 542-4910
F: (602) 542-2273
E: PHarrington@azdes.gov

ARKANSAS
Mr. Artee Williams
Director
Department of Workforce Services
P.O. Box 2981
Little Rock, AR 72203
P: (501) 682-2121
F: (501) 682-2273
E: artee.williams@arkansas.gov

CALIFORNIA
Mr. Patrick Henning
Director
Employment Development Department
800 Capitol Mall, Room 5000
Sacramento, CA 95814
P: (916) 654-8210
F: (916) 657-5294
E: PHenning@edd.ca.gov

COLORADO
Mr. Don J. Mares
Executive Director
Department of Labor & Employment
1515 Arapahoe Street, Suite 375
Denver, CO 80202
P: (303) 318-8000
F: (303) 318-8048
E: don.mares@state.co.us

CONNECTICUT
Ms. Patricia Mayfield
Commissioner
Department of Labor
200 Folly Brook Boulevard
Wethersfield, CT 06109
P: (860) 263-6505
F: (860) 263-6529
E: patricia.mayfield@po.state.ct.us

DELAWARE
Mr. Robert Strong
Director
Division of Employment & Training
Department of Labor
4425 North Market Street, Room 328
Wilmington, DE 19802
P: (302) 761-8129
F: (302) 577-3996
E: robert.strong@state.de.us

DISTRICT OF COLUMBIA
Ms. Summer Spencer
Acting Director
Department of Employment Services
609 H Street, NE
Washington, DC 20002
P: (202) 724-7000

FLORIDA
Ms. Monesia Brown
Director
Agency for Workforce Innovation
107 East Madison Street
Suite 100, Caldwell Building
Tallahassee, FL 32399
P: (850) 245-7298
F: (850) 921-3223
E: monesia.brown@awi.state.fl.us

GEORGIA
Mr. Michael L. Thurmond
Commissioner
Department of Labor
Sussex Place, Room 600
148 International Boulevard, Northeast
Atlanta, GA 30303
P: (404) 232-3001
F: (404) 232-3017
E: commissioner@dol.state.ga.us

GUAM
Ms. Maria Connelley
Director
Department of Labor
414 West Soledad, Suite 400
GCIC Building, P.O. Box 9970
Tamuning, GU 96931
P: (671) 475-7046
F: (671) 475-7045

HAWAII
Ms. Elaine Young
Administrator
Department of Labor & Industrial Relations
830 Punchbowl Street
Suite 329
Honolulu, HI 96813
P: (808) 586-8812
F: (808) 586-8822

IDAHO
Mr. Roger B. Madsen
Director
Department of Commerce & Labor
317 West Main Street
Boise, ID 83735
P: (208) 332-3579
F: (208) 334-6430
E: rmadsen@cl.idaho.gov

ILLINOIS
Mr. James P. Sledge
Director
Department of Employment Security
33 South State Street
Chicago, IL 60602
P: (312) 793-5700
F: (312) 793-9834
E: james.sledge@illinois.gov

INDIANA
Mr. Andrew Penca
Commissioner
Department of Workforce Development
Indiana Government Center, South
10 North Senate Avenue, Room SE 302
Indianapolis, IN 46204
P: (317) 232-7676
F: (317) 233-1670

IOWA
Mr. David Neil
Interim Director
Department of Workforce Development
1000 East Grand Avenue
Des Moines, IA 50319
P: (515) 281-8067
F: (515) 281-4698
E: dave.neil@iwd.iowa.gov

KANSAS
Mr. David Kerr
Secretary
Department of Commerce
1000 Southwest Jackson Street, Suite 100
Topeka, KS 66612
P: (785) 296-2741
F: (785) 296-3665

KENTUCKY
Mr. Andrew Frauenhoffer
Executive Director
Office of Employment & Training
275 East Main Street
Frankfort, KY 40621
P: (502) 564-5331
F: (502) 564-7452
E: andrew.frauenhoffer@ky.gov

Employment Services

LOUISIANA
Ms. Anne Soileau
Director
Department of State Civil Service
P.O. Box 94111
Capitol Station
Baton Rouge, LA 70804
P: (225) 342-8069
F: (225) 342-8058
E: asoileau@dscs.state.la.us

MAINE
Ms. Larinda Meade
Director
Bureau of Employment Services
55 State House Station
Augusta, ME 04333
P: (207) 624-6390
E: larinda.meade@maine.gov

MARYLAND
Ms. Cynthia Kollner
Acting Executive Director
Department of Budget & Management
Office of Personnel Services & Benefits
301 West Preston Street, Room 609
Baltimore, MD 21201
P: (410) 767-4716
F: (410) 333-5262
E: ckollner@dbm.state.md.us

MICHIGAN
Mr. David A. Plawecki
Deputy Director
Department of Labor & Economic Growth
Cadillac Place, Suite 13-650
3024 West Grand Boulevard
Detroit, MI 48202
P: (313) 456-2403
F: (313) 456-2424
E: PlaweckiDave@michigan.gov

MINNESOTA
Hon. Dan McElroy
Commissioner
Department of Employment & Economic Development
1st National Bank Building
332 Minnesota Street, Suite E200
St. Paul, MN 55101
P: (651) 259-7119
F: (651) 296-4772
E: dan.mcelroy@state.mn.us

MISSISSIPPI
Ms. Tommye Dale Favre
Executive Director
Department of Employment Security
P.O. Box 1699
Jackson, MS 39215
P: (601) 321-6100
F: (601) 321-6104
E: tdfavre@mdes.ms.gov

MISSOURI
Mr. Roderick Nunn
Director
Division of Workforce Development
P.O. Box 1087
Jefferson City, MO 65102
P: (573) 751-3349
F: (573) 751-8162
E: rod.nunn@ded.mo.gov

MONTANA
Mr. Keith Kelly
Commissioner
Department of Labor & Industry
P.O. Box 1728
Helena, MT 59624
P: (406) 444-2840
F: (406) 444-1394
E: kkelly@mt.gov

NEBRASKA
Mr. Fernando "Butch" Lecuona III
Commissioner of Labor
Department of Labor
Department of Labor
P.O. Box 94600
Lincoln, NE 68509
P: (402) 471-2600
F: (402) 471-9867
E: flecuona@dol.state.ne.us

NEVADA
Ms. Cynthia A. Jones
Administrator
Employment Security Division
Employment Security Division
500 East Third Street, Suite 260
Carson City, NV 89713
P: (775) 684-3909
F: (775) 684-3910
E: cajones@nvdetr.org

NEW HAMPSHIRE
Mr. Richard S. Brothers
Commissioner
Department of Employment Security
32 South Main Street
Concord, NH 03301
P: (603) 228-4000
F: (603) 228-4145
E: richard.s.brothers@nhes.nh.gov

NEW JERSEY
Mr. Gary Altman
Director
One-Stop Programs & Services Division
Second Floor, P.O. Box 055
Trenton, NJ 08625
P: (609) 292-5005
F: (609) 633-2556

Ms. Tamara Thomas
Deputy Assistant Commissioner
One-Stop Programs & Services Division
Second Floor, P.O. Box 055
Trenton, NJ 08625
P: (609) 292-5005
F: (609) 633-2556

NEW MEXICO
Ms. Betty Sparrow Davis
Cabinet Secretary
Department of Labor
401 Broadway, Northeast
P.O. Box 1928
Albuquerque, NM 87103
P: (505) 841-8405
F: (505) 841-8491
E: bdoris@state.nm.us

NEW YORK
Ms. Patricia Smith
Commissioner
Department of Labor
345 Hudson Street
Albany, NY 10014
P: (518) 457-2741
F: (518) 457-6908
E: nysdol@labor.state.ny.us

NORTH CAROLINA
Mr. Harry E. Payne Jr.
Chair
Employment Security Commission
P.O. Box 25903
Raleigh, NC 27611
P: (919) 733-7546
F: (919) 733-1129
E: harry.payne@ncmail.net

NORTH DAKOTA
Ms. Maren L. Daley
Executive Director
Job Service North Dakota
1000 East Divide Avenue
P.O. Box 5507
Bismarck, ND 58506
P: (701) 328-2836
F: (701) 328-1612
E: mdaley@nd.gov

NORTHERN MARIANA ISLANDS
Mr. Alfred A. Pangelinan
Director of Employment Services
Department of Labor
Afetnas Square
Caller Box 10007
Saipan, MP 96950
P: (670) 236-0926
F: (670) 236-0994

OHIO
Mr. Patrick J. Power
Deputy Director
Office of Unemployment Compensation
Rhodes Tower
30 East Broad Street, 32nd Floor
Columbus, OH 43215
P: (614) 995-7066
F: (614) 466-6873

OKLAHOMA
Mr. Jon Brock
Executive Director
Employment Security Commission
2401 North Lincoln Boulevard
Will Rogers Memorial Office Building
Oklahoma City, OK 73105
P: (405) 557-7201
F: (405) 557-7174
E: jon.brock@oesc.state.ok.us

Mr. Oscar B. Jackson Jr.
Cabinet Secretary for Administration & Human Resources
Office of Personnel Management
2101 North Lincoln Boulevard
Room G-80
Oklahoma City, OK 73105
P: (405) 521-6301
F: (405) 522-0694
E: oscar.jackson@opm.state.ok.us

OREGON
Mr. Tom Erhardt
Administrator
Business & Employment Services
Employment Department
875 Union Street, Northeast
Salem, OR 97311
P: (503) 947-1207
F: (503) 947-1658
E: thomas.m.erhardt @state.or.us

PENNSYLVANIA
Ms. Naomi Wyatt
Deputy Secretary
Bureau of Human Resource Management & Development
Governor's Office of Administration
517 Finance Buidling
Harrisburg, PA 17110
P: (717) 787-8191
F: (717) 783-4429

PUERTO RICO
Ms. Maria Del Carmen Fuentes
Administrator
Right to Work Administration
Department of Labor & Human Resources
505 Munoz Rivera Avenue, P.O. Box 364452
Hato Rey, PR 00936
P: (787) 754-5151 Ext. 2000
F: (787) 758-0690
E: mfuentes@adt.govierno.pr

RHODE ISLAND
Ms. Adelita Orefice
Director
Department of Labor & Training
1511 Pontiac Avenue
Cranston, RI 02920
P: (401) 462-8870
F: (401) 462-8872
E: aorefice@dlt.state.ri.us

SOUTH CAROLINA
Mr. Roosevelt Ted Halley
Executive Director
Employment Security Commission
P.O. Box 995
Columbia, SC 29202
P: (803) 737-2617
F: (803) 737-2629
E: thalley@sces.org

SOUTH DAKOTA
Ms. Marcia Hultman
Deputy Secretary
One-Stop Career Center
Kneip Building
700 Governors Drive
Pierre, SD 57501
P: (605) 773-3101
F: (605) 773-4211
E: marcia.hultman @state.sd.us

TENNESSEE
Mr. James G. Neeley
Commissioner
Department of Labor & Workforce Development
Andrew Johnson Tower, 8th Floor
Nashville, TN 37243
P: (615) 741-6642
F: (615) 741-5078
E: james.neeley@state.tn.us

TEXAS
Mr. Larry Temple
Executive Director
Workforce Commission
TWC Building
101 East 15th Street, Room 618
Austin, TX 78778
P: (512) 463-0735
F: (512) 475-2321
E: larry.temple @twc.state.tx.us

U.S. VIRGIN ISLANDS
Mr. Albert Bryant Jr.
Commissioner
Department of Labor
2203 Church Street
Christiansted, VI 00820
P: (340) 773-1994
F: (340) 773-0094

UTAH
Ms. Tani Pack Downing
Executive Director
Department of Workforce Services
140 East 300 South
Salt Lake City, UT 84145
P: (801) 526-9210
F: (801) 526-9211
E: tdowning@utah.gov

VIRGINIA
Ms. Dolores A. Esser
Commissioner
Employment Commission
703 East Main Street
Richmond, VA 23219
P: (804) 786-3001
F: (804) 225-3923
E: dee.esser @vec.virginia.gov

WASHINGTON
Ms. Karen Turner Lee
Commissioner
Employment Security Department
P.O. Box 9046
Olympia, WA 98507
P: (360) 902-9301
F: (360) 902-9383
E: klee@esd.wa.gov

Ms. Eva Santos
Director
Department of Personnel
P.O. Box 47500
Olympia, WA 98504
P: (360) 664-6350
F: (360) 753-1003
E: evas@dop.wa.gov

WISCONSIN
Mr. Bill Clingan
Administrator
Division of Workforce Solutions
201 East Washington Avenue
Madison, WI 53707
P: (608) 266-6824

WYOMING
Ms. Cindy Pomeroy
Director
Department of Employment
1510 East Pershing Boulevard
Cheyenne, WY 82002
P: (307) 777-7672
F: (307) 777-5805
E: cpomer@state.wy.us

Energy

Develops and administers programs relating to energy conservation, alternative energy research and development, and energy information.

ALABAMA
Ms. Terri Adams
Division Director
Energy, Weatherization & Technology Division
401 Adams Avenue
P.O. Box 5690
Montgomery, AL 36103
P: (334) 242-5292
F: (334) 242-0552
E: terria@adeca.state.al.us

ALASKA
Ms. Rebecca Garrett
Program Manager
Alaska Energy Authority
P.O. Box 101020
4300 Boniface Parkway
Anchorage, AK 99510
P: (907) 269-4624
F: (907) 269-3044
E: rgarrett@aidea.org

AMERICAN SAMOA
Mr. Reupena Tagaloa
Director
Territorial Energy Office
American Samoa Government
Samoa Energy House, Tauna
Pago Pago, AS 96799
P: (684) 699-5015
F: (684) 699-2835
E: rtagaloa@blueskynet.as

ARIZONA
Mr. Jim Arwood
Director
Energy Office
1700 West Washington, Suite 220
Phoenix, AZ 85007
P: (602) 771-1139
F: (602) 771-1203
E: jima@azcommerce.com

ARKANSAS
Mr. Chris Benson
Director
Energy Office
Department of Economic Development
One Capitol Mall
Little Rock, AR 72201
P: (501) 682-8065
F: (501) 682-2703
E: cbenson@1800arkansas.com

CALIFORNIA
Mr. B.B. Blevins
Executive Director
Energy Commission
1516 9th Street
Sacramento, CA 95814
P: (916) 654-4996
E: bblevins
@energy.state.ca.us

COLORADO
Mr. Tom Plant
Executive Director
Governor's Energy Office
225 East 16th Avenue, Suite 650
Denver, CO 80203
P: (303) 866-2401
F: (303) 866-2930
E: tom.plant@state.co.us

CONNECTICUT
Mr. John A. Mengacci
Undersecretary
Energy Research & Policy Development Unit
450 Capitol Avenue MS#52 ENR
P.O. Box 341441
Hartford, CT 06134
P: (860) 418-6374
F: (860) 418-6495
E: john.mengacci
@po.state.ct.us

DELAWARE
Mr. Charlie T. Smisson Jr.
State Energy Coordinator
Energy Office
146 South Governors Avenue
Dover, DE 19904
P: (302) 739-1530
F: (302) 739-1527
E: charlie.smisson
@state.de.us

DISTRICT OF COLUMBIA
Mr. Charles J. Clinton
Director
Energy Office
2000 14th Street, Northwest
Room 300E
Washington, DC 20009
P: (202) 673-6710
F: (202) 673-6725
E: chuck.clinton@dc.gov

FLORIDA
Mr. Allan Guyet
Director
Energy Office
2600 Blairstone Road, MS-19
Tallahassee, FL 32399
P: (850) 245-8002
F: (850) 245-8003
E: allan.guyet
@dep.state.fl.us

Mr. Alexander Mack
Manager
Department of Environmental Protection/Energy Office
2600 Blairstone Road, MS-19
Tallahassee, FL 32399
P: (850) 245-8002
F: (850) 245-8003
E: alexander.mack
@dep.state.fl.us

GEORGIA
Ms. Elizabeth S. Robertson
Director
Division of Energy Resources
233 Peachtree Street, Northeast
Harris Tower, Suite 900
Atlanta, GA 30303
P: (404) 584-1007
F: (404) 584-1008
E: esr@gefa.ga.gov

GUAM
Ms. Lorilee Crisostomo
Administrator
Energy Office
17-3304/15-6101 Mariner Avenue, Tiyan
P.O. Box 22439
Barrigada, GU 96921
P: (671) 475-1658
F: (671) 734-5910
E: lorilee@guamcell.net

HAWAII
Mr. Maurice H. Kaya
Chief Technology Officer
DBEDT, Strategic Industries Division
235 South Beretania Street, Room 502
P.O. Box 2359
Honolulu, HI 96804
P: (808) 587-3812
F: (808) 586-2536
E: mkaya@dbedt.hawaii.gov

IDAHO
Mr. Robert W. Hoppie
Administrator
Energy Division
322 East Front Street
P.O. Box 83720
Boise, ID 83720
P: (208) 287-4807
F: (208) 287-6700
E: bob.hoppie
@idwr.idaho.gov

ILLINOIS
Mr. Hans Detweiler
Deputy Director of Energy & Recycling
Department of Commerce & Economic Opportunity
620 East Adams
Springfield, IL 62701
P: (312) 814-2266
E: hans_detweiler
@commerce.state.il.us

INDIANA
Mr. Brandon Seitz
Policy Director
Energy Policy Division
Department of Commerce
1 North Capitol, Suite 700
Indianapolis, IN 46204
P: (317) 232-7578
F: (317) 232-8995
E: bseitz@lg.in.gov

IOWA
Mr. Brian J. Tormey
Bureau Chief
Energy and Waste Management Bureau
Wallace State Office Building
East 9th & Grand Avenue
Des Moines, IA 50319
P: (515) 281-8927
F: (515) 281-8895
E: brian.tormey
@dnr.state.ia.us

KANSAS
Mr. Jim Ploger
Director of Energy Efficiency & Renewable Energy
Corporation Commission
Energy Office
1500 Southwest Arrowhead Road
Topeka, KS 66604
P: (785) 271-3349
F: (785) 271-3268
E: j.ploger@kcc.state.ks.us

KENTUCKY
Mr. John Davies
Director
Division of Renewable Energy & Energy Efficiency
Office of Energy Policy
663 Teton Trail
Frankfort, KY 40601
P: (502) 564-7192
F: (502) 564-7484
E: john.davies@ky.gov

LOUISIANA
Mr. Mike French
Director
LDNR/Technology Assessment Division
P.O. Box 44156
617 North 3rd Street
Baton Rouge, LA 70804
P: (225) 342-1275
F: (225) 342-1397
E: mike.french@la.gov

MAINE
Mr. Denis Bergeron
Director
Division of Energy Programs
Office of the Governor
One State House Station
Augusta, ME 04333
P: (207) 287-3318
F: (207) 287-1039
E: Denis.Bergeron@maine.gov

Ms. Beth Nagusky
Director of Energy Independence
Office of the Governor
One State House Station
Augusta, ME 04333
P: (207) 287-4315
F: (207) 287-1039
E: beth.nagusky@maine.gov

MARYLAND
Mr. Frederick Davis
Director
Energy Administration
1623 Forest Drive, Suite 300
Annapolis, MD 21403
P: (410) 260-7655
F: (410) 974-2250
E: fdavis@energy.state.md.us

MASSACHUSETTS
Mr. David L. O'Connor
Commissioner
Division of Energy Resources
100 Cambridge Street, Suite 1020
Boston, MA 02114
P: (617) 727-4732
F: (617) 727-0030
E: david.oconnor@state.ma.us

MICHIGAN
Mr. Tom Martin
Director
Energy Office
611 West Ottawa, 4th Floor
P.O. Box 30221
Lansing, MI 48909
P: (517) 241-6280
F: (517) 241-6229

MINNESOTA
Ms. Janet Streff
Manager
State Energy Office
Department of Commerce
85 7th Place East, Suite 500
St. Paul, MN 55101
P: (651) 297-2545
F: (651) 297-7891
E: janet.streff@state.mn.us

MISSISSIPPI
Mr. Kenneth Calvin
Director
Energy Division
510 George Street, Suite 300
P.O. Box 849
Jackson, MS 39205
P: (601) 359-6600
F: (601) 359-6642
E: kcalvin@mississippi.org

MISSOURI
Ms. Anita C. Randolph
Director
Energy Center
1101 Riverside Drive
P.O. Box 176
Jefferson City, MO 65102
P: (573) 751-2254
F: (573) 526-2124
E: anita.randolph@dnr.mo.gov

MONTANA
Mr. Tom Livers
Deputy Director
Department of Environmental Quality
1100 North Last Chance Gulch
Room 401-H
P.O. Box 200901
Helena, MT 59620
P: (406) 841-4632
F: (406) 841-4386
E: tlivers@mt.gov

NEBRASKA
Mr. Larry Pearce
Deputy Director
State Energy Office
1111 "O" Street, Suite 223
P.O. Box 95085
Lincoln, NE 68508
P: (402) 471-2867
F: (402) 471-3064
E: lpearce@neo.ne.gov

NEVADA
Dr. Hatice Gecol
Director
Office of Energy
727 Fairview Drive, Suite F
Carson City, NV 89701
P: (775) 687-9700
F: (775) 687-9714
E: gecol@dbi.state.nv.us

NEW HAMPSHIRE
Ms. Amy Ignatius
Director
Office of Energy & Planning
57 Regional Drive
Concord, NH 03301
P: (603) 271-2705
F: (603) 271-2615
E: amy.ignatius@nh.gov

NEW JERSEY
Mr. Michael Winka
Director
Office of Clean Energy
Board of Public Utilities
2 Gateway Center
Newark, NJ 07102
P: (609) 777-3335
F: (609) 777-3330
E: michael.winka@bpu.state.nj.us

NEW MEXICO
Mr. Fernando Martinez
Director
Energy Conservation & Management Division
1220 St. Francis Drive
Santa Fe, NM 87505
P: (505) 476-3312
F: (505) 476-3322
E: fernando.r.martinez@state.nm.us

NEW YORK
Mr. Brian Henderson
Program Director
State Energy Research & Development Authority
17 Columbia Circle
Albany, NY 12203
P: (518) 862-1090 Ext. 3305
F: (518) 862-1091
E: bmh@nyserda.org

Mr. Peter Smith
President
State Energy Research & Development Authority
17 Columbia Circle
Albany, NY 12203
P: (518) 862-1090 Ext. 3320
F: (518) 862-1091
E: prs@nyserda.org

NORTH CAROLINA
Mr. Larry Shirley
Director
State Energy Office
Department of Administration
1340 Mail Service Center
Raleigh, NC 27699
P: (919) 733-1889
F: (919) 733-2953
E: larry.shirley@ncmail.net

NORTH DAKOTA
Kim C. Christianson
Energy Program Manager
Division of Community Services
1600 East Century Avenue, Suite 2
P.O. Box 2057
Bismarck, ND 58502
P: (701) 328-4137
F: (701) 328-5320
E: kchristianson@state.nd.us

Mr. Paul Govig
Director
Division of Community Services
1600 East Century Avenue, Suite 2
P.O. Box 2057
Bismarck, ND 58502
P: (701) 328-4499
F: (701) 328-5320
E: pgovig@state.nd.us

Energy

NORTHERN MARIANA ISLANDS
Ms. Thelma B. Inos
Acting Energy Director
Commonwealth of the Northern Mariana Islands
Energy Division
P.O. Box 340
Saipan, MP 96950
P: (670) 664-4480
F: (670) 664-4483
E: energy@vzpacifica.net

OHIO
Ms. Sara E. Ward
Chief
Office of Energy Efficiency
77 South High Street, 26th Floor
P.O. Box 1001
Columbus, OH 43216
P: (614) 466-6797
F: (614) 466-1864
E: sward@odod.state.oh.us

OKLAHOMA
Mr. Vaughn Clark
Director
Office of Community Development
P.O. Box 26980
900 North Stiles
Oklahoma City, OK 73126
P: (405) 815-5370
F: (405) 815-5377
E: vaughn_clark@odoc.state.ok.us

OREGON
Mr. Michael W. Grainey
Director
Department of Energy
625 Marion Street, Northeast
Salem, OR 97301
P: (503) 378-5489
F: (503) 373-7806
E: michael.w.grainey@state.or.us

PENNSYLVANIA
Mr. Daniel Desmond
Deputy Secretary
Office of Energy & Technology Deployment
Rachel Carson State Office Building
400 Market Street, 15th Floor
Harrisburg, PA 17105
P: (717) 783-0540
F: (717) 783-0546
E: ddesmond@state.pa.us

PUERTO RICO
Mr. Javier Mendez
Administrator
Energy Affairs Administration
P.O. Box 9066600
Puerta De Tierra Station
San Juan, PR 00936
P: (787) 724-8777 Ext. 4015
F: (717) 721-3089
E: quintanaj@caribe.net

RHODE ISLAND
Mr. Andrew Dzykewicz
Commissioner
Office of Energy Resources
1 Capitol Hill, 2nd Floor
Providence, RI 02908
P: (401) 222-7524
F: (401) 222-1260
E: adzykewicz@gov.state.ri.us

SOUTH CAROLINA
Mr. Mitch Perkins
Director
Energy Office
1201 Main Street, Suite 1010
Columbia, SC 29201
P: (803) 737-9822
F: (803) 737-9846
E: mperkins@gs.sc.gov

SOUTH DAKOTA
Ms. Michele Farris
State Energy Manager
Energy Management Office
Bureau of Administration
523 East Capitol Avenue
Pierre, SD 57501
P: (605) 773-3899
F: (605) 773-5980
E: michele.farris@state.sd.us

TENNESSEE
Mr. Brian Hensley
Director
Energy Division
Tennessee Tower
312 8th Avenue, North, 9th Floor
Nashville, TN 37243
P: (615) 741-2994
F: (615) 741-5070
E: brian.hensley@state.tn.us

TEXAS
Mr. William E. Taylor
Director
State Energy Conservation Office
111 East 17th Street, 11th Floor
Austin, TX 78701
P: (512) 463-1931
F: (512) 475-2569
E: dub.taylor@cpa.state.tx.us

U.S. VIRGIN ISLANDS
Mr. Bevan R. Smith Jr.
Director
Energy Office
Dept. of Planning & Natural Resources
#45 Mars Hill
Fredrickstead, St. Croix, VI 00840
P: (340) 773-1082
F: (340) 772-2133
E: bsmith@vienergy.org

UTAH
Ms. Laura Nelson
State Energy Director
State Energy Program
1594 West North Temple, Suite 110
P.O. Box 146100
Salt Lake City, UT 84114
P: (801) 538-8802
F: (801) 538-4795
E: lsnelson@utah.gov

VERMONT
Mr. Robert Ide
Director
Energy Efficiency Division
Department of Public Service
112 State Street, Drawer 20
Montpelier, VT 05620
P: (802) 828-4009
F: (802) 828-2342
E: robert.ide@state.vt.us

VIRGINIA
Mr. John Warren
Director
Division of Energy
Department of Mines, Minerals & Energy
202 North 9th Street, 8th Floor
Richmond, VA 23219
P: (804) 692-3216
F: (804) 692-3238
E: john.warren@dmme.virginia.gov

WASHINGTON
Mr. Jacob Fey
Director
Washington State University Energy Program
925 Plum Street, Southeast, Building #4
P.O. Box 43165
Olympia, WA 98504
P: (360) 956-2002
F: (360) 956-2010
E: feyj@energy.wsu.edu

Mr. Tony Usibelli
Division Director
Energy Policy Office
925 Plum Street, Southeast, Building 4
P.O. Box 43173
Olympia, WA 98504
P: (360) 956-2125
F: (360) 956-2180
E: tonyu@cted.wa.gov

WEST VIRGINIA
Mr. Jeff F. Herholdt Jr.
Manager
Energy Efficiency Office
Building 6, Room 645
State Capitol Complex
Charleston, WV 25305
P: (304) 558-0350
F: (304) 558-0362
E: jherholdt@wvdo.org

WISCONSIN
Ms. Judy Ziewacz
Executive Director
Governor's Office of Energy Independence
17 West Main, Office 429
Madison, WI 53702
P: (608) 261-0685
F: (608) 261-8427
E: judy.ziewacz@wisconsin.gov

WYOMING
Mr. Thomas Fuller
Director of State Energy Programs
Business Council
214 West 15th Street
Cheyenne, WY 82003
P: (307) 777-2804
F: (307) 777-2837
E: Tom.Fuller@Wybusiness.Org

Environmental Protection

Oversees the overall quality of the environment by coordinating and managing the state's pollution control programs and planning, permit granting and regulation of standards.

Information provided by:

Environmental Council of the States
R. Steven Brown
Executive Director
444 North Capitol Street, NW
Suite 445
Washington, DC 20001
P: (202) 624-3660
F: (202) 624-3666
sbrown@sso.org
www.ecos.org

ALABAMA
Mr. Onis Trey Glenn III
Director
Department of Environmental Management
1400 Coliseum Boulevard
P.O. Box 301463
Montgomery, AL 36110
P: (334) 271-7710
F: (334) 279-3043

ALASKA
Mr. Larry Hartig
Commissioner
Department of Environmental Conservation
410 Willoughby Avenue, Suite 303
Juneau, AK 99801
P: (907) 465-5065

ARIZONA
Mr. Stephen A. Owens
Director
Department of Environmental Quality
1110 West Washington Street
Phoenix, AZ 85007
P: (602) 771-2203
F: (602) 771-2218

ARKANSAS
Mr. Marcus C. Devine
Director
Department of Environmental Quality
8001 National Drive
P.O. Box 8913
Little Rock, AR 72209
P: (501) 682-0959
F: (501) 682-0798

CALIFORNIA
Ms. Linda Adams
Secretary
Environmental Protection Agency
1001 I Street, 25th Floor
Sacramento, CA 95814
P: (916) 445-3846
F: (916) 445-6401

Mr. Dan Skopec
Under Secretary
Environmental Protection Agency
1001 I Street, 25th Floor
Sacramento, CA 95814
P: (916) 323-3708
F: (916) 445-6401

COLORADO
Mr. James B. Martin
Executive Director
Department of Public Health & Environment
4300 Cherry Creek Drive, South, OE-B2
Denver, CO 80246
P: (303) 692-2011
F: (303) 691-7702

CONNECTICUT
Ms. Amey Marrella
Deputy Commissioner
Department of Environmental Protection
79 Elm Street
Hartford, CT 06106
P: (860) 424-3009
F: (860) 424-4054

Ms. Gina McCarthy
Commissioner
Department of Environmental Protection
79 Elm Street
Hartford, CT 06106
P: (860) 424-3009
F: (860) 424-4054
E: gina.mccarthy@po.state.ct.us

DELAWARE
Mr. John A. Hughes
Secretary
Department of Natural Resources & Environmental Control
89 Kings Highway
P.O. Box 1401
Dover, DE 19903
P: (302) 739-9000
F: (302) 739-6242
E: John.Hughes@state.de.us

Mr. Robert J. Zimmerman
Department of Natural Resources & Environmental Control
Office of the Secretary
89 Kings Highway
Dover, DE 19901
P: (302) 739-4403
F: (302) 739-6242

DISTRICT OF COLUMBIA
Ms. Elizabeth Berry
Acting Director
Department of the Environment
51 N Street, Northeast, 6th Floor
Washington, DC 20002
P: (202) 535-2600
F: (202) 535-1359

FLORIDA
Mr. Michael Sole
Secretary
Department of Environmental Protection
3900 Commonwealth Boulevard
Mail Station 10
Tallahassee, FL 32399
P: (850) 245-2011
F: (850) 245-2021

GEORGIA
Dr. Carol A. Couch
Director
Environmental Protection Division
205 Butler Street, Southeast
1152 East Tower
Atlanta, GA 30334
P: (404) 656-4713
F: (404) 651-5778

HAWAII
Mr. Laurence K. Lau
Deputy Director for Environmental Health
Department of Health
1250 Punchbowl Street, 3rd Floor
P.O. Box 3378
Honolulu, HI 96801
P: (808) 586-4424
F: (808) 586-4368

IDAHO
Ms. Toni Hardesty
Director
Department of Environmental Quality
1410 North Hilton
Boise, ID 83706
P: (208) 373-0240
F: (208) 373-0417
E: toni.hardesty@deq.idaho.gov

ILLINOIS
Mr. Doug P. Scott
Director
Environmental Protection Agency
1021 North Grand Avenue, East
P.O. Box 19276
Springfield, IL 62794
P: (217) 782-9540
F: (217) 782-9039

INDIANA
Mr. Thomas Easterly
Commissioner
Department of Environmental Management
100 North Senate Avenue, MC 50-01
P.O. Box 6015
Indianapolis, IN 46206
P: (317) 232-8611
F: (317) 233-6647

IOWA
Mr. Wayne Gieselman
Division Administrator
Environmental Services Division
4th Floor Wallace Building
502 East 9th Street
Des Moines, IA 50319
P: (515) 281-5817
F: (515) 281-8895

KANSAS
Mr. Ronald F. Hammerschmidt
Director, Division of Environment
Department of Health & Environment
1000 Southwest Jackson, Suite 400
Topeka, KS 66612
P: (785) 296-1535
F: (785) 296-8464

KENTUCKY
Mr. Lloyd Cress
Commissioner
Department for Environmental Protection
14 Reilly Road
Frankfort, KY 40601
P: (502) 564-2150
F: (502) 564-4245

Environmental Protection

LOUISIANA
Mr. Mike D. McDaniel
Secretary
Department of Environmental Quality
602 North Fifth Street, #1022
P.O. Box 4301
Baton Rouge, LA 70821
P: (225) 219-3950
F: (225) 219-3970

MAINE
Mr. David P. Littell
Commissioner
Department of Environmental Protection
State House Station 17
Augusta, ME 04333
P: (207) 287-2812
F: (207) 287-2814
E: david.p.littell@maine.gov

MARYLAND
Ms. Shari Wilson
Secretary
Department of the Environment
1800 Washington Boulevard
Baltimore, MD 21230
P: (410) 537-3084
F: (410) 537-3888

MASSACHUSETTS
Mr. Ian A. Bowles
Secretary
Executive Office of Environmental Affairs
100 Cambridge Street, 9th Floor
Boston, MA 02114
P: (617) 626-1101
F: (617) 626-1181

Ms. Arleen O'Donnell
Acting Commissioner
Department of Environmental Protection
One Winter Street, 2nd Floor
Boston, MA 02108
P: (617) 292-5975
F: (617) 574-6880

MICHIGAN
Mr. Steven E. Chester
Director
Department of Environmental Quality
525 West Allegan Street
P.O. Box 30473
Lansing, MI 48909
P: (517) 373-7917
F: (517) 241-7401

MINNESOTA
Mr. Brad Moore
Commissioner
Pollution Control Agency
520 Lafayette Road
St. Paul, MN 55155
P: (651) 296-7301
F: (651) 296-6334
E: Brad.Moore@pca.state.mn.us

MISSISSIPPI
Ms. Trudy H. Fisher
Executive Director
Department of Environmental Quality
2380 Highway 80 West
P.O. Box 20305
Jackson, MS 39289
P: (601) 961-5100
F: (601) 961-5093
E: trudy_fisher@deq.state.ms.us

MISSOURI
Mr. Doyle Childers
Director
Department of Natural Resources
205 Jefferson Street
P.O. Box 176
Jefferson City, MO 65102
P: (573) 751-4732
F: (573) 751-7627

MONTANA
Mr. Richard Opper
Director
Department of Environmental Quality
1520 East Sixth Avenue
P.O. Box 200901
Helena, MT 59620
P: (406) 444-6701
F: (406) 444-4386
E: ropper@mt.gov

NEBRASKA
Mr. Michael J. Linder
Director
Department of Environmental Quality
1200 N Street, Suite 400
P.O. Box 98922
Lincoln, NE 68509
P: (402) 471-0275
F: (402) 471-2909

NEVADA
Mr. Leo Drozdoff
Administrator
Division of Environmental Protection
901 South Stewart, Suite 4001
Carson City, NV 89701
P: (775) 687-9301
F: (775) 687-5856
E: ldrozdof@ndep.nv.gov

Mr. Tom Porta
Department Administrator
Division of Environmental Protection
901 South Stewart Street, Suite 4001
Carson City, NV 89701
P: (775) 687-9416
F: (775) 687-5856

NEW HAMPSHIRE
Mr. Thomas Burack
Commissioner
Department of Environmental Services
Six Hazen Drive
P.O. Box 95
Concord, NH 03302
P: (603) 271-2958
F: (603) 271-2867

NEW JERSEY
Ms. Lisa P. Jackson
Commissioner
Department of Environmental Protection
P.O. Box 402
401 East State Street, 7th Floor
Trenton, NJ 08625
P: (609) 777-4327
F: (609) 292-7695

NEW YORK
Mr. Alexander "Pete" Grannis (D)
Commissioner
Department of Environmental Conservation
625 Broadway
Albany, NY 12207
P: (518) 402-8540
F: (518) 474-5450

NORTH CAROLINA
Mr. William G. Ross Jr.
Secretary
Department of Environment & Natural Resources
512 North Salisbury Street
1601 Mail Service Center
Raleigh, NC 27699
P: (919) 733-4101
F: (919) 733-4299
E: bill.ross@ncmail.net

NORTH DAKOTA
Mr. L. David Glatt
Chief
Environmental Health Section
Department of Health
1200 Missouri Avenue, P.O. Box 5520
Bismarck, ND 58506
P: (701) 328-5152
F: (701) 328-5200

OHIO
Mr. Chris Korleski
Director
Environmental Protection Agency
Lazarus Government Center
122 South Front Street, 6th Floor
Columbus, OH 43215
P: (614) 644-2782
F: (614) 644-3184

OKLAHOMA
Mr. Steven A. Thompson
Executive Director
Department of Environmental Quality
707 North Robinson, Suite 7100
P.O.Box 1677
Oklahoma City, OK 73101
P: (405) 702-7163
F: (405) 702-7101

OREGON
Ms. Stephanie Hallock
Director
Department of Environmental Quality
811 Southwest 6th Avenue
Portland, OR 97204
P: (503) 229-5300
F: (503) 229-6762

PENNSYLVANIA
Ms. Kathleen McGinty
Secretary
Department of Environmental Protection
400 Market Street, 16th Floor
P.O. Box 2063
Harrisburg, PA 17105
P: (717) 787-2814
F: (717) 705-4980

Ms. Barbara Sexton
Special Deputy Secretary
Department of Environmental Protection
Rachel Carson State Office Building
16th Floor, 400 Market Street
Harrisburg, PA 17101
P: (717) 772-1856
F: (717) 705-4980

PUERTO RICO
Mr. Javier Velez-Arocho
Secretary
Department of Natural & Environmental Resources
P.O. Box 366147
San Juan, PR 00936
P: (787) 767-8056
F: (787) 767-8122

RHODE ISLAND
Dr. W. Michael Sullivan
Director
Department of Environmental Management
235 Promenade Street, 4th Floor
Providence, RI 02908
P: (401) 222-2771
F: (401) 222-6802

SOUTH CAROLINA
Mr. Robert W. King Jr.
Deputy Commissioner
Department of Health & Environmental Control
2600 Bull Street
Columbia, SC 29201
P: (803) 896-8940
F: (803) 896-8941

SOUTH DAKOTA
Mr. Steve M. Pirner
Secretary
Department of Environment & Natural Resources
Foss Building
523 East Capitol Avenue
Pierre, SD 57501
P: (605) 773-5559
F: (605) 773-6035
E: steve.pirner@state.sd.us

TENNESSEE
Mr. Jim Fyke
Commissioner
Department of Environment & Conservation
1st Floor, L & C Annex
401 Church Street
Nashville, TN 37243
P: (615) 532-0106
F: (615) 532-0120

Mr. Paul Sloan
Deputy Commissioner
Department of Environment & Conservation
1st Floor, L & C Annex
Nashville, TN 37243
P: (615) 532-0102
F: (615) 532-0120
E: paul.sloan@state.tn.us

TEXAS
Ms. Kathleen Hartnett-White
Chair
Commission on Environmental Quality
12100 Park 35 Circle (MC 100)
P.O. Box 13087 (MC 100)
Austin, TX 78711
P: (512) 239-5510
F: (512) 239-5533

Mr. Larry R. Soward
Commissioner
Commission on Environmental Quality
12100 Park 35 Circle
P.O. Box 13087 (MC 100)
Austin, TX 78711
P: (512) 239-5500
F: (512) 239-5533

UTAH
Dr. Dianne R. Nielson
Executive Director
Department of Environmental Quality
168 North 1950 West
P.O. Box 144810
Salt Lake City, UT 84114
P: (801) 536-4404
F: (801) 536-0061

Mr. William Sinclair
Deputy Director
Department of Environmental Quality
168 North 1950 West
Salt Lake City, UT 84116
P: (801) 536-4405
F: (801) 536-0061

VERMONT
Mr. Jeffrey Wennberg
Commissioner, Department of Environmental Conservation
Agency of Natural Resources
103 South Main Street, Center Building
Waterbury, VT 05671
P: (802) 241-3808
F: (802) 244-5141

VIRGINIA
Mr. David K. Paylor
Director
Department of Environmental Quality
629 East Main Street
P.O. Box 10009
Richmond, VA 23240
P: (804) 698-4390
F: (804) 698-4019
E: dkpaylor@deq.virginia.gov

WASHINGTON
Mr. Jay Manning
Director
Department of Ecology
300 Desmond Drive, Southeast
P.O. Box 47600
Olympia, WA 98504
P: (360) 407-7001
F: (360) 407-6989

WEST VIRGINIA
Ms. Stephanie Timmermeyer
Cabinet Secretary
Department of Environmental Protection
601 57th Street Southeast
Charleston, WV 25304
P: (304) 926-0499 ext.1545
F: (304) 926-0447

WISCONSIN
Mr. P. Scott Hassett
Secretary
Department of Natural Resources
101 South Webster Street
Madison, WI 53703
P: (608) 266-0865
F: (608) 266-6983

WYOMING
Mr. John V. Corra
Director
Department of Environmental Quality
122 West 25th Street, 4W
Cheyenne, WY 82002
P: (307) 777-7937
F: (307) 777-7682
E: jcorra@state.wy.us

Equal Employment Opportunity

Enforces laws promoting equal employment opportunity in the state.

ALABAMA
Ms. Phyllis Kennedy
Director
Department of Industrial Relations
649 Monroe Street
Room 2204
Montgomery, AL 36131
P: (334) 242-8990
F: (334) 242-3960
E: Phyllis.Kennedy@dir.alabama.gov

ALASKA
Ms. Penny Beiler
EEO Program Manager
Department of Administration
P.O. Box 110201
Juneau, AK 99811
P: (907) 465-8482
F: (907) 465-2576

AMERICAN SAMOA
Mr. Puni Penei Sewell
Director
Department of Human Resources
American Samoa Government
Pago Pago, AS 96799
P: (683) 644-4485
F: (684) 633-1139
E: sewells_l@hotmail.com

ARIZONA
Mr. Manuel Cisneros
Director
Office of Equal Opportunity
1700 West Washington
State Capitol, WW, Room 156
Phoenix, AZ 85007
P: (602) 542-3711
F: (602) 542-3712
E: EqualOpportunity@az.gov

ARKANSAS
Mr. Freddy Jacobs
Manager
Equal Opportunity
Employment Security Division
2 Capitol Mall
Little Rock, AR 72201
P: (501) 682-3106
F: (501) 682-3748
E: freddy.jacobs@arkansas.gov

CALIFORNIA
Mr. Walter Johnson
Chief
Equal Employment Opportunity Office
800 Capitol Mall
Sacramento, CA 95814
P: (916) 654-8434
F: (916) 654-9371

COLORADO
Mr. Wendell Pryor
Director
Civil Rights Division
1560 Broadway
Suite 1050
Denver, CO 80202
P: (303) 894-2997
F: (303) 894-7830
E: wendell.pryor@dora.state.co.us

CONNECTICUT
Mr. Raymond Pech
Executive Director
Equal Opportunity Unit
21 Grand Street
Hartford, CT 06106
P: (860) 541-3400
F: (860) 246-5068
E: raymond.pech@po.state.ct.us

DELAWARE
Mr. Gregory T. Chambers
State Affirmative Action Coordinator
Office of State Personnel
820 North French Street
Wilmington, DE 19801
P: (302) 577-8977
F: (302) 577-3996
E: gchambers@state.de.us

DISTRICT OF COLUMBIA
Mr. Gustavo F. Velasquez
Director
Office of Human Rights
441 4th Street, Northwest
Suite 570N
Washington, DC 20001
P: (202) 727-4559
F: (202) 727-9589

FLORIDA
Mr. Derrick Daniel
Executive Director
Commission on Human Relations
2009 Appalache Parkway
Suite 100
Tallahassee, FL 32301
P: (850) 488-7082
F: (850) 488-5291
E: fchrinfo@fchr.myflorida.com

GEORGIA
Mr. Gordon Joyner
Administrator
Commission on Equal Opportunity
Suite 710, International Tower
229 Peachtree Street, North East
Atlanta, GA 30303
P: (404) 656-1736
F: (404) 656-4399

GUAM
Ms. Maria Connelley
Director
Department of Labor
414 West Soledad, Suite 400
GCIC Building, P.O. Box 9970
Tamuning, GU 96931
P: (671) 475-7046
F: (671) 475-7045

HAWAII
Mr. William D. Hoshijo
Executive Director
Civil Rights Commission
830 Punchbowl Street
Suite 411
Honolulu, HI 96813
P: (808) 586-8636
F: (808) 586-8655
E: info@hicrc.org

IDAHO
Ms. Leslie Goddard
Director
Human Rights Commission
1109 Main Street
Owyhee Plaza, Suite 400
Boise, ID 83720
P: (208) 334-2873
F: (208) 334-2664
E: lgoddard@ihrc.idaho.gov

ILLINOIS
Mr. Rocco Claps
Director
Department of Human Rights
100 West Randolph
Suite 10-100
Chicago, IL 60601
P: (312) 814-6200
F: (312) 814-1436

INDIANA
Ms. Lavenia Haskett
Program Director
Personnel Department
402 West Washington
Room W161
Indianapolis, IN 46204
P: (317) 232-4555
F: (317) 233-0236

IOWA
Mr. Ralph Rosenberg
Executive Director
Civil Rights Commission
Grimes State Office Building
400 East 14th Street
Des Moines, IA 50319
P: (515) 281-4121
F: (515) 242-5840
E: ralph.rosenberg@icrc.state.ia.us

KANSAS
Mr. Jim Garner
Secretary
Department of Labor
401 Southwest Topeka Boulevard
Topeka, KS 66603
P: (785) 296-7474
F: (785) 368-6294
E: jim.garner@dol.ks.gov

Mr. William V. Minner
Executive Director
Human Rights Commission
900 Southwest Jackson Street
Suite 851-S
Topeka, KS 66612
P: (785) 296-3206
F: (785) 296-0589

KENTUCKY
Ms. Yvette Smith
Executive Director
Office of Equal Employment Opportunity & Contract Compliance
320 Capitol Annex
Frankfort, KY 40601
P: (502) 564-2874
F: (502) 564-1065

LOUISIANA
Mr. John Warner Smith
Secretary of Labor
Department of Labor
P.O. Box 94094
1001 North 23rd Street
Baton Rouge, LA 70804
P: (225) 342-3011
F: (225) 342-3778
E: jwsmith@ldol.state.la.us

MAINE
Ms. Laurel J. Shippee
State Equal Employment Opportunity Coordinator
Bureau of Human Resources
4 State House Station
Augusta, ME 04333
P: (207) 624-7761

MARYLAND
Mr. Henry B. Ford
Executive Director
Commission on Human Relations
6 Saint Paul Street, 9th Floor
Baltimore, MD 21202
P: (410) 767-8563
F: (410) 333-1841
E: hford@mail.mchr.state.md.us

MASSACHUSETTS
Ms. Sandra E. Borders
Director
Office of Diversity & Equal Opportunity
One Ashburton Place, Room 213
Boston, MA 02108
P: (617) 727-7441
F: (617) 727-0568

MICHIGAN
Ms. Linda V. Parker
Director
Department of Civil Rights
Capitol Tower Building
Suite 800
Lansing, MI 48933
P: (517) 335-3165
F: (517) 241-0546
E: parkerlv@michigan.gov

MINNESOTA
Ms. Velma Korbel
Commissioner
Department of Human Rights
190 East 5th Street
Suite 700
St. Paul, MN 55101
P: (651) 296-9038
F: (651) 296-1736
E: velma.korbel@state.mn.us

MISSISSIPPI
Mr. Jim Nelson Jr.
Director
Equal Opportunity Department
1520 West Capitol
P.O. Box 1699
Jackson, MS 39215
P: (601) 969-7420
F: (601) 961-7405
E: jnelson@sos.state.ms.us

MISSOURI
Ms. Donna Cavitte
Director
Commission on Human Rights
3315 West Truman Boulevard
P.O. Box 1129
Jefferson City, MO 65102
P: (573) 751-3325
F: (573) 751-2905
E: donna.cavitte@dolir.mo.gov

MONTANA
Mr. Randy Morris
Administrator
State Personnel Division
P.O. Box 200127
Helena, MT 59620
P: (406) 444-3894
F: (406) 444-0703
E: ramorris@mt.gov

NEBRASKA
Ms. Anne Hobbs
Executive Director
Equal Opportunity Commission
301 Centennial Mall Sourth, 5th Floor
P.O. Box 94934
Lincoln, NE 68509
P: (402) 471-2024
F: (402) 471-4059

NEVADA
Ms. Deborah Madison
Executive Director
Equal Rights Commission
1515 East Tropicana, Suite 590
Las Vegas, NV 89119
P: (702) 486-7616
F: (702) 486-7054
E: demadison@nvdetr.org

NEW HAMPSHIRE
Ms. Katharine Daly
Executive Director
Commission for Human Rights
2 Chennell Drive
Concord, NH 03301
P: (603) 271-6838
F: (603) 271-6339
E: katharine.daly@nh.gov

NEW JERSEY
Ms. Deborah Boykin-Greenberg
Acting Director
Division of Equal Employment Opportunity & Affirmative Action
P.O. Box 315
44 South Clinton Avenue
Trenton, NJ 08625
P: (609) 777-0919
F: (609) 292-7067

NEW MEXICO
Ms. Francie Cordova
Director
Human Rights Division
Department of Labor
1596 Pacheco Street
Santa Fe, NM 87505
P: (505) 827-6838
F: (505) 827-6878

NEW YORK
Ms. Nancy Groenwegen
Commissioner
Department of Civil Service
State Office Campus, Building 1
Albany, NY 12239
P: (518) 457-6212
F: (518) 457-7547

NORTH CAROLINA
Ms. Nellie Riley
Director
Office of State Personnel
116 West Jones Street
1331 Mail Service Center
Raleigh, NC 27699
P: (919) 733-0205
F: (919) 733-0653
E: nelli.riley@ncmail.net

NORTH DAKOTA
Ms. Lisa Fair McEvers
Commissioner of Labor
Department of Labor
600 East Boulevard Avenue, Department 406
Bismarck, ND 58505
P: (701) 328-2660
F: (701) 328-2031
E: labor@nd.gov

NORTHERN MARIANA ISLANDS
Ms. Matilde A. Rosario
Chief
Office of Personnel Management
P.O. Box 5153 CHRB
Saipan, MP 96950
P: (670) 233-1272
F: (670) 234-1013

OHIO
Mr. Hugh Quill
Director
Department of Administrative Services
30 East Broad Street, Suite 4040
Columbus, OH 43215
P: (614) 466-6511
F: (614) 644-8151
E: hugh.quill@das.state.oh.us

OKLAHOMA
Ms. Brenda Thornton
Director
Equal Opportunity & Workforce Diversity
Office of Personnel Management
2101 North Lincoln Boulevard
Oklahoma City, OK 73105
P: (405) 521-3082
F: (405) 524-6942

OREGON
Hon. Dan Gardner (D)
Labor Commissioner
Bureau of Labor & Industries
800 Northeast Oregon Street, #32
Suite 1045
Portland, OR 97232
P: (503) 731-4070
F: (503) 731-4103
E: dan.gardner@state.or.us

PENNSYLVANIA
Mr. Stephen Schmerin
Secretary
Department of Labor & Industry
Labor and Industry Building, Room 1700
Harrisburg, PA 17121
P: (717) 787-5279
F: (717) 787-8826
E: sschmerin@state.pa.us

PUERTO RICO
Ms. Maria Del Carmen Fuentes
Administrator
Right to Work Administration
Department of Labor & Human Resources
505 Munoz Rivera Avenue, P.O. Box 364452
Hato Rey, PR 00936
P: (787) 754-5151 Ext. 2000
F: (787) 758-0690
E: mfuentes@adt.govierno.pr

Equal Employment Opportunity

RHODE ISLAND
Ms. Adelita Orefice
Director
Department of Labor & Training
1511 Pontiac Avenue
Cranston, RI 02920
P: (401) 462-8870
F: (401) 462-8872
E: aorefice@dlt.state.ri.us

SOUTH CAROLINA
Mr. Jesse Washington Jr.
Commissioner
Human Affairs Commission
P.O. Box 4490
Columbia, SC 29204
P: (803) 737-7800
E: jesse@schac.state.sc.us

SOUTH DAKOTA
Ms. Sandy Zinter
Commissioner
Bureau of Personnel
State Capitol
500 East Capitol Avenue
Pierre, SD 57501
P: (605) 773-4918
F: (605) 773-4344
E: sandy.zinter@state.sd.us

TENNESSEE
Ms. Evelyn Gaines
Affirmative Action Officer
Department of Labor & Workforce Development
500 James Robertson Parkway
Nashville, TN 37243
P: (615) 253-1331
F: (615) 741-3203

TEXAS
Mr. Robert Gomez
Director
Civil Rights Division
Texas Workforce Commission
101 East 15th Street
Austin, TX 78778
P: (512) 463-4432
E: robert.gomez@twc.state.tx.us

U.S. VIRGIN ISLANDS
Mr. Albert Bryant Jr.
Commissioner
Department of Labor
2203 Church Street
Christiansted, VI 00820
P: (340) 773-1994
F: (340) 773-0094

UTAH
Ms. Heather Morrison
Director
Anti-Discrimination & Labor Division
160 East 300 South, 3rd Floor
P.O. Box 146630
Salt Lake City, UT 84114
P: (801) 530-6921
F: (801) 530-7609
E: hmorrison@utah.gov

VERMONT
Mr. David Tucker
Director
State Economic Opportunity Office
103 South Main Street
Waterbury, VT 05671
P: (802) 241-2450
F: (802) 241-1225

VIRGINIA
Mrs. Sara Redding Wilson
Director
Department of Human Resource Management
101 North 14th Street, 12th Floor
Richmond, VA 23219
P: (804) 225-2237
F: (804) 371-7401
E: sara.wilson@dhrm.virginia.gov

WASHINGTON
Mr. Roy Standifer
Administrator
Affirmative Action Program
P.O. Box 47500
Olympia, WA 98504
P: (360) 664-6228
E: roys@dop.wa.gov

WEST VIRGINIA
Mr. Jim Sago
Director
Equal Employment Opportunity Office
#1 Player's Club Drive, Suite 501
Charleston, WV 25311
P: (304) 558-0400
F: (304) 558-3861

WISCONSIN
Mr. Demetri Fisher
Administrator
Division of Affirmative Action
P.O. Box 7855
Madison, WI 53707
P: (608) 266-3017
F: (608) 267-4592

WYOMING
Hon. Patrick J. Crank (D)
Attorney General
Office of the Attorney General
State Capitol Building
Cheyenne, WY 82002
P: (307) 777-7841
F: (307) 777-6869

Ethics

Administers and enforces the state ethics laws applying to public officials.

ALABAMA
Mr. James L. Sumner
Director
Ethics Commission
100 North Union Street, Suite 104
Montgomery, AL 36104
P: (334) 242-2806
F: (334) 242-0248

ALASKA
Ms. Joyce Anderson
Administrator
Committee on Legislative Ethics
P.O. Box 101468
Anchorage, AK 99510
P: (907) 269-0150
F: (907) 269-0152
E: ethics_committee@legis.state.ak.us

ARIZONA
Hon. Janet Napolitano (D)
Governor
Office of the Governor
State Capitol
1700 West Washington Street
Phoenix, AZ 85007
P: (602) 542-4331
F: (602) 542-1381

ARKANSAS
Mr. Graham Sloan
Director
State Ethics Commission
910 West 2nd Street, Suite 100
Little Rock, AR 72201
P: (501) 682-9600
F: (501) 682-9606
E: graham.sloan@mail.state.ar.us

CALIFORNIA
Mr. Mark Krausse
Executive Director
Fair Political Practices Commission
428 J Street, Suite 620
Sacramento, CA 95814
P: (916) 322-5660
F: (916) 322-0886

CONNECTICUT
Mr. Benjamin Bycel
Executive Director
Office of State Ethics
18-20 Trinity Street, Suite 205
Hartford, CT 06106
P: (860) 566-4472
F: (860) 566-3806
E: benjamin.bycel@ct.gov

DELAWARE
Ms. Janet Wright
Commission Counsel
Public Integrity Commission
Margaret O'Neill Building
410 Federal Street, Suite 3
Dover, DE 19901
P: (302) 739-2399
F: (302) 739-2398

DISTRICT OF COLUMBIA
Mr. Charles Lowery
Executive Director
Board of Elections & Ethics
441 Fourth Street, Northwest
Suite 250N
Washington, DC 20001
P: (202) 727-2525

FLORIDA
Mr. Phillip Claypool
Executive Director
Commission on Ethics
P.O. Drawer 15709
Tallahassee, FL 32317
P: (904) 488-7864
F: (904) 488-3077

GEORGIA
Mr. C. Theodore Lee
Executive Secretary
State Ethics Commission
205 Jesse Hill Jr. Drive, South East
Suite 478, East Tower
Atlanta, GA 30334
P: (404) 463-1980
F: (404) 463-1988
E: ethics@ethics.state.ga.us

GUAM
Mr. Gerald A. Taitano
Executive Director
Elections Commission
GCIC Building, Suite 200
414 West Soledad Avenue
Hagatna, GU 96910
P: (671) 477-9791
F: (671) 477-1895

HAWAII
Mr. Daniel J. Mollway
Executive Director
State Ethics Commission
P.O. Box 616
Honolulu, HI 96809
P: (808) 587-0460
F: (808) 587-0470
E: ethics@hawaiiethics.org

IDAHO
Hon. Lawrence Wasden (R)
Attorney General
Office of the Attorney General
P.O. Box 83720
Boise, ID 83720
P: (208) 334-2400
F: (208) 334-3446

INDIANA
Ms. Mary Lee Comer
Director
State Ethics Commission
150 West Market Street, Suite 414
Indianapolis, IN 46204
P: (317) 232-3850
F: (317) 232-0707

IOWA
Mr. W. Charles Smithson
Executive Director & Legal Counsel
Ethics & Campaign Disclosure Board
510 East 12th Street, Suite 1A
Des Moines, IA 50319
P: (515) 281-3489
F: (515) 281-3701
E: charlie.smithson@iowa.gov

KANSAS
Ms. Carol Williams
Executive Director
Governmental Ethics Commission
109 Southwest 9th Street, 5th Floor
Topeka, KS 66612
P: (785) 296-4219
F: (785) 296-2548

KENTUCKY
Ms. Jill LeMaster
Executive Director
Executive Branch Ethics Commission
258 Capitol Annex
Frankfort, KY 40601
P: (502) 564-7954
F: (502) 564-2686
E: jill.lemaster@ky.gov

Mr. Anthony Wilhoit
Executive Director
Legislative Ethics Commission
22 Mill Creek Park
Frankfort, KY 40601
P: (502) 573-2863
F: (502) 573-2929
E: tony.wilhoit@lrc.state.ky.us

LOUISIANA
Mr. R. Gray Sexton
Executive Director
Ethics Administration
2415 Quail Drive, Third Floor
Baton Rouge, LA 70808
P: (225) 763-8777
F: (225) 763-8780

MAINE
Mr. Jonathan Wayne
Executive Director
Commission on Governmental Ethics & Election Practices
125 State House Station
Augusta, ME 04333
P: (207) 287-4179
F: (207) 287-6775

MARYLAND
Ms. Suzanne S. Fox
Executive Director
State Ethics Commission
45 Calvert Street, 1st Floor
Annapolis, MD 21401
P: (410) 260-7770
E: sfox@gov.state.md.us

MASSACHUSETTS
Mr. E. George Daher
Chair
Ethics Commission
One Ashburton Place
Boston, MA 02108
P: (617) 727-0600

MICHIGAN
Ms. Janet McClelland
Deputy Director
State Board of Ethics
400 South Pine Street
P.O. Box 30002
Lansing, MI 48909
P: (517) 373-9276
F: (517) 373-3103
E: mcclellandj@michigan.gov

Ethics

MINNESOTA
Ms. Jeanne Olson
Executive Director
Campaign Finance & Public Disclosure Board
Centennial Office Building, Suite 190
658 Cedar Street
St. Paul, MN 55155
P: (651) 296-1721
F: (651) 296-1722
E: jeanne.olson@state.mn.us

MISSISSIPPI
Mr. Tom Hood
Executive Director
Ethics Commission
P.O. Box 22746
Jackson, MS 39225
P: (601) 359-1285
F: (601) 354-6253
E: info@ethics.state.ms.us

MISSOURI
Mr. Robert F. Connor
Executive Director
Ethics Commission
P.O. Box 1254
Jefferson City, MO 65102
P: (573) 751-2020
F: (573) 526-4506
E: robert.connor@mec.mo.gov

MONTANA
Mr. Dennis Unsworth
Commissioner
Office of the Commissioner of Political Practices
1205 Eighth Avenue
P.O. Box 202401
Helena, MT 59620
P: (406) 444-2942
F: (406) 444-1643
E: dunsworth@mt.gov

NEBRASKA
Mr. Frank Daley
Executive Director
Accountability & Disclosure Commission
P.O. Box 95086
Lincoln, NE 68509
P: (402) 471-2522
F: (402) 471-6599

NEVADA
Mr. L. Patrick Hearn
Executive Director
Commission on Ethics
3476 Executive Pointe Way, Suite 16
Carson City, NV 89706
P: (775) 687-5469
F: (775) 687-1279
E: phearn@ethics.state.nv.us

NEW HAMPSHIRE
Hon. Kelly Ayotte (R)
Attorney General
Department of Justice
State House Annex
33 Capitol Street
Concord, NH 03301
P: (603) 271-3658
F: (603) 271-2110

NEW JERSEY
Ms. Rita L. Strmensky
Executive Director
State Ethics Commission
P.O. Box 082
28 West State Street, Room 1407
Trenton, NJ 08625
P: (609) 292-1892
F: (609) 633-9252
E: ethics@eces.state.nj.us

NEW MEXICO
Hon. Mary Herrera (D)
Secretary of State
Office of the Secretary of State
325 Don Gaspar, Suite 300
State Capitol Annex, North
Santa Fe, NM 87503
P: (505) 827-3600
F: (505) 827-3634
E: MaryE.Herrera@state.nm.us

Mr. Daniel A. Ivey-Soto
Director of Elections/Legal Counsel
Bureau of Elections
State Capitol Annex North
325 Don Gaspar, Suite 300
Santa Fe, NM 87503
P: (505) 827-3600
F: (505) 827-8403
E: Elections@state.nm.us

NEW YORK
Mr. Karl J. Sleight
Executive Director
Ethics Commission
39 Columbia Street
Albany, NY 12207
P: (518) 432-8208
F: (518) 432-8255
E: ethics@dos.state.ny.us

NORTH CAROLINA
Mr. Perry Newson
Executive Director
Board of Ethics
116 West Jones Street
1324 Mail Service Center
Raleigh, NC 27699
P: (919) 733-2780
F: (919) 733-2785
E: perry.newson@ncmail.net

NORTH DAKOTA
Mr. Ryan Berstein
Legal Counsel
Governor's Office
600 East Boulevard Avenue, 1st Floor
Bismark, ND 58505
P: (701) 328-2200
F: (701) 328-2205
E: governor@nd.gov

NORTHERN MARIANA ISLANDS
Hon. Matthew T. Gregory
Attorney General
Office of the Attorney General
Capitol Hil, Caller Box 10007
Saipan, MP 95960
P: (670) 664-2341
F: (670) 664-2349
E: matt@gregoryfirm.com

OHIO
Mr. David Freel
Executive Director
Ethics Commission
8 East Long Street, 10th Floor
Columbus, OH 43215
P: (614) 466-7093
F: (614) 466-8368
E: ethics@ethics.state.oh.us

OKLAHOMA
Ms. Marilyn Hughes
Executive Director
Ethics Commission
State Capitol Building, Room B-5
2300 North Lincoln Boulevard
Oklahoma City, OK 73105
P: (405) 521-3451
F: (405) 521-4905

PENNSYLVANIA
Mr. John J. Contino
Exeuctive Director
State Ethics Commission
Room 309, Finance Building
P.O. Box 11470
Harrisburg, PA 17108
P: (717) 783-1610
F: (717) 787-0806

PUERTO RICO
Mr. Hiram Morales-Lugo
Executive Director
Office of Governmental Ethics
P.O. Box 194629
San Juan, PR 00919
P: (787) 766-4400
F: (787) 754-0977

RHODE ISLAND
Mr. Kent Willever
Executive Director
Ethics Commission
40 Fountain Street
Providence, RI 02903
P: (401) 222-3790
F: (401) 272-3382

SOUTH CAROLINA
Mr. Herbert Hayden Jr.
Executive Director
State Ethics Commission
5000 Thurmond Mall, Suite 250
Columbia, SC 29201
P: (803) 253-4192
F: (803) 253-7539
E: herb@ethics.state.sc.us

TENNESSEE
Mr. Drew Rawlins
Executive Director
Registry of Election Finance
404 James Robertson Parkway, 16th Floor
Nashville, TN 37243
P: (615) 741-7959
F: (615) 532-8905

TEXAS
Mr. David A. Reisman
Executive Director
Ethics Commission
201 East 14th Street, 10th Floor
P.O. Box 12070
Austin, TX 78711
P: (512) 463-5800
F: (512) 463-5777

U.S. VIRGIN ISLANDS
Mr. Elliott M. Davis
Solicitor General
Solicitor General's Office
34-38 Kron Prindsens Gade
GERS Building, 2nd Floor
St. Thomas, VI 00802
P: (340) 774-5666
F: (340) 776-3494
E: edavis@doj.vi.gov

UTAH
Hon. Mark L. Shurtleff (R)
Attorney General
Office of the Attorney General
State Capitol Complex, Suite E320
Salt Lake City, UT 84114
P: (801) 538-1191
F: (801) 538-1121
E: MSHURTLEFF@utah.gov

WASHINGTON
Ms. Vicki Rippie
Executive Director
Public Disclosure Commission
711 Capitol Way, Room 206
P.O. Box 40908
Olympia, WA 98504
P: (360) 586-4838
F: (360) 753-1112
E: vrippie@pdc.wa.gov

WEST VIRGINIA
Mr. Lewis G. Brewer
Executive Director
Ethics Commission
210 Brooks Street, Suite 300
Charleston, WV 25301
P: (304) 558-0664
F: (304) 558-2169
E: lbrewer@wvadmin.gov

WISCONSIN
Mr. R. Roth Judd
Executive Director
Ethics Board
44 East Mifflin Street, Suite 601
Madison, WI 53703
P: (608) 266-8123
F: (608) 264-9309

WYOMING
Hon. Max Maxfield (R)
Secretary of State
Office of the Secretary of State
State Capitol
Cheyenne, WY 82002
P: (307) 777-5333
F: (307) 777-6217
E: Secofstate@state.wy.us

Facilities Management

Maintains, constructs, designs, renovates and delivers basic services to state-owned facilities.

Information provided by:

National Association of State Facilities Administrators
Marcia Stone
Association Manager
2760 Research Park Drive
P.O. Box 11910
Lexington, KY 40578
P: (859) 244-8181
F: (859) 244-8001
nasfa@nasfa.net
www.nasfa.net

ALASKA
Mr. Joel St. Aubin
Chief
Department of Transportation & Public Facilities
Public Facilities Branch
2200 East 42nd Avenue
Anchorage, AK 99508
P: (907) 269-0823
F: (907) 269-0805
E: joel_staubin@dot.state.ak.us

AMERICAN SAMOA
Mr. Vaivao Logotaeao Etelagi
President
Development Bank of American Samoa
P.O. Box 9
Pago Pago, AS 96799
P: (684) 633-4031
F: (684) 633-1163

ARIZONA
Mr. Ellis Jones
General Manager
General Services Division
100 North 15th Avenue, Suite 202
Phoenix, AZ 85007
P: (602) 364-0403
F: (602) 542-1926
E: ellis.jones@azdoa.gov

ARKANSAS
Ms. Anita L. Murrell
Director
Building Authority
501 Woodlane, Suite 600
Little Rock, AR 72201
P: (501) 682-5558
F: (501) 682-5547
E: amurrell@aba.state.ar.us

Mr. Craig Parsons
DHS, Facilities Manager
Department of Human Services
Department of Health & Human Services
Slot W345, P.O. Box 1437
Little Rock, AR 72203
P: (501) 682-6551
F: (501) 682-1483
E: craig.parsons@arkansas.gov

Mr. Ronald A. Snead
Assistant Director
Special Projects
Employment Security Department
1 Pershing Circle Drive, North Little Rock, AR 72114
P: (501) 682-2033
F: (501) 682-3144
E: ron.snead.aesd@mail.state.ar.us

Mr. Dale Woodall
General Services Manager
Developmental Disabilities Services
Department of Health & Human Services
Slot N505, P.O. Box 1437
Little Rock, AR 72203
P: (501) 682-8709
F: (501) 682-8679
E: dale.woodall@arkansas.gov

CALIFORNIA
Mr. Michael Bocchicchio
Assistant Vice President
University of California, Facilities Administration
1111 Franklin Street
6th Floor, Suite 6201
Oakland, CA 94607
P: (510) 987-0777
F: (510) 987-0752
E: mike.bocchicchio@ucop.edu

Mr. Glenn Yee
Chief
Department of Transportation
1515 River Park Drive, Suite 200
Sacramento, CA 95815
E: glenn_yee@dot.ca.gov

CONNECTICUT
Mr. Manuel Becerra
Administrator
Department of Public Works
Facilities Management
165 Capitol Avenue, Room G-39
Hartford, CT 06106
P: (860) 713-5624
F: (860) 713-7262
E: manuel.becarra@po.state.ct.us

DELAWARE
Mr. Robert Furman
Division Director
Division of Facilities Management
Department of Administrative Services
540 South Dupont Highway, Suite 1
Dover, DE 19901
P: (302) 739-5644
F: (302) 739-6148
E: robert.furman@state.de.us

DISTRICT OF COLUMBIA
Mr. Sheldon Greenberg
Building Management Specialist
U.S. General Services Administration
Office of Governmentwide Policy
1800 F Street, Northwest (MPE)
Washington, DC 20405
P: (202) 841-4868
F: (202) 219-0104
E: sheldon.greenberg@gsa.gov

FLORIDA
Mr. Tim Dimond
Director
Facilities Management
Suite 315, Building 4050
4050 Esplanade Way
Tallahassee, FL 32399
P: (850) 414-9712
E: tim.dimond@dms.myflorida.com

GEORGIA
Ms. Gena L. Abraham
Director
State Financing & Investment Commission
Construction Division
2nd Floor, 270 Washington Street
Atlanta, GA 30334
P: (404) 463-5600
F: (404) 656-6006
E: gabraham@gsfic.ga.gov

Mr. J. Ray Crawford Jr.
Interim Executive Director
Building Authority
1 Martin Luther King, Jr. Drive, Southwest
Atlanta, GA 30334
P: (404) 656-3253
F: (404) 657-0337
E: ray.crawford@gw.gba.state.ga.us

Mr. Danny Elijah
Project Engineer
Department of Corrections
Engineering & Construction Services
P.O. Box 17765
Atlanta, GA 30316
P: (404) 635-4671
F: (404) 635-4669
E: elijad00@dcor.state.ga.us

ILLINOIS
Ms. Jan Grimes
Executive Director
Captial Development Board
W.G. Stratton Building, 3rd Floor
Springfield, IL 62706
P: (217) 782-8725
E: jgrimes@cdb.state.il.us

Mr. Bruce Washington
Deputy Director
Department of Central Management Services
Property Management
WMG Stratton Building, 7th Floor
Springfield, IL 62706
P: (217) 785-0562

Mr. Ron Wright
Senior Executive Assistant
Capital Development Board
W.G. Stratton Building, 3rd Floor
401 South Spring Street
Springfield, IL 62706
P: (217) 782-8532
F: (217) 524-4208
E: ron.wright@Illinois.gov

IOWA
Mr. Lee Hammer
Director
Facilities Support
Department of Transportation
800 Lincoln Way
Ames, IA 50010
P: (515) 239-1327
F: (515) 239-1964
E: lee.hammer@dot.iowa.gov

KANSAS
Ms. Marilyn L. Jacobson
Interim Director
Division of Facilities Management
Landon State Office Building
900 Southwest Jackson
Topeka, KS 66612
P: (785) 296-2037

KENTUCKY
Mr. Jim Abbott
Commissioner
Department for Facilities & Support Services
Room 76, 702 Capital Avenue
Frankfort, KY 40601
P: (502) 564-0402
F: (502) 564-6822
E: james.abbott@ky.gov

Mr. Jamie Link
Acting Commissioner
Department of Facilities Management
Capitol Annex, Room 76
702 Capitol Avenue
Frankfort, KY 40601
P: (502) 564-1026
E: jamie.link@ky.gov

LOUISIANA
Mr. William Morrison
Assistant Director
Office of Facility Planning & Control
Division of Administration
P.O. Box 94095
Baton Rouge, LA 70804
P: (225) 342-0855
F: (225) 342-7624
E: bill.morrison@la.gov

MAINE
Mr. Barry Cote
Superintendent of Buildings
Property Management Division
Bureau of General Services
76 State House Station
Augusta, ME 04333
P: (207) 287-4151
F: (207) 287-4845
E: barry.cote@maine.gov

Mr. Gordon Nelson
Director of Property Management
Division of Property Management
5734 Hilltop Commons, Suite 103
Orono, ME 04469
P: (207) 581-4799
F: (207) 581-4714
E: gordon.nelson@umit.maine.edu

MASSACHUSETTS
Ms. Hope Davis
Director
Division of Capitol Asset Management
1 Ashburton Place, 15th Floor
Boston, MA 02108
P: (617) 727-4030
F: (617) 727-4043
E: hope.davis@state.ma.us

Mr. William Tivnan
Director
Office of Finance & Administration
Division of Capital Asset Management
One Ashburton Place, 15th Floor
Boston, MA 02108
F: (617) 727-5363
E: bill.tivnan@dcp.state.ma.us

MICHIGAN
Mr. George Hakim
Director
Infrastructure Services
Department of Management & Budget
1st Floor, Cass Building
Lansing, MI 48909
P: (517) 373-3670
F: (517) 373-1638
E: hakimg@michigan.gov

Mr. Tom Saxton
Acting Director
Facilities Administration
Department of Management & Budget
P.O. Box 30026
Lansing, MI 48909
P: (517) 373-3809
F: (517) 335-1638
E: saxtont@michigan.gov

Mr. Robert Winter
Physical Plant Supervisor
Department of Management & Budget
IS Operations Division
1st Floor, Mason, P.O. Box 30026
Lansing, MI 48909
P: (517) 373-7184
F: (517) 373-7052
E: winterr1@michigan.gov

MINNESOTA
Ms. Heidi M. Myers
State Architect
Division of State Building & Construction
301 Centennial Office Building
358 Cedar Street
St. Paul, MN 55155
P: (651) 201-2370
E: heidi.myers@state.mn.us

MISSISSIPPI
Mr. David Anderson
Director
Bureau of Building, Grounds & Real Property Management
1401 Suite B, 501 Northwest Street
Jackson, MS 39201
P: (601) 359-3898
F: (601) 359-2470
E: andersd@dfa.state.ms.us

Mr. Paul J. Barlow
Assistant Director
Department of Finance & Administration
Bureau of Buildings
501 Northwest Street, Suite 1401-B
Jackson, MS 39201
P: (601) 359-3621
F: (601) 359-2470
E: barlowp@dfa.state.ms.us

MISSOURI
Mr. Edwin Bybee
Director of Planning & Budget Unit
Division of Design & Construction
Harry S. Truman State Office Building
P.O. Box 809
Jefferson City, MO 65102
P: (573) 751-2015
F: (573) 751-7277
E: ed.bybee@oa.mo.gov

Mr. David Mosby
Director
Division of Facilities Management
Room 730, 301 West High Street
P.O. Box 809
Jefferson City, MO 65102
P: (573) 751-1034
F: (573) 526-9828
E: dave.mosby@oa.mo.gov

MONTANA
Mr. Russ Katherman
Contract Administrator
Architecture & Engineering Division
P.O. Box 200103
1520 East 6th Avenue
Helena, MT 59620
P: (406) 444-3332
F: (406) 444-3399
E: rkatherman@mt.gov

NEBRASKA
Mr. Larry Eckles
Administrator
State Building Division
The Executive, Suite 509
521 South 14th Street
Lincoln, NE 68508
P: (402) 471-3191
F: (402) 471-0403
E: larry.eckles@email.state.ne.us

Mr. Jason Kress
Capitol Facilities Manager
Department of Roads
5001 South 14th Street
P.O. Box 94759
Lincoln, NE 68509
P: (402) 479-3746
F: (402) 479-3902
E: jasonkress@dor.state.ne.us

Mr. Stephen Robinson
Administrator
Department of Administration Services
State Building Division
521 South 14th Street, Suite 509
Lincoln, NE 68508
P: (402) 471-3191
E: srobinso@notes.state.ne.us

Facilities Management

Mr. Jim Schmailzl
Manager
Department of Roads
Operations & Maintenance Division
5001 South 14th
Lincoln, NE 68509
P: (402) 479-4787
F: (402) 479-4567
E: jschmail@dor.state.ne.us

NEVADA
Mr. Mike Rice
Manager
State Public Works Board
515 East Musser Street, Suite 102
Carson City, NV 89701
E: mcrife@spwb.state.nv.us

NEW JERSEY
Mr. Anthony Mazzella
Executive Director
State Capitol Joint Management Commission
50 West State Street, 2nd Floor
P.O. Box 200
Trenton, NJ 08625
P: (609) 984-0976
F: (609) 984-6858

NEW MEXICO
Mr. Selby L. Lucero
Deputy Director
Building Services Division
Room 1022, 1100 South St. Francis Drive
P.O. Drawer 26110
Santa Fe, NM 87502
P: (505) 827-2068
F: (505) 827-2349
E: selby.lucero@state.nm.us

NEW YORK
Mr. Martin Gilroy
Director
Real Property Management
Corning Tower, 39th Floor
Empire State Plaza
Albany, NY 12242
P: (518) 474-6057
F: (518) 474-1523
E: martin.gilroy@ogs.state.ny.us

NORTH CAROLINA
Mr. Gregory Driver
Director
Consulting Services Section
State Construction Office
301 North Wilmington Street
Raleigh, NC 27601
P: (919) 807-4100
F: (919) 807-4110
E: gregory.driver@ncmail.net

Mr. Speros J. Fleggas
Director
Department of Administration
State Construction Office
1307 Mail Service Center
Raleigh, NC 27699
P: (919) 807-4100
F: (919) 807-4110
E: speros.fleggas@ncmail.net

NORTH DAKOTA
Mr. Joel Leapaldt
State Facility Planner
Division of Facility Management
4th Floor, State Capitol Building
600 East Boulevard Avenue
Bismarck, ND 58505
P: (701) 328-1968
F: (701) 328-3230
E: jleapaldt@state.nd.us

NORTHERN MARIANA ISLANDS
Hon. Timothy P. Villagomez (C)
Lieutenant Governor
Commonwealth Utilities Corporation
Executive Director's Office
Joeten Dandan Building, P.O. Box 501220
Saipan, MP 96950
P: (670) 235-7025
F: (670) 235-6145
E: cucedo@gtepacifica.net

OHIO
Mr. Larry Ayres
Administrator of Properties & Facilities
Department of Administrative Services
Division of General Services
4200 Surface Road
Columbus, OH 43288
P: (614) 387-1300
F: (614) 728-2400
E: larry.ayres@das.state.oh.us

Mr. Dan Barr
Administrator of Properties & Facilities
Division of General Services
4200 Surface Road
Columbus, OH 43288

OKLAHOMA
Mr. Harold Munson
Construction/Maintenance Administrator II
Department of Central Services
Facilities Services Division
Will Rogers Building, P.O. Box 53187
Oklahoma City, OK 73152
P: (405) 522-6742
F: (405) 340-9178
E: harold_munson@dcs.state.ok.us

OREGON
Ms. Virginia K. Carey
Facilities Manager
Department of Transportation
Support Services/Facilities Management
885 Airport Road, Southeast, Building X
Salem, OR 97301
P: (503) 986-5800
F: (503) 986-5780
E: virginia.k.carey@odot.state.or.us

Mr. Bill Foster
Interim Facilities Manager
Department of Administrative Services
Division of Facilities
1225 Ferry Street, Southeast
Salem, OR 97310
P: (503) 378-2865
F: (503) 373-7210
E: bill.i.foster@state.or.us

PUERTO RICO
Ms. Leila Hernandez Umpierre
Acting Executive Director
Public Building Authority
Minillas Station
P.O. Box 41029
San Juan, PR 00940
P: (787) 721-5540
F: (787) 728-4670

SOUTH CAROLINA
Mr. Allen R. Carter
Interim Acting Director
Office of State Engineer
Procurement Services Division
1201 Main Street, Suite 600
Columbia, SC 29201
P: (803) 737-0776
F: (803) 737-0639
E: acarter@mmo.state.sc.us

TENNESSEE
Mr. Michael A. Fitts
State Architect
Capital Projects/Real Property Management
Tennessee Tower, Suite 2100
312 Eighth Avenue, North
Nashville, TN 37243
P: (615) 741-4201
F: (615) 741-6189
E: mike.fitts@state.tn.us

Mr. Charles Garrett
Assistant Commissioner
Capitol Projects/Real Property Management
Tennessee Tower, Suite 2200
312 Eighth Avenue, North
Nashville, TN 37243
P: (615) 741-7865
F: (615) 741-7599
E: charles.garrett@state.tn.us

TEXAS
Mr. William E. Taylor
Director
State Energy Office
111 East 17th Street, 11th Floor
Austin, TX 78701
P: (512) 463-1931
F: (512) 475-2569
E: dub.taylor@cpa.state.tx.us

UTAH
Mr. Bruce Whittington
Assistant Director
Department of Administrative Services
Facilities, Construction & Management
4130 State Office Bulding
Salt Lake City, UT 84114
P: (801) 538-3547
F: (801) 538-3378
E: bwhittington@utah.gov

VERMONT
Ms. Laurel LaFramboise
Program Specialist
Maintenance & Aviation Division
Agency of Transportation
National Life Building, 1 Drawer 33
Montpelier, VT 05633
P: (802) 828-2604
F: (802) 828-2848
E: laurel.laframboise@state.vt.us

Mr. Thomas J. Sandretto
Deputy Commissioner
Department of Buildings & General Services
2 Governor Aiken Avenue, Drawer 33
Montpelier, VT 05633
P: (802) 828-3515
F: (802) 828-3533
E: tom.sandretto@state.vt.us

VIRGINIA
Mr. Bert Jones
Director
Division of Engineering & Buildings
805 East Broad Street, Room 101
Richmond, VA 23219
P: (804) 786-3263
F: (804) 371-7934
E: bert.jones@dgs.virginia.gov

WASHINGTON
Mr. Robert A. Bippert
Senior Deputy Assistant Director
Buildings, Grounds & Real Estate Division
230 General Administration Building
P.O. Box 41015
Olympia, WA 98504
P: (360) 902-7395
F: (360) 586-9088
E: bippert@ga.wa.gov

WEST VIRGINIA
Mr. Robert Ferguson
Secretary
Department of Administration
1900 Kanawha Boulevard, East
Charleston, WV 25305
P: (304) 558-4331
F: (304) 558-2999
E: rferguson@wvadmin.gov

Mr. David Oliverio
Director
General Services
Building 1, Room MB-60
Charleston, WV 25305
P: (304) 558-1301
F: (304) 558-2334
E: davido@wvadmin.gov

WISCONSIN
Mr. Robert Cramer
Administrator
Division of State Facilities
7th Floor, 101 East Wilson Street
P.O. Box 7866
Madison, WI 53707
P: (608) 266-1031
F: (608) 267-2710
E: robert.cramer@wisconsin.gov

WYOMING
Mr. Joe McCord
Facilities Manager
Department of Administration
Division of Facilities Management
801 West 20th Street
Cheyenne, WY 82002
P: (307) 777-7760
F: (307) 777-6273
E: jmccor@state.wy.us

Mr. Raymond Vigil Jr.
Manager of Facilities
Department of Transportation
5300 Bishop Boulevard
Cheyenne, WY 82009
P: (307) 777-4474
F: (307) 777-3801
E: raymond.vigil@dot.state.wy.us

Federal Liaison

The individual, typically based in Washington D.C., who serves as the chief representative of state government in the nation's capital, and works to promote state-federal relations.

For more information contact:

National Governors Association
Ray Scheppach
Executive Director
Hall of States
444 North Capitol Street
Washington, DC 20001
P: (202) 624-5300
F: (202) 624-5313
www.nga.org

ALASKA
Mr. John Katz
Director
Governor's Washington Office
444 North Capitol Street, Suite 336
Washington, DC 20001
P: (202) 624-5858
F: (202) 624-5857

AMERICAN SAMOA
Ms. Janice Lipsen
Washington Representative
Washington, DC Office
1101 Vermont Avenue, Northwest
Suite 403
Washington, DC 20005
P: (202) 408-4998
F: (202) 408-4997

ARIZONA
Mr. Brian De Vallance
Director
Governor's Washington Office
444 North Capitol Street, Suite 428
Washington, DC 20001
P: (202) 220-1396
F: (202) 624-1475

CALIFORNIA
Ms. Linda Ulrich
Director
Washington, DC Office
444 North Capitol Street, Suite 134
Washington, DC 20001
P: (202) 624-5270
F: (202) 624-5280

CONNECTICUT
Ms. Julie Williams
Director
Governor's Washington Office
444 North Capitol Street, Suite 317
Washington, DC 20001
P: (202) 347-4535
F: (202) 347-7151

DELAWARE
Ms. Kate Finnerty
Director
Washington, DC Office
444 North Capitol Street, Suite 230
Washington, DC 20001
P: (202) 624-7724
F: (202) 624-5495

FLORIDA
Mr. Kerry Feehery
Director
Washington, DC Office
444 North Capitol Street, Suite 349
Washington, DC 20001
P: (202) 624-5885
F: (202) 624-5886

GEORGIA
Mr. Pat Wilson
Director of Federal Affairs
Washington, DC Office
400 North Capitol Street, Suite 376
Washington, DC 20001
P: (202) 624-3681
F: (202) 624-3682

ILLINOIS
Ms. Margaret Larson
Director
Washington, DC Office
444 North Capitol Street, Suite 400
Washington, DC 20001
P: (202) 624-7760
F: (202) 724-0689

INDIANA
Ms. Debbie Hohlt
Federal Representative
Washington, DC Office
1455 Pennsylvania Avenue, Northwest
Suite 1140
Washington, DC 20004
P: (202) 624-1474
F: (202) 833-1587

IOWA
Mr. Jon Murphy
Director
Office of State-Federal Relatioı
400 North Capitol Street, Suite 359
Washington, DC 20001
P: (202) 624-5444
F: (202) 624-8189

KANSAS
Mr. Adam Nordstrom
Washington Representative for the Governor
Washington, DC Office
500 New Jersey Avenue, Northwest
Suite400
Washington, DC 20001
P: (202) 715-2923
F: (202) 638-1045

KENTUCKY
Ms. Kristi Craig
Director
Governor's Washington Office
444 North Capitol Street, Suite 224
Washington, DC 20001
P: (202) 220-1350
F: (202) 220-1359

LOUISIANA
Mr. Clyde Henderson
Director
Office of State-Federal Relatioı
444 North Capitol Street, Suite 372
Washington, DC 20001
P: (202) 434-4795
F: (202) 434-8054

MARYLAND
Ms. Dana Thompson
Director
Governor's Washington Office
444 North Capitol Street, Suite 311
Washington, DC 20001
P: (202) 624-1430
F: (202) 783-3061

MASSACHUSETTS
Ms. Susan Liss
Director
Office of State-Federal Relatioı
444 North Capitol Street, Suite 208
Washington, DC 20001
P: (202) 624-7713
F: (202) 624-7714

MICHIGAN
Mr. Dan Beattie
Director
Governor's Washington Office
444 North Capitol Street, Suite 411
Washington, DC 20001
P: (202) 624-5840
F: (202) 624-5841

MINNESOTA
Mr. Jason Rohloff
Director of Federal Affairs
Governor's Washington Office
400 North Capitol Street, Suite 380
Washington, DC 20001
P: (202) 624-5308
F: (202) 624-5425

NEVADA
Mr. Ryan McGinness
Washington Office
444 North Capitol Street, Suite 209
Washington, DC 20001
P: (202) 624-5405
F: (202) 624-8181

NEW JERSEY
Mr. Jarrod Koenig
Washington Representative
Governor's Washington Office
444 North Capitol Street, Suite 201
Washington, DC 20001
P: (202) 638-0631
F: (202) 638-2296

NEW MEXICO
Mr. Tony Martinez
Office Director
Governor's Washington Office
444 North Capitol Street, Suite 400
Washington, DC 20001
P: (202) 220-1348
F: (202) 220-1349

NEW YORK
Mr. Derek Douglas
Director
Governor's Washington Office
444 North Capitol Street, Suite 301
Washington, DC 20001
P: (202) 434-7100
F: (202) 434-7110

NORTH CAROLINA
Mr. Jim McCleskey
Director
Governor's Washington Office
444 North Capitol Street, Suite 332
Washington, DC 20001
P: (202) 624-5830
F: (202) 624-5836

NORTH DAKOTA
Ms. Krista Carman
Washington Representative
Washington, DC Office
444 North Capitol Street, Suite 224
Washington, DC 20001
P: (202) 624-5471
F: (202) 478-0811

OHIO
Mr. Drew McCracken
Director
Washington Office
444 North Capitol Street, Suite 546
Washington, DC 20001
P: (202) 624-5844
F: (202) 624-5847

OREGON
Ms. Sarah Bittleman
Director
Washington Office
444 North Capitol Street, Suite 400
Washington, DC 20001
P: (202) 624-7765
F: (202) 624-7785

PENNSYLVANIA
Mr. Peter A. Peyser Jr.
Washington Representative
Washington, DC Office
600 New Hampshire Avenue, Northwest
Washington, DC 20037
P: (202) 772-5806
F: (202) 772-1660

PUERTO RICO
Mr. Eduardo Bhatia
Executive Director
Federal Affairs Administration
1100 17th Street, Northwest, Suite 800
Washington, DC 20036
P: (202) 778-0710
F: (202) 822-0916

SOUTH CAROLINA
Ms. Blair Goodrich
Policy Analyst
Governor's Washington Office
444 North Capitol Street, Suite 203
Washington, DC 20001
P: (202) 624-7784
F: (202) 624-7800

TEXAS
Mr. Ed Perez
Executive Director
Office of State-Federal Relatioı
122 C Street, Northwest, Suite 200
Washington, DC 20001
P: (202) 638-3927
F: (202) 628-1943

VERMONT
Mr. Craig Pattee
Washington Representative
Washington, DC Office
412 First Street, Southeast
Washington, DC 20003
P: (202) 484-4019
F: (202) 484-0609

VIRGINIA
Mr. Alfonso Lopez
Director
Virginia Liaison Office
444 North Capitol Street, Suite 214
Washington, DC 20001
P: (202) 783-1769
F: (202) 783-7687

WASHINGTON
Mr. Mark Rupp
Director
Washington, DC Office
444 North Capitol Street, Suite 411
Washington, DC 20001
P: (202) 624-3691
F: (202) 624-5841

WISCONSIN
Ms. Jen Jinks
Director
Washington Office
444 North Capitol Street, Suite 613
Washington, DC 20001
P: (202) 624-5870
F: (202) 624-5871

Finance

Responsible for multiple financial functions (budget, payroll, accounting, revenue estimation.)

ALABAMA
Mr. Jim Main
Director
Department of Finance
600 Dexter Avenue, Suite N-105
Montgomery, AL 36130
P: (334) 242-7160
F: (334) 353-3300
E: jim.main
@finance.alabama.gov

ALASKA
Ms. Kim Garnero
Division Director
Division of Finance
333 Willoughby Avenue, 10th Floor
Juneau, AK 99811
P: (907) 465-3435
F: (907) 465-2169
E: kim_garnero
@admin.state.ak.us

AMERICAN SAMOA
Hon. Velega Savali
Treasurer
Department of Treasury
American Samoa Government
Pago Pago, AS 96799
P: (684) 633-4155
F: (684) 633-4100

ARIZONA
Mr. D. Clark Partridge
State Comptroller
Department of Administration
100 North 15th Avenue, Suite 302
Phoenix, AZ 85007
P: (602) 542-5405
F: (602) 542-5749
E: clark.partridge
@azdoa.gov

ARKANSAS
Mr. Richard Weiss
Director
Department of Finance & Administration
1509 West 7th Street, Room 401
DFA Building
Little Rock, AR 72201
P: (501) 682-2242
F: (501) 682-1029
E: richard.weiss
@dfa.state.ar.us

CALIFORNIA
Mr. Mike Genest
Director
Department of Finance
State Capitol, 1st Floor
Sacramento, CA 95814
P: (916) 445-4141

COLORADO
Ms. Leslie M. Shenefelt
State Controller
Division of Finance & Procurement
633 17th Street, Suite 1500
Denver, CO 80203
P: (303) 866-6200
F: (303) 866-4233
E: leslie.shenefelt
@state.co.us

CONNECTICUT
Mr. Robert Genuario
Secretary
Office of Policy & Management
450 Capitol Avenue
Hartford, CT 06106
P: (860) 418-6500
E: robert.genuario
@po.state.ct.us

DELAWARE
Mr. Richard S. Cordrey
Secretary of Finance
Department of Finance
Carvel State Building, 8th Floor
820 North French Street
Wilmington, DE 19801
P: (302) 577-8984
F: (302) 577-8982
E: marybeth.wilson
@state.de.us

DISTRICT OF COLUMBIA
Dr. Natwar M. Gandhi
Chief Financial Officer
Office of the Chief Financial Officer
1350 Pennsylvania Avenue, Northwest
Suite 203
Washington, DC 20004
P: (202) 727-2476
F: (202) 727-1643
E: ocfo@dc.gov

FLORIDA
Hon. Alex Sink (D)
Chief Financial Officer
Department of Financial Services
Fletcher Building, Suite 516
200 East Gaines Street
Tallahassee, FL 32399
P: (850) 413-2850
F: (850) 413-2950
E: alex.sink@fldfs.com

GEORGIA
Hon. W. Daniel Ebersole
Director, Office of Treasury & Fiscal Services
Office of Treasury & Fiscal Services
200 Piedmont Avenue
Suite 1202, West Tower
Atlanta, GA 30334
P: (404) 656-2168
F: (404) 656-9048
E: OTFSweb@otfs.ga.gov

GUAM
Ms. Lourdes M. Perez
Director
Department of Administration
P.O. Box 884
Agana, GU 96932
P: (671) 475-1250
F: (671) 477-6788

HAWAII
Hon. Georgina K. Kawamura
Director of Finance
Department of Budget & Finance
P.O. Box 150
Honolulu, HI 96810
P: (808) 586-1518
F: (808) 586-1976
E: Hi.BudgetandFinance
@hawaii.gov

IDAHO
Mr. Brad Foltman
Administrator
Division of Financial Management
Statehouse
P.O. Box 83720
Boise, ID 83720
P: (208) 334-3900
F: (208) 334-2438
E: bfoltman@dfm.idaho.gov

ILLINOIS
Ms. Ginger Ostro
Director
Governor's Office of Management & Budget
108 State House
Springfield, IL 60706
P: (217) 782-4520
F: (217) 524-1514

INDIANA
Mr. Charles E. Schalliol
Director
State Budget Agency
200 West Washington Street
Room 212
Indianapolis, IN 46204
P: (317) 232-0696

IOWA
Mr. Mark Schuling
Director
Department of Revenue
Hoover Building
1305 East Walnut Street
Des Moines, IA 50319
P: (515) 281-3204
E: mark.schuling
@idrf.state.ia.us

KANSAS
Mr. Robert Mackey
Director
Division of Accounts & Reports
900 Southwest Jackson Street, Room 351-S
Topeka, KS 66612
P: (785) 296-2314
F: (785) 296-6841
E: bob.mackey
@da.state.ks.us

KENTUCKY
Mr. Bradford L. Cowgill
State Budget Director
Office of State Budget Director
702 Capital Avenue, Room 284
Frankfort, KY 40601
P: (502) 564-7300
F: (502) 564-6684
E: Brad.Cowgill@ky.gov

Mr. John Farris
Secretary
Finance & Administration Cabinet
702 Capitol Avenue, Room 383
Frankfort, KY 40601
P: (502) 564-4240
F: (502) 564-6785

LOUISIANA
Mr. Gene Knecht
Director
Office of Finance & Support Services
1201 North Third Street
Claiborne Building, Suite 6-180
Baton Rouge, LA 70804
P: (225) 342-0700
F: (225) 342-2606
E: Gene.Knecht@la.gov

MAINE
Ms. Rebecca Wyke
Commissioner
Department of Administrative & Financial Services
76 State House Station
Augusta, ME 04333
P: (207) 624-7800
F: (207) 624-7804
E: rebeccawyke@maine.gov

MARYLAND
Ms. T. Eloise Foster
Secretary
Department of Budget & Management
45 Calvert Street, 1st Floor
Annapolis, MD 21401
P: (410) 260-7041
F: (410) 974-2585
E: efoster@dbm.state.md.us

MASSACHUSETTS
Ms. Leslie A. Kirwan
Secretary
Executive Office for Administration & Finance
State House, Room 373
Boston, MA 02133
P: (617) 727-2040
F: (617) 727-2779
E: leslie.a.kirwan@state.ma.us

MICHIGAN
Mr. Robert L. Emerson
Budget Director
Office of the State Budget
111 South Capitol
Lansing, MI 48913
P: (517) 373-7560
F: (517) 241-5428

MINNESOTA
Mr. Tom J. Hanson
Commissioner
Department of Finance
Centennial Office Building, Suite 400
658 Cedar Street
St. Paul, MN 55155
P: (651) 201-8010
F: (651) 296-7714
E: Tom.J.Hanson@state.mn.us

MISSISSIPPI
Ms. Leila Malatesta
Director
Office of Fiscal Management
P.O. Box 1060
501 North West Street, Suite 1101-B
Jackson, MS 39201
P: (601) 359-3538
F: (601) 359-3896
E: malatel@dfa.state.ms.us

Mr. J.K. Stringer Jr.
Executive Director/State Fiscal Officer
Department of Finance & Administration
P.O. Box 267
Jackson, MS 39205
P: (601) 359-3402
F: (601) 359-2405
E: stringer@dfa.state.ms.us

MISSOURI
Mr. Michael N. Keathley
Commissioner
Office of Administration
State Capitol, Room 125
Jefferson City, MO 65102
P: (573) 751-1851

MONTANA
Mr. Paul Christofferson
Administrator
Financial Services Division, Department of Administration
P.O. Box 200102
Helena, MT 59620
P: (406) 444-4609
F: (406) 444-2812
E: pachristofferson@mt.gov

Mr. David Ewer
Director
Office of Budget & Program Planning
State Capitol, Room 277
P.O. Box 200802
Helena, MT 59620
P: (406) 444-3616
F: (406) 444-4670
E: dewer@mt.gov

NEBRASKA
Mr. Carlos Castillo
Director
Department of Administrative Services
State Capitol, Suite 1315
Lincoln, NE 68509
P: (402) 471-2331
E: carlos.castillo@email.state.ne.us

NEVADA
Mr. Andrew K. Clinger
Director
Department of Administration
209 East Musser Street, Room 200
Carson City, NV 89701
P: (775) 684-0222
F: (775) 684-0260
E: aclinger@budget.state.nv.us

NEW HAMPSHIRE
Mr. Donald S. Hill
Commissioner
Department of Administrative Services
25 Capitol Street, Room 120
Concord, NH 03301
P: (603) 271-3201
F: (603) 271-6600
E: don.hill@nh.gov

NEW JERSEY
Ms. Charlene Holzbaur
Director
Office of Management & Budget
Department of Treasury
P.O. Box 221
Trenton, NJ 08625
P: (609) 292-6746
F: (609) 633-8179
E: charlene.holzbaur@treas.state.nj.us

NEW MEXICO
Ms. Katherine B. Miller
Cabinet Secretary
Department of Finance & Administration
180 Bataan Memorial Building
407 Galisteo Street
Santa Fe, NM 87501
P: (505) 827-4985
F: (505) 827-4984

NORTH CAROLINA
Mr. David McCoy
State Budget Officer
Office of State Budget & Management
116 West Jones Street
20320 Mail Service Center
Raleigh, NC 27699
P: (919) 807-4700
F: (919) 733-0640
E: david.mccoy@ncmail.net

NORTH DAKOTA
Ms. Sheila Peterson
Director
Fiscal Management Division
600 East Boulevard Avenue
Department 110
Bismarck, ND 58505
P: (701) 328-4904
F: (701) 328-3230

Ms. Pam Sharp
Director
Office of Management & Budget
600 East Boulevard, 4th Floor
Bismarck, ND 58505
P: (701) 328-4904
F: (701) 328-3230
E: psharp@nd.gov

NORTHERN MARIANA ISLANDS
Mr. Eloy S. Inos
Secretary of Finance
Department of Finance
P.O. Box 5234 CHRB
Saipan, MP 96950
P: (670) 664-1100
F: (670) 664-1115
E: eloyinos@aol.com

OHIO
Ms. J. Pari Sabety
Director
Office of Budget & Management
30 East Broad Street, 34th Floor
Columbus, OH 43215
P: (614) 466-4034
F: (614) 644-3147
E: pari.sabety@obm.state.oh.us

OKLAHOMA
Mr. Tony Hutchinson
Director
Office of State Finance
2300 North Lincoln Boulevard, Suite 122
Oklahoma City, OK 73105
P: (405) 521-2141
F: (405) 522-3902

OREGON
Mr. George Naughton
Administrator
Department of Administrative Services
155 Cottage Street, Northeast
Salem, OR 97301
P: (503) 378-3106
F: (503) 378-2322
E: george.naughton@state.or.us

PENNSYLVANIA
Mr. Michael Masch
Secretary
Office of the Budget
Office of the Governor
207 Finance Building
Harrisburg, PA 17101
P: (717) 787-9945
F: (717) 787-4523
E: mmasch@state.pa.us

Finance

PUERTO RICO
Mr. Jose Guillermo Davila
Director
Office of Budget & Management
254 Cruz Street
P.O. Box 9023228
San Juan, PR 00902
P: (787) 725-9420
F: (787) 721-8329

RHODE ISLAND
Ms. Rosemary Booth Gallogly
Executive Director/State Budget Officer
Budget Office
One Capitol Hill
Providence, RI 02908
P: (401) 222-6300
E: roseb@budget.state.ri.us

SOUTH CAROLINA
Hon. Thomas Ravenel (R)
State Treasurer
Office of the Treasurer
P.O. Box 11778
Columbia, SC 29211
P: (803) 734-2101
F: (803) 734-2690
E: treasurer@sto.sc.gov

Mr. Henry J. White
Executive Director
Office of General Services
Budget & Control
P.O. Box 12444
Columbia, SC 29211
P: (803) 734-2320
F: (803) 734-2117

Mr. Henry J. White
Executive Director
State Budget & Control Board
Budget & Control
P.O. Box 12444
Columbia, SC 29211
P: (803) 734-2320
F: (803) 734-2117

SOUTH DAKOTA
Mr. Jason Dilges
Commissioner
Bureau of Finance & Management
State Capitol
500 East Capitol Avenue
Pierre, SD 57501
P: (605) 773-3411
F: (605) 773-4711
E: jason.dilges@state.sd.us

TENNESSEE
Mr. Dave Goetz Jr.
Commissioner
Division of the Budget
State Capitol, 1st Floor
600 Charlotte Avenue
Nashville, TN 37243
P: (615) 741-2401
F: (615) 741-9872

TEXAS
Ms. Susan Combs
Comptroller of Public Accounts
Office of the Comptroller of Public Accounts
P.O. Box 13528, Capitol Station
Austin, TX 78711
P: (512) 463-4444
F: (512) 475-0450
E: scombs@cpa.state.tx.us

UTAH
Mr. John Reidhead
Director
Division of Finance
2110 State Office Building
Salt Lake City, UT 84114
P: (801) 538-3095
F: (801) 538-3244
E: jreidhead@utah.gov

VERMONT
Mr. Jim Reardon
Commissioner
Department of Finance & Management
109 State Street
Montpelier, VT 05602
P: (802) 828-2376
F: (802) 828-2428
E: jim.reardon@state.vt.us

VIRGINIA
Hon. Jody M. Wagner
Secretary of Finance
Office of the Secretary of Finance
P.O. Box 1475
Richmond, VA 23218
P: (804) 786-1148
F: (804) 692-0676
E: jody.wagner@governor.virginia.gov

WASHINGTON
Mr. Victor Moore
Director
Office of Financial Management
P.O. Box 43113
Olympia, WA 98504
P: (360) 902-0530
F: (360) 664-2832
E: victor.moore@ofm.wa.gov

WEST VIRGINIA
Mr. James Alsop
Director
Department of Revenue
P.O. Box 963
Charleston, WV 25305
P: (304) 558-0211
F: (304) 558-2324
E: ralsop@tax.state.wv.us

WISCONSIN
Mr. David Schmiedicke
State Budget Director
Division of Executive Budget & Finance
101 East Wilson Street, 10th Floor
P.O. Box 7864
Madison, WI 53707
P: (608) 266-1035
F: (608) 267-0626

WYOMING
Hon. Rita Meyer (R)
State Auditor
Office of the State Auditor
Room 114, Capitol Building
Cheyenne, WY 82002
P: (307) 777-7831
F: (307) 777-6983
E: rita.meyer@state.wy.us

Firearms

Conducts background checks for firearm purchases, issues weapon permits, regulates firearm sales, and oversees all other matters relating to the buying and selling of firearms within the state.

ALASKA
Mr. Walt Monegan
Commissioner
Department of Public Safety
5700 East Tudor Road
Anchorage, AK 99507
P: (907) 269-5086
F: (907) 269-4543

AMERICAN SAMOA
Mr. Sotoa Savali
Commissioner
Department of Public Safety
American Samoa Government
P.O. Box 3699
Pago Pago, AS 96799
P: (684) 633-1111
F: (684) 633-7296

CALIFORNIA
Mr. Randy Rossi
Chief
Bureau of Firearms
P.O. Box 820200
Sacramento, CA 94203
P: (916) 263-6275

COLORADO
Mr. Robert Cantwell
Director
Bureau of Investigation
Department of Public Safety
690 Kipling Street
Lakewood, CO 80215
P: (303) 239-4201
F: (303) 235-0568

CONNECTICUT
Mr. Philip Dukes
Chairman
Board of Firearms Permit Examiners
505 Hudson Street
Hartford, CT 06106
P: (860) 566-7078
F: (860) 566-7079
E: susan.mazzoccoli@po.state.ct.us

FLORIDA
Mr. Gerald Bailey
Commissioner
Department of Law Enforcement
P.O. Box 1489
Tallahassee, FL 32302
P: (850) 410-7001

GEORGIA
Mr. Vernon Keenan
Director
Bureau of Investigation
3121 Panthersville Road
PO Box 370808
Decatur, GA 30037
P: (404) 244-2600

ILLINOIS
Mr. Larry Trent
Director
State Police
125 East Monroe Street, Room 107
Springfield, IL 62794
P: (217) 782-7263
F: (217) 785-2821
E: larry_trent@isp.state.il.us

INDIANA
Dr. Paul Whitesell
Superintendent
State Police
100 North Senate Avenue, Room N340
Indianapolis, IN 46204
P: (317) 232-8241

KANSAS
Hon. Paul Morrison (D)
Attorney General
Office of the Attorney General
120 Southwest 10th Avenue, 2nd Floor
Topeka, KS 66612
P: (785) 296-2215
F: (785) 296-6296

Mr. Larry Welch
Director
Bureau of Investigation
1620 Southwest Tyler Street
Topeka, KS 66612
P: (785) 296-8200
F: (785) 296-6781

KENTUCKY
Mr. John Adams
Commissioner
Department of State Police
919 Versailles Road
Frankfort, KY 40601
P: (502) 695-6303
F: (502) 573-1479

LOUISIANA
Col. Henry Whitehorn
Superintendent of State Police
Department of Public Safety & Corrections
7919 Independence Boulevard
P.O. Box 66614
Baton Rouge, LA 70896
P: (225) 925-6118
F: (225) 925-3742
E: hwhitehorn@dps.state.la.us

MAINE
Col. Craig A. Poulin
Chief
State Police
36 Hospital Street
Augusta, ME 04333
P: (207) 624-7200
F: (207) 624-7042
E: craig.a.poulin@maine.gov

MASSACHUSETTS
Col. Mark F. Delaney
Superintendent
State Police
470 Worcester Road
Framingham, MA 01702
P: (508) 820-2300
F: (617) 727-6874

MINNESOTA
Mr. Michael Campion
Commissioner
Department of Public Safety
Bremer Tower, Suite 1000
445 Minnesota Street
St. Paul, MN 55101
P: (651) 201-7000
F: (651) 297-5728
E: michael.campion@state.mn.us

MONTANA
Hon. Mike McGrath (D)
Attorney General
Department of Justice
Department of Justice
P.O. Box 201401
Helena, MT 59620
P: (406) 444-2026
F: (404) 444-3549
E: contactdoj@mt.gov

NEBRASKA
Maj. Bryan Tuma
State Patrol
P.O. Box 94907
Lincoln, NE 68509
P: (402) 471-4545
F: (402) 479-4002

NEW HAMPSHIRE
Mr. John J. Barthelmes
Commissioner
Department of Safety
33 Hazen Drive
Concord, NH 03305
P: (603) 271-2791
F: (603) 271-3903
E: jbarthelmes@safety.state.nh.us

NORTH DAKOTA
Col. Bryan Klipfel
Superintendent
Highway Patrol
600 East Boulevard Avenue
Department 504
Bismarck, ND 58505
P: (701) 328-2455
F: (701) 328-1717
E: bklipfel@nd.gov

NORTHERN MARIANA ISLANDS
Mr. Pedro C. Muna
Commander
Department of Public Safety
Caller Box 10007, Capitol Hill
Saipan, MP 96950
P: (670) 664-9070
F: (670) 664-9067

OHIO
Mr. Henry Guzman
Director
Department of Public Safety
1970 West Broad Street
P.O. Box 182081
Columbus, OH 43218
P: (614) 466-3383
F: (614) 466-0433

OREGON
Mr. Dave Schmierbach
Forensics Division Director
State Police
255 Capitol Street, Northeast
Room 400
Salem, OR 97310
P: (503) 378-3720

SOUTH CAROLINA
Mr. Robert M. Stewart
Chief
State Law Enforcement Division
P.O. Box 21398
Columbia, SC 29221
P: (803) 896-7001

Firearms

U.S. VIRGIN ISLANDS
Mr. Elton Lewis
Commissioner
Police Department
Alexander Farrelly Criminal Justice Ctr.
Charlotte Amalie
St. Thomas, VI 00802
P: (340) 774-2211
F: (340) 715-5517
E: elton.lewis@us.army.mil

UTAH
Mr. Edward McConkie
Bureau Chief
Bureau of Criminal Identification
Department of Public Safety
3888 West 5400 South
Salt Lake City, UT 84118
P: (801) 965-4571
F: (801) 965-4749
E: edmcconkie@utah.gov

VIRGINIA
Col. W. Steven Flaherty
Superintendent
Department of State Police
7700 Midlothian Turnpike
P.O. Box 27472
Richmond, VA 23235
P: (804) 674-2087
F: (804) 674-2132
E: supt@vsp.virginia.gov

WISCONSIN
Mr. Gary Hamblin
Administrator
Division of Law Enforcement Services
17 West Main Street #839
P.O. Box 7857
Madison, WI 53707
P: (608) 261-7052
F: (608) 266-1656

WYOMING
Mr. Forrest Bright
Director
Division of Criminal Investigation
316 West 22nd Street
Cheyenne, WY 82002
P: (307) 777-7181
F: (307) 777-7252

Fish and Wildlife

Protects and manages fish and wildlife resources and enforces the state's fish and game laws.

Information provided by:

International Association of Fish and Wildlife Agencies
Matt Hogan
Executive Director
444 North Capitol Street NW
Suite 725
Washington, DC 20001
P: (202) 624-7890
F: (202) 624-7891
info@fishwildlife.org
www.fishwildlife.org

ALABAMA
Mr. M. N. Pugh
Director
Division of Wildlife & Freshwater Fisheries
64 North Union Street
Montgomery, AL 36130
P: (334) 242-3849
F: (334) 242-3032

ALASKA
Mr. Denby Lloyd
Acting Commissioner
Department of Fish & Game
P.O. Box 25526
Juneau, AK 99802
P: (907) 465-6141
F: (907) 465-2332

AMERICAN SAMOA
Mr. Philip Langford
Marine & Wildlife Resources Department
P.O. Box 3730
Pago Pago, AS 96799
P: (684) 633-4456
F: (684) 633-5944

ARIZONA
Mr. Duane Shroufe
Director
Game & Fish Department
2222 West Greenway Road
Phoenix, AZ 85023
P: (602) 789-3278
F: (602) 789-3299

ARKANSAS
Mr. Scott Henderson
Director
Game & Fish Commission
#2 Natural Resources Drive
Little Rock, AR 72205
P: (501) 223-6305
F: (501) 223-6448

CALIFORNIA
Mr. Ryan Broddrick
Director
Department of Fish & Game
P.O. Box 944209
Sacramento, CA 94244
P: (916) 653-7667
F: (916) 653-1856

COLORADO
Mr. Bruce McCloskey
Director
Division of Wildlife
6060 Broadway
Denver, CO 80216
P: (303) 291-7208
F: (303) 294-0874

CONNECTICUT
Mr. Edward C. Parker
Chief
Bureau of Natural Resources
Department of Environmental Protection
79 Elm Street
Hartford, CT 06106
P: (860) 424-3010
F: (860) 424-4078

DELAWARE
Mr. Patrick Emory
Director
Division of Fish & Wildlife
89 Kings Highway
Dover, DE 19901
P: (302) 739-9910
F: (302) 739-6157

DISTRICT OF COLUMBIA
Mr. M. Jon Siemien
Acting Program Manager
Fisheries & Wildlife Division
Environmental Health Administration
51 North Street, Northeast, 5th Floor
Washington, DC 20002
P: (202) 535-2273
F: (202) 535-1373

FLORIDA
Mr. Kenneth Haddad
Executive Director
Fish & Wildlife Conservation Commission
620 South Meridian Street
Tallahassee, FL 32399
P: (850) 488-2975
F: (850) 921-5786

GEORGIA
Mr. Dan Forster
Director
Wildlife Resources Division
2070 U.S. Highway 278, Southeast
Social Circle, GA 30025
P: (770) 918-6401
F: (706) 557-3030

GUAM
Mr. Mitchell P. Warner
Division of Aquatic & Wildlife Resources
Department of Agriculture
192 Dairy Road
Mangilao, GU 96923
P: (671) 735-3984
F: (671) 734-6570

HAWAII
Mr. Peter T. Young
Chair
Department of Land & Natural Resources
P.O. Box 621
Honolulu, HI 96809
P: (808) 587-0401
F: (808) 587-0390

IDAHO
Mr. Cal Groen
Director
Fish & Game Department
Box 25, 600 South Walnut
Boise, ID 83707
P: (208) 334-5159
F: (208) 334-4885

ILLINOIS
Mr. Sam Flood
Acting Director
Department of Natural Resources
One Natural Resources Way
Springfield, IL 62702
P: (217) 785-0075
F: (217) 785-9236

INDIANA
Mr. Glen Salmon
Director
Division of Fish & Wildlife
Department of Natural Resources
402 West Washington Street, Room W-273
Indianapolis, IN 46204
P: (317) 232-4091
F: (317) 232-8150

IOWA
Mr. Richard Leopold
Director
Department of Natural Resources
East 9th & Grand Avenue
Des Moines, IA 50319
P: (515) 281-5385
F: (515) 281-6794
E: richard.leopold@dnr.state.ia.us

KANSAS
Mr. Keith Sexson
Assistant Secretary, Wildlife Operations
Department of Wildlife & Parks
512 Southeast 25th Avenue
Pratt, KS 67124
P: (316) 672-5911
F: (316) 672-6020

KENTUCKY
Dr. Jonathan Gassett
Commissioner
Department of Fish & Wildlife Resources
One Sportsman's Lane
Frankfort, KY 40601
P: (502) 564-7109
F: (502) 564-6508

LOUISIANA
Mr. Bryant Hammett
Secretary
Department of Wildlife & Fisheries
P.O. Box 98000
Baton Rouge, LA 70898
P: (225) 765-2623
F: (225) 765-2607

MAINE
Mr. R. Dan Martin
Commissioner
Department of Inland Fisheries & Wildlife
284 State Street, Station #41
Augusta, ME 04333
P: (207) 287-5202
F: (207) 287-6395

Fish and Wildlife

MARYLAND
Mr. Paul Peditto
Director
Wildlife & Heritage Service
Department of Natural Resources
580 Taylor Avenue, E-1
Annapolis, MD 21401
P: (410) 260-8549
F: (410) 260-8595

MASSACHUSETTS
Mr. Wayne MacCallum
Director
Division of Fisheries & Wildlife
One Rabbit Hill Road
Westborough, MA 01581
P: (508) 389-6300
F: (508) 389-7890

MICHIGAN
Ms. Rebecca A. Humphries
Director
Department of Natural Resources
P.O. Box 30028
Lansing, MI 48909
P: (517) 373-2329
F: (517) 335-4242
E: humphrir@michigan.gov

MINNESOTA
Mr. Dave Schad
Director
Division of Fish & Wildlife
Department of Natural Resources
500 Lafayette Road
St. Paul, MN 55155
P: (651) 259-5180
F: (651) 297-7272

MISSISSIPPI
Dr. Sam Polles
Executive Director
Department of Wildlife, Fisheries & Parks
1505 Eastover Drive
Jackson, MS 39211
P: (601) 432-2001
F: (601) 432-2236

MISSOURI
Mr. John D. Hoskins
Director
Department of Conservation
P.O. Box 180
Jefferson City, MO 65102
P: (573) 522-4115
F: (573) 751-4467

MONTANA
Mr. M. Jeff Hagener
Director
Department of Fish, Wildlife & Parks
1420 East 6th Avenue
P.O. Box 200701
Helena, MT 59620
P: (406) 444-3186
F: (406) 444-4952

NEBRASKA
Mr. Rex Amack
Director
Game & Parks Commission
2200 North 33rd, Box 30370
Lincoln, NE 68510
P: (402) 471-5539
F: (402) 471-5528

NEVADA
Mr. Kenneth Mayer
Administrator
Department of Wildlife
1100 Valley Road
Reno, NV 89512
P: (775) 688-1599
F: (775) 688-1595

NEW HAMPSHIRE
Mr. Lee Perry
Executive Director
Fish & Game Department
11 Hazen Drive
Concord, NH 03301
P: (603) 271-3422
F: (603) 271-1438

NEW JERSEY
Mr. Dave Chanda
Director
Division of Fish & Wildlife
P.O. Box 400
Trenton, NJ 08625
P: (609) 292-9410
F: (609) 292-8207

NEW MEXICO
Dr. Bruce Thompson
Director
Game & Fish Department
One Wildlife Way
Santa Fe, NM 87507
P: (505) 476-8008
F: (505) 476-8124

NEW YORK
Mr. Gerry Barnhart
Director
Division of Fish, Wildlife & Marine Resources
Department of Environmental Conservation
625 Broadway, 5th Floor
Albany, NY 12233
P: (518) 402-8924
F: (518) 402-8925

NORTH CAROLINA
Mr. Richard Hamilton
Executive Director
Wildlife Resources Commission
1722 Mail Service Center
1751 Varsity Drive, Room 451
Raleigh, NC 27695
P: (919) 707-0010

NORTH DAKOTA
Mr. Terry Steinwand
Commissioner
Game & Fish Department
100 North Bismarck Expressway
Bismarck, ND 58501
P: (701) 328-6300
F: (701) 328-6352

NORTHERN MARIANA ISLANDS
Mr. Richard B. Seman
Secretary
Department of Lands & Natural Resources
P.O. Box 10007
Saipan, MP 96950
P: (670) 322-9834
F: (670) 322-2633
E: dlnrgov@vzpacifica.net

OHIO
Mr. Steven A. Gray
Chief
Division of Wildlife
2045 Morse Road, Building G
Columbus, OH 43229
P: (614) 265-6304
F: (614) 262-1143

OKLAHOMA
Mr. Greg Duffy
Director
Department of Wildlife Conservation
P.O. Box 53465
Oklahoma City, OK 73152
P: (405) 521-4660
F: (405) 521-6505

OREGON
Mr. Virgil Moore
Director
Department of Fish & Wildlife
3406 Cherry Avenue, Northeast
Salem, OR 97303
P: (503) 947-6044
F: (503) 947-6042

PENNSYLVANIA
Dr. Douglas Austen
Executive Director
Fish & Boat Commission
P.O. Box 67000
Harrisburg, PA 17106
P: (717) 705-7801
F: (717) 705-7802

Mr. Carl Roe
Executive Director
Game Commission
2001 Elmerton Avenue
Harrisburg, PA 17110
P: (717) 787-3633
F: (717) 772-0502

PUERTO RICO
Mr. Miguel A. Garcia
Director, Division of Wildlife
Department of Natural Resources
P.O. Box 9066600
San Juan, PR 00906
P: (787) 723-3090
F: (787) 724-0365

Mr. Craig G. Lilyestrom
Director, Marine Resources Division
Department of Natural Resources
PDA 3 1/2 Ave. Munoc Rivera
Puerta De Tierra Station, PO Box 9066600
San Juan, PR 00906
P: (787) 723-3090
F: (787) 724-0365

RHODE ISLAND
Mr. Michael Lapisky
Acting Chief
Division of Fish & Wildlife
4808 Tower Hill Road
Wakefield, RI 02879
P: (401) 789-3094
F: (401) 783-4460

SOUTH CAROLINA
Mr. John E. Frampton
Director
Department of Natural Resources
P.O. Box 167
Columbia, SC 29202
P: (803) 734-4007
F: (803) 734-6310
E: framptonj@dnr.sc.gov

SOUTH DAKOTA
Mr. Jeff Vonk
Secretary
Department of Game Fish & Parks
523 East Capitol Avenue
Pierre, SD 57501
P: (605) 773-3387
F: (605) 773-6245

TENNESSEE
Mr. Gary T. Myers
Executive Director
Wildlife Resources Agency
P.O. Box 40747
Nashville, TN 37204
P: (615) 781-6552
F: (615) 781-6551

TEXAS
Mr. Robert L. Cook
Executive Director
Parks & Wildlife Department
4200 Smith School Road
Austin, TX 78744
P: (512) 389-4802
F: (512) 389-4814

U.S. VIRGIN ISLANDS
Dr. Barbara Kojis
Director
Division of Fish & Wildlife
Dept. of Planning & Natural Resources
6291 Estate Nazareth 101
St. Thomas, VI 00802
P: (340) 775-6762
F: (340) 775-3972

UTAH
Mr. Jim Karpowitz
Director
Division of Wildlife Resources
1594 West North Temple, Suite 2110
P.O. Box 146301
Salt Lake City, UT 84114
P: (801) 538-4703
F: (801) 538-4709

VERMONT
Mr. Wayne Laroche
Commissioner
Department of Fish & Wildlife
103 South Main Street, 10 South
Waterbury, VT 05671
P: (802) 241-3730
F: (802) 241-3295

VIRGINIA
Mr. J. Carlton Courter III
Director
Department of Game & Inland Fisheries
4010 West Broad Street, Box 11104
Richmond, VA 23230
P: (804) 367-9231
F: (804) 367-0405
E: james.courter@vdacs.virginia.gov

WASHINGTON
Dr. Jeff Koenings
Director
Department of Fish & Wildlife
600 Capitol Way North
Olympia, WA 98501
P: (360) 902-2225
F: (360) 902-2947

WEST VIRGINIA
Mr. Curtis Taylor
Chief
Wildlife Resources Section
Division of Natural Resources
1900 Kanawha Boulevard, East
Charleston, WV 25305
P: (304) 558-2771
F: (304) 558-3147

WISCONSIN
Mr. P. Scott Hassett
Secretary
Department of Natural Resources
101 South Webster Street
Madison, WI 53703
P: (608) 266-0865
F: (608) 266-6983

WYOMING
Mr. Terry Cleveland
Director
Game & Fish Department
5400 Bishop Boulevard
Cheyenne, WY 82006
P: (307) 777-4501
F: (307) 777-4699

Gaming Officials

Head of the entity that administers and regulates state gaming laws.

ALASKA
Mr. Jeff Prather
Gaming Group Supervisor
Tax Division
Department of Revenue
P.O. Box 110420
Juneau, AK 99811
P: (907) 465-3410
F: (907) 465-2375

ARIZONA
Mr. Paul Bullis
Director
Department of Gaming
202 East Earll Drive, #200
Phoenix, AZ 85012
P: (602) 604-1801
F: (602) 255-3883

CALIFORNIA
Hon. Edmund G. Brown Jr. (D)
Attorney General
Office of the Attorney General
1300 I Street, Suite 1740
Sacramento, CA 95814
P: (916) 445-9555
F: (916) 323-5341

COLORADO
Mr. Ron Kammerzell
Director
Division of Gaming
Department of Revenue
1881 Pierce Street
Lakewood, CO 80214
P: (303) 205-1314
F: (303) 205-1342
E: ron.kammerzell@spike.dor.state.co.us

CONNECTICUT
Mr. Paul A. Young
Executive Director
Division of Special Revenue
555 Russell Road
Newington, CT 06111
P: (860) 594-0501
F: (860) 594-0696
E: paul.young@po.state.ct.us

DELAWARE
Mr. Wayne Lemons
Director
State Lottery Office
1575 McKee Road, Suite 102
Dover, DE 19904
P: (302) 739-5291
F: (302) 739-6706

FLORIDA
Ms. Holly Benson
Secretary
Department of Business & Professional Regulations
1940 North Monroe Street
Tallahassee, FL 32399
P: (850) 487-1395
F: (850) 488-1830
E: secretary@dpbr.state.fl.us

GEORGIA
Mr. Vernon Keenan
Director
Bureau of Investigation
3121 Panthersville Road
PO Box 370808
Decatur, GA 30037
P: (404) 244-2600

GUAM
Mr. Artemio B. Illagan
Acting Director
Department of Revenue & Taxation
13-1 Mariner Drive, Tiyan
P.O. Box 23607
Barrigada, GU 96921
P: (671) 475-1817
F: (671) 472-2643

ILLINOIS
Mr. Mark Ostrowski
Administrator
Gaming Board
160 North LaSalle, Suite 300
Chicago, IL 60601
P: (312) 814-4700
F: (312) 814-4602

INDIANA
Mr. Ernest Yelton
Executive Director
Gaming Commission
115 West Washington Street, Room 950S
Indianapolis, IN 46204
P: (317) 233-0046
F: (317) 233-0047

IOWA
Mr. Jack P. Ketterer
Administrator
Racing & Gaming Commission
717 East Court
Suite B
Des Moines, IA 50309
P: (515) 281-7352
F: (515) 242-6560
E: irgc@iowa.gov

KANSAS
Mr. Steve Martino
Executive Director
Racing & Gaming Commission
700 Southwest Harrison Street
Topeka, KS 66611
P: (785) 296-5800
F: (785) 296-0900

Mr. John McElroy
Executive Director
State Gaming Agency
700 Southwest Harrison Street
Topeka, KS 66603
P: (785) 368-6202
F: (785) 291-3798

Mr. Ed Van Petten
Executive Director
Kansas Lottery
128 North Kansas Avenue
Topeka, KS 66603
P: (785) 296-5700
F: (785) 296-5712

KENTUCKY
Mr. Arthur L. Gleason Jr.
President & CEO
State Lottery Board
1011 West Main Street
Louisville, KY 40202
P: (502) 560-1500
F: (502) 560-1532

Ms. Lisa Underwood
Executive Director
Horse Racing Authority
4063 Iron Works Pike, Building B
Lexington, KY 40511
P: (859) 246-2040
F: (859) 246-2039
E: lisa.underwood@ky.gov

LOUISIANA
Lt. Col. Dane Morgan
Deputy Superintendent
Bureau of Investigations
7919 Independence Boulevard
Baton Rouge, LA 70806
P: (225) 763-5756

MAINE
Ms. Anne Jordan
Commissioner
Department of Public Safety
42 State House Station
Augusta, ME 04333
P: (207) 624-9435
F: (207) 287-3842
E: dan.walters@maine.gov

MARYLAND
Ms. Alison L. Asti
Acting Executive Director
Stadium Authority
333 West Camden Street
Suite 500
Baltimore, MD 21201
P: (410) 333-1560
F: (410) 333-1888

MASSACHUSETTS
Mr. Daniel Crane
Director
Office of Consumer Affairs & Business Regulation
Ten Park Plaza, Suite 5170
Boston, MA 02116
P: (617) 973-8700
F: (617) 973-8798

MICHIGAN
Mr. Dan Gustafson
Director
Gaming Control Board
1500 Abbott Road, Suite 400
East Lansing, MI 48823
P: (517) 241-0040
F: (517) 241-0510

MINNESOTA
Mr. Clint Harris
Executive Director
State Lottery
2645 Long Lake Road
Roseville, MN 55113
P: (651) 635-8100
F: (651) 297-7496

MISSISSIPPI
Mr. Larry Gregory
Executive Director
Gaming Commission
202 East Pearl
P.O. Box 23577
Jackson, MS 39225
P: (601) 351-2800
F: (601) 351-2843
E: lgregory@mgc.state.ms.us

MISSOURI
Mr. Gene McNary
Director
Gaming Commission
3417 Knipp Dirve
Jefferson City, MO 65109
P: (573) 526-4083
F: (573) 526-1999
E: gene.mcnary
@mgc.dps.mo.gov

MONTANA
Hon. Mike McGrath (D)
Attorney General
Office of the Attorney General
Department of Justice
P.O. Box 201401
Helena, MT 59620
P: (406) 444-2026
F: (404) 444-3549
E: contactdoj@mt.gov

NEBRASKA
Mr. Doug Ewald
Tax Commissioner
Department of Revenue
P.O. Box 94818
Lincoln, NE 68509
P: (402) 471-2971
F: (402) 471-5608

NEVADA
Mr. Dennis Neilander
Chair
Gaming Control Board
1919 East College Parkway
Carson City, NV 89706
P: (775) 684-7700
F: (775) 684-5817
E: dneilander
@gcb.state.nv.us

NEW HAMPSHIRE
Mr. Rick Wisler
Executive Director
Lottery Commission
P.O. Box 1208
Concord, NH 03302
P: (603) 271-3391
F: (603) 271-1160
E: rickey.a.wisler
@lottery.nh.gov

NEW JERSEY
Ms. Yvonne G. Maher
Acting Director
Division of Gaming
Enforcement
140 East Front Street
P.O. Box 047
Trenton, NJ 08625
P: (609) 292-9394
F: (609) 633-7355

NEW MEXICO
Mr. John Monforte
Executive Director
Gaming Control Board
4900 Alameda Boulevard,
Northeast
Albuquerque, NM 87113
P: (505) 841-9700
F: (505) 841-9725

NEW YORK
Mr. Daniel Hogan
Chair
Racing & Wagering Board
Corning Tower, 41st Floor
Empire State Plaza
Albany, NY 12242
P: (518) 474-5991
F: (518) 486-9179

NORTH DAKOTA
Mr. Keith Lauer
Director
Gaming Division
Office of Attorney General
600 East Boulevard Avenue,
17th Floor
Bismarck, ND 58505
P: (701) 328-4848
F: (701) 328-3535
E: klauer@nd.gov

NORTHERN MARIANA ISLANDS
Dr. Ignacio T. Dela Cruz
Secretary
Department of Lands & Natural
Resources
Caller Box 10007, Capitol Hill
Saipan, MP 96950
P: (670) 322-9830
F: (670) 322-2633
E: dlnrgov@vzpacifica.net

OHIO
Mr. Sam Zonak
Executive Director
Racing Commission
Vern Riffe Center
77 South High Street, 18th Floor
Columbus, OH 43215
P: (614) 466-2757
F: (614) 466-1900
E: sam.zonak@rc.state.oh.us

OREGON
Capt. Bob Sundstrom
Director
Gaming Enforcement Division
255 Capitol Street, Northeast
4th Floor
Salem, OR 97310
P: (503) 378-3725 Ext. 4127
F: (503) 378-8282

PENNSYLVANIA
Mr. Thomas Decker
Chair
Gaming Control Board
P.O. Box 69060
Harrisburg, PA
P: (717) 346-8300

PUERTO RICO
Mr. Guillermo J. Cabret
Director
Gaming Division
P.O. Box 9023960
San Juan, PR 00902
P: (787) 721-2400
F: (787) 724-3009
E: logarcia@prtourism.com

SOUTH CAROLINA
Mr. John E. Frampton
Director
Department of Natural
Resources
P.O. Box 167
Columbia, SC 29202
P: (803) 734-4007
F: (803) 734-6310
E: framptonj@dnr.sc.gov

SOUTH DAKOTA
Mr. Larry Eliason
Executive Secretary
Gaming Commission
Department of Revenue &
Regulation
118 East Missouri
Pierre, SD 57501
P: (605) 773-6050
F: (605) 773-6053
E: larry.eliason
@state.sd.us

U.S. VIRGIN ISLANDS
Ms. Eileen Peterson
Chair
Casino Control Commission
#5 Orange Grove
Christiansted
St. Croix, VI 00820
P: (340) 773-3616
F: (340) 773-3136

VERMONT
Mr. Alan Yandow
Executive Director
Lottery Commission
1311 U.S. Route 302 - Berlin
P.O. Box 420
Barre, VT 05641
P: (802) 479-5686
F: (802) 479-4294

VIRGINIA
Mr. Harry Durham
Interim Director
Department of Charitable
Gaming
Monroe Building, 17th Floor
101 North 14th Street
Richmond, VA 23219
P: (804) 786-1681
F: (804) 786-1079
E: harry.durham
@dcg.virginia.gov

WASHINGTON
Mr. Rick Day
Director
Gambling Commission
P.O. Box 42400
Olympia, WA 98504
P: (360) 486-3440
F: (360) 486-3629

WEST VIRGINIA
Mr. James Alsop
Director
Department of Revenue
P.O. Box 963
Charleston, WV 25305
P: (304) 558-0211
F: (304) 558-2324
E: ralsop@tax.state.wv.us

Geographic Information Systems

Coordinates geographic information systems within state government.

ALABAMA
Mr. Nick Tew Jr.
State Geologist/Oil & Gas Supervisor
State Oil & Gas Board/Geological Survey
P.O. Box 869999
420 Hackberry Lane
Tuscaloosa, AL 35486
P: (205) 247-3679
F: (205) 349-2861
E: ntew@gsa.state.al.us

ALASKA
Mr. Richard McMahon
Section Chief
Land Records Information Section
Department of Natural Resources
550 West 7th Avenue, Suite 706
Anchorage, AK 99501
P: (907) 269-8836
F: (907) 269-8920
E: Richard_McMahon@dnr.state.ak.us

ARIZONA
Mr. Gene Trobia
State Cartographer
Geographic Information Council
State Land Department
1616 West Adams Street
Phoenix, AZ 85007
P: (602) 542-3190
F: (602) 542-2600
E: gtrobia@land.az.gov

ARKANSAS
Mr. Shelby Johnson
Geographic Information Coordinator
Geographic Information Office
124 West Capitol Avenue, Suite 200
Little Rock, AR 72201
P: (501) 682-2767
F: (501) 682-2040
E: shelby.johnson@arkansas.gov

CALIFORNIA
Mr. John Ellison
Agency Technology Officer
California Resources Agency
1416 9th Street, Suite 1311
Sacramento, CA 95814
P: (916) 653-2238
F: (916) 653-7738
E: john.ellison@resources.ca.gov

COLORADO
Mr. Jon Gottsegen
State GIS Coordinator
Department of Local Affairs
1313 Sherman Street, Room 521
Denver, CO 80203
P: (303) 866-3925
F: (303) 866-2660
E: jon.gottsegen@state.co.us

CONNECTICUT
Mr. Steve Fish
Director
Office of Information Management
Department of Environmental Protection
79 Elm Street
Hartford, CT 06106
P: (860) 424-3642
F: (860) 424-4058
E: steve.fish@po.state.ct.us

DELAWARE
Mr. Michael Mahaffie
GIS Coordinator
Office of State Planning Coordination
540 South DuPont Highway, Suite 7
Dover, DE 19901
P: (302) 739-3090
F: (302) 831-3579
E: mike.mahaffie@state.de.us

DISTRICT OF COLUMBIA
Mr. Vivek Kundra
Director
Chief Technology Office
441 4th Street, Northwest
Suite 930-S
Washington, DC 20001
P: (202) 727-2277
F: (202) 727-6857

GEORGIA
Mr. Eric McRae
Program Coordinator
Information Technology Outreach Services
Carl Vinson Institute of Government
1180 East Broad Street, Suite 2058
Athens, GA 30602
P: (706) 542-5308
F: (706) 542-6535
E: mcrae@cviog.itos.uga.edu

HAWAII
Mr. Craig Tasaka
GIS Program Manager
Department of Business, Economic Development & Tourism
Office of Planning
P.O. Box 2359
Honolulu, HI 96804
P: (808) 587-2894
F: (808) 587-2899
E: ctasaka@dbedt.hawaii.gov

IDAHO
Mr. Nathan Bentley
State GIS Coordinator
Department of Administration
650 West State, Room 100
P.O. Box 83720-0042
Boise, ID 83702
P: (208) 332-1879
F: (208) 332-1884
E: nbentley@adm.idaho.gov

ILLINOIS
Mr. Rob Krumm
Geologist/GIS Manager
State Geological Survey
615 East Peabody Drive
Champaign, IL 61820
P: (217) 333-4085
F: (217) 333-2830
E: krumm@isgs.uiuc.edu

Ms. Sheryl G. Oliver
GIS Coordinator
Department of Natural Resources
1 Natural Resources Way
Springfield, IL 62702
P: (217) 785-8586
F: (217) 782-5016
E: soliver@dnrmail.state.il.us

INDIANA
Dr. Jill Saligoe-Simmel
Executive Director
Indiana Geographic Information Council, Inc.
107 Kenwood Circle
Indianapolis, IN 46260
P: (317) 815-8455
E: jsaligoe@iupui.edu

IOWA
Mr. Brad Cutler
Golden Hills Resource Conservation & Development
712 South Highway 6
P.O. Box 189
Oakland, IA 51560
P: (712) 482-3029
F: (712) 482-5590

Mr. Alan D. Jensen
State GIS Coordinator
Geographic Information Council
Iowa State University
105 West Adams Street, Suite A
Creston, IA 50801
P: (641) 782-8426
F: (641) 782-7213
E: adjensen@iastate.edu

KANSAS
Mr. Ivan Weichert
GIS Director
Kansas Information Technology Office
Landon State Office Building
900 Southwest Jackson Street, Room 807
Topeka, KS 66612
P: (785) 296-0257
F: (785) 296-1168
E: Ivan.Weichert@da.state.ks.us

KENTUCKY
Mr. Kenny Ratliff
Director
Division of Geographic Information
403 Wapping Street, Suite 340
Frankfort, KY 40601
P: (502) 573-1450
F: (502) 573-1475
E: kennyd.ratliff@ky.gov

LOUISIANA
Mr. Joe Holmes
GIS Manager
GIS Center
Department of Environmental Quality
602 North 5th Street
Baton Rouge, LA 70802
P: (225) 219-3348
F: (225) 219-3374
E: Joe.Holmes@LA.gov

Mr. Craig Johnson
Director
Geographic Information Center
Louisiana State University
E-313 Howe Russell Building
Baton Rouge, LA 70803
P: (225) 578-3479
F: (225) 578-7289
E: cjohnson@lsu.edu

MAINE
Mr. Daniel Walters
GIS Administrator
Office of Information Technology
Office of Geographic Information Systems
145 State House Station
Augusta, ME 04333
P: (207) 624-9435
F: (207) 287-3842
E: dan.walters@maine.gov

MARYLAND
Mr. Ken Miller
Director
Watershed Information Services
Tawes State Office Building E-2
580 Taylor Avenue
Annapolis, MD 21401
P: (410) 260-8751
F: (410) 260-8759
E: kenmiller@dnr.state.md.us

MASSACHUSETTS
Mr. Christian Jacqz
Director
Massachusetts GIS
Office of Environmental Affairs
251 Causeway Street, 5th Floor
Boston, MA 02114
P: (614) 626-1057
F: (614) 626-1249
E: Christian.Jacqz@state.ma.us

MICHIGAN
Mr. Eric Swanson
Director
Center for Geographic Information
111 South Capitol Avenue, 10th Floor
Lansing, MI 48933
P: (517) 373-7916
E: swansone@michigan.gov

MINNESOTA
Mr. David Arbeit
Director
Land Management Information Center
Department of Administration
658 Cedar Street, Room 300
St. Paul, MN 55155
P: (651) 201-2460
F: (651) 296-3698
E: david.arbeit@state.mn.us

Mr. Will Craig
Associate Director
Center for Urban & Regional Affairs
University of Minnesota
301 South 19th Avenue, Suite 330
Minneapolis, MN 55455
P: (612) 625-3321
F: (612) 626-0273
E: wcraig@umn.edu

MISSISSIPPI
Mr. Claude Johnson
Director
Strategic Services Division
Information Technology Services
301 North Lamar Street, Suite 508
Jackson, MS 39201
P: (601) 359-2748
F: (601) 354-6016
E: johnson@its.state.ms.us

Mr. Jim Steil
Director
Institutions of Higher Learning
MARIS
3825 Ridgewood Road
Jackson, MS 39211
P: (601) 432-6354
F: (601) 432-6893
E: Jsteil@ihl.state.ms.us

MISSOURI
Mr. Ryan Lanclos
Chief Information Officer
Department of Agriculture
P.O. Box 630
Jefferson City, MO 65102
P: (573) 751-5518
E: ryan.lanclos@mda.mo.gov

Mr. Tony Spicci
GIS Supervisor
Resource Science Division
Department of Conservation
1110 South College Avenue
Columbia, MO 65201
P: (573) 882-9909 Ext. 3295
F: (573) 882-4517
E: Tony.Spicci@mdc.mo.gov

MONTANA
Mr. Stu Kirkpatrick
Bureau Chief
Geographic Information Services Bureau
Weinstein Building
101 North Rodney
Helena, MT 59620
P: (406) 444-9013
F: (406) 444-1255
E: skirkpatrick@mt.gov

NEBRASKA
Mr. Larry K. Zink
GIS Coordinator
GIS Steering Committee
DAS-DOC
521 South 14th Street, Suite 300
Lincoln, NE 65808
P: (402) 471-3206
F: (402) 471-3339
E: lzink@notes.state.ne.us

NEVADA
Mr. Ronald H. Hess
GIS Supervisor, Executive Secretary
State Mapping Advisory Committee
Nevada Bureau of Mines & Geology
University of Nevada-Reno, MS 178
Reno, NV 89557
P: (775) 784-6691 Ext. 121
F: (775) 784-1709
E: rhess@unr.edu

NEW HAMPSHIRE
Mr. Ken Gallager
Principal Planner
Office of Energy & Planning
57 Regional Drive
Concord, NH 03301
P: (603) 271-1773
F: (603) 271-2615
E: ken.gallager@nh.gov

NEW JERSEY
Ms. Suzy Hess
GIS Specialist
Office of GIS
200 Riverview Plaza
P.O. Box 212
Trenton, NJ 08625
P: (609) 633-8946
F: (609) 633-0200
E: suzy.hess@oit.state.nj.us

Mr. Andy Rowan
Geographic Information Officer
Office of Geographic Information Systems
Office of Information Technology
200 Riverview Plaza, P.O. Box 212
Trenton, NJ 08611
P: (609) 633-0276
F: (609) 633-0200
E: andrew.rowan@oit.state.nj.us

NEW MEXICO
Ms. Amelia M. Budge
Clearinghouse Manager
Earth Data Analysis Center
1 University of New Mexico
MSC01 1110
Albuquerque, NM 87131
P: (505) 277-3622
F: (505) 277-3614
E: abudge@edac.unm.edu

NEW YORK
Mr. Bill Johnson
Manager of GIS & Critical Infrastructure Coordination
Office of Cyber Security & Critical Infrastructure Coordination
30 South Pearl Street, Floor 11
Albany, NY 12207
P: (518) 473-5755
F: (518) 473-5848
E: william.johnson@cscic.state.ny.us

NORTH CAROLINA
Mr. Tim Johnson
Director
Center for Geographic Information & Analysis
20322 Mail Service Center
Raleigh, NC 27699
P: (919) 715-0711
F: (919) 715-0725
E: tim.r.johnson@ncmail.net

Zsolt Nagy
Program Manager
Center for Geographic Information & Analysis
301 North Wilmington Street, Suite 700
Raleigh, NC 27601
P: (919) 733-2090
F: (919) 715-0725
E: zsolt.nagy@ncmail.net

Geographic Information Systems

NORTH DAKOTA
Mr. Bob Nutsch
GIS Coordinator
Information Technology Department
600 East Boulevard Avenue
Department 112
Bismarck, ND 58505
P: (701) 328-3212
F: (701) 328-3000
E: bnutsch@nd.gov

OHIO
Mr. Stuart R. Davis
Administrator, Enterprise Shared Services
Service Delivery Division
Office of Information Technology
77 South High Street, Room 1990
Columbus, OH 43215
P: (614) 644-3923
F: (614) 728-5297
E: stu.davis@ohio.gov

OKLAHOMA
Mr. Mike Sharp
Director of IT
Conservation Commission
2800 North Lincoln Boulevard
Suite 160
Oklahoma City, OK 73105
P: (405) 521-4813
F: (405) 521-6686
E: mike.sharp@conservation.ok.gov

Ms. May Yuan
Director
Center for Spacial Analysis
100 East Boyd Street, SEC 684
Norman, OK 73019
P: (405) 325-4871
F: (405) 325-6090
E: myuan@ou.edu

OREGON
Mr. Cy Smith
Statewide GIS Coordinator
Geospatial Enterprise Office
Department of Administrative Services
1225 Ferry Street, Southeast
Salem, OR 97301
P: (503) 378-6066
F: (503) 373-1424
E: cy.smith@state.or.us

PENNSYLVANIA
Mr. Jim Knudson
Director
Bureau of Geospatial Technologies
Office for Information Technology
P.O. Box 1438
Harrisburg, PA 17105
P: (717) 705-9844
F: (717) 705-9112
E: jknudson@state.pa.us

Dr. Jay G. Parrish
Director & State Geologist
Bureau of Topographic & Geologic Survey
Dept of Conservation & Natural Resources
3240 Schoolhouse Road
Middletown, PA 17057
P: (717) 702-2053
F: (717) 702-2065
E: jayparrish@state.pa.us

SOUTH CAROLINA
Mr. Jim Scurry
Program Director
Technology Development
Department of Natural Resources
1000 Assembly Street, Suite 134
Columbia, SC 29201
P: (803) 734-9494
F: (803) 734-7001
E: scurryj@dnr.sc.gov

Ms. Lynn Shirley
GIS Manager
Department of Geography
State Mapping Advisory Committee
Callcott Building, 709 Bull Street
Columbia, SC 29208
P: (803) 777-4590
E: lynn@sc.edu

SOUTH DAKOTA
Mr. Ron Knecht
GIS Coordinator
Bureau of Information & Telecommunications
Kneip Building
700 Governors Drive
Pierre, SD 57501
P: (605) 773-4642
F: (605) 773-6040
E: ron.knecht@state.sd.us

TENNESSEE
Mr. Dennis Pedersen
Director, GIS Services
Office for Information Resources
312 8th Avenue, North, Floor 16
Nashville, TN 37243
P: (615) 253-4799
F: (615) 532-0471
E: dennis.pedersen@state.tn.us

TEXAS
Mr. Dustin Lanier
Director
Strategic Initiatives Division
300 West 15th Street, Suite 1300
P.O. Box 13564
Austin, TX 78701
P: (512) 305-9076
F: (512) 475-4759

UTAH
Mr. Dennis Goreham
Manager
Automated Geographic Reference Center
Department of Technology Services
1 State Office Building, Room 5130
Salt Lake City, UT 84114
P: (801) 538-3163
F: (801) 538-3317
E: dgoreham@utah.gov

Ms. Jeannie Watanabe
State Data Administrator
Office of Chief Information Officer
5110 State Office Building
Salt Lake City, UT 84114
P: (801) 538-9543
F: (801) 538-1547
E: jwatanabe@utah.gov

VERMONT
Mr. David Brotzman
Executive Director
Center for Geographic Information, Inc.
58 South Main Street, Suite 2
Waterbury, VT 05676
P: (802) 882-3003
F: (802) 882-3001
E: davidb@vcgi.org

VIRGINIA
Mr. Steve Marzolf
State Coordinator
Information Technologies Agency
Geographic Information Network
110 South 7th Street, Suite 135
Richmond, VA 23219
P: (804) 371-0015
F: (804) 371-2795
E: steve.marzolf@vita.virginia.go

WASHINGTON
Mr. Jeff Holm
WAGIC Coordinator
Management & Oversight of Strategic Technologies Division
Department of Information Services
P.O. Box 42445
Olympia, WA 98504
P: (360) 902-3447
F: (360) 902-2982
E: jeffh@dis.wa.gov

WEST VIRGINIA
Mr. Kurt Donaldson
Project Manager
GIS Technical Center
West Virginia University
P.O. Box 6300
Morgantown, WV 26506
P: (304) 293-5603 Ext. 4336
F: (304) 293-6522
E: kdonalds@wvu.edu

Mr. Craig A. Neidig
State GIS Coordinator
Geological & Economic Survey
1124 Smith Street, Suite LM-10
Charleston, WV 25301
P: (304) 558-4218
F: (304) 558-4963
E: cneidig@gis.state.wv.us

WISCONSIN
Mr. Ted Koch
State Cartographer
State Cartographer's Office
University of Wisconsin-Madison
550 North Park Street, Room 384
Madison, WI 53706
P: (608) 262-6852
F: (608) 262-5205
E: tkoch@wisc.edu

Mr. Jerry Sullivan
GIS Data Specialist
Division of Enterprise Technology
Department of Administration
101 East Wilson, Floor 8
Madison, WI 53707
P: (608) 264-6109
F: (608) 266-5519
E: jerry.sullivan@doa.state.wi.us

WYOMING
Mr. Jeffrey Hamerlinck
Director
WYGISC
1000 East University Avenue
Department 4008
Laramie, WY 82072
P: (307) 766-2736
F: (307) 766-2744
E: itasca@uwyo.edu

Geological Survey

Conducts research on the state's terrain, mineral resources, and possible geological hazards such as earthquakes, faults, etc.

ALABAMA
Mr. Nick Tew Jr.
State Geologist/Oil & Gas Supervisor
Geological Survey of Alabama
P.O. Box 869999
420 Hackberry Lane
Tuscaloosa, AL 35486
P: (205) 247-3679
F: (205) 349-2861
E: ntew@gsa.state.al.us

ALASKA
Mr. Robert F. Swenson
Acting Director & State Geologist
Division of Geological & Geophysical Surveys
Department of Natural Resources
3354 College Road
Fairbanks, AK 99709
P: (907) 451-5001
F: (907) 451-5223
E: robert_swenson@dnr.state.ak.us

ARIZONA
Dr. Lee Allison
Director & State Geologist
Geological Survey
416 West Congress Street, Suite 100
Tucson, AZ 85701
P: (520) 770-3500
F: (520) 770-3505
E: lee.allison@azgs.az.gov

ARKANSAS
Ms. Bekki White
State Geologist & Director
Geological Commission
Vardelle Parham Geology Center
3815 West Roosevelt Road
Little Rock, AR 72204
P: (501) 296-1877
F: (501) 663-7360
E: bekki.white@mail.state.ar.us

CALIFORNIA
Dr. John Parrish
State Geologist
Geological Survey
801 K Street, MS 12-01
Sacramento, CA 95814
P: (916) 445-1923
F: (916) 445-5718
E: john.parrish@conservation.ca.gov

COLORADO
Mr. Vincent Matthews
State Geologist
Geological Survey
1313 Sherman Street, Room 715
Denver, CO 80203
P: (303) 866-3028
F: (303) 866-2461
E: vince.matthews@state.co.us

DELAWARE
Mr. John H. Talley
State Geologist & Director
Geological Survey
University of Delaware
Newark, DE 19716
P: (302) 831-2833
F: (302) 831-3579
E: waterman@UDel.edu

FLORIDA
Mr. Walter Schmidt
Chief & State Geologist
Geological Survey
903 West Tennessee Street
Tallahassee, FL 32304
P: (850) 488-4191
F: (850) 488-8086
E: Walt.Schmidt@dep.state.fl.us

GEORGIA
Mr. William G. Smith
Program Manager
Geological Survey Branch
19 Martin Luther King Jr. Drive, SW
Room 400
Atlanta, GA 30334
P: (404) 656-3214
F: (404) 657-8379

HAWAII
Mr. Kevin L. Gooding
Acting State Geologist
Commission on Water Resource Management
P.O. Box 621, 1151 Punchbowl Street
Kalanimoku Building, Room 227
Honolulu, HI 96809
P: (808) 587-0263
F: (808) 587-0219
E: kevin.l.gooding@hawaii.gov

IDAHO
Mr. Roy M. Breckenridge
State Geologist
Geological Survey
University of Idaho, Morrill Hall Room 332
Moscow, ID 83844
P: (208) 885-7991
F: (208) 885-5826
E: roybreck@uidaho.edu

ILLINOIS
Dr. William W. Shilts
Chief
State Geological Survey
121 Natural Resources Building
615 East Peabody Drive
Champaign, IL 61820
P: (217) 333-5111
F: (217) 244-7004
E: shilts@isgs.uiuc.edu

INDIANA
Dr. John C. Steinmetz
Director & State Geologist
Geological Survey
Indiana University
611 North Walnut Grove
Bloomington, IN 47405
P: (812) 855-5067
F: (812) 855-2862
E: jsteinm@indiana.edu

IOWA
Mr. Robert L. Libra
State Geologist
Geological Survey Bureau/IDNR
Department of Natural Resources
109 Trowbridge Hall
Iowa City, IA 52242
P: (319) 335-1585
F: (319) 335-2754
E: blibra@igsb.uiowa.edu

KANSAS
Mr. William Harrison
Director & State Geologist
Geological Survey
1930 Constant Avenue, Campus West
The University of Kansas
Lawrence, KS 66047
P: (785) 864-2070
F: (785) 864-5317
E: harrison@kgs.ku.edu

KENTUCKY
Mr. James C. Cobb
State Geologist & Director
Geological Survey
228 Mining & Mineral Resources Building
University of Kentucky
Lexington, KY 40506
P: (859) 257-5500
F: (859) 257-1147
E: cobb@uky.edu

LOUISIANA
Mr. Chacko J. John
Director & State Geologist
Geological Survey
Louisiana State University
3079 Energy, Coast & Environment Bldg.
Baton Rouge, LA 70803
P: (225) 578-5320
F: (225) 578-3662
E: cjohn@lsu.edu

MAINE
Mr. Robert G. Marvinney
Director & State Geologist
Geological Survey
22 State House Station
Augusta, ME 04333
P: (207) 287-2804
F: (207) 287-2353
E: robert.g.marvinney@maine.gov

MARYLAND
Mr. Emery T. Cleaves
Director & State Geologist
Geological Survey
2300 St. Paul Street
Baltimore, MD 21218
P: (410) 554-5500
F: (410) 554-5502
E: ecleaves@dnr.state.md.us

MASSACHUSETTS
Mr. Stephen B. Mabee
State Geologist
Department of Geosciences
611 North Pleasant Street
University of Massachusetts
Amherst, MA 01003
P: (413) 545-4814
F: (413) 545-1200
E: sbmabee@geo.umass.edu

MICHIGAN
Mr. Harold R. Fitch
State Geologist
Office of Geological Survey
Box 30256
525 West Allegan
Lansing, MI 48909
P: (517) 241-1548
F: (517) 241-1601
E: fitchh@michigan.gov

MINNESOTA
Mr. Harvey Thorleifson
Professor & Director
Geological Survey
University of Minnesota
2642 University Avenue West, Room 104
St. Paul, MN 55114
P: (612) 627-4780
F: (612) 627-4778
E: thorleif@umn.edu

MISSISSIPPI
Mr. Michael Bograd
Acting State Geologist
Office of Geology
P.O. Box 20307
Jackson, MS 39289
P: (601) 961-5500
F: (601) 961-5521
E: michael_bograd@deq.state.ms.us

MISSOURI
Ms. Mimi Garstang
Director & State Geologist
Geological Survey & Resource Assessment Division
111 Fairgrounds Road
P.O. Box 250
Rolla, MO 65402
P: (573) 368-2101
F: (573) 368-2111
E: mimi.garstang@dnr.mo.gov

MONTANA
Mr. Edmond G. Deal
Director & State Geologist
Bureau of Mines & Geology
Montana Tech
1300 West Park Street
Butte, MT 59701
P: (406) 496-4167
F: (406) 496-4451
E: edeal@mtech.edu

NEBRASKA
Mr. Mark S. Kuzila
Director
Conservation & Survey Division
113 Nebraska Hall
University of Nebraska
Lincoln, NE 68588
P: (402) 472-3471
F: (402) 472-4608
E: mkuzila1@unl.edu

NEVADA
Dr. Jonathan G. Price
Director & State Geologist
Bureau of Mines & Geology
University of Nevada, Reno, MS 178
Reno, NV 89557
P: (775) 784-6691 Ext. 126
F: (775) 784-1709
E: jprice@unr.edu

NEW HAMPSHIRE
Mr. David R. Wunsch
State Geologist & Director
Geological Survey
Department of Environmental Services
29 Hazen Drive
Concord, NH 03302
P: (603) 271-6482
F: (603) 271-3305
E: dwunsch@des.state.nh.us

NEW JERSEY
Dr. Karl Muessig
State Geologist
Geological Survey
Department of Environmental Protection
P.O. Box 427
Trenton, NJ 08625
P: (609) 292-1185
F: (609) 633-1004
E: karl.muessig@dep.state.nj.us

NEW MEXICO
Dr. Peter A. Scholle
Director & State Geologist
Bureau of Geology & Mineral Resources
Institute of Mining & Technology
801 Leroy Place
Socorro, NM 87801
P: (505) 835-5294
F: (505) 835-6333
E: scholle1@nmt.edu

NEW YORK
Mr. William Kelly
State Geologist & Chief
State Geological Survey
New York State Museum
3140 Cultural Education Center
Albany, NY 12230
P: (518) 474-7559
F: (518) 486-2034
E: wkelly@mail.nysed.gov

NORTH CAROLINA
Mr. James D. Simons
Director & State Geologist
Geological Survey
Division of Land Resources
1612 Mail Service Center
Raleigh, NC 27699
P: (919) 733-3833
F: (919) 715-8801
E: jim.simons@ncmail.net

NORTH DAKOTA
Mr. Ed Murphy
Director & State Geologist
Geological Survey
600 East Boulevard Avenue
Bismarck, ND 58505
P: (701) 328-8000
F: (701) 328-8010
E: emurphy@nd.gov

OHIO
Mr. Lawrence H. Wickstrom
State Geologist & Division Chief
Division of Geological Survey
Department of Natural Resources
2045 Morse Road, Building C
Columbus, OH 43229
P: (614) 265-6598
F: (614) 644-3439
E: larry.wickstrom@dnr.state.oh.us

OKLAHOMA
Dr. Charles J. Mankin
Director
Geological Survey
100 East Boyd, Room N-131
Norman, OK 73019
P: (405) 325-3031
F: (405) 325-7069
E: cjmankin@ou.edu

OREGON
Ms. Vicki McConnell
Director & State Geologist
Department of Geology & Mineral Industries
800 Northeast Oregon Street
Suite 965
Portland, OR 97232
P: (971) 673-1550
F: (971) 673-1562
E: vicki.mcconnell@dogami.state.or.us

PENNSYLVANIA
Dr. Jay G. Parrish
Director & State Geologist
Bureau of Topographic & Geologic Survey
Dept of Conservation & Natural Resources
3240 Schoolhouse Road
Middletown, PA 17057
P: (717) 702-2053
F: (717) 702-2065
E: jayparrish@state.pa.us

PUERTO RICO
Mr. Javier Velez-Arocho
Secretary
Department of Natural & Environmental Resources
P.O. Box 366147
San Juan, PR 00936
P: (787) 767-8056
F: (787) 767-8122

RHODE ISLAND
Dr. Jon C. Boothroyd
State Geologist
Geological Survey
9 East Alumni Ave., 314 Woodward Hall
University of Rhode Island
Kingston, RI 02881
P: (401) 874-2191
F: (401) 874-2190
E: Jon_Boothroyd@uri.edu

Geological Survey

SOUTH CAROLINA
Mr. C. W. Clendenin Jr.
State Geologist & Chief
Geological Survey
5 Geology Road
Columbia, SC 29210
P: (803) 896-7708
F: (803) 896-7695
E: clendeninb@dnr.sc.gov

SOUTH DAKOTA
Mr. Derric L. Iles
State Geologist
Geological Survey Program,
Department of Environment &
Natural Resources
Akeley-Lawrence Science
Center
414 East Clark Street
Vermillion, SD 57069
P: (605) 677-5227
F: (605) 677-5895
E: derric.iles@usd.edu

TENNESSEE
Mr. Ronald P. Zurawski
State Geologist
Division of Geology
401 Church Street
L & C Tower, 13th Floor
Nashville, TN 37243
P: (615) 532-1500
F: (615) 532-1517
E: ronald.zurawski
@state.tn.us

TEXAS
Dr. Scott W. Tinker
State Geologist & Director
Bureau of Economic Geology
University of Texas At Austin
University Station, Box X
Austin, TX 78713
P: (512) 471-1534
F: (512) 471-0140
E: scott.tinker
@beg.utexas.edu

UTAH
Mr. Rick Allis
Director & State Geologist
Geological Survey
1594 West North Temple, Suite
3110
P.O. Box 146100
Salt Lake City, UT 84114
P: (801) 537-3301
F: (801) 537-3400
E: rickallis@utah.gov

VERMONT
Mr. Laurence R. Becker
State Geologist & Director
Geological Survey, Department
of Environmental Conservation
Agency of Natural Resources
103 South Main Street, Logue
Cottage
Waterbury, VT 05671
P: (802) 241-3496
F: (802) 241-3273
E: laurence.becker
@state.vt.us

VIRGINIA
Mr. Edward E. Erb
State Geologist Director
Department of Mines, Minerals
& Energy
Division of Mineral Resources
900 Natural Resources Drive,
Suite 500
Charlottesville, VA 22903
P: (434) 951-6350
F: (434) 951-6366
E: ed.erb@dmme.virginia.gov

WASHINGTON
Mr. Ron Teissere
State Geologist & Division
Manager
Division of Geology & Earth
Resources
1111 Washington Street SE,
Room 148
P.O. Box 47007
Olympia, WA 98504
P: (360) 902-1440
F: (360) 902-1785
E: ron.teissere@wadnr.gov

WEST VIRGINIA
Mr. Michael E. Hohn
Director & State Geologist
Geological & Economic Survey
1 Mont Chateau Road
Morgantown, WV 26508
P: (304) 594-2331
F: (304) 594-2575
E: hohn@geosrv.wvnet.edu

WISCONSIN
Mr. James M. Robertson
Director & State Geologist
Geological & Natural History
Survey
3817 Mineral Point Road
Madison, WI 53705
P: (608) 262-1705
F: (608) 262-8086
E: jmrober1@wisc.edu

WYOMING
Mr. Ron Surdam
Director & State Geologist
State Geological Survey
P.O. Box 1347
University Station
Laramie, WY 82073
P: (307) 766-2286
F: (307) 766-2605
E: rsurdam@uwyo.edu

Governor

Information provided by:

National Governors Association
Ray Scheppach
Executive Director
Hall of the States
444 North Capitol Street
Suite 267
Washington, DC 20001
P: (202) 624-5300
F: (202) 624-5313
www.nga.org

The Council of State Governments
Dan Sprague
Executive Director
2760 Research Park Drive
Lexington, KY 40511
P: (859) 244-8000
F: (859) 244-8001
www.csg.org

ALABAMA
Hon. Bob Riley (R)
Governor
Office of the Governor
State Capitol
600 Dexter Avenue
Montgomery, AL 36130
P: (334) 242-7100
F: (334) 353-0004

ALASKA
Hon. Sarah H. Palin (R)
Governor
Office of the Governor
State Capitol
P.O. Box 110001
Juneau, AK 99811
P: (907) 465-3500
F: (907) 465-3532

AMERICAN SAMOA
Hon. Togiola T.A. Tulafono (D)
Governor
Office of the Governor
Executive Office Building
Third Floor, Utulei
Pago Pago, AS 96799
P: (684) 633-4116
F: (684) 633-2269

ARIZONA
Hon. Janet Napolitano (D)
Governor
Office of the Governor
State Capitol
1700 West Washington Street
Phoenix, AZ 85007
P: (602) 542-4331
F: (602) 542-1381

ARKANSAS
Hon. Mike Beebe (D)
Governor
Office of the Governor
250 State Capitol Building
Little Rock, AR 72201
P: (501) 682-2345
F: (501) 682-3597

CALIFORNIA
Hon. Arnold Schwarzenegger (R)
Governor
Office of the Governor
State Capitol
Sacramento, CA 95814
P: (916) 445-2841
F: (916) 445-4633
E: governor@governor.ca.gov

COLORADO
Hon. Bill Ritter (D)
Governor
Office of the Governor
136 State Capitol
Denver, CO 80203
P: (303) 866-2471
F: (303) 866-2003

CONNECTICUT
Hon. M. Jodi Rell (R)
Governor
Office of the Governor
210 Capitol Avenue
Hartford, CT 06106
P: (800) 406-1527
E: Governor.Rell@po.state.ct.us

DELAWARE
Hon. Ruth Ann Minner (D)
Governor
Office of the Governor
Legislative Hall
Dover, DE 19902
P: (302) 577-3210

DISTRICT OF COLUMBIA
Hon. Adrian Fenty (D)
Mayor
Office of the Mayor
John A. Wilson Building
1350 Pennsylvania Avenue, Northwest
Washington, DC 20004
P: (202) 727-2980

FLORIDA
Hon. Charlie Crist (R)
Governor
Office of the Governor
The Capitol
Tallahassee, FL 32399
P: (850) 488-7146
F: (850) 487-0801
E: Charlie.Crist@myflorida.com

GEORGIA
Hon. Sonny Perdue (R)
Governor
Office of the Governor
Office of the Governor
Georgia State Capitol
Atlanta, GA 30334
P: (404) 656-1776

GUAM
Hon. Felix Perez Camacho (R)
Governor
Office of the Governor
Executive Chamber
P.O. Box 2950
Agana, GU 96932
P: (671) 472-8931
F: (671) 477-4826

HAWAII
Hon. Linda Lingle (R)
Governor
Office of the Governor
State Capitol
Executive Chambers
Honolulu, HI 96813
P: (808) 586-0034
F: (808) 586-0006

IDAHO
Hon. C.L. Butch Otter (R)
Governor
Office of the Governor
P.O. Box 83720
Boise, ID 83720
P: (208) 334-2100
F: (208) 334-2175

ILLINOIS
Hon. Rod R. Blagojevich (D)
Governor
Office of the Governor
207 State House
Springfield, IL 62706
P: (217) 782-0244
F: (217) 524-4049

INDIANA
Hon. Mitch Daniels (R)
Governor
Office of the Governor
Office of the Governor
Statehouse
Indianapolis, IN 46204
P: (317) 232-4567
F: (317) 232-3443

IOWA
Hon. Chet Culver (D)
Governor
Office of the Governor
State Capitol
Des Moines, IA 50319
P: (515) 281-5211
F: (515) 281-6611

KANSAS
Hon. Kathleen Sebelius (D)
Governor
Office of the Governor
State Capitol
300 Southwest 10th Avenue, Suite 212S
Topeka, KS 66612
P: (785) 296-3232

KENTUCKY
Hon. Ernie Fletcher (R)
Governor
Office of the Governor
700 Capitol Avenue
Suite 100
Frankfort, KY 40601
P: (502) 564-2611
F: (502) 564-2517

LOUISIANA
Hon. Kathleen Blanco (D)
Governor
Office of the Governor
P.O. Box 94004
Baton Rouge, LA 70804
P: (225) 342-0991
F: (225) 342-7099

MAINE
Hon. John Baldacci (D)
Governor
Office of the Governor
#1 State House Station
Augusta, ME 04333
P: (207) 287-3531
F: (207) 287-1034
E: governor@maine.gov

Governor

MARYLAND
Hon. Martin O'Malley (D)
Governor
Office of the Governor
State House
Office of the Governor
Annapolis, MD 21401
P: (410) 974-3901
F: (410) 974-3275

MASSACHUSETTS
Hon. Deval Patrick (D)
Governor
Office of the Governor
State House, Room 360
Boston, MA 02133
P: (617) 725-4005
F: (617) 727-9725

MICHIGAN
Hon. Jennifer Granholm (D)
Governor
Office of the Governor
P.O. Box 30013
Lansing, MI 48909
P: (517) 335-7858
F: (517) 335-6863

MINNESOTA
Hon. Tim Pawlenty (R)
Governor
Office of the Governor
130 State Capitol
75 Rev. Dr. Martin Luther King Jr. Blvd.
St. Paul, MN 55155
P: (651) 296-3391
F: (651) 296-2089
E: tim.pawlenty@state.mn.us

MISSISSIPPI
Hon. Haley Barbour (R)
Governor
Office of the Governor
P.O. Box 139
Jackson, MS 39205
P: (601) 359-3150
F: (601) 359-3741

MISSOURI
Hon. Matt Blunt (R)
Governor
Office of the Governor
State Capitol, Room 216
Jefferson City, MO 65101
P: (573) 751-3222

MONTANA
Hon. Brian Schweitzer (D)
Governor
Office of the Governor
State Capitol
Helena, MT 59620
P: (406) 444-3111
F: (406) 444-5529

NEBRASKA
Hon. Dave Heineman (R)
Governor
Office of the Governor
P.O. Box 94848
Lincoln, NE 68509
P: (402) 471-2244
F: (402) 471-6031

NEVADA
Hon. James A. Gibbons (R)
Governor
Office of the Governor
Capitol Building
101 N. Carson Street
Carson City, NV 89701
P: (775) 684-5670
F: (775) 684-5683

NEW HAMPSHIRE
Hon. John Lynch (D)
Governor
Office of the Governor
Office of the Governor
25 Capitol Street, Room 212
Concord, NH 03301
P: (603) 271-7532
F: (603) 271-7680

NEW JERSEY
Hon. Jon S. Corzine (D)
Governor
Office of the Governor
The State House
P.O. Box 001
Trenton, NJ 08625
P: (609) 292-6000

NEW MEXICO
Hon. Bill Richardson (D)
Governor
Office of the Governor
State Capitol, 4th Floor
Santa Fe, NM 87300
P: (505) 827-3000

NEW YORK
Hon. Eliot Spitzer (D)
Governor
Office of the Governor
State Capitol
Albany, NY 12224
P: (518) 474-8390

NORTH CAROLINA
Hon. Michael Easley (D)
Governor
Office of the Governor
Office of the Governor
20301 Mail Service Center
Raleigh, NC 27699
P: (919) 733-4240
F: (919) 733-2120

NORTH DAKOTA
Hon. John Hoeven (R)
Governor
Office of the Governor
600 East Boulevard Avenue
Department 101
Bismarck, ND 58505
P: (701) 328-2200
F: (701) 328-2205
E: governor@nd.gov

NORTHERN MARIANA ISLANDS
Hon. Benigno R. Fitial (C)
Governor
Office of the Governor
Caller Box 10007
Saipan, MP 96950
P: (670) 664-2280
F: (670) 664-2211

OHIO
Hon. Ted Strickland (D)
Governor
Office of the Governor
77 South High Street
Riffe Center
Columbus, OH 43215
P: (614) 466-3555
F: (614) 466-9354

OKLAHOMA
Hon. Brad Henry (D)
Governor
Office of the Governor
Capitol Building, Room 212
2300 North Lincoln Boulevard
Oklahoma City, OK 73105
P: (405) 521-2342
F: (405) 521-3353

OREGON
Hon. Ted Kulongoski (D)
Governor
Office of the Governor
State Capitol, Room 160
900 Court Street, North
Salem, OR 97301
P: (503) 378-4582
F: (503) 378-6827

PENNSYLVANIA
Hon. Edward G. Rendell (D)
Governor
Office of the Governor
225 Main Capitol Building
Harrisburg, PA 17120
P: (717) 787-2500

PUERTO RICO
Hon. Aníbal Acevedo Vilá (PDP)
Governor
Office of the Governor
La Fortaleza
P.O. Box 9020082
San Juan, PR 00902
P: (787) 721-7000

RHODE ISLAND
Hon. Donald L. Carcieri (R)
Governor
Office of the Governor
State House
Room 115
Providence, RI 02903
P: (401) 222-2080
F: (401) 222-8096

SOUTH CAROLINA
Hon. Mark Sanford (R)
Governor
Office of the Governor
P.O. Box 11829
Columbia, SC 29211
P: (803) 734-9400

SOUTH DAKOTA
Hon. Mike Rounds (R)
Governor
Office of the Governor
500 East Capitol Avenue
Pierre, SD 57501
P: (605) 773-3212
F: (605) 773-5844

TENNESSEE
Hon. Phil Bredesen (D)
Governor
Office of the Governor
State Capitol
Nashville, TN 37243
P: (615) 741-2001
F: (615) 532-9711
E: phil.bredesen@state.tn.us

TEXAS
Hon. Rick Perry (R)
Governor
Office of the Governor
P.O. Box 12428
Austin, TX 78711
P: (512) 463-2000
F: (512) 463-1849

U.S. VIRGIN ISLANDS
Hon. John De Jongh (D)
Governor
Office of the Governor
Government House, 21-22
Kongens Gade, Charlotte Amalie
St. Thomas, VI 00802
P: (340) 774-0001
F: (340) 774-1361

UTAH
Hon. Jon Huntsman Jr. (R)
Governor
Office of the Governor
East Office Building, Suite E220
P.O. Box 142220
Salt Lake City, UT 84114
P: (801) 538-1000
F: (801) 538-1528

VERMONT
Hon. James H. Douglas (R)
Governor
Office of the Governor
109 State Street
Pavilion Office Building
Montpelier, VT 05609
P: (802) 828-3333
F: (802) 828-3339

VIRGINIA
Hon. Timothy M. Kaine (D)
Governor
Office of the Governor
Patrick Henry Building, 3rd
Floor
1111 East Broad Street
Richmond, VA 23219
P: (804) 786-2211
F: (804) 371-6351

WASHINGTON
Hon. Christine Gregoire (D)
Governor
Office of the Governor
Office of the Governor
P.O. Box 40002
Olympia, WA 98504
P: (360) 902-4111
F: (360) 753-4110

WEST VIRGINIA
Hon. Joe Manchin III (D)
Governor
Office of the Governor
1900 Kanawha Street
Charleston, WV 25305
P: (304) 558-2000
E: governor@wvgov.org

WISCONSIN
Hon. Jim Doyle (D)
Governor
Office of the Governor
115 East State Capitol
Madison, WI 53707
P: (608) 266-1212

WYOMING
Hon. Dave Freudenthal (D)
Governor
Office of the Governor
State Capitol Building, Room
124
Cheyenne, WY 82002
P: (307) 777-7434
F: (307) 632-3909
E: governor@state.wy.us

Governor's Chief of Staff

Manages the office of the governor and assists in all duties performed by the governor.

Information provided by:

National Governors Association
Ray Scheppach
Executive Director
Hall of the States
444 North Capitol Street
Suite 267
Washington, DC 20001
P: (202) 624-5300
F: (202) 624-5313
www.nga.org

ALABAMA
Mr. Dave Stewart
Chief of Staff
Office of the Governor
State Capitol
600 Dexter Avenue
Montgomery, AL 36130
P: (334) 242-7100
F: (334) 242-0937

ALASKA
Mr. Mike Tibbles
Chief of Staff
Office of the Governor
State Capitol
P.O. Box 110001
Juneau, AK 99811
P: (907) 465-3500
F: (907) 465-3532

AMERICAN SAMOA
Mr. Pati Faiai
Chief of Staff
Office of the Governor
Executive Office Building
Pago Pago, AS 96799
P: (684) 633-4116
F: (684) 633-2269

ARIZONA
Mr. Dennis Burke
Chief of Staff for Policy
Office of the Governor
1700 West Washington
Phoenix, AZ 85007
P: (602) 542-4331
F: (602) 542-7601

Mr. Alan Stephens
Chief of Staff for Operations
Office of the Governor
1700 West Washington
Phoenix, AZ 85007
P: (602) 542-4331
F: (602) 542-7601

ARKANSAS
Mr. Morril Harriman
Chief of Staff
Office of the Governor
State Capitol, Room 250
Little Rock, AR 72201
P: (501) 682-2345
F: (501) 682-1382

CALIFORNIA
Ms. Susan Kennedy
Chief of Staff
Office of the Governor
State Capitol
Sacramento, CA 95814
P: (916) 445-2841
F: (916) 445-4633

COLORADO
Mr. Jim Carpenter
Chief of Staff
Office of the Governor
136 State Capitol
Denver, CO 80203
P: (303) 866-2471
F: (303) 866-2003

CONNECTICUT
Ms. M. Lisa Moody
Chief of Staff
Office of the Governor
210 Capitol Avenue
Hartford, CT 06106
P: (800) 406-1527
F: (860) 524-7395

DELAWARE
Mr. Mark T. Brainard
Chief of Staff
Office of the Governor
Tatnall Building
William Penn Street
Dover, DE 19901
P: (302) 744-4101
F: (302) 739-2775

FLORIDA
Mr. George Lemieux
Chief of Staff
Office of the Governor
The Capitol
Tallahassee, FL 32399
P: (850) 488-2272
F: (850) 922-4292

GEORGIA
Mr. Ed Holcombe
Chief of Staff
Office of the Governor
142 State Capitol
Atlanta, GA 30334
P: (404) 656-1776
F: (404) 656-5947

GUAM
Mr. J. George Bamba
Chief of Staff
Office of the Governor
Executive Chamber, P.O. Box 2950
Hagatna, GU 96932
P: (671) 472-8931
F: (671) 477-4826

HAWAII
Mr. Robert Awana
Chief of Staff
Office of the Governor
State Capitol
Executive Chambers
Honolulu, HI 96813
P: (808) 586-0034
F: (808) 586-0006

IDAHO
Mr. Jeff Malmen
Chief of Staff
Office of the Governor
P.O. Box 83720
Boise, ID 83720
P: (208) 334-2100
F: (208) 334-2175

ILLINOIS
Mr. John Harris
Chief of Staff
Office of the Governor
State Capitol
207 Statehouse
Springfield, IL 62706
P: (217) 782-6830
F: (217) 524-4049

INDIANA
Mr. Earl Goode
Chief of Staff
Office of the Governor
State House
Indianapolis, IN 46204
P: (317) 232-4567
F: (317) 232-3443

IOWA
Mr. Patrick Dillon
Chief of Staff
Office of the Governor
State Capitol
Des Moines, IA 50319
P: (515) 281-5211
F: (515) 281-6611

KANSAS
Mr. Troy Findley
Chief of Staff
Office of the Governor
State Capitol, 2nd Floor
Topeka, KS 66612
P: (785) 296-3232
F: (785) 296-7973

KENTUCKY
Mr. Stan Cave
Chief of Staff
Office of the Governor
The Capitol Building
700 Capital Avenue, Suite 100
Frankfort, KY 40601
P: (502) 564-2611
F: (502) 564-0437

LOUISIANA
Mr. Jimmy Clarke
Chief of Staff
Office of the Governor
P.O. Box 94004
Baton Rouge, LA 70804
P: (225) 342-7015
F: (225) 342-7099

MAINE
Ms. Jane Lincoln
Chief of Staff
Office of the Governor
Office of the Governor
1 State House Station
Augusta, ME 04333
P: (207) 287-3531
F: (207) 287-1034

MARYLAND
Mr. Michael Enright
Chief of Staff
Office of the Governor
State House
100 State Circle
Annapolis, MD 21401
P: (410) 974-3901
F: (410) 974-3275

MASSACHUSETTS
Mr. Doug Rubin
Chief of Staff
Office of the Governor
State House, Room 360
Boston, MA 02133
P: (617) 725-4000
F: (617) 727-9725

MICHIGAN
Ms. Mary A. Lannoye
Chief of Staff
Office of the Governor
P.O. Box 30013
Lansing, MI 48909
P: (517) 373-3400
F: (517) 335-6863

MINNESOTA
Mr. Matt Kramer
Chief of Staff
Office of the Governor
130 State Capitol
75 Martin Luther King Jr. Boulevard
St. Paul, MN 55155
P: (651) 296-3391
F: (651) 296-2089

MISSISSIPPI
Mr. Charlie Williams
Chief of Staff
Office of the Governor
P.O. Box 139
Jackson, MS 39205
P: (601) 359-3150
F: (601) 359-3741

MISSOURI
Mr. Ed Martin
Chief of Staff
Office of the Governor
Missouri Capitol Building, Room 216
Jefferson City, MO 65101
P: (573) 751-3222
F: (573) 526-3291

MONTANA
Mr. Bruce Nelson
Chief of Staff
Office of the Governor
P.O. Box 200801
State Capitol
Helena, MT 59620
P: (406) 444-3111
F: (406) 444-5529

NEBRASKA
Mr. Larry Bare
Chief of Staff
Office of the Governor
P.O. Box 94848
Lincoln, NE 68509
P: (402) 471-2244
F: (402) 471-6031

NEVADA
Mr. Michael Dayton
Chief of Staff
Office of the Governor
State Capitol
101 North Carson Street
Carson City, NV 89701
P: (775) 684-5670
F: (775) 684-5683

NEW HAMPSHIRE
Mr. Rich Sigel
Chief of Staff
Office of the Governor
State House, Room 208
107 North Main Street
Concord, NH 03301
P: (603) 271-2121
F: (603) 271-7680

NEW JERSEY
Mr. Thomas Shea
Chief of Staff
Office of the Governor
125 West State Street
P.O. Box 001
Trenton, NJ 08625
P: (609) 292-6000
F: (609) 777-2922

NEW MEXICO
Mr. James Jimenez
Chief of Staff
Office of the Governor
State Capitol, Fourth Floor
Santa Fe, NM 87501
P: (505) 476-2200
F: (505) 476-2226

NEW YORK
Mr. Rich Baum
Secretary To the Governor
Office of the Governor
State Capitol
Albany, NY 12224
P: (518) 474-7516

NORTH DAKOTA
Mr. William Goetz
Chief of Staff
Office of the Governor
State Capitol
600 East Boulevard Avenue, Dept. 101
Bismarck, ND 58505
P: (701) 328-2200
F: (701) 328-2205

NORTHERN MARIANA ISLANDS
Ms. Esther Fleming
Special Assistant for Administration
Office of the Governor
Caller Box 10007, Capitol Hill
Saipan, MP 96950
P: (670) 664-2280
F: (670) 664-2211

OHIO
Mr. John Haseley
Chief of Staff
Office of the Governor
77 South High Street, 30th Floor
Columbus, OH 43215
P: (614) 466-3555
F: (614) 466-9354

OKLAHOMA
Mr. Gerald Adams
Chief of Staff
Office of the Governor
State Capitol Building
2300 Lincoln Boulevard, Suite 212
Oklahoma City, OK 73105
P: (405) 521-2342
F: (405) 521-3353

OREGON
Mr. Chip Terhune
Chief of Staff
Office of the Governor
900 Court Street, Northeast, Room 254
Salem, OR 97301
P: (503) 378-3111
F: (503) 378-8970

PENNSYLVANIA
Mr. John H. Estey
Chief of Staff
Office of the Governor
Room 225, Main Capitol Building
Harrisburg, PA 17120
P: (717) 787-2500
F: (717) 772-8284

PUERTO RICO
Mr. Jorge Silva Puras
Chief of Staff
Office of the Governor
La Fortaleza
P.O. Box 9020082
San Juan, PR 00902
P: (787) 721-7000
F: (787) 721-5072

RHODE ISLAND
Mr. Brian Stern
Chief of Staff
Office of the Governor
State House
Providence, RI 02903
P: (401) 222-2080
F: (401) 222-5729

SOUTH CAROLINA
Mr. Tom Davis
Chief of Staff
Office of the Governor
P.O. Box 12267
Columbia, SC 29211
P: (803) 734-2100
F: (803) 734-5167

SOUTH DAKOTA
Mr. Rob Skjonsberg
Chief of Staff
Office of the Governor
500 East Capitol Avenue
Pierre, SD 57501
P: (605) 773-3212
F: (605) 773-5844

TENNESSEE
Mr. Stuart Brunson
Deputy To the Governor
Office of the Governor
State Capitol
Nashville, TN 37243
P: (615) 741-2001
F: (615) 532-9711

TEXAS
Ms. Deirdre Delisi
Chief of Staff
Office of the Governor
P.O. Box 12428
Austin, TX 78711
P: (512) 463-2000
F: (512) 463-5571

U.S. VIRGIN ISLANDS
Mr. Louis Penn
Chief of Staff
Office of the Governor
Government House, 21-22 Kongens Gade
Charlotte Amalie
St. Thomas, VI 00802
P: (340) 774-0001
F: (340) 693-4374

UTAH
Mr. Neil Ashdown
Chief of Staff
Office of the Governor
East Office Building, Suite E-220
Salt Lake City, UT 84114
P: (801) 538-1000
F: (801) 538-1528

Governor's Chief of Staff

VERMONT
Mr. Tim Hayward
Chief of Staff
Office of the Governor
109 State Street
Montpelier, VT 05609
P: (802) 828-3333
F: (802) 828-3339

VIRGINIA
Mr. William H. Leighty
Chief of Staff
Office of the Governor
Patrick Henry Building
1111 East Broad Street, 3rd Floor
Richmond, VA 23219
P: (804) 786-2211
F: (804) 371-6353

WASHINGTON
Mr. Thomas Fitzsimmons
Chief of Staff
Office of the Governor
P.O. Box 40002
Olympia, WA 98504
P: (360) 902-4111
F: (360) 753-4110

WEST VIRGINIA
Mr. Larry Puccio
Chief of Staff
Office of the Governor
State Capitol Complex
Charleston, WV 25305
P: (304) 558-2000
F: (304) 342-7025

WISCONSIN
Ms. Susan Goodwin
Chief of Staff
Office of the Governor
115 East State Capitol
P.O. Box 7863
Madison, WI 53707
P: (608) 266-1212
F: (608) 267-8983

WYOMING
Mr. Christopher Boswell
Chief of Staff
Office of the Governor
State Capitol Building
Room 124
Cheyenne, WY 82002
P: (307) 777-7434
F: (307) 632-3909

Governor's Legislative Director

Oversees the governor's legislative priorities, aids in legislative administration, and assists the governor in all other legislative matters.

Information provided by:

National Governors Association
Ray Scheppach
Executive Director
Hall of the States
444 North Capitol Street
Suite 267
Washington, DC 20001
P: (202) 624-5300
F: (202) 624-5313
www.nga.org

ALABAMA
Robin Stone
State-Legislative Relations
Office of the Governor
State Capitol
600 Dexter Avenue
Montgomery, AL 36130
P: (334) 242-7100
F: (334) 242-0937

ALASKA
Mr. John Bitney
Director of Legislative Affairs
State-Legislative Relations
State Capitol
P.O. Box 110001
Juneau, AK 99811
P: (907) 465-3500
F: (907) 465-3532

AMERICAN SAMOA
Tuiefano M. Vaela'a
Legislative Liaison
State-Legislative Relations
Office of the Governor
Executive Office Building
Pago Pago, AS 96799
P: (684) 633-4116
F: (684) 633-2269

ARIZONA
Mr. Mike Haener
State-Legislative Relations
Office of the Governor
1700 West Washington
Phoenix, AZ 85007
P: (602) 542-4331
F: (602) 542-7601

CALIFORNIA
Chris Kahn
Legislative Affairs Secretary
State-Legislative Relations
Office of the Governor
State Capitol
Sacramento, CA 95814
P: (916) 445-2841
F: (916) 445-4633

COLORADO
Ms. Mary Kay Hogan
Legislative Director
State-Legislative Relations
Office of the Governor
136 State Capitol
Denver, CO 80203
P: (303) 866-2471
F: (303) 866-2003

DELAWARE
Mr. Joseph Schoell
Legal Counsel To the Governor
Office of the Governor
Tatnall Building
William Penn Street
Dover, DE 19901
P: (302) 744-4101
F: (302) 739-2775

FLORIDA
Mr. Towson Fraser
Legislative Affairs Director
State-Federal Relations
Office of the Governor
The Capitol
Tallahassee, FL 32399
P: (850) 488-2272
F: (850) 922-4292

GEORGIA
Mr. Chad Holland
State-Legislative Relations
Office of the Governor
142 State Capitol
Atlanta, GA 30334
P: (404) 656-1776
F: (404) 656-5947

GUAM
Mr. J. George Bamba
Chief of Staff
State-Legislative Relations
Executive Chamber, P.O. Box 2950
Hagatna, GU 96932
P: (671) 472-8931
F: (671) 477-4826

HAWAII
Ms. Linda Smith
Senior Advisor - Policy
State-Legislative Relations
Office of the Governor
State Capitol, Executive Chambers
Honolulu, HI 96813
P: (808) 586-0034
F: (808) 586-0006

IDAHO
Mr. Bob Wells
State-Legislative Relations
Office of the Governor
P.O. Box 83720
Boise, ID 83720
P: (208) 334-2100
F: (208) 334-2175

ILLINOIS
Mr. Joe Handley
Director of Legislative Affairs
State-Legislative Relations
Office of the Governor
State Capitol, 207 Statehouse
Springfield, IL 62706
P: (217) 782-6830
F: (217) 524-4049

INDIANA
Mr. John Okeson
State-Legislative Relations
Office of the Governor
State House
Indianapolis, IN 46204
P: (317) 323-4567
F: (317) 232-3443

KANSAS
Mr. Jeremy Anderson
Director of Government Affairs
State-Legislative Relations
Office of the Governor
State Capitol, 2nd Floor
Topeka, KS 66612
P: (785) 296-3232
F: (785) 296-7973

KENTUCKY
Stacy Bassett
Legislative Liaison
Office of the Governor
The Capitol Building
700 Capital Avenue, Suite 100
Frankfort, KY 40601
P: (502) 564-2611
F: (502) 564-0437

LOUISIANA
Maj. Gen. Hunt Downer (D)
Legislative Director
State-Legislative Relations
Office of the Governor
P.O. Box 94004
Baton Rouge, LA 70804
P: (225) 342-7015
F: (225) 342-7099

MAINE
Ms. Jane Lincoln
Chief of Staff
State-Legislative Relations
Office of the Governor
1 State House Station
Augusta, ME 04333
P: (207) 287-3531
F: (207) 287-1034

MARYLAND
Mr. Joe Bryce
Legislative & Policy Director
State-Legislative Relations
Office of the Governor
State House, 100 State Circle
Annapolis, MD 21401
P: (410) 974-3901
F: (410) 974-3275

MICHIGAN
Mr. Tim Hughes
Director of Legislative Affairs
State-Legislative Relations
Office of the Governor
P.O. Box 30013
Lansing, MI 48909
P: (517) 373-3400
F: (517) 335-6863

MINNESOTA
Rima Kawas
State-Legislative Relations
Office of the Governor
130 State Capitol
75 Rev. Dr. Martin Luther King Jr. Blvd.
St. Paul, MN 55155
P: (651) 296-3391
F: (651) 296-2089

MISSISSIPPI
Mr. Neely Carlton
Legislative Affairs & Counselor
State-Legislative Relations
Office of the Governor
P.O. Box 139
Jackson, MS 39205
P: (601) 359-3150
F: (601) 359-3741

Governor's Legislative Director

Mr. Andrew Ketchings
State-Legislative Relations
Office of the Governor
Office of the Governor
P.O. Box 139
Jackson, MS 39205
P: (601) 359-3150
F: (601) 359-3741

MISSOURI
Mr. Todd Smith
Legislative Director
State-Legislative Relations
Office of the Governor
Capitol Building, Room 216
Jefferson City, MO 65101
P: (573) 751-3222
F: (573) 526-3291
E: Todd.Smith@senate.mo.gov

NEVADA
Mr. Steve Robinson
Deputy Chief of Staff/Legislative Director
State-Legislative Relations
Office of the Governor
State Capitol, 101 North Carson Street
Carson City, NV 89701
P: (775) 684-5670
F: (775) 684-5683

NEW MEXICO
Mr. Eric Witt
Director of Legislative & Political Affairs
State-Legislative Relations
Office of the Governor
State Capitol, Fourth Floor
Santa Fe, NM 87501
P: (505) 476-2200
F: (505) 476-2226

NORTH CAROLINA
Mr. Franklin Freeman
Senior Assistant for Governmental Affairs
State-Legislative Relations
Office of the Governor
20301 Mail Service Center
Raleigh, NC 27699
P: (919) 733-5811
F: (919) 733-2120

Ms. Susan Rabon
Special Assistant for Administration
State-Legislative Relations
Office of the Governor
20301 Mail Service Center
Raleigh, NC 27699
P: (919) 733-5811
F: (919) 733-2120

NORTH DAKOTA
Mr. William Goetz
Chief of Staff
State-Legislative Relations
State Capitol
600 East Boulevard Avenue, Dept. 101
Bismarck, ND 58505
P: (701) 328-2200
F: (701) 328-2205

Mr. Don Larson
State-Legislative Relations
Office of the Governor
State Capitol
600 East Boulevard Avenue, Dept. 101
Bismarck, ND 58505
P: (701) 328-2200
F: (701) 328-2205

NORTHERN MARIANA ISLANDS
Mr. Ramon Mafnas
Policy Director
State-Legislative Relations
Office of the Governor
Caller Box 10007, Capitol Hill
Saipan, MP 96950
P: (670) 664-2280
F: (670) 664-2211

OHIO
Mr. Kent Markus
Chief Legal Counsel
State-Legislative Relations
Office of the Governor
77 South High Street, 30th Floor
Columbus, OH 43215
P: (614) 466-3555
F: (614) 466-9354

OKLAHOMA
Ms. Kristi Ice
Director of Policy & Legislative Liaison
State-Legislative Relations
State Capitol Building
2300 Lincoln Boulevard, Suite 212
Oklahoma, OK 73105
P: (405) 521-2342
F: (405) 521-3353

OREGON
Ms. Teresa Miller
Legislative Director
State-Legislative Relations
Office of the Governor
900 Court Street, Northeast, Room 254
Salem, OR 97301
P: (503) 378-3111
F: (503) 378-8970

PENNSYLVANIA
Mr. Steve Crawford
Secretary, Office of Legislative Affairs
State-Legislative Relations
Office of the Governor
Room 225, Main Capitol Building
Harrisburg, PA 17120
P: (717) 787-2500
F: (717) 772-8284

PUERTO RICO
Mr. Jose L. Galarza-Garcia
Advisor To the Governor on Legislative Affairs
State-Legislative Relations
Office of the Governor
La Fortaleza, P.O. Box 9020082
San Juan, PR 00902
P: (787) 721-7000
F: (787) 721-5072

RHODE ISLAND
Mr. Mike Cronan
Director of Legislative Relations
State-Legislative Relations
Office of the Governor
State House
Providence, RI 02903
P: (401) 222-2080
F: (401) 273-5729

SOUTH CAROLINA
Mr. Tom Davis
Chief of Staff
State-Legislative Relations
P.O. Box 12267
Columbia, SC 29211
P: (803) 734-2100
F: (803) 734-5167

SOUTH DAKOTA
Mr. Jim Soyer
State-Legislative Relations
Office of the Governor
500 East Capitol Avenue
Pierre, SD 57501
P: (605) 773-3212
F: (605) 773-5844

TENNESSEE
Mr. Robert Gowan
Senior Advisor for Legislation/Policy
State-Legislative Relations
Office of the Governor
State Capitol
Nashville, TN 37243
P: (615) 741-2001
F: (615) 532-9711

TEXAS
Mr. Dan Shelley
Director of Legislative Affairs
State-Legislative Relations
Office of the Governor
P.O. Box 12428
Austin, TX 78711
P: (512) 463-2000
F: (512) 463-5571

UTAH
Mr. Michael Mower
Legislative Liaison/Constituent Affairs
State-Legislative Relations
Office of the Governor
East Office Building, Suite E-220
Salt Lake City, UT 84114
P: (801) 538-1000
F: (801) 538-1528

VERMONT
Ms. Betsy Bishop
Deputy Chief of Staff
State-Legislative Relations
Office of the Governor
109 State Street
Montpelier, VT 05609
P: (802) 828-3333
F: (802) 828-3339

VIRGINIA
Mr. William H. Murray
State-Legislative Relations
Office of the Governor
Patrick Henry Building
1111 East Broad Street, 3rd Floor
Richmond, VA 23219
P: (804) 786-2211
F: (804) 786-6351

WASHINGTON
Mr. Marty Brown
Director of Legislative Affairs
State-Legislative Relations
Office of the Governor
P.O. Box 40002
Olympia, WA 98504
P: (360) 902-4111
F: (360) 753-4110

WEST VIRGINIA
Mr. Jim Pitrolo
Legislative Director
State-Legislative Relations
Office of the Governor
1900 Kanawha Boulevard, East
Charleston, WV 25305
P: (304) 558-2000
F: (304) 342-7025

WISCONSIN
Mr. Ron Hermes
Legislative Director
Office of the Governor
115 East State Capitol, P.O. Box 7863
Madison, WI 53707
P: (608) 266-1212
F: (608) 267-8983

Governor's Media Contacts

Issues press releases on behalf of the governor, acts as a liaison with the media and public, and serves as the governor's spokesperson.

Information provided by:

National Governors Association
Ray Scheppach
Executive Director
Hall of the States
444 North Capitol Street
Suite 267
Washington, DC 20001
P: (202) 624-5300
F: (202) 624-5313
www.nga.org

ALABAMA
Mr. Jeff Emerson
Communications Director
Office of the Governor
State Capitol
600 Dexter Avenue
Montgomery, AL 36130
P: (334) 242-7150
F: (334) 242-0937

ALASKA
Ms. Meghan Stapleton
Press Secretary &
Communications Director
Office of the Governor
State Capitol
P.O. Box 110001
Juneau, AK 99811
P: (907) 465-4031

AMERICAN SAMOA
Mr. Stan Sorenson
Press Officer
Office of the Governor
Executive Office Building
Third Floor
Pago Pago, AS 96799
P: (684) 633-4116
F: (684) 633-2269

ARIZONA
Ms. Jeanine L'Ecuyer
Director of Communications
Office of the Governor
1700 West Washington
Phoenix, AZ 85007
P: (602) 542-4331
F: (602) 542-7601

ARKANSAS
Mr. Zac Wright
Director of Communications
Office of the Governor
State Capitol, Room 250
Little Rock, AR 72201
P: (501) 993-6354

CALIFORNIA
Mr. Adam Mendelsohn
Communications Director
Office of the Governor
State Capitol, First Floor
Sacramento, CA 95814
P: (916) 445-4571
F: (916) 445-4633

COLORADO
Mr. Evan Dreyer
Director of Communications
Office of the Governor
State Capitol, Room 127
Denver, CO 80203
P: (303) 866-2471

CONNECTICUT
Mr. Chris Cooper
Communications Director
Office of the Governor
State Capitol
210 Capitol Avenue
Hartford, CT 06106
P: (860) 524-7313
F: (860) 524-7395

DELAWARE
Ms. Kate Bailey
Communications Director
Office of the Governor
Tatnall Building
William Penn Street
Dover, DE 19901
P: (302) 577-8229
F: (302) 739-2775

FLORIDA
Ms. Vivian Myretus
Director of Communications
Office of the Governor
State Capitol, Room 206
Tallahassee, FL 32399
P: (850) 488-5394

GEORGIA
Mr. Dan McLagan
Communications Director
Office of the Governor
State Capitol, Room 100
Atlanta, GA 30334
P: (404) 656-1776
F: (404) 656-5947

GUAM
Ms. Erica Perez
Director of Communications &
Press Secretary
Office of the Governor
Executive Chamber
P.O. Box 2950
Hagatna, GU 96932
P: (671) 472-8931
F: (671) 477-4826

HAWAII
Mr. Lenny Klompus
Senior Advisor -
Communications
Office of the Governor
State Capitol
415 South Beretania Street
Honolulu, HI 96813
P: (808) 586-0034
F: (808) 586-0006

IDAHO
Mr. Mark Warbis
Communications Director
Office of the Governor
State Capitol
700 West Jefferson, 2nd Floor
Boise, ID 83720
P: (208) 334-2100

ILLINOIS
Ms. Abby Ottenhoff
Director of Communications
Office of the Governor
James R. Thompson Center
100 West Randolph, Suite
16-100
Chicago, IL 60601
P: (312) 814-3158

INDIANA
Ms. Jane Jankowski
Press Secretary & Interim
Communications Director
Office of the Governor
206 State House
Indianapolis, IN 46204
P: (317) 232-6122
F: (317) 232-3443

IOWA
Mr. Brad Anderson
Communications Director
Office of the Governor
State Capitol
Des Moines, IA 50319
P: (515) 281-5211

KANSAS
Ms. Nicole Corcoran
Director of Communications
Office of the Governor
State Capitol, 2nd Floor
Topeka, KS 66612
P: (785) 368-8500
F: (785) 296-7973

KENTUCKY
Mr. Brett Hall
Director of Communications &
Planning
Office of the Governor
State Capitol
700 Capital Avenue, Suite 100
Frankfort, KY 40601
P: (502) 564-2611
F: (502) 564-0437

LOUISIANA
Ms. Marie Centanni
Press Secretary
Office of the Governor
P.O. Box 94004
Baton Rouge, LA 70804
P: (225) 342-9037

MAINE
Mr. David Farmer
Communications Director
Office of the Governor
State House, Station 1
Augusta, ME 04333
P: (207) 287-3138
F: (207) 287-1034

MARYLAND
Mr. Steve Kearney
Director of Communications
Office of the Governor
State House
Annapolis, MD 21401
P: (410) 974-2316

MASSACHUSETTS
Mr. Kyle Sullivan
Press Secretary
Office of the Governor
State House, Room 265
Boston, MA 02133
P: (617) 725-4000

MICHIGAN
Ms. Genna Beaudoin Gent
Communications Director
Office of the Governor
P.O. Box 30013
Lansing, MI 48909
P: (517) 335-6397
F: (517) 335-6949

MINNESOTA
Mr. Brian McClung
Press Secretary
Office of the Governor
State Capitol, Room 130
75 Rev. Dr. Martin Luther King Jr. Blvd.
St. Paul, MN 55155
P: (651) 296-0061
F: (651) 296-2089

MISSISSIPPI
Mr. Buddy Bynum
Director of Communications
Office of the Governor
P.O. Box 139
Jackson, MS 39205
P: (601) 359-3150
F: (601) 359-3741

MISSOURI
Mr. Rich Chrismer
Deputy Chief of Staff for Communications
Office of the Governor
State Capitol
P.O. Box 720
Jefferson City, MO 65101
P: (573) 751-0290

MONTANA
Ms. Sarah Elliot
Director of Communications
Office of the Governor
State Capitol
Helena, MT 59620
P: (406) 444-9725
F: (406) 444-5529

NEBRASKA
Mr. Jennifer Hein
Director of Communications
Office of the Governor
P.O. Box 94848
Lincoln, NE 68509
P: (402) 471-1967
F: (402) 471-6031

NEVADA
Mr. Brent Boynton
Director of Communications
Office of the Governor
State Capitol
101 North Carson Street
Carson City, NV 89701
P: (775) 684-5670

NEW HAMPSHIRE
Mr. Colin Manning
Press Secretary
Office of the Governor
State House
Concord, NH 03301
P: (603) 271-2121

NEW JERSEY
Ms. Ivette Mendez
Press Secretary
Office of the Governor
125 West State Street
P.O. Box 001
Trenton, NJ 08625
P: (609) 292-2600
F: (609) 777-2922

NEW MEXICO
Mr. Paul Shipley
Director of Communications
Office of the Governor
State Capitol, Fourth Floor
Santa Fe, NM 87501
P: (505) 476-2202
F: (505) 476-2226

NEW YORK
Mr. Darren Dopp
Director of Communications
Office of the Governor
State Capitol, Room 200
Albany, NY 12224
P: (518) 474-8418

NORTH CAROLINA
Ms. Sherri Johnson
Director of Communications
Office of the Governor
20301 Mail Service Center
Raleigh, NC 27699
P: (919) 733-0301
F: (919) 733-5166

NORTH DAKOTA
Mr. Don Canton
Communications Director & Policy Advisor
Office of the Governor
State Capitol
600 East Boulevard Avenue, Dept. 101
Bismarck, ND 58505
P: (701) 328-2200
F: (701) 328-2205

NORTHERN MARIANA ISLANDS
Mr. Peter A. Callaghan
Press Secretary
Office of the Governor
Capitol Hill
Saipan, MP 96950
P: (670) 664-2276
F: (670) 664-2211

OHIO
Mr. Jess Goode
Communications Director
Office of the Governor
77 South High Street, 30th Floor
Columbus, OH 43215
P: (614) 644-0957

OKLAHOMA
Mr. Paul Sund
Director of Communications
Office of the Governor
State Capitol
Oklahoma City, OK 73105
P: (405) 521-2342
F: (405) 521-3354

OREGON
Ms. Anna Richter Taylor
Communications Director
Office of the Governor
State Capitol
900 Court Street, Northeast, Room 254
Salem, OR 97301
P: (503) 378-3111
F: (503) 378-8970

PENNSYLVANIA
Mr. Ronald Jury
Director of Communications & Press Secretary
Office of the Governor
Main Capitol Building, Room 308
Harrisburg, PA 17120
P: (717) 783-1116
F: (717) 772-8284

PUERTO RICO
Ms. Juanita Colombani Lopez
Director of Communications
Office of the Governor
La Fortaleza
San Juan, PR 00902
P: (787) 721-3005
F: (787) 721-5072

RHODE ISLAND
Mr. Steve Kass
Director of Communications
Office of the Governor
State House
Providence, RI 02903
P: (401) 222-2080
F: (401) 273-5729

SOUTH CAROLINA
Ms. Marisa Crawford
Communications Director
Office of the Governor
P.O. Box 11829
Columbia, SC 29211
P: (803) 734-5254

SOUTH DAKOTA
Mr. Mitch Krebs
Press Secretary
Office of the Governor
500 East Capitol
Pierre, SD 57501
P: (605) 773-5706

TENNESSEE
Mr. Bob Corney
Communications Director & Special Assistant To the Governor
Office of the Governor
State Capitol, Room G-9
Nashville, TN 37243
P: (615) 741-3763
F: (615) 532-9711

TEXAS
Ms. Kathy Walt
Press Secretary
Office of the Governor
P.O. Box 12428
Austin, TX 78711
P: (412) 463-1826
F: (512) 463-5571

U.S. VIRGIN ISLANDS
Mr. Jean P. Greaux Jr.
Communications Director
Office of the Governor
Government House, 21-22 Kongens Gade
Charlotte Amalie
St. Thomas, VI 00802
P: (340) 774-0294
F: (340) 774-1361

UTAH
Mr. Michael Mower
Legislative Liaison/Constituent Affairs
Office of the Governor
Office of the Governor
East Office Building, Suite E-220
Salt Lake City, UT 84114
P: (801) 538-1000
F: (801) 538-1528

VERMONT
Mr. Jason Gibbs
Director of Communications
Office of the Governor
109 State Street
Montpelier, VT 05609
P: (802) 828-3333
F: (802) 828-3339

Governor's Media Contacts

VIRGINIA
Ms. Delacey Skinner
Director of Communications
Office of the Governor
Patrick Henry Building, 3rd Floor
1111 East Broad Street
Richmond, VA 23219
P: (804) 692-0145
F: (804) 371-6353

WASHINGTON
Ms. Holly Armstrong
Communications Director
Office of the Governor
416 4th Avenue, Southwest
Olympia, WA 98504
P: (360) 902-4136
F: (360) 753-4110

WEST VIRGINIA
Ms. Lara Ramsburg
Communications Director & Speechwriter
Office of the Governor
State Capitol
Charleston, WV 25305
P: (304) 558-3830
F: (304) 342-7025

WISCONSIN
Mr. Matt Canter
Communications Director
Office of the Governor
115 East, State Capitol
Madison, WI 53702
P: (608) 266-2169

WYOMING
Mr. Rob Black
Press Secretary
Office of the Governor
State Capitol
Cheyenne, WY 82002
P: (307) 777-7434
F: (307) 632-3909

Hazardous Waste Management

Develops and maintains a comprehensive hazardous waste management program in the state.

ALABAMA
Mr. Stephen Cobb
Chief
Hazardous Waste Branch
1400 Coliseum Boulevard
Montgomery, AL 36110
P: (334) 271-7739
F: (334) 279-3050

ALASKA
Ms. Kim Stricklan
Program Manager
Solid Waste Management Program
Department of Environmental Conservation
555 Cordova Street
Anchorage, AK 99501
P: (907) 269-1099
F: (907) 269-7510

ARIZONA
Ms. Amanda Stone
Waste Programs Division Director
Department of Environmental Quality
1110 West Washington
Phoenix, AZ 85007
P: (602) 771-4208
F: (602) 771-2302
E: stone.amanda@azdeq.gov

ARKANSAS
Mr. Mike Bates
Chief
Hazardous Waste Division
P.O. Box 8913
Little Rock, AR 72209
P: (501) 682-0831
F: (501) 682-0565
E: bates@adeq.state.ar.us

CALIFORNIA
Mr. Mark Leary
Executive Director
Integrated Waste Management Board
1001 I Street
Sacramento, CA 95814
P: (916) 341-6544
F: (916) 319-7319
E: mleary@ciwmb.ca.gov

CONNECTICUT
Ms. Gina McCarthy
Commissioner
Department of Environmental Protection
79 Elm Street
Hartford, CT 06106
P: (860) 424-3009
F: (860) 424-4054
E: gina.mccarthy@po.state.ct.us

DELAWARE
Ms. Nancy C. Marker
Program Manager II
Solid Waste & Hazardous Management Branch
89 Kings Highway
Dover, DE 19901
P: (302) 739-9403
F: (302) 739-3491

DISTRICT OF COLUMBIA
Dr. Gregg A. Pane
Director and State Health Officer
Department of Health
825 North Capitol Street, Northeast
Suite 4400
Washington, DC 20002
P: (202) 442-5999
F: (202) 442-4788
E: doh@dc.gov

FLORIDA
Mr. Raoul Clarke
Environmental Administrator
Department of Environmental Protection
2600 Blairstone Road, MS 4555
Tallahassee, FL 32399
P: (850) 245-8750
F: (850) 245-8811
E: raoul.clarke@dep.state.fl.us

GEORGIA
Mr. Mark Smith
Branch Chief
Hazardous Waste Management Branch
2 Martin Luther King, Jr. Drive, SE
Suite 1154 East
Atlanta, GA 30334
P: (404) 656-7802
F: (404) 651-9425

GUAM
Ms. Lorilee Crisostomo
Administrator
Environmental Protection Agency
17-3304/15-6101 Mariner Avenue, Tiyan
P.O. Box 22439
Barrigada, GU 96921
P: (671) 475-1658
F: (671) 734-5910
E: lorilee@guamcell.net

HAWAII
Mr. Steven Chang
Branch Chief
Solid & Hazardous Waste Branch
919 Ala Moana Boulevard
Room 212
Honolulu, HI 96814
P: (808) 586-4226
E: schang@eha.health.state.hi.us

IDAHO
Mr. Orville Green
Administrator
Waste & Remediation Division
1410 North Hilton
Boise, ID 83706
P: (208) 373-0148
F: (208) 373-0154
E: orville.green@deq.idaho.gov

ILLINOIS
Dr. George Vander Velde
Director
Waste Management & Research Center
One East Hazelwood Drive
Champaign, IL 61820
P: (217) 333-8940
F: (217) 333-8944
E: gvvelde@wmrc.vivc.edu

INDIANA
Mr. Bruce Palin
Assistant Commissioner
Department of Environmental Management
100 North Senate Avenue
Room N1154
Indianapolis, IN 46204
P: (317) 233-6591
F: (317) 232-3403
E: bpalin@dem.state.in.us

IOWA
Mr. Brian J. Tormey
Bureau Chief
Energy & Waste Management Bureau
Wallace State Office Building
East 9th & Grand Avenue
Des Moines, IA 50319
P: (515) 281-8927
F: (515) 281-8895
E: brian.tormey@dnr.state.ia.us

KANSAS
Mr. William Bider
Director
Bureau of Waste Management
1000 Southwest Jackson Street
Suite 320
Topeka, KS 66612
P: (785) 296-1600
F: (785) 296-8909

KENTUCKY
Mr. Bruce Scott
Director
Division of Waste Management
14 Reilly Road
Frankfort, KY 40601
P: (502) 564-7042
F: (502) 564-7091
E: bruce.scott@ky.gov

LOUISIANA
Ms. Linda Levy
Administrator
Environmental Assistance Division
Department of Environmental Quality
P.O. Box 4313
Baton Rouge, LA 70821
P: (225) 219-3241
F: (225) 219-3309
E: deqassistance@la.gov

MAINE
Mr. Mark Hyland
Director
Bureau of Remediation & Waste Management
Department of Environmental Protection
17 State House Station
Augusta, ME 04333
P: (207) 287-2651
F: (207) 287-7826
E: Mark.Hyland@maine.gov

Hazardous Waste Management

MARYLAND
Mr. Horacio Tablada
Director
Waste Management Division
Department of Environment
1800 Washington Boulevard
Baltimore, MD 21230
P: (410) 631-3304
F: (410) 631-3321
E: htablada@mde.state.md.us

MASSACHUSETTS
Ms. Arleen O'Donnell
Acting Commissioner
Department of Environmental Protection
One Winter Street, 2nd Floor
Boston, MA 02108
P: (617) 292-5975
F: (617) 574-6880

MICHIGAN
Mr. George Bruchmann
Chief
Waste & Hazardous Materials Division
525 West Allegan
Lansing, MI 48913
P: (517) 335-2690

MINNESOTA
Mr. Brad Moore
Commissioner
Pollution Control Agency
520 Lafayette Road
St. Paul, MN 55155
P: (651) 296-7301
F: (651) 296-6334
E: Brad.Moore@pca.state.mn.us

MISSISSIPPI
Mr. Mark Williams
Chief
Solid Waste Policy, Planning & Grants Branch
P.O. Box 10385
Jackson, MS 39289
P: (601) 961-5304
F: (601) 961-5785
E: mark_williams@deq.state.ms.us

MISSOURI
Mr. Bob Geller
Director
DEQ Hazardous Waste Program
P.O. Box 176
1738 East Elm Street
Jefferson City, MO 65102
P: (573) 751-2747
F: (573) 751-7869
E: bob.geller@dnr.mo.gov

MONTANA
Mr. Dan McGowan
Administrator
Disaster & Emergency Services
Department of Military Affairs
P.O. Box 4789
Ft. Harrison, MT 59636
P: (406) 841-3911
F: (406) 841-3965
E: dmcgowan@mt.gov

NEBRASKA
Mr. Michael J. Linder
Director
Department of Environmental Quality
1200 N Street, Suite 400
P.O. Box 98922
Lincoln, NE 68509
P: (402) 471-0275
F: (402) 471-2909

NEVADA
Mr. Eric Noack
Bureau Chief
Bureau of Waste Management
901 South Stewart Street, Suite 4001
Carson City, NV 89701
P: (775) 687-9366
E: enoack@ndep.nv.gov

NEW HAMPSHIRE
Mr. Anthony P. Giunta
Director
Department of Environmental Services
29 Hazen Drive
P.O. Box 95
Concord, NH 03301
P: (603) 271-2905
F: (603) 271-2456
E: aguinta@des.state.nh.us

NEW JERSEY
Mr. Frank Coolick
Administrator
Division of Solid & Hazardous Waste
401 East State Street
P.O. Box 414
Trenton, NJ 08625
P: (609) 984-1418
F: (609) 777-0769

NEW MEXICO
Mr. James Bearzi
Bureau Chief
Hazardous Waste Bureau
2905 Rodeo Park Drive East, Building 1
Santa Fe, NM 87505
P: (505) 476-6016
F: (505) 476-6030
E: james.bearzi@state.nm.us

NEW YORK
Mr. Alexander "Pete" Grannis (D)
Commissioner
Department of Environmental Conservation
625 Broadway
Albany, NY 12207
P: (518) 402-8540
F: (518) 474-5450

NORTH CAROLINA
Ms. Elizabeth Cannon
Waste Management Division
401 Oberlin Road, Suite 150
Raleigh, NC 27605
P: (919) 508-8400
F: (919) 715-3605
E: elizabeth.cannon@ncmail.net

NORTH DAKOTA
Mr. Scott Radig
Director
Division of Waste Management
918 East Divide Avenue, 3rd Floor
Bismark, ND 58501
P: (701) 328-5166
F: (701) 328-5200
E: sradig@nd.gov

NORTHERN MARIANA ISLANDS
Mr. Gregorio Guerrero
Director
Emergency Management Office
Office of the Governor
P.O. Box 10007
Saipan, MP 96950
P: (670) 322-8002
F: (670) 322-7743
E: gguerrero@cnmiemo.gov.mp

OHIO
Mr. Michael Savage
Division Chief
Division of Hazardous Waste Management
50 West Town Street, Suite 700
Columbus, OH 43215
P: (614) 644-2917
E: mike.savage@epa.state.oh.us

OKLAHOMA
Mr. Scott Thompson
Director
Land Protection Division
P.O. Box 1677
Oklahoma City, OK 73118
P: (405) 702-5100
F: (405) 702-5101
E: scott.thompson@deq.state.ok.us

OREGON
Ms. Karen Whisler
Division Administrator
Department of Environmental Quality
811 South West 6th Avenue
Portland, OR 97204
P: (503) 229-5918
F: (503) 229-6124
E: hw@deq.state.or.us

PENNSYLVANIA
Mr. Richard Shipman
Division Chief
Division of Hazardous Waste Management
P.O. Box 8471
Harrisburg, PA 17105
P: (717) 787-6239
F: (717) 787-0884

PUERTO RICO
Mr. Jose Negron
Interim Director
Solid Waste Management Authority
P.O. Box 40285
San Juan, PR 00918
P: (787) 765-7575
F: (787) 753-2220

RHODE ISLAND
Mr. Leo Hellested
Chief
Office of Waste Management
235 Promenade Street
Providence, RI 02908
P: (401) 222-2797
F: (401) 222-3812
E: hellested@dem.ri.gov

SOUTH CAROLINA
Mr. Patrick Walker
Chief
Bureau of Land & Waste Management
Dept. of Health & Environmental Control
2600 Bull Street
Columbia, SC 29201
P: (803) 896-4000
F: (803) 896-4001
E: walkerpt@dhec.sc.gov

SOUTH DAKOTA
Ms. Vonni Kallemeyn
Administrator
Waste Management Program
Foss Building
523 East Capitol Avenue
Pierre, SD 57501
P: (605) 773-3153
F: (605) 773-6035
E: vonni.kallemeyn@state.sd.us

TENNESSEE
Mr. Mike Apple
Director
Division of Solid & Hazardous Waste Management
401 Church Street, 5th Floor
Nashville, TN 37243
P: (615) 532-0780
F: (615) 532-0886

TEXAS
Ms. Jacqueline S. Hardee
Director
Waste Permits Division
P.O. Box 13087
Austin, TX 78711
P: (512) 239-4150
F: (512) 239-5533

U.S. VIRGIN ISLANDS
Mr. Aaron Hutchins
Director
Division of Environmental Protection
Cyril E. King Airport
Terminal Building, 2nd Floor
St. Thomas, VI 00802
P: (340) 774-3320
F: (340) 714-9549

UTAH
Mr. Dennis R. Downs
Director
Division of Solid & Hazardous Waste
288 North 1460 West
P.O. Box 144880
Salt Lake City, UT 84114
P: (801) 538-6785
F: (801) 538-6715
E: ddowns@utah.gov

VERMONT
Mr. P. Howard Flanders
Director
Waste Management Division
103 South Main Street
Waterbury, VT 05671
P: (802) 241-3888
F: (802) 241-3296
E: p.howard.flanders@anr.state.vt.us

VIRGINIA
Mr. David K. Paylor
Director
Department of Environmental Quality
629 East Main Street
P.O. Box 10009
Richmond, VA 23240
P: (804) 698-4390
F: (804) 698-4019
E: dkpaylor@deq.virginia.gov

WASHINGTON
Mr. Darin Rice
Program Manager
Hazardous Waste & Toxic Reduction Division
P.O. Box 47600
Olympia, WA 98504
P: (360) 407-6724
F: (360) 407-6715
E: dric461@ecy.wa.gov

WEST VIRGINIA
Mr. Ken Ellison
Director
Division of Land Restoration
601 57th Street, Southeast
Charleston, WV 25304
P: (304) 926-0499 Ext. 1263
E: kellison@wvdep.org

WISCONSIN
Mr. Al Shea
Administrator
Air & Waste Division
P.O. Box 7921
Madison, WI 53707
P: (608) 266-5896
F: (608) 267-2768

WYOMING
Mr. John V. Corra
Director
Department of Environmental Quality
122 West 25th Street, 4W
Cheyenne, WY 82002
P: (307) 777-7937
F: (307) 777-7682
E: jcorra@state.wy.us

Health Services

Manages the development, administration and delivery of all health programs.

ALABAMA
Dr. Donald Williamson
State Health Officer
Department of Public Health
201 Monroe Street
Montgomery, AL 36104
P: (334) 206-5200
F: (334) 206-5609

ALASKA
Ms. Karleen K. Jackson
Commissioner
Health & Social Services
P.O. Box 110601
Juneau, AK 99811
P: (907) 465-3030
F: (907) 465-3068

AMERICAN SAMOA
Mr. Utoofili Asofa'afetai Maga
Director
Department of Health
American Samoa Government
Pago Pago, AS 96799
P: (684) 633-4606
F: (684) 633-5379

ARIZONA
Ms. Susan Gerard
Director
Department of Health Services
150 North 18th Avenue
Phoenix, AZ 85007
P: (602) 542-1001
F: (602) 543-0883

ARKANSAS
Mr. John Selig
Director
Department of Health & Human Services
P.O. Box 1437, Slot S201
Little Rock, AR 72203
P: (501) 682-8650
F: (501) 682-6836
E: John.Selig@arkansas.gov

CALIFORNIA
Ms. Sandra Louise Shewry
Director
Department of Health Services
1501 Capitol Avenue, Suite 6001
Sacramento, CA 95814
P: (916) 440-7400
F: (916) 657-1156
E: sshewry@dhs.ca.gov

COLORADO
Mr. Jim Martin
Executive Director
Department of Public Health & Environment
4300 Cherry Creek Drive, South
Denver, CO 80246
P: (303) 692-2012
F: (303) 691-7702

CONNECTICUT
Mr. J. Robert Galvin
Commissioner
Department of Public Health
410 Capitol Avenue
Hartford, CT 06106
P: (860) 509-7101
F: (860) 509-7111
E: Robert.Galvin@po.state.ct.us

DELAWARE
Mr. Vincent P. Meconi
Secretary
Department of Health & Social Services
Herman M. Holloway, Sr. Campus
1901 North DuPont Highway, Main Building
New Castle, DE 19720
P: (302) 255-9040
E: Vincent.Meconi@state.de.us

FLORIDA
Ms. Ana Viamonte Ros
Secretary
Department of Health
4052 Bald Cypress Way, Bin #A00
Tallahassee, FL 32399
P: (850) 245-4321
F: (850) 414-7613
E: secretary@doh.state.fl.us

GEORGIA
Dr. Stuart T. Brown
Director
Division of Public Health
Two Peachtree Street, Northwest
Atlanta, GA 30303
P: (404) 657-2700

GUAM
Mr. Arthur U. San Agustin
Director
Department of Health & Social Services
123 Chalan Kareta, Route 10
Mangilao, GU 96923
P: (671) 735-7102
F: (671) 734-5910
E: chiefdsc@dphss.govguam.net

HAWAII
Dr. Chiyome Leinaala Fukino
Director
Department of Health
1250 Punchbowl Street
Honolulu, HI 96813
P: (808) 586-4400
F: (808) 586-4444

IDAHO
Mr. Richard Armstrong
Director
Department of Health & Welfare
450 West State Street
Pete T. Cenarrusa Building
Boise, ID 83720
P: (208) 334-5500
F: (208) 334-6558

ILLINOIS
Dr. Eric E. Whitaker
Director
Department of Public Health
535 West Jefferson, 5th Floor
Springfield, IL 62761
P: (217) 782-4977

INDIANA
Ms. Judith Monroe
Commissioner
State Department of Health
2 North Meridian Street
3rd Floor
Indianapolis, IN 46204
P: (317) 233-7400

IOWA
Mr. Tom Newton
Director
Department of Public Health
Lucas Building
321 East 12th Street
Des Moines, IA 50319
P: (515) 281-7689
F: (515) 281-4958

KANSAS
Mr. Rod Bremby
Secretary of Health & Environment
Department of Health & Environment
1000 Southwest Jackson Street
Suite 540
Topeka, KS 66612
P: (785) 296-0461
F: (785) 368-6368

KENTUCKY
Mr. Mark Birdwhistell
Secretary
Cabinet for Health & Family Services
275 East Main Street, 5W-A
Frankfort, KY 40601
P: (502) 564-7042
F: (502) 564-7091

LOUISIANA
Dr. Fred Cerise
Secretary
Department of Health & Hospitals
628 North 4th Street
P.O. Box 629
Baton Rouge, LA 70821
P: (225) 342-9500
F: (225) 342-5568

MAINE
Ms. Brenda M. Harvey
Acting Commissioner
Department of Human Services
11 State House Station
Augusta, ME 04333
P: (207) 287-2736
F: (207) 287-3005
E: brenda.harvey@maine.gov

MARYLAND
Mr. John M. Colmers
Secretary
Department of Mental Health & Hygiene
201 West Preston Street, 5th Floor
Baltimore, MD 21201
P: (410) 767-4639

MASSACHUSETTS
Mr. John Auerbach
Commissioner
Department of Public Health
250 Washington Street
Boston, MA 02108
P: (617) 624-6000

MICHIGAN
Ms. Janet Olszewski
Director
Department of Community Health
Capitol View Building
201 Townsend Street
Lansing, MI 48913
P: (517) 373-3740
F: (517) 373-4288
E: olszewskijd@michigan.gov

MINNESOTA
Ms. Dianne Mandernach
Commissioner
Department of Health
625 Robert Street, North
Box 64975
St. Paul, MN 55164
P: (651) 201-5810
F: (651) 201-4986
E: dianne.mandernach
@state.mn.us

MISSISSIPPI
Dr. Brian W. Amy
State Health Officer
State Department of Health
P.O. Box 1700
Jackson, MS 39215
P: (601) 576-7400
E: bamy@msdh.state.ms.us

MISSOURI
Ms. Jane Drummond
Director
Department of Health & Human Services
920 Wildwood
P.O. Box 570
Jefferson City, MO 65102
P: (573) 751-6001
F: (573) 751-6041
E: jane.drummond
@dhss.mo.gov

MONTANA
Ms. Joan Miles
Director
Department of Public Health & Human Services
111 North Sanders, Room 301/308
P.O. Box 4210
Helena, MT 59604
P: (406) 444-5622
F: (406) 444-1970

NEBRASKA
Ms. Joann Schaefer
Director
Department of Health & Human Services
Regulation & Licensure
P.O. Box 95007
Lincoln, NE 68509
P: (402) 471-8566
F: (402) 471-9449
E: roxie.anderson
@hhss.ne.us

NEVADA
Mr. Michael Willden
Director
Department of Health & Human Services
505 East King Street, Room 600
Carson City, NV 89706
P: (775) 684-4000
F: (775) 684-4010
E: mwillden@dhhs.nv.gov

NEW HAMPSHIRE
Mr. John A. Stephen
Commissioner
Department of Health & Human Services
129 Pleasant Street
Concord, NH 03301
P: (603) 271-4331
F: (603) 271-4912
E: jstephen
@dhhs.state.nh.us

NEW JERSEY
Dr. Fred M. Jacobs
Commissioner
Department of Health & Senior Services
P.O. Box 360
Trenton, NJ 08625
P: (609) 292-7837
F: (609) 292-0053
E: Fred.Jacobs
@doh.state.nj.us

NEW MEXICO
Ms. Michelle Lujan Grisham
Cabinet Secretary
Department of Health
1190 St. Francis Drive
Santa Fe, NM 87502
P: (505) 827-2613
F: (505) 827-2530

NEW YORK
Mr. Richard Daines
Acting Commissioner
Department of Health
Corning Tower Building
Empire State Plaza
Albany, NY 12237
P: (518) 474-2011
F: (518) 474-1449

NORTH CAROLINA
Ms. Carmen Hooker-Odom
Secretary
Department of Health & Human Services
2001 Mail Service Center
Raleigh, NC 27699
P: (919) 733-4534
F: (919) 715-4645
E: carmen.hookerodom
@ncmail.net

NORTH DAKOTA
Dr. Terry Dwelle
State Health Officer
Department of Health
600 East Boulevard Avenue, 2nd Floor
Judicial Wing
Bismarck, ND 58505
P: (701) 328-2372
F: (701) 328-4727
E: tdwelle@nd.gov

NORTHERN MARIANA ISLANDS
Mr. Joseph P. Villagomez
Secretary of Public Health
Department of Public Health
P.O. Box 500409
Saipan, MP 96950
P: (670) 236-8201
F: (670) 234-8930
E: jkvsaipan@aol.com

OHIO
Dr. Alvin D. Jackson
Director of Health
Department of Health
246 North High Street
Columbus, OH 43216
P: (614) 466-2253
F: (614) 466-5866

OKLAHOMA
Dr. James Michael Crutcher
Commissioner
State Department of Health
1000 Northeast 10th Street
Oklahoma City, OK 73117
P: (405) 271-5600

OREGON
Ms. Susan Allan
Assistant Director
DHS - Public Health
800 Oregon Street
Portland, OR 97232
P: (971) 673-1298
F: (971) 673-1361
E: dhs.info@state.or.us

PENNSYLVANIA
Dr. Calvin B. Johnson
Secretary
Department of Health
Health & Welfare Building
Harrisburg, PA 17108
P: (717) 787-6436
F: (717) 787-0191
E: prankin@state.pa.us

PUERTO RICO
Dr. Rosa Perez
Secretary of Health
Department of Health
P.O. Box 70184
San Juan, PR 00936
P: (787) 274-7604
F: (787) 250-6547
E: rperez@salud.gov.pr

RHODE ISLAND
Dr. David R. Gifford
Director
Department of Health
3 Capitol Hill, Room 104
Providence, RI 02908
P: (401) 222-2827
F: (401) 222-1272
E: health@ri.gov

SOUTH CAROLINA
Ms. Susan Bowling
Acting Director
Department of Health & Human Services
1801 Main Street
P.O. Box 8206
Columbia, SC 29202
P: (803) 898-2504
F: (803) 898-4515

SOUTH DAKOTA
Ms. Doneen Hollingsworth
Secretary
Department of Health
Hayes Building
600 East Capitol Avenue
Pierre, SD 57501
P: (605) 773-3361
F: (605) 773-5683
E: doh.info@state.sd.us

TENNESSEE
Ms. Susan R. Cooper
Commissioner
Department of Health
425 Fifth Avenue, North
Cordell Hull Building, 3rd Floor
Nashville, TN 37247
P: (615) 741-3111
F: (615) 741-6230

TEXAS
Dr. Eduardo J. Sanchez
Commissioner
Department of Health Services
1100 West 49th Street
Austin, TX 78456
P: (512) 458-7375

Health Services

U.S. VIRGIN ISLANDS
Ms. Darlene Carty
Commissioner
Department of Health
48 Sugar Estate
Charlotte Amalie
St. Thomas, VI 00802
P: (340) 774-0117
F: (340) 774-4001
E: darlene.carty
@usvi-doh.org

UTAH
Dr. David Sundwall
Executive Director
Department of Health
288 North 1460 West
P.O. Box 141000
Salt Lake City, UT 84114
P: (801) 538-6111
F: (801) 538-6306
E: dsundwall@utah.gov

VERMONT
Ms. Sharon Moffatt
Acting Commissioner
Department of Health
108 Cherry Street
Burlington, VT 05402
P: (802) 863-7280
F: (802) 865-7754
E: smoffat@vdh.state.vt.us

VIRGINIA
Dr. Robert B. Stroube
Commissioner
Department of Health
109 Governor Street, 13th Floor
Richmond, VA 23219
P: (804) 864-7009
F: (804) 864-7022
E: robert.stroube
@vdh.virginia.gov

WASHINGTON
Ms. Mary C. Selecky
Secretary
Department of Health
P.O. Box 47890
Olympia, WA 98504
P: (360) 236-4030
F: (360) 586-7424
E: secretary@doh.wa.gov

WEST VIRGINIA
Ms. Martha Yeager Walker
Cabinet Secretary
Department of Health & Human Resources
Capitol Complex Building 3, Room 206
1900 Kanawha Boulevard, East
Charleston, WV 25305
P: (304) 558-0684
F: (304) 558-1130
E: marthaywalker@wvdhrr.org

WISCONSIN
Mr. Kevin Hayden
Secretary
Department of Health & Family Services
1 West Wilson Street, Room 650
Madison, WI 53702
P: (608) 266-9622
E: haydekr@dhfs.state.wi.us

WYOMING
Dr. Brent D. Sherard
Director
Department of Health
Hathaway Building, 1st Floor
2300 Capitol Avenue
Cheyenne, WY 82002
P: (307) 777-7656
F: (307) 777-5648

Higher Education

Serves as coordinating and planning agency for state-supported post-secondary education.

ALABAMA
Mr. Michael E. Malone
Executive Director
Commission on Higher Education
P.O. Box 302000
Montgomery, AL 36130
P: (334) 242-1998
F: (334) 242-0268
E: mmalone@ache.state.al.us

ALASKA
Ms. Diane Barrans
Executive Director
Commission on Postsecondary Education
P.O. Box 110505
Juneau, AK 99811
P: (907) 465-6740
F: (907) 465-3293
E: diane_barrans@acpe.state.ak.us

Mr. Mark Hamilton
President
University of Alaska System
P.O. Box 755000
Fairbanks, AK 99775
P: (907) 450-8000
F: (907) 450-8012
E: sypres@alaska.edu

ARIZONA
Mr. Joel Sideman
Executive Director
Board of Regents
2020 North Central Avenue
Suite 230
Phoenix, AZ 85004
P: (602) 229-2500
F: (602) 229-2555
E: jsideman@asu.edu

ARKANSAS
Dr. Linda Beene
Director
Department of Higher Education
114 East Capitol Avenue
Little Rock, AR 72201
P: (501) 371-2000
F: (501) 371-2003
E: llbeene@adhe.arknet.edu

CALIFORNIA
Mr. Murray Haberman
Executive Director
Postsecondary Education Commission
770 L Street, Suite 1160
Sacramento, CA 95814
P: (916) 445-1000
F: (916) 327-4417
E: mhaberman@cpec.ca.gov

COLORADO
Mr. David Skaggs
Executive Director
Department of Higher Education
1380 Lawrence Street, Suite 1200
Denver, CO 80204
P: (303) 866-2723
F: (303) 866-4266

CONNECTICUT
Ms. Valerie F. Lewis
Commissioner
Department of Higher Education
61 Woodland Street
Hartford, CT 06105
P: (860) 947-1800
F: (860) 947-1310
E: vlewis@ctdhe.org

DELAWARE
Ms. Maureen Laffey
Director
Higher Education Commission
820 North French Street
Wilmington, DE 19801
P: (302) 577-3240
F: (302) 577-6765
E: mlaffey@doe.k12.de.us

DISTRICT OF COLUMBIA
Dr. Deborah Gist
Director
State Office of Education
441 4th Street, NW
Suite 350-N
Washington, DC 20001
P: (202) 727-6436
F: (202) 727-2834

FLORIDA
Mr. Mark Rosenberg
Chancellor
State University System of Florida
Turlington Building, Suite 1614
325 West Gaines Street
Tallahassee, FL 32399
P: (850) 245-0466
F: (850) 245-9685
E: chancellor@flbog.org

GEORGIA
Mr. Erroll B. Davis Jr.
Chancellor
Board of Regents
University System of Georgia
270 Washington Street, Southwest
Atlanta, GA 30334
P: (404) 656-2202
F: (404) 657-6979
E: chancellor@usg.edu

HAWAII
Mr. David McClain
Interim President
Board of Regents
University of Hawaii
2444 Dole Street, Bachman Hall 202
Honolulu, HI 96822
P: (808) 956-8207
F: (808) 956-5286
E: mcclain@hawaii.edu

IDAHO
Mr. Dwight Johnson
Interim Executive Director
Office of the State Board of Education
P.O. Box 83720
Boise, ID 83720
P: (208) 332-1591
F: (208) 334-2632
E: dwight.johnson@osbe.idaho.gov

ILLINOIS
Ms. Judy Erwin
Executive Director
Board of Higher Education
431 East Adams, 2nd Floor
Springfield, IL 62701
P: (217) 782-2551
F: (217) 782-8548
E: erwin@ibhe.org

INDIANA
Mr. Stanley G. Jones
Commissioner
Commission for Higher Education
101 West Ohio Street, Suite 550
Indianapolis, IN 46204
P: (317) 464-4400
F: (317) 464-4410
E: sjones@che.state.in.us

IOWA
Mr. Gary Steinke
Executive Director
Board of Regents
11260 Aurora Avenue
Urbandale, IA 50322
P: (515) 281-6426
F: (515) 281-6420
E: gwstein@iastate.edu

KANSAS
Mr. Reginald L. Robinson
President & CEO
Board of Regents
1000 Southwest Jackson Street, Suite 520
Topeka, KS 66612
P: (785) 296-3421
F: (785) 296-0983
E: rrobinson@ksbor.org

KENTUCKY
Dr. Thomas D. Layzell
President
Council on Postsecondary Education
1024 Capital Center Drive, Suite 320
Frankfort, KY 40601
P: (502) 573-1555
F: (502) 573-1535
E: tom.layzell@ky.gov

LOUISIANA
Dr. E. Joseph Savoie
Commissioner of Higher Education
Board of Regents
P.O. Box 3677
Baton Rouge, LA 70821
P: (225) 342-4253
F: (225) 342-9318
E: commish@regents.state.la.us

MAINE
Mr. Terrance McTaggert
Chancellor
University of Maine System
107 Maine Avenue
Bangor, ME 04401
P: (207) 287-2132
F: (207) 287-2335
E: earle.shettleworth@maine.gov

MARYLAND
Mr. James E. Lyons Sr.
Secretary of Higher Education
Higher Education Commission
839 Bestgale Road, Suite 400
Annapolis, MD 21401
P: (410) 260-4516
F: (410) 260-3200
E: jlyons@mhec.state.md.us

MASSACHUSETTS
Dr. Patricia Plummer
Chancellor
Board of Higher Education
One Ashburton Place, Room 1401
Boston, MA 02108
P: (617) 994-6901
F: (617) 994-6397
E: pplummer@bhe.mass.edu

Higher Education

MINNESOTA
Ms. Susan Heegaard
Director
Office of Higher Education
1450 Energy Park Drive, Suite 350
St. Paul, MN 55108
P: (651) 642-0567
F: (651) 642-0675
E: susan.heegaard@state.mn.us

Mr. James H. McCormick
Chancellor
State Colleges & Universities
Wells Fargo Place
30 East 7th Street, Suite 350
St. Paul, MN 55101
P: (651) 296-8012
F: (651) 296-0872
E: james.mccormick@so.mnscu.edu

MISSISSIPPI
Mr. Thomas Meredith
Commissioner of Higher Education
State Institutions of Higher Learning
Board of Trustees
3825 Ridgewood Road
Jackson, MS 39211
P: (601) 432-6623
F: (601) 432-6972
E: tmeredith@ihl.state.ms.us

MISSOURI
Dr. Robert Stein
Commissioner of Higher Education
Department of Higher Education
3515 Amazonas Drive
Jefferson City, MO 65109
P: (573) 751-2361
F: (573) 751-8835
E: robert.stein@dhe.mo.gov

MONTANA
Ms. Sheila Stearns
Commissioner of Higher Education
University System
46 North Last Chance Gulch
P.O. Box 23201
Helena, MT 59620
P: (406) 444-6570
F: (406) 444-1469
E: sstearns@montana.edu

NEBRASKA
Dr. Marshall A. Hill
Executive Director
Coordinating Commission for Postsecondary Education
140 North 8th Street, Suite 300
P.O. Box 95005
Lincoln, NE 68509
P: (402) 471-2847
F: (402) 471-2886
E: Marshall.Hill@ccpe.ne.gov

NEVADA
Mr. James E. Rogers
Chancellor
System of Higher Education
System Administration North
2601 Enterprise Road
Reno, NV 89512
P: (775) 784-4905
F: (775) 784-1127
E: Chancellor@nevada.edu

NEW HAMPSHIRE
Ms. Kathryn G. Dodge
Executive Director
Postsecondary Education Commission
3 Barrell Court, Suite 300
Concord, NH 03301
P: (603) 271-2555
F: (603) 271-2696
E: kdodge@pec.state.nh.us

Dr. Stephen J. Reno
Chancellor
University System
Dunlap Center
25 Concord Road
Durham, NH 03824
P: (603) 862-0908
F: (603) 862-1800
E: sreno@unh.edu

NEW JERSEY
Ms. Jeanne M. Oswald
Deputy Executive Director
Commission on Higher Education
20 West State Street, 7th Floor
P.O. Box 542
Trenton, NJ 08625
P: (609) 292-8916
F: (609) 292-7225
E: joswald@che.state.nj.us

NEW MEXICO
Ms. Beverlee J. McClure
Secretary of Higher Education
Higher Education Department
1068 Cerrillos Road
Santa Fe, NM 87505
P: (505) 476-6500
F: (505) 476-6511
E: Beverlee.McClure@state.nm.us

NEW YORK
Ms. Johanna Duncan-Poitier
Deputy Commissioner
State Education Department
Office of the Professions
89 Washington Avenue
Albany, NY 12234
P: (518) 474-3862
F: (518) 474-1449
E: jpoitier@mail.nysed.gov

NORTH CAROLINA
Mr. Erskine B. Bowles
President
University of North Carolina
910 Raleigh Road
P.O. Box 2688
Chapel Hill, NC 27515
P: (919) 962-1000
F: (919) 843-9695
E: ebowles@northcarolina.edu

NORTHERN MARIANA ISLANDS
Dr. Rita H. Inos
Chair
Board of Regents
Northern Marianas College
P.O. Box 501250
Saipan, MP 96950
P: (670) 234-5498
F: (670) 234-1270

OHIO
Dr. E. Garrison Walters
Interim Chancellor
Board of Regents
30 East Broad Street, 36th Floor
Columbus, OH 43215
P: (614) 466-6000
F: (614) 466-5866
E: gwalters@regents.state.oh.us

OKLAHOMA
Mr. Glenn D. Johnson Jr.
Chancellor
State Regents for Higher Education
655 Research Parkway, Suite 200
Oklahoma City, OK 73104
P: (405) 225-9100
F: (405) 225-9230

OREGON
Mr. George Pernsteiner
Acting Chancellor
University System
P.O. Box 3175
Eugene, OR 97403
P: (541) 346-5700
F: (541) 346-5764
E: george_pernsteiner@ous.edu

PENNSYLVANIA
Dr. Judy G. Hample
Chancellor
State System of Higher Education
2986 North 2nd Street
Harrisburg, PA 17110
P: (717) 720-4000
F: (717) 720-4011
E: jhample@passhe.edu

PUERTO RICO
Ms. Viviana Abreu
Executive Director
Council on Higher Education
P.O. Box 19900
San Juan, PR 00910
P: (787) 724-7100
F: (787) 721-6447
E: vi_abreu@ces.gobierno.pr

Mr. Justo Reyes-Torres
Executive Director
Council on Higher Education
P.O. Box 19900
San Juan, PR 00910
P: (787) 724-7100
F: (787) 721-6447
E: ju_reyes@ces.gobierno.pr

RHODE ISLAND
Dr. Jack R. Warner
Commissioner
Board of Governors for Higher Education
301 Promenade Street
Providence, RI 02908
P: (401) 222-6560
F: (401) 222-2545
E: jwarner@etal.uri.edu

SOUTH CAROLINA
Mr. Conrad Festa
Executive Director
Commission on Higher Education
1333 Main Street, Suite 200
Columbia, SC 29201
P: (803) 737-2260
F: (803) 737-2297
E: cfesta@che.sc.gov

Dr. Gail M. Morrison
Acting Executive Director
Commission on Higher Education
1333 Main Street, Suite 200
Columbia, SC 29201
P: (803) 737-0056
F: (803) 737-2297
E: gmorrison@che.sc.gov

SOUTH DAKOTA
Dr. Robert T. Perry
Executive Director
Board of Regents
306 East Capitol Avenue, Suite 200
Pierre, SD 57501
P: (605) 773-3455
F: (605) 773-5320
E: tadp@sdbor.edu

TENNESSEE
Dr. Richard G. Rhoda
Executive Director
Higher Education Commission
404 James Robertson Parkway
Parkway Towers, Suite 1900
Nashville, TN 37243
P: (615) 741-3605
F: (615) 741-6230
E: richard.rhoda@state.tn.us

TEXAS
Dr. Raymund Paredes
Commissioner
Higher Education Coordinating Board
P.O. Box 12788
Austin, TX 78711
P: (512) 427-6101
F: (512) 427-6127
E: raymund.paredes@thecb.state.tx.us

UTAH
Mr. Richard E. Kendell
Commissioner
State Board of Regents
Board of Regents Building, The Gateway
60 South 400 West
Salt Lake City, UT 84101
P: (801) 321-7103
F: (801) 321-7199
E: rkendell@utahsbr.edu

VERMONT
Dr. Robert G. Clarke
Chancellor
State Colleges
P.O. Box 359
Park Street, Stanley Hall
Waterbury, VT 05676
P: (802) 241-2526
F: (802) 241-3369
E: robert.clarke@quark.vsc.edu

Mr. Daniel Mark Fogel
President
University of Vermont
Waterman Building
Burlington, VT 05405
P: (802) 656-3186
F: (802) 656-1363
E: daniel.fogel@uvm.edu

VIRGINIA
Dr. Daniel J. LaVista
Executive Director
State Council of Higher Education for Virginia
101 North 14th Street
Richmond, VA 23219
P: (804) 225-2600
F: (804) 225-2604
E: DanielLaVista@schev.edu

WASHINGTON
Ms. Anne Daley
Executive Director
Higher Education Coordinating Board
P.O. Box 43430
Olympia, WA 98504
P: (360) 753-7810
F: (360) 753-7808
E: annd@hecb.wa.gov

WEST VIRGINIA
Dr. Brian Noland
Chancellor
Higher Education Policy Commission
1018 Kanawha Boulevard, East, Suite 700
Charleston, WV 25301
P: (304) 558-0699
F: (304) 558-1011
E: noland@hepc.wvnet.edu

WISCONSIN
Mr. Kevin P. Reilly
President
University of Wisconsin System
1700 Van Hise Hall
1220 Linden Drive
Madison, WI 53706
P: (608) 262-2321
F: (608) 262-3985
E: kreilly@uwsa.edu

WYOMING
Mr. Thomas Buchanan
President
University of Wyoming
Box 3434
Laramie, WY 82071
P: (307) 766-4121
F: (307) 766-2271
E: tombuch@uwyo.edu

Dr. James O. Rose
Executive Director
Community College Commission
2020 Carey Avenue, 8th Floor
Cheyenne, WY 82002
P: (307) 777-7763
F: (307) 777-6567
E: jrose@commission.wcc.edu

Historic Preservation

Surveys, restores and preserves structures and/or sites of historical or architectural significance in the state.

ALABAMA
Dr. Ed C. Bridges
Director
Department of Archives & History
624 Washington Avenue
Montgomery, AL 36130
P: (334) 242-4441
E: ed.bridges@archives.alabama.gov

Ms. Elizabeth Brown
Interim State Historic Preservation Officer
Historical Commission
468 South Perry Street
Montgomery, AL 36130
P: (334) 242-3184
F: (334) 240-3477

ALASKA
Ms. Judith Bittner
State Historic Preservation Officer
Office of History & Archeology
Department of Natural Resources
550 West 7th Avenue, Suite 1310
Anchorage, AK 99501
P: (907) 269-8721
F: (907) 269-8908
E: judyb@dnr.state.ak.us

AMERICAN SAMOA
Mr. John Enright
Historic Preservation Officer
Executive Offices of the Governor
American Samoa Government
Historic Preservation Office
Pago Pago, AS 96799
P: (684) 633-2384
F: (684) 633-2367
E: enright@samoatelco.com

ARIZONA
Mr. James W. Garrison
State Historic Preservation Officer
State Parks
1300 West Washington
Phoenix, AZ 85007
P: (602) 542-4174
F: (602) 542-4180
E: jgarrison@pr.state.az.us

ARKANSAS
Ms. Cathie Matthews
State Historic Preservation Officer
Department of Arkansas Heritage
323 Center Street
Suite 1500
Little Rock, AR 72201
P: (501) 324-9150
F: (501) 324-9154
E: cathie@arkansasheritage.org

CALIFORNIA
Mr. Milford Wayne Donaldson
State Historic Preservation Officer
Office of Historic Preservation
Department of Parks & Recreation
P.O. Box 942896
Sacramento, CA 94296
P: (916) 653-6624
F: (916) 653-9824
E: mwdonaldson@parks.ca.gov

COLORADO
Ms. Georgianna Contiguglia
State Historic Preservation Officer
Historical Society
1300 Broadway
Denver, CO 80203
P: (303) 866-3355
F: (303) 866-4464

CONNECTICUT
Ms. Jennifer Aniskovich
Executive Director
Commission on Culture & Tourism
755 Main Street
One Financial Plaza
Hartford, CT 06103
P: (860) 566-4770
F: (860) 566-5078
E: janiskovich@ctarts.org

DELAWARE
Mr. Timothy A. Slavin
State Historic Preservation Officer
Division of Historical & Cultural Affairs
21 The Green
Dover, DE 19901
P: (302) 739-5313
F: (302) 739-6711
E: timothy.slavin@state.de.us

FLORIDA
Mr. Frederick Gaske
State Historic Preservation Officer & Division Director
Division of Historical Resources
Department of State
500 S. Bronough St., Room 305
Tallahassee, FL 32399
P: (850) 245-6300
E: fgaske@dos.state.fl.us

GEORGIA
Mr. Noel A. Holcomb
Commissioner
Department of Natural Resources
2 Marting Luther King Jr. Drive SE
Suite 1252 East Tower
Atlanta, GA 30334
P: (404) 656-3500
F: (404) 656-0770

Mr. W. Ray Luce
Deputy State Historic Preservation Officer
Historical Preservation Division
34 Peachtree Street Northwest
Suite 1600
Atlanta, GA 30303
P: (404) 651-5061
F: (404) 657-1040
E: ray_luce@dnr.state.ga.us

HAWAII
Ms. Melanie Chinen
Administrator
State Historic Preservation Division
601 Kamokila Boulevard, Suite 555
Kapolei, HI 96707
P: (808) 692-8015

Mr. Allan A. Smith
Interim Director
Department of Land & Natural Resources
1151 Punchbowl Street
Honolulu, HI 96813
P: (808) 587-0401
F: (808) 587-0390

IDAHO
Mr. Keith Petersen
Interim State Historic Preservation Officer
State Historical Society
2205 Old Penitentiary Road
Boise, ID 83712
P: (208) 334-2682

ILLINOIS
Mr. William L. Wheeler
State Historic Preservation Officer & Associate Director
Historic Preservation Agency
One Old State Capitol Plaza
Springfield, IL 62701
P: (217) 785-4512
F: (217) 524-7525

INDIANA
Mr. Robert E. Carter Jr.
Director
Department of Natural Resources
402 West Washington Street
Government Center South, Room W256
Indianapolis, IN 46204
P: (317) 232-4020
F: (317) 233-6811

IOWA
Ms. Cyndi Pederson
Executive Director
Historical Society of Iowa
Capitol Complex
East 6th & Locust Street
Des Moines, IA 50319
P: (515) 281-7471
E: cyndi.pederson@iowa.gov

KANSAS
Ms. Jennie Chinn
State Historic Preservation Officer & Executive Director
State Historical Society
6425 Southwest 6th Avenue
Topeka, KS 66615
P: (785) 272-8681 Ext. 210
F: (785) 272-8682
E: jchinn@kshs.org

KENTUCKY
Ms. Donna M. Neary
Executive Director
Heritage Council
300 Washington Street
Frankfort, KY 40601
P: (502) 564-7005
F: (502) 564-5820
E: donna.neary@ky.gov

LOUISIANA
Mr. Jonathan Fricker
Director
Division of Historical Preservation
P.O. Box 44247
Baton Rouge, LA 70804
P: (225) 342-8160
F: (225) 342-8173

MAINE
Mr. Earle G. Shettleworth Jr.
State Historic Preservation Officer
Historic Preservation Commission
55 Capitol Street
Station 65
Augusta, ME 04333
P: (207) 287-2132
F: (207) 287-2335
E: earle.shettleworth@maine.gov

MARYLAND
Mr. J. Rodney Little
State Historic Preservation Officer
Historical Trust
100 Community Place
3rd Floor
Crownsville, MD 21032
P: (410) 514-7600
F: (410) 514-7678
E: rlittle@mdp.state.md.us

MASSACHUSETTS
Ms. Brona Simon
State Historic Preservation Officer & Executive Director
Historical Commission
220 Morrissey Boulevard
Boston, MA 02125
P: (617) 727-8470
F: (617) 727-5128
E: Brona.Simon@state.ma.us

MICHIGAN
Mr. Brian D. Conway
State Historic Preservation Officer
Historic Preservation Office
702 West Kalamazoo Street
P.O. Box 30740
Lansing, MI 48909
P: (517) 373-1630
F: (517) 335-0348
E: conwaybd@michigan.gov

MINNESOTA
Dr. Nina Archabal
State Historic Preservation Officer
Historical Society
345 Kellogg Boulevard West
St. Paul, MN 55102
P: (651) 296-2747
F: (651) 296-1004

MISSISSIPPI
Mr. H.T. Holmes
State Historic Preservation Officer
Department of Archives & History
P.O. Box 571
Jackson, MS 39205
P: (601) 576-6850
E: hholmes@mdah.state.ms.us

MISSOURI
Mr. Doyle Childers
Director
Department of Natural Resources
205 Jefferson Street
P.O. Box 176
Jefferson City, MO 65102
P: (573) 751-4732
F: (573) 751-7627

Mr. Mark A. Miles
Director
State Historic Preservation Office
P.O. Box 176
Jefferson City, MO 65102
P: (573) 751-7858
F: (573) 526-2852
E: mark.miles@dnr.mo.gov

MONTANA
Dr. Stan Wilmoth
Acting State Historic Preservation Officer
State Historic Preservation Office
1410 8th Avenue
P.O. Box 201202
Helena, MT 59620
P: (406) 444-7719
F: (406) 444-6575
E: swilmoth@mt.gov

NEBRASKA
Mr. Michael Smith
Director & State Historic Preservation Officer
State Historical Society
P.O. Box 82554
1500 R Street
Lincoln, NE 68501
P: (402) 471-4745
F: (402) 471-3100
E: msmith@nebraskahistory.org

NEVADA
Mr. Ronald M. James
State Historic Preservation Officer
Historic Preservation Office
100 North Stewart Street
Capitol Complex
Carson City, NV 89701
P: (775) 684-3440
F: (775) 684-3442
E: ron@unr.edu

NEW HAMPSHIRE
Mr. James McConaha
Director & State Historic Preservation Officer
Division of Historical Resources
19 Pillsbury Street
2nd Floor
Concord, NH 03301
P: (603) 271-6435
F: (603) 271-3433
E: james.mcconaha@dcr.nh.gov

NEW JERSEY
Ms. Dorothy P. Guzzo
Administrator
Historic Preservation Office
501 East State Street, 3rd Floor
P.O. Box 404
Trenton, NJ 08625
P: (609) 984-0176
F: (609) 984-0578
E: dorothy.guzzo@dep.state.nj.us

Ms. Lisa P. Jackson
Commissioner
Department of Environmental Protection
P.O. Box 402
401 East State Street, 7th Floor
Trenton, NJ 08625
P: (609) 777-4327
F: (609) 292-7695

NEW MEXICO
Ms. Kak Slick
Director
Historic Preservation Division
Department of Cultural Affairs
407 Galisteo Street
Santa Fe, NM 87501
P: (505) 827-6320
F: (505) 827-6338
E: katherine.slick@state.nm.us

NEW YORK
Ms. Carol Ash
Acting Commissioner
Parks, Recreation & Historic Preservation
Agency Building 1
Empire State Plaza
Albany, NY 12238
P: (518) 474-0443

NORTH CAROLINA
Dr. Jeffrey J. Crow
Deputy Secretary & State Historic Preservation Officer
Division of Archives & History
4610 Mail Service Center
109 East Jones Street
Raleigh, NC 27699
P: (919) 807-7280
F: (919) 733-8807
E: jeff.crow@ncmail.net

NORTH DAKOTA
Mr. Merlan E. Paaverud Jr.
State Historical Preservation Officer
State Historical Society
612 East Boulevard Avenue
Bismarck, ND 58505
P: (701) 328-2666
F: (701) 328-3710
E: mpaaverud@nd.gov

NORTHERN MARIANA ISLANDS
Mr. Roy Sablan
Director & Historic Preservation Officer
Department of Community & Cultural Affairs
Caller Box 10007, Capital Hill
Saipan, MP 96950
P: (670) 664-2120
F: (670) 664-2139
E: administration@cda.gov.mp

Historic Preservation

OHIO
Ms. Rachel M. Tooker
State Historic Preservation Officer
Historic Preservation Office
Ohio Historical Society
567 East Hudson Street
Columbus, OH 43211
P: (614) 298-2000
F: (614) 298-2037
E: rtooker@ohiohistory.org

OKLAHOMA
Dr. Bob L. Blackburn
State Historic Preservation Officer
Historical Society
2401 North Laird Avenue
Oklahoma City, OK 73105
P: (405) 521-5202
E: bblackburn@okhistory.org

OREGON
Mr. Roger Roper
Deputy State Historic Preservation Officer
State Historic Preservation Office
725 Summer Street, Northeast
Suite C
Salem, OR 97301
P: (503) 986-0677
E: roger.roper@state.or.us

Mr. Tim Wood
State Historic Preservation Officer
Parks & Recreation Department
725 Summer Street, Northeast,
Suite C
Salem, OR 97301
P: (503) 986-0718
F: (503) 986-0796
E: tim.wood@state.or.us

PENNSYLVANIA
Ms. Barbara Franco
State Historic Preservation Officer
Historical & Museum Commission
300 North Street
Harrisburg, PA 17120
P: (717) 787-3362
F: (717) 787-9924

PUERTO RICO
Ms. Aida Belen Rivera Ruiz
State Historic Preservation Officer
Historic Preservation Office
P.O. Box 9066581
San Juan, PR 00906
P: (787) 721-3737
F: (787) 722-3773
E: abrivera@prshpo.gobierno.pr

RHODE ISLAND
Mr. Edward Sanderson
Executive Director
Historic Preservation & Heritage Commission
Old State House
150 Benefit Street
Providence, RI 02903
P: (401) 222-4130
F: (401) 222-2968

SOUTH CAROLINA
Dr. Rodger E. Stroup
State Historic Preservation Officer
Department of Archives & History
8301 Parklane Road
Columbia, SC 29223
P: (803) 896-6187
F: (803) 896-6167

SOUTH DAKOTA
Mr. Jay D. Vogt
State Historic Preservation Officer
State Historical Preservation Office
Cultural Heritage Center
900 Governors Drive
Pierre, SD 57501
P: (605) 773-3458
F: (605) 773-6041
E: jay.vogt@state.sd.us

TENNESSEE
Mr. Jim Fyke
Commissioner
Department of Environment & Conservation
1st Floor, L & C Annex
401 Church Street
Nashville, TN 37243
P: (615) 532-0106
F: (615) 532-0120

Mr. E. Patrick McIntyre Jr.
Executive Director
Historical Commission
2941 Lebanon Road
Nashville, TN 37243
P: (615) 532-1550
F: (615) 532-0120

TEXAS
Mr. Lawrence F. Oaks
Executive Director
Historical Commission
P.O. Box 12276
Austin, TX 78711
P: (512) 463-6100
F: (512) 463-8222
E: l.oaks@thc.state.tx.us

U.S. VIRGIN ISLANDS
Mr. Dean C. Plaskett
State Historic Preservation Officer
Department of Planning & Natural Resources
17 Kongens
St. Thomas, VI 00802
P: 340-776-8605
F: 340-776-7236

UTAH
Mr. Phillip F. Notarianni
Director
Department of Community & Culture
State History
300 Rio Grande
Salt Lake City, UT 84101
P: (801) 533-3515
F: (801) 533-3503
E: pnotarianni@utah.gov

VERMONT
Ms. Jane Lendway
State Historic Preservation Officer
Division for Historic Preservation
National Life Building
Drawer 20
Montpelier, VT 05620
P: (802) 828-3211
E: jane.lendway@state.vt.us

VIRGINIA
Ms. Kathleen S. Kilpatrick
Director
Department of Historic Resources
2801 Kensington Avenue
Richmond, VA 23221
P: (804) 367-2323
F: (804) 367-2391
E: Kathleen.Kilpatrick@dhr.virginia.gov

WASHINGTON
Dr. Allyson Brooks
State Historic Preservation Officer
Office of Archaeology & Historic Preservation
P.O. Box 48343
Olympia, WA 98504
P: (360) 586-3066
F: (360) 586-3067
E: allyson.brooks@dahp.wa.gov

WEST VIRGINIA
Ms. Susan Pierce
Director
State Historic Preservation Office
1900 Kanawha Boulevard, East
Charleston, WV 25305
P: (304) 558-0240
E: susan.pierce@wvculture.org

WISCONSIN
Dr. Michael E. Stevens
State Historic Preservation Officer
Historical Society
816 State Street
Madison, WI 53706
P: (608) 264-6464
F: (608) 264-6504
E: mestevens@whs.wisc.edu

WYOMING
Ms. Sara Needles
Interim State Historic Preservation Officer
State Historic Preservation Office
2301 Central Avenue, 3rd Floor
Cheyenne, WY 82002
P: (307) 777-7697
F: (307) 777-6421
E: sneedl@state.wy.us

Housing Finance

Administers the state's housing assistance programs, provides low and moderate income housing by financing low interest loans.

ALABAMA
Mr. Robert Strickland
Director
Housing Finance Authority
P.O. Box 230909
Montgomery, AL 36123
P: (334) 244-9200
F: (334) 244-9214

ALASKA
Mr. Dan Fauske
Executive Director/CEO
Housing Finance Corporation
P.O. Box 101020
Anchorage, AK 99510
P: (907) 330-8452
F: (907) 338-9218

AMERICAN SAMOA
Mr. Vaivao Logotaeao Etelagi
President
Development Bank of American Samoa
P.O. Box 9
Pago Pago, AS 96799
P: (684) 633-4031
F: (684) 633-1163

Mr. Ute Abe Malae
President
Development Bank of American Samoa
American Samoa Government
P.O. Box 9
Pago Pago, AS 96799
P: (684) 633-4031
F: (684) 633-1163

ARIZONA
Ms. Sheila Harris
Director
Department of Housing
1700 West Washington, Suite 210
Phoenix, AZ 85007
P: (602) 771-1000

ARKANSAS
Mr. Mac Dodson
Director
Development Finance Authority
423 Main Street, Suite 500
Little Rock, AR 72201
P: (501) 682-5900
F: (501) 682-5939
E: mdodson@adfa.state.ar.us

CALIFORNIA
Ms. Theresa Parker
Executive Director
Housing Finance Agency
1121 L Street
Sacramento, CA 95814
P: (916) 322-3991

COLORADO
Ms. Kathi Williams
Director
Division of Housing
Department of Local Affairs
1313 Sherman, Room 518
Denver, CO 80203
P: (303) 866-2033
F: (303) 866-4077

CONNECTICUT
Mr. Gary E. King
President/Executive Director
Housing Finance Authority
999 West Street
Rocky Hill, CT 06067
P: (860) 721-9501
E: info@chfa.org

DELAWARE
Ms. Saundra Ross Johnson
Director
State Housing Authority
18 The Green
Dover, DE 19901
P: (302) 739-4263
F: (302) 739-6122

DISTRICT OF COLUMBIA
Ms. Leila Funucane Edmonds
Acting Director
Department of Housing & Community Development
801 North Capitol Street, NE
8th Floor
Washington, DC 20002
P: (202) 442-7210
F: (202) 442-9280

FLORIDA
Mr. Stephen P. Auger
Executive Director
Housing Finance Corporation
227 North Bronough Street, Suite 5000
Tallahassee, FL 32301
P: (850) 488-4197
F: (850) 488-9809

GEORGIA
Ms. Carmen Chubb
Division Director
Housing Finance Division
60 Executive Park South, North East
Room 228
Atlanta, GA 30329
P: (404) 679-0607
E: cchubb@dca.state.ga.us

GUAM
Mr. Jose Guevara
Acting President
Housing Corporation
ITC Building, Suite 535
590 So. Marine Drive, P.O. Box 3457
Hagatna, GU 96932
P: (671) 647-4143
F: (674) 649-4144

HAWAII
Mr. Dan Davidson
Executive Director
Housing Finance & Development Corporation
677 Queen Street, Suite 300
Honolulu, HI 96813
P: (808) 587-0610

IDAHO
Mr. Gerald M. Hunter
Executive Director
Housing & Finance Association
P.O. Box 7899
Boise, ID 83707
P: (208) 331-4889
F: (208) 331-4804
E: geraldh@ihfa.org

ILLINOIS
Ms. Deshana Forney
Executive Director
Housing Development Authority
401 North Michigan Avenue, Suite 900
Chicago, IL 60611
P: (312) 836-5314
F: (312) 836-5313

INDIANA
Ms. Sherry Seiwert
Executive Director
Housing & Community Development Authority
30 South Meridian
Suite 1000
Indianapolis, IN 46204
P: (317) 232-7777
F: (317) 232-7778

IOWA
Mr. Bret Mills
Executive Director
Iowa Finance Authority
100 East Grand Avenue
Suite 250
Des Moines, IA 50309
P: (512) 242-4858
F: (515) 242-4957
E: bret.mills@ifa.state.ia.us

KANSAS
Mr. Steve Weatherford
Director
Development Finance Authority
555 South Kansas Avenue
Suite 202
Topeka, KS 66603
P: (785) 357-4445
F: (785) 357-4478

KENTUCKY
Mr. Ben Cook
CEO
Housing Corporation
1231 Louisville Road
Frankfort, KY 40601
P: (502) 564-7630
F: (502) 564-5708
E: bcook@kyhousing.org

LOUISIANA
Mr. Milton Bailey
President
Housing Finance Agency
2415 Quail Drive
Baton Rouge, LA 70808
P: (225) 763-8700
F: (225) 763-8710

MAINE
Ms. Dale McCormick
Director
State Housing Authority
89 State House Station
Augusta, ME 04333
P: (207) 626-4600

MARYLAND
Mr. Raymond A. Skinner
Director
Department of Housing Community Development
100 Community Place
Crownsville, MD 21032
P: (410) 514-7001
E: skinner@mdhousing.org

Housing Finance

MASSACHUSETTS
Mr. Thomas Gleason
Executive Director
MassHousing
One Beacon Street
Boston, MA 02108
P: (617) 854-1000
F: (617) 854-1029

MICHIGAN
Mr. Michael R. DeVos
Executive Director
Michigan State Housing
Develpment Authority
735 East Michigan Avenue
P.O. Box 30044
Lansing, MI 48912
P: (517) 373-8370
F: (517) 335-4797
E: devosm@michigan.gov

MINNESOTA
Mr. Tim Marx
Commissioner
Housing Finance Agency
400 Sibley Street, Suite 300
St. Paul, MN 55101
P: (651) 296-5738
F: (651) 296-8139
E: tim.marx@state.mn.us

MISSISSIPPI
Ms. Diane Bolen
Executive Director
Home Corporation
P.O. Box 23369
Jackson, MS 39225
P: (601) 718-4600
F: (601) 354-7076
E: dbolen@mshc.com

MISSOURI
Mr. Pete Ramsel
Acting Executive Director
Housing Development
Commission
3435 Broadway
Kansas City, MO 64111
P: (816) 759-6606
F: (816) 759-6608
E: Pete.Ramsel@ded.mo.gov

MONTANA
Mr. Anthony Preite
Director
Department of Commerce
301 South Park
P.O. Box 200501
Helena, MT 59620
P: (406) 841-2704
F: (406) 841-2701
E: tpreite@mt.gov

NEBRASKA
Mr. Richard Baier
Director
Department of Economic
Development
P.O. Box 94666
Lincoln, NE 68509
P: (402) 471-3111
F: (402) 471-3778

NEVADA
Mr. Charles L. Horsey III
Administrator
Housing Division
1802 North Carson Street, Suite
154
Carson City, NV 89701
P: (775) 687-2031
F: (775) 687-4040
E: chorsey
@nvhousing.state.nv.us

NEW HAMPSHIRE
Ms. Claira P. Monier
Executive Director
Housing Finance Authority
32 Constitution Drive
Bedford, NH 03110
P: (603) 472-8623
F: (603) 472-8501
E: cmonier@nhhfa.org

NEW JERSEY
Ms. Marge Della Vecchia
Executive Director
Housing & Mortgage Finance
Agency
637 South Clinton Avenue
P.O. Box 18550
Trenton, NJ 08650
P: (609) 278-7400
F: (609) 278-1754

NEW MEXICO
Mr. Jay Czar
Executive Director
Mortgage Finance Authority
334 Fourth Street Southwest
Albuquerque, NM 87102
P: (505) 767-2210
F: (505) 243-3289
E: jczar@housingnm.org

NEW YORK
Ms. Priscilla Almodovar
President & CEO
Housing Finance Agency
641 Lexington Avenue
New York, NY 10022
P: (212) 688-4000
F: (518) 486-6935

NORTH CAROLINA
Mr. Robert Kucab
Director
Housing Finance Agency
3508 Bush Street
Raleigh, NC 27609
P: (919) 877-5600
F: (919) 877-5701
E: arkucab@nchfa.com

NORTH DAKOTA
Mr. Mike Anderson
Executive Director
Housing Finance Agency
P.O. Box 1535
Bismarck, ND 58502
P: (701) 328-8080
F: (701) 328-8090
E: info@ndhfa.nd.gov

NORTHERN MARIANA ISLANDS
Mr. Thomas C. Duenas
Executive Director
Housing Corporation
P.O. Box 502149
Saipan, MP 96950
P: (670) 234-6245
F: (670) 234-7144
E: administration
@cda.gov.mp

OHIO
Mr. William Graves
Deputy Director
Community Development
Division
77 South High Street, 24th Floor
Columbus, OH 43215
P: (614) 466-3144

OKLAHOMA
Mr. Dennis Shockley
Executive Director
Housing Finance Agency
100 North West 63rd Street,
Suite 200
P.O. Box 26720
Oklahoma City, OK 73126
P: (405) 848-1144
F: (405) 840-1109

OREGON
Mr. Victor Merced
Director
Housing & Community Services
P.O. Box 14508
725 Summer Street, Northeast,
Suite B
Salem, OR 97301
P: (503) 986-2005
F: (503) 378-2897
E: info@hcs.state.or.us

PENNSYLVANIA
Mr. Brian A. Hudson Sr.
Executive Director
Housing Finance Agency
211 North Front Street
P.O. Box 8029
Harrisburg, PA 17105
P: (717) 780-3911
F: (717) 780-4026
E: bhudson@phfa.org

PUERTO RICO
Mr. Carlos D. Rivas
Executive Director
Housing Finance Authority
235 Arterial Hostos
Suite 1201, North Tower
Hato Rey, PR 00918
P: (787) 765-7577 Ext. 4573
F: (787) 620-3521

RHODE ISLAND
Ms. Noreen Shawcross
Executive Director
Housing Resources Commission
One Capitol Hill, 3rd Floor
Providence, RI 02903
P: (401) 222-5766
F: (401) 222-2803
E: nshawcross
@gw.doa.state.ri.us

SOUTH CAROLINA
Mr. Andy Laurent
Executive Director
State Housing Finance
Development Authority
300-C Outlet Point Boulevard
Columbia, SC 29210
P: (803) 896-9001
F: (803) 896-8583

SOUTH DAKOTA
Mr. Mark Lauseng
Executive Director
Housing Development
Authority
P.O. Box 1237
Pierre, SD 57501
P: (605) 773-3181
F: (605) 773-5154
E: mark@sdhda.org

TENNESSEE
Mr. Ted R. Fellman
Executive Director
Housing Development Agency
404 James Robertson Parkway,
Room 1114
Nashville, TN 37243
P: (615) 741-2400
F: (615) 741-9634

TEXAS
Mr. Michael Gerber
Executive Director
Department of Housing & Community Affairs
221 East 11th Street
P.O. Box 13941
Austin, TX 78711
P: (512) 475-3932

U.S. VIRGIN ISLANDS
Mr. Clifford Graham
Executive Director
Housing Finance Authority
3202 Demarara #3
Frenchtown Plaza, Suite 200
St. Thomas, VI 00802
P: (340) 774-4432
F: (340) 775-7913
E: vihfa@vihfa.gov

UTAH
Mr. William H. Erickson
President & CEO
Housing Corporation
2479 South Lake Park Boulevard
West Valley City, UT 84120
P: (801) 902-8200
F: (801) 359-1701
E: werickson@uthc.org

VERMONT
Ms. Sarah Carpenter
Executive Director
Housing Finance Agency
1 Burlington Square
P.O. Box 408
Burlington, VT 05402
P: (802) 864-5743
F: (802) 864-5746

VIRGINIA
Ms. Susan F. Dewey
Executive Director
Housing Development Authority
600 South Belvidere Street
Richmond, VA 23230
P: (804) 343-5701
F: (804) 783-6704
E: susan.dewey@vhda.com

Mr. William C. Shelton
Director
Department of Housing & Community Development
The Jackson Center
501 North 2nd Street
Richmond, VA 23219
P: (804) 371-7002
F: (804) 371-6524
E: bill.shelton@dhcd.virginia.gov

WASHINGTON
Mr. Kim Herman
Executive Director
Housing Finance Commission
1000 2nd Avenue, Suite 2700
Seattle, WA 98104
P: (206) 464-7139
F: (206) 587-5113

WEST VIRGINIA
Mr. Joe Hatfield
Executive Director
Housing Development Fund
814 Virginia Street, East
Charleston, WV 25301
P: (304) 345-6475
F: (304) 345-4828

WISCONSIN
Mr. Antonio Riley
Executive Director
Housing & Economic Development Authority
201 West Washington Avenue, Suite 700
P.O. Box 1728
Madison, WI 53703
P: (608) 266-2893
F: (608) 267-1099

WYOMING
Mr. George Axlund
Executive Director
Community Development Authority
P.O. Box 634
Casper, WY 82601
P: (307) 265-0603
F: (307) 266-5414

Human Services

Manages the development, administration, and delivery of all human and social service programs.

ALABAMA
Dr. Page Walley
Commissioner
Department of Human Resources
Gordon Persons Building, Suite 2104
50 North Ripley Street
Montgomery, AL 36130
P: (334) 242-1310
F: (334) 242-1086

ALASKA
Ms. Karleen K. Jackson
Commissioner
Health & Social Services
P.O. Box 110601
Juneau, AK 99811
P: (907) 465-3030
F: (907) 465-3068

AMERICAN SAMOA
Mr. Talia Fa'afetai I'aulualo
Director
Department of Human & Social Services
American Samoa Government
Pago Pago, AS 96799
P: (684) 633-1187
F: (684) 633-7449

ARIZONA
Ms. Susan Gerard
Director
Department of Health Services
150 North 18th Avenue
Phoenix, AZ 85007
P: (602) 542-1001
F: (602) 543-0883

ARKANSAS
Mr. John Selig
Director
Department of Health & Human Services
P.O. Box 1437, Slot S201
Little Rock, AR 72203
P: (501) 682-8650
F: (501) 682-6836
E: John.Selig@arkansas.gov

CALIFORNIA
Ms. S. Kimberly Belshe
Secretary
Health & Human Services Agency
1600 Ninth Street, Room 460
Sacramento, CA 95814
P: (916) 654-3345
F: (916) 654-3343

COLORADO
Ms. Karen Legault Beye
Executive Director
Department of Human Services
1575 Sherman Street
Denver, CO 80203
P: (303) 866-5700
F: (303) 866-4740

CONNECTICUT
Mr. Michael Starkowski
Commissioner
Department of Social Services
25 Sigourney Street
Hartford, CT 06106
P: (860) 424-5008

DELAWARE
Mr. Vincent P. Meconi
Secretary
Department of Health & Social Services
Herman M. Holloway, Sr. Campus
1901 North DuPont Highway, Main Building
New Castle, DE 19720
P: (302) 255-9040
E: Vincent.Meconi@state.de.us

DISTRICT OF COLUMBIA
Ms. Kate Jesberg
Interim Director
Department of Human Services
64 New York Avenue, NE
6th Floor
Washington, DC 20001
P: (202) 671-4200
F: (202) 671-4381

FLORIDA
Mr. Bob Butterworth
Secretary
Department of Children & Families
1317 Winewood Boulevard
Building 1, Room 202
Tallahassee, FL 32399
P: (850) 487-1111
F: (850) 922-2993

GEORGIA
Ms. B. J. Walker
Commissioner
Department of Human Resources
2 Peachtree Street, Northwest
Room 29-250
Atlanta, GA 30303
P: (404) 463-3390
F: (404) 651-8669

GUAM
Mr. Arthur U. San Agustin
Director
Department of Health & Social Services
123 Chalan Kareta, Route 10
Mangilao, GU 96923
P: (671) 735-7102
F: (671) 734-5910
E: chiefdsc@dphss.govguam.net

HAWAII
Ms. Lillian B. Koller
Director
Department of Human Services
P.O. Box 339
Honolulu, HI 96809
P: (808) 586-4997
F: (808) 586-4890

IDAHO
Mr. Richard Armstrong
Director
Department of Health & Welfare
450 West State Street
Pete T. Cenarrusa Building
Boise, ID 83720
P: (208) 334-5500
F: (208) 334-6558

ILLINOIS
Dr. Carol L. Adams
Director
Department of Human Services
100 South Grand Avenue, East
3rd Floor
Springfield, IL 62762
P: (217) 557-1601
F: (217) 557-1647

INDIANA
Mr. E. Mitch Roob Jr.
Cabinet Secretary
Family & Social Services Administration
402 West Washington Street, Room W461
Indianapolis, IN 46206
P: (317) 233-4454
F: (317) 233-4693

IOWA
Mr. Kevin Concannon
Director
Department of Human Services
Hoover Building
1305 East Walnut Street
Des Moines, IA 50319
P: (515) 281-5454
F: (515) 281-4980

KANSAS
Mr. Don Jordan
Secretary
Department of Social & Rehabilitation Services
915 Southwest Harrison Street
Topeka, KS 66612
P: (785) 296-3274
F: (785) 296-4685

KENTUCKY
Mr. Mark Birdwhistell
Secretary
Cabinet for Health & Family Services
275 East Main Street, 5W-A
Frankfort, KY 40601
P: (502) 564-7042
F: (502) 564-7091

LOUISIANA
Ms. Ann Williamson
Secretary
Department of Social Services
755 Third Street
P.O. Box 3776
Baton Rouge, LA 70821
P: (225) 342-0286
F: (225) 342-8636
E: Ann.Williamson@dss.state.la.us

MAINE
Ms. Brenda M. Harvey
Acting Commissioner
Department of Human Services
11 State House Station
Augusta, ME 04333
P: (207) 287-2736
F: (207) 287-3005
E: brenda.harvey@maine.gov

MARYLAND
Ms. Brenda Donald
Secretary
Department of Human Resources
311 West Saratoga Street
Baltimore, MD 21201
P: (410) 767-7109
E: bdonald@dhr.state.md.us

MASSACHUSETTS
Dr. JudyAnn Bigby
Secretary
Executive Office of Health & Human Services
One Ashburton Place, Room 1109
Boston, MA 02108
P: (617) 727-7600
F: (617) 727-5134

MICHIGAN
Ms. Marianne Udow
Director
Department of Human Services
P.O. Box 30037
Lansing, MI 48909
P: (517) 373-1121
F: (517) 335-6101
E: udowm@michigan.gov

MINNESOTA
Mr. Cal Ludeman
Commissioner
Department of Human Services
Human Services Building
540 Cedar Street
St. Paul, MN 55155
P: (651) 431-2907
F: (651) 431-7443
E: cal.ludeman@state.mn.us

MISSISSIPPI
Mr. Donald Taylor
Executive Director
Department of Human Services
750 North State Street
Jackson, MS 39202
P: (601) 359-4500

MISSOURI
Ms. Jane Drummond
Director
Department of Health & Human Services
920 Wildwood
P.O. Box 570
Jefferson City, MO 65102
P: (573) 751-6001
F: (573) 751-6041
E: jane.drummond@dhss.mo.gov

MONTANA
Ms. Joan Miles
Director
Department of Public Health & Human Services
111 North Sanders, Room 301/308
P.O. Box 4210
Helena, MT 59604
P: (406) 444-5622
F: (406) 444-1970

NEBRASKA
Ms. Chris Peterson
CEO
Department of Health & Human Services
P.O. Box 95044
Lincoln, NE 68509
P: (402) 471-3121

NEVADA
Mr. Michael Willden
Director
Department of Health & Human Services
505 East King Street, Room 600
Carson City, NV 89706
P: (775) 684-4000
F: (775) 684-4010
E: mwillden@dhhs.nv.gov

NEW HAMPSHIRE
Mr. John A. Stephen
Commissioner
Department of Health & Human Services
129 Pleasant Street
Concord, NH 03301
P: (603) 271-4331
F: (603) 271-4912
E: jstephen@dhhs.state.nh.us

NEW JERSEY
Mr. Kevin M. Ryan
Commissioner
Department of Human Services
222 South Warren Street
P.O. Box 700
Trenton, NJ 08625
P: (609) 292-3717

Ms. Jennifer Velez
Acting Commissioner
Department of Human Services
P.O. Box 726
Trenton, NJ 08625
P: (609) 292-0901

NEW MEXICO
Ms. Pamela S. Hyde
Cabinet Secretary
Department of Human Services
2009 South Pacheco, Pollon Plaza
P.O. Box 2348
Santa Fe, NM 87504
P: (505) 827-7750
F: (505) 827-3185

NEW YORK
Mr. David Hansell
Commissioner
Office of Temporary & Disability Assistance
40 North Pearl Street
Albany, NY 12243
P: (518) 408-3847
F: (518) 486-9179

NORTH CAROLINA
Ms. Carmen Hooker-Odom
Secretary
Department of Health & Human Services
2001 Mail Service Center
Raleigh, NC 27699
P: (919) 733-4534
F: (919) 715-4645
E: carmen.hookerodom@ncmail.net

NORTH DAKOTA
Ms. Carol K. Olson
Executive Director
Department of Human Services
600 East Boulevard Avenue
3rd Floor - Judicial Wing
Bismarck, ND 58505
P: (701) 328-2310
F: (701) 328-2359
E: socols@nd.gov

NORTHERN MARIANA ISLANDS
Mr. Joseph P. Villagomez
Secretary of Public Health
Department of Public Health
P.O. Box 500409
Saipan, MP 96950
P: (670) 236-8201
F: (670) 234-8930
E: jkvsaipan@aol.com

OHIO
Ms. Helen Jones-Kelley
Director
Department of Job & Family Services
30 East Broad Street, 31st Floor
Columbus, OH 43215
P: (614) 466-6282
F: (614) 466-2815
E: jonesh@odjfs.state.oh.us

OKLAHOMA
Mr. Howard Hendrick
Secretary
Department of Human Services
P.O. Box 25352
Oklahoma City, OK 73125
P: (405) 521-3646
F: (405) 521-6684

OREGON
Dr. Bruce Goldberg
Director
Department of Human Services
500 Summer Street, Northeast
4th Floor, E-15
Salem, OR 97301
P: (503) 945-5944
F: (503) 378-2897
E: dhs.info@state.or.us

PENNSYLVANIA
Ms. Estelle B. Richman
Secretary
Department of Public Welfare
Health & Welfare Building, Room 333
Harrisburg, PA 17105
P: (717) 787-2600
F: (717) 772-2062

PUERTO RICO
Mr. Felix Matos Rodriguez
Secretary
Department of the Family
P.O. Box 11398
San Juan, PR 00910
P: (787) 294-4900
F: (787) 294-0732

RHODE ISLAND
Mr. Gary Alexander
Acting Director
Department of Human Services
Louis Pasteur Building
600 New London Avenue
Craston, RI 02920
P: (401) 462-2121
F: (401) 462-3677

SOUTH CAROLINA
Ms. Kathleen M. Hayes
Director
Department of Social Services
P.O. Box 1520
Columbia, SC 29202
P: (803) 898-7360
F: (803) 898-7277

SOUTH DAKOTA
Mr. Jerry Hofer
Secretary
Department of Human Services
Hillsview Plaza
C/o 500 East Capitol Avenue
Pierre, SD 57501
P: (605) 773-5990
F: (605) 773-5483
E: jerry.hofer@state.sd.us

Human Services

TENNESSEE
Ms. Virginia T. Lodge
Commissioner
Department of Human Services
Citizens Plaza, 15th Floor
400 Deaderick Street
Nashville, TN 37248
P: (615) 313-4700
F: (615) 741-4165

TEXAS
Mr. Albert Hawkins
Executive Commissioner
Health and Human Services
Commission
P.O. Box 13247
Austin, TX 78711
P: (512) 424-6603
F: (512) 424-6587

Ms. Adelaide Horn
Commissioner
Department of Aging &
Disablility Services
P.O. Box 149030
Austin, TX 78714
P: (512) 438-3030
F: (512) 438-4220

U.S. VIRGIN ISLANDS
Ms. Sedonie Halbert
Commissioner
Department of Human Services
Knud Hansen Complex,
Building A
1303 Hospital Grounds
St. Thomas, VI 00802
P: (340) 774-0930
F: (340) 774-3466

VERMONT
Ms. Cynthia D. LaWare
Commissioner
Agency of Human Services
103 South Main Street
Waterbury, VT 05671
P: (802) 241-2220
F: (802) 241-2979

VIRGINIA
Ms. Marilyn B. Tavenner
Secretary
Department of Health & Human
Services
1111 East Broad Street
Patrick Henry Building
Richmond, VA 23219
P: (804) 786-7765
F: (804) 371-6984
E: marilyn.tavenner
@governor.virginia.gov

WASHINGTON
Ms. Robin Arnold-Williams
Secretary
Department of Social & Health
Services
P.O. Box 45010
Olympia, WA 98504
P: (360) 902-7800

WEST VIRGINIA
Ms. Martha Yeager Walker
Cabinet Secretary
Department of Health & Human
Resources
Capitol Complex Building 3,
Room 206
1900 Kanawha Boulevard, East
Charleston, WV 25305
P: (304) 558-0684
F: (304) 558-1130
E: marthaywalker@wvdhrr.org

WISCONSIN
Mr. Kevin Hayden
Secretary
Department of Health & Family
Services
1 West Wilson Street, Room 650
Madison, WI 53702
P: (608) 266-9622
E: haydekr@dhfs.state.wi.us

WYOMING
Mr. Tony Lewis
Interim Director of Family
Services
Department of Family Services
Hathaway Building, 3rd Floor
2300 Capitol Avenue
Cheyenne, WY 82002
P: (307) 777-7561
F: (307) 777-7747

Information Systems

Provides statewide computer services or coordinates the operation of various data processing systems within state government.

ALABAMA
Mr. Eugene J. Akers
Manager
Office of Planning & Development
Information Services Division
64 North Union Street
Montgomery, AL 36130
P: (334) 353-4363
F: (334) 242-3228

ALASKA
Ms. Jan Moyer
Deputy Director
Information Technology Group
Department of Administration
P.O. Box 110206
Juneau, AK 99811
P: (907) 465-5169
F: (907) 465-3450
E: Janet_Moyer@admin.state.ak.us

AMERICAN SAMOA
Mr. Faleseu Eliu Paopao
Director
Department of Commerce
American Samoa Government
Executive Office Building, Utulei
Pago Pago, AS 96799
P: (684) 633-5155
F: (684) 633-4195

Hon. Velega Savali
Treasurer
Department of Treasury
American Samoa Government
Pago Pago, AS 96799
P: (684) 633-4155
F: (684) 633-4100

ARIZONA
Mr. Patrick Quain
Assistant Director
Information Services Division
100 North 15th Avenue, Suite 400
Phoenix, AZ 85007
P: (602) 542-2250
F: (602) 542-4272

ARKANSAS
Ms. Claire Bailey
Interim Executive Chief Information Officer
Department of Information Systems
#1 Capitol Mall, 3rd Floor
Little Rock, AR 72203
P: (501) 682-9990
F: (501) 682-9465
E: claire.bailey@arkansas.gov

CALIFORNIA
Mr. P.K. Agarwal
Director
Department of Technology Services
P.O. Box 1810
Rancho Cordova, CA 95741
P: (916) 657-9974

CONNECTICUT
Ms. Diane S. Wallace
Chief Information Officer
Department of Information Technology
101 East River Drive
East Hartford, CT 06108
P: (860) 622-2419
F: (860) 291-8665
E: diane.wallace@ct.gov

DELAWARE
Mr. Thomas M. Jarrett
Chief Information Officer
Department of Technology & Information
801 Silver Lake Boulevard
Dover, DE 19904
P: (302) 739-9629
F: (302) 739-1442
E: thomas.jarrett@state.de.us

DISTRICT OF COLUMBIA
Mr. Vivek Kundra
Director
Chief Technology Office
441 4th Street, Northwest
Suite 930-S
Washington, DC 20001
P: (202) 727-2277
F: (202) 727-6857

GEORGIA
Mr. Tom Wade
Executive Director and State Chief Information Officer
Technology Authority
100 Peachtree Street, Northwest
Suite 2300
Atlanta, GA 30303
P: (404) 463-2340
F: (404) 463-2380
E: twade@gta.ga.gov

GUAM
Ms. Lourdes M. Perez
Director
Department of Administraiton
P.O. Box 884
Agana, GU 96932
P: (671) 475-1250
F: (671) 477-6788

HAWAII
Mr. Lester Nakamura
Administrator
Information & Communications Services Division
DAGS
P.O. Box 119
Honolulu, HI 96810
F: (808) 586-1922
E: lnakamura@state.hi.us

IDAHO
Mr. Keith Johnson
Director
Department of Administration
650 West State Street, Room 100
P.O. Box 83720
Boise, ID 83720
P: (208) 332-1824
F: (208) 334-2307
E: keith.johnson@adm.idaho.gov

Mr. Joe Roche
Administrator
Division of Information Technology & Communications Services
Department of Administration
650 West State Street, Room 100
Boise, ID 83720
P: (208) 332-1841
F: (208) 334-2307
E: joe.roche@adm.idaho.gov

ILLINOIS
Ms. Lana Kains
Division Manager
Information Services Division
120 West Jefferson, 3rd Floor
Springfield, IL 62702
P: (217) 524-6895

INDIANA
Mr. Gerry Weaver
Chief Information Officer
Office of Technology
100 North Senate Avenue, Room N551
Indianapolis, IN 46204
P: (317) 232-3172
F: (317) 232-0748
E: gweaver@iot.in.gov

IOWA
Ms. Mollie K. Anderson
Director
Department of Administrative Services
Hoover Building, 3rd Floor
1305 East Walnut
Des Moines, IA 50319
P: (515) 281-5360
F: (515) 281-6140
E: mollie.anderson@iowa.gov

KANSAS
Ms. Denise Moore
Chief Information Technology Officer
Division of Information Services & Communications
Department of Administration
900 Southwest Jackson Street, Room 751-S
Topeka, KS 66612
P: (785) 296-3463
F: (785) 296-1168
E: denise.moore@da.state.ks.us

KENTUCKY
Mr. Mark Rutledge
Chief Information Officer
Commonwealth Office of Technology
Finance & Administration Cabinet
702 Capitol Avenue, Suite 258
Frankfort, KY 40601
P: (502) 564-1201
F: (502) 564-0421
E: mark.rutledge@ky.gov

LOUISIANA
Dr. Allen L. Doescher
Deputy Chief Information Officer
Division of Administration
Office of Information Technology
P.O. Box 94095
Baton Rouge, LA 70804
P: (225) 342-7105
F: (225) 219-4994
E: allen.doescher@la.gov

MAINE
Mr. Richard F. Hinkley
Director
Bureau of Information Services
145 State House Station
Augusta, ME 04333
P: (207) 624-7840

Information Systems

MARYLAND
Mr. Ellis L. Kitchen
Chief Information Officer
Office of Information Technology
Department of Budget & Management
45 Calvert Street
Annapolis, MD 21401
P: (410) 260-2994
F: (410) 974-5615
E: ekitchen@dbm.state.md.us

MASSACHUSETTS
Ms. Bethann Pepoli
Acting Chief Information Officer
Information Technology Division
1 Ashburton Place, Floor 8
Boston, MA 02108
P: (617) 626-4529
F: (617) 727-3766
E: bethann.pepoli@state.ma.us

MICHIGAN
Ms. Teri M. Takai
Director and Chief Information Officer
Department of Information Technology
111 South Capitol Avenue, Floor 8
Romney Building
Lansing, MI 48913
P: (517) 373-1006
F: (517) 373-8213
E: takait@michigan.gov

MINNESOTA
Ms. Dana Badgerow
Commissioner
Department of Administration
200 Administration Building
50 Sherburne Avenue
St. Paul, MN 55155
P: (651) 201-2555
F: (651) 297-7909
E: dana.badgerow@state.mn.us

MISSISSIPPI
Mr. David L. Litchliter
Executive Director
Department of Information Technology Services
301 North Lamar Street, Suite 508
Jackson, MS 39201
P: (601) 359-1395
F: (601) 354-6016
E: david.litchliter@its.state.ms.us

MISSOURI
Mr. Dan Ross
Chief Information Officer
Office of Information Technology
301 West High Street, Room 280
Jefferson City, MO 65102
P: (573) 526-7746
F: (573) 526-0132
E: dan.ross@oa.mo.gov

MONTANA
Mr. Dick Clark
Chief Information Officer
Information Technology Services Division
Department of Administration
P.O. Box 200113
Helena, MT 59620
P: (406) 444-2700
F: (406) 444-2701
E: dclark@mt.gov

NEBRASKA
Ms. Brenda L. Decker
Chief Information Officer
Department of Administrative Services
Office of the CIO
521 South 14th Street, Suite 300
Lincoln, NE 68508
P: (402) 471-3717
F: (402) 471-4864
E: bdecker@notes.state.ne.us

NEVADA
Mr. Dan Stockwell
Chief Information Officer
Department of Information Technology
505 East King Street, Room 403
Carson City, NV 89701
P: (775) 687-1294
F: (775) 684-5846
E: stockwell@doit.state.nv.us

NEW JERSEY
Mr. Adel W. Ebeid
Chief Information Officer
Office of Information Technology
200/300 Riverview Plaza
P.O. Box 212
Trenton, NJ 08625
P: (609) 984-4082
F: (609) 633-9100
E: abel.ebeid@oit.state.nj.us

NEW MEXICO
Mr. Roy Soto
Chief Information Officer
Office of the Chief Information Officer
5301 Central Avenue, Northeast Suite 1500
Albuquerque, NM 87108
P: (505) 841-6605
F: (505) 841-4780
E: Roy.Soto@state.nm.us

NEW YORK
Mr. John Egan
Commissioner
Office of General Services
Corning Tower Building, 41st Floor
Empire State Plaza
Albany, NY 12242
P: (518) 474-5991
F: (518) 473-6814

NORTH CAROLINA
Mr. George Bakolia
Chief Information Officer
Office of Information Technology Services
P.O. Box 17209
Raleigh, NC 27619
P: (919) 981-2680
F: (919) 981-2548
E: george.bakolia@ncmail.net

NORTH DAKOTA
Ms. Lisa Feldner
Chief Information Officer
Information Technology Department
600 East Boulevard Avenue, Room 103
Bismarck, ND 58505
P: (701) 328-1000
F: (701) 328-0301
E: lfeldner@nd.gov

NORTHERN MARIANA ISLANDS
Mr. Joe I. Quitugua
Director
Commonwealth of Northern Mariana Islands
P.O. Box 5234 CHRB
Saipan, MP 96950
P: (670) 664-1400
F: (670) 664-1415
E: finanedp02@gtepacifica.net

OHIO
Mr. R. Steve Edmonson
Chief Information Officer
Department of Administrative Services
30 East Broad Street, Floor 39
Columbus, OH 43215
P: (614) 644-6446
F: (614) 644-9382
E: steve.edmonson@oit.ohio.gov

OKLAHOMA
Mr. Joe Fleckinger
Director
Information Services Division
Office of State Finance
2209 North Central Avenue
Oklahoma City, OK 73105
P: (405) 522-4026
F: (405) 522-3042
E: joe.fleckinger@osf.ok.gov

OREGON
Mr. Dugan Petty
Interim Chief Information Officer
Enterprise Information Strategy & Policy (EISPD)
Department of Administrative Services
955 Center Street, Northeast, Room 470
Salem, OR 97301
P: (503) 378-3160
F: (503) 378-4351
E: dugan.petty@state.or.us

PENNSYLVANIA
Ms. Kristen Miller
Chief Information Officer
Office for Information Technology
Office of Information Technology
209 Finance Building
Harrisburg, PA 17120
P: (717) 214-1915
F: (717) 783-4374
E: krismiller@state.pa.us

RHODE ISLAND
Ms. Beverly Najarian
Director
Division of Information Technology
1 Capitol Hill
Providence, RI 02908
P: (401) 222-2280
F: (401) 222-6436
E: bnajarian@admin.ri.gov

SOUTH CAROLINA
Dr. Jim Bryant
Chief Information Officer
Office ofthe Chief Information Officer
Budget & Control Board
4430 Broad River Road
Columbia, SC 29210
P: (803) 896-0520
F: (803) 896-0789
E: jabryant@cio.sc.gov

SOUTH DAKOTA
Mr. Otto Doll
Commissioner
Bureau of Information & Telecommunications
Kneip Building
700 Governors Drive
Pierre, SD 57501
P: (605) 773-4165
F: (605) 773-6040
E: otto.doll@state.sd.us

TENNESSEE
Mr. Bill Ezell
Chief Information Officer
Office for Information Resources
William R. Snodgrass Tennessee Towers
16th Floor, 312 8th Avenue, North
Nashville, TN 37243
P: (615) 741-3700
F: (615) 532-0471
E: bill.ezell@state.tn.us

TEXAS
Mr. Brian Rawson
Director
Department of Information Resources
300 West 15th Street, Suite 1300
P.O. Box 13564
Austin, TX 78701
P: (512) 463-9909
F: (512) 475-4759
E: brian.rawson@dir.state.tx.us

U.S. VIRGIN ISLANDS
Mr. John George
Director, Chief Information Technology Officer
Information Technology
1050 Norre Gade, #5
Charlotte Amalie, VI 00801
P: (340) 774-1013
F: (340) 774-1490

UTAH
Mr. Stephen Fletcher
Chief Information Officer & Executive Director
Department of Technology Services
1 State Office Building, Floor 6
P.O. Box 141172
Salt Lake City, UT 84114
P: (801) 538-3298
F: (801) 538-3622
E: sfletcher@utah.gov

VERMONT
Mr. Thomas Murray
Commissioner & Chief Information Officer
Department of Information & Innovation
133 State Street, Floor 5
Montpelier, VT 05633
P: (802) 828-4141
F: (802) 828-3398
E: thomas.murray@state.vt.us

VIRGINIA
Mr. Aneesh P. Chopra
Secretary of Technology
Office of the Secretary of Technology
1111 East Broad Street
Patrick Henry Building
Richmond, VA 23219
P: (804) 786-9579
F: (804) 786-9584
E: aneesh.chopra@governor.virginia.gov

WASHINGTON
Mr. Gary Robinson
Chief Information Officer
Department of Information Services
1110 Jefferson Street, Southeast
P.O. Box 42445
Olympia, WA 98504
P: (360) 902-3500
F: (360) 664-0733
E: garyr@dis.wa.gov

WEST VIRGINIA
Ms. Helen Wilson
Director
Information Services & Communications Division
Building 6, Room 110
1900 Kanawha Boulevard, East
Charleston, WV 25305
P: (304) 558-8918
F: (304) 558-8887
E: hwilson@gwmail.state.wv.us

WISCONSIN
Mr. Oskar Anderson
Chief Information Officer
Division of Enterprise Technology
Department of Administration
P.O. Box 7844
Madison, WI 53707
P: (608) 264-9502
F: (608) 267-0626
E: oskar.anderson@wisconsin.gov

WYOMING
Mr. Earl Atwood
Administrator
Division of Information Technology
Department of A & I
2001 Capitol Avenue
Cheyenne, WY 82002
P: (307) 777-5600
F: (307) 777-6725
E: earl.atwood@wy.gov

Insurance

Licenses and regulates insurance agents and insurance and title companies in the state.

ALABAMA
Mr. Walter Bell
Commissioner
Department of Insurance
201 Monroe Street, Suite 1700
Montgomery, AL 36130
P: (334) 269-3550
F: (334) 241-4192

ALASKA
Ms. Linda Hall
Director
Division of Insurance
550 West 7th Avenue, Suite 1560
Anchorage, AK 99501
P: (907) 269-7900
F: (907) 269-7912

AMERICAN SAMOA
Mr. Elisara Togia'i
Insurance Commissioner
Office of the Governor
American Samoa Government
Pago Pago, AS 96799
P: (684) 633-4116
F: (684) 633-2269
E: perriliz@samoatelco.com

ARIZONA
Ms. Christina Urias
Director
Department of Insurance
2910 North 44th Street, 2nd Floor
Ste. 210
Phoenix, AZ 85018
P: (602) 912-8400

ARKANSAS
Ms. Julie Benafield Bowman
Commissioner
Insurance Department
1200 West 3rd
Little Rock, AR 72201
P: (501) 682-2600
F: (501) 682-2618

COLORADO
Mr. Marcy Morrison
Commissioner
Division of Insurance
Department of Regulatory Agencies
1560 Broadway, Suite 8500
Denver, CO 80203
P: (303) 894-7499
F: (303) 894-7455

CONNECTICUT
Ms. Susan F. Cogswell
Commissioner
Insurance Department
153 Market Street, 7th Floor
Hartford, CT 06103
P: (860) 297-3800
F: (860) 566-7410
E: susan.cogswell@po.state.ct.us

DELAWARE
Mr. Matthew Denn
Commissioner
Office of the Insurance Commissioner
Rodney Building
841 Silver Lake Boulevard
Dover, DE 19901
P: (302) 739-4251
F: (302) 739-5280

DISTRICT OF COLUMBIA
Mr. Thomas Hampton
Director
Department of Insurance, Securities & Banking
810 1st Street, Northeast
Suite 701
Washington, DC 20002
P: (202) 442-7773
F: (202) 535-1196

FLORIDA
Hon. Alex Sink (D)
Chief Financial Officer
Department of Financial Services
Fletcher Building, Suite 516
200 East Gaines Street
Tallahassee, FL 32399
P: (850) 413-2850
F: (850) 413-2950
E: alex.sink@fldfs.com

GEORGIA
Hon. John W. Oxendine (R)
Commissioner
Department of Insurance
2 Martin Luther King, Jr. Drive
Ste. 704, West Tower
Atlanta, GA 30334
P: (404) 656-2070
F: (404) 657-8542
E: executive@mail.oci.state.ga.us

GUAM
Mr. Artemio B. Illagan
Acting Director
Department of Revenue & Taxation
13-1 Mariner Drive, Tiyan
P.O. Box 23607
Barrigada, GU 96921
P: (671) 475-1817
F: (671) 472-2643

HAWAII
Mr. Jeffrey P. Schmidt
Insurance Commissioner
Division of Insurance
P.O. Box 3614
Honolulu, HI 96811
P: (808) 586-2799
F: (808) 586-2806

IDAHO
Mr. William W. Deal
Director
Department of Insurance
700 West State Street, 3rd Floor
P.O. Box 83720
Boise, ID 83720
P: (208) 334-4250
F: (208) 334-4398

ILLINOIS
Mr. Michael T. McRaith
Director
Division of Insurance
320 West Washington, 4th Floor
Springfield, IL 62767
P: (217) 782-4515
F: (217) 782-5020

INDIANA
Mr. James D. Atterholt
Commissioner
Department of Insurance
311 W. Washington St.
Rm. 300
Indianapolis, IN 46240
P: (317) 232-2385
F: (317) 232-5251

IOWA
Ms. Susan E. Voss
Commissioner
Insurance Division
330 Maple Street
Des Moines, IA 50319
P: (515) 281-5523

KANSAS
Hon. Sandy Praeger (R)
Commissioner of Insurance
Insurance Department
420 Southwest 9th Street
Topeka, KS 66612
P: (785) 296-3071
F: (785) 296-2283

KENTUCKY
Ms. Julie Mix McPeak
Executive Director
Office of Insurance
P.O. Box 517
Frankfort, KY 40602
P: (502) 564-3630
F: (502) 564-1453

LOUISIANA
Mr. James J. Donelon
Commissioner
Department of Insurance
1702 North 3rd Street
Baton Rouge, LA 70802
P: (225) 342-5900
F: (225) 342-4652

MAINE
Ms. Anne L. Head
Director
Office of Licensing & Regulation
Professional & Financial Regulation
35 State House Station, Gardiner Annex
Augusta, ME 04333
P: (207) 624-8633
F: (207) 624-8637
E: anne.l.head@maine.gov

MARYLAND
Mr. R. Stephen Orr
Commissioner
Insurance Administration
525 Saint Paul Place
Annapolis, MD 21202
P: (410) 468-2090
F: (410) 468-2020

MASSACHUSETTS
Ms. Nonnie S. Burnes
Commissioner
Division of Insurance
1 South Station
Boston, MA 02110
P: (617) 521-7301
F: (617) 521-7758

MICHIGAN
Ms. Linda A. Watters
Commissioner
Office of Financial & Insurance Services
Department of Labor & Economic Growth
611 West Ottawa Street, Third Floor
Lansing, MI 48933
P: (877) 999-6442
F: (517) 241-3953
E: ofis-sec-info@michigan.gov

MINNESOTA
Mr. Glenn Wilson
Commissioner
Department of Commerce
85 7th Place East, Suite 500
St. Paul, MN 55101
P: (651) 296-6025
F: (651) 282-2568
E: glenn.wilson@state.mn.us

MISSISSIPPI
Mr. George Dale
Commissioner
Department of Insurance
1804 Sillers Building
P.O. Box 79
Jackson, MS 39205
P: (601) 359-3569
F: (601) 359-2474
E: george.dale
@mid.state.ms.us

MISSOURI
Mr. Douglas M. Ommen
Director
Department of Insurance, Financial Institutions & Professional Registration
301 West High Street
P.O. Box 690
Jefferson City, MO 65102
P: (573) 751-1927
F: (573) 751-1165
E: doug.ommen
@insurance.mo.gov

MONTANA
Hon. John Morrison (D)
State Auditor
Insurance Division
840 Helena Avenue
Helena, MT 59601
P: (406) 444-2040
F: (406) 444-3497

NEBRASKA
Mr. Tim Wagner
Director
Department of Insurance
941 O Street
Lincoln, NE 68508
P: (402) 471-2201
F: (402) 471-4610

NEVADA
Ms. Alice Molasky-Arman
Commissioner
Division of Insurance
788 Fairview Drive #300
Carson City, NV 89701
P: (775) 687-4270
F: (775) 687-3937
E: icommish@doi.state.nv.us

NEW HAMPSHIRE
Mr. Roger A. Sevigny
Commissioner
Department of Insurance
21 South Fruit Street, Suite 14
Concord, NH 03301
P: (603) 271-7973
F: (603) 271-1406
E: roger.sevigny@ins.nh.gov

NEW JERSEY
Mr. Steven M. Goldman
Commissioner
Department of Banking & Insurance
P.O. Box 325
Trenton, NJ 08625
P: (609) 292-5360
F: (609) 663-3601
E: commissioner
@dobi.state.nj.us

NEW MEXICO
Mr. Morris J. Chavez
Superintendent of Insurance
Insurance Division
P.O. Box 1269
Santa Fe, NM 87501
P: (505) 827-4297
F: (505) 827-4734

NEW YORK
Mr. Eric Dinallo
Superintendent
Insurance Department
One Commerce Plaza
Albany, NY 12257
P: (212) 480-2289
F: (212) 803-3715

NORTH CAROLINA
Mr. James E. Long
Commissioner of Insurance
Department of Insurance
430 North Salisbury Street
P.O. Box 2638
Raleigh, NC 27611
P: (919) 733-7343
F: (919) 733-6495
E: jlong@ncdoi.net

NORTH DAKOTA
Mr. Jim Poolman
Commissioner
Insurance Department
600 East Boulevard Avenue, 5th Floor
Bismarck, ND 58505
P: (701) 328-2440
F: (701) 328-4880
E: jpoolman@nd.gov

NORTHERN MARIANA ISLANDS
Mr. James A. Santos
Director
Department of Commerce
Caller Box 10007, Capital Hill
Saipan, MP 96950
P: (670) 664-3000
F: (670) 664-3070
E: commercedept
@vzpacifica.net

OHIO
Ms. Mary Jo Hudson
Director
Department of Insurance
2100 Stella Court
Columbus, OH 43215
P: (614) 644-2658
F: (614) 644-3743

OKLAHOMA
Ms. Kim Holland
Insurance Commissioner
Department of Insurance
P.O. Box 53408
Oklahoma City, OK 73152
P: (405) 521-2668
F: (405) 521-6635

OREGON
Mr. Joel Ario
Insurance Administrator
Insurance Division
350 Winter Street, Northeast
Room 430
Salem, OR 97301
P: (503) 947-7980
F: (503) 378-4351
E: dcbs.insmail@state.or.us

PENNSYLVANIA
Mr. Randy Rohrbaugh
Acting Commissioner
Insurance Department
1326 Strawberry Square
Harrisburg, PA 17120
P: (717) 783-0442
F: (717) 772-1969

PUERTO RICO
Ms. Dorelisse Juarbe Jimenez
Commissioner
Offcie of the Commissioner of Insurance
P.O. Box 8330
San Juan, PR 00910
P: (787) 722-8686
F: (787) 722-4400

RHODE ISLAND
Mr. Joseph Torti III
Superintendent of Insurance & Associate Director
Division of Insurance
233 Richmond Street
Providence, RI 02903
P: (401) 222-2223
F: (401) 222-5475

SOUTH CAROLINA
Mr. Scott H. Richardson
Department of Insurance
P.O. Box 100105
Columbia, SC 29202
P: (803) 737-6805

SOUTH DAKOTA
Mr. Merle Scheiber
Director
Division of Insurance
Anderson Building
445 East Capitol Avenue
Pierre, SD 57501
P: (605) 773-3563
F: (605) 773-5369
E: merle.scheiber
@state.sd.us

TENNESSEE
Ms. Leslie A. Newman
Commissioner
Department of Commerce & Insurance
500 James Robertson Parkway
Nashville, TN 37243
P: (615) 741-2241
F: (615) 532-5934

TEXAS
Mr. Mike Geeslin
Commissioner of Insurance
Department of Insurance
P.O. Box 149104
Austin, TX 78714
P: (512) 463-6464
F: (512) 475-2005

UTAH
Mr. Kent Michie
Commissioner
Department of Insurance
3110 State Office Building
Salt Lake City, UT 84114
P: (801) 538-3840
F: (801) 538-3829
E: kmichie@utah.gov

VERMONT
Ms. Paulette J. Thabault
Commissioner
Department of Banking, Insurance, Securities & Health Care
89 Main Street
Drawer 20
Montpelier, VT 05620
P: (802) 828-3301
F: (802) 828-3306

VIRGINIA
Mr. Alfred W. Gross
Commissioner
Bureau of Insurance
State Corporation Commission
1300 East Main Street, P.O. Box 1157
Richmond, VA 23218
P: (804) 371-9225
F: (804) 371-9348
E: al.gross
@scc.virginia.gov

Insurance

WASHINGTON
Mr. Mike Kreidler
Commissioner
Office of the Insurance Commissioner
5000 Capitol Blvd.
P.O. Box 40255
Olympia, WA 98504
P: (360) 664-3154
F: (360) 586-3535

WEST VIRGINIA
Ms. Jane Cline
Commissioner
Insurance Commission
1124 Smith Street
Charleston, WV 25301
P: (304) 558-3029
F: (304) 558-0412
E: jane.cline@wvinsurance.gov

WISCONSIN
Mr. Sean Dilweg
Commissioner
Office of the Commissioner of Insurance
121 East Wilson Street
Madison, WI 53702
P: (608) 266-3782
F: (608) 261-8579

WYOMING
Mr. Ken Vines
Commissioner of Insurance
Insurance Department
Herschler Building, 3E
122 West 25th Street
Cheyenne, WY 82002
P: (307) 777-7401
F: (307) 777-5895

International Trade

Promotes state exports, attracts overseas investments in the state and directs trade and investment missions.

ALABAMA
Mr. Neal Wade
Director
Development Office
401 Adams Avenue, 6th Floor
Suite 670
Montgomery, AL 36130
P: (334) 353-1717
F: (334) 242-5669
E: waden@ado.state.al.us

AMERICAN SAMOA
Mr. Faleseu Eliu Paopao
Director
Department of Commerce
American Samoa Government
Executive Office Building, Utulei
Pago Pago, AS 96799
P: (684) 633-5155
F: (684) 633-4195

ARIZONA
Mr. Armando Bras
Director
International Trade & Investment Division
1700 West Washington, Suite 600
Phoenix, AZ 85007
P: (602) 771-1158

Mr. Seth Mones
Deputy Director
Department of Commerce
1700 West Washington, Suite 600
Phoenix, AZ 85007
P: (602) 771-1162

ARKANSAS
Mr. Alan McVey
Deputy Director
Department of Economic Development
#1 Capitol Mall
Room 4C-300
Little Rock, AR 72201
P: (501) 682-7350
F: (501) 682-7394
E: amcvey@1800Arkansas.com

CALIFORNIA
Mr. Garret Ashley
Undersecretary, International Trade
Business, Transportation & Housing Agency
980 9th Street, Suite 250
Sacramento, CA 95814
P: (916) 323-5400
F: (916) 324-5791

COLORADO
Mr. Don Elliman
Director
Office of Economic Development & International Trade
1625 Broadway, Suite 1710
Denver, CO 80202
P: (303) 898-3840
F: (303) 898-3848

CONNECTICUT
Mr. Ronald Angelo
Deputy Commissioner
Department of Economic & Community Development
505 Hudson Street
Hartford, CT 06106
F: (860) 270-8000

DELAWARE
Mr. John Pastor
Director - International Trade Section
International Trade Section
Carvel State Building, 10th Floor
820 French Street
Wilmington, DE 19801
P: (302) 577-8466
F: (302) 577-8499

FLORIDA
Ms. Keisha Rice
Deputy Director
Office of Tourism, Trade & Economic Development
The Capitol, Room 2001
Tallahassee, FL 32399
P: (850) 487-2568
F: (850) 487-3014

GEORGIA
Mr. Kenneth C. Stewart
Commissioner
Department of Economic Development
75 Fifth Street, Northwest, Suite 1200
Atlanta, GA 30308
P: (404) 962-4000
F: (404) 962-4001

GUAM
Mr. Anthony Blaz
Administrator
Economic Development & Commerce Authority
ITC Building, Suite 226
590 South Marine Drive
Tamuning, GU 96913
P: (671) 647-4375
F: (671) 472-5003

HAWAII
Mr. Theodore E. Liu
Director
Department of Business, Economic Development & Tourism
P.O. Box 2359
Honolulu, HI 96804
P: (808) 586-2355
F: (808) 586-2377

IDAHO
Hon. Jim Risch (R)
Lieutenant Governor
Office of the Lieutenant Governor
Room 225, State Capitol
Boise, ID 83720
P: (208) 334-2200
F: (208) 334-3259

ILLINOIS
Mr. Rajinder Bedi
Managing Director
Office of Trade & Investment
James R. Thompson Center, 3-400
100 West Randolph Street
Chicago, IL 60601
P: (312) 814-6872
E: RBedi@ildceo.net

INDIANA
Mr. Nathan J. Feltman
Secretary of Commerce
Economic Development Corporation
One North Capitol Avenue, Suite 700
Indianapolis, IN 46204
P: (317) 232-8992
F: (317) 233-5123
E: nfeltman@iedc.in.gov

IOWA
Mr. Jeff Rossate
Division Administrator
Business Development Division
200 East Grand Avenue
Des Moines, IA 50319
P: (515) 242-4707
E: jeff.rossate@iowalifechanging.com

KANSAS
Mr. John Watson
Director
Trade Development Division
1000 Southwest Jackson Street
Suite 100
Topeka, KS 66612
P: (785) 296-4027
F: (785) 296-5263

KENTUCKY
Mr. Mark Peachey
Director
International Trade Division
Old Capitol Annex Building
300 West Broadway
Frankfort, KY 40601
P: (502) 564-7140
F: (502) 564-3256
E: mark.peachey@ky.gov

LOUISIANA
Mr. Larry Collins
Director of International Trade
International Services Division
P.O. Box 94185
Baton Rouge, LA 70804
P: (225) 342-4323
F: (225) 342-5389
E: lcollins@la.gov

MAINE
Ms. Janine Bisaillon-Cary
Executive Director
International Trade Center
511 Congress Street
Portland, ME 04101
P: (207) 287-2711
E: bartlett.h.stoodley@maine.gov

MARYLAND
Ms. Nancy Wallace
Director
Department of Business & Economic Development
International Development
217 East Redwood Street
Baltimore, MD 21202
P: (410) 767-0680
E: nwallace@choosemaryland.org

MASSACHUSETTS
Ms. Christa Bleyleben
Director
Office of International Trade & Investment
10 Park Plaza, Suite 4510
Boston, MA 02116
P: (617) 973-8618
F: (617) 227-3488
E: christa.bleyleben@state.ma.us

International Trade

MINNESOTA
Mr. Anthony M. Lorusso
Executive Director
Trade Office
1st National Bank Building, Suite E200
332 Minnesota Street
St. Paul, MN 55101
P: (651) 297-4657
F: (651) 296-3555
E: tony.lorusso@state.mn.us

MISSISSIPPI
Ms. Liz Cleveland
Manager
International Trade Office
P.O. Box 849
Jackson, MS 39205
P: (601) 359-6672
F: (601) 359-3613
E: lcleveland@mississippi.org

MISSOURI
Mr. Kevin Stover
Manager
International Trade Office
Truman Building, Room 720
P.O. Box 118
Jefferson City, MO 65102
P: (573) 751-4962
F: (573) 526-1567
E: Kevin.Stover@ded.mo.gov

MONTANA
Mr. Anthony Preite
Director
Department of Commerce
301 South Park
P.O. Box 200501
Helena, MT 59620
P: (406) 841-2704
F: (406) 841-2701
E: tpreite@mt.gov

NEBRASKA
Mr. Richard Baier
Director
Department of Economic Development
P.O. Box 94666
Lincoln, NE 68509
P: (402) 471-3111
F: (402) 471-3778

NEVADA
Mr. Alan Di Stefano
Director of Global Trade & Investment
Commission on Economic Development
108 East Proctor Street
Carson City, NV 89701
P: (775) 687-4325
F: (775) 687-4450
E: ccintl@bizopp.state.nv.us

NEW HAMPSHIRE
Ms. Dawn Wivell
Director
Office of International Commerce
17 New Hampshire Avenue
Portsmouth, NH 03801
P: (603) 334-6074
F: (603) 334-6110
E: dwivell@dred.state.nh.us

NEW JERSEY
Ms. Virginia S. Bauer
CEO & Secretary
Commerce, Economic Growth & Tourism Commission
20 West State Street
Trenton, NJ 08625
P: (609) 292-2444
F: (609) 292-0082
E: Virginia.Bauer@commerce.state.nj.us

NEW MEXICO
Mr. Rick Homans
Director
Economic Development Department
1100 South St. Francis Drive, Suite 1060
Joseph Montoya Building
Santa Fe, NM 87505
P: (505) 476-3736
F: (505) 827-0328
E: edd.info@state.nm.us

NEW YORK
Mr. Patrick Foye
Commissioner
Empire State Development
633 Third Avenue
New York, NY 10017
P: (212) 803-3700
F: (518) 474-2474

NORTH CAROLINA
Mr. Peter Cunningham
Director
Department of Commerce
4320 Mail Service Center
Raleigh, NC 27699
P: (919) 733-7193
F: (919) 733-0110
E: pcunninham@det.commerce.state.nc.us

NORTH DAKOTA
Mr. Shane Goettle
Director
Commerce Department
1600 East Century Avenue, Suite 2
P.O. Box 2057
Bismarck, ND 58502
P: (701) 328-5300
F: (701) 328-5320

NORTHERN MARIANA ISLANDS
Mr. James A. Santos
Director
Department of Commerce
Caller Box 10007, Capital Hill
Saipan, MP 96950
P: (670) 664-3000
F: (670) 664-3070
E: commercedept@vzpacifica.net

OHIO
Mr. Kirk Merritt
International Trade Director
International Trade Division
Ohio Department of Development
77 South High Street
Columbus, OH 43215
P: (614) 466-5017
F: (614) 463-1540
E: itd@odod.ohio.gov

OKLAHOMA
Mr. Barry Clark
Director
Global Business Services
700 North Greenwood Avenue
Suite 1400
Tulsa, OK 74106
P: (918) 594-8588
F: (918) 594-8413

OREGON
Mr. Michael Doyle
Director
International Division
121 Southwest Salmon Street, Suite 205
One World Trade Center
Portland, OR 97204
P: (503) 229-6054
F: (503) 229-5050
E: Oregon.trade@state.or.us

PENNSYLVANIA
Ms. Joe M. Hoeffel
Office of International Business Development
Commonwealth Keystone Building
4th Floor
Harrisburg, PA 17120
P: (717) 787-3003
F: (717) 787-6866

PUERTO RICO
Mr. Ricardo Rivera
Interim Secretary
Department of Economic Development & Commerce
P.O. Box 362350
Hato Rey, PR 00918
P: (787) 758-4747
F: (787) 753-6874

RHODE ISLAND
Ms. Maureen Mezei
Director
International Trade Office
1 West Exchange Street
Providence, RI 02903
P: (401) 278-9100
E: info@riedc.com

SOUTH CAROLINA
Mr. Clarke Thompson
International Trade Director
Department of Commerce
P.O. Box 927
Columbia, SC 29201
P: (803) 737-0438
F: (803) 806-3508

SOUTH DAKOTA
Mr. Richard Benda
Secretary
Department of Tourism & Economic Development
Capitol Lake Plaza
711 East Wells Avenue
Pierre, SD 57501
P: (605) 773-3301
F: (605) 773-3256
E: richard.benda@state.sd.us

TENNESSEE
Mr. Paul LaGrange
Assistant Commissioner, Business Development
Department of Economic & Community Development
312 8th Avenue North, 11th Floor
Nashville, TN 37243
P: (615) 741-3282
F: (615) 741-5829
E: paul.lagrange@state.tn.us

TEXAS
Ms. Tracye McDaniel
Executive Director
Economic Development
P.O. Box 12428
Austin, TX 78711
P: (512) 936-0101
F: (512) 936-0303

U.S. VIRGIN ISLANDS
Mr. Frank Schulterbrandt
Chief Executive Officer
Economic Development Authority
1050 Norre Gade
P.O. Box 305038
St. Thomas, VI 00803
P: (340) 774-0100
F: (340) 779-7153

UTAH
Mr. Doug Clark
Director
Governor's Office of Economic Development
324 South State Street, Suite 500
Salt Lake City, UT 84111
P: (801) 538-8873
F: (801) 538-8888
E: dougclark@utah.gov

VIRGINIA
Mr. Jeffrey R. Anderson
Executive Director
Economic Development Partnership
901 East Byrd Street
P.O. Box 798
Richmond, VA 23218
P: (804) 371-8109
F: (804) 371-6524
E: janderson@yesvirginia.org

WASHINGTON
Ms. Juli Wilkerson
Director
Office of Community, Trade & Economic Development
906 Columbia Street, Southwest
P.O. Box 42525
Olympia, WA 98501
P: (360) 725-4011
F: (360) 586-8440
E: juliw@cted.wa.gov

WEST VIRGINIA
Mr. Stephen Spence
Executive Director
Development Office
Capitol Complex Building 6, Room 553
1900 Kanawha Boulevard East
Charleston, WV 25305
P: (304) 558-2234
F: (304) 558-0449
E: sspence@wvdo.org

WISCONSIN
Ms. Mary Regel
Administrator, Division of International Development
Division of International Exports
201 West Washington Ave.
Madison, WI 53703
P: (608) 266-1767
F: (608) 266-5551
E: mregel@wisconsin.gov

WYOMING
Mr. Tucker Fagan
Chief Executive Officer
Business Council
214 West 15th Street
Cheyenne, WY 82002
P: (307) 777-2800
F: (307) 777-2837

Juvenile Rehabilitation

Administers rehabilitative facilities and programs for delinquent youth committed by the courts.

ALABAMA
Mr. Walter Wood
Director
Department of Youth Services
P.O. Box 66
Mount Meigs, AL 36057
P: (334) 215-3800
F: (334) 215-1453
E: walter.wood@dys.alabama.gov

ALASKA
Mr. Steve McComb
Director
Division of Juvenile Justice
Department of Health & Social Services
P.O. Box 110635
Juneau, AK 99507
P: (907) 269-5086
F: (907) 269-4543

AMERICAN SAMOA
Mr. Sotoa Savali
Commissioner
Department of Public Safety
American Samoa Government
P.O. Box 3699
Pago Pago, AS 96799
P: (684) 633-1111
F: (684) 633-7296

ARIZONA
Mr. Michael D. Branham
Director
Department of Juvenile Corrections
Central Administration Office
1624 West Adams
Phoenix, AZ 85007
P: (602) 542-4302
F: (602) 542-5156

ARKANSAS
Mr. Greg Rivet
Interim Director
Division of Youth Services
P.O. Box 1437, Slot S501
Little Rock, AR 72203
P: (501) 682-8755
F: (501) 682-1351
E: greg.rivet@arkansas.gov

CALIFORNIA
Mr. Bernard Warner
Chief Deputy Secretary
Division of Juvenile Justice
1515 S Street, Suite 502 South
Sacramento, CA 95814
P: (916) 323-2848
F: (916) 323-5584

COLORADO
Mr. John Gomez
Director
Division of Youth Corrections
4255 S. Knox Court
Denver, CO 80236
P: (303) 866-7390
F: (303) 866-7344

CONNECTICUT
Mr. Joseph D'Alesio
Executive Director of Operations
Office of the Chief Court Administrator
231 Capitol Avenue
Hartford, CT 06106
P: (860) 757-2102
E: joseph.dalesio@jud.state.ct.us

DELAWARE
Mr. Perry Phelps
Director
Division of Youth Rehabilitative Services
1825 Faulkland Road
Wilmington, DE 19805
P: (302) 633-2620
F: (302) 739-5966

FLORIDA
Mr. Walt McNeil
Secretary
Department of Juvenile Justice
2737 Centerview Drive
Tallahassee, FL 32399
P: (850) 413-7313

GEORGIA
Mr. Albert Murray
Commissioner
Department of Juvenile Justice
3408 Covington Highway
Decatur, GA 30032
P: (404) 508-7200
F: (404) 508-7289

GUAM
Mr. Christopher Duenas
Acting Director
Department of Youth Affairs
P.O. Box 23672
GMF, GU 96921
P: (671) 735-5010
F: (671) 734-7536

HAWAII
Ms. Martha T. Torney
Executive Director
Office of Youth Services
820 Mililani Street, Suite 817
Honolulu, HI 96813
P: (808) 587-5706
F: (808) 587-5734

IDAHO
Mr. Brent Reinke
Director
Department of Juvenile Corrections
1299 North Orchard Street, Suite 110
Boise, ID 83706
P: (208) 658-2000
F: (208) 327-7404
E: breinke@asca.net

ILLINOIS
Mr. Roger E. Walker Jr.
Director
Department of Corrections
1301 Concordia Court
P.O. Box 19277
Springfield, IL 62794
P: (217) 522-2666
F: (217) 522-8719
E: rwalker@asca.net

INDIANA
Ms. Tanya Johnson
Director
Youth Division
Criminal Justice Institute
One North Capitol Avenue, Suite 1000
Indianapolis, IN 46204
P: (317) 234-4387
E: tjohnson@cji.in.gov

IOWA
Ms. Mary Nelson
Division Administrator
Department of Behavioral, Developmental, & Protective Services
Hoover Building, 5th Floor
1305 East Walnut Street
Des Moines, IA 50319
P: (515) 281-5521
F: (515) 242-6036
E: mnelson1@dhs.state.ia.us

KANSAS
Mr. Russ Jennings
Commissioner
Juvenile Justice Authority
714 Southwest Jackson Street, Suite 300
Topeka, KS 66603
P: (785) 296-4213
F: (785) 296-1412

KENTUCKY
Ms. Bridgette Skaggs Brown
Commissioner
Department of Juvenile Justice
1025 Capital Center Drive, 3rd Floor
Frankfort, KY 40601
P: (502) 573-2738
F: (502) 573-4308

LOUISIANA
Mr. Simon Gonsoulin
Deputy Secretary
Office of Youth Development
7919 Independence Boulevard
P.O. Box 66458
Baton Rouge, LA 70896
P: (225) 287-7900
F: (225) 287-7969

MAINE
Mr. Bartlett H. Stoodley
Associate Commissioner
Juvenile Services Division
111 State House Station
Augusta, ME 04333
P: (207) 287-2711
E: bartlett.h.stoodley@maine.gov

MARYLAND
Mr. Donald W. DeVore
Secretary
Department of Juvenile Services
120 West Fayette Street
Baltimore, MD 21201
P: (410) 230-3100
F: (410) 333-4199

MASSACHUSETTS
Ms. Jane E. Tewksbury
Commissioner
Department of Youth Services
27 Wormwood Street, Suite 400
Boston, MA 02110
P: (617) 727-7575
F: (617) 727-0696

MICHIGAN
Mr. Leonard B. Dixon
Director
Bureau of Juvenile Justice
235 South Grand Avenue
Lansing, MI 48909
P: (517) 335-3489
F: (517) 241-5632

MINNESOTA
Ms. Joan Fabian
Commissioner
Department of Corrections
1450 Energy Park Drive, Suite 200
St. Paul, MN 55108
P: (651) 361-7226
F: (651) 642-0414
E: Joan.Fabian@state.mn.us

MISSOURI
Mr. Tim Decker
Director
Division of Youth Services
221 West High Street
P.O. Box 447
Jefferson City, MO 65102
P: (573) 751-3324
F: (573) 526-4494
E: tim.decker@dss.mo.gov

MONTANA
Mr. Mike Ferriter
Director
Department of Corrections
1539 11th Avenue
P.O. Box 201301
Helena, MT 59620
P: (406) 444-4913
F: (406) 444-4920
E: mferriter@asca.net

NEBRASKA
Mr. Scott Adams
Director
Department of Health & Human Services
P.O. Box 95044
Lincoln, NE 68509
P: (402) 471-3121
E: roger.lempke@ne.ngb.army.mil

NEVADA
Ms. Amy Merget
Chief
Juvenile Justice Programs
620 Belrose, Suite 107
Las Vegas, NV 89107
P: (702) 486-5980
F: (702) 486-5087
E: asmerget@dcfs.state.nv.us

NEW HAMPSHIRE
Mr. Rodney Forey
Director
Division for Juvenile Justice Services
1056 North River Road
Manchester, NH 03104
P: (603) 625-5471
F: (603) 624-0512

NEW JERSEY
Mr. Howard L. Beyer
Executive Director
Juvenile Justice Commission
1001 Spruce Street, Suite 202
P.O. Box 107
Trenton, NJ 08625
P: (609) 292-1400
F: (609) 943-4611

NEW MEXICO
Mr. Roger Gillespie
Director
Juvenile Justice Services
Children, Youth & Families Department
P.O. Drawer 5160
Santa Fe, NM 87502
P: (505) 827-7632

NEW YORK
Ms. Gladys Carrion
Commissioner
Office of Children & Family Services
Capitol View Office Park
52 Washington Street
Rensselaer, NY 12144
P: (518) 474-5522

NORTH CAROLINA
Mr. George L. Sweat
Secretary
Department of Juvenile Justice & Delinquency Prevention
410 South Salisbury Street
1801 Mail Service Center
Raleigh, NC 27699
P: (919) 733-3388
F: (919) 733-1045
E: george.sweat@ncmail.net

NORTH DAKOTA
Ms. Lisa Bjergaard
Director
Department of Corrections & Rehabilitation
Division of Juvenile Services
P.O. Box 1898
Bismarck, ND 58502
P: (701) 328-6390
F: (701) 328-6651

NORTHERN MARIANA ISLANDS
Ms. Debra Inos
Director
Division of Youth Services
Caller Box 10007, Capital Hill
Saipan, MP 96950
P: (670) 664-2550
F: (670) 664-2560

OHIO
Mr. Thomas J. Stickrath
Director
Department of Youth Services
51 North High Street
Columbus, OH 43215
P: (614) 466-8783
F: (614) 752-9078

OKLAHOMA
Mr. Gary Bolin
Interim Director
Office of Juvenile Affairs
3812 North Santa Fe, Suite 400
Oklahoma City, OK 73118
P: (405) 530-2800
F: (405) 530-2890

Mr. Robert E. Christian
Executive Director
Office of Juvenile Affairs
3812 North Santa Fe, Suite 400
Oklahoma City, OK 73118
P: (405) 530-2806
F: (405) 530-2890
E: gene.christian@oja.ok.gov

OREGON
Mr. Bob Jester
Director
Oregon Youth Authority
530 Center Street, Northeast
Suite 200
Salem, OR 97301
P: (503) 373-7205
F: (503) 373-7622
E: oya.info@state.or.us

PUERTO RICO
Mr. Julio R. Gonzalez Rodriguez
Administrator
Juvenile Institutions Administration
P.O. Box 19175
San Juan, PR 00910
P: (787) 767-9600
F: (787) 765-3394

RHODE ISLAND
Mr. Warren Hurlbut
Superintendent
Juvenile Correctional Services
101 Friendship Street
Providence, RI 02903
P: (401) 462-7201

SOUTH CAROLINA
Mr. William Byars
Director
Department of Juvenile Justice
4900 Broad River Road
P.O. Box 21069
Columbia, SC 29221
P: (803) 896-9479
F: (803) 896-9767
E: byarsw@main.djj.state.sc.us

SOUTH DAKOTA
Ms. Virgena Wieseler
Administrator
Office of Child Protection Services
Kneip Building
700 Governors Drive
Pierre, SD 57505
P: (605) 773-3227
F: (605) 773-6834
E: virgena.wieseler@state.sd.us

TENNESSEE
Dr. Viola Miller
Commissioner
Department of Children's Services
Cordell Hull Building, 7th Floor
710 James Robertson Parkway
Nashville, TN 37243
P: (615) 741-9699
F: (615) 532-8079

TEXAS
Ms. Vicki Spriggs
Executive Director
Juvenile Probation Commission
P.O. Box 13547
Austin, TX 78711
P: (512) 424-6682
F: (512) 424-6717

U.S. VIRGIN ISLANDS
Ms. Sedonie Halbert
Commissioner
Department of Human Services
Knud Hansen Complex, Building A
1303 Hospital Grounds
St. Thomas, VI 00802
P: (340) 774-0930
F: (340) 774-3466

Juvenile Rehabilitation

UTAH
Mr. Dan Maldonado
Director
Division of Juvenile Justice Services
Department of Human Services
120 North 200 West, Suite 419
Salt Lake City, UT 84103
P: (801) 538-8224
F: (801) 538-4334
E: dmaldona@utah.gov

VERMONT
Ms. Cindy Walcott
Deputy Commissioner
Family Services Division
Department for Children & Families
103 South Main Street
Waterbury, VT 05671
P: (802) 241-2131
F: (802) 241-2407

VIRGINIA
Mr. Barry R. Green
Director
Department of Juvenile Justice
700 Centre, 4th Floor
7th & Franklin Streets
Richmond, VA 23219
P: (804) 371-0704
F: (804) 371-0773
E: barry.green@djj.virginia.gov

WASHINGTON
Mr. John Clayton
Interim Assistant Secretary
Juvenile Rehabilitation Administration
P.O. Box 45045
Olympia, WA 98504
P: (360) 902-7804
F: (360) 902-7848

WEST VIRGINIA
Mr. Dale Humphreys
Director
Division of Juvenile Services
1200 Quarrier Street, 2nd Floor
Charleston, WV 25301
P: (304) 558-9800
F: (304) 558-6032
E: dhumphreys@djs.state.wv.us

WISCONSIN
Mr. Charles Tubbs
Administrator
Division of Juvenile Corrections
3099 East Washington Avenue
P.O. Box 8930
Madison, WI 53708
P: (608) 240-5901
F: (608) 240-3370
E: charles.tubbs@doc.state.wi.us

WYOMING
Mr. Tony Lewis
Interim Director of Family Services
Department of Family Services
Hathaway Building, 3rd Floor
2300 Capitol Avenue
Cheyenne, WY 82002
P: (307) 777-7561
F: (307) 777-7747

Labor

Overall responsibility for administering and enforcing the state's labor laws.

Information provided by:

National Association of Government Labor Officials
Piper Plummer
Association Manager
P.O. Box 11910
Lexington, KY 40578
P: (859) 244-8121
F: (859) 244-8001
pplummer@csg.org
www.naglo.org

ALABAMA
Mr. Jim Bennett
Commissioner
Department of Labor
P.O. Box 303500
Montgomery, AL 36130
P: (334) 242-3460
F: (334) 240-3417
E: jbennett
@alalabor.state.al.us

ALASKA
Mr. Clark "Click" Bishop
Commissioner
Department of Labor
P.O. Box 21149
Juneau, AK 99802
P: (907) 465-2700
F: (907) 465-2784
E: commissioner_labor
@labor.state.ak.us

ARIZONA
Mr. Orlando J. Macias
Director of Labor & Wage
State Labor Department
P.O. Box 19070
Phoenix, AZ 85007
P: (602) 542-4515
F: (602) 542-8097
E: laboradmin
@ica.state.az.us

ARKANSAS
Mr. James Salkeld
Director
Department of Labor
10421 West Markham Street
Suite 100
Little Rock, AR 72205
P: (501) 682-4541
F: (501) 682-4535
E: james.salkeld
@arkansas.gov

CALIFORNIA
Ms. Victoria L. Bradshaw
Secretary
Labor & Workforce Development Agency
801 K Street, Suite 2101
Sacramento, CA 95814
P: (916) 327-9064
F: (916) 327-9158
E: victoria.bradshaw
@labor.ca.gov

COLORADO
Mr. Don J. Mares
Executive Director
Department of Labor & Employment
1515 Arapahoe Street, Suite 375
Denver, CO 80202
P: (303) 318-8000
F: (303) 318-8048
E: don.mares@state.co.us

CONNECTICUT
Ms. Patricia Mayfield
Commissioner
Department of Labor
200 Folly Brook Boulevard
Wethersfield, CT 06109
P: (860) 263-6505
F: (860) 263-6529
E: patricia.mayfield
@po.state.ct.us

DELAWARE
Mr. Thomas B. Sharp
Secretary of Labor
Department of Labor
4425 North Market Street, 4th Floor
Wilmington, DE 19802
P: (302) 761-8000
F: (302) 761-6621
E: tom.sharp@state.de.us

DISTRICT OF COLUMBIA
Ms. Susan O. Gilbert
Interim Director
Department of Employment Services
Employment Security Building
500 H Street, Northeast
Washington, DC 20210
P: (202) 724-7100
F: (202) 724-6111
E: susan.gilbert@dc.gov

FLORIDA
Ms. Holly Benson
Secretary
Department of Business & Professional Regulation
1940 North Monroe Street
Tallahassee, FL 32399
P: (850) 487-1395
F: (850) 488-1830
E: secretary
@dpbr.state.fl.us

GEORGIA
Mr. Earl Everett
Director of Safety & Engineering
Department of Labor
1700 Century Circle, Suite 100
Atlanta, GA 30345
P: (404) 679-0687
F: (404) 982-3405
E: earl.everett
@dol.state.ga.us

Mr. Michael L. Thurmond
Commissioner
Department of Labor
Sussex Place, Room 600
148 International Boulevard, Northeast
Atlanta, GA 30303
P: (404) 232-3001
F: (404) 232-3017
E: commissioner
@dol.state.ga.us

GUAM
Ms. Maria Connelley
Director
Department of Labor
414 West Soledad, Suite 400
GCIC Building, P.O. Box 9970
Tamuning, GU 96931
P: (671) 475-7046
F: (671) 475-7045

HAWAII
Mr. Nelson B. Befitel
Director
Department of Labor & Industrial Relations
Princess Keelikolani Building
830 Punchbowl Street, Room 321
Honolulu, HI 96813
P: (808) 586-8844
F: (808) 586-9099
E: dlir.director@hawaii.gov

IDAHO
Mr. Roger B. Madsen
Director
Department of Commerce & Labor
317 West Main Street
Boise, ID 83735
P: (208) 332-3579
F: (208) 334-6430
E: rmadsen@cl.idaho.gov

ILLINOIS
Ms. Catherine Shannon
Director
Department of Labor
160 North LaSalle Street, Suite C-1300
Chicago, IL 60601
P: (312) 793-1808
F: (312) 793-5257
E: catherine.shannon
@illinois.gov

INDIANA
Ms. Lori A. Torres
Commissioner
Department of Labor
Indiana Government Center-South
402 West Washington Street, Room W-195
Indianapolis, IN 46204
P: (317) 232-2378
F: (317) 233-5381
E: ltorres@dol.in.gov

IOWA
Mr. Steve Slater
Interim Labor Commissioner
Division of Labor
1000 East Grand Avenue
Des Moines, IA 50319
P: (515) 281-3447
F: (515) 281-4698

KANSAS
Mr. Jim Garner
Secretary
Department of Labor
401 Southwest Topeka Boulevard
Topeka, KS 66603
P: (785) 296-7474
F: (785) 368-6294
E: jim.garner@dol.ks.gov

KENTUCKY
Mr. Philip Anderson
Commissioner
Department of Labor
1047 US Highway 127 South
Suite 4
Frankfort, KY 40602
P: (502) 564-3070
F: (502) 564-5387
E: philip.anderson@ky.gov

Labor

LOUISIANA
Mr. John Warner Smith
Secretary of Labor
Department of Labor
P.O. Box 94094
1001 North 23rd Street
Baton Rouge, LA 70804
P: (225) 342-3011
F: (225) 342-3778
E: jwsmith@ldol.state.la.us

MAINE
Ms. Laura Fortman
Commissioner of Labor
Department of Labor
P.O. Box 259
Augusta, ME 04332
P: (207) 287-3787
F: (207) 287-5292
E: laura.fortman@maine.gov

Mr. William A. Peabody
Director
Department of Labor
Bureau of Labor Standards
45 State House Station
Augusta, ME 04333
P: (207) 624-6400
F: (207) 624-6449
E: william.a.peabody@maine.gov

MARYLAND
Mr. Thomas E. Perez
Secretary
Department of Labor, Licensing & Regulation
500 North Calvert Street, Room 401
Baltimore, MD 21202
P: (410) 230-6020
F: (410) 333-0853
E: tperez@dllr.state.md.us

MASSACHUSETTS
Ms. Suzanne M. Bump
Director
Department of Workforce Development
1 Ashburton Place, Room 2112
Boston, MA 02108
P: (617) 727-6573
F: (617) 727-1090
E: suzanne.m.bump@state.ma.us

Mr. George Noel
Director
Department of Labor
600 Washington Street, 7th Floor
Boston, MA 02111
P: (617) 788-3610
F: (617) 727-7470
E: george.noel@dia.state.ma.us

MICHIGAN
Mr. Douglas J. Kalinowski
Deputy Director
Department of Labor & Economic Growth
P.O. Box 30004
Lansing, MI 48909
P: (517) 373-1820
F: (517) 373-3728
E: dkalin@michigan.gov

MINNESOTA
Mr. Scott Brener
Commissioner
Department of Labor & Industry
443 Lafayette Road, North
St. Paul, MN 55155
P: (651) 284-5010
F: (651) 284-5721
E: scott.brener@state.mn.us

MISSISSIPPI
Ms. Tommye Dale Favre
Executive Director
Department of Employment Security
P.O. Box 1699
Jackson, MS 39215
P: (601) 321-6100
F: (601) 321-6104
E: tdfavre@mdes.ms.gov

MISSOURI
Ms. Alice A. Bartlett
Director
Labor & Industrial Relations Commission
P.O. Box 59
Jefferson City, MO 65102
P: (573) 751-3215
F: (573) 751-4945
E: lirc@dolir.mo.gov

Mr. Rod Chapel
Director
Department of Labor & Industrial Relations
P.O. Box 504
421 East Dunklin Street
Jefferson City, MO 65102
P: (573) 751-9691
F: (573) 751-4135
E: diroffice@dolir.mo.gov

Mr. John J. Hickey
Director
Labor & Industrial Relations Commission
P.O. Box 59
Jefferson City, MO 65102
P: (573) 751-2461
F: (573) 751-7806
E: lirc@dolir.mo.gov

MONTANA
Mr. Jerry Keck
Administrator
Employment Relations Division
Department of Labor & Industry
P.O. Box 8011
Helena, MT 59604
P: (406) 444-1555
E: jkeck@mt.gov

Mr. Keith Kelly
Commissioner
Department of Labor & Industry
P.O. Box 1728
Helena, MT 59624
P: (406) 444-2840
F: (406) 444-1394
E: kkelly@mt.gov

NEBRASKA
Mr. Fernando "Butch" Lecuona III
Commissioner of Labor
Workforce Development
Department of Labor
P.O. Box 94600
Lincoln, NE 68509
P: (402) 471-2600
F: (402) 471-9867
E: flecuona@dol.state.ne.us

NEVADA
Mr. Michael Tanchek
Commissioner
Department of Business & Industry
Office of the Labor Commissioner
555 East Washington Avenue, Suite 4100
Las Vegas, NV 89101
P: (702) 486-2650
F: (702) 486-2660
E: mtanchek@laborcommissioner.com

NEW HAMPSHIRE
Mr. George N. Copadis
Commissioner of Labor
Department of Labor
95 Pleasant Street
Concord, NH 03301
P: (603) 271-3171
F: (603) 271-6852
E: gcopadis@labor.state.nh.us

NEW JERSEY
Mr. David J. Socolow
Commissioner
Department of Labor
P.O. Box 110
Trenton, NJ 08625
P: (609) 292-2975
F: (609) 633-9271
E: janet.sliwinkski@dol.state.nj.us

NEW MEXICO
Ms. Betty D. Sparrow
Secretary
Department of Labor
P.O. Box 1928
Albuquerque, NM 87103
P: (505) 841-8409
F: (505) 841-8491
E: betty.sparrow@state.nm.us

NEW YORK
Ms. Patricia Smith
Commissioner
State Department of Labor
345 Hudson Street
Albany, NY 10014
P: (518) 457-2741
F: (518) 457-6908
E: nysdol@labor.state.ny.us

NORTH CAROLINA
Ms. Cherie K. Berry
Commissioner
Department of Labor
1101 Mail Service Center
4 West Edenton Street
Raleigh, NC 27699
P: (919) 733-7166
F: (919) 733-6197
E: cberry@mail.dol.state.nc.us

NORTH DAKOTA
Ms. Lisa Fair McEvers
Commissioner of Labor
Department of Labor
600 East Boulevard Avenue,
Department 406
Bismarck, ND 58505
P: (701) 328-2660
F: (701) 328-2031
E: labor@nd.gov

OHIO
Mr. Gordon Gatien
Superintendent
Division of Labor & Worker Safety
Wage & Hour Bureau
77 South High Street, 22nd Floor
Columbus, OH 43215
P: (614) 644-2239
F: (614) 728-8639
E: gordon.gatien@wagehour.com.state.oh.us

OKLAHOMA
Mr. Lloyd L. Fields
Commissioner of Labor
Department of Labor
4001 North Lincoln Boulevard
Oklahoma City, OK 73105
P: (405) 528-1500
F: (405) 528-5751
E: lfields@oklaosf.state.ok.us

OREGON
Hon. Dan Gardner (D)
Labor Commissioner
Bureau of Labor & Industries
800 Northeast Oregon Street, #32
Suite 1045
Portland, OR 97232
P: (503) 731-4070
F: (503) 731-4103
E: dan.gardner@state.or.us

PENNSYLVANIA
Mr. Patrick Beaty
Deputy Secretary for Unemployment Compensation Program
Department of Labor & Industry
Labor & Industry Building
7th & Forester Streets, Suite 1700
Harrisburg, PA 17121
P: (717) 787-3756
F: (717) 787-8826
E: pbeaty@state.pa.us

Mr. Stephen Schmerin
Secretary
Department of Labor & Industry
Labor and Industry Building, Room 1700
Harrisburg, PA 17121
P: (717) 787-5279
F: (717) 787-8826
E: sschmerin@state.pa.us

PUERTO RICO
Mr. Roman M. Velasco Gonzalez
Secretary
Department of Labor
Prudencio Rivera-Martinez Building
505 Munoz Rivera Avenue, 21st Floor
Hato Rey, PR 00918
P: (787) 754-2119
F: (787) 753-9550

RHODE ISLAND
Ms. Adelita Orefice
Director
Department of Labor & Training
1511 Pontiac Avenue
Cranston, RI 02920
P: (401) 462-8870
F: (401) 462-8872
E: aorefice@dlt.state.ri.us

SOUTH CAROLINA
Ms. Adrienne R. Youmans
Director
Department of Labor, Licensing & Regulation
P.O. Box 11329
Columbia, SC 29211
P: (803) 896-4300
F: (803) 896-4393
E: youmansa@llr.sc.gov

SOUTH DAKOTA
Ms. Pamela Roberts
Secretary of Labor
Department of Labor
700 Governors Drive
Pierre, SD 57501
P: (605) 773-3101
F: (605) 773-4211
E: pamela.roberts@state.sd.us

TENNESSEE
Mr. James G. Neeley
Commissioner
Department of Labor & Workforce Development
Andrew Johnson Tower, 8th Floor
Nashville, TN 37243
P: (615) 741-6642
F: (615) 741-5078
E: james.neeley@state.tn.us

TEXAS
Mr. Larry Temple
Executive Director
Workforce Commission
TWC Building
101 East 15th Street, Room 618
Austin, TX 78778
P: (512) 463-0735
F: (512) 475-2321
E: larry.temple@twc.state.tx.us

U.S. VIRGIN ISLANDS
Mr. Albert Bryan Jr.
Commissioner
Department of Labor
2203 Church Street
Christiansted, St. Croix, VI 00820
P: (340) 773-1994 ext.230
F: (340) 773-0094
E: abryan@vidol.gov

UTAH
Ms. Sherrie Hayashi
Commissioner
Labor Commission
P.O. Box 146600
Salt Lake City, UT 84114
P: (801) 530-6880
F: (801) 530-6804
E: ahayashi@utah.gov

VERMONT
Mr. Tom Douse
Deputy Commissioner
Department of Labor
P.O. Box 488
Montpelier, VT 05601
P: (802) 828-4301
F: (802) 828-4022
E: tdouse@labor.state.vt.us

VIRGINIA
Mr. C. Ray Davenport
Commissioner
Department of Labor & Industry
13 South 13th Street
Richmond, VA 23219
P: (804) 786-2377
F: (804) 371-6524
E: ray.davenport@doli.virginia.gov

WASHINGTON
Ms. Judy Schurke
Acting Director
Department of Labor & Industries
P.O. Box 44001
Olympia, WA 98504
P: (360) 902-4200
F: (360) 902-4202

WEST VIRGINIA
Mr. David M. Mullins
Commissioner
Division of Labor
Bureau of Commerce, Room B-749
State Capitol Complex, Building 6
Charleston, WV 25305
P: (304) 558-7890
F: (304) 558-3797
E: dmullins@labor.state.wv.us

WISCONSIN
Ms. Roberta Gassman
Secretary
Department of Workforce Development
P.O. Box 7946
Madison, WI 53707
P: (608) 267-9692
F: (608) 266-1784
E: roberta.gassman@dwd.state.wi.us

WYOMING
Ms. Cindy Pomeroy
Director
Department of Employment
1510 East Pershing Boulevard
Cheyenne, WY 82002
P: (307) 777-7672
F: (307) 777-5805
E: cpomer@state.wy.us

Law Enforcement

Conducts state-level criminal investigations.

ALABAMA
Col. Chris Murphy
Director
Department of Public Safety
P.O. Box 1511
Montgomery, AL 36102
P: (334) 242-4394
F: (334) 242-0512
E: director@alalinc.net

ALASKA
Mr. Walt Monegan
Commissioner
Department of Public Safety
5700 East Tudor Road
Anchorage, AK 99507
P: (907) 269-5086
F: (907) 269-4543

AMERICAN SAMOA
Mr. Sotoa Savali
Commissioner
Department of Public Safety
American Samoa Government
P.O. Box 3699
Pago Pago, AS 96799
P: (684) 633-1111
F: (684) 633-7296

ARIZONA
Mr. Roger Vanderpool
Director
Department of Public Safety
2102 West Encanto Boulevard
P.O. Box 6638
Phoenix, AZ 85005
P: (602) 223-2359
F: (602) 223-2917

ARKANSAS
Col. Steve Dozier
Director
State Police
#1 State Police Plaza Drive
Little Rock, AR 72209
P: (501) 618-8200
F: (501) 618-8222
E: steve.dozier
@asp.arkansas.gov

CALIFORNIA
Hon. Edmund G.
Brown Jr. (D)
Attorney General
Office of the Attorney General
1300 I Street, Suite 1740
Sacramento, CA 95814
P: (916) 445-9555
F: (916) 323-5341

COLORADO
Mr. Robert Cantwell
Director
Bureau of Investigation
Department of Public Safety
690 Kipling Street
Lakewood, CO 80215
P: (303) 239-4201
F: (303) 235-0568

CONNECTICUT
Mr. Kevin Kane
Chief State's Attorney
Division of Criminal Justice
300 Corporate Place
Rocky Hill, CT 06067
P: (860) 258-5800
F: (860) 258-5858

DELAWARE
Col. Thomas F. Macleish
Superintendent
State Police
P.O. Box 430
Dover, DE 19901
P: (302) 739-5901
F: (302) 739-5966
E: Thomas.Macleish
@state.de.us

DISTRICT OF COLUMBIA
Ms. Cathy L. Lanier
Chief of Police
Metropolitan Police Department
300 Indiana Avenue, NW
Room 5080
Washington, DC 20001
P: (202) 727-4218
F: (202) 727-9524

FLORIDA
Mr. Gerald Bailey
Commissioner
Department of Law
Enforcement
P.O. Box 1489
Tallahassee, FL 32302
P: (850) 410-7001

GEORGIA
Mr. Vernon Keenan
Director
Bureau of Investigation
3121 Panthersville Road
PO Box 370808
Decatur, GA 30037
P: (404) 244-2600

GUAM
Mr. Paul Suba
Commander
Police Department
233 Central Avenue
Tiyan, GU 96913
P: (671) 475-8512
F: (671) 472-2825

HAWAII
Mr. James L. Propotnick
Deputy Director for Law
Enforcement
Law Enforcement Division
Department of Public Safety
919 Ala Moana Boulevard, 4th
Floor
Honolulu, HI 96814
P: (808) 587-2562
F: (808) 581-1282

IDAHO
Col. Jerry Russell
Director
State Police
P.O. Box 700
Meridian, ID 83680
P: (208) 884-7003
F: (208) 884-7090

ILLINOIS
Mr. Larry Trent
Director
State Police
125 East Monroe Street, Room
107
Springfield, IL 62794
P: (217) 782-7263
F: (217) 785-2821
E: larry_trent
@isp.state.il.us

INDIANA
Dr. Paul Whitesell
Superintendent
State Police
100 North Senate Avenue,
Room N340
Indianapolis, IN 46204
P: (317) 232-8241

IOWA
Mr. Eugene T. Meyer
Commissioner
Department of Public Safety
215 East 7th Street
Des Moines, IA 50319
P: (515) 725-6182

KANSAS
Col. William Seck
Superintendent
Highway Patrol
122 Southwest 7th Street
Topeka, KS 66603
P: (785) 296-6800
F: (785) 296-3049
E: wseck
@mail.khp.state.ks.us

Mr. Larry Welch
Director
Bureau of Investigation
1620 Southwest Tyler Street
Topeka, KS 66612
P: (785) 296-8200
F: (785) 296-6781

KENTUCKY
Mr. John Adams
Commissioner
Department of State Police
919 Versailles Road
Frankfort, KY 40601
P: (502) 695-6303
F: (502) 573-1479

LOUISIANA
Lt. Col. Dane Morgan
Deputy Superintendent
Bureau of Investigations
7919 Independence Boulevard
Baton Rouge, LA 70806
P: (225) 763-5756

MAINE
Hon. G. Steven Rowe (D)
Attorney General
Office of the Attorney General
State House Station 6
Augusta, ME 04333
P: (207) 626-8800

MARYLAND
Col. Thomas E. Hutchins
Superintendent
Department of State Police
1201 Reisterstown Road
Pikesville, MD 21208
P: (410) 653-4219
F: (410) 653-4269
E: superintendent@mdsp.org

MASSACHUSETTS
Col. Mark F. Delaney
Superintendent
State Police
470 Worcester Road
Framingham, MA 01702
P: (508) 820-2300
F: (617) 727-6874

MICHIGAN
Col. Peter C. Munoz
Director
State Police
714 South Harrison Road
East Lansing, MI 48823
P: (517) 336-6158
F: (517) 336-6551

MINNESOTA
Mr. Michael Campion
Commissioner
Department of Public Safety
Bremer Tower, Suite 1000
445 Minnesota Street
St. Paul, MN 55101
P: (651) 201-7000
F: (651) 297-5728
E: michael.campion@state.mn.us

MISSISSIPPI
Mr. George Phillips
Commissioner
Department of Public Safety
P.O. Box 958
Jackson, MS 39205
P: (601) 987-1212
F: (601) 987-1488
E: commissioner@mdps.state.ms.us

MISSOURI
Mr. Larry Crawford
Director
Department of Corrections
2729 Plaza Drive
Jefferson City, MO 65109
P: (573) 526-6607
F: (573) 751-4099
E: lcrawford@asca.net

MONTANA
Hon. Mike McGrath (D)
Attorney General
Department of Justice
Department of Justice
P.O. Box 201401
Helena, MT 59620
P: (406) 444-2026
F: (404) 444-3549
E: contactdoj@mt.gov

NEBRASKA
Maj. Bryan Tuma
State Patrol
P.O. Box 94907
Lincoln, NE 68509
P: (402) 471-4545
F: (402) 479-4002

NEVADA
Mr. John Douglas
Chief
Investigations Division
Department of Public Safety
555 Wright Way
Carson City, NV 89711
P: (775) 684-7412
F: (775) 687-4405
E: jdouglas@dps.state.nv.us

NEW HAMPSHIRE
Col. Frederick H. Booth
Director
Division of State Police
33 Hazen Drive
Concord, NH 03305
P: (603) 271-2450
F: (603) 271-2527
E: fbooth@safety.state.nh.us

NEW MEXICO
Mr. Farron W. Segotta
State Police Chief/Deputy
Secretary of Operations
Department of Public Safety
4491 Cerrillos Road
P.O. Box 1628
Santa Fe, NM 87501
P: (505) 827-9219
F: (505) 827-3395
E: faron.segotta@state.nm.us

NEW YORK
Mr. Preston Felton
Interim Superintendent
State Police
1220 Washington Avenue,
Building 22
Albany, NY 12226
P: (518) 457-6721

NORTH CAROLINA
Ms. Robin Pendergraft
Director
State Bureau of Investigation
3320 Garner Road
Raleigh, NC 27610
P: (919) 662-4500
F: (919) 662-4523
E: rpendergrat@jus.state.nc.us

NORTH DAKOTA
Mr. Jerry Kemmet
Director
Bureau of Criminal
Investigation
Office of Attorney General
P.O. Box 1054
Bismark, ND 58505
P: (701) 328-5500
F: (701) 328-5510
E: jkemmet@nd.gov

Col. Bryan Klipfel
Superintendent
Highway Patrol
600 East Boulevard Avenue
Department 504
Bismarck, ND 58505
P: (701) 328-2455
F: (701) 328-1717
E: bklipfel@nd.gov

NORTHERN MARIANA ISLANDS
Hon. Matthew T. Gregory
Attorney General
Office of the Attorney General
Capitol Hil, Caller Box 10007
Saipan, MP 95960
P: (670) 664-2341
F: (670) 664-2349
E: matt@gregoryfirm.com

OHIO
Mr. Henry Guzman
Director
Department of Public Safety
1970 West Broad Street
P.O. Box 182081
Columbus, OH 43218
P: (614) 466-3383
F: (614) 466-0433

OKLAHOMA
Mr. Kevin Ward
Secretary of Safety & Security
Department of Public Safety
P.O. Box 11415
Oklahoma City, OK 73136
P: (405) 425-2424
F: (405) 425-2324

OREGON
Mr. Ronald C. Ruecker
Superintendent
State Police
400 Public Service Building
255 Capitol Street, Northeast,
4th Floor
Salem, OR 97310
P: (503) 378-3720
F: (503) 378-8282
E: osp.ghq@state.or.us

PENNSYLVANIA
Col. Jeffrey B. Miller
Commissioner
State Police
1800 Elmerton Avenue
Harrisburg, PA 17110
P: (717) 783-5558
F: (717) 787-2948

PUERTO RICO
Mr. Pedro A. Toledo Davila
Superintendent
Puerto Rico Police
P.O. Box 70166
San Juan, PR 00936
P: (787) 793-1234
F: (787) 781-0080

RHODE ISLAND
Col. Brendan P. Doherty
Superintendent
State Police
311 Danielson Pike
North Scituate, RI 02857
P: (401) 444-1000
F: (401) 444-1105

Maj. Steven M. O'Donnell
Acting Superintendent
State Police
311 Danielson Pike
North Scituate, RI 02857
P: (401) 444-1000
F: (401) 444-1105
E: sodonnell@risp.state.ri.us

SOUTH CAROLINA
Mr. Robert M. Stewart
Chief
State Law Enforcement Division
P.O. Box 21398
Columbia, SC 29221
P: (803) 896-7001

SOUTH DAKOTA
Mr. Jim Vlahakis
Director
Division of Criminal
Investigation
Attorney General's Office
1302 East Highway 14, Suite 5
Pierre, SD 57501
P: (605) 773-3331
F: (605) 773-4629
E: jim.vlahakis@state.sd.us

TENNESSEE
Mr. Mark Gwyn
Director
Bureau of Investigation
901 R.S. Gass Boulevard
Nashville, TN 37216
P: (615) 744-4000

Law Enforcement

TEXAS
Mr. Timothy Braaten
Executive Director
Commission on Law Enforcement Officer Standards & Education
6330 U.S. Highway 290 East, Suite 200
Austin, TX 78723
P: (512) 936-7711
F: (512) 936-7766

U.S. VIRGIN ISLANDS
Mr. Elton Lewis
Commissioner
Police Department
Alexander Farrelly Criminal Justice Ctr.
Charlotte Amalie
St. Thomas, VI 00802
P: (340) 774-2211
F: (340) 715-5517
E: elton.lewis@us.army.mil

UTAH
Col. Lance Davenport
Colonel
Department of Public Safety
Utah Highway Patrol
4501 South 2700 West
Salt Lake City, UT 84119
P: (801) 965-4379
F: (801) 965-4716
E: ldavenport@utah.gov

VERMONT
Maj. Kerry L. Sleeper
Commissioner of Public Safety
Department of Public Safety
103 South Main Street
Waterbury, VT 05671
P: (802) 244-8718
F: (802) 244-5551
E: ksleeper@dps.state.vt.us

VIRGINIA
Col. W. Steven Flaherty
Superintendent
Department of State Police
7700 Midlothian Turnpike
P.O. Box 27472
Richmond, VA 23235
P: (804) 674-2087
F: (804) 674-2132
E: supt@vsp.virginia.gov

WASHINGTON
Mr. John R. Batiste
Chief
State Patrol
General Administration Building
P.O. Box 42600
Olympia, WA 98504
P: (360) 753-6540

WEST VIRGINIA
Col. David Lemmon
Superintendent
State Police
725 Jefferson Road
South Charleston, WV 25309
P: (304) 746-2111
F: (304) 746-2230
E: dlemmon@wvsp.state.wv.us

WISCONSIN
Mr. James Warren
Administrator
Division of Criminal Investigation
17 West Main Street
Madison, WI 53707
P: (608) 266-1671
F: (608) 267-2777

WYOMING
Mr. Forrest Bright
Director
Division of Criminal Investigation
316 West 22nd Street
Cheyenne, WY 82002
P: (307) 777-7181
F: (307) 777-7252

Law Library

Legal resource for the state's highest court.

ALABAMA
Mr. Timothy A. Lewis
Director
State Law Library
300 Dexter Avenue
Montgomery, AL 36104
P: (334) 242-4347
F: (334) 242-4484
E: director@alalinc.net

ALASKA
Ms. Catherine Lemann
Law Librarian
State Court Law Library
303 K Street
Anchorage, AK 99501
P: (907) 264-0583
F: (907) 264-0733

AMERICAN SAMOA
Hon. Afa Ripley Jr.
Attorney General
Office of the Attorney General
American Samoa Government
Executive Office Building, Utulei
Pago Pago, AS 96799
P: (684) 633-4163
F: (684) 633-1838

ARIZONA
Ms. Gladys Ann Wells
Director
State Library, Archives & Public Records
Archives & Public Records
State Capitol, Room 200
Phoenix, AZ 85007
P: (602) 542-4035
F: (602) 542-4972
E: gawells@lib.az.us

ARKANSAS
Ms. Ava Hicks
Director
Supreme Court Library
Justice Building, 1st Floor North
625 Marshall
Little Rock, AR 72201
P: (501) 682-2147
F: (501) 682-6877
E: ava.hicks@mail.state.ar.us

CALIFORNIA
Ms. Mary Sawyer
Law Librarian
Office of the Attorney General
1300 I Street, 11th Floor
Sacramento, CA 95814
P: (916) 327-7865

COLORADO
Mr. Dan Cordova
Librarian
State Law Library, Judicial Branch
State Judicial Building, #B112
2 East 14th Avenue
Denver, CO 80203
P: (303) 837-3720
F: (303) 864-4510

CONNECTICUT
Ms. Carol Trinchitella
Serials Librarian
State Library
231 Capitol Avenue
Hartford, CT 06106
P: (860) 757-6562
E: ctrinchitella@cslib.org

DELAWARE
Ms. Karen Parrott
Law Librarian
State Law Library
414 Federal Street, #100
Dover, DE 19901
P: (302) 739-5467
F: (302) 739-6721

DISTRICT OF COLUMBIA
Ms. Letty Limbach
Librarian
DC Court of Appeals
500 Indiana Avenue, Northwest
Washington, DC 20001
P: (202) 879-2767

FLORIDA
Ms. Billie J. Blaine
Librarian
Supreme Court Library
500 South Duvall Street
Tallahassee, FL 32399
P: (850) 488-8919
F: (850) 922-5219

GUAM
Ms. Margaret Tarnate
Territorial Law Library
141 San Ramon Street
Hagatna, GU 96910
P: (671) 472-8062
F: (671) 472-1246

HAWAII
Ms. Ann Koto
Law Librarian
Supreme Court Law Library
417 South King Street
Room 119
Honolulu, HI 96813
P: (808) 539-4964
F: (808) 539-4974

IDAHO
Mr. Rick Visser
Librarian
Law Library
451 West State Street
Boise, ID 83720
P: (208) 334-3316
F: (208) 334-4019
E: rvisser@idcourts.net

ILLINOIS
Ms. Brenda Larison
Director
Courts of Illinois
Supreme Court Building
200 East Capitol Avenue
Springfield, IL 62706
P: (217) 782-2425
F: (217) 782-5287

INDIANA
Ms. Terri Ross
Law Librarian
State Supreme Court
200 West Washington Street, Room 316
Indianapolis, IN 46204
P: (317) 232-2557
F: (317) 232-8372
E: tross@courts.state.in.us

IOWA
Mr. Cory Quist
Law Librarian
State Law Library
State Library of Iowa
1112 East Grand Avenue
Des Moines, IA 50319
P: (515) 281-4307
F: (515) 281-5405
E: cory.quist@lib.state.ia.us

KANSAS
Mr. Fred Knecht
Law Librarian
Supreme Court Law Library
301 Southwest 10th Avenue
Topeka, KS 66612
P: (785) 296-3257
F: (785) 296-1863

LOUISIANA
Ms. Carol Billings
Director
Law Library
400 Royal Street, 2nd Floor
New Orleans, LA 70130
P: (504) 310-2400
F: (504) 568-5069
E: library@lasc.org

MAINE
Ms. Lynn E. Randall
State Law Librarian
State Law & Legislative Reference Library
43 State House Station
Augusta, ME 04333
P: (207) 287-1600
F: (207) 287-6467

MARYLAND
Mr. Michael S. Miller
Director
State Law Library
361 Rowe Boulevard
Annapolis, MD 21401
P: (410) 260-1432
F: (410) 974-2063

MASSACHUSETTS
Mr. Stephen A. Fulchino
State Librarian
State Library
State House, Room 341
24 Beacon Street
Boston, MA 02133
P: (617) 727-2590
F: (617) 727-5819

MICHIGAN
Ms. Susan Adamczak
Administrator
State Law Library
G. Mennen Williams Bldg., 1st Floor
525 West Ottawa Street
Lansing, MI 48933
P: (517) 373-0630
F: (517) 373-7130
E: sadamczak@michigan.gov

MINNESOTA
Ms. Barbara Golden
State Law Librarian
State Law Library
25 Rev. Dr. Martin Luther King Jr. Blvd.
St. Paul, MN 55155
P: (651) 296-2775
F: (651) 296-6740
E: barb.golden@courts.state.mn.us

MISSISSIPPI
Mr. Charles Pearce
State Librarian
State Law Library
P.O. Box 1040
Jackson, MS 39215
P: (601) 359-3672
F: (601) 359-2912
E: cpearce@mssc.state.ms.us

Law Library

MONTANA
Ms. Judith A. Meadows
Director & State Law Librarian
State Law Library
P.O. Box 203004
Helena, MT 59620
P: (406) 444-3660
F: (406) 444-3603
E: jmeadows@mt.gov

NEBRASKA
Ms. Janice Walker
Court Administrator
Supreme Court
P.O. Box 98910
Lincoln, NE 68509
P: (402) 471-2755

NEVADA
Ms. Kathleen Harrington
Law Librarian
Supreme Court Law Library
Supreme Court Building
201 South Carson Street #100
Carson City, NV 89701
P: (775) 684-1640
F: (775) 684-1662
E: klharrin@clan.lib.nv.us

NEW HAMPSHIRE
Ms. Mary Searles
Law Librarian
State Law Library
Supreme Court Building
One Noble Drive
Concord, NH 03301
P: (603) 271-3777
F: (603) 271-2168

NEW MEXICO
Mr. Robert Mead
State Law Librarian
Supreme Court Law Library
P.O. Box L
Santa Fe, NM 87504
P: (505) 827-4854
F: (505) 827-4852

NORTH CAROLINA
Mr. Tom Davis
Librarian
Supreme Court Library
Justice Building, Room 500
2 East Morgan Street
Raleigh, NC 27601
P: (919) 831-5709
F: (919) 831-5732
E: tpd@sc.state.nc.us

NORTH DAKOTA
Mr. Ted Smith
Law Librarian
Supreme Court Law Library
600 East Boulevard Avenue, 2nd Floor
Judicial Wing
Bismarck, ND 58505
P: (701) 328-4594
F: (701) 328-3609
E: TSmith@ndcourts.gov

NORTHERN MARIANA ISLANDS
Ms. Margarita M. Palacios
Court Administrator
Supreme Court
P.O. Box 2165
Saipan, MP 96950
P: (670) 236-9800
F: (670) 236-9701
E: supreme.court@saipan.com

OHIO
Mr. Kenneth Kozlowski
Director
Law Library
Supreme Court of Ohio
65 South Front Street, 11th Floor
Columbus, OH 43215
P: (614) 387-9680
F: (614) 387-9689

OKLAHOMA
Ms. Louisa Voden
Legislative Reference Director
Cartwright Memorial Library
State Capitol, Room B-8
2300 North Lincoln Boulevard
Oklahoma City, OK 73105
P: (405) 522-3413
F: (405) 521-2753

OREGON
Mr. Joe Stephens
Director
State Law Library
1163 State Street
Salem, OR 97301
P: (503) 986-5644
F: (503) 986-5623

PENNSYLVANIA
Ms. Caryn Carr
Library Director
Bureau of State Library
Room 318, Forum Building
Harrisburg, PA 17105
P: (717) 783-5968
F: (717) 772-8268
E: cacarr@state.pa.us

RHODE ISLAND
Ms. Karen Quinn
Chief Law Librarian
State Law Library
Frank Licht Judicial Complex
250 Benefit Street
Providence, RI 02903
P: (401) 222-3275
F: (401) 222-3865
E: kquinn@courts.state.ri.us

SOUTH CAROLINA
Ms. Janet Meyer
Librarian
Supreme Court Library
Supreme Court Building
1231 Gervais Street
Columbia, SC 29201
P: (803) 734-1080
F: (803) 734-0519

SOUTH DAKOTA
Ms. Sheri Anderson
Chief of Legal Research
Unified Judicial System
State Capitol
500 East Capitol Avenue
Pierre, SD 57501
P: (605) 773-4898
F: (605) 773-4898
E: sheri.anderson@ujs.state.sd.us

TENNESSEE
Mr. Stephen Jackson
Librarian
Supreme Court Library
Supreme Court Building
Nashville, TN 37243
P: (615) 741-2016
F: (615) 741-7186

TEXAS
Mr. Tony Estrada
Director
State Law Library
P.O. Box 12367
Austin, TX 78711
P: (512) 463-1722
F: (512) 463-1728
E: tony.estrada@sll.state.tx.us

U.S. VIRGIN ISLANDS
Ms. Janet Lloyd
Law Librarian
Law Library
5400 Veteran's Drive
St. Thomas, VI 00802
P: (340) 774-6680
F: (340) 776-9889

UTAH
Ms. Jessica Van Buren
Director
Courts - State Law Library
450 South State Street
P.O. Box 140220
Salt Lake City, UT 84114
P: (801) 238-7991
F: (801) 238-7993
E: JESSICAVB@email.utcourts.gov

VERMONT
Ms. Sybil Brigham McShane
State Librarian
Department of Libraries
Pavillion Office Building
Montpelier, VT 05609
P: (802) 828-3265
F: (802) 828-2199
E: sybil.mcshane@dol.state.vt.us

VIRGINIA
Mr. Karl Hade
Executive Secretary
Supreme Court
Supreme Court Building, 3rd Floor
100 North Ninth Street
Richmond, VA 23219
P: (804) 786-6455
F: (804) 786-4542
E: khade@courts.state.va.us

WASHINGTON
Ms. Kay Newman
State Law Librarian
State Law Library
Temple of Justice
P.O. Box 40751
Olympia, WA 98504
P: (360) 357-2136

WEST VIRGINIA
Ms. Kaye L. Maerz
Supreme Court Law Librarian
State Law Library
State Capitol, Room E-404
1900 Kanawha Boulevard, East
Charleston, WV 25305
P: (304) 558-2607
F: (304) 558-3673

WISCONSIN
Ms. Jane Colwin
State Law Librarian
State Law Library
120 Martin Luther King Jr. Boulevard
Madison, WI 53703
P: (608) 266-1600
F: (608) 267-2319

WYOMING
Ms. Kathy Carlson
State Law Librarian
State Law Library
Supreme Court & Library Building
2301 Capitol Avenue
Cheyenne, WY 82002
P: (307) 777-7509
F: (307) 777-7040
E: kcarls@state.wy.us

Licensing (Occupational and Professional)

Licenses and regulates the function of various professions in the state. Since there are hundreds of autonomous boards in the states, it is the centralized agencies that are represented in this listing.

Information provided by:

Council on Licensure, Enforcement and Regulation
Pam Brinegar
Executive Director
403 Marquis Avenue
Suite 100
Lexington, KY 40502
P: (859) 269-1901
F: (859) 269-1943
pbrinegar@mis.net
www.clearhq.org

ALASKA
Mr. Rick Urion
Director
Division of Professional Licensing
P.O. Box 110806
Juneau, AK 99811
P: (907) 465-2534
F: (907) 465-2974
E: rick_urion@commerce.state.ak.us

CALIFORNIA
Ms. Charlene Zettel
Director
Department of Consumer Affairs
1625 North Market Boulevard, Suite 5308
Sacramento, CA 95834
P: (916) 574-8211
F: (916) 574-8613
E: charlene_zettel@dca.ca.gov

COLORADO
Ms. Rosemary McCool
Division Director
Division of Registrations
Department of Regulatory Agencies
1560 Broadway, Suite 1350
Denver, CO 80202
P: (303) 894-7711
F: (303) 894-7692
E: rose.mccool@dora.state.co.us

Mr. Tambor Williams
Executive Director
Department of Regulatory Agencies
1560 Broadway, Suite 1550
Denver, CO 80202
P: (303) 894-7866
F: (303) 894-7866
E: tambor.williams@dora.state.co.us

CONNECTICUT
Ms. Wendy H. Furniss
Bureau Chief
Bureau of Healthcare Systems
Department of Public Health
P.O. Box 340308
Hartford, CT 06134
P: (860) 509-7405
F: (860) 509-7539
E: wendy.furniss@po.state.ct.us

DELAWARE
Mr. James L. Collins
Director
Division of Professional Regulation
Department of Administrative Services
861 Silver Lake Boulevard, Suite 203
Dover, DE 19904
P: (302) 744-4501
F: (302) 739-2711
E: james.l.collins@state.de.us

Ms. J. Kay Warren
Deputy Director
Division of Professional Regulation
Department of Administrative Services
861 Silverlake Boulevard, Suite 203
Dover, DE 19904
P: (302) 744-4503
F: (302) 739-2711
E: kay.warren@state.de.us

DISTRICT OF COLUMBIA
Dr. Patrick J. Canavan
Director
Department of Consumer & Regulatory Affairs
941 North Capitol Street, Northeast
Washington, DC 20002
P: (202) 442-8947
F: (202) 442-9445
E: patrick.canavan@dc.gov

Dr. Gregg A. Pane
Director and State Health Officer
Department of Health
825 North Capitol Street, Northeast
Suite 4400
Washington, DC 20002
P: (202) 442-5999
F: (202) 442-4788
E: doh@dc.gov

Feseha Woldu
Administrator
Department of Health
Professional Licensing Administration
717 14th Street, Northwest, Suite 600
Washington, DC 20005
P: (202) 724-8927
E: feseha.woldu@dc.gov

FLORIDA
Dr. M. Rony Francois
Secretary
Department of Health
4052 Bald Cypress Way, Bin #A00
Tallahassee, FL 32399
P: (850) 245-4444
F: (850) 414-7613
E: secretary@doh.state.fl.us

Ms. Lucy C. Gee
Division Director
Division of Medical Quality Assurance
Department of Health
4052 Bald Cypress Way, Bin #C01
Tallahassee, FL 32399
P: (850) 488-0595
F: (850) 414-7613
E: lucy_gee@doh.state.fl.us

Ms. Simone Marstiller
Secretary
Department of Business & Professional Regulation
1940 North Monroe Street
Tallahassee, FL 32399
P: (850) 413-0755
F: (850) 487-9529
E: simone.marstiller@dbpr.state.fl.us

GEORGIA
Ms. Mollie L. Fleeman
Division Director
Professional Licensing Boards Division
Office of Secretary of State
237 Coliseum Drive
Macon, GA 31217
P: (478) 207-1320
F: (478) 207-1363
E: mfleeman@sos.state.ga.us

HAWAII
Mr. Noe Noe Tom
Division Administrator
Department of Commerce & Consumer Affairs
Professional Licensing Division
P.O. Box 3469
Honolulu, HI 96801
P: (808) 586-2690
F: (808) 586-2689
E: pvl@dcca.hawaii.gov

IDAHO
Ms. Rayola Jacobsen
Bureau Chief
Bureau of Occupational Licenses
1109 Main Street, Suite 220
Boise, ID 83702
P: (208) 334-3233
F: (208) 334-3945
E: rjacobsen@ibol.idaho.gov

ILLINOIS
Mr. Daniel E. Bluthardt
Director
Division of Professional Regulation
320 West Washington Street, 3rd Floor
Springfield, IL 62786
P: (217) 782-9405
F: (217) 558-6001
E: jwatson@idfpr.com

INDIANA
Frances L. Kelly
Executive Director
Professional Licensing Agency
402 West Washington Street, Room W072
Indianapolis, IN 46204
P: (317) 232-2960
F: (317) 232-2312
E: fkelly@pla.in.gov

IOWA
Ms. Lois Churchill
Bureau Chief
Bureau of Professional Licensure
Department of Public Health
321 East 12th Street, 5th Floor
Des Moines, IA 50266
P: (515) 281-6385
F: (515) 281-3121
E: lchurchi@idph.state.ia.us

Ms. Shari Fett
Bureau Chief
Professional Licensing Division
Department of Commerce
1920 Southeast Hulsizer Road
Ankeny, IA 50021
P: (515) 281-7447
F: (515) 281-7411
E: shari.fett@iowa.gov

KENTUCKY
Mr. John C. Parrish
Executive Director
Division of Occupations & Professions
Finance & Administration Cabinet
P.O. Box 1360
Frankfort, KY 40601
P: (502) 564-3296 Ext. 224
F: (502) 564-4818
E: john.parrish@ky.gov

MAINE
Ms. Anne L. Head
Director
Office of Licensing & Registration
Professional & Financial Regulation
35 State House Station, Gardiner Annex
Augusta, ME 04333
P: (207) 624-8633
F: (207) 624-8637
E: anne.l.head@maine.gov

MARYLAND
Dr. James D. Fielder Jr.
Secretary
Department of Labor, Licensing & Regulation
500 North Calvert Street, Room 401
Baltimore, MD 21202
P: (410) 230-6020
F: (410) 333-0853
E: jfielder@dllr.state.md.us

Mr. Harry Loleas
Deputy Commissioner
Department of Labor, Licensing & Regulation
500 North Calvert Street, 3rd Floor
Baltimore, MD 21202
P: (410) 230-6226
F: (410) 333-6314
E: hloleas@dllr.state.md.us

Mr. S. Anthony McCann
Secretary
Department of Health & Mental Hygiene
201 West Preston Street
Baltimore, MD 21201
P: (410) 767-6860
F: (410) 767-6489

MASSACHUSETTS
Mr. George K. Weber
Director
Division of Professional Licensure
Office of Consumer Affairs
239 Causeway Street
Boston, MA 02114
P: (617) 727-3074
F: (617) 727-2197
E: george.k.weber@state.ma.us

MICHIGAN
Ms. Melanie Brim
Director
Bureau of Health Professions
Department of Community Health
P.O. Box 30670
Lansing, MI 48909
P: (517) 373-8068
F: (517) 241-3082
E: mbbrim@michigan.gov

Mr. Andrew L. Metcalf
Director
Bureau of Commerical Services
Department of Labor & Economic Growth
P.O. Box 30018
Lansing, MI 48909
P: (517) 241-9223
F: (517) 241-9280
E: ametca@michigan.gov

MISSOURI
Mr. David Broeker
Division Director
Division of Professional Registration
P.O. Box 1335
Jefferson City, MO 65102
P: (573) 751-1081
F: (573) 751-4176
E: david.broeker@pr.mo.gov

MONTANA
Mr. James F. Brown
Division Administrator
Business Standards Division
Department of Labor & Industry
P.O. Box 200517
Helena, MT 59620
P: (406) 841-2042
F: (406) 841-2305
E: jbrown@state.mt.us

NEBRASKA
Ms. Helen L. Meeks
Credentialing Division Administrator
Department of Health & Human Services
Regulation & Licensure
P.O. Box 94986
Lincoln, NE 68509
P: (402) 471-0179
F: (402) 471-3577
E: Helen.Meeks@hhss.ne.gov

Ms. Joann Schaefer
Director
Department of Health & Human Services
Regulation & Licensure
P.O. Box 95007
Lincoln, NE 68509
P: (402) 471-8566
F: (402) 471-9449
E: roxie.anderson@hhss.ne.us

NEW JERSEY
Ms. Kimberly S. Ricketts
Director
Division of Consumer Affairs
Office of Attorney General
P.O. Box 45027
Newark, NJ 07101
P: (973) 504-6200
F: (973) 273-8035
E: askconsumeraffairs@lps.state.nj.us

NEW MEXICO
Mr. Edward J. Lopez
Superintendent
Regulation & Licensing Department
Office of the Superintendent
2550 Cerrillos Road
Santa Fe, NM 87504
P: (505) 476-4508
F: (505) 476-4511
E: ed.lopez@state.nm.us

NEW YORK
Ms. Johanna Duncan-Poitier
Deputy Commissioner
State Education Department
Office of the Professions
89 Washington Avenue
Albany, NY 12234
P: (518) 474-3862
F: (518) 474-1449
E: jpoitier@mail.nysed.gov

OREGON
Ms. Susan K. Wilson
Administrator
Health Licensing Agency
700 Summer Street, Northeast, Suite 320
Salem, OR 97301
P: (503) 378-8667
F: (503) 585-9114
E: susan.k.wilson@state.or.us

PENNSYLVANIA
Mr. Basil L. Merenda
Commissioner
Bureau of Professional & Occupational Affairs
Department of State
P.O. Box 2649
Harrisburg, PA 17105
P: (717) 783-7192
F: (717) 783-0510
E: ra-bpoa@state.pa.us

Licensing (Occupational and Professional)

RHODE ISLAND
Mr. Charles Alexandre
Chief
Office of Health Professions Regulation
Department of Health
3 Capitol Hill, Room 205
Providence, RI 02908
P: (401) 222-5700
F: (401) 222-3352
E: charliea@doh.state.ri.us

Dr. David R. Gifford
Director
Department of Health
3 Capitol Hill, Room 104
Providence, RI 02908
P: (401) 222-2827
F: (401) 222-1272
E: health@ri.gov

SOUTH CAROLINA
Ms. Adrienne R. Youmans
Director
Department of Labor, Licensing & Regulation
P.O. Box 11329
Columbia, SC 29211
P: (803) 896-4300
F: (803) 896-4393
E: youmansa@llr.sc.gov

SOUTH DAKOTA
Ms. Doneen Hollingsworth
Secretary
Department of Health
Hayes Building
600 East Capitol Avenue
Pierre, SD 57501
P: (605) 773-3361
F: (605) 773-5683
E: doh.info@state.sd.us

TENNESSEE
Mr. Robbie H. Bell
Director
Division of Health Related Boards
1st Floor, Cordell Hull Building
425 5th Avenue, North
Nashville, TN 37247
P: (615) 741-2040
F: (615) 532-5369
E: robbie.bell@state.tn.us

TEXAS
Mr. Richard Bays
Assistant Commissioner
Department of State Health Services
Regulatory Services
1100 West 49th Street
Austin, TX 78756
P: (512) 458-7338
E: jrichard.bays@tdh.state.tx.us

Ms. Linda Jackson-Kirby
Administrative Assistant
Department of State Health Services
Professional Licensing & Certification
8407 Wall Street, Suite S-420
Austin, TX 78754
P: (512) 834-6628 Ext. 2729
F: (512) 834-6677
E: linda.kirby@dshs.state.tx.us

Mr. William Kuntz
Executive Director
Department of Licensing & Regulation
P.O. Box 12157
Austin, TX 78711
P: (512) 463-3173
F: (512) 475-2874
E: bill@license.state.tx.us

Ms. Dede McEachern
Director of Licensing
Department of Licensing & Regulation
P.O. Box 12157
Austin, TX 78711
P: (512) 475-2896
F: (512) 475-2871
E: dede@license.state.tx.us

Ms. Debbie Peterson
Director
Professional Licensing & Certification Unit
Department of State Health Services
1100 West 49th Street
Austin, TX 78756
P: (512) 834-6628

UTAH
Mr. J. Craig Jackson
Director
Division of Occupational & Professional Licensing
Department of Commerce
P.O. Box 146741
Salt Lake City, UT 84114
P: (801) 530-6039
F: (801) 530-6511
E: cjackson@utah.gov

VERMONT
Mr. Christopher D. Winters
Director
Office of Professional Regulation
Secretary of State's Office
26 Terrace Street, Drawer 09
Montpelier, VT 05609
P: (802) 828-2458
F: (802) 828-2496
E: cwinters@sec.state.vt.us

VIRGINIA
Mr. Jay W. DeBoer
Director
Department of Professional & Occupational Regulation
3600 West Broad Street
Richmond, VA 23230
P: (804) 367-8519
F: (804) 367-9537
E: jay.deboer@dpor.virginia.gov

Ms. Sandra Whitley Ryals
Director
Department of Health Professions
6603 West Broad Street, 5th Floor
Richmond, VA 23230
P: (804) 662-9919
F: (804) 662-9114
E: robert.nebiker@dhp.virginia.gov

WASHINGTON
Ms. Laurie A. Jinkins
Assistant Secretary
Health Systems Quality Assurance
Department of Health
P.O. Box 47850
Olympia, WA 98504
P: (360) 236-4600
F: (360) 236-4626
E: laurie.jinkins@doh.wa.gov

Ms. Liz Luce
Director
Department of Licensing
1125 Washington Street, Southeast
P.O. Box 9020
Olympia, WA 98507
P: (360) 902-3933
F: (360) 902-4042
E: doldirector@dol.wa.gov

Ms. Mary C. Selecky
Secretary
Department of Health
P.O. Box 47890
Olympia, WA 98504
P: (360) 236-4030
F: (360) 586-7424
E: secretary@doh.wa.gov

WISCONSIN
Ms. Celia M. Jackson
Secretary
Department of Regulation & Licensing
1400 East Washington Avenue
P.O. Box 8935
Madison, WI 53708
P: (608) 266-8609
F: (608) 267-0644
E: becky.fry@drl.state.wi.us

Ms. Sandra Rowe
Deputy Secretary
Department of Regulation & Licensing
1400 East Washington Avenue
P.O. Box 8935
Madison, WI 53708
P: (608) 267-2435
F: (608) 261-2381
E: sandra.rowe@drl.state.wi.us

Lieutenant Governor

The statewide elected official who is next in line of succession to the governorship. (In Maine, New Hampshire, New Jersey, Tennessee and West Virginia, the presidents (or speakers) of the Senate are the next in line of succession to the governorship. In Tennessee, the speaker of the Senate bears the statutory title of lieutenant governor. In Arizona, Oregon, and Wyoming, the secretary of state is next in line of succession to the governorship.)

Information provided by:

National Lieutenant Governors Association
Julia Nienaber Hurst
Executive Director
71 Cavalier Boulevard
Suite 124
Florence, KY 41042
P: (859) 283-1400
F: (859) 244-8001
jhurst@csg.org
www.ngla.us

ALABAMA
Hon. Jim Folsom Jr. (D)
Lieutenant Governor
Office of the Lieutenant Governor
Suite 725, 11 South Union Street
Montgomery, AL 36130
P: (334) 242-7900
F: (334) 242-4661

ALASKA
Hon. Sean R. Parnell (R)
Lieutenant Governor
Office of the Lieutenant Governor
550 West 7th Street, Suite 1700
Anchorage, AK 99501
P: (907) 269-7460

AMERICAN SAMOA
Hon. Ipulasi Aito Sunia (D)
Lieutenant Governor
Office of the Lieutenant Governor
Office of the Lieutenant Governor
Territory of American Samoa
Pago Pago, AS 96799
P: (684) 633-4116
F: (684) 633-2269

ARKANSAS
Hon. Bill Halter (D)
Lieutenant Governor
Office of the Lieutenant Governor
270 State Capitol
Little Rock, AR 72201
P: (501) 682-2144
F: (501) 682-2894

CALIFORNIA
Hon. John Garamendi (D)
Lieutenant Governor
Office of the Lieutenant Governor
State Capitol, Room 1114
Sacramento, CA 95814
P: (916) 445-8994
F: (916) 323-4998

COLORADO
Hon. Barbara O'Brien (D)
Lieutenant Governor
Office of the Lieutenant Governor
130 State Capitol
Denver, CO 80203
P: (303) 866-2087
F: (303) 866-5469

CONNECTICUT
Hon. Michael C. Fedele (R)
Lieutenant Governor
Office of the Lieutenant Governor
State Capitol, Room 304
Hartford, CT 06106
P: (860) 524-7384
F: (860) 524-7304

DELAWARE
Hon. John Carney Jr. (D)
Lieutenant Governor
Office of the Lieutenant Governor
Tatnall Building, 3rd Floor
Dover, DE 19901
P: (302) 744-4333
F: (302) 739-6965

FLORIDA
Hon. Jeffrey D. Kottkamp (R)
Lieutenant Governor
Office of the Lieutenant Governor
The State Capitol
Tallahassee, FL 32399
P: (850) 488-7146
F: (850) 487-0801
E: Jeff.Kottkamp@myflorida.com

GEORGIA
Hon. Casey Cagle (R)
Lieutenant Governor
Office of the Lieutenant Governor
240 State Capitol
Atlanta, GA 30334
P: (404) 656-5030
F: (404) 656-6739

GUAM
Hon. Michael Cruz (R)
Lieutenant Governor
Office of the Lieutenant Governor
R.J. Bordallo Governor's Complex
P.O. Box 2950
Hagatna, GU 96932
P: (671) 475-9380
F: (671) 477-2007
E: mcruz@guamocd.org

HAWAII
Hon. James "Duke" Aiona Jr. (R)
Lieutenant Governor
Office of the Lieutenant Governor
Executive Chambers
State Capitol
Honolulu, HI 96813
P: (808) 586-0255
F: (808) 586-0231

IDAHO
Hon. Jim Risch (R)
Lieutenant Governor
Office of the Lieutenant Governor
Room 225, State Capitol
Boise, ID 83720
P: (208) 334-2200
F: (208) 334-3259

ILLINOIS
Hon. Patrick Quinn (D)
Lieutenant Governor
Office of the Lieutenant Governor
214 State House
Springfield, IL 62706
P: (217) 782-7884
F: (217) 524-6262

INDIANA
Hon. Becky Skillman (R)
Lieutenant Governor
Office of the Lieutenant Governor
State Capitol, Room 333
Indianapolis, IN 46204
P: (317) 232-4545
F: (317) 232-4788

IOWA
Hon. Patty Judge (D)
Lieutenant Governor
Office of the Lieutenant Governor
State Capitol, Room 9
Des Moines, IA 50319
P: (515) 281-0225
F: (515) 281-6611

KANSAS
Hon. Mark V. Parkinson (D)
Lieutenant Governor
Office of the Lieutenant Governor
State Capitol
300 Southwest 10th Avenue, Suite 222S
Topeka, KS 66612
P: (785) 296-2213
F: (785) 296-5669

KENTUCKY
Hon. Stephen Pence (R)
Lieutenant Governor
Office of the Lieutenant Governor
700 Capitol Avenue
Suite 142
Frankfort, KY 40601
P: (502) 564-2611
F: (502) 564-2849

LOUISIANA
Hon. Mitch Landrieu (D)
Lieutenant Governor
Office of the Lieutenant Governor
Pentagon Court Barracks
900 North 3rd Street, P.O. Box 44243
Baton Rouge, LA 70804
P: (225) 342-7009
F: (225) 342-1949

MARYLAND
Hon. Anthony G. Brown (D)
Lieutenant Governor
Office of the Lieutenant Governor
100 State Circle
Annapolis, MD 21401
P: (410) 974-3591
F: (410) 974-5882

MASSACHUSETTS
Hon. Timothy Murray (D)
Lieutenant Governor
Office of the Lieutenant Governor
Office of the Lieutenant Governor
Room 360
Boston, MA 02133
P: (617) 725-4005
F: (617) 727-9725

Lieutenant Governor

MICHIGAN
Hon. John D. Cherry Jr. (D)
Lieutenant Governor
Office of the Lieutenant Governor
P.O. Box 30013
Lansing, MI 48909
P: (517) 373-6800
F: (517) 241-3956

MINNESOTA
Hon. Carol L. Molnau (R)
Lieutenant Governor & Commissioner, Department of Transportation
Office of the Lieutenant Governor
130 State Capitol
75 Rev. Dr. Martin Luther King Jr. Blvd.
St. Paul, MN 55155
P: (651) 296-3391
F: (651) 296-2089

MISSISSIPPI
Hon. Amy Tuck (R)
Lieutenant Governor
Office of the Lieutenant Governor
New Capitol, Room 315
P.O. Box 1018
Jackson, MS 39215
P: (601) 359-3200
F: (601) 359-3935
E: ltgov@mail.senate.state.ms.us

MISSOURI
Hon. Peter Kinder (R)
Lieutenant Governor
Office of the Lieutenant Governor
State Capitol, Room 224
Jefferson City, MO 65101
P: (573) 751-4727
F: (573) 751-9422
E: ltgov@mail.mo.gov

MONTANA
Hon. John C. Bohlinger (R)
Lieutenant Governor
Office of the Lieutenant Governor
Capitol Station, Room 207
Helena, MT 59620
P: (406) 444-5665
F: (406) 444-4648

NEBRASKA
Hon. Rick Sheehy (R)
Lieutenant Governor
Office of the Lieutenant Governor
State Capitol, Room 2315
P.O.Box 94863
Lincoln, NE 68509
P: (402) 471-2256
F: (402) 471-6031

NEVADA
Hon. Brian K. Krolicki (R)
Lieutenant Governor
Office of the Lieutenant Governor
Capitol Complex
Carson City, NV 89701
P: (775) 684-5637
F: (775) 684-5782
E: nvltgov@govmail.state.nv.us

NEW MEXICO
Hon. Diane D. Denish (D)
Lieutenant Governor
Office of the Lieutenant Governor
State Capitol, Suite 417
Santa Fe, NM 87501
P: (505) 476-2250
F: (505) 476-2257

NEW YORK
Hon. David A. Paterson (D)
Lieutenant Governor
Office of the Lieutenant Governor
Executive Chamber
State Capitol
Albany, NY 12224
P: (518) 474-4623
F: (518) 486-4170

NORTH CAROLINA
Hon. Beverly Perdue (D)
Lieutenant Governor
Office of the Lieutenant Governor
310 North Blount Boulevard
20301 Mail Service Center
Raleigh, NC 27699
P: (919) 733-7350
F: (919) 733-6595

NORTH DAKOTA
Hon. Jack Dalrymple (R)
Lieutenant Governor
Office of the Lieutenant Governor
State Capitol
Bismarck, ND 58505
P: (701) 328-4222
F: (701) 328-2205

NORTHERN MARIANA ISLANDS
Hon. Timothy P. Villagomez (C)
Lieutenant Governor
Office of the Lieutenant Governor
Executive Director's Office
Joeten Dandan Building, P.O. Box 501220
Saipan, MP 96950
P: (670) 235-7025
F: (670) 235-6145
E: cucedo@gtepacifica.net

OHIO
Hon. Lee Fisher (D)
Lieutenant Governor
Office of the Lieutenant Governor
77 South High Street,30th Floor
Columbus, OH 43215
P: (614) 466-3679
F: (614) 644-0575

OKLAHOMA
Hon. Jari Askins (D)
Lieutenant Governor
Office of the Lieutenant Governor
State Capitol, Room 211
Oklahoma City, OK 73105
P: (405) 521-2161
F: (405) 525-2702

PENNSYLVANIA
Hon. Catherine Baker Knoll (D)
Lieutenant Governor
Office of the Lieutenant Governor
200 Main Capitol Building
Harrisburg, PA 17120
P: (717) 787-3300
F: (717) 783-0150
E: **lieutenant-governor@state.pa.us

RHODE ISLAND
Hon. Elizabeth H. Roberts (D)
Lieutenant Governor
Office of the Lieutenant Governor
116 State House
Providence, RI 02903
P: (401) 222-2371
F: (401) 222-2012
E: riltgov@ltgov.ri.gov

SOUTH CAROLINA
Hon. R. Andre Bauer (R)
Lieutenant Governor
Office of the Lieutenant Governor
P.O. Box 142
Columbia, SC 29202
P: (803) 734-2080
F: (803) 734-2082

SOUTH DAKOTA
Hon. Dennis Daugaard (R)
Lieutenant Governor
Office of the Lieutenant Governor
500 East Capitol Street
Pierre, SD 57501
P: (605) 773-3212
F: (605) 773-4711

TENNESSEE
Hon. Ron Ramsey (R) (elected by the Senate)
Senate President/Lieutenant Governor
Office of the Lieutenant Governor
One Legislative Plaza
Nashville, TN 37219
P: (615) 741-4524
F: (615) 741-4990
E: lt.gov.ron.ramsey@legislature.state.tn.us

TEXAS
Hon. David Dewhurst (R)
Lieutenant Governor
Office of the Lieutenant Governor
Capitol Station
P.O. Box 12068
Austin, TX 78711
P: (512) 463-0001
F: (512) 463-0677

U.S. VIRGIN ISLANDS
Hon. Gregory Francis (D)
Lieutenant Governor
Office of the Lieutenant Governor
1131 Kings Street, Suite 101
St. Croix, VI 00802
P: (340) 773-6449
F: (340) 773-0330

UTAH
Hon. Gary R. Herbert (R)
Lieutenant Governor
Office of the Lieutenant Governor
203 State Capitol
Salt Lake City, UT 84114
P: (801) 538-1520
F: (801) 538-1557
E: GHERBERT@utah.gov

VERMONT
Hon. Brian Dubie (R)
Lieutenant Governor
Office of the Lieutenant Governor
115 State Street
Montpelier, VT 05633
P: (802) 828-2226
F: (802) 828-3198

VIRGINIA
Hon. Bill Bolling (R)
Lieutenant Governor
Office of the Lieutenant Governor
102 Governor Street
Richmond, VA 23219
P: (804) 786-2078
F: (804) 786-7514
E: ltgov@ltgov.virginia.gov

WASHINGTON
Hon. Brad Owen (D)
Lieutenant Governor
Office of the Lieutenant Governor
416 14th Avenue, Southwest
Olympia, WA 98504
P: (360) 786-7700
F: (360) 786-7749
E: ltgov@leg.wa.gov

WEST VIRGINIA
Hon. Earl Ray Tomblin (D)
Senate President/Lieutenant Governor
West Virginia Legislature
Room 229, Main Unit
Capitol Complex
Charleston, WV 25305
P: (304) 357-7801
F: (304) 357-7839
E: spres@mail.wvnet.edu

WISCONSIN
Hon. Barbara Lawton (D)
Lieutenant Governor
Office of the Lieutenant Governor
Room 19 East State Capitol
Madison, WI 53702
P: (608) 266-3516
F: (608) 267-3571

Lobby Law Administration

Administers registration and reporting requirements for lobbyists.

ALABAMA
Hon. Beth Chapman (R)
Secretary of State
Office of the Secretary of State
State House
600 Dexter Avenue
Montgomery, AL 36104
P: (334) 242-7205
F: (334) 242-4993
E: beth.chapman@sos.alabama.gov

ALASKA
Ms. Brooke Miles
Director
Public Offices Commission
2221 East Northern Lights Boulevard
Room 128
Anchorage, AK 99508
P: (907) 276-4176
F: (907) 276-7018
E: brooke_miles@admin.state.ak.us

ARIZONA
Hon. Jan Brewer (R)
Secretary of State
Office of the Secretary of State
7th Floor, State Capitol
1700 West Washington Street
Phoenix, AZ 85007
P: (520) 628-6583
F: (520) 628-6938
E: lglenn@azsos.gov

ARKANSAS
Hon. Charlie Daniels (D)
Secretary of State
Office of the Secretary of State
256 State Capitol Building
Little Rock, AR 72201
P: (501) 682-1010
F: (501) 682-3510
E: larowland@sosmail.state.ar.us

CALIFORNIA
Ms. Caren Daniels-Meade
Chief
Political Reform Division
1500 11th Street, 5th Floor
Sacramento, CA 95814
P: (916) 657-2166
F: (916) 653-3214

DELAWARE
Ms. Janet Wright
Commission Counsel
Public Integrity Commission
Margaret O'Neill Building
410 Federal Street, Suite 3
Dover, DE 19901
P: (302) 739-2399
F: (302) 739-2398

DISTRICT OF COLUMBIA
Ms. Cecily Collier-Montgomery
Director
Office of Campaign Finance
2000 14th Street, Northwest
Suite 433
Washington, DC 20009
P: (202) 671-0547
F: (202) 671-0658

FLORIDA
Mr. Phillip Claypool
Executive Director
Commission on Ethics
P.O. Drawer 15709
Tallahassee, FL 32317
P: (904) 488-7864
F: (904) 488-3077

GEORGIA
Mr. C. Theodore Lee
Executive Secretary
State Ethics Commission
205 Jesse Hill Jr. Drive, South East
Suite 478, East Tower
Atlanta, GA 30334
P: (404) 463-1980
F: (404) 463-1988
E: ethics@ethics.state.ga.us

HAWAII
Mr. Daniel J. Mollway
Executive Director
State Ethics Commission
P.O. Box 616
Honolulu, HI 96809
P: (808) 587-0460
F: (808) 587-0470
E: ethics@hawaiiethics.org

IDAHO
Hon. Ben T. Ysursa (R)
Secretary of State
Office of the Secretary of State
State Capitol, Room 203
Boise, ID 83720
P: (208) 334-2300
F: (208) 334-2282
E: bysursa@sos.idaho.gov

ILLINOIS
Ms. Jacqueline Price
Director
Department of Index
111 East Monroe
Springfield, IL 62756
P: (217) 782-0645
F: (217) 524-0930

INDIANA
Ms. Sarah L. Nagy
Executive Director
Lobby Registration Commission
251 North Illinois Street, Suite 975
Indianapolis, IN 46204
P: (317) 232-9860
F: (317) 233-0077
E: snagy@lrc.state.in.us

IOWA
Mr. Michael E. Marshall
Secretary of the Senate
General Assembly
State Capitol
East 12th & Grand Avenue
Des Moines, IA 50319
P: (515) 281-5307
E: Mike.Marshall@legis.state.ia.us

KANSAS
Mr. Brad Bryant
Deputy Assistant for Elections
Office of the Secretary of State - Elections
120 Southwest 10th Avenue
Memorial Hall
Topeka, KS 66612
P: (785) 296-4575
F: (785) 368-8033

KENTUCKY
Hon. Trey Grayson (R)
Secretary of State
Office of the Secretary of State
700 Capitol Avenue, Suite 152
Frankfort, KY 40601
P: (502) 564-3490
F: (502) 564-5687
E: sos.secretary@ky.gov

LOUISIANA
Mr. R. Gray Sexton
Executive Director
Ethics Administration
2415 Quail Drive, Third Floor
Baton Rouge, LA 70808
P: (225) 763-8777
F: (225) 763-8780

MARYLAND
Ms. Suzanne S. Fox
Executive Director
State Ethics Commission
45 Calvert Street, 1st Floor
Annapolis, MD 21401
P: (410) 260-7770
E: sfox@gov.state.md.us

MASSACHUSETTS
Hon. William Francis Galvin (D)
Secretary of the Commonwealth
Office of the Secretary of the Commonwealth
State House, Room 337
Boston, MA 02133
P: (617) 727-9180
F: (617) 742-4722
E: cis@sec.state.ma.us

MICHIGAN
Mr. Christopher M. Thomas
Director
Bureau of Elections
Mutual Building, 4th Floor
208 North Capitol Avenue
Lansing, MI 48918
P: (517) 373-2540
F: (517) 241-2784

MINNESOTA
Ms. Jeanne Olson
Executive Director
Campaign Finance & Public Disclosure Board
Centennial Office Building, Suite 190
658 Cedar Street
St. Paul, MN 55155
P: (651) 296-1721
F: (651) 296-1722
E: jeanne.olson@state.mn.us

Hon. Mark Ritchie (DFL)
Secretary of State
Office of the Secretary of State
180 State Office Building
100 Constitution Avenue
St. Paul, MN 55155
P: (651) 296-2803
F: (651) 297-5844
E: secretary.state@state.mn.us

MISSISSIPPI
Mr. Jay Eads
Assistant Secretary of State for Elections
Elections Division
P.O. Box 136
401 Mississippi Street
Jackson, MS 39205
P: (601) 359-6368
F: (601) 359-5019

MISSOURI
Mr. Robert F. Connor
Executive Director
Ethics Commission
P.O. Box 1254
Jefferson City, MO 65102
P: (573) 751-2020
F: (573) 526-4506
E: robert.connor@mec.mo.gov

Ms. Liz Ziegler
General Council
Ethics Commission
P.O. Box 1254
Jefferson City, MO 65102
P: (573) 751-2020
E: lziegler@mec.mo.gov

MONTANA
Mr. Dennis Unsworth
Commissioner
Office of the Commissioner of Political Practices
1205 Eighth Avenue
P.O. Box 202401
Helena, MT 59620
P: (406) 444-2942
F: (406) 444-1643
E: dunsworth@mt.gov

NEBRASKA
Mr. Patrick J. O'Donnell
Clerk of the Legislature
State Legislature
State Capitol, Room 2018
P.O. Box 94604
Lincoln, NE 68509
P: (402) 471-2271
F: (402) 471-2126
E: podonnell@leg.ne.gov

NEVADA
Mr. Lorne J. Malkiewich
Director
Legislative Counsel Bureau
Legislative Counsel Bureau
401 South Carson Street
Carson City, NV 89701
P: (775) 684-6800
F: (775) 684-6600
E: malkiewich@lcb.state.nv.us

NEW HAMPSHIRE
Hon. William M. Gardner (D)
Secretary of State
Office of the Secretary of State
State House, Room 204
Concord, NH 03301
P: (603) 271-3242
F: (603) 271-6316
E: kladd@sos.state.nh.us

NEW JERSEY
Dr. Frederick M. Herrmann
Executive Director
Election Law Enforcement Commission
P.O. Box 185
Trenton, NJ 08625
P: (609) 292-8700
F: (609) 777-1457

NEW MEXICO
Hon. Mary Herrera (D)
Secretary of State
Office of the Secretary of State
325 Don Gaspar, Suite 300
State Capitol Annex, North
Santa Fe, NM 87503
P: (505) 827-3600
F: (505) 827-3634
E: MaryE.Herrera@state.nm.us

NEW YORK
Mr. David M. Grandeau
Executive Director
Temporary State Commission on Lobbying
Empire State Plaza
Agency Building 2
Albany, NY 12223
P: (518) 474-7126

NORTH CAROLINA
Hon. Elaine F. Marshall (D)
Secretary of State
Office of the Secretary of State
P.O. Box 29622
Raleigh, NC 27626
P: (919) 807-2005
F: (919) 807-2010
E: Secretary@sosnc.com

NORTH DAKOTA
Hon. Alvin A. Jaeger (R)
Secretary of State
Office of the Secretary of State
600 East Boulevard Avenue
Department 108
Bismark, ND 58505
P: (701) 328-2900
F: (701) 328-2992
E: sos@nd.gov

OHIO
Mr. Tony W. Bledsoe
Legislative Inspector General
Office of the Legislative Inspector General
50 West Broad Street, Suite 1308
Columbus, OH 43215
P: (614) 728-5100
F: (614) 728-5074
E: info@jlec-olig.state.oh.us

OKLAHOMA
Ms. Marilyn Hughes
Executive Director
Ethics Commission
State Capitol Building, Room B-5
2300 North Lincoln Boulevard
Oklahoma City, OK 73105
P: (405) 521-3451
F: (405) 521-4905

PENNSYLVANIA
Mr. Mark R. Corrigan
Secretary of the Senate
State Legislature
462 Capitol Building
Senate Box 203053
Harrisburg, PA 17120
P: (717) 787-5920
E: secretary@os.pasen.gov

SOUTH CAROLINA
Hon. Mark Hammond (R)
Secretary of State
Office of the Secretary of State
P.O. Box 11350
Columbia, SC 29211
P: (803) 734-2170
F: (803) 734-1661
E: rdaggerhart@sos.sc.gov

Mr. Herbert Hayden Jr.
Executive Director
State Ethics Commission
5000 Thurmond Mall, Suite 250
Columbia, SC 29201
P: (803) 253-4192
F: (803) 253-7539
E: herb@ethics.state.sc.us

SOUTH DAKOTA
Hon. Chris Nelson (R)
Secretary of State
Office of the Secretary of State
State Capitol
500 East Capitol Avenue
Pierre, SD 57501
P: (605) 773-3537
F: (605) 773-6580
E: sdsos@state.sd.us

TENNESSEE
Mr. Drew Rawlins
Executive Director
Registry of Elections Finance
404 James Robertson Parkway, 16th Floor
Nashville, TN 37243
P: (615) 741-7959
F: (615) 532-8905

TEXAS
Ms. Ann McGeehan
Division Director
Elections Division
Office of the Secretary of State
P.O. Box 12697
Austin, TX 78711
P: (512) 463-9871
F: (512) 475-2811

UTAH
Hon. Gary R. Herbert (R)
Lieutenant Governor
Office of the Lieutenant Governor
203 State Capitol
Salt Lake City, UT 84114
P: (801) 538-1520
F: (801) 538-1557
E: GHERBERT@utah.gov

VERMONT
Hon. Deborah L. Markowitz (D)
Secretary of State
Office of the Secretary of State
26 Terrace Street
Montpelier, VT 05609
P: (802) 828-2148
F: (802) 828-2496
E: dmarkowitz@sec.state.vt.us

VIRGINIA
Hon. Katherine K. Hanley (D)
Secretary of the Commonwealth
Office of the Secretary of the Commonwealth
1111 East Broad Street, 4th Floor
Patrick Henry Building
Richmond, VA 23201
P: (804) 786-2441
F: (804) 371-0017
E: kate.hanley@governor.virginia.gov

WASHINGTON
Ms. Vicki Rippie
Executive Director
Public Disclosure Commission
711 Capitol Way, Room 206
P.O. Box 40908
Olympia, WA 98504
P: (360) 586-4838
F: (360) 753-1112
E: vrippie@pdc.wa.gov

Lobby Law Administration

WEST VIRGINIA
Mr. Lewis G. Brewer
Executive Director
Ethics Commission
210 Brooks Street, Suite 300
Charleston, WV 25301
P: (304) 558-0664
F: (304) 558-2169
E: lbrewer@wvadmin.gov

WISCONSIN
Mr. R. Roth Judd
Executive Director
Ethics Board
44 East Mifflin Street, Suite 601
Madison, WI 53703
P: (608) 266-8123
F: (608) 264-9309

WYOMING
Hon. Max Maxfield (R)
Secretary of State
Office of the Secretary of State
State Capitol
Cheyenne, WY 82002
P: (307) 777-5333
F: (307) 777-6217
E: Secofstate@state.wy.us

Lottery

Administers the state lottery system.

ARIZONA
Mr. Art Macias
Executive Director
State Lottery
4740 East University Drive
Phoenix, AZ 85034
P: (480) 921-4400
F: (480) 921-4488

CALIFORNIA
Ms. Joan M. Borucki
Director
State Lottery
600 North 10th Street
Sacramento, CA 95814
P: (916) 323-7095
F: (916) 323-7087

COLORADO
Ms. Margaret Gordon
Director
State Lottery
212 West 3rd Street
Suite 210 (P.O. Box 7)
Pueblo, CO 81003
P: (719) 546-5200
F: (719) 546-5208

CONNECTICUT
Mr. James Vance
President & CEO
State Lottery Corporation
270 John Downey Drive
New Britain, CT 06051
P: (860) 348-4000
F: (860) 348-4015

DELAWARE
Mr. Wayne Lemons
Director
State Lottery
1575 McKee Road, Suite 102
Dover, DE 19904
P: (302) 739-5291
F: (302) 739-6706

DISTRICT OF COLUMBIA
Ms. Jeanette A. Michael
Executive Director
Lottery & Charitable Games Control Board
2101 Martin Luther King Jr. Avenue, SE
Washington, DC 20020
P: (202) 645-8000
F: (202) 645-7914

FLORIDA
Mr. Leo DiBenigno
Secretary
State Lottery
250 Marriott Drive
Tallahassee, FL 32301
P: (850) 487-7777
F: (850) 487-7709

GEORGIA
Ms. Margaret R. DeFrancisco
President & CEO
State Lottery Corporation
Inforum, Suite 3000
250 Williams Street
Atlanta, GA 30303
P: (404) 215-5000
F: (404) 215-8871

IDAHO
Mr. Jeffrey R. Anderson
Director
State Lottery
1199 Shoreline Lane, Suite 100
P.O. Box 6537
Boise, ID 83707
P: (208) 334-2600
F: (208) 334-2610

ILLINOIS
Ms. Jodie Winnett
Acting Superintendent
State Lottery
100 West Randolph, Suite 7-274
Chicago, IL 60601
P: (312) 793-3026
F: (312) 793-5514

INDIANA
Ms. Kathryn Densborn
Executive Director
State Lottery
Pan Am Plaza
201 South Capitol Avenue, Suite 1100
Indianapolis, IN 46225
P: (317) 264-4800
F: (317) 264-4908

IOWA
Dr. Edward J. Stanek II
Chief Executive Officer
State Lottery Authority
2323 Grand Avenue
Des Moines, IA 50312
P: (515) 725-7900
F: (515) 725-7882

KANSAS
Mr. Ed Van Petten
Executive Director
State Lottery
128 North Kansas Avenue
Topeka, KS 66603
P: (785) 296-5700
F: (785) 296-5712

KENTUCKY
Mr. Arthur L. Gleason Jr.
President & CEO
State Lottery Corporation
1011 West Main Street
Louisville, KY 40202
P: (502) 560-1500
F: (502) 560-1532

LOUISIANA
Ms. Rose Hudson
President
State Lottery Corporation
555 Laurel Street
Baton Rouge, LA 70801
P: (225) 297-2000
F: (225) 297-2005

MAINE
Mr. Dan A. Gwadosky
Director
State Lottery
#8 State House Station
Augusta, ME 04333
P: (207) 287-3721
F: (207) 287-6769
E: dgwadosky@maine.gov

MARYLAND
Mr. Buddy Roogow
Executive Director
State Lottery
Montgomery Park Business Center
1800 Washington Boulevard, Suite 330
Baltimore, MD 21230
P: (410) 230-8790
F: (410) 230-8728
E: broogow@msla.state.md.us

MASSACHUSETTS
Mr. Mark J. Cavanaugh
Executive Director
State Lottery Commission
60 Columbian Street
Braintree, MA 02184
P: (781) 849-5555
F: (781) 849-5546

MICHIGAN
Mr. Gary C. Peters
Commissioner
Bureau of State Lottery
101 East Hillsdale
P.O. Box 30023
Lansing, MI 48909
P: (517) 335-5600
F: (517) 335-5651

MINNESOTA
Mr. Clint Harris
Executive Director
State Lottery
2645 Long Lake Road
Roseville, MN 55113
P: (651) 635-8100
F: (651) 297-7496

MISSOURI
Mr. Larry Jansen
Executive Director
State Lottery
P.O. Box 1603
Jefferson City, MO 65102
P: (573) 751-4050
F: (573) 522-1630

MONTANA
Mr. George Parisot
Director
State Lottery
2525 North Montana Avenue
P.O. Box 200544
Helena, MT 59620
P: (406) 444-5825
F: (406) 444-5830

NEBRASKA
Mr. Jim Haynes
Acting Director
State Lottery
P.O. Box 98901
301 Centennial Mall South, 2nd Floor
Lincoln, NE 68509
P: (402) 471-6100
F: (402) 471-6108

NEW HAMPSHIRE
Mr. Rick Wisler
Executive Director
State Lottery Commission
P.O. Box 1208
Concord, NH 03302
P: (603) 271-3391
F: (603) 271-1160
E: rickey.a.wisler@lottery.nh.gov

NEW JERSEY
Mr. William T. Jourdain
Acting Executive Director
State Lottery
P.O. Box 041
Trenton, NJ 08625
P: (609) 599-5800
F: (609) 599-5935

Lottery

NEW MEXICO
Mr. Tom Romero
CEO
State Lottery
P.O. Box 93130
Albuquerque, NM 87199
P: (505) 342-7600
F: (505) 342-7512

NEW YORK
Mr. Robert McLaughlin
Director
State Lottery
1 Broadway Center
P.O. Box 7500
Schenectady, NY 12301
P: (518) 388-3400
F: (518) 486-6852

NORTH CAROLINA
Mr. Tom Shaheen
Executive Director
Education Lottery
2100 Yonkers Road
Raleigh, NC 27604
P: (919) 301-3300
F: (919) 715-8825
E: tshaheen@lotterync.net

OHIO
Mr. Mike Dolan
Executive Director
State Lottery Commission
615 West Superior Avenue
Cleveland, OH 44113
P: (216) 774-5900

OKLAHOMA
Mr. James Scroggins
Executive Director
State Education Lottery
3817 North Santa Fe
Oklahoma City, OK 73112
P: (405) 521-0520
F: (405) 521-0528

OREGON
Mr. Dale Penn
Director
State Lottery
P.O. Box 12649
Salem, OR 97309
P: (503) 540-1000
F: (503) 540-1001

PENNSYLVANIA
Mr. Ed Trees
Executive Director
State Lottery
2850 Turnpike Industrial Drive
Middletown, PA 17057
P: (717) 986-4699

PUERTO RICO
Ms. Hilda Ramos Maldonado
Auxiliary Director
Loteria Electronica
383 Avenue Roosevelt, Suite 110
San Juan, PR 00918
P: (787) 759-8686
F: (787) 763-8463

RHODE ISLAND
Mr. Gerald Aubin
Executive Director
State Lottery
1425 Pontiac Avenue
Cranston, RI 02920
P: (401) 463-6500
F: (401) 463-5669

SOUTH CAROLINA
Mr. Ernie Passailaigue
Executive Director
State Education Lottery
1333 Main Street
Suite 400
Columbia, SC 29201
P: (803) 737-2002
F: (803) 737-2005

SOUTH DAKOTA
Mr. Norman Lingle
Director
State Lottery
Department of Revenue & Regulation
P.O. Box 7107
Pierre, SD 57501
P: (605) 773-5770
F: (605) 773-5786
E: norman.lingle@state.sd.us

TENNESSEE
Ms. Rebecca Paul Hargrove
President & CEO
Education Lottery Corporation
Plaza Tower, Metrocenter
200 Athens Way, Suite 200
Nashville, TN 37228
P: (615) 324-6500
F: (615) 324-6512

TEXAS
Mr. Anthony Sadberry
Acting Executive Director
State Lottery Commission
P.O. Box 16630
Austin, TX 78761
P: (512) 344-5000
F: (512) 478-3682

U.S. VIRGIN ISLANDS
Mr. Paul Flemming
Executive Director
State Lottery
8A Ross Estate
Barbel Plaza
St. Thomas, VI 00802
P: (340) 774-2502 Ext. 25
F: (340) 776-4730

VERMONT
Mr. Alan Yandow
Executive Director
Lottery Commission
1311 U.S. Route 302 - Berlin
P.O. Box 420
Barre, VT 05641
P: (802) 479-5686
F: (802) 479-4294

VIRGINIA
Ms. Shelia Hill-Christian
Executive Director
Virginia Lottery
900 East Main Street
Pocahontas Building
Richmond, VA 23219
P: (804) 692-7000
F: (804) 692-7102
E: schristian@valottery.virginia.gov

WASHINGTON
Mr. Christopher Liu
Director
State Lottery
814 East 4th Avenue
Olympia, WA 98506
P: (360) 664-4800
F: (360) 586-1039

WEST VIRGINIA
Mr. John C. Musgrave
Director
State Lottery
P.O. Box 2067
Charleston, WV 25327
P: (304) 558-0500
F: (304) 558-3321
E: jmusgrave@tax.state.wv.us

WISCONSIN
Mr. Michael J. Edmonds
Director
State Lottery
P.O. Box 8941
Madison, WI 53708
P: (608) 261-8800
F: (608) 264-6644

Medicaid

Administers the medical assistance program that finances medical care for income assistance recipients and other eligible medically needy persons.

ALABAMA
Ms. Carol Herrmann-Steckel
Commissioner
Medicaid Agency
501 Dexter Avenue
P.O. Box 5624
Montgomery, AL 36103
P: (334) 293-5500

ALASKA
Ms. Ellie Fitzjarrald
Director
Division of Public Assistance
Department of Health & Social Services
P.O. Box 110640
Juneau, AK 99811
P: (907) 465-2680
F: (907) 465-5154

AMERICAN SAMOA
Mr. Andy Puletasi
Medicaid Program Director
Medicaid Program
LBJ Tropical Medical Center
Pago Pago, AS 96799
P: (684) 633-4590
F: (684) 633-1869

ARIZONA
Mr. Anthony D. Rodgers
Director
Health Care Cost Containment System
801 East Jefferson
Phoenix, AZ 85034
P: (602) 417-4680

ARKANSAS
Mr. Roy Jeffus
Director
Division of Medical Services
P.O. Box 1437, Slot S-401
Little Rock, AR 72203
P: (501) 682-8292
F: (501) 682-1197
E: roy.jeffus@medicaid.state.ar.us

CALIFORNIA
Ms. Sandra Louise Shewry
Director
Department of Health Services
1501 Capitol Avenue, Suite 6001
Sacramento, CA 95814
P: (916) 440-7400
F: (916) 657-1156
E: sshewry@dhs.ca.gov

COLORADO
Ms. Joan Henneberry
Executive Director
Department of Health Care Policy & Financing
1570 Grant Street
Denver, CO 80203
P: (303) 866-2993
F: (303) 866-4411

CONNECTICUT
Mr. Michael Starkowski
Commissioner
Department of Social Services
25 Sigourney Street
Hartford, CT 06106
P: (860) 424-5008

DELAWARE
Mr. Harry Hill
Director
Division of Medicaid & Medical Assistance
Department of Health & Social Services
1901 North DuPont Highway, Lewis Bldg.
New Castle, DE 19720
P: (302) 255-9626

DISTRICT OF COLUMBIA
Dr. Gregg A. Pane
Director and State Health Officer
Department of Health
825 North Capitol Street, Northeast
Suite 4400
Washington, DC 20002
P: (202) 442-5999
F: (202) 442-4788
E: doh@dc.gov

FLORIDA
Mr. Tom Arnold
Deputy Secretary for Medicaid
Agency for Healthcare Administration
2727 Mahan Drive
M.S. 8
Tallahassee, FL 32308
P: (850) 488-3560
F: (850) 488-2520

GEORGIA
Mr. Mark Trail
Director
Division of Medical Assistance
Two Peachtree Street, Northwest
Atlanta, GA 30303
P: (404) 651-8681

HAWAII
Mr. Wesley Mun
Acting Administrator
Med-Quest Division
Department of Human Services
P.O. Box 700190
Kapolei, HI 96709
P: (808) 692-8050
F: (808) 692-8155

IDAHO
Ms. Leslie Clement
Administrator
Division of Medicaid
Department of Health & Welfare
3232 Elder Street
Boise, ID 83705
P: (208) 364-5747
F: (208) 364-1811

ILLINOIS
Ms. Ann Marie Murphy
Medicaid Director
Medical Programs
Department of Public Aid
201 South Grand Avenue, East
Springfield, IL 62763
P: (217) 782-2570
F: (217) 782-5672

INDIANA
Mr. Jeff Wells
Director
Office of Medicaid Policy & Planning
402 West Washington Street, Room W461
Indianapolis, IN 46204
P: (317) 234-2407

IOWA
Ms. Ann Wiebers
Administrator
Division of Financial, Health & Work Supports
FHWS-5th Floor
1305 East Walnut
Des Moines, IA 50319
P: (515) 281-3131
F: (515) 281-7791

KANSAS
Dr. Marcia Nielsen
Director
Health Policy Authority
Landon State Office Building, 10th Floor
Topeka, KS 66612
P: (785) 296-3981
F: (785) 296-4813

KENTUCKY
Mr. Glenn Jennings
Commissioner
Department for Medicaid Services
275 East Main Street, 6W-A
Frankfort, KY 40621
P: (502) 564-4321
F: (502) 564-0509

LOUISIANA
Mr. Jerry Phillips
Director
Bureau of Health Services Financing
1207 Capitol Access Road
P.O. Box 91030
Baton Rouge, LA 70821
P: (225) 342-3891
F: (225) 342-9508

MAINE
Ms. Christine Zukas-Lessard
Medicaid Director
Bureau of Medical Services
Statehouse Station # 11
249 Western Avenue
Augusta, ME 04333
P: (207) 287-2674
F: (207) 287-2675

MARYLAND
Mr. John M. Colmers
Secretary
Department of Mental Health & Hygiene
201 West Preston Street, 5th Floor
Baltimore, MD 21201
P: (410) 767-4639

MASSACHUSETTS
Mr. Thomas Dehner
Acting Medicaid Director
Office of Medicaid
Office of Medicaid
One Ashburton Place, Room 1109
Boston, MA 02108
P: (617) 573-1770
F: (617) 573-1894

Medicaid

MICHIGAN
Mr. Paul Reinhart
Sr. Deputy Director
Department of Community Health
320 South Walnut
Lansing, MI 48913
P: (517) 241-7882
F: (517) 335-5007

MINNESOTA
Ms. Christine Bronson
Director
Health Care Operations
Department of Human Services
540 Cedar Street
St. Paul, MN 55155
P: (651) 431-2914
F: (651) 431-7443
E: christine.bronson@state.mn.us

MISSISSIPPI
Mr. Bob Robinson
Medicaid Director
Division of Medicaid
Office of the Governor
239 North Lamar Street
Jackson, MS 39201
P: (601) 359-6050
F: (601) 359-6048

MISSOURI
Mr. Steven E. Renne
Interim Director
Division of Medical Services
615 Howerton Court
P.O. Box 6500
Jefferson City, MO 65102
P: (573) 751-6922
F: (573) 751-6564
E: steven.e.renne@dss.mo.gov

MONTANA
Mr. John Chappuis
Deputy Director
Department of Public Health & Human Services
111 North Sanders, Room 301/308
P.O. Box 4210
Helena, MT 59604
P: (406) 444-4084
F: (406) 444-1970

NEBRASKA
Ms. Mary Steiner
Medicaid Administrator
Department of Finance & Support
P.O. Box 95026
Lincoln, NE 68509
P: (402) 471-3121

NEVADA
Mr. Charles Duarte
Administrator
Division of Health Care Financing & Policy
100 East Williams
Suite 116
Carson City, NV 89710
P: (775) 684-3678
F: (775) 684-3893
E: cduarte@ahcfp.state.nv.us

NEW HAMPSHIRE
Mr. Norman Cordell
Medicaid Director
Health Policy & Medicaid
Office of Commissioner
129 Pleasant Street
Concord, NH 03301
P: (603) 271-4297
F: (603) 271-8431

NEW JERSEY
Mr. John R. Guhl
Director
Division of Medical Assistance & Health Services
P.O. Box 700
Trenton, NJ 08625
P: (609) 292-3717

NEW MEXICO
Ms. Pamela S. Hyde
Cabinet Secretary
Human Services Department
2009 South Pacheco, Pollon Plaza
P.O. Box 2348
Santa Fe, NM 87504
P: (505) 827-7750
F: (505) 827-3185

NEW YORK
Mr. Brian Wing
Deputy Commissioner & Director
Office of Medicaid Management
Empire State Plaza
Room 1466, Corning Tower Building
Albany, NY 12237
P: (518) 474-3018
F: (518) 486-6852

NORTH CAROLINA
Dr. Allen Dobson
Assistant Secretary for Health Policy & Medical Assistance
Division of Medical Assistance
1985 Umstead Drive
2517 Mail Service Center
Raleigh, NC 27699
P: (919) 733-4534
F: (919) 715-4675
E: allen.dobson@ncmail.net

NORTH DAKOTA
Mr. David Zentner
Director
Medical Services
600 East Boulevard Avenue
Bismarck, ND 58505
P: (701) 328-3194
F: (701) 328-1544

NORTHERN MARIANA ISLANDS
Ms. Helen Sablan
Administrator
Medicaid Program
Department of Public Health
P.O. Box 500409
Saipan, MP 96950
P: (670) 664-4884
F: (670) 664-4885
E: dlnrgov@vzpacifica.net

OHIO
Ms. Cristal Thomas
Medicaid Director
Ohio Health Plans
Department of Job & Family Services
30 East Broad Street, 31st Floor
Columbus, OH 43266
P: (614) 466-4443
F: (614) 752-3986

OKLAHOMA
Mr. Mike Fogarty
CEO
Health Care Authority
4545 North Lincoln Boulevard
Suite 124
Oklahoma City, OK 73105
P: (405) 522-7417
F: (405) 522-7471

Ms. Lynn V. Mitchell
Chief Medical Officer, Medicaid Director
Health Care Authority
4545 North Lincoln Boulevard
Suite 124
Oklahoma City, OK 73105
P: (405) 522-7365
F: (405) 530-3218

OREGON
Ms. Lynn Read
Director
DHS - Office of Medical Assistance Programs
500 Summer Street, Northeast
3rd Floor, E-49
Salem, OR 97310
P: (503) 945-5769
F: (503) 373-7689
E: dhs.info@state.or.us

Mr. James D. Toews
Interim Director
Senior & Disabled Services Division
500 Summer Street, Northeast
1st Floor, E-02
Salem, OR 97301
P: (503) 945-5811
F: (503) 373-7823
E: dhs.info@state.or.us

PENNSYLVANIA
Mr. Michael Nardone
Acting Deputy Secretary
Office of Medical Assistance Programs
P.O. Box 2675
Harrisburg, PA 17105
P: (717) 787-1870
F: (717) 787-4639

PUERTO RICO
Ms. Wendy Matos-Negron
Director
Office of Economic Assistance
P.O. Box 70184
San Juan, PR 00936
P: (787) 250-0453
F: (787) 250-0990

RHODE ISLAND
Mr. John Young
Associate Director
Division of Health Care Quality
Furand Building
600 New London Avenue
Cranston, RI 02920
P: (401) 462-3575

SOUTH CAROLINA
Ms. Susan Bowling
Acting Director
Department of Health & Human Services
1801 Main Street
P.O. Box 8206
Columbia, SC 29202
P: (803) 898-2504
F: (803) 898-4515

SOUTH DAKOTA
Mr. Larry Iversen
Administrator
Office of Medical Services
Kneip Building
700 Governors Drive
Pierre, SD 57501
P: (605) 773-3495
F: (605) 773-5246
E: larry.iverson
@state.sd.us

TENNESSEE
Mr. Darin Gordon
Deputy Commissioner
Bureau of TennCare
Department of Finance & Administration
310 Great Circle Road
Nashville, TN 37243
P: (615) 597-6419

TEXAS
Mr. David Balland
Associate Commissioner
Medicaid/CHIP Program
P.O. Box 13247
Austin, TX 78711
P: (512) 491-1867

U.S. VIRGIN ISLANDS
Ms. Patricia Berry-Quetel
Executive Director
Bureau of Health Insurance & Medical Assistance
3730 Estate Altona
Frostco Center, Suite 302
St. Thomas, VI 00802
P: (340) 774-4624
F: (340) 774-4918

UTAH
Ms. Paula McGuire
Bureau Director
Medicaid Operations
Division of Health Care Financing
288 North 1460 West
Salt Lake City, UT 84116
P: (801) 538-6719
F: (801) 538-6099
E: pmcguire@utah.gov

VERMONT
Mr. Joshua Slen
Director
Office of Vermont Health Access
312 Hurricane Lane
Williston, VT 05495
P: (802) 879-5901
F: (802) 879-5962
E: joshuas
@wpgate1.ahs.state.vt.us

VIRGINIA
Mr. Patrick Finnerty
Director
Department of Medical Assistance Services
600 East Broad Street, Suite 1300
Richmond, VA 23219
P: (804) 662-9333
F: (804) 662-7035
E: patrick.finnerty
@dmas.virginia.gov

WASHINGTON
Ms. Kathy Leitch
Assistant Secretary
Aging & Adult Services Administration
Mail Stop 45050
14th and Jefferson, Office Building 2
Olympia, WA 98504
P: (360) 902-7797
F: (360) 902-7848
E: leitckj@dshs.wa.gov

Mr. Doug Porter
Assistant Secretary
Medical Assistance Administration
623 8th Avenue Southeast
Building 2
Olympia, WA 98504
P: (360) 902-7807
F: (360) 902-7885

WEST VIRGINIA
Mr. Leonard Kelley
Deputy Commissioner
Bureau for Medical Services
Department of Health & Human Services
350 Capitol Street, Room 251
Charleston, WV 25301
P: (304) 558-1784
F: (304) 558-1451

WISCONSIN
Mr. Jason Helgerson
Administrator
Division of Health Care Financing
1 West Wilson Street, Room 350
Madison, WI 53701
P: (608) 266-8922
F: (608) 266-1096

WYOMING
Ms. Iris Oleske
State Medicaid Director
Office of Medicaid
154 Hathaway Building
2300 Capitol Avenue
Cheyenne, WY 82002
P: (307) 777-7848
F: (307) 777-6964

Mental Health and Mental Retardation

Administers the mental services of the state and/or plans and coordinates programs for persons with mental illness.

ALABAMA
Mr. John Houston
Commissioner
Department of Mental Health & Mental Retardation
100 North Union Street
P.O. Box 301410
Montgomery, AL 36130
P: (334) 242-3107
F: (334) 242-0684
E: john.houston@mh.alabama.gov

ALASKA
Ms. Stacy Toner
Acting Director
Division of Behavioral Health
Department of Health & Social Services
P.O. Box 110620
Juneau, AK 99801
P: (907) 465-3370
F: (907) 465-5864
E: stacy_toner@health.state.ak.us

AMERICAN SAMOA
Mr. Talia Fa'afetai I'aulualo
Director
Department of Human & Social Services
American Samoa Government
Pago Pago, AS 96799
P: (684) 633-1187
F: (684) 633-7449

ARIZONA
Mr. Eddy Broadway
Deputy Director
Division of Behavioral Health Services
Department of Health Services
150 North 18th Avenue, Suite 200
Phoenix, AZ 85007
P: (602) 364-4567
F: (602) 364-4570
E: broadwed@azdhs.gov

ARKANSAS
Mr. Jay Bradford
Director
Division of Behavioral Health Services
4313 West Markham
Little Rock, AR 72205
P: (501) 686-9594
F: (501) 686-9182
E: jay.bradford@arkansas.gov

CALIFORNIA
Dr. Stephen W. Mayberg
Director
Department of Mental Health
1600 9th Street, Room 151
Sacramento, CA 95814
P: (916) 654-2309
F: (916) 654-3198
E: stephen.mayberg@dmh.ca.gov

COLORADO
Ms. Deborah Trout
Director
Division of Mental Health Services
Department of Human Services
1575 Sherman Street
Denver, CO 80203
P: (303) 866-2806
F: (303) 866-7428

CONNECTICUT
Dr. Thomas A. Kirk Jr.
Commissioner
Department of Mental Health & Addiction Services
410 Capitol Avenue, MS#14COM
Hartford, CT 06106
P: (860) 418-6700
F: (860) 418-6691
E: thomas.kirk@po.state.ct.us

DELAWARE
Ms. Renata J. Henry
Director
Division of Substance Abuse & Mental Health
Department of Health & Social Services
1901 North Dupont Highway
New Castle, DE 19720
P: (302) 255-9398
F: (302) 255-4427
E: Renata.Henry@state.de.us

DISTRICT OF COLUMBIA
Mr. Stephen Baron
Director
Department of Mental Health
64 New York Avenue, Northeast
4th Floor
Washington, DC 20002
P: (202) 673-3433
F: (202) 673-3433

FLORIDA
Dr. Rod Hall
Director of Mental Health
Substance Abuse & Mental Health
1317 Winewood Boulevard
Building 6, Room 275
Tallahassee, FL 32399
P: (850) 413-0935
F: (850) 487-2239
E: rod_hall@dcf.state.fl.us

GEORGIA
Ms. Gwendolyn B. Skinner
Division Director
Division of Mental Health, Developmental Disabilities & Addictive Diseases
Department of Human Resources
2 Peachtree Street, Suite 22.224
Atlanta, GA 30303
P: (404) 657-2260
F: (404) 657-1137
E: gbskinner@dhr.ga.gov

GUAM
Dr. Andrea Leitheiser
Director
Department of Mental Health & Substance Abuse
790 Governor Carlos G. Camacho Road
Tamuning, GU 96913
P: (671) 647-5330
F: (671) 649-6948

HAWAII
Ms. Michelle R. Hill
Deputy Director
Behavioral Health Administration
1250 Punchbowl Street
P.O. Box 3378
Honolulu, HI 96813
P: (808) 586-4416
F: (808) 586-4444
E: mrhill@mail.health.state.hi.us

IDAHO
Mr. Raymond M. Millar
Program Manager, Adult Mental Health
Division of Family & Community Services
Department of Health & Welfare
450 West State Street, 5th Floor
Boise, ID 83720
P: (208) 334-6500
F: (208) 332-7331
E: millarr@idhw.idaho.gov

ILLINOIS
Ms. Lori Rickman Jones
Director
Mental Health Services
Department of Human Services
160 North La Salle Street, Suite S-1004
Chicago, IL 60601
P: (312) 814-3784

INDIANA
Ms. Cathy Boggs
Director
Division of Mental Health & Addiction
402 West Washington St., Room W-353
Indianapolis, IN 46204
P: (317) 232-4319
F: (317) 233-3472
E: cathy.boggs@fssa.in.gov

IOWA
Mr. Kevin Concannon
Director
Department of Human Services
Hoover State Office Building
1305 East Walnut Street, 5th Floor
Des Moines, IA 50319
P: (515) 281-5452
F: (515) 281-4980
E: kconcan@dhs.state.ia.us

KANSAS
Mr. Steve Erikson
Director of Mental Health
Department of Social & Rehabilitation Services
Docking State Officce Building
915 Southwest Harrison, 10th Floor
Topeka, KS 66612
P: (785) 296-7272
F: (785) 296-6142
E: sxxe@srskansas.org

KENTUCKY
Ms. Donna Hillman
Director
Division of Mental Health & Substance Abuse
100 Fair Oaks Lane, 4E-D
Frankfort, KY 40621
P: (502) 564-4456
F: (502) 564-9010

LOUISIANA
Dr. Cheryll Bowers-Stephens
Assistant Secretary
Office of Mental Health
Department of Health & Hospitals
P.O. Box 4049, Bin #12
Baton Rouge, LA 70821
P: (225) 342-2540
F: (225) 342-5066
E: cstephen@dhh.la.gov

MAINE
Ms. Sabra Burdick
Acting Deputy Director
Department of Programs Health & Human Services
11 State House Station
Augusta, ME 04333
P: (207) 287-4223
F: (207) 287-3005
E: sabra.burdick@maine.gov

MARYLAND
Mr. John M. Colmers
Secretary
Department of Mental Health & Hygiene
201 West Preston Street, 5th Floor
Baltimore, MD 21201
P: (410) 767-4639

MASSACHUSETTS
Dr. Elizabeth Childs
Commissioner
Department of Mental Health
25 Staniford Street
Boston, MA 02114
P: (617) 626-8123
F: (617) 626-8131
E: Elizabeth.Childs@dmh.state.ma.us

MICHIGAN
Mr. Patrick Barrie
Deputy Director
Mental Health & Substance Abuse Administration
Department of Community Health
320 South Walnut Street
Lansing, MI 48913
P: (517) 335-0196
F: (517) 335-4798
E: barriep@michigan.gov

MINNESOTA
Ms. Sharon Autio
Director
Mental Health Program Division
Human Services Building
P.O. Box 64981
St. Paul, MN 55164
P: (651) 431-2228
F: (651) 431-7418
E: sharon.autio@state.mn.us

MISSISSIPPI
Mr. Edwin C. LeGrand III
Deputy Executive Director
Department of Mental Health
1101 Robert E. Lee Building
239 North Lamar Street
Jackson, MS 39201
P: (601) 359-6243
F: (601) 359-5330
E: edlegrand@dmh.state.ms.org

MISSOURI
Dr. Joe Parks
Division Director
Comprehensive Psychiatric Services/Alcohol & Drug Abuse
1706 East Elm Street
P.O. Box 687
Jefferson City, MO 65102
P: (573) 751-3035
F: (573) 751-7815
E: joe.parks@dmh.mo.gov

MONTANA
Ms. Lou Thompson
Chief
Mental Health Services
555 Fuller Avenue
P.O. Box 202905
Helena, MT 59620
P: (406) 444-9657
F: (406) 444-4435
E: lothompson@mt.gov

NEBRASKA
Mr. Ron Sorensen
Administrator, Behavioral Health Services
Division of Behavioral Health
Department of Health & Human Services
P.O. Box 98925
Lincoln, NE 68509
P: (402) 479-5517
F: (402) 479-5162
E: Ron.Sorenson@hhss.ne.gov

NEVADA
Dr. Carlos Brandenburg
Administrator
Division of Mental Health & Developmental Services
Department of Human Resources
505 East King Street, Room 602
Carson City, NV 89701
P: (775) 684-5943
F: (775) 684-5966
E: cbrandenburg@dhr.state.nv.us

NEW HAMPSHIRE
Ms. Nancy Rollins
Director, Division of Community Based Services
Bureau of Behavioral Health
Department of Health & Human Services
105 Pleasant Street, Main Building
Concord, NH 03301
P: (603) 271-8560
F: (603) 271-5058
E: nrollins@dhhs.state.nh.us

NEW JERSEY
Mr. Kevin Martone
Assistant Commissioner
Division of Mental Health Services
P.O. Box 700
Trenton, NJ 08625
P: (609) 292-3717
F: (609) 777-0662
E: dmhsmail@dhs.state.nj.us

NEW MEXICO
Ms. Catherine Kinney
Behavioral Health Services Division
Department of Health
1190 South St. Francis Drive
Santa Fe, NM 87502
P: (505) 827-2658
F: (505) 827-2530

NEW YORK
Mr. Michael Hogan
Acting Commissioner
Office of Mental Health
44 Holland Avenue
Albany, NY 12229
P: (518) 474-4403
F: (518) 457-3207
E: coevsec@omh.state.ny.us

NORTH CAROLINA
Mr. Michael Moseley
Director
Division of Mental Health, Developmental Disabilities & Substance Abuse
Division of Mental Health
3007 Mail Service Center
Raleigh, NC 27699
P: (919) 733-4670 Ext. 231
F: (919) 733-9455
E: michael.moseley@ncmail.net

NORTH DAKOTA
Ms. JoAnne D. Hoesel
Director
Division of Mental Health & Substance Abuse
Department of Human Services
600 East Boulevard, Room 302
Bismarck, ND 58505
P: (701) 328-8924
F: (701) 328-3538
E: sohoej@nd.gov

NORTHERN MARIANA ISLANDS
Ms. Josephine T. Sablan
Director
Mental Health & Social Services
P.O. Box 500409
Saipan, MP 96950

OHIO
Mr. Donald Anderson
Acting Director
Department of Mental Health
30 East Broad Street, 8th Floor
Columbus, OH 43215
P: (614) 466-2337
F: (614) 752-9453
E: andersondc@mh.state.oh.us

Mental Health and Mental Retardation

OKLAHOMA
Mr. Rand Baker
Interim Secretary of Health & Commissioner
Department of Mental Health & Substance Abuse Services
P.O. Box 53277
Oklahoma City, OK 73152
P: (405) 522-3908
F: (405) 522-3650

OREGON
Mr. Robert E. Nikkel
Administrator
Office of Mental Health & Addiction Services
500 Summer Street, Northeast
3rd Floor, E86
Salem, OR 97301
P: (503) 945-9704
F: (503) 373-7327
E: dhs.info@state.or.us

PENNSYLVANIA
Ms. Joan L. Erney
Deputy Secretary
Office of Mental Health & Substance Abuse Services
P.O. Box 2675, Health & Welfare Building
7th & Forster Streets, Room 502
Harrisburg, PA 17105
P: (717) 787-6443
F: (717) 787-5394
E: joerney@state.pa.us

PUERTO RICO
Mr. Jose Luis Galarza
Administrator
Mental Health & Anti-Addiction Services Administration
Ave Barbosa 414
P.O. Box 21414
San Juan, PR 00928
P: (787) 763-7575
F: (787) 765-5888
E: jgalarza@assmca.gobierno.pr

RHODE ISLAND
Dr. Ellen R. Nelson
Director
Department of Mental Health, Retardation & Hospitals
14 Harrington Road
Barry Hall
Cranston, RI 02920
P: (401) 462-3201
F: (401) 462-3204

SOUTH CAROLINA
Mr. John McGill
State Director
Department of Mental Health
2414 Bull Street, Suite 321
P.O. Box 485
Columbia, SC 29202
P: (803) 898-8319
F: (803) 898-8586

SOUTH DAKOTA
Ms. Amy Iversen-Pollreisz
Director
Division of Mental Health
Hillsview Plaza
C/o 500 East Capitol
Pierre, SD 57501
P: (605) 773-5991
F: (605) 773-7076
E: amy.iversen-pollreisz@state.sd.us

TENNESSEE
Ms. Virginia Trotter Betts
Commissioner
Department of Mental Health & Developmental Disabilities
Cordell Hull Building, 3rd Floor
425 Fifth Avenue, North
Nashville, TN 37243
P: (615) 532-6500
F: (615) 532-6514
E: virginiatrotter.betts@state.tn.us

TEXAS
Dr. Dave Wanser
Deputy Commissioner
Behavioral & Community Health
Department of State Health Services
1100 West 49th Street, M-751
Austin, TX 78756
P: (512) 458-7376
F: (512) 458-7477
E: dave.wanser@dshs.state.tx.us

U.S. VIRGIN ISLANDS
Ms. Denese Marshall
Director
Department of Mental Health, Alcoholism & Drug Dependency Services
Barbell Plaza South
St. Thomas, VI 00802
P: (340) 774-4888
F: (340) 774-4701
E: denese.marshall@usvi-doh.org

UTAH
Mr. Mark Payne
Director
Division of Substance Abuse & Mental Health
Department of Human Services
120 North 200 West, #209
Salt Lake City, UT 84103
P: (801) 538-3939
F: (801) 538-4696
E: mpayne@utah.gov

VERMONT
Mr. Michael Hartman
Deputy Commissioner
Agency of Human Services
Division of Mental Health
108 Cherry Street
Burlington, VT 05401
P: (802) 951-1258
F: (802) 951-1275
E: mhartma@vdh.state.vt.us

VIRGINIA
Dr. James S. Reinhard
Commissioner
Department of Mental Health, Mental Retardation & Substance Abuse Services
1220 Bank Street
P.O. Box 1797
Richmond, VA 23218
P: (804) 786-3921
F: (804) 371-6638
E: james.reinhard@co.dmhmrsas.virginia.gov

WASHINGTON
Mr. Richard E. Kellogg
Director
Mental Health Division
P.O. Box 45320
Olympia, WA 98504
P: (360) 902-0790
F: (360) 902-0809

WEST VIRGINIA
Mr. John Bianconi
Commissioner
Bureau for Behavioral Health & Health Facilities
Department of Health & Human Resources
350 Capitol Street, Room 350
Charleston, WV 25301
P: (304) 558-0298
F: (304) 558-2230
E: jbianconi@wvdhhr.org

WISCONSIN
Ms. Joyce Bohn Allen
Director
Bureau of Mental Health & Substance Abuse Services
1 West Wilson Street, Room 434
P.O. Box 7851
Madison, WI 53707
P: (608) 266-1351
F: (608) 266-1533
E: allenjb@dhfs.state.wi.us

WYOMING
Mr. Rodger McDaniel
Deputy Director
Division of Mental Health
Department of Health
6101 Yellowstone Road, Room 220
Cheyenne, WY 82002
P: (307) 777-5698
F: (307) 777-5849

Minority Affairs

Serves as an advocate for state minority communities and promotes minority business enterprises within the state.

AMERICAN SAMOA
Mr. Talia Fa'afetai I'aulualo
Director
Department of Human & Social Services
American Samoa Government
Pago Pago, AS 96799
P: (684) 633-1187
F: (684) 633-7449

ARIZONA
Mr. Seth Mones
Deputy Director
Department of Commerce
1700 West Washington, Suite 600
Phoenix, AZ 85007
P: (602) 771-1162

CONNECTICUT
Ms. Anne Gnazzo
Commissioner
Department of Administrative Services
165 Capitol Avenue, Room 491
Hartford, CT 06106
P: (860) 713-5100
F: (860) 713-7481
E: anne.gnazzo@po.state.ct.us

ILLINOIS
Mr. N. Keith Chambers
Executive Director
Human Rights Commission
100 West Randolph Street, Suite 5-100
Chicago, IL 60601
P: (312) 814-6269
F: (312) 814-6517

INDIANA
Ms. Claudia Cummings
Deputy Commissioner
Minority & Women's Business Enterprises
402 West Washington Street
Room W469
Indianapolis, IN 46204
P: (317) 232-3061
F: (317) 233-6921

IOWA
Mr. Ralph Rosenberg
Executive Director
Civil Rights Commission
Grimes State Office Building
400 East 14th Street
Des Moines, IA 50319
P: (515) 281-4121
F: (515) 242-5840
E: ralph.rosenberg@icrc.state.ia.us

KANSAS
Ms. Danielle Dempsey-Swopes
Executive Director
African-American Affairs Commission
Landon State Office Building, Room 100-N
Topeka, KS 66603
P: (785) 296-4874
F: (785) 296-1984

Mr. Elias Garcia
Executive Director
Hispanic & Latino American Affairs Committee
Landon State Office Building, Room 101-N
Topeka, KS 66603
P: (785) 296-3465
F: (785) 296-8118

KENTUCKY
Mr. Troy Body
Executive Director
Governor's Office of Minority Empowerment
700 Capital Avenue, Suite 132
Frankfort, KY 40601
P: (502) 564-2611
F: (502) 564-0437

LOUISIANA
Mr. Richard Chambers
Deputy Commissioner
Minority Affairs
P.O. Box 94214
Baton Rouge, LA 70802
P: (225) 342-8395
E: richambers@ldi@state.la.us

MAINE
Ms. Laurel J. Shippee
State Equal Employment Opportunity Coordinator
Bureau of Human Resources
4 State House Station
Augusta, ME 04333
P: (207) 624-7761

MARYLAND
Ms. Sharon Roberson Pinder
Executive Director
Office of Minority Affairs
6 Saing Paul Street, Suite 1502
Baltimore, MD 21202
P: (410) 767-8232
E: spinder@oma.state.md.us

MASSACHUSETTS
Ms. Sandra E. Borders
Director
Office of Diversity & Equal Opportunity
One Ashburton Place, Room 213
Boston, MA 02108
P: (617) 727-7441
F: (617) 727-0568

MICHIGAN
Ms. Linda V. Parker
Director
Department of Civil Rights
Capitol Tower Building
Suite 800
Lansing, MI 48933
P: (517) 335-3165
F: (517) 241-0546
E: parkerlv@michigan.gov

MINNESOTA
Ms. Velma Korbel
Commissioner
Department of Human Rights
190 East 5th Street
Suite 700
St. Paul, MN 55101
P: (651) 296-9038
F: (651) 296-1736
E: velma.korbel@state.mn.us

MISSOURI
Ms. Donna M. White
Director
Office of Supplier & Workforce Diversity
Truman Building, Room 630
P.O. Box 809
Jefferson City, MO 65102
P: (573) 751-8130
F: (573) 522-8078
E: Donna.White@oa.mo.gov

MONTANA
Mr. Anthony Preite
Director
Department of Commerce
301 South Park
P.O. Box 200501
Helena, MT 59620
P: (406) 841-2704
F: (406) 841-2701
E: tpreite@mt.gov

NORTH DAKOTA
Ms. Lisa Fair McEvers
Commissioner of Labor
Department of Labor
600 East Boulevard Avenue, Department 406
Bismarck, ND 58505
P: (701) 328-2660
F: (701) 328-2031
E: labor@nd.gov

OHIO
Mr. Aaron Wheeler Sr.
Chair
Civil Rights Commission
1111 East Broad Street, Suite 301
Columbus, OH 43205
P: (614) 466-6715
F: (614) 644-8776

OKLAHOMA
Mr. Oscar B. Jackson Jr.
Cabinet Secretary for Administration & Human Resources
Cabinet for Administration & Human Resources
2101 North Lincoln Boulevard
Room G-80
Oklahoma City, OK 73105
P: (405) 521-6301
F: (405) 522-0694
E: oscar.jackson@opm.state.ok.us

OREGON
Ms. Lydia Muniz
Advocate for Minority, Women & Emerging Small Business
Office of the Governor
155 Cottage Street, Northeast
Salem, OR 97301
P: (503) 373-1224
F: (503) 378-3139
E: lydia.muniz@state.or.us

SOUTH CAROLINA
Ms. Janie A. Davis
Executive Director
Commission for Minority Affairs
6904 North Main Street, Suite 107
Columbia, SC 29203
P: (803) 333-9621
F: (803) 333-9627
E: jdavis@cfma.state.sc.us

Minority Affairs

SOUTH DAKOTA
Mr. Roger Campbell
Director
Tribal Governmental Relations
Capitol Lake Plaza
711 East Wells Avenue
Pierre, SD 57501
P: (605) 773-3415
F: (605) 773-6592
E: roger.campbell
@state.sd.us

UTAH
Ms. Luz Robles
Director
Office of Ethnic Affairs
Department of Community & Culture
324 South State, Suite 500
Salt Lake City, UT 84111
P: (801) 538-8753
F: (801) 538-8678
E: lrobles@utah.gov

VIRGINIA
Mr. Stacy L. Burrs
Director
Department of Minority Business Enterprise
1100 East Main Street, Suite 300
Richmond, VA 23219
P: (804) 786-6585
F: (804) 371-7359
E: stacy.burrs
@dmbe.virginia.gov

WEST VIRGINIA
Ms. Ivin Lee
Executive Director
Human Rights Commission
1321 Plaza East
Room 104-106
Charleston, WV 25301
P: (304) 558-2616
F: (304) 558-2248
E: ivinlee@wvdhhr.org

WISCONSIN
Mr. Demetri Fisher
Administrator
Division of Affirmative Action
P.O. Box 7855
Madison, WI 53707
P: (608) 266-3017
F: (608) 267-4592

Motor Vehicle Administration

Issues and maintains all records related to motor vehicle registration, operators' licenses and certificates of titles in the state.

ALABAMA
Col. Chris Murphy
Director
Department of Public Safety
P.O. Box 1511
Montgomery, AL 36102
P: (334) 242-4394
F: (334) 242-0512
E: director@alalinc.net

ALASKA
Mr. Duane Bannock
Director
Division of Motor Vehicles
Department of Administration
1300 West Benson Boulevard
Anchorage, AK 99503
P: (907) 269-5559
F: (907) 269-3762
E: duane_bannock
@admin.state.ak.us

Maj. Doug Norris
Deputy Director
State Troopers
5700 East Tudor Road
Anchorage, AK 99507
P: (907) 269-5511
F: (907) 337-2059

AMERICAN SAMOA
Mr. Sotoa Savali
Commissioner
Department of Public Safety
American Samoa Government
P.O. Box 3699
Pago Pago, AS 96799
P: (684) 633-1111
F: (684) 633-7296

ARIZONA
Ms. Stacey K. Stanton
Director
Motor Vehicle Division
1801 West Jefferson
Phoenix, AZ 85007
P: (602) 712-8152
F: (602) 712-6539
E: sstanton@azdot.gov

Mr. Roger Vanderpool
Director
Department of Public Safety
2102 West Encanto Boulevard
P.O. Box 6638
Phoenix, AZ 85005
P: (602) 223-2359
F: (602) 223-2917

ARKANSAS
Mr. Roger Duren
Administrator of Motor Vehicles
Revenue Division
P.O. Box 1272
Little Rock, AR 72203
P: (501) 682-4630
F: (501) 682-1116
E: roger.duren
@rev.state.ar.us

Mr. Mike Munns
Assistant Commissioner of Revenue
Revenue Division
P.O. Box 1272
Little Rock, AR 72203
P: (501) 682-7052
F: (501) 682-1683
E: mike.munns
@rev.state.ar.us

Ms. Susan O. Sims
Acting Administrator of Driver Services
Office of Driver Services
P.O. Box 1272
Little Rock, AR 72203
P: (501) 682-7060
F: (501) 682-7688
E: susan.sims
@rev.state.ar.us

Mr. John H. Theis
Assistant Commissioner of Revenue
Revenue Division
P.O. Box 1272
Little Rock, AR 72203
P: (501) 682-7000
F: (501) 682-1161
E: john.theis
@rev.state.ar.us

CALIFORNIA
Mr. Mike Brown
Commissioner
Highway Patrol
Business, Trans. & Housing Agency
2555 First Avenue
Sacramento, CA 95818
P: (916) 657-7152
F: (916) 657-7324

Mr. George Valverde
Director
Department of Motor Vehicles
2415 First Avenue
Sacramento, CA 95818
P: (916) 657-6940
F: (916) 657-7393

COLORADO
Ms. Kirstie Nucon
Director
Motor Carrier Services Division
Department of Revenue
1881 Pierce Street
Lakewood, CO 80214
P: (303) 205-8300
F: (303) 205-5764

Ms. Joan Vecchi
Senior Director
Motor Vehicle Business Group
1881 Pierce Street, Room 100
Lakewood, CO 80214
P: (303) 205-5935

CONNECTICUT
Mr. Robert Ward
Commissioner
Division of State Police
1111 Country Club Road
Middletown, CT 06457
P: (860) 685-8090
F: (860) 685-8475

DELAWARE
Col. Thomas F. Macleish
Superintendent
State Police
P.O. Box 430
Dover, DE 19901
P: (302) 739-5901
F: (302) 739-5966
E: Thomas.Macleish
@state.de.us

Mr. Michael D. Shahan
Director
Division of Motor Vehicles
P.O. Box 698
Dover, DE 19903
P: (302) 744-2510
F: (302) 739-3152
E: mike.shahan@state.de.us

DISTRICT OF COLUMBIA
Ms. Lucinda Babers
Director
Department of Motor Vehicles
95 M Street, SW
Washington, DC 20004
P: (202) 727-2200
F: (202) 727-1010

FLORIDA
Col. Christopher Knight
Director
Division of Highway Patrol
2900 Apalachee Parkway
Neil Kirkman Building
Tallahassee, FL 32399
P: (850) 488-4885
F: (850) 922-0148
E: knight.chris
@hsmv.state.fl.us

Ms. Sandra C. Lambert
Director
Division of Driver Licenses
2900 Apalachee Parkway
Neil Kirkland Building
Tallahassee, FL 32399
P: (850) 414-2426
F: (850) 410-0231
E: Lambert.Sandra
@hsmv.state.fl.us

Ms. Electra
Theodorides-Bustle
Executive Director
Department of Highway Safety & Motor Vehicles
Neil Kirkman Building
2900 Apalachee Parkway
Tallahassee, FL 32399
P: (850) 487-3132
F: (850) 922-6274

GEORGIA
Mr. Greg Dozier
Commissioner
Department of Driver Services
P.O. Box 80447
Conyers, GA 30013
P: (678) 413-8650

Mr. Douglas Hooper
Director
Motor Vehicle Division
P.O. Box 16909
Atlanta, GA 30321
P: (404) 362-6440

GUAM
Mr. Frank R. Blaz
Director
Motor Vehicle Division
P.O. Box 23607
GMF, GU 96921
P: (671) 477-5107

Motor Vehicle Administration

HAWAII
Mr. Barry Fukunaga
Interim Director of Transportation
Department of Transportation
869 Punchbowl Street, Room 509
Honolulu, HI 96813
P: (808) 587-2150
F: (808) 587-2167

IDAHO
Mr. Tom Fry
Registration Program Coordinator
Division of Motor Vehicles
P.O. Box 7129
Boise, ID 83707
P: (208) 334-8679
F: (208) 334-8542
E: tfry@itd.idaho.gov

Col. Jerry Russell
Director
State Police
P.O. Box 700
Meridian, ID 83680
P: (208) 884-7003
F: (208) 884-7090

ILLINOIS
Mr. Ernie Dannenberger
Director
Vehicle Services Department
Room 312 Howlett Building
501 South Second Street
Springfield, IL 62756
P: (217) 785-3000
F: (217) 785-4727
E: edannenberger@ilsos.net

Mr. Brad Demuzio
Director
Department of Police
322 East Adams
Springfield, IL 62701
P: (217) 782-7126
F: (217) 524-8020
E: BDemuzio@ilsos.net

Mr. Carl Forn
Director
Department of Accounting Revenue
248 Howlett Building
Springfield, IL 62756
P: (217) 782-4779
F: (217) 782-1691
E: cforn@ilsos.net

Mr. Gary Lazzerini
Director, Metro
Driver Services Department
17 North State Street
Suite 1100
Chicago, IL 60602
P: (312) 814-2975
F: (312) 814-2974
E: glazzerini@ilsos.net

Mr. Michael Mayer
Director of Driver Services
Driver Services Department
2701 South Dirksen Parkway
Springfield, IL 62723
P: (217) 785-0963
F: (217) 785-2472
E: mmayer@lisos.net

Mr. Milton R. Sees
Acting Secretary
Department of Transportation
3215 Executive Park Drive
Springfield, IL 62764
P: (217) 782-5597
F: (217) 782-6828

Mr. Michael R. Stout
Director
Division of Traffic Safety
Department of Transportation
3215 Executive Park Drive
Springfield, IL 62794
P: (217) 782-4972
F: (217) 782-9159
E: stoutmr@dot.il.gov

Mr. Larry Trent
Director
State Police
125 East Monroe Street, Room 107
Springfield, IL 62794
P: (217) 782-7263
F: (217) 785-2821
E: larry_trent@isp.state.il.us

INDIANA
Mr. Ronald L. Stiver
Commissioner
Bureau of Motor Vehicles
100 North Senate Avenue, N440
Indianapolis, IN 46204
P: (317) 233-2349

Dr. Paul Whitesell
Superintendent
State Police
100 North Senate Avenue, Room N340
Indianapolis, IN 46204
P: (317) 232-8241

IOWA
Ms. Shirley E. Andre
Director
Motor Vehicle Division
100 Euclid Avenue, Park Fair Mall
P.O. Box 9204
Des Moines, IA 50306
P: (515) 237-3121
F: (515) 237-3355
E: shirley.andre@dot.state.ia.us

Col. Robert O. Garrison
Chief
State Patrol
Wallace State Office Building
502 East 9th Street
Des Moines, IA 50319
P: (515) 281-5824

Mr. Eugene T. Meyer
Commissioner
Department of Public Safety
215 East 7th Street
Des Moines, IA 50319
P: (515) 725-6182

KANSAS
Ms. Carmen Alldritt
Director
Division of Motor Vehicles
Robert B. Docking Office Building
First Floor
Topeka, KS 66626
P: (785) 296-3601
F: (785) 291-3755
E: carmen_alldritt@kdor.state.ks.us

Lt. Col. Terry Maple
Assistant Superintendent
Highway Patrol
122 Southwest 7th Street
Topeka, KS 66603
P: (785) 296-6800
F: (785) 296-3049
E: tmaple@mail.khp.state.ks.us

Col. William Seck
Superintendent
Highway Patrol
122 Southwest 7th Street
Topeka, KS 66603
P: (785) 296-6800
F: (785) 296-3049
E: wseck@mail.khp.state.ks.us

KENTUCKY
Mr. Roy V. Mundy II
Commissioner
Department of Vehicle Regulation
Second Floor, TCOB
200 Mero Street
Frankfort, KY 40622
P: (502) 564-7000
F: (502) 564-6403
E: Roy.Mundy@ky.gov

Mr. Bill Nighbert
Secretary
Transportation Cabinet
200 Mero Street
Frankfort, KY 40622
P: (502) 564-4890
F: (502) 564-9540

LOUISIANA
Ms. Kay Hodges
Commissioner
Office of Motor Vehicles
7979 Independence Boulevard
Baton Rouge, LA 70806
P: (225) 925-6161
F: (225) 925-6735
E: khodges@dps.state.la.us

Col. Henry Whitehorn
Superintendent of State Police
Department of Public Safety & Corrections
7919 Independence Boulevard
P.O. Box 66614
Baton Rouge, LA 70896
P: (225) 925-6118
F: (225) 925-3742
E: hwhitehorn@dps.state.la.us

MAINE
Ms. Catherine Curtis
Deputy Secretary of State
Bureau of Motor Vehicles
101 Hospital Street
State House Station #29
Augusta, ME 04333
P: (207) 287-4900

Col. Craig A. Poulin
Chief
State Police
36 Hospital Street
Augusta, ME 04333
P: (207) 624-7200
F: (207) 624-7042
E: craig.a.poulin@maine.gov

MARYLAND
Col. Thomas E. Hutchins
Superintendent
State Police
1201 Reisterstown Road
Pikesville, MD 21208
P: (410) 653-4219
F: (410) 653-4269
E: superintendent@mdsp.org

Mr. John T. Kuo
Administrator
Motor Vehicle Administration
6601 Ritchie Highway Northeast
Room 200
Glen Burnie, MD 21062
P: (410) 768-7274
F: (410) 768-7506
E: jkuo@mdot.state.md.us

MASSACHUSETTS
Mr. Kevin Burke
Secretary
Executive Office of Public Safety
One Ashburton Place, Suite 2133
Boston, MA 02108
P: (617) 727-7775
F: (617) 727-4764

Ms. Anne L. Collins
Registrar
Registry of Motor Vehicles
One Copley Place
Boston, MA 02116
P: (617) 351-9992
F: (617) 351-9971

MICHIGAN
Hon. Terri Lynn Land (R)
Secretary of State
Office of the Secretary of State
430 West Allegan Street, 4th Floor
Lansing, MI 48918
P: (517) 373-2510
F: (517) 373-0727
E: secretary@michigan.gov

Col. Peter C. Munoz
Director
State Police
714 South Harrison Road
East Lansing, MI 48823
P: (517) 336-6158
F: (517) 336-6551

Mr. Michael Wartella
Administration Director
Department of State
7064 Crowner Drive
Lansing, MI 48918
P: (517) 322-3448
F: (517) 322-5032
E: WartellaM1@michigan.gov

MINNESOTA
Col. Mark A. Dunaski
Chief
State Patrol
444 Cedar Street
Suite 130, Town Square
St. Paul, MN 55101
P: (651) 201-7117
E: mark.dunaski@state.mn.us

Ms. Patricia McCormack
Director
Driver & Vehicle Services Division
445 Minnesota Street
Suite 195
St. Paul, MN 55101
P: (651) 201-7580
F: (651) 296-3141
E: patricia.mccormack@state.mn.us

MISSISSIPPI
Mr. Joe Blount
Chair
State Tax Commission
P.O. Box 22828
Jackson, MS 39225
P: (601) 923-7411
F: (601) 923-7423
E: jblount@mstc.state.ms.us

Mr. George Phillips
Commissioner
Department of Public Safety
P.O. Box 958
Jackson, MS 39205
P: (601) 987-1212
F: (601) 987-1488
E: commissioner@mdps.state.ms.us

MISSOURI
Ms. Julie Allen
Director
Motor Vehicle & Driver Licensing Division
Harry S. Truman State Office Building
P.O. Box 629
Jefferson City, MO 65105
P: (573) 526-1824
F: (573) 526-4774
E: Julie.A.Allen@dor.mo.gov

MONTANA
Col. Paul K. Grimstad
Chief Administrator
Highway Patrol Division
2550 Prospect Avenue
P.O. Box 201419
Helena, MT 59620
P: (406) 444-3780
F: (406) 444-4169
E: mhphqcontact@mt.gov

Mr. Dean Roberts
Administrator
Motor Vehicle Division
Scott Hart Building, 2nd Floor
303 N. Roberts, P.O. Box 201430
Helena, MT 59620
P: (406) 444-1773
F: (406) 444-1631
E: mvd@mt.gov

Mr. Dennis Sheehy
Administrator
Motor Carrier Services Division
2701 Prospect Avenue
P.O. Box 201001
Helena, MT 59620
P: (406) 444-7638
E: dsheehy@mt.gov

NEBRASKA
Ms. Beverly Neth
Director
Department of Motor Vehicles
301 Centennial Mall South
Lincoln, NE 68509
P: (402) 471-3900
F: (402) 471-9594
E: bneth@notes.state.ne.us

Maj. Bryan Tuma
State Patrol
P.O. Box 94907
Lincoln, NE 68509
P: (402) 471-4545
F: (402) 479-4002

NEVADA
Mr. Phillip A. Galeoto
Director
Department of Public Safety
555 Wright Way
Carson City, NV 89711
P: (775) 684-4808
F: (775) 684-4809

Ms. Ginny Lewis
Director
Department of Motor Vehicles
555 Wright Way
Carson City, NV 89711
P: (775) 684-4549
F: (775) 684-4692
E: Glewis@dmv.state.nv.us

Col. Chris Perry
Chief
Highway Patrol
555 Wright Way
Carson City, NV 89711
P: (775) 687-5300
E: cperry@dps.state.nv.us

NEW HAMPSHIRE
Mr. John J. Barthelmes
Commissioner
Department of Safety
33 Hazen Drive
Concord, NH 03305
P: (603) 271-2791
F: (603) 271-3903
E: jbarthelmes@safety.state.nh.us

Ms. Virginia C. Beecher
Director
Division of Motor Vehicles
Department of Safety
33 Hazen Drive
Concord, NH 03305
P: (603) 271-2484
F: (603) 271-3903
E: vbeecher@safety.state.nh.us

NEW JERSEY
Ms. Sharon A. Harrington
Chief Administrator
Motor Vehicle Commission
P.O. Box 160
Trenton, NJ 08666
P: (609) 292-6500
F: (609) 777-4171
E: sharon.harrington@dot.state.nj.us

NEW MEXICO
Ms. Jan Goodwin
Secretary
Taxation & Revenue Department
1100 South St. Francis Drive
P.O. Box 630
Santa Fe, NM 87504
P: (505) 827-0341
F: (505) 827-0331
E: jgoodwin@state.nm.us

Motor Vehicle Administration

Mr. Ken Ortiz
Director
Motor Vehicle Division
1100 South St. Francis Drive, Room 2107
Santa Fe, NM 87501
P: (505) 827-2296
F: (505) 827-2397
E: k2ortiz@state.nm.us

Mr. Keith M. Perry
Deputy Director
Motor Vehicle Division
Joseph M. Montoya Building
P.O. Box 1028
Santa Fe, NM 87504
P: (505) 476-3547
F: (505) 827-2397
E: kperry@state.nm.us

NEW YORK
Mr. Preston Felton
Interim Superintendent
State Police
1220 Washington Avenue, Building 22
Albany, NY 12226
P: (518) 457-6721

Mr. David Swarts
Commissioner
Department of Motor Vehicles
6 Empire State Plaza
Albany, NY 12228
P: (518) 473-9324
F: (518) 402-9016

NORTH CAROLINA
Mr. George E. Tatum
Commissioner
Division of Motor Vehicles
1100 New Bern Avenue
Room 220-DMV Building
Raleigh, NC 27697
P: (919) 861-3015
F: (919) 733-0126
E: gtatum@dot.state.nc.us

NORTH DAKOTA
Col. Bryan Klipfel
Superintendent
Highway Patrol
600 East Boulevard Avenue
Department 504
Bismarck, ND 58505
P: (701) 328-2455
F: (701) 328-1717
E: bklipfel@nd.gov

Mr. Keith Magnusson
Deputy Director
Driver & Vehicle Services
Department of Transportation
608 East Boulevard Avenue
Bismarck, ND 58505
P: (701) 328-2727
F: (701) 328-1420
E: kmagnuss@nd.gov

Ms. Lorrie Pavlicek
Director
Division of Motor Vehicles
Department of Transportation
608 E. Boulevard Avenue
Bismarck, ND 58505
P: (701) 328-2725

Mr. Francis G. Ziegler
Director
Department of Transportation
608 East Boulevard Avenue
Bismarck, ND 58505
P: (701) 328-2581
F: (701) 328-1420

NORTHERN MARIANA ISLANDS
Ms. Juana Delon Guerrero
Officer in Charge
Department of Public Safety
Saipan, MP 96950

OHIO
Col. Richard H. Collins
Superintendent
State Highway Patrol
1970 West Broad Street
PO Box 182074
Columbus, OH 43223
P: (614) 466-9144

Mr. Henry Guzman
Director
Department of Public Safety
1970 West Broad Street
P.O. Box 182081
Columbus, OH 43218
P: (614) 466-3383
F: (614) 466-0433

Mr. Mike Rankin
Registrar
Bureau of Motor Vehicles
1970 West Broad Street
P.O. Box 16520
Columbus, OH 43216
P: (614) 387-3000
F: (614) 261-9601

OKLAHOMA
Mr. Russ Nordstrom
Director
Motor Vehicle Division
2501 North Lincoln Boulevard
Oklahoma City, OK 73194
P: (405) 521-3221
F: (405) 521-6937
E: rnordstrom@eris.oktax.state.ok.us

OREGON
Mr. Gregg Dal Ponte
Deputy Director
Motor Carrier Transportation Branch
550 Capitol, Northeast
Salem, OR 97310
P: (503) 378-6351
F: (503) 378-6880
E: gregg.l.dalponte@odot.state.or.us

Ms. Lorna Youngs
Department of Motor Vehicles Administrator
Driver & Motor Vehicle Services Division
1905 Lana Avenue, Northeast
Salem, OR 97314
P: (503) 945-5100
F: (503) 945-5254
E: lorna.c.youngs@odot.state.or.us

PENNSYLVANIA
Mr. Allen Biehler
Secretary of Transportation
Department of Transportation
400 North Street
Commonwealth Keystone Building
Harrisburg, PA 17120
P: (717) 787-2838
F: (717) 787-5491

Col. Jeffrey B. Miller
Commissioner
State Police
1800 Elmerton Avenue
Harrisburg, PA 17110
P: (717) 783-5558
F: (717) 787-2948

PUERTO RICO
Mr. Carlos Gonzalez Miranda
Secretary
Department of Transportation & Public Works
P.O. Box 41269
Minillas Station
Santurce, PR 00940
P: (787) 722-2929
F: (787) 725-1620

Mr. Pedro A. Toledo Davila
Superintendent
Puerto Rico Police
P.O. Box 70166
San Juan, PR 00936
P: (787) 793-1234
F: (787) 781-0080

RHODE ISLAND
Col. Brendan P. Doherty
Superintendent
State Police
311 Danielson Pike
North Scituate, RI 02857
P: (401) 444-1000
F: (401) 444-1105

Mr. Charles F. Dolan
Administrator
Division of Motor Vehicles
286 Main Street
Pawtucket, RI 02860
P: (401) 721-2690
F: (401) 721-2697
E: charlesd@dmv.state.ri.us

Maj. Steven M. O'Donnell
Acting Superintendent
State Police
311 Danielson Pike
North Scituate, RI 02857
P: (401) 444-1000
F: (401) 444-1105
E: sodonnell@risp.state.ri.us

SOUTH CAROLINA
Ms. Marcia Adams
Executive Director
Department of Motor Vehicles
P.O. Box 1498
Columbia, SC 29216
P: (803) 737-1782
F: (803) 737-1785
E: marcia.adams@scdmv.net

Col. Russell F. Roark III
Commander
Highway Patrol
5400 Broad River Road
Columbia, SC 29212
P: (803) 896-7888
F: (803) 896-7922

Mr. James K. Schweitzer
Director
Department of Public Safety
P.O. Box 1993
10311 Wilson Boulevard
Blythewood, SC 29016
P: (803) 896-7932
F: (803) 896-7881
E: jamesschweitzer@scdps.net

SOUTH DAKOTA
Mr. Tom Dravland
Secretary
Department of Public Safety
118 West Capitol Avenue
Pierre, SD 57501
P: (605) 773-3178
F: (605) 773-3018
E: tom.dravland@state.sd.us

Ms. Cynthia D. Gerber
Director
Driver Licensing
Department of Public Safety
118 West Capitol Avenue
Pierre, SD 57501
P: (605) 773-4846
F: (605) 773-3018
E: cindy.gerber@state.sd.us

Ms. Debra Hillmer
Director
Division of Motor Vehicles
Anderson Building
445 East Capitol Avenue
Pierre, SD 57501
P: (605) 773-5747
F: (605) 773-2549
E: debra.hillmer
@state.sd.us

Col. Daniel C. Mosteller
Superintendent
Division of Highway Patrol
Department of Public Safety
118 West Capitol Avenue
Pierre, SD 57501
P: (605) 773-3105
F: (605) 773-6046
E: dan.mosteller
@state.sd.us

TENNESSEE
Mr. Robert S. McKee
Executive Director
Motor Vehicle Commission
500 James Robertson Parkway
Second Floor
Nashville, TN 37243
P: (615) 741-2711
F: (615) 741-0651
E: bob.mckee@state.tn.us

Ms. Wanda Moore
Director
Driver License Issuance
Department of Safety
1150 Foster Avenue
Nashville, TN 37249
P: (615) 253-5221

Col. Mike Walker
Chief
Highway Patrol
1150 Foster Avenue
Nashville, TN 37249
P: (615) 251-5175
F: (615) 532-1051

TEXAS
Ms. Rebecca Davio
Director
Vehicle Titles & Registration
Division
Department of Transportation
125 East 11th Street
Austin, TX 78701
P: (512) 465-7570
F: (512) 467-5909

Col. Thomas A. Davis Jr.
Director
Department of Public Safety
P.O. Box 4087
Austin, TX 78773
P: (512) 424-2000
E: thomas.davis
@txdps.state.tx.us

U.S. VIRGIN ISLANDS
Mr. Elton Lewis
Commissioner
Police Department
Alexander Farrelly Criminal
Justice Ctr.
Charlotte Amalie
St. Thomas, VI 00802
P: (340) 774-2211
F: (340) 715-5517
E: elton.lewis@us.army.mil

UTAH
Mr. Brad L. Simpson
Division Director
Division of Motor Vehicles
Tax Commission
210 North 1950 West
Salt Lake City, UT 84134
P: (801) 297-7687
F: (801) 297-7697
E: bsimpson@utah.gov

VERMONT
Col. James W. Baker
Director
State Police
103 South Main Street
Waterbury, VT 05671
P: (802) 244-7345

Ms. Bonnie L. Rutledge
Commissioner
Department of Motor Vehicles
120 State Street
Montpelier, VT 05602
P: (802) 828-2011
F: (802) 828-2170
E: bonnie.rutledge
@state.vt.us

Maj. Kerry L. Sleeper
Commissioner of Public Safety
Department of Public Safety
103 South Main Street
Waterbury, VT 05671
P: (802) 244-8718
F: (802) 244-5551
E: ksleeper@dps.state.vt.us

VIRGINIA
Mr. D.B. Smit
Commissioner
Department of Motor Vehicles
P.O. Box 27412
Richmond, VA 23269
P: (804) 367-6606
F: (804) 367-2296
E: DB.Smit@dmv.virginia.gov

WASHINGTON
Mr. John R. Batiste
Chief
State Patrol
General Administration Building
P.O. Box 42600
Olympia, WA 98504
P: (360) 753-6540

Ms. Liz Luce
Director
Department of Licensing
1125 Washington Street,
Southeast
P.O. Box 9020
Olympia, WA 98507
P: (360) 902-3933
F: (360) 902-4042
E: doldirector@dol.wa.gov

WEST VIRGINIA
Mr. Joseph Cicchirillo
Commissioner
Division of Motor Vehicles
Building 3, Capitol Complex
1900 Kanawha Boulevard, East
Charleston, WV 25317
P: (304) 558-3900

WISCONSIN
Mr. David L. Collins
Superintendent
Division of State Patrol
4802 Sheboygan Avenue, Room
551
P.O. Box 7912
Madison, WI 53707
P: (608) 266-0454
F: (608) 267-4495
E: david.collins
@dot.state.wi.us

Ms. Lynne Judd
Administrator
Division of Motor Vehicles
4802 Sheboygan Avenue
Madison, WI 53702
P: (608) 266-7079
F: (608) 267-6974

WYOMING
Col. John Cox
Director
Department of Transportation
5300 Bishop Boulevard
Cheyenne, WY 82009
P: (307) 777-4484
F: (307) 777-4163

Col. Sam Powell
Administrator
Highway Patrol
5300 Bishop Boulevard
Cheyenne, WY 82009
P: (307) 777-4301
F: (307) 777-4288

Natural Resources

Formulates and coordinates policies to protect, develop, utilize, restore and enhance the state's natural resources.

ALABAMA
Mr. Barnett Lawley
Commissioner
Department of Conservation & Natural Resources
64 North Union Street, Suite 449
Montgomery, AL 36130
P: (334) 242-3486
F: (334) 242-3489

ALASKA
Mr. Tom Irwin
Commissioner
Department of Natural Resources
400 Willoughby Avenue, 5th Floor
Juneau, AK 99801
P: (907) 465-2400
F: (907) 465-3886

AMERICAN SAMOA
Mr. Ufagafa Ray Tulafono
Director
Department of Marine & Wildlife Resources
American Samoa Government
Pago Pago, AS 96799
P: (684) 633-4456
F: (684) 633-5590

ARIZONA
Mr. William Dowdle
Director of Natural Resources
State Land Department
1616 West Adams
Phoenix, AZ 85007
P: (602) 542-4625

ARKANSAS
Ms. Sandi Formica
Chief
Department of Environmental Quality
8001 National Drive
Little Rock, AR 72201
P: (501) 682-0020
F: (501) 682-0010
E: formica@adeq.state.ar.us

CALIFORNIA
Mr. Lester Snow
Director
Department of Water Resources
1416 Ninth Street
Sacramento, CA 95814
P: (916) 653-7007
F: (916) 653-5028
E: ddeanda@water.ca.gov

COLORADO
Mr. Harris Sherman
Executive Director
Department of Natural Resources
1313 Sherman Street
Centennial Building, 7th Floor
Denver, CO 80203
P: (303) 866-3311
F: (303) 866-2115

CONNECTICUT
Ms. Gina McCarthy
Commissioner
Department of Environmental Protection
79 Elm Street
Hartford, CT 06106
P: (860) 424-3009
F: (860) 424-4054
E: gina.mccarthy@po.state.ct.us

DELAWARE
Mr. John A. Hughes
Secretary
Department of Natural Resources & Environmental Control
89 Kings Highway
P.O. Box 1401
Dover, DE 19903
P: (302) 739-9000
F: (302) 739-6242
E: John.Hughes@state.de.us

FLORIDA
Mr. Michael Sole
Secretary
Department of Environmental Protection
3900 Commonwealth Boulevard
Mail Station 10
Tallahassee, FL 32399
P: (850) 245-2011
F: (850) 245-2021

GEORGIA
Mr. Noel A. Holcomb
Commissioner
Department of Natural Resources
2 Marting Luther King Jr. Drive SE
Suite 1252 East Tower
Atlanta, GA 30334
P: (404) 656-3500
F: (404) 656-0770

GUAM
Mr. Paul C. Bassler
Director
Department of Agriculture
192 Dairy Road
Mangilao, GU 96923
P: (671) 734-3942
F: (671) 734-6569

HAWAII
Mr. Allan A. Smith
Interim Director
Department of Land & Natural Resources
1151 Punchbowl Street
Honolulu, HI 96813
P: (808) 587-0401
F: (808) 587-0390

IDAHO
Ms. Toni Hardesty
Director
Department of Environmental Quality
1410 North Hilton
Boise, ID 83706
P: (208) 373-0240
F: (208) 373-0417
E: toni.hardesty@deq.idaho.gov

ILLINOIS
Mr. Sam Flood
Acting Director
Department of Natural Resources
One Natural Resources Way
Springfield, IL 62702
P: (217) 785-0075
F: (217) 785-9236

INDIANA
Mr. Robert E. Carter Jr.
Director
Department of Natural Resources
402 West Washington Street
Government Center South, Room W256
Indianapolis, IN 46204
P: (317) 232-4020
F: (317) 233-6811

IOWA
Mr. Richard Leopold
Director
Department of Natural Resources
East 9th & Grand Avenue
Des Moines, IA 50319
P: (515) 281-5385
F: (515) 281-6794
E: richard.leopold@dnr.state.ia.us

KANSAS
Ms. Susan Allen
Special Assistant/Legislative Liaison
Governor's Office
State Capitol, 2nd Floor
Topeka, KS 66612
P: (785) 368-8500
F: (785) 368-8788

KENTUCKY
Ms. Susan C. Bush
Commissioner
Department for Natural Resources
#2 Hudson Hollow
Frankfort, KY 40601
P: (502) 564-6940
F: (502) 564-5698

LOUISIANA
Mr. Scott Angelle
Secretary
Department of Natural Resources
P.O. Box 94396
Baton Rouge, LA 70804
P: (225) 342-2710
F: (225) 342-3442
E: info@dnr.state.la.us

MAINE
Mr. Patrick K. McGowan
Commissioner
Department of Conservation
22 State House Station
Augusta, ME 04333
P: (207) 287-4900

MARYLAND
Mr. John R. Griffin
Secretary
Department of Natural Resources
Tawes State Office Building, C4
580 Taylor Avenue
Annapolis, MD 21401
P: (410) 260-8101
E: jgriffin@dnr.state.md.us

MASSACHUSETTS
Ms. Priscilla H. Geigis
Acting Commissioner
Department of Conservation & Recreation
20 Somerset Street
Boston, MA 02108
P: (617) 722-5500
F: (617) 727-0891

MICHIGAN
Ms. Rebecca A. Humphries
Director
Department of Natural Resources
P.O. Box 30028
Lansing, MI 48909
P: (517) 373-2329
F: (517) 335-4242
E: humphrir@michigan.gov

MINNESOTA
Mr. Mark Holsten
Commissioner
Department of Natural Resources
500 Lafayette Road
P.O. Box 37
St. Paul, MN 55155
P: (651) 259-5555
F: (651) 296-4799
E: mark.holsten@state.mn.us

MISSISSIPPI
Ms. Trudy H. Fisher
Executive Director
Department of Environmental Quality
2380 Highway 80 West
P.O. Box 20305
Jackson, MS 39289
P: (601) 961-5100
F: (601) 961-5093
E: trudy_fisher@deq.state.ms.us

MISSOURI
Mr. Doyle Childers
Director
Department of Natural Resources
205 Jefferson Street
P.O. Box 176
Jefferson City, MO 65102
P: (573) 751-4732
F: (573) 751-7627

MONTANA
Mr. M. Jeff Hagener
Director
Department of Fish, Wildlife & Parks
1420 East 6th Avenue
P.O. Box 200701
Helena, MT 59620
P: (406) 444-3186
F: (406) 444-4952

Ms. Mary Sexton
Director
Department of Natural Resources & Conservation
1625 11th Avenue
Helena, MT 59620
P: (406) 444-2074
F: (406) 444-2684
E: msexton@mt.gov

NEBRASKA
Ms. Ann Bleed
Acting Director
Department of Natural Resources
P.O. Box 94676
Lincoln, NE 68509
P: (402) 471-2363
F: (402) 471-2900

NEVADA
Mr. Allen Biaggi
Director
Department of Conservation & Natural Resources
901 South Stewart, Suite 5001
Carson City, NV 89701
P: (775) 684-2700
F: (775) 684-2715
E: abiaggi@dcnr.nv.gov

NEW HAMPSHIRE
Mr. George Bald
Commissioner
Department of Resources & Economic Development
P.O. Box 1856
Concord, NH 03302
P: (603) 271-2411
F: (603) 271-2629
E: gbald@dred.state.nh.us

NEW JERSEY
Mr. John Sacco
Acting Chief
Office of Natural Resource Restoration
501 East State Street, 3rd Floor
P.O. Box 404
Trenton, NJ 08625
P: (609) 984-5475
F: (609) 984-0836

NEW MEXICO
Ms. Joanna Prukop
Cabinet Secretary
Energy, Minerals & Natural Resources Department
1220 South Saint Francis Drive
Santa Fe, NM 87505
P: (505) 476-3200
F: (505) 476-3220

NEW YORK
Mr. Alexander "Pete" Grannis (D)
Commissioner
Department of Environmental Conservation
625 Broadway
Albany, NY 12207
P: (518) 402-8540
F: (518) 474-5450

NORTH CAROLINA
Mr. William G. Ross Jr.
Secretary
Department of Environment & Natural Resources
512 North Salisbury Street
1601 Mail Service Center
Raleigh, NC 27699
P: (919) 733-4101
F: (919) 733-4299
E: bill.ross@ncmail.net

NORTH DAKOTA
Mr. Michael McKenna
Chief
Conservation & Communications Division
Game & Fish Department
100 North Bismarck Expressway
Bismarck, ND 58501
P: (701) 328-6332
F: (701) 328-6352
E: mmckenna@nd.gov

NORTHERN MARIANA ISLANDS
Dr. Ignacio T. Dela Cruz
Secretary
Department of Lands & Natural Resources
Caller Box 10007, Capitol Hill
Saipan, MP 96950
P: (670) 322-9830
F: (670) 322-2633
E: dlnrgov@vzpacifica.net

OHIO
Mr. Sean D. Logan
Director
Department of Natural Resources
1930 Belcher Drive
Columbus, OH 43224
P: (614) 265-6879

OKLAHOMA
Mr. Miles Tolbert
Secretary of Environment
Office of the Secretary of Environment
3800 North Classen Boulevard
Oklahoma City, OK 73118
P: (405) 530-8995
F: (405) 530-8999

OREGON
Mr. Michael Carrier
Natural Resources Advisor
Office of the Governor
160 State Capitol
900 Court Street, Northeast
Salem, OR 97301
P: (503) 378-3548
F: (503) 378-6827

PENNSYLVANIA
Mr. Michael DiBerardinis
Secretary
Department of Conservation & Natural Resources
Rachel Carson State Office Building
P.O. Box 8767
Harrisburg, PA 17105
P: (717) 772-9084
F: (717) 772-9106

PUERTO RICO
Hon. Javier Velez Arocho
Secretary
Department of Natural & Environmental Resources
Puerta De Tierra Station
P.O. Box 9066600
San Juan, PR 00906
P: (787) 724-8774
F: (787) 723-4255

RHODE ISLAND
Mr. Larry Mouradjian
Associate Director
Bureau of Natural Resources
235 Promenade Street
Providence, RI 02908
P: (401) 222-4700 Ext. 2414
F: (401) 222-3162
E: larry.mouradjian@dem.ri.gov

SOUTH CAROLINA
Mr. John E. Frampton
Director
Department of Natural Resources
P.O. Box 167
Columbia, SC 29202
P: (803) 734-4007
F: (803) 734-6310
E: framptonj@dnr.sc.gov

Natural Resources

SOUTH DAKOTA
Mr. Steve M. Pirner
Secretary
Department of Environment & Natural Resources
Foss Building
523 East Capitol Avenue
Pierre, SD 57501
P: (605) 773-5559
F: (605) 773-6035
E: steve.pirner@state.sd.us

TENNESSEE
Mr. Jim Fyke
Commissioner
Department of Environment & Conservation
1st Floor, L & C Annex
401 Church Street
Nashville, TN 37243
P: (615) 532-0106
F: (615) 532-0120

TEXAS
Mr. Larry R. Soward
Commissioner
Commission on Environmental Quality
12100 Park 35 Circle
P.O. Box 13087 (MC 100)
Austin, TX 78711
P: (512) 239-5500
F: (512) 239-5533

U.S. VIRGIN ISLANDS
Mr. Dean C. Plaskett
State Historic Preservation Officer
Department of Planning & Natural Resources
17 Kongens
St. Thomas, VI 00802
P: 340-776-8605
F: 340-776-7236

UTAH
Mr. Michael R. Styler
Executive Director
Department of Natural Resources
1594 West North Temple, Suite 3710
P.O. Box 145610
Salt Lake City, UT 84114
P: (801) 538-7201
F: (801) 538-7315
E: mikestyler@utah.gov

VERMONT
Mr. George Crombie
Secretary
Agency of Natural Resources
103 South Main Street
Waterbury, VT 05671
P: (802) 241-3600
F: (802) 244-1102

VIRGINIA
Hon. L. Preston Bryant Jr. (R)
Secretary
Office of Natural Resources
1111 East Broad Street
Patrick Henry Building
Richmond, VA 23218
P: (804) 786-0044
F: (804) 371-8333
E: preston.bryant@governor.virginia.gov

WASHINGTON
Mr. Doug Sutherland
Commissioner of Public Lands
Department of Natural Resources
P.O. Box 47001
Olympia, WA 98504
P: (360) 902-1000
F: (360) 902-1775

WEST VIRGINIA
Mr. Frank Jezioro
Director
Natural Resources
Capitol Complex, Building 3
1900 Kanawha Boulevard, East
Charleston, WV 25305
P: (304) 558-2754
F: (304) 558-2768
E: fjezioro@wvdnr.gov

WISCONSIN
Mr. P. Scott Hassett
Secretary
Department of Natural Resources
101 South Webster Street
Madison, WI 53703
P: (608) 266-0865
F: (608) 266-6983

WYOMING
Mr. Grant Stumbough
Manager
Natural Resources & Policy Division
Department of Agriculture
2219 Carey Avenue
Cheyenne, WY 82002
P: (307) 777-6579
F: (307) 777-6593
E: gstumb@state.wy.us

Occupational Safety

Enforces safety standards for the protection of employees in places of employment.

ALABAMA
Mr. Jim Bennett
Commissioner
Department of Labor
P.O. Box 303500
Montgomery, AL 36130
P: (334) 242-3460
F: (334) 240-3417
E: jbennett
@alalabor.state.al.us

ALASKA
Mr. Grey Mitchell
Director
Department of Labor & Workforce Development
Division of Labor Standards & Safety
P.O. Box 21149
Juneau, AK 99802
P: (907) 465-4855
F: (907) 465-6012

AMERICAN SAMOA
Mr. Puni Penei Sewell
Director
Department of Human Resources
American Samoa Government
Pago Pago, AS 96799
P: (683) 644-4485
F: (684) 633-1139
E: sewells_1@hotmail.com

ARIZONA
Mr. Larry J. Etchechury
Director
Industrial Commission
800 West Washington Street
P.O. Box 19070
Phoenix, AZ 85007
P: (602) 542-4411
F: (602) 542-7889
E: letchechury
@ica.state.az.us

ARKANSAS
Mr. James Salkeld
Director
Department of Labor
10421 West Markham Street
Suite 100
Little Rock, AR 72205
P: (501) 682-4541
F: (501) 682-4535
E: james.salkeld
@arkansas.gov

CALIFORNIA
Mr. Len Welsh
Acting Chief
Division of Occupational Safety & Health
Department of Industrial Relations
1515 Clay Street, Suite 1901
Oakland, CA 94612
P: (510) 286-7000
F: (510) 286-7088

COLORADO
Mr. Richard Gonzales
Executive Director
Department of Personnel & Administration
1600 Broadway, Suite 1030
Denver, CO 80202
P: (303) 866-6559
E: rich.gonzales
@state.co.us

CONNECTICUT
Ms. Patricia Mayfield
Commissioner
Department of Labor
200 Folly Brook Boulevard
Wethersfield, CT 06109
P: (860) 263-6505
F: (860) 263-6529
E: patricia.mayfield
@po.state.ct.us

DELAWARE
Mr. James Cagle
Director
Division of Industrial Affairs
4425 North Market Street
Wilmington, DE 19802
P: (302) 761-8200
F: (302) 739-6242

DISTRICT OF COLUMBIA
Ms. Summer Spencer
Acting Director
Department of Employment Services
609 H Street, NE
Washington, DC 20002
P: (202) 724-7000

FLORIDA
Mr. Tanner Holloman
Director
Division of Workers' Compensation
200 East Gaines Street
Tallahassee, FL 32399
P: (850) 413-1600
E: tanner.holloman
@fldfs.com

GEORGIA
Mr. Earl Everett
Director of Safety & Engineering
Safety Engineering Division
1700 Century Circle, Suite 100
Atlanta, GA 30345
P: (404) 679-0687
F: (404) 982-3405
E: earl.everett
@dol.state.ga.us

GUAM
Ms. Maria Connelley
Director
Department of Labor
414 West Soledad, Suite 400
GCIC Building, P.O. Box 9970
Tamuning, GU 96931
P: (671) 475-7046
F: (671) 475-7045

HAWAII
Ms. Jennifer Shishido
Administrator
Occupational Safety & Health Division
830 Punchbowl Street
Room 425
Honolulu, HI 96813
P: (808) 586-9116
F: (808) 586-9104

IDAHO
Mr. James M. Alcorn
Manager
State Insurance Fund
1215 West State Street
Boise, ID 83720
P: (208) 332-2100
F: (208) 334-2607
E: jalcorn@isif.state.id.us

INDIANA
Ms. Lori A. Torres
Commissioner
Department of Labor
Indiana Government Center-South
402 West Washington Street, Room W-195
Indianapolis, IN 46204
P: (317) 232-2378
F: (317) 233-5381
E: ltorres@dol.in.gov

IOWA
Mr. Steve Slater
Interim Labor Commissioner
Division of Labor Services
1000 East Grand Avenue
Des Moines, IA 50319
P: (515) 281-3447
F: (515) 281-4698

KANSAS
Mr. Jim Garner
Secretary
Department of Labor
401 Southwest Topeka Boulevard
Topeka, KS 66603
P: (785) 296-7474
F: (785) 368-6294
E: jim.garner@dol.ks.gov

Mr. Steve Zink
Director
Industrial Safety & Health Division
512 West 6th Street
Topeka, KS 66603
P: (785) 296-6324
F: (785) 296-1775

KENTUCKY
Mr. Steve Morrison
Executive Director
Office of Occupational Safety & Health
1047 US Highway 127 South, Suite 4
Frankfort, KY 40601
P: (502) 564-3070
F: (502) 696-1902

LOUISIANA
Ms. Karen Winfrey
Assistant Secretary of Labor
Office of Workers' Compensation
P.O. Box 94094
Baton Rouge, LA 70804
P: (225) 342-3111
F: (225) 342-5665
E: os@ldol.state.la.us

MAINE
Mr. David Wacker
Director
Workplace Safety & Health Division
45 State House Station
Augusta, ME 04333
P: (207) 624-6400
E: david.e.wacker@maine.gov

MARYLAND
Ms. Cheryl Kammerman
Assistant Commissioner
Occupational Safety & Health
1100 North Eutaw Street, Room 613
Baltimore, MD 21201
P: (410) 767-2190

Occupational Safety

MASSACHUSETTS
Mr. Kevin Burke
Secretary
Executive Office of Public Safety
One Ashburton Place, Suite 2133
Boston, MA 02108
P: (617) 727-7775
F: (617) 727-4764

MICHIGAN
Mr. Douglas J. Kalinowski
Deputy Director
Occupational Safety & Health Administration
P.O. Box 30004
Lansing, MI 48909
P: (517) 373-1820
F: (517) 373-3728
E: dkalin@michigan.gov

MISSOURI
Mr. Allen Dillingham
Director
Division of Labor Standards
3315 West Truman Boulevard, Room 205
P.O. Box 449
Jefferson City, MO 65102
P: (573) 751-3403
F: (573) 751-3721
E: allen.dillingham@dolir.mo.gov

MONTANA
Mr. Keith Kelly
Commissioner
Department of Labor & Industry
P.O. Box 1728
Helena, MT 59624
P: (406) 444-2840
F: (406) 444-1394
E: kkelly@mt.gov

NEBRASKA
Mr. Fernando "Butch" Lecuona III
Commissioner of Labor
Department of Labor
Department of Labor
P.O. Box 94600
Lincoln, NE 68509
P: (402) 471-2600
F: (402) 471-9867
E: flecuona@dol.state.ne.us

NEVADA
Mr. Charles Verre
Chief Administrative Officer
Division of Industrial Relations
788 Fairview Drive, Suite 300
400 West King Street, Suite 400
Carson City, NV 89703
P: (775) 486-9087

NEW HAMPSHIRE
Mr. George N. Copadis
Commissioner of Labor
Department of Labor
95 Pleasant Street
Concord, NH 03301
P: (603) 271-3171
F: (603) 271-6852
E: gcopadis@labor.state.nh.us

NEW JERSEY
Dr. Eddy A. Bresnitz
State Epidemiologist/Deputy Commissioner
Division of Epidemiology, Environmental & Occupational Health
P.O. Box 369
Trenton, NJ 08625
P: (609) 588-7465

NEW YORK
Ms. Patricia Smith
Commissioner
Department of Labor
345 Hudson Street
Albany, NY 10014
P: (518) 457-2741
F: (518) 457-6908
E: nysdol@labor.state.ny.us

NORTH CAROLINA
Ms. Cherie K. Berry
Commissioner
Department of Labor
1101 Mail Service Center
4 West Edenton Street
Raleigh, NC 27699
P: (919) 733-7166
F: (919) 733-6197
E: cberry@mail.dol.state.nc.us

NORTH DAKOTA
Mr. Wally Kalmbach
Director
Loss Prevention
Workers Compensation Bureau
500 East Front Avenue
Bismarck, ND 58504
P: (701) 328-3886
F: (701) 328-3820
E: wkalmbac@nd.gov

NORTHERN MARIANA ISLANDS
Mr. Gil M. San Nicolas
Secretary
Department of Labor
Caller Box 10007
Saipan, MP 96950
P: (670) 322-9834
F: (670) 322-2633

OHIO
Ms. Kimberly A. Zurz
Director of Commerce
Department of Commerce
77 South High Street, 23rd Floor
Columbus, OH 43215
P: (614) 466-3636
F: (614) 752-5078
E: kim.zurz@com.state.oh.us

OKLAHOMA
Ms. Diana Jones
Director of OSHA
Department of Labor
4001 North Lincoln
Oklahoma City, OK 73105
P: (405) 528-1500
F: (405) 528-5751
E: djones@oklaosf.state.ok.us

OREGON
Mr. Michael Wood
Administrator
Occupational Safety & Health Division
350 Winter Street Northeast
Room 430
Salem, OR 97301
P: (503) 378-3272
F: (503) 947-7461

PENNSYLVANIA
Mr. Charles J. Sludden Jr.
Director
Bureau of Occupational & Industrial Safety
Labor & Industry Building, Room 1613
Harrisburg, PA 17120
P: (717) 787-3323

PUERTO RICO
Mr. Roman M. Velasco Gonzalez
Secretary
Department of Labor
Prudencio Rivera-Martinez Building
505 Munoz Rivera Avenue, 21st Floor
Hato Rey, PR 00918
P: (787) 754-2119
F: (787) 753-9550

RHODE ISLAND
Ms. Adelita Orefice
Director
Occupational Safety & Health
1511 Pontiac Avenue
Cranston, RI 02920
P: (401) 462-8870
F: (401) 462-8872
E: aorefice@dlt.state.ri.us

SOUTH CAROLINA
Ms. Adrienne R. Youmans
Director
Labor, Licensing & Regulation
P.O. Box 11329
Columbia, SC 29211
P: (803) 896-4300
F: (803) 896-4393
E: youmansa@llr.sc.gov

SOUTH DAKOTA
Mr. James E. Marsh
Director
Division of Labor & Management
Kneip Building
700 Governors Drive
Pierre, SD 57501
P: (605) 773-3681
F: (605) 773-4211
E: james.marsh@state.sd.us

TENNESSEE
Mr. John Winkler
Administrator
Occupational Safety & Health Administration
710 James Robertson Parkway, 3rd Floor
Nashville, TN 37243
P: (615) 741-7115
F: (615) 253-1623

TEXAS
Dr. Eduardo J. Sanchez
Commissioner
Department of Health Services
1100 West 49th Street
Austin, TX 78456
P: (512) 458-7375

U.S. VIRGIN ISLANDS
Mr. Albert Bryant Jr.
Commissioner
Department of Labor
2203 Church Street
Christiansted, VI 00820
P: (340) 773-1994
F: (340) 773-0094

UTAH
Mr. Bill Adams
Safety & Health Manager
Occupational Safety & Health Division
Labor Commission
160 East 300 South
Salt Lake City, UT 84114
P: (801) 530-6897
F: (801) 530-7606
E: wadams@utah.gov

VERMONT
Mr. Robert McLeod
Manager
Division of Occupational Safety & Health Administration
North Building, National Life
Montpelier, VT 05620
P: (802) 828-2765
F: (802) 828-2748
E: robert.mcleod@labind.state.vt.us

VIRGINIA
Mr. C. Ray Davenport
Commissioner
Department of Labor & Industry
13 South 13th Street
Richmond, VA 23219
P: (804) 786-2377
F: (804) 371-6524
E: ray.davenport@doli.virginia.gov

WASHINGTON
Mr. Stephen Cant
Assistant Director
Division of Occupational Safety & Health
P.O. Box 44600
Olympia, WA 98504
P: (360) 902-5495
F: (360) 902-5529

WEST VIRGINIA
Mr. David M. Mullins
Commissioner
Division of Labor
Bureau of Commerce, Room B-749
State Capitol Complex, Building 6
Charleston, WV 25305
P: (304) 558-7890
F: (304) 558-3797
E: dmullins@labor.state.wv.us

WISCONSIN
Mr. Greg Jones
Administrator
Safety & Buildings Division
P.O. Box 7969
Madison, WI 53707
P: (608) 266-1816
F: (608) 266-3080

WYOMING
Ms. Cindy Pomeroy
Director
Department of Employment
1510 East Pershing Boulevard
Cheyenne, WY 82002
P: (307) 777-7672
F: (307) 777-5805
E: cpomer@state.wy.us

Oil & Gas Regulation

Regulates the drilling, operation, maintenance and abandonment of oil and gas wells in the state.

ALABAMA
Mr. Nick Tew Jr.
State Geologist/Oil & Gas Supervisor
Geological Survey of Alabama
P.O. Box 869999
420 Hackberry Lane
Tuscaloosa, AL 35486
P: (205) 247-3679
F: (205) 349-2861
E: ntew@gsa.state.al.us

ALASKA
Mr. Kevin Banks
Acting Director
Division of Oil & Gas
Department of Natural Resources
550 West 7th Avenue, Suite 800
Anchorage, AK 99501
P: (907) 269-8800
F: (907) 269-8938

ARIZONA
Dr. Lee Allison
Director & State Geologist
Geological Survey
416 West Congress Street, Suite 100
Tucson, AZ 85701
P: (520) 770-3500
F: (520) 770-3505
E: lee.allison@azgs.az.gov

ARKANSAS
Mr. Larry Bengal
Director
Oil & Gas Commission
P.O. Box 1472
El Dorado, AR 71731
P: (870) 862-4965
F: (870) 862-8823
E: Larry.Bengal@aogc.state.ar.us

CALIFORNIA
Mr. Hal Bopp
Oil & Gas Supervisor
Division of Oil, Gas & Geothermal Resources
801 K Street, MS 20-20
Sacramento, CA 95814
P: (916) 323-1777
F: (916) 323-0424

COLORADO
Mr. Brian Macke
Director
Oil & Gas Conservation Commission
1120 Lincoln Street, Suite 801
Denver, CO 80203
P: (303) 894-2100, Ext. 122
F: (303) 894-2109
E: Brian.Macke@cogcc.state.co.us

CONNECTICUT
Mr. Donald W. Downes
Chair
Department of Public Utility Control
10 Franklin Square
New Britain, CT 06051
P: (860) 827-2801
F: (860) 827-2806
E: donald.downes@po.state.ct.us

DELAWARE
Mr. John A. Hughes
Secretary
Department of Natural Resources & Environmental Control
89 Kings Highway
P.O. Box 1401
Dover, DE 19903
P: (302) 739-9000
F: (302) 739-6242
E: John.Hughes@state.de.us

FLORIDA
Mr. Walter Schmidt
Chief & State Geologist
Geological Survey
903 West Tennessee Street
Tallahassee, FL 32304
P: (850) 488-4191
F: (850) 488-8086
E: Walt.Schmidt@dep.state.fl.us

GEORGIA
Mr. William G. Smith
Program Manager
Geological Survey Branch
19 Martin Luther King Jr. Drive, SW
Room 400
Atlanta, GA 30334
P: (404) 656-3214
F: (404) 657-8379

GUAM
Ms. Lorilee Crisostomo
Administrator
Environmental Protection Agency
17-3304/15-6101 Mariner Avenue, Tiyan
P.O. Box 22439
Barrigada, GU 96921
P: (671) 475-1658
F: (671) 734-5910
E: lorilee@guamcell.net

Mr. Lawrence Perez
Director
Department of Public Works
542 North Marine Drive
Tamuning, GU 96913
P: (671) 646-3131
F: (671) 649-6178
E: dpwdir@mail.gov.gu

ILLINOIS
Mr. Al Clayborne
Acting Supervisor
Division of Oil & Gas
One Natural Resources Way
Springfield, IL 62702
P: (217) 782-7756
E: aclayborne@dnrmail.state.il.us

INDIANA
Mr. Herschel McDivitt
Director
Oil & Gas Division
402 West Washington Street, Room W293
Indianapolis, IN 46204
P: (317) 232-4058

IOWA
Mr. John Norris
Chair
Utilities Board
350 Maple Street
Des Moines, IA 50319
P: (515) 281-5167
F: (515) 281-8821

KANSAS
Mr. Maurice L. Korphage
Director
Conservation Division
130 South Market, Room 2078
Wichita, KS 67202
P: (316) 337-6200
F: (316) 337-6211

KENTUCKY
Mr. Rick Bender
Director
Division of Oil & Gas
1025 Capital Center Drive, Suite 201
P.O. Box 2244
Frankfort, KY 40601
P: (502) 573-0147
F: (502) 573-0152
E: rick.bender@ky.gov

LOUISIANA
Dr. Madhurendu B. Kumar
Director
Geological Oil & Gas Division
617 North Third Street
P.O. Box 94275
Baton Rouge, LA 70804
P: (225) 342-5501
F: (225) 342-8199
E: ooc-info@dnr.state.la.us

MAINE
Mr. Mark Hyland
Director
Bureau of Remediation & Waste Management
Department of Environmental Protection
17 State House Station
Augusta, ME 04333
P: (207) 287-2651
F: (207) 287-7826
E: Mark.Hyland@maine.gov

MARYLAND
Mr. Herbert Meade
Program Administrator
Oil Control Program
2500 Broening Highway
Baltimore, MD 21224
P: (410) 631-3386
F: (410) 631-3092
E: hmeade@mde.state.md.us

MASSACHUSETTS
Ms. Arleen O'Donnell
Acting Commissioner
Department of Environmental Protection
One Winter Street, 2nd Floor
Boston, MA 02108
P: (617) 292-5975
F: (617) 574-6880

MICHIGAN
Mr. Harold R. Fitch
State Geologist
Office of Geological Survey
Box 30256
525 West Allegan
Lansing, MI 48909
P: (517) 241-1548
F: (517) 241-1601
E: fitchh@michigan.gov

MINNESOTA
Mr. LeRoy Koppendrayer
Chair
Public Utilities Commission
Suite 350, 121 7th Place East
St. Paul, MN 55101
P: 651-296-0402
F: (651) 297-7073
E: Leroy.koppendrayer@state.mn.us

MISSISSIPPI
Ms. Lisa Ivshin
Executive Director
Oil & Gas Board
500 Greymont Avenue, Suite E
Jackson, MS 39202
P: (601) 354-7112
F: (601) 354-6873
E: livshin@ogb.state.ms.us

MISSOURI
Mr. Scott Kaden
Geologist
DNR Geological Survey Program
111 Fairgrounds Road
P.O. Box 250
Rolla, MO 65402
P: (573) 368-2100
F: (573) 368-2111
E: Scott.Kaden@dnr.mo.gov

MONTANA
Mr. Tom Richmond
Division Administrator & Petroleum Engineer
Board of Oil & Gas
2535 St. Johns Avenue
Billings, MT 59102
P: (406) 656-0040
F: (406) 655-6015

NEBRASKA
Mr. William H. Sydow
Director
Oil & Gas Conservation Commission
P.O. Box 399
Sidney, NE 69162
P: (308) 254-6919
F: (308) 254-6922

NEVADA
Mr. Alan Coyner
Administrator
Division of Minerals
901 South Stewart
Carson City, NV 89701
P: (775) 684-7040
F: (775) 684-7052
E: acoyner@govmail.state.nv.us

NEW HAMPSHIRE
Mr. David R. Wunsch
State Geologist & Director
Geological Survey
Department of Environmental Services
29 Hazen Drive
Concord, NH 03302
P: (603) 271-6482
F: (603) 271-3305
E: dwunsch@des.state.nh.us

NEW JERSEY
Mr. Jim P. Giuliano
Director
Division of Reliability & Security
Board of Public Utilities
2 Gateway Center, 8th Floor
Newark, NJ 07102
P: (201) 648-2026
F: (201) 648-2242

NEW YORK
Mr. Alexander "Pete" Grannis (D)
Commissioner
Department of Environmental Conservation
625 Broadway
Albany, NY 12207
P: (518) 402-8540
F: (518) 474-5450

NORTH CAROLINA
Mr. William G. Ross Jr.
Secretary
Department of Environment & Natural Resources
512 North Salisbury Street
1601 Mail Service Center
Raleigh, NC 27699
P: (919) 733-4101
F: (919) 733-4299
E: bill.ross@ncmail.net

NORTH DAKOTA
Mr. Lynn D. Helms
Director
Oil & Gas Division
Industrial Commission
600 East Boulevard Avenue
Bismarck, ND 58505
P: (701) 328-8020
F: (701) 328-8022
E: ldh@saturn.ndic.nd.gov

OHIO
Ms. Kimberly A. Zurz
Director of Commerce
Department of Commerce
77 South High Street, 23rd Floor
Columbus, OH 43215
P: (614) 466-3636
F: (614) 752-5078
E: kim.zurz@com.state.oh.us

OKLAHOMA
Ms. Lori Wrotenbery
Director
Oil & Gas Conservation Division
Jim Thorpe Building, Room 255
2101 North Lincoln Boulevard
Oklahoma City, OK 73105
P: (405) 521-2302
F: (405) 521-3099

OREGON
Mr. Robert A. Houston
Natural Resource Specialist
Department of Geology & Mineral Industries
229 Broadalbin Street, Southwest
Albany, OR 97321
P: (541) 967-2039
E: Robert.A.Houston@mlrr.oregongeology.com

PENNSYLVANIA
Mr. David C. Hogeman
Director
Bureau of Oil and Gas Management
Rachael Carson Office Bldg., 5th Floor
P.O. Box 8765
Harrisburg, PA 17105
P: (717) 772-2199
F: (717) 772-2291

PUERTO RICO
Mr. Javier Mendez
Administrator
Energy Affairs Administration
P.O. Box 9066600
Puerta De Tierra Station
San Juan, PR 00936
P: (787) 724-8777 Ext. 4015
F: (717) 721-3089
E: quintanaj@caribe.net

RHODE ISLAND
Mr. Elia Germani
Chair
Public Utilities Commission
89 Jefferson Boulevard
Providence, RI 02888
P: (401) 941-4500 Ext. 170
F: (401) 941-1691
E: egermani@puc.state.ri.us

SOUTH CAROLINA
Mr. Bud Badr
Chief
Hydrology Section
Land, Water & Conservation Division
1000 Assembly Street
Columbia, SC 29201
P: (803) 734-6362
F: (803) 734-9200
E: badrb@dnr.sc.gov

SOUTH DAKOTA
Ms. Mary Jo Joens
Administrator
Oil & Gas Division
State Capitol
500 East Capitol Avenue
Pierre, SD 57501
P: (605) 773-3303
F: (605) 773-5520
E: maryjo.joens@state.sd.us

TENNESSEE
Mr. Mike Burton
Assistant Supervisor
Oil & Gas Board
L & C Tower, 13th Floor
401 Church Street
Nashville, TN 37243
P: (615) 532-0166
F: (615) 532-1517
E: Michael.K.Burton@state.tn.us

TEXAS
Mr. Tommie Seitz
Director
Oil & Gas Division
Railroad Commissioner
P.O. Box 12967
Austin, TX 78711
P: (512) 463-6810

UTAH
Mr. John R. Baza
Director
Division of Oil, Gas & Mining
1594 West North Temple, Suite 1210
P.O. Box 145801
Salt Lake City, UT 84114
P: (801) 538-5334
F: (801) 359-3940
E: johnbaza@utah.gov

VERMONT
Mr. George Crombie
Secretary
Agency of Natural Resources
103 South Main Street
Waterbury, VT 05671
P: (802) 241-3600
F: (802) 244-1102

Oil & Gas Regulation

VIRGINIA
Mr. George P. Willis
Director
Department of Mines, Minerals & Energy
200 North Ninth Street, 8th Floor
Richmond, VA 23219
P: (804) 692-3200
F: (804) 692-3237
E: bo.willis@dmme.virginia.gov

WASHINGTON
Mr. Ron Teissere
State Geologist & Division Manager
Geology & Earth Resources
1111 Washington Street SE, Room 148
P.O. Box 47007
Olympia, WA 98504
P: (360) 902-1440
F: (360) 902-1785
E: ron.teissere@wadnr.gov

WEST VIRGINIA
Mr. James Martin
Chief
Office of Oil & Gas
601 57th Street, Southeast
Charleston, WV 25304
P: (304) 926-0499
F: (304) 926-0452
E: jmartin@wvdep.org

WISCONSIN
Mr. Robert Norcross
Administrator
Electric Division
P.O. Box 7839
Madison, WI 53707
P: (608) 266-0699
F: (608) 267-1381
E: robert.norcross@psc.state.wi.us

WYOMING
Mr. Donald Likwartz
State Oil & Gas Supervisor
Oil & Gas Conservation Commission
P.O. Box 2640
777 West 1st Street
Casper, WY 82602
P: (307) 234-7147
F: (307) 234-5306

Ombudsman

Investigates citizens' complaints about the administrative acts of any state agency.

ALABAMA
Ms. Patricia Simpkins
Director of Constituent Services
Office of the Governor
600 Dexter Avenue
Montgomery, AL 36104
P: (334) 242-7100
F: (334) 353-0004

ALASKA
Ms. Linda Lord-Jenkins
Ombudsman
Office of the Ombudsman
P.O. Box 102636
Anchorage, AK 99510
P: (907) 269-5290
F: (907) 269-5291

ARIZONA
Mr. Patrick Shannahan
Ombudsman for the State
Office of the Ombudsman - Citizen's Aide
3737 North 7th Street, Suite 209
Phoenix, AZ 85014
P: (602) 277-7292
F: (602) 277-7312
E: ombuds@azoca.org

ARKANSAS
Mr. Chris Masingill
Director of Agency & Constituency Affairs
Office of the Governor
State Capitol, Suite 120
Little Rock, AR 72201
P: (501) 682-2345
F: (501) 682-3596
E: chris.masingill@governor.arkansas.gov

CALIFORNIA
Ms. Elaine M. Howle
State Auditor
Office of the State Auditor
555 Capitol Mall, Suite 300
Sacramento, CA 95814
P: (916) 445-0255
F: (916) 322-7801
E: elaineh@bsa.ca.gov

HAWAII
Mr. Robin K. Matsunaga
Ombudsman
Office of the Ombudsman
Kehuanaca Building
465 South King Street, 4th Floor
Honolulu, HI 96813
P: (808) 587-0770
F: (808) 587-0773

IOWA
Mr. William C. Angrick II
Ombudsman
Office of Citizen's Aide
Ola Babcock Miller Building
1112 East Grand Avenue
Des Moines, IA 50319
P: (515) 281-3592
F: (515) 242-6007
E: ombudsman@legis.state.ia.us

KANSAS
Ms. Gwen Sims
Chief Ombudsman
Office of the Ombudsman
700 Southwest Jackson Street
Suite 503
Topeka, KS 66603
P: (785) 296-5295
F: (785) 296-2643

KENTUCKY
Mr. Erwin Lewis
Executive Director
Department of Public Advocacy
100 Fair Oaks Lane, Suite 302
Frankfort, KY 40601
P: (502) 564-8006
F: (502) 564-7890
E: ernie.lewis@ky.gov

LOUISIANA
Ms. Linda Sadden
State Long-Term Care Ombudsman
Office of the Long-Term Care Ombudsman
P.O. Box 80374
Baton Rouge, LA 70897
P: (225) 342-9722
F: (225) 342-7144
E: lasadden@goea.state.la.us

MASSACHUSETTS
Mr. Ron Bell
Director
Public Liasion Office
Office of the Governor
State House, Room 280
Boston, MA 02133
P: (617) 725-4005
F: (617) 727-9725

MISSISSIPPI
Ms. Anniece McLemore
State LTC Ombudsman
Division of Aging
Department of Human Services
750 North State Street
Jackson, MS 39202
P: (601) 359-4927

MISSOURI
Hon. Peter Kinder (R)
Lieutenant Governor
Office of the Lieutenant Governor
State Capitol, Room 224
Jefferson City, MO 65101
P: (573) 751-4727
F: (573) 751-9422
E: ltgov@mail.mo.gov

MONTANA
Mr. Bob Schleicher
Citizen's Advocate
Office of the Citizen's Advocate
State Capitol, Room 232
P.O. Box 200803
Helena, MT 59620
P: (406) 444-3468
F: (406) 444-4151
E: citizensadvocate@mt.gov

NEBRASKA
Mr. Marshall Lux
Ombudsman
State Legislature
P.O. Box 94604
Lincoln, NE 68509
P: (402) 471-2035

NEVADA
Mr. Dale Liebherr
Chief Investigator
General Investigations Unit
100 North Carson Street
Carson City, NV 89701
P: (775) 684-1153
F: (775) 684-1108
E: dwliebhe@ag.state.nv.us

NEW HAMPSHIRE
Mr. Billy J. Hagy
Director
Governor's Commission on Disability, Client Assistance Program
57 Regional Drive
Concord, NH 03301
P: (603) 271-4175
F: (603) 271-2837
E: bhagy@nh.gov

NEW JERSEY
Mr. Ronald Chen
Public Advocate
Department of the Public Advocate
240 West State Street
P.O. Box 851
Trenton, NJ 08625
P: (609) 826-5090
F: (609) 984-4747

NEW MEXICO
Mr. Carlos Acosta
Ombudsman
Office of the Lieutenant Governor
State Capitol, Room 417
Santa Fe, NM 87503
P: (505) 827-3050
F: (505) 827-3057

NORTH CAROLINA
Ms. Linda Povlich
Assistant Secretary for Internet & Community Resources
Department of Health & Human Services
2001 Mail Service Center
Raleigh, NC 27699
P: (919) 733-4534
F: (919) 715-6645
E: linda.povlich@ncmail.net

NORTH DAKOTA
Ms. Monty Rauser
Director
Constituent Services
Office of the Governor
600 East Boulevard Avenue
Bismarck, ND 58505
P: (701) 328-2200
F: (701) 328-2205
E: governor@nd.gov

NORTHERN MARIANA ISLANDS
Mr. James Benedetto
Office of the Attorney General
P.O. Box 502452
Saipan, MP 96950
P: (670) 664-2333
F: (670) 664-2349
E: ombudsman@federal.com

OREGON
Ms. Liz Kiren
Citizens' Representative
Office of the Governor
900 Court Street, Northeast
Room 160
Salem, OR 97301
P: (503) 378-4582
F: (503) 378-4863

Ombudsman

PUERTO RICO
Mr. Carlos Lopez-Nieves
Ombudsman
Office of the Ombudsman
P.O. Box 41088
San Juan, PR 00940
P: (787) 724-7373
F: (787) 724-7386

SOUTH DAKOTA
Mr. Aaron Miller
Special Assistant To the Governor
Constituent Services
State Capitol
500 East Capitol Avenue
Pierre, SD 57501
P: (605) 773-3661
F: (605) 773-4711
E: aaron.miller@state.sd.us

U.S. VIRGIN ISLANDS
Mr. Julien Harley
St. John Administrator
Office of the Governor
P.O. Box 488
Cruz Bay
St. Johns, VI 00830
P: (340) 776-6484
F: (340) 776-6992

UTAH
Mr. Michael Mower
Legislative Liaison/Constituent Affairs
Office of the Governor - Constituent Services
Office of the Governor
East Office Building, Suite E-220
Salt Lake City, UT 84114
P: (801) 538-1000
F: (801) 538-1528

VERMONT
Ms. Joan Bagalio
Public Information Officer
Office of the Governor
109 State Street
Montpelier, VT 05609
P: (802) 828-3333
F: (802) 828-3339
E: joan.bagalio@state.vt.us

VIRGINIA
Mr. Marc D. Cheatham
Director
Office of Constituent Services
202 North Ninth Street, 1st Floor
P.O. Box 1475
Richmond, VA 23219
P: (804) 786-2211
F: (804) 371-6351
E: marc.cheatham@governor.virginia.gov

WASHINGTON
Hon. Brian Sonntag (D)
State Auditor
State Auditor's Office
P.O. Box 40021
Olympia, WA 98504
P: (360) 902-0360
F: (360) 753-0646
E: sonntagb@sao.wa.gov

Parks and Recreation

Manages the state's parks, historical sites and recreational areas.

ALABAMA
Mr. Mark Easterwood
Director
State Parks
64 North Union Street
Montgomery, AL 36130
P: (334) 242-3334
F: (334) 353-8629

ALASKA
Ms. Chris Degernes
Director
Division of Parks & Outdoor Recreation
Departmentof Natural Resources
550 West 7th Avenue, Suite 1380
Anchorage, AK 99501
P: (907) 269-8700
F: (907) 269-8907

ARIZONA
Mr. Kenneth E. Travous
Executive Director
State Parks
1300 West Washington
Phoenix, AZ 85007
P: (602) 542-4174
F: (602) 542-4188

ARKANSAS
Mr. Greg Butts
Director
State Parks
One Capitol Mall
Little Rock, AR 72201
P: (501) 682-7743
F: (501) 682-1364

CALIFORNIA
Ms. Ruth Coleman
Director
Department of Parks & Recreation
1416 Ninth Street, Room 1405
Sacramento, CA 95814
P: (916) 653-8380
F: (916) 657-3903

COLORADO
Mr. Lyle Laverty
Director
Division of Parks & Outdoor Recreation
1313 Sherman Street, Suite 618
Denver, CO 80203
P: (303) 866-2884
F: (303) 866-3206

CONNECTICUT
Ms. Pamela Aey Adams
Director
DEP, State Parks Division
79 Elm Street, 6th Floor
Hartford, CT 06106
P: (860) 424-3203
F: (860) 424-4070

DELAWARE
Mr. Charles A. Salkin
Director
Division of Parks & Recreation
89 Kings Highway
Dover, DE 19901
P: (302) 739-4401
F: (302) 739-3817

FLORIDA
Mr. Mike Bullock
Director
State Parks
3900 Commonwealth Boulevard
Mail Station 500
Tallahassee, FL 32399
P: (850) 245-3029
F: (850) 245-3041

GEORGIA
Ms. Becky Kelley
Director
State Parks & Historic Sites Division
2 Martin Luther King, Jr. Drive, SE
Suite 1352, East Tower
Atlanta, GA 30334
P: (404) 656-9448
F: (404) 651-5871

GUAM
Mr. Joseph Duenas
Director
Department of Parks & Recreation
542 North Marine Drive
Tamuning, GU 96913
P: (671) 646-3131
F: (671) 649-6178

HAWAII
Mr. Dan Quinn
Administrator
Division of State Parks
P.O. Box 621
Honolulu, HI 96809
P: (808) 587-0290
F: (808) 587-0311

IDAHO
Mr. Robert L. Meinen
Director
Department of Parks & Recreation
P.O. Box 83720
5657 Warm Springs Avenue
Boise, ID 83720
P: (208) 514-2251
F: (208) 334-5232
E: bmeinen@idpr.state.id.us

ILLINOIS
Mr. Tony Mayville
Director
Office of Land Management & Education
Department of Natural Resources
One Natural Resources Way
Springfield, IL 62702
P: (217) 782-6752
F: (217) 524-5612

INDIANA
Mr. Dan Bortner
Director
Division of State Parks & Reservoirs
402 West Washington Street
Room W-298
Indianapolis, IN 46204
P: (317) 232-4124
F: (317) 232-4132

IOWA
Mr. Kevin Szcodronski
Bureau Chief
Parks & Preserves Bureau
Department of Natural Resources
Wallace State Office Building
Des Moines, IA 50319
P: (515) 281-8674
F: (515) 281-6794

KANSAS
Mr. Jerold R. Hover
Director
Division of State Parks
512 Southeast 25th Avenue
Pratt, KS 67124
P: (620) 672-5911
F: (620) 672-2972

KENTUCKY
Mr. J. T. Miller
Commissioner
Department of Parks
500 Mero Street
Capitol Plaza Tower, 10th Floor
Frankfort, KY 40601
P: (502) 564-2172
E: jt.miller@ky.gov

LOUISIANA
Mr. Stuart Johnson
Assistant Secretary
Office of State Parks
P.O. Box 44426
Baton Rouge, LA 70804
P: (225) 342-8111
F: (225) 342-8107

MAINE
Mr. David Soucy
Director
Bureau of Parks & Lands
22 State House Station
Augusta, ME 04333
P: (207) 287-4960
F: (207) 287-3823

MARYLAND
Mr. Richard P. Barton
Superintendent
State Park Service
580 Taylor Avenue
Tawes State Office Building E-3
Annapolis, MD 21401
P: (410) 260-8186
F: (410) 260-8191

MASSACHUSETTS
Mr. Ken Foley
Acting Director
Department of Conservation & Recreation
Division of State Parks & Recreation
251 Causeway St. 9th Floor
Boston, MA 02114
P: (617) 626-4986
F: (617) 626-1351

MICHIGAN
Mr. Ronald Olson
Chief
Parks & Recreation Division
P.O. Box 30257
Lansing, MI 48909
P: (517) 335-4827
F: (517) 373-4625

MINNESOTA
Mr. Courtland Nelson
Director
Division of Parks & Recreation
500 Lafayette Road
St. Paul, MN 55155
P: (651) 259-5591
F: (651) 297-1157
E: courtland.nelson@state.mn.us

Parks and Recreation

MISSISSIPPI
Dr. Sam Polles
Executive Director
Wildlife, Fisheries & Parks
1505 Eastover Drive
Jackson, MS 39211
P: (601) 432-2001
F: (601) 432-2236

MISSOURI
Mr. Douglas K. Eiken
Director
Division of State Parks
P.O. Box 176
Jefferson City, MO 65101
P: (573) 751-9392
F: (573) 526-7716
E: Doug.Eiken@dnr.mo.gov

MONTANA
Mr. Joe Maurier
Parks Administrator
Parks Division
1420 East 6th Avenue
P.O. Box 200701
Helena, MT 59620
P: (406) 444-3750
F: (406) 444-4952

NEBRASKA
Mr. Roger L. Kuhn
Assistant Director
Parks Division
Game & Parks Commission
P.O. Box 30370
Lincoln, NE 68503
P: (402) 471-5512
F: (402) 471-5528

NEVADA
Mr. David K. Morrow
Administrator
Division of State Parks
901 South Stewart Street, 5th Floor
Carson City, NV 89701
P: (775) 684-2770
F: (775) 687-2777

NEW HAMPSHIRE
Ms. Allison McLean
Director
Division of Parks & Recreation
172 Pembroke Road
P.O. Box 1856
Concord, NH 03302
P: (603) 271-3556
F: (603) 271-3553
E: amclean@dred.state.nh.us

NEW JERSEY
Mr. Jose Fernandez
Director
Division of Parks & Forestry
P.O. Box 404
501 East State Street, 4th Floor
Trenton, NJ 08625
P: (609) 292-2733
F: (609) 984-0503

NEW MEXICO
Mr. Dave Simon
Director
State Park Division
1220 South Saint Francis Drive
P.O. Box 1147
Santa Fe, NM 87504
P: (505) 476-3357
F: (505) 476-3361

NEW YORK
Ms. Carol Ash
Acting Commissioner
Parks, Recreation & Historic Preservation
Agency Building 1
Empire State Plaza
Albany, NY 12238
P: (518) 474-0443

NORTH CAROLINA
Mr. Lewis Ledford
Director
Division of Parks & Recreation
1615 Mail Service Center
Raleigh, NC 27699
P: (919) 715-8710
F: (919) 715-3085

NORTH DAKOTA
Mr. Douglass A. Prchal
Director
Parks & Recreation Department
1600 East Century Avenue
Suite #3
Bismarck, ND 58503
P: (701) 328-5361
F: (701) 328-5363

NORTHERN MARIANA ISLANDS
Mr. Anthony T. Benavente
Director
Division of Parks & Grounds
Saipan, MP 96950

OHIO
Mr. Dan West
Chief
Division of Parks & Recreation
2045 Morse Road
Building C-3
Columbus, OH 43229
P: (614) 265-6511
F: (614) 261-8407

OKLAHOMA
Mr. Jeff Erwin
Director
State Parks, Resorts & Golf
P.O. Box 52002
Oklahoma City, OK 73152
P: (405) 521-3790
F: (405) 521-2428

OREGON
Mr. Tim Wood
State Historic Preservation Officer
Parks & Recreation Department
725 Summer Street, Northeast, Suite C
Salem, OR 97301
P: (503) 986-0718
F: (503) 986-0796
E: tim.wood@state.or.us

PENNSYLVANIA
Mr. John Norbeck
Director
Bureau of State Parks
P.O. Box 8551
Harrisburg, PA 17105
P: (717) 787-6640
F: (717) 787-8817

SOUTH CAROLINA
Mr. Phil Gaines
Director
State Park Service
1205 Pendleton Street, Suite 251
Columbia, SC 29201
P: (803) 734-0345
F: (803) 734-1017
E: pgaines@scprt.com

SOUTH DAKOTA
Mr. Doug Hofer
Director
Division of Parks & Recreation
Foss Building
523 East Capitol Avenue
Pierre, SD 57501
P: (605) 773-3391
F: (605) 773-6245
E: doug.hofer@state.sd.us

TEXAS
Mr. Walter Dabney
Division Director
State Parks
4200 Smith School Road
Austin, TX 78744
P: (512) 389-4966
F: (512) 389-4960

UTAH
Ms. Mary Tullius
Director
Division of State Parks & Recreation
1594 West North Temple, Suite 116
P.O. Box 146001
Salt Lake City, UT 89114
P: (801) 538-7336
F: (801) 538-7378
E: marytullius@utah.gov

VERMONT
Mr. Jonathan Wood
Commissioner
Department of Forests, Parks & Recreation
103 South Main Street
Waterbury, VT 05671
P: (802) 241-3670
F: (802) 244-1481
E: jonathan.wood@state.vt.us

VIRGINIA
Mr. Joe Elton
Director
Division of State Parks
Department of Conservation & Recreation
203 Governor Street, Suite 306
Richmond, VA 23219
P: (804) 786-4375
F: (804) 786-9294
E: joe.elton@dcr.virginia.gov

WASHINGTON
Mr. Rex Derr
Director
State Parks & Recreation Commission
P.O. Box 42650
Olympia, WA 98504
P: (360) 902-8501
F: (360) 902-8681

WEST VIRGINIA
Mr. Kenneth Caplinger
Acting Chief
Parks & Recreation
Capitol Complex, Building 3,
Room 713
Charleston, WV 25305
P: (304) 558-2764
F: (304) 558-0077

WISCONSIN
Mr. Bill Morrissey
Director
Bureau of Parks & Recreation
P.O. Box 7921
Madison, WI 53707
P: (608) 266-2185
F: (607) 267-7474

WYOMING
Mr. Patrick Green
Director
Division of State Parks &
Historic Sites
2301 Central Avenue
Barrett Building, 4th Floor
Cheyenne, WY 82002
P: (307) 777-6324
F: (307) 777-6005

Parole and Probation (Adult)

Determines whether paroles should be granted or revoked and supervises adult parolees and probationers.

For more information contact:

American Probation & Parole Association
Carl Wicklund
Executive Director
P.O. Box 11910
Lexington, KY 40578
P: (859) 244-8203
F: (859) 244-8001
cwicklund@csg.org
www.appa-net.org

ALABAMA
Mr. William C. Segrest
Executive Director
Board of Pardons & Paroles
500 Monroe Street
P.O. Box 302405
Montgomery, AL 36130
P: (334) 242-8700
F: (334) 242-1809
E: william.segrest@paroles.alabama.gov

ALASKA
Ms. Donna White
Director
Parole Board
Department of Corrections
4500 Diplomacy Drive, Suite 109
Anchorage, AK 99508
P: (907) 269-7367
F: (907) 269-7365

AMERICAN SAMOA
Mr. Sotoa Savali
Commissioner
Department of Public Safety
American Samoa Government
P.O. Box 3699
Pago Pago, AS 96799
P: (684) 633-1111
F: (684) 633-7296

ARIZONA
Mr. Duane Belcher Sr.
Chair & Executive Director
Board of Executive Clemency
1645 West Jefferson Street, Suite 101
Phoenix, AZ 85007
P: (602) 542-5656
F: (602) 542-5680

ARKANSAS
Mr. Dan Roberts
Deputy Director, Parole and Probation
Department of Community Correction
Two Union National Plaza
105 West Capitol
Little Rock, AR 72201
P: (501) 682-9510
F: (501) 682-9513

CALIFORNIA
Mr. James Tilton
Secretary
Department of Corrections & Rehabilitation
P.O. Box 942883
Sacramento, CA 95815
P: (916) 323-6001
F: (916) 442-2637
E: jtilton@asca.net

COLORADO
Ms. Jeaneene Miller
Director
Divisions of Adult Parole, Community Corrections & YOS
12157 West Cedar Drive
Lakewood, CO 80228
P: (303) 763-2420
E: jeaneene.miller@doc.state.co.us

CONNECTICUT
Mr. Robert Farrell
Chair
Adult Services
936 Silas Deane Highway
Wethersfield, CT 06109
P: (860) 721-2100

DELAWARE
Mr. Dwight F. Holden
Chairperson
Board of Parole
Carvel State Office Building
820 North French Street, 5th Floor
Wilmington, DE 19801
P: (302) 577-5233
F: (302) 577-3501

DISTRICT OF COLUMBIA
Mr. Paul A. Quander
Director
Court Services & Offender Supervision Agency
633 Indiana Avenue, Northwest
Washington, DC 20005
P: (202) 220-5300
F: (202) 220-5466

GEORGIA
Mr. Garland R. Hunt
Chair
Board of Pardons & Paroles
2 Martin Luther King Jr. Drive, SE
Suite 458, Balcony Level, East Tower
Atlanta, GA 30334
P: (404) 657-9350

GUAM
Mr. Edward A. Alvarez
Chief Probation Officer
Probation Services Division
Superior Court of Guam
120 West O'Brien Drive
Hagatna, GU 96910
P: (671) 475-3448
F: (671) 477-4944

HAWAII
Mr. Albert Tufono
Chair
Paroling Authority
1177 Alakea Street, Ground Floor
Honolulu, HI 96813
P: (808) 587-1310
F: (808) 587-1314

IDAHO
Ms. Olivia Craven
Executive Director
Commission of Pardons & Parole
P.O. Box 83720
Statehouse Mail
Boise, ID 83720
P: (208) 334-2520

ILLINOIS
Mr. Jesse Montgomery
Deputy Director of Parole
Parole Division
1301 Concordia Court
P.O. Box 19277
Springfield, IL 62794
P: (217) 522-2666

INDIANA
Mr. Raymond W. Rizzo
Chair
Parole Board
IGC-South, Room E321
302 West Washington Street
Indianapolis, IN 46204
P: (317) 232-5737
F: (317) 232-5738

IOWA
Ms. Jeanette Bucklew
Deputy Director, Offender Services
Department of Corrections
Capitol Annex
523 East 12th Street
Des Moines, IA 50319
P: (515) 242-5713

KANSAS
Mr. Paul Feleciano Jr.
Chair
Parole Board
900 Southwest Jackson, Room 452-S
Topeka, KS 66612
P: (785) 296-3469
F: (785) 296-7949

KENTUCKY
Mr. Ted Kuster
Chair
Parole Board
P.O. Box 2400
Frankfort, KY 40601
P: (502) 564-3620
F: (502) 564-8995
E: ted.kuster@ky.gov

LOUISIANA
Ms. Genie Powers
Director
Division of Probation & Parole
P.O. Box 94304
Baton Rouge, LA 70804
P: (225) 342-6609
F: (225) 342-3087

MAINE
Mr. Harold Doughty
Associate Commissioner for Community Corrections
Department of Corrections
111 State House Station
Augusta, ME 04333
P: (207) 287-2711

MARYLAND
Ms. Judith Sachwald
Director
Division of Parole & Probation
6776 Reisterstown Road, Suite 305
Baltimore, MD 21215
P: (410) 585-3525
F: (410) 764-4091
E: jsachwald@dpscs.state.md.us

MASSACHUSETTS
Ms. Maureen Walsh
Chair
Parole Board
P.O. Box 647
Medfield, MA 02052
P: (508) 242-8001
F: (508) 242-8200

MICHIGAN
Mr. John Rubitschun
Chair
Parole Board
P.O. Box 30003
Lansing, MI 48909
P: (517) 373-0270
F: (517) 335-0039

MINNESOTA
Ms. Joan Fabian
Commissioner
Department of Corrections
1450 Energy Park Drive, Suite 200
St. Paul, MN 55108
P: (651) 361-7226
F: (651) 642-0414
E: Joan.Fabian@state.mn.us

MISSISSIPPI
Mr. Glenn Hamilton
Chair
State Parole Board
201 West Capitol Street
Suite 800
Jackson, MS 39201
P: (601) 354-7716
F: (601) 354-7725
E: ghamilton@mdoc.state.ms.us

MISSOURI
Mr. William Seibert Jr.
Chairman
Division of the Board of Parole & Probation
1511 Christy Drive
Jefferson City, MO 65101
P: (573) 751-8488
F: (573) 751-8501
E: william.seibert@doc.mo.gov

MONTANA
Mr. Craig Thomas
Executive Director
Board of Pardons & Parole
300 Maryland Avenue
Deer Lodge, MT 59722
P: (406) 846-1404
F: (406) 846-3512

NEBRASKA
Ms. Esther Casmer
Chair
Board of Parole
P.O. Box 94661
State House Station
Lincoln, NE 68509
P: (402) 471-2156
F: (402) 471-2453

NEVADA
Mr. John Gonska
Chief
Department of Parole & Probation
215 East Bonanza Road
Las Vegas, NV 89101
P: (702) 486-3001
F: (702) 486-3040
E: jgonska@dps.state.nv.us

NEW HAMPSHIRE
Mr. Michael McAlister
Acting Director
Division of Field Services
Department of Corrections
P.O. Box 1806
Concord, NH 03302
P: (603) 271-5652

NEW JERSEY
Mr. Michael Dowling
Executive Director
State Parole Board
P.O. Box 862
Trenton, NJ 08625
P: (609) 292-4257
F: (609) 943-4769

NEW MEXICO
Ms. Charlene Knipfing
Director
Probation & Parole Division
4337 State Road 14
P.O. Box 27116
Santa Fe, NM 87502
P: (505) 827-8830
F: (505) 827-8679

NEW YORK
Mr. George Alexander
Chair
Division of Parole
97 Central Avenue
Albany, NY 12206
P: (518) 473-9548
F: (212) 345-6670

NORTH CAROLINA
Mr. Theodis Beck
Secretary
Department of Corrections
214 West Jones Street, MSC 4201
Shore Building
Raleigh, NC 27603
P: (919) 716-3700
F: (919) 716-3794
E: tbeck@doc.state.nc.us

NORTH DAKOTA
Mr. Warren Emmer
Director
Department of Corrections & Rehabilitation
Field Services Division
P.O. Box 5521
Bismarck, ND 58506
P: (701) 328-6190
F: (701) 328-6186
E: wemmer@nd.gov

NORTHERN MARIANA ISLANDS
Ms. Ursula L. Aldan
Chief Probation Officer
Superior Court
P.O. Box 500137
Saipan, MP 96950
P: (670) 236-9865
F: (670) 236-9866
E: ualdan@hotmail.com

Mr. Eugene Villagomez
Chief Parole Officer
Board of Parole
P.O. Box 502641
Saipan, MP 95950
P: (670) 664-3300
F: (670) 664-3310
E: ualdan@hotmail.com

OHIO
Mr. Harry Hageman
Deputy Director
Division of Parole & Community Services
1050 Freeway Drive, North
Columbus, OH 43229
P: (614) 752-1235
F: (614) 752-1251

OKLAHOMA
Mr. Terry Jenks
Executive Director
Pardon & Parole Board
120 North Robinson Avenue, Suite 900W
Oklahoma City, OK 73102
P: (405) 602-5863
F: (405) 602-6437
E: terry.jenks@ppb.state.ok.us

OREGON
Mr. Aaron East
Executive Director
Board of Parole & Post-Prison Supervision
2575 Center Street, Northeast
Suite 100
Salem, OR 97301
P: (503) 945-9009
F: (503) 373-7558

PENNSYLVANIA
Ms. Catherine C. McVey
Chair
Board of Probation & Parole
1101 South Front Street
Riverfront Office Center
Harrisburg, PA 17104
P: (717) 787-5699

PUERTO RICO
Mr. Enrique Garcia-Garcia
President
Parole Board
Minillas Station
P.O. Box 40945
San Juan, PR 00940
P: (787) 754-8115 Ext. 241
F: (787) 754-8181

RHODE ISLAND
Ms. Lisa S. Holley
Chair
Parole Board
Varley Building
40 Howard Street
Providence, RI 02920
P: (401) 462-0900
F: (401) 462-0915

SOUTH CAROLINA
Mr. Samuel B. Glover
Director
Department of Probation, Parole & Pardon Services
2221 Devine Street, Suite 600
P.O. Box 50666
Columbia, SC 29250
P: (803) 734-9220
F: (803) 734-9440

Parole and Probation (Adult)

SOUTH DAKOTA
Mr. Ed Ligtenberg
Executive Director
Board of Pardons and Paroles
P.O. Box 5911
Sioux Falls, SD 57117
P: (605) 367-5040
F: (605) 367-5025
E: ed.ligtenberg@state.sd.us

TENNESSEE
Mr. Charles M. Traughber
Chair
Board of Probation & Parole
404 James Robertson Parkway
Suite 1300
Nashville, TN 37243
P: (615) 741-1673
F: (615) 532-8098

TEXAS
Ms. Rissie L. Owens
Chair
Board of Pardons & Parole
P.O. Box 13084
Austin, TX 78711
P: (512) 936-6351
F: (512) 463-8120

U.S. VIRGIN ISLANDS
Hon. Verne A. Hodge
Presiding Judge
Territorial Court
P.O. Box 70
St. Thomas, VI 00804
P: (340) 774-6680
F: (340) 777-8187

Mr. Chesley Roebuck
Chair
Board of Parole
P.O. Box 2668
St. Thomas, VI 00802
P: (340) 778-2036
F: (340) 778-1637

UTAH
Mr. William Fowlke
Director
Division of Adult Probation & Parole
Department of Corrections
14717 South Minuteman Drive
Draoer, UT 84020
P: (801) 545-5908
F: (801) 565-5911
E: wfowlke@utah.gov

VERMONT
Ms. Linda Shambo
Executive Director
Parole Board
103 South Main Street
Waterbury, VT 05671
P: (802) 241-2294
F: (802) 241-3969
E: lindas@doc.state.vt.us

VIRGINIA
Ms. Helen H. Fahey
Chair
Parole Board
6900 Atmore Drive
Richmond, VA 23225
P: (804) 674-3081
F: (804) 674-3284
E: faheyhf@vadocs.state.va.us

WASHINGTON
Ms. Jeralita P. Costa
Chair
Indeterminate Sentence Review Board
4317 6th Avenue, Southeast
P.O. Box 40907
Olympia, WA 98504
P: (360) 493-9266
F: (360) 493-9287

WEST VIRGINIA
Mr. Dennis Foreman
Chair
Parole Board
112 California Avenue
Room 307
Charleston, WV 25305
P: (304) 558-6366

WISCONSIN
Mr. Alfonso Graham
Chair
Parole Commission
3099 East Washington Avenue
P.O. Box 7960
Madison, WI 53707
P: (608) 240-7280
F: (608) 240-7299

WYOMING
Mr. Patrick M. Anderson
Executive Director
Board of Parole
3120 Old Faithful, Suite 100
Cheyenne, WY 82002
P: (307) 777-5444
E: pander@state.wy.us

Personnel

Formulates, implements, and enforces personnel management policies and procedures for the state.

Information provided by:

National Association of State Personnel Executives
Leslie Scott
Association Manager
P.O. Box 11910
Lexington, KY 40578
P: (859) 244-8182
F: (859) 244-8001
lscott@csg.org
www.naspe.net

ALABAMA
Jackie Graham
Personnel Director
State Personnel Department
313 Folsom Administration Building
64 North Union Street, Suite 300
Montgomery, AL 36130
P: (334) 353-4076
F: (334) 353-3320
E: jgraham @personnel.state.al.us

ALASKA
Ms. Dianne Kiessel
Director
Division of Personnel
P.O. Box 110201
333 Willoughby Avenue, 10th Floor
Juneau, AK 99911
P: (907) 465-4429
F: (907) 465-3415
E: dianne_kiesel @admin.state.ak.us

AMERICAN SAMOA
Mr. Puni Penei Sewell
Director
Department of Human Resources
American Samoa Government
Pago Pago, AS 96799
P: (683) 644-4485
F: (684) 633-1139
E: sewells_l@hotmail.com

Eneliko Sofa'i
Deputy Director
American Samoa Government
Department of Human Resources
Pago Pago, AS 96799
P: (684) 633-4485
F: (684) 633-1139

ARIZONA
Ms. Kathy Peckardt
Human Resources Director
Department of Administration
100 North 15th Avenue
Suite 261
Phoenix, AZ 85007
P: (602) 542-8378
F: (602) 542-2796
E: kathy.peckardt @ad.state.az.us

ARKANSAS
Ms. Kay Barnhill
Interim State Personnel Administrator
Office of Personnel Administration
Department of Finance & Administration
1509 West 7th Street
Little Rock, AR 72201
P: (501) 682-1753
F: (501) 682-5104
E: kay.barnhill @dfa.state.ar.us

CALIFORNIA
Ms. Laura M. Aguilera
Deputy Executive Director
State Personnel Board
801 Capitol Mall
Sacramento, CA 95814
P: (916) 653-1028
F: (916) 653-8147
E: laguilera@spb.ca.gov

Ms. Suzanne M. Ambrose
Executive Officer
State Personnel Board
801 Capitol Mall
Sacramento, CA 95814
P: (916) 653-1028
F: (916) 653-8147
E: sambrose@spb.ca.gov

COLORADO
Mr. David Kaye
Director
Division of Human Resources
Department of Personnel & Administration
1313 Sherman Street, # 122
Denver, CO 80203
P: (303) 866-2393
F: (303) 866-2021
E: david.kaye@state.co.us

CONNECTICUT
Dr. Pamela L. Libby
Director
Human Resource Management
165 Capitol Avenue, Room 411
Hartford, CT 06106
P: (860) 713-5204
F: (860) 622-2965
E: pamela.libby @po.state.ct.us

DELAWARE
Mr. Joseph Hickey
Deputy Director
Human Resource Management
Carvel State Office Building, 10th Floor
820 North French Street
Wilmington, DE 19801
P: (302) 557-8977
F: (302) 557-3996
E: joseph.hickey @state.de.us

Dr. Dana Jefferson
Director
Human Resource Management
Carvel Office Building, 10th Floor
820 North French Street
Wilmington, DE 19801
P: (302) 577-8977
F: (302) 577-3996
E: dana.jefferson @state.de.us

DISTRICT OF COLUMBIA
Brender L. Gregory
Director
Department of Human Resources
One Judiciary Square
441 4th Street, NW, Suite 300S
Washington, DC 20001
P: (202) 671-1300
F: (202) 727-6827
E: brender.gregory@dc.gov

FLORIDA
Ms. Libby Farmer
Deputy Director
Department of Management Services
Division of Human Resource Management
4050 Esplanade Way
Tallahassee, FL 32399
P: (850) 921-7931
F: (850) 922-6642
E: libby.farmer @dms.myflorida.com

Ms. Sharon Larson
Director
Division of Human Resource Management
Department of Management Services
4050 Esplanade Way
Tallahassee, FL 32399
P: (850) 921-8275
F: (850) 922-6642
E: sharon.larson @dms.myflorida.com

GEORGIA
Mr. Frank Heiny
Deputy Commissioner
Georgia Merit System
2 Martin Luther King, Jr. Drive, SW
West Tower, Room 504
Atlanta, GA 30334
P: (404) 656-2705
F: (404) 656-5979
E: fheiny@gms.state.ga.us

Mr. Raymond E. Stevenson
Commissioner
Georgia Merit System
2 Martin Luther King, Jr. Drive, SW
West Tower, Room 504
Atlanta, GA 30334
P: (404) 656-2705
F: (404) 656-5979
E: steve.stevenson @gms.state.ga.us

GUAM
Ms. Rebecca T. Quintanilla
Deputy Director
Department of Administration
P.O. Box 884
Agana, GU 96932
P: (671) 475-1250
F: (671) 477-6788

Mr. Michael Reidy
Director
Department of Administration
P.O. Box 884
Agana, GU 96932
P: (671) 475-1250
F: (671) 477-6788
E: mreidy@ns.gov.gu

Personnel

HAWAII
Ms. Cindy S. Inouye
Deputy Director
Department of Human Resource Development
State Office Tower
235 South Beretania Street, 14th Floor
Honolulu, HI 96813
P: (808) 587-1110
F: (808) 587-1106
E: cindy.s.inouye@hawaii.gov

Ms. Marie C. Laderta
Director
Department of Human Resources Development
235 South Beretania Street, 14th Floor
State Office Tower
Honolulu, HI 96813
P: (808) 587-1100
F: (808) 587-1106
E: marie.c.laderta@hawaii.gov

IDAHO
Ms. Judie Wright
Bureau Chief
Division of Financial Management
700 West Jefferson, Room 122
P.O. Box 83720
Boise, ID 83720
P: (208) 854-3054
E: jwright@dfm.idaho.gov

INDIANA
Mr. Jack Borgerding
Deputy Director
State Personnel Department
401 West Washington Street
Indianapolis, IN 46204
P: (317) 232-3065
E: jborgerding@spd.in.gov

Ms. Debra Minott
Director
Dept. of Personnel
402 Washington Street
Indianapolis, IN 46204
P: (317) 234-3830
F: (317) 232-3089
E: dminott@spd.in.gov

IOWA
Ms. Nancy Berggren
Chief Operating Officer
Human Resources Enterprise, Department of Administrative Services
400 East 14th Street
Grimes State Office Building
Des Moines, IA 50319
P: (515) 281-5064
F: (515) 242-6450
E: nancy.berggren@iowa.gov

KANSAS
Mr. George Vega
Director
Department of Administration
Division of Personnel Services
900 Southwest Jackson, Room 951-S
Topeka, KS 66612
P: (785) 296-2541
F: (785) 296-3655
E: george.vega@da.state.ks.us

KENTUCKY
Mr. Brian Crall
Secretary
Personnel Cabinet
200 Fair Oaks Lane, Suite 516
Frankfort, KY 40601
P: (502) 564-7430
E: brian.crall@ky.gov

Mr. Wayne Harman
Deputy Secretary
Personnel Cabinet
200 Fair Oaks Lane, Suite 516
Frankfort, KY 40601
P: (502) 564-7430
F: (502) 564-7603
E: waynea.harman@ky.gov

LOUISIANA
Mr. Steve J. Hebert
Administrator
Human Resource Division
Department of State Civil Service
P.O. Box 94111
Baton Rouge, LA 70804
P: (225) 342-8297
F: (225) 342-6074
E: steve.hebert@la.gov

Ms. Jean Jones
Deputy Director
Department of State Civil Service
P.O. Box 94111
Baton Rouge, LA 70804
P: (225) 342-8540
F: (225) 342-2386
E: jean.jones@la.gov

Ms. Anne Soileau
Director
Department of State Civil Service
P.O. Box 94111
Capitol Station
Baton Rouge, LA 70804
P: (225) 342-8069
F: (225) 342-8058
E: asoileau@dscs.state.la.us

MAINE
Ms. Alicia Kellogg
Director
Bureau of Human Resources
114 State House Station
220 Capitol Street
Augusta, ME 04330
P: (207) 287-6780
E: alicia.kellogg@maine.gov

Mr. Philip Schlegel
Merit System Coordinator
Bureau of Human Resources
State House Station 4
Cross Office Building
Augusta, ME 04333
P: (207) 287-4427
F: (207) 287-4414
E: philip.j.schlegel@state.me.us

MARYLAND
Ms. Cynthia Kollner
Acting Executive Director
Department of Budget & Management
Office of Personnel Services & Benefits
301 West Preston Street, Room 609
Baltimore, MD 21201
P: (410) 767-4716
F: (410) 333-5262
E: ckollner@dbm.state.md.us

MASSACHUSETTS
Mr. Paul Dietl
Interim Director
Human Resources Division
1 Ashburton Palce, Room 301
Boston, MA 02108
P: (617) 878-9705
F: (617) 727-1175
E: paul.d.dietl@massmail.state.ma.us

MICHIGAN
Mr. James D. Farrell
Director
Department of Civil Service
400 South Pine Street
P.O. Box 30002
Lansing, MI 48909
P: (517) 373-3020
F: (517) 373-3103
E: farrellj1@michigan.gov

Ms. Janet McClelland
Deputy Director
Department of Civil Service
400 South Pine Street
P.O. Box 30002
Lansing, MI 48909
P: (517) 373-9276
F: (517) 373-3103
E: mcclellandj@michigan.gov

MINNESOTA
Ms. Patricia Anderson
Commissioner
Department of Employee Relations
200 Centennial Building
658 Cedar Street
St. Paul, MN 55155
P: (651) 296-3095
F: (651) 296-1990
E: patricia.anderson@state.mn.us

MISSISSIPPI
Mr. Hollis Baugh
Assistant Personnel Director
Recruiting & Selection
301 North Lamar Street
Jackson, MS 39201
P: (601) 359-2749
F: (601) 355-2729
E: hbaugh@spb.state.ms.us

Mr. Frederick Matthes
Assistant Personnel Director
Classification & Compensation
301 North Lamar Street
Jackson, MS 39201
P: (601) 359-2769
F: (601) 359-2729
E: fmatthes@spb.state.ms.us

Mr. John Mulholland
Deputy Director
State Personnel Board
301 North Lamar Street, Suite 100
Jackson, MS 39201
P: (601) 359-2702
F: (601) 359-2729
E: jmulholl@spb.state.ms.us

Mr. Donald R. Thompson
Director
State Personnel Board
301 North Lamar Street, Suite 100
Jackson, MS 39201
P: (601) 359-2702
F: (601) 359-2729
E: dthompson@spb.state.ms.us

MISSOURI
Mr. Chester White
Director
Office of Administration
Division of Personnel
P.O. Box 388
Jefferson City, MO 65102
P: (573) 751-3053
F: (573) 751-8641
E: chester.white@oa.mo.gov

MONTANA
Mr. Randy Morris
Administrator
Division of Personnel
P.O. Box 200127
Helena, MT 59620
P: (406) 444-3894
F: (406) 444-0703
E: ramorris@mt.gov

Ms. Paula Stoll
Chief, Labor Relations Bureau
Division of Personnel
P.O. Box 200127
Mitchell Building, Room 130
Helena, MT 59620
P: (406) 444-3819
F: (406) 444-0544
E: pstoll@state.mt.us

NEBRASKA
Mr. Mike McCrory
Director
Department of Administrative Services
State Personnel
P.O. Box 94905
Lincoln, NE 68509
P: (409) 471-2833
F: (402) 471-3754
E: mmccrory@notes.state.ne.us

Mr. William Wood
Labor Relations Administrator
DAS Employee Relations
301 Centennial Mall, South
P.O. Box 95061
Lincoln, NE 68509
P: (402) 471-4106
F: (402) 471-3394
E: wwood@notes.state.ne.us

NEVADA
Mr. Mark Anastas
Interim Director
Department of Personnel
209 East Musser Street, Room 101
Carson City, NV 89710
P: (775) 684-0131
F: (775) 684-0124
E: manastas@govmail.state.nv.us

Mr. Peter Long
Chief Personnel Executive
Field Services Division
Department of Personnel
209 East Musser Street, Room 101
Carson City, NV 89701
P: (775) 684-0121
F: (775) 684-0122
E: plong@govmail.state.nv.us

NEW HAMPSHIRE
Ms. Karen Levchuk
Director
Division of Personnel
25 Capitol Street
Concord, NH 03301
P: (603) 271-1420
E: karen.levchuk@nh.gov

Ms. Sara Willingham
Manager
Employee Relations
Division of Personnel
25 Capitol Street
Concord, NH 03301
P: (603) 271-3359
F: (603) 271-1422
E: swillin@admin.state.nh.us

NEW JERSEY
Mr. Rolando Torres Jr.
Commissioner
Department of Personnel
44 South Clinton Avenue
Trenton, NJ 08625
P: (609) 292-4145
F: (609) 984-3631
E: rolando.torres@dop.state.nj.us

NEW MEXICO
Sandra Perez
Director
Office of State Personnel
2600 Cerrillos Road
Santa Fe, NM 87505
P: (505) 476-7751
F: (505) 476-7806
E: sandra.perez@state.nm.us

NEW YORK
Ms. Nancy Groenwegen
Commissioner
Department of Civil Service
State Office Campus, Building 1
Albany, NY 12239
P: (518) 457-6212
F: (518) 457-7547

NORTH CAROLINA
Mr. Carl Goodwin
Office of Personnel
116 West Jones Street
Raleigh, NC 27603
P: (919) 733-7108
F: (919) 715-9750
E: carl.goodwin@ncosp.net

Mr. Thomas Wright
Director
Office of Personnel
116 West Jones Street
Raleigh, NC 27603
P: (919) 733-7108
F: (919) 715-9750
E: thomas.wright@ncmail.net

NORTH DAKOTA
Mr. Ken Purdy
Compensation Manager
Human Resource Management Services Division
State Capitol, 14th Floor
600 East Boulevard Avenue
Bismarck, ND 58505
P: (701) 328-4739
F: (701) 328-1475
E: kpurdy@state.nd.us

Ms. Laurie Sterioti-Hammeren
Director
Human Resource Management Services Division
State Capitol, 14th Floor
600 East Boulevard Avenue, Dept. 113
Bismarck, ND 58505
P: (701) 328-4735
F: (701) 328-1475
E: lhammeren@state.nd.us

OHIO
Ms. Nancy Kelly
Acting Deputy Director
Department of Administrative Services
Human Resources Division
100 East Broad Street, 15th Floor
Columbus, OH 43266
P: (614) 466-3455
F: (614) 728-2785
E: brenda.oyer@das.state.oh.us

OKLAHOMA
Mr. Hank Batty
Deputy Administrator for Programs
Office of Personnel Management
2101 North Lincoln Boulevard, Room G-80
Oklahoma City, OK 73105
P: (405) 521-6303
F: (405) 522-0694
E: hank.batty@opm.state.ok.us

Mr. Oscar B. Jackson Jr.
Cabinet Secretary for Administration & Human Resources
Office of Personnel Management
2101 North Lincoln Boulevard Room G-80
Oklahoma City, OK 73105
P: (405) 521-6301
F: (405) 522-0694
E: oscar.jackson@opm.state.ok.us

OREGON
Ms. Denise L. Hall
Manager
Human Resource Systems, Services & Audits
Human Resource Services Division
155 Cottage Street, Northeast, U-30
Salem, OR 97301
P: (503) 373-7320
F: (503) 378-5734
E: denise.l.hall@state.or.us

Personnel

Ms. Susan Wilson
Administrator
Human Resource Services Division
Department of Administrative Services
155 Cottage Street, Northeast
Salem, OR 97310
P: (503) 378-3020
F: (503) 373-7684
E: susan.wilson@state.or.us

PENNSYLVANIA
Mr. Ralph Winters
Director
Bureau of Classification, Compensation & Workforce Support
Office of Adminsitration
517 Finance Building
Harrisburg, PA 17120
P: (717) 787-5966
F: (717) 783-4429
E: rwinters@state.pa.us

Ms. Naomi Wyatt
Deputy Secretary
Human Resources & Management
Governor's Office of Administration
517 Finance Buidling
Harrisburg, PA 17110
P: (717) 787-8191
F: (717) 783-4429

PUERTO RICO
Ms. Marta Beltran
Administrator
Human Resources, Administrative Office
Ponce De Leon Avenue, 1507
P.O. Box 8476
San Juan, PR 00910
P: (787) 706-5967
F: (787) 706-5697

RHODE ISLAND
Mr. Anthony A. Bucci
Personnel Administrator
Office of Personnel Administration
1 Capitol Hill
Providence, RI 02908
P: (401) 222-2160
F: (401) 222-6391
E: anthonyb@hr.ri.gov

SOUTH CAROLINA
Mr. Chris Byrd
Assistant Director
Budget & Control Board
The Capitol Complex
1201 Main Street, Suite 800
Columbia, SC 29201
P: (803) 737-0900
F: (803) 737-0968
E: cbyrd@ohr.sc.gov

Ms. Joye Lang
Assistant Director
Budget & Control Board
Office of Human Resources
1401 Senate Street
Columbia, SC 29201
P: (803) 734-9080
F: (803) 734-9098
E: jlang@ohr.sc.gov

Mr. Samuel Wilkins
Director
Office of Human Resources
Budget & Control Board
1201 Main Street, Suite 1000
Columbia, SC 29201
P: (803) 737-0904
F: (803) 737-3529
E: swilkins@ohr.sc.gov

SOUTH DAKOTA
Ms. Sandra Jorgensen
Director
Compensation, Bureau of Personnel
PMB 0141-1
500 East Capitol
Pierre, SD 57501
P: (605) 773-4918
F: (605) 773-4344
E: sandy.jorgensen@state.sd.us

TENNESSEE
Ms. Deborah E. Story
Commissioner
Department of Personnel
505 Deaderick Street
James K. Polk Building, 2nd Floor
Nashville, TN 37243
P: (615) 741-2958
E: deborah.story@state.tn.us

U.S. VIRGIN ISLANDS
Mr. Milton E. Potter
Assistant Director
Division of Personnel
GERS Complex, 3rd Floor
48B-50C Kronprinsdens Gade
St. Thomas, VI 00820
P: (340) 774-8588
F: (340) 714-5040
E: rodriquez41@yahoo.com

Mr. Kevin Rodriquez
Assistant Director
Division of Personnel
GERS Complex, 3rd Floor
48B-50C Kronprinsdens Gade
St. Thomas, VI 00820
P: (340) 744-8588
F: (340) 714-5040
E: rodriquez41@yahoo.com

UTAH
Mr. Jeff Herring
Executive Director
Department of Human Resource Management
State Office Building, Room 2120
Salt Lake City, UT 84114
P: (801) 538-3403
F: (801) 538-3081
E: jherring@utah.gov

VERMONT
Ms. Harriet Johnson
Assistant To the Commissioner
Department of Human Resources
110 State Street, Drawer 20
Montpelier, VT 05620
P: (802) 828-3491
F: (802) 828-3409
E: harriet.johnson@state.vt.us

Ms. Linda P. McIntire
Commissioner
Department of Human Resources
110 State Street, Drawer 20
Montpelier, VT 05620
P: (802) 828-3491
F: (802) 828-3409
E: linda.mcintire@per.state.vt.us

VIRGINIA
Mrs. Sara Redding Wilson
Director
Human Resource Management
101 North 14th Street, 12th Floor
Richmond, VA 23219
P: (804) 225-2237
F: (804) 371-7401
E: sara.wilson@dhrm.virginia.gov

WASHINGTON
Ms. Eva Santos
Director
Department of Personnel
P.O. Box 47500
Olympia, WA 98504
P: (360) 664-6350
F: (360) 753-1003
E: evas@dop.wa.gov

WEST VIRGINIA
Mr. Lowell "Tim" Basford
Assistant Director
Classification & Compensation
State Capitol Complex
Building 6, Room 404
Charleston, WV 25305
P: (304) 558-3950
F: (304) 558-1587
E: tbasford@wvadmin.gov

Ms. Tari Crouse
Assistant Director
Division of Personnel
Department of Administration
1900 Kanawha Boulevard, East
Charleston, WV 25305
P: (304) 558-3950
F: (304) 558-1587
E: tcrouse@wvadmin.gov

Ms. Billie Jo Streyle-Anderson
Director
Division of Personnel
1900 Kanawha Boulevard, East
Building 6, Room 416
Charleston, WV 25305
P: (304) 558-3950
F: (304) 558-1399
E: bstreyleanderson@wvadmin.gov

Mr. James D. Wells
Assistant Director
Division of Personnel
1900 Kanawha Boulevard, East
Building 6, Room 416
Charleston, WV 25305
P: (304) 558-3950
F: (304) 558-1587
E: jwells@wvadmin.gov

WISCONSIN

Ms. Patricia M. Almond
Division Administrator
Office of State Employment Relations
101 East Wilson Street
P.O. Box 7855
Madison, WI 53707
P: (608) 266-1499
F: (608) 267-1000
E: patricia.almond@wisconsin.gov

Ms. Jennifer Donnelly
Director
Office of State Employment Relations
101 East Wilson Street
P.O. Box 7855
Madison, WI 53707
P: (608) 266-9820
F: (608) 267-1014
E: jennifer.donnelly@wisconsin.gov

Yer Vang
Executive Assistant
Office of State Employment Relations
101 East Wilson Street, 4th Floor
P.O. Box 7855
Madison, WI 53707
P: (608) 266-9820
F: (608) 267-1014
E: yer.vang@wisconsin.gov

WYOMING

Mr. Dean Fausset
Selection, Recruitment & Training Manager
Administration & Information
Human Resources Division
Emerson Building, 2001 Capitol Avenue
Cheyenne, WY 82001
P: (307) 777-6738
F: (307) 777-6562
E: dfauss@state.wy.us

Mr. Brian Foster
Administrator
Human Resources Division
Administration & Information
Emerson Building, 2001 Capitol Avenue
Cheyenne, WY 82001
P: (307) 777-6713
F: (307) 777-6562
E: bfoste2@state.wy.us

Ms. Kate Selby
Classification & Compensation Manager
Administration & Information
Human Resources Division
2001 Capitol Avenue, Emerson Building
Cheyenne, WY 82001
P: (307) 777-6728
F: (307) 777-6562
E: kselby@state.wy.us

Port Authority

Agency housed under the department of transportation that oversees coastal transportation, international transportation, shipping, and all other acts involving state ports.

ALABAMA
Mr. James K. Lyons
Director/CEO
State Docks
P.O. Box 1588
Mobile, AL 36633
P: (251) 441-7107
E: jlyons@asdd.com

AMERICAN SAMOA
Mr. Fofo Tuitele
Acting Director
Department of Port Administration
American Samoa Government
Pago Pago, AS 96799
P: (684) 633-4251
F: (684) 633-5281

GEORGIA
Mr. Doug Marchand
Executive Director
Ports Authority
P.O. Box 2406
Savannah, GA 31402
P: (912) 964-3874
F: (912) 964-3921
E: dmarchand@gaports.com

HAWAII
Dr. Glenn M. Okimoto
Harbors Administrator
Harbors Division
79 South Nimitz Highway Rm. 310
Honolulu, HI 96813
P: (808) 587-1927

INDIANA
Mr. Rich Cooper
Executive Director
Port Commission
150 West Market Street, Room 100
Indianapolis, IN 46204
P: (317) 232-9202

KANSAS
Ms. Debra L. Miller
Secretary of Transportation
Department of Transportation
700 Southwest Harrison Street
Topeka, KS 66612
P: (785) 296-3461
F: (785) 296-1095

LOUISIANA
Mr. Edmond J. Preau
Assistant Secretary
Office of Public Works & Intermodal Transportation
Dept. of Transportation & Development
P.O. Box 94245
Baton Rouge, LA 70804
P: (225) 274-4106
F: (225) 274-4110
E: epreau@dotd.louisiana.gov

MAINE
Mr. Brian Nutter
Director
Port Authority
16 State House Station
Augusta, ME 04333
P: (207) 624-3564

MARYLAND
Mr. F. Brooks Royster
Executive Director
Port Administration
401 Pratt Street
Baltimore, MD 21202
P: (410) 385-4401
E: broyster@mdot.state.md.us

MASSACHUSETTS
Mr. Thomas J. Kinton Jr.
Director
Port Authority
One Harborside Drive, Suite 200S
East Boston, MA 02128
P: (617) 568-5000

MINNESOTA
Hon. Carol L. Molnau (R)
Lieutenant Governor & Commissioner, Department of Transportation
Department of Transportation
395 John Ireland Blvd. Room 423
St. Paul, MN 55155
P: (651) 207-2930
F: (651) 296-3587

MISSISSIPPI
Mr. Mark L. McAndrews
Port Director
Pascagoula Port Authority
P.O. Box 70
Pascagoula, MS 39568
P: (228) 762-4041
F: (228) 762-7476
E: mmcandrews@portofpascagoula.com

NEW HAMPSHIRE
Mr. Geno Marconi
Director
Division of Ports & Harbors
P.O. Box 369
Portsmouth, NH 03802
P: (603) 436-8500
F: (603) 436-2780

NEW YORK
Mr. Anthony Shorris
Executive Director
The Port Authority
225 Park Avenue South
New York, NY 10003
P: (212) 435-7241
F: (518) 402-9016

NORTH CAROLINA
Mr. Thomas Eagar
Executive Director
State Ports Authority
2202 Burnett Boulevard
P.O. Box 9002
Wilmington, NC 28401
P: (910) 343-6232
F: (910) 343-6237

NORTHERN MARIANA ISLANDS
Mr. Lee Cabrera
Executive Director
Commonwealth Ports Authority
P.O. Box 501055
Saipan, MP 96950
P: (670) 664-3500
F: (670) 234-5962

OHIO
Mr. James G. Beasley
Director
Department of Transportation
1980 West Broad Street
Columbus, OH 43223
P: (614) 466-8990

OKLAHOMA
Mr. Bob Portiss
Director
Port of Catoosa
5350 Cimarron Road
Catoosa, OK 74015
P: (918) 266-2291
F: (918) 266-7678
E: bob@tulsaport.com

Mr. Scott Robinson
Director
Port of Muskogee
4901 Harold Scoggins Drive
Muskogee, OK 74403
P: (918) 682-7886
F: (918) 683-4811
E: Scott@muskogeeport.com

SOUTH CAROLINA
Mr. Bernard S. Groseclose Jr.
President and CEO
Ports Authority
176 Concord Street
P.O. Box 22287
Charleston, SC 29413
P: (843) 577-8600

U.S. VIRGIN ISLANDS
Mr. Darlan Brin
Executive Director
Port Authority
P.O. Box 301707
St. Thomas, VI 00803
P: (340) 774-1629
F: (340) 774-0025
E: dbrin@viport.com

UTAH
Mr. Richard Clasby
Director, Motor Carriers
Department of Transportation - Ports of Entry
4501 South 2700 West
P.O. Box 148240
Salt Lake City, UT 84119
P: (801) 965-4156
F: (801) 965-4847
E: rclasby@utah.gov

VIRGINIA
Mr. Jerry L. Bridges
Executive Director
Port Authority
600 World Trade Center
Norfolk, VA 23510
P: (757) 683-2103
F: (757) 683-8500
E: jbridges@portofvirginia.com

WISCONSIN
Mr. Ron Adams
Director
Railroads & Harbors Bureau
P.O. Box 7914
Madison, WI 53707
P: (608) 266-2941
F: (608) 267-3567

Public Defender

Represents indigent criminal defendants who desire to appeal their convictions to the state's intermediate appellate court or court of last resort.

ALASKA
Mr. Quinlan Steiner
Director
Public Defender Agency
Department of Administration
900 West 5th Avenue, Suite 200
Anchorage, AK 99501
P: (907) 334-4400
F: (907) 269-5476

ARKANSAS
Ms. Didi Sallings
Director
Public Defender Commission
101 East Capitol, Suite 201
Little Rock, AR 72201
P: (501) 682-9070
F: (501) 682-9073

CALIFORNIA
Mr. Michael Hersek
State Public Defender
Office of the State Public Defender
221 Main Street, 10th Floor
San Francisco, CA 94105
P: (415) 904-5600
F: (415) 904-5635

COLORADO
Mr. Douglas Wilson
State Public Defender
Office of the State Public Defender
110 16th Street
Petroleum Building, Suite 800
Denver, CO 80202
P: (303) 620-4888
F: (303) 620-4931

CONNECTICUT
Mr. Gerard Smyth
Chief Public Defender
Division of Public Services
One Hartford Square West
Hartford, CT 06106
P: (860) 509-6429

DELAWARE
Mr. Lawrence Sullivan
Public Defender
Public Defender's Office
New Castle County Courthouse
500 North King Street
Wilmington, DE 19801
P: (302) 577-5200
F: (302) 577-3995

DISTRICT OF COLUMBIA
Mr. Avis Buchanan
Director
Public Defender Service
633 Indiana Avenue, Northwest
Washington, DC 20004
P: (202) 628-1200
F: (202) 824-2423

FLORIDA
Mr. Sheldon Gusky
Executive Director
Public Defender Association
P.O. Box 11057
Tallahassee, FL 32302
P: (850) 488-6850
F: (850) 488-4720
E: sgusky@st.flpda.org

GEORGIA
Hon. Thurbert E. Baker (D)
Attorney General
Office of the Attorney General
40 Capitol Square, SW
Atlanta, GA 30334
P: (404) 656-3300

GUAM
Ms. Kathleen Maher
Director
Public Defenders Service Commission
200 Judicial Center Annex
110 West O'Brien Drive
Hagatna, GU 96910
P: (671) 475-3100
F: (671) 477-5844

HAWAII
Mr. John M. Tonaki
Public Defender
Office of the Public Defender
1130 North Nimitz Highway
Suite A-254
Honolulu, HI 96817
P: (808) 586-2200
F: (808) 586-2222

IDAHO
Ms. Molly J. Huskey
State Appellate Public Defender
Public Defendents Office
3647 Lake Harbor Lane
Boise, ID 83703
P: (208) 334-2712
F: (208) 334-2985
E: mhusky@sapd.state.id.us

ILLINOIS
Mr. Ted Gottfried
State Appellate Defender
Office of the State Appellate Defender
400 South 9th Street, Suite 201
Springfield, IL 62701
P: (217) 782-7203
F: (217) 782-5385

INDIANA
Ms. Susan K. Carpenter
Public Defender
Office of the State Public Defender
1 North Capitol Avenue
8th Floor
Indianapolis, IN 46204
P: (317) 232-2475
F: (317) 232-2307
E: spd@iquest.net

IOWA
Mr. Tom Becker
State Public Defender
State Public Defender Office
Lucas Building, 4th Floor
321 East 12th Street
Des Moines, IA 50319
P: (515) 242-6158
F: (515) 281-7289

KANSAS
Ms. Patricia A. Scalia
Executive Director
Board of Indigents' Defense Services
701 Southwest Jackson Street, 3rd Floor
Topeka, KS 66603
P: (785) 296-1833
F: (785) 296-7418

KENTUCKY
Mr. Erwin Lewis
Executive Director
Department of Public Advocacy
100 Fair Oaks Lane, Suite 302
Frankfort, KY 40601
P: (502) 564-8006
F: (502) 564-7890
E: ernie.lewis@ky.gov

LOUISIANA
Mr. Edward Greenlee
Director
Indigent Defense Assistance Board
1010 Common Street, Suite 2710
New Orleans, LA 70112
P: (504) 568-8530
F: (504) 568-8499
E: egreenlee@lidab.com

MARYLAND
Ms. Nancy Forster
Public Defender
Office of the State Public Defender
William Donald Schefer Tower
6 St. Paul Street, Suite 1400
Baltimore, MD 21202
P: (410) 767-8479
F: (410) 333-8496

MASSACHUSETTS
Mr. Andrew Silverman
Deputy Chief Counsel
Public Defender Division
Committee for Public Counsel Services
44 Bromfield Street
Boston, MA 02108
P: (617) 482-6212
F: (617) 988-8495

MICHIGAN
Mr. James Neuhard
Director
State Appellate Defender Office
3300 Panapscot Building
645 Griswald
Detroit, MI 48226
P: (313) 256-9833

MINNESOTA
Mr. John Stuart
State Public Defender
Office of the State Public Defender
331 Second Avenue South, Suite 900
Minneapolis, MN 55401
P: (612) 373-2728
E: John.Stuart@pubdef.state.mn.us

MISSOURI
Mr. J. Marty Robinson
State Public Defender
State Public Defender System
3402 Buttonwood Drive
Columbia, MO 65201
P: (573) 882-9855
F: (573) 882-9740
E: public.defender@mspd.mo.gov

Public Defender

MONTANA
Ms. Randi Hood
Chief Public Defender
Office of the State Public Defender
44 West Park Street
Butte, MT 59701
P: (406) 496-6082
F: (406) 496-6080

NEBRASKA
Mr. James Mowbray
Chief Counsel
Commission on Public Advocacy
P.O. Box 98932
Lincoln, NE 68509
P: (402) 471-7774

NEVADA
Mr. Steven G. McGuire
State Public Defender
Office of the Public Defender
511 East Robinson Street, Suite 1
Carson City, NV 89701
P: (775) 687-4880 EXT. 230
F: (775) 687-4993
E: smcguire@govmail.state.nv.us

NEW HAMPSHIRE
Mr. Christopher Keating
Executive Director
Public Defender Program
117 North State Street
Concord, NH 03301
P: (603) 224-1236
F: (603) 226-4299
E: ckeating@nhpd.org

NEW JERSEY
Ms. Yvonne Smith Segars
Public Defender
Office of the Public Defender
25 Market Street, 1st Floor
N-Wing
P.O. Box 850
Trenton, NJ 08625
P: (609) 292-7087
F: (609) 777-1795

NEW MEXICO
Mr. John Bigelow
Chief Public Defender
Public Defender Department
301 North Guadalupe Street, Suite 101
Santa Fe, NM 87501
P: (505) 827-3931
F: (505) 827-3999

NORTH CAROLINA
Mr. Malcolm Ray Hunter
Executive Director
Office of Indigent Defense Services
123 West Main Street, Suite 400
Durham, NC 27701
P: (919) 560-3380
F: (919) 560-3332
E: malcolm.r.hunter@nccourts.org

NORTH DAKOTA
Hon. Wayne Stenehjem (R)
Attorney General
Office of the Attorney General
State Capitol
600 East Boulevard Avenue, Dept. 125
Bismarck, ND 58505
P: (701) 328-2210
F: (701) 328-2226
E: ndag@nd.gov

NORTHERN MARIANA ISLANDS
Ms. Elisa Long
Office of the Public Defender
Caller Box 10007, Capitol Hill
Saipan, MP 96950
P: (670) 234-2421
F: (670) 234-1009

OHIO
Mr. David H. Bodiker
Public Defender
Office of the Public Defender
8 East Long Street, 11th Floor
Columbus, OH 43215
P: (614) 466-5394
F: (614) 644-9972

OKLAHOMA
Mr. James D. Bednar
Executive Director
Indigent Defense System
P.O. Box 926
Norman, OK 73070
P: (405) 801-2601
F: (405) 801-2649

OREGON
Mr. David Groom
Public Defender
Office of the Public Defender
1320 Capitol Street, Northeast #200
Salem, OR 97303
P: (503) 378-3349
F: (503) 375-9701
E: webmaster@opd.state.or.us

RHODE ISLAND
Mr. John Hardiman
Public Defender
Office of the Public Defender
160 Pine Street
Providence, RI 02903
P: (401) 222-3492

SOUTH CAROLINA
Mr. Daniel T. Stacey
Chief Attorney
Office of Appellate Defense
1122 Lady Street, Suite 940
Columbia, SC 29201
P: (803) 734-1330

SOUTH DAKOTA
Hon. Larry Long (R)
Attorney General
Office of the Attorney General
1302 East Highway 14, Suite 1
Pierre, SD 57501
P: (605) 773-3215
F: (605) 773-4106
E: larry.long@state.sd.us

U.S. VIRGIN ISLANDS
Mr. Thurston McKelvin
Federal Public Defender
Office of the Public Defender
P.O. Box 3450
Christiansted
St. Croix, VI 00820
P: (340) 773-3585
F: (340) 773-3742

VERMONT
Mr. Mathew Valerio
Defender General
Office of the Defender General
14-16 Baldwin Street
Montpelier, VT 05620
P: (802) 828-3168
F: (802) 828-3163
E: mvalerio@defgen.state.vt.us

VIRGINIA
Mr. David J. Johnson
Executive Director
Public Defender Commission
701 East Franklin Street, #1416
Richmond, VA 23219
P: (804) 225-3297
F: (804) 371-8326

WEST VIRGINIA
Mr. John A. Rogers
Executive Director
Public Defender Services
1900 Kanawha Boulevard, East
Charleston, WV 25305
P: (304) 348-3905
F: (304) 558-1098
E: jrogers@wvpds.org

WISCONSIN
Mr. Nicholas Chiarkas
State Public Defender
Office of the State Public Defender
315 North Henry, 2nd Floor
Madison, WI 53707
P: (608) 266-0087
F: (608) 267-0584

WYOMING
Ms. Diane Lozano
State Public Defender
State Public Defenders Office
2020 Carey Avenue, 3rd Floor
Cheyenne, WY 82002
P: (307) 777-7137
F: (307) 777-6253

Public Lands

Manages state-owned lands.

ALABAMA
Mr. James H. Griggs
Director
State Lands Division
64 North Union Street, Room 464
Montgomery, AL 36130
P: (334) 242-3484
F: (334) 242-0999

ALASKA
Mr. Tom Irwin
Commissioner
Department of Natural Resources
400 Willoughby Avenue, 5th Floor
Juneau, AK 99801
P: (907) 465-2400
F: (907) 465-3886

ARIZONA
Mr. Mark Winkleman
State Land Commissioner
State Land Department
1616 West Adams Street
Phoenix, AZ 85007
P: (602) 542-4621

ARKANSAS
Hon. Mark Wilcox
Commissioner of State Lands
Office of the Commissioner
State Capitol, Room 109
Little Rock, AR 72201
P: (501) 324-9222
F: (501) 324-9421
E: land@aristotle.net

COLORADO
Mr. Britt Weygandt
President
Board of Land Commissioners
Department of Natural Resources
1313 Sherman Street, 6th Floor
Denver, CO 80203
P: (303) 866-3454
F: (303) 866-3152

CONNECTICUT
Ms. Gina McCarthy
Commissioner
Department of Environmental Protection
79 Elm Street
Hartford, CT 06106
P: (860) 424-3009
F: (860) 424-4054
E: gina.mccarthy@po.state.ct.us

DELAWARE
Mr. Charles A. Salkin
Director
Division of Parks & Recreation
89 Kings Highway
Dover, DE 19901
P: (302) 739-4401
F: (302) 739-3817

FLORIDA
Ms. Deborah Poppell
Director
Department of Environmental Protection
State Lands
3900 Commonwealth Boulevard, MS 100
Tallahassee, FL 32399
P: (850) 245-2555
F: (850) 245-2572

GEORGIA
Mr. Noel A. Holcomb
Commissioner
Department of Natural Resources
2 Marting Luther King Jr. Drive SE
Suite 1252 East Tower
Atlanta, GA 30334
P: (404) 656-3500
F: (404) 656-0770

GUAM
Mr. Terezo Mortera
Director
Department of Land Management
855 West Marine Corps, Route 1, Anigua
P.O. Box 2950
Hagatna, GU 96932
P: (671) 475-5252
F: (671) 649-6178

HAWAII
Mr. Allan A. Smith
Interim Director
Department of Land & Natural Resources
1151 Punchbowl Street
Honolulu, HI 96813
P: (808) 587-0401
F: (808) 587-0390

IDAHO
Mr. George Bacon
Director
Department of Lands
954 West Jefferson
Boise, ID 83720
P: (208) 334-0200
F: (208) 334-2339
E: gbacon@idl.idaho.gov

ILLINOIS
Mr. Tim Hickmann
Director
Office of Land Management & Education
1 Natural Resources Way
Springfield, IL 62702
P: (217) 782-6752
F: (217) 524-5612
E: thickmann@dnrmail.state.il.us

INDIANA
Mr. John Davis
Deputy Director
Division of Land Acquisition
402 West Washington Street, Room W256
Indianapolis, IN 46204
P: (317) 232-4025
F: (317) 233-6811
E: jdavis@dnr.state.in.us

IOWA
Mr. Kenneth Herring
Administrator
Division of Conservation & Recreation
Department of Natural Resources
East Ninth & Grand Avenue
Des Moines, IA 50319
P: (515) 281-5529
F: (515) 281-6794

KANSAS
Mr. Mike Hayden
Secretary
Department of Wildlife & Parks
1020 South Kansas Avenue
Suite 200
Topeka, KS 66612
P: (785) 296-2281
F: (785) 296-6953

LOUISIANA
Mr. Charles St. Romain
Administrator
State Land Office
P.O. Box 44124
Baton Rouge, LA 70804
P: (225) 342-4575
E: charles.stromain@la.gov

MAINE
Mr. Thomas Morrison
Director
Buruea of Parks & Lands
22 State House Station
Augusta, ME 04333
P: (207) 287-3061

MARYLAND
Ms. Pamela Lunsford
Director
Capital Grants & Loans Administration
580 Taylor Avenue
Annapolis, MD 21401
P: (410) 260-8447
F: (410) 260-8404
E: plunsford@dnr.state.md.us

MASSACHUSETTS
Ms. Priscilla H. Geigis
Acting Commissioner
Department of Conservation & Recreation
20 Somerset Street
Boston, MA 02108
P: (617) 722-5500
F: (617) 727-0891

MICHIGAN
Mr. Ronald Olson
Chief
Parks & Recreation Division
P.O. Box 30257
Lansing, MI 48909
P: (517) 335-4827
F: (517) 373-4625

MINNESOTA
Mr. Mark Holsten
Commissioner
Department of Natural Resources
500 Lafayette Road
P.O. Box 37
St. Paul, MN 55155
P: (651) 259-5555
F: (651) 296-4799
E: mark.holsten@state.mn.us

MISSISSIPPI
Mr. Gerald McWhorter
Assistant Secretary of State for Public Lands
Public Lands Division
P.O. Box 136
Jackson, MS 39205
P: (601) 359-6373
F: (601) 359-1461
E: gmcwhorter@sos.state.ms.us

MISSOURI
Mr. Douglas K. Eiken
Director
Division of State Parks
P.O. Box 176
Jefferson City, MO 65101
P: (573) 751-9392
F: (573) 526-7716
E: Doug.Eiken@dnr.mo.gov

Public Lands

MONTANA
Ms. Mary Sexton
Director
Department of Natural Resources & Conservation
1625 11th Avenue
Helena, MT 59620
P: (406) 444-2074
F: (406) 444-2684
E: msexton@mt.gov

NEVADA
Ms. Pamela B. Wilcox
Administrator
State Lands Division
333 West Nye Lane, Room 118
Carson City, NV 89706
P: (775) 687-4363
F: (775) 687-3783
E: pwilcox@lands.nv.gov

NEW HAMPSHIRE
Mr. Philip Bryce
Director
Division of Forests & Lands
P.O. Box 1856
Concord, NH 03302
P: (603) 271-2214
F: (603) 271-6488
E: pbryce@dred.state.nh.us

NEW MEXICO
Mr. Patrick H. Lyons
Commissioner of Public Lands
State Land Office
310 Old Santa Fe Trail
P.O. Box 1148
Santa Fe, NM 87504
P: (505) 827-5760
F: (505) 827-5766

NEW YORK
Mr. Alexander "Pete" Grannis (D)
Commissioner
Department of Environmental Conservation
625 Broadway
Albany, NY 12207
P: (518) 402-8540
F: (518) 474-5450

NORTH CAROLINA
Mr. William G. Ross Jr.
Secretary
Department of Environment & Natural Resources
512 North Salisbury Street
1601 Mail Service Center
Raleigh, NC 27699
P: (919) 733-4101
F: (919) 733-4299
E: bill.ross@ncmail.net

NORTH DAKOTA
Mr. Gary D. Preszler
Land Commissioner
Land Department
P.O. Box 5523
Bismarck, ND 58506
E: gpreszle@nd.gov

NORTHERN MARIANA ISLANDS
Mr. John S. Del Rosario
Secretary
Department of Public Lands
Caller Box 10007, Capital Hill
Saipan, MP 96950
P: (670) 234-3751
F: (670) 234-3755
E: jrosario@pticom.com

OHIO
Mr. Sean D. Logan
Director
Department of Natural Resources
1930 Belcher Drive
Columbus, OH 43224
P: (614) 265-6879

OKLAHOMA
Mr. Scott Thompson
Director
Land Protection Division
P.O. Box 1677
Oklahoma City, OK 73118
P: (405) 702-5100
F: (405) 702-5101
E: scott.thompson@deq.state.ok.us

OREGON
Ms. Louise Solliday
Acting Director
Department of State Lands
775 Summer Street, Northeast
Suite 100
Salem, OR 97301
P: (503) 378-3805 Ext. 224
F: (503) 378-4844
E: louise.solliday@dsl.state.or.us

PENNSYLVANIA
Mr. John Norbeck
Director
Bureau of State Parks
P.O. Box 8551
Harrisburg, PA 17105
P: (717) 787-6640
F: (717) 787-8817

PUERTO RICO
Mr. Jose O. Fabre Laboy
Executive Director
Department of Agriculture
Apartado 10163
Santurce, PR 00909
P: (787) 721-2120
F: (787) 723-8512

RHODE ISLAND
Dr. W. Michael Sullivan
Director
Department of Environmental Management
235 Promenade Street, 4th Floor
Providence, RI 02908
P: (401) 222-2771
F: (401) 222-6802

SOUTH CAROLINA
Mr. M. Richbourg Robinson
Director
Office of General Services
Budget & Control Board
1201 Main Street, Suite 420
Columbia, SC 29201
P: (803) 737-3880

SOUTH DAKOTA
Hon. Jarrod Johnson
Commissioner
School & Public Lands
State Capitol
500 East Capitol Avenue
Pierre, SD 57501
P: (605) 773-3303
E: jarrod.johnson@state.sd.us

TENNESSEE
Mr. Ken Givens
Commissioner
Department of Agriculture
Melrose Station
P.O. Box 40627
Nashville, TN 37204
P: (615) 837-5100
F: (615) 837-5333

U.S. VIRGIN ISLANDS
Ms. Kim Aska
Manager
Property & Procurement Division
5400 Veteran's Drive
St. Thomas, VI 00802
P: (340) 774-6680
F: (340) 776-9889

Mr. Darlan Brin
Executive Director
Port Authority
P.O. Box 301707
St. Thomas, VI 00803
P: (340) 774-1629
F: (340) 774-0025
E: dbrin@viport.com

Mr. Dean C. Plaskett
State Historic Preservation Officer
Department of Planning & Natural Resources
17 Kongens
St. Thomas, VI 00802
P: 340-776-8605
F: 340-776-7236

UTAH
Mr. Joel Frandsen
State Forester/Director
Division of Forestry, Fire & State Lands
1594 West North Temple, Suite 3520
P.O. Box 145703
Salt Lake City, UT 84114
P: (801) 538-5530
F: (801) 533-4111
E: joelfrandsen@utah.gov

VERMONT
Mr. George Crombie
Secretary
Agency of Natural Resources
103 South Main Street
Waterbury, VT 05671
P: (802) 241-3600
F: (802) 244-1102

VIRGINIA
Mr. Richard F. Sliwoski
Director
Department of General Services
202 North 9th Street, Room 209
Richmond, VA 23219
P: (804) 786-3263
F: (804) 371-7934
E: richard.sliwoski@dgs.virginia.gov

WASHINGTON
Mr. Doug Sutherland
Commissioner of Public Lands
Department of Natural Resources
P.O. Box 47001
Olympia, WA 98504
P: (360) 902-1000
F: (360) 902-1775

WEST VIRGINIA
Mr. Joe Scarberry
Acting Chief
Real Estate Management
Division of Natural Resources
State Capitol Building 3, Room 643
Charleston, WV 25305
P: (304) 558-3225

WYOMING
Ms. Lynne Boomgaarden
Director of Lands and Investments
Office of State Lands & Investments
Herschler Building, 3rd Floor
Cheyenne, WY 82003
P: (307) 777-7331
F: (307) 777-5400

Public Safety

Provides information and services to insure the protection and safety of citizens and property.

ALABAMA
Col. Chris Murphy
Director
Department of Public Safety
P.O. Box 1511
Montgomery, AL 36102
P: (334) 242-4394
F: (334) 242-0512
E: director@alalinc.net

ALASKA
Mr. Walt Monegan
Commissioner
Department of Public Safety
5700 East Tudor Road
Anchorage, AK 99507
P: (907) 269-5086
F: (907) 269-4543

AMERICAN SAMOA
Mr. Sotoa Savali
Commissioner
Department of Public Safety
American Samoa Government
P.O. Box 3699
Pago Pago, AS 96799
P: (684) 633-1111
F: (684) 633-7296

ARIZONA
Mr. Roger Vanderpool
Director
Department of Public Safety
2102 West Encanto Boulevard
P.O. Box 6638
Phoenix, AZ 85005
P: (602) 223-2359
F: (602) 223-2917

CALIFORNIA
Mr. Mike Brown
Commissioner
Highway Patrol
Business, Trans. & Housing Agency
2555 First Avenue
Sacramento, CA 95818
P: (916) 657-7152
F: (916) 657-7324

COLORADO
Mr. Peter Weir
Executive Director
Department of Public Safety
700 Kipling Street, Suite 3000
Lakewood, CO 80215
P: (303) 239-4398
F: (303) 239-4670
E: Public.Safety@cdps.state.co.us

CONNECTICUT
Mr. John Danaher
Commissioner
Department of Public Safety
1111 Country Club ROad
Middletown, CT 06457
P: (860) 685-8000
F: (860) 685-8354

DELAWARE
Mr. David B. Mitchell
Director of Homeland Security
Department of Safety & Homeland Security
330 Transportation Circle
P.O. Box 818
Dover, DE 19901
P: (302) 744-2680
F: (302) 739-4874

DISTRICT OF COLUMBIA
Ms. Cathy L. Lanier
Chief of Police
Metropolitan Police Department
300 Indiana Avenue, NW
Room 5080
Washington, DC 20001
P: (202) 727-4218
F: (202) 727-9524

FLORIDA
Mr. Gerald Bailey
Commissioner
Department of Law Enforcement
P.O. Box 1489
Tallahassee, FL 32302
P: (850) 410-7001

GEORGIA
Col. Bill Hitchens
Commissioner
Department of Public Safety
P.O. Box 1456
Atlanta, GA 30371
P: (404) 624-7477
F: (404) 624-6706

GUAM
Mr. Lawrence Perez
Director
Department of Public Safety
542 North Marine Drive
Tamuning, GU 96913
P: (671) 646-3131
F: (671) 649-6178
E: dpwdir@mail.gov.gu

HAWAII
Mr. Frank J. Lopez
Acting Director
Department of Public Safety
919 Ala Moana Boulevard, Room 400
Honolulu, HI 96814
P: (808) 587-1350
F: (808) 587-1421
E: flopez@asca.net

IDAHO
Col. Jerry Russell
Director
State Police
P.O. Box 700
Meridian, ID 83680
P: (208) 884-7003
F: (208) 884-7090

ILLINOIS
Col. Jill Morgenthaler
Deputy Chief of Staff for Public Safety
Office of the Governor
Capitol Building, Room 205
Springfield, IL 62706
P: (217) 524-1423

INDIANA
Dr. Paul Whitesell
Superintendent
State Police
100 North Senate Avenue, Room N340
Indianapolis, IN 46204
P: (317) 232-8241

IOWA
Mr. Eugene T. Meyer
Commissioner
Department of Public Safety
215 East 7th Street
Des Moines, IA 50319
P: (515) 725-6182

KANSAS
Maj. Gen. Tod M. Bunting
Adjutant General
Adjutant General's Department
2800 Southwest Topeka Boulevard
Topeka, KS 66611
P: (913) 274-1001
F: (913) 274-1682

KENTUCKY
Brig. Gen. Norman E. Arflack
Secretary
Justice & Public Safety Cabinet
125 Holmes Street
Frankfort, KY 40601
P: (502) 564-7554
F: (502) 564-4840

LOUISIANA
Mr. Richard L. Stalder
Secretary
Department of Public Safety & Corrections
P.O. Box 94304, Capitol Station
Baton Rouge, LA 70804
P: (225) 342-6956
F: (225) 342-2486
E: rstalder@asca.net

Col. Henry Whitehorn
Superintendent of State Police
Department of Public Safety & Corrections
7919 Independence Boulevard
P.O. Box 66614
Baton Rouge, LA 70896
P: (225) 925-6118
F: (225) 925-3742
E: hwhitehorn@dps.state.la.us

MAINE
Ms. Anne Jordan
Commissioner
Department of Public Safety
42 State House Station
Augusta, ME 04333
P: (207) 624-9435
F: (207) 287-3842
E: dan.walters@maine.gov

MARYLAND
Mr. Gary D. Maynard
Secretary
Department of Public Safety & Correctional Services
300 East Joppa Road, Suite 1000
Towson, MD 21286
P: (410) 339-5005
F: (410) 339-4243

MASSACHUSETTS
Mr. Thomas G. Gatzunis
Commissioner
Department of Public Safety
One Ashburton Place, Room 1301
Boston, MA 02108
P: (617) 727-3200
F: (617) 227-1754
E: thomas.gatzunis@state.ma.us

MINNESOTA
Mr. Michael Campion
Commissioner
Department of Public Safety
Bremer Tower, Suite 1000
445 Minnesota Street
St. Paul, MN 55101
P: (651) 201-7000
F: (651) 297-5728
E: michael.campion
@state.mn.us

MISSISSIPPI
Mr. George Phillips
Commissioner
Department of Public Safety
P.O. Box 958
Jackson, MS 39205
P: (601) 987-1212
F: (601) 987-1488
E: commissioner
@mdps.state.ms.us

MISSOURI
Mr. Mark S. James
Director
Department of Public Safety
301 West High Street
Truman Building, Room 870
Jefferson City, MO 65102
P: (573) 751-4905
F: (573) 751-5399
E: Mark.James@dps.mo.gov

MONTANA
Mr. Dan McGowan
Administrator
Disaster & Emergency Services
Department of Military Affairs
P.O. Box 4789
Ft. Harrison, MT 59636
P: (406) 841-3911
F: (406) 841-3965
E: dmcgowan@mt.gov

NEBRASKA
Maj. Bryan Tuma
State Patrol
P.O. Box 94907
Lincoln, NE 68509
P: (402) 471-4545
F: (402) 479-4002

NEVADA
Mr. Phillip A. Galeoto
Director
Department of Public Safety
555 Wright Way
Carson City, NV 89711
P: (775) 684-4808
F: (775) 684-4809

NEW HAMPSHIRE
Mr. John J. Barthelmes
Commissioner
Department of Safety
33 Hazen Drive
Concord, NH 03305
P: (603) 271-2791
F: (603) 271-3903
E: jbarthelmes
@safety.state.nh.us

NEW MEXICO
Mr. John Denko
Cabinet Secretary
Department of Public Safety
4491 Cerrillos Road
P.O. Box 1628
Santa Fe, NM 87504
P: (505) 827-3370

NEW YORK
Ms. Denise O'Donnell
Commissioner
Division of Criminal Justice Services
4 Tower Place
Stuyvesant Plaza
Albany, NY 12203
P: (518) 457-1260
F: (518) 473-1271

NORTH CAROLINA
Mr. Bryan E. Beatty
Secretary
Department of Crime Control & Public Safety
512 North Salisbury Street
4701 Mail Service Center
Raleigh, NC 27699
P: (919) 733-2126
F: (919) 715-8477
E: bbeatty
@nccrimecontrol.org

NORTH DAKOTA
Col. Bryan Klipfel
Superintendent
Highway Patrol
600 East Boulevard Avenue
Department 504
Bismarck, ND 58505
P: (701) 328-2455
F: (701) 328-1717
E: bklipfel@nd.gov

NORTHERN MARIANA ISLANDS
Ms. Rebecca Warfield
Commissioner
Department of Public Safety
Caller Box 10007, Capital Hill
Saipan, MP 96950
P: (670) 664-9022
F: (670) 664-9027
E: doris@cjpa.gov.mp

OHIO
Mr. Henry Guzman
Director
Department of Public Safety
1970 West Broad Street
P.O. Box 182081
Columbus, OH 43218
P: (614) 466-3383
F: (614) 466-0433

OKLAHOMA
Mr. Kevin Ward
Secretary of Safety & Security
Department of Public Safety
P.O. Box 11415
Oklahoma City, OK 73136
P: (405) 425-2424
F: (405) 425-2324

OREGON
Mr. Ken Murphy
Director
Emergency Management
3225 State Street
P.O. Box 14370
Salem, OR 97309
P: (503) 378-2911
F: (503) 373-7833
E: kmurphy@oem.state.or.us

PUERTO RICO
Mr. Pedro A. Toledo Davila
Superintendent
Puerto Rico Police
P.O. Box 70166
San Juan, PR 00936
P: (787) 793-1234
F: (787) 781-0080

SOUTH CAROLINA
Mr. James K. Schweitzer
Director
Department of Public Safety
P.O. Box 1993
10311 Wilson Boulevard
Blythewood, SC 29016
P: (803) 896-7932
F: (803) 896-7881
E: jamesschweitzer
@scdps.net

SOUTH DAKOTA
Mr. Tom Dravland
Secretary
Department of Public Safety
118 West Capitol Avenue
Pierre, SD 57501
P: (605) 773-3178
F: (605) 773-3018
E: tom.dravland@state.sd.us

TEXAS
Capt. Franklin William
Captain
Patrol & Security Operations
Department of Public Safety
P.O. Box 4087
Austin, TX 78773
P: (512) 424-2000

U.S. VIRGIN ISLANDS
Mr. Elton Lewis
Commissioner
Police Department
Alexander Farrelly Criminal Justice Ctr.
Charlotte Amalie
St. Thomas, VI 00802
P: (340) 774-2211
F: (340) 715-5517
E: elton.lewis@us.army.mil

UTAH
Mr. Scott Duncan
Commissioner
Department of Public Safety
4501 South 2700 West
Salt Lake City, UT 84119
P: (801) 965-4463
F: (801) 965-4608
E: sduncan@utah.gov

VERMONT
Maj. Kerry L. Sleeper
Commissioner of Public Safety
Department of Public Safety
103 South Main Street
Waterbury, VT 05671
P: (802) 244-8718
F: (802) 244-5551
E: ksleeper@dps.state.vt.us

VIRGINIA
Hon. John W. Marshall
Secretary of Public Safety
Office of the Secretary of Public Safety
1111 East Broad Street
Patrick Henry Building
Richmond, VA 23219
P: (804) 786-5351
F: (804) 371-6381
E: john.marshall
@governor.virginia.gov

WASHINGTON
Mr. John R. Batiste
Chief
State Patrol
General Administration Building
P.O. Box 42600
Olympia, WA 98504
P: (360) 753-6540

Public Safety

WEST VIRGINIA
Mr. James Spears
Secretary
Department of Military Affairs
& Public Safety
State Capitol Complex
Building 6, Room 122
Charleston, WV 25305
P: (304) 558-2930
F: (304) 558-6221
E: jspears@wvdmaps.gov

WISCONSIN
Mr. James Warren
Administrator
Division of Criminal
Investigation
17 West Main Street
Madison, WI 53707
P: (608) 266-1671
F: (608) 267-2777

Public Utility Regulation

Supervises and regulates the electric, gas, telephone and water utilities in the state.

Information provided by:

National Association of Regulatory Utility Commissioners
Charles D. Gray
Executive Director
1101 Vermont Avenue NW, Suite 200
Washington, DC 20005
P: (202) 898-2208
F: (202) 898-2213
cgray@naruc.org
www.naruc.org

ALABAMA
Mr. Jim Sullivan
President
Public Service Commission
100 North Union Street, Suite 800
Montgomery, AL 36101
P: (334) 242-5207
F: (334) 242-0921
E: jsullivan@psc.state.al.us

ALASKA
Ms. Kate Giard
Chair
Regulatory Commission of Alaska
701 West 8th Avenue, Suite 300
Anchorage, AK 99501
P: (907) 276-6222
F: (907) 276-0160
E: kate_giard@rca.state.ak.us

ARIZONA
Mr. Jeff Hatch-Miller
Chair
Corporation Commission
1200 West Washington Street
Phoenix, AZ 85007
P: (602) 542-3625
F: (602) 542-3669
E: jhatch@cc.state.az.us

ARKANSAS
Ms. Sandra L. Hochstetter
Chair
Public Service Commission
P.O. Box 400
Little Rock, AR 72203
P: (501) 682-1455
F: 501-682-5731
E: sandyh@psc.state.ar.us

CALIFORNIA
Mr. Michael R. Peevey
President
Public Utilities Commission
505 Van Ness Avenue
San Francisco, CA 94102
P: (415) 703-3703
F: (415) 703-5091
E: mrp@cpuc.ca.gov

COLORADO
Mr. Ron Binz
Chairman
Public Utility Commission
Logan Tower, Office Level 2
1580 Logan Street
Denver, CO 80203
P: (303) 894-2000
F: (303) 894-2065

CONNECTICUT
Mr. Donald W. Downes
Chair
Department of Public Utility Control
10 Franklin Square
New Britain, CT 06051
P: (860) 827-2801
F: (860) 827-2806
E: donald.downes@po.state.ct.us

DELAWARE
Ms. Arnetta McRae
Chair
Public Service Commission
861 Silver Lake Boulevard
Dover, DE 19904
P: (302) 739-4247
F: (302) 739-4849

DISTRICT OF COLUMBIA
Ms. Agnes A. Yates
Chair
Public Service Commission
1333 H Street, Northwest
2nd Floor, West Tower
Washington, DC 20005
P: (202) 626-5115
F: (202) 626-9212
E: ayates@dcpsc.org

FLORIDA
Ms. Lisa Polak Edgar
Chair
Public Service Commission
2540 Shumard Oak Boulevard
Gerald Gunter Building
Tallahassee, FL 32399
P: (850) 413-6044
F: (850) 413-6019
E: lisa.edgar@psc.state.fl.us

GEORGIA
Mr. Robert B. Baker
Chair
Public Service Commission
244 Washington Street
Atlanta, GA 30334
P: (404) 656-4514
F: (404) 657-2980
E: bbaker@psc.state.ga.us

HAWAII
Mr. Carlito P. Caliboso
Chair
Public Utilities Commission
465 South King Street
Kekuanao'a Building, No. 103
Honolulu, HI 96813
P: (808) 586-2020
F: (808) 586-2066
E: ccaliboso@hawaii.gov

IDAHO
Mr. Paul Kjellander
President
Public Utilities Commission
P.O. Box 83720
Boise, ID 83720
P: (208) 334-2898
F: (208) 334-3762
E: paul.kjellander@puc.idaho.gov

ILLINOIS
Mr. Charles E. Box
Chair
Commerce Commission
160 North LaSalle Street, Suite C-800
Chicago, IL 60601
P: (312) 814-2859
F: (312) 814-1818
E: cbox@icc.illinois.gov

INDIANA
Mr. David Lott Hardy
Chair
Utility Regulatory Commission
Suite E306, Government Center, South
302 West Washington Street
Indianapolis, IN 46204
P: (317) 232-2702
F: (317) 232-6758
E: dlhardy@urc.IN.gov

IOWA
Mr. John Norris
Chair
Utilities Board
350 Maple Street
Des Moines, IA 50319
P: (515) 281-5167
F: (515) 281-8821

KANSAS
Mr. Brian J. Moline
Chair
Corporation Commission
1500 Southwest Arrowhead Road
Topeka, KS 66604
P: (785) 271-3166
F: (785) 271-3354
E: b.moline@kcc.state.ks.us

KENTUCKY
Mr. Mark David Goss
Chair
Public Service Commission
211 Sower Boulevard
P.O. Box 615
Frankfort, KY 40602
P: (502) 564-3940
F: (502) 564-8992
E: mark.goss@ky.gov

LOUISIANA
Mr. James M. Field
Chair
Public Service Commission
P.O. Box 91154
Baton Rouge, LA 70821
P: (225) 342-6900
F: 225-342-6912
E: cynthiat@lpsc.org

MAINE
Mr. Kurt Adams
Chair
Public Utilities Commission
242 State Street
State House Station 18
Augusta, ME 04333
P: (207) 287-3831
F: (207) 287-1039
E: kurt.adams@maine.gov

MARYLAND
Mr. Kenneth D. Schisler
Chair
Public Service Commission
16th Floor, 6 St. Paul Street
Baltimore, MD 21202
P: (410) 767-8073
F: (410) 333-6495
E: kschisler@psc.state.md.us

Public Utility Regulation

MASSACHUSETTS
Ms. Judith F. Judson
Chair
Department of Telecommunications & Energy
One South Station
Boston, MA 02110
P: (617) 305-3520
F: (617) 345-9102
E: judith.judson@state.ma.us

MICHIGAN
Mr. J. Peter Lark
Chair
Public Service Commission
Mercantile Building, 6545 Mercantile Way
P.O. Box 30221
Lansing, MI 48909
P: (517) 241-6190
F: (517) 241-6189
E: jplark@michigan.gov

MINNESOTA
Mr. LeRoy Koppendrayer
Chair
Public Utilities Commission
Suite 350, 121 7th Place East
St. Paul, MN 55101
P: 651-296-0402
F: (651) 297-7073
E: Leroy.koppendrayer@state.mn.us

MISSISSIPPI
Mr. Dorlos "Bo" Robinson
Chair
Public Service Commission
501 North West Street
201A Woolfolk State Office Building
Jackson, MS 39201
P: 601-961-5450
F: (601) 961-5476
E: bo.robinson@psc.state.ms.us

MISSOURI
Mr. Jeff Davis
Chair
Public Service Commission
P.O. Box 360
Truman State Office Building
Jefferson City, MO 65102
P: (573) 751-3233
F: (573) 526-7341
E: jeff.davis@psc.mo.gov

MONTANA
Mr. Greg Jergeson
Chair
Public Service Commission
1701 Prospect Avenue
Helena, MT 59620
P: (406) 444-6166
F: (406) 444-7618
E: gjergeson@mt.gov

NEBRASKA
Mr. Rod Johnson
Chair
Public Service Commission
300 The Atrium, 1200 N Street
P.O. Box 94927
Lincoln, NE 68509
P: 402-471-0212
F: 402-471-0233
E: rod.johnson@psc.ne.gov

NEVADA
Mr. Donald L. Soderberg
Chair
Public Utilities Commission
1150 East William Street
Carson City, NV 89701
P: (775) 684-6007
F: 775-687-8726
E: soderber@puc.state.nv.us

NEW HAMPSHIRE
Mr. Thomas B. Getz
Chair
Public Utilities Commission
10 Fruit Street, Suite 10
Concord, NH 03301
P: (603) 271-2442
F: (603) 271-3878
E: tom.getz@puc.nh.gov

NEW JERSEY
Ms. Jeanne M. Fox
President
Board of Public Utilities
Two Gateway Center, 8th Floor
Newark, NJ 07102
P: (973) 648-2013
F: 973-648-4195
E: jeanne.fox@bpu.state.nj.us

NEW MEXICO
Mr. Ben R. Lujan
Chair
Public Regulation Commission
P.O. Box 1269
Santa Fe, NM 87504
P: (505) 827-4533
F: 505-476-0167
E: benrlujan@state.nm.us

NEW YORK
Ms. Patricia Acampora
Chair
Public Service Commission
Three Empire State Plaza
Albany, NY 12223
P: 518-474-7080
F: 518-474-0421

NORTH CAROLINA
Mr. Edward Finley Jr.
Chair
Utilities Commission
4325 Mail Service Center
Raleigh, NC 27699
P: (919) 733-6067
F: (919) 733-7300
E: finley@ncuc.net

NORTH DAKOTA
Ms. Susan Wefald
Chair
Public Service Commission
State Capitol Building
600 East Boulevard, Department 408
Bismarck, ND 58505
P: (701) 328-4559
F: (701) 328-2410
E: swefald@state.nd.us

OHIO
Mr. Alan R. Schriber
Chair
Public Utilities Commission
180 East Broad Street
Columbus, OH 43215
P: (614) 466-3204
F: (614) 995-3690
E: Alan.schriber@puc.state.oh.us

OKLAHOMA
Mr. Jeff Cloud
Chair
Corporation Commission
Jim Thorpe Office Building
P.O. Box 52000-2000
Oklahoma City, OK 73152
P: (405) 521-2264
F: (405) 522-1623
E: j.cloud@occemail.com

OREGON
Mr. Lee Beyer
Chair
Public Utility Commission
550 Capitol Street, Northeast
Salem, OR 97310
P: (503) 378-6611
F: (503) 378-5505
E: Lee.beyer@state.or.us

PENNSYLVANIA
Mr. Wendell F. Holland
Chair
Public Utility Commission
400 North Street, 3rd Floor
Harrisburg, PA 17105
P: (717) 787-1031
F: (717) 783-0698
E: wfh@state.pa.us

RHODE ISLAND
Mr. Elia Germani
Chair
Public Utilities Commission
89 Jefferson Boulevard
Providence, RI 02888
P: (401) 941-4500 Ext. 170
F: (401) 941-1691
E: egermani@puc.state.ri.us

SOUTH CAROLINA
Mr. John Howard
Chair
Public Service Commission
P.O. Drawer 11649
Columbia, SC 29211
P: (803) 896-5220
F: (803) 896-5188
E: butch.howard@psc.state.sc.us

SOUTH DAKOTA
Mr. Dustin Johnson
Chair
Public Utilities Commission
State Capitol
500 East Capitol
Pierre, SD 57501
P: (605) 773-3201
F: (605) 773-3809
E: dustin.johnson@state.sd.us

TENNESSEE
Ms. Sara Kyle
Chair
Regulatory Authority
460 James Robertson Parkway
Nashville, TN 37243
P: (615) 741-3125
F: (615) 741-7491
E: sarah.kyle@state.tn.us

TEXAS
Mr. Paul Hudson
Chair
Public Utility Commission
1701 North Congress Avenue
P.O. Box 12967
Austin, TX 78711
P: (512) 936-7015
F: (512) 936-7018
E: Paul.Hudson@puc.state.tx.us

UTAH
Mr. Ric Campbell
Chair
Public Service Commission
160 East 300 South
P.O. Box 45585
Salt Lake City, UT 84145
P: (801) 530-6716
F: (801) 530-6796
E: rcampbell@utah.gov

VERMONT
Mr. James Volz
Chair
Public Service Board
112 State Street, 4th Floor
Montpelier, VT 05620
P: (802) 828-2358
F: (802) 828-3351
E: jvolz@psb.state.vt.us

VIRGINIA
Mr. Mark C. Christie
Chair
State Corporation Commission
Tyler Building
P.O. Box 1197
Richmond, VA 23218
P: (804) 371-9608
F: (804) 371-9376
E: mark.christie
@scc.state.va.us

WASHINGTON
Mr. Mark Sidran
Chair
Utilities & Transportation
Commission
Chandler Plaza Building
P.O. Box 47250
Olympia, WA 98504
P: (360) 664-1173
E: msidran@wutc.wa.gov

WEST VIRGINIA
Mr. John McKinney
Chair
Public Service Commission
201 Brooks Street
P.O. Box 812
Charleston, WV 25323
P: (304) 340-0307
F: (304) 340-3758
E: jmckinney
@psc.state.wv.us

WISCONSIN
Mr. Daniel R. Ebert
Chair
Public Service Commission
P.O. Box 7854
Madison, WI 53707
P: (608) 267-7897
F: (608) 266-1401
E: daniel.ebert
@psc.state.wi.us

WYOMING
Mr. Steve Furtney
Chair
Public Service Commission
2515 Warren Avenue, Suite 300
Cheyenne, WY 82002
P: (307) 777-7427
F: (307) 777-5700
E: sfurtn@state.wy.us

Purchasing

Central screening and acquisition point for supplies, equipment, and/or services for state agencies.

Information provided by:

National Association of State Procurement Officials
Jack Gallt
Association Director
201 East Main Street
Suite 1405
Lexington, KY 40507
P: (859) 514-9159
F: (859) 514-9188
naspo@amrms.com
www.naspo.org

ALABAMA
Mr. Isaac Kervin
Purchasing Director
Division of Purchasing
P.O. Box 302620
100 North Union Street, Suite 192
Montgomery, AL 36130
P: (334) 242-7250
F: (334) 242-4419
E: isaac.kervin@purchasing.alabama.gov

ALASKA
Mr. Vern Jones
Chief Procurement Officer
Division of General Services
Department of Administration
P.O. Box 110210
Juneau, AK 99811
P: (907) 465-5684
F: (907) 465-2189
E: Vern_jones@admin.state.ak.us

AMERICAN SAMOA
Mr. Laau Seui
Director
Office of Material Management
P.O. Box 1329
Pago Pago, AS 96799

ARIZONA
Ms. Jean A. Clark
State Procurement Administrator
Department of Administration
State Procurement Office
100 North 15th Avenue, Suite 104
Phoenix, AZ 85007
P: (602) 542-9136
F: (602) 542-5508
E: jean.clark@azdoa.gov

ARKANSAS
Mr. Joe Giddis
Director
Office of State Procurement
Department of Finance & Administration
1509 West 7th Street, Suite 300
Little Rock, AR 72201
P: (501) 324-9312
F: (501) 324-9311
E: joe.giddis@dfa.state.ar.us

CALIFORNIA
Ms. Rita Hamilton
Deputy Director
Procurement Division
Department of General Services
707 Third Street, 2nd Floor
West Sacramento, CA 95605
P: (916) 375-4417
F: (916) 375-4505
E: rita.hamilton@dgs.ca.gov

COLORADO
Mr. John Utterback
Purchasing Director
Department of Personnel & Administration
State Purchasing
633 17th Street, Suite 1520
Denver, CO 80202
P: (303) 866-6181
F: (303) 894-7445
E: john.utterback@state.co.us

CONNECTICUT
Ms. Carol Wilson
Director of Procurement
Department of Administrative Services
P.O. Box 150414
165 Capitol Avenue
Hartford, CT 06106
P: (860) 713-5093
F: (860) 713-7484
E: carol.wilson@ct.gov

DELAWARE
Mr. Blaine Herrick
Contracting Administrator
Government Support Services
Office of Management & Budget
100 Enterprise Place, Suite 4
Dover, DE 19904
P: (302) 857-4552
F: (302) 739-3779
E: blaine.herrick@state.de.us

DISTRICT OF COLUMBIA
Mr. Oscar Rodriguez
Interim Chief Procurement Officer
Office of Contracting & Procurement
District of Columbia Government
441 4th Street, Northwest, Suite 800 S
Washington, DC 20001
P: (202) 724-4242
F: (202) 727-3229
E: oscar.rodriguez@dc.gov

FLORIDA
Mr. Charles W. Covington
Director of State Purchasing
Department of Management Services
4050 Esplanade Way
Tallahassee, FL 32399
P: (850) 487-3964
F: (850) 414-6122
E: charles.covington@dms.myflorida.com

GEORGIA
Mr. Tim Gibney
Assistant Commissioner, Procurement
Department of Administrative Services
200 Piedmont Avenue, Suite 1308
West Floyd Building
Atlanta, GA 30334
P: (404) 656-2291
F: (404) 657-8444
E: tgibney@doas.ga.gov

GUAM
Mr. Lorenzo Aflague
Chief Procurement Officer
General Services Agency
P.O. Box FG
Agana, GU 96910
P: (671) 477-1725
F: (671) 472-4217

HAWAII
Mr. Aaron Fujioka
Administrator
State Procurement Office
1151 Punchbowl Street, Room 416
Honolulu, HI 96813
P: (808) 586-0554
F: (808) 586-0570
E: aaron.fujioka@hawaii.gov

IDAHO
Ms. Bobbi Eckerle
Administrator
Division of Purchasing
5569 Kendall Street
P.O. Box 83720
Boise, ID 83720
P: (208) 332-1604
F: (208) 327-7320
E: bobbi.eckerle@adm.idaho.gov

ILLINOIS
Mr. Mike Smith
Chief Operating Official
Department of Central Management Services
405 William G. Stratton Building
Springfield, IL 62706
P: (217) 557-8253
F: (217) 558-1759
E: Mike.Smith@illinois.gov

INDIANA
Mr. Rob Wynkoop
Deputy Commissioner
Department of Administration
402 West Washington Street
IGCS, Room W468
Indianapolis, IN 46204
P: (317) 232-3185
F: (317) 232-7312
E: rwynkoop@idoa.in.gov

IOWA
Ms. Debbie O'Leary
Division Administrator
General Services Enterprise-Purchasing
Department of Administrative Services
Hoover State Office Building, Level A
Des Moines, IA 50319
P: (515) 281-8384
F: (515) 242-5974
E: debbie.oleary@iowa.gov

KANSAS
Mr. Chris Howe
Director of Purchases
Division of Purchases
Landon State Office Building
900 SW Jackson Street, Room 102N
Topeka, KS 66612
P: (785) 296-2374
F: (785) 296-7240
E: chris.howe@da.ks.gov

LOUISIANA
Ms. Denise Lea
Director
Office of State Purchasing & Travel
P.O. Box 94095
301 Main Street, 13th Floor
Baton Rouge, LA 70804
P: (225) 342-8057
F: (225) 342-8688
E: denise.lea@la.gov

MAINE
Ms. Betty Lamoreau
Director
Division of Purchases
State Office Building
State House Station #9
Augusta, ME 04333
P: (207) 624-7331
F: (207) 287-6578
E: Betty.M.Lamoreau@maine.gov

MARYLAND
Mr. Mark Pemberton
Assistant Secretary
Office of Procurement & Logistics
Department of General Services
301 West Preston Street, Room M-6
Baltimore, MD 21201
P: (410) 767-4429
E: mark.pemberton@dgs.state.md.us

MASSACHUSETTS
Ms. Ellen L. Phillips
Deputy State Purchasing Agent
Operational Services Division
John W. McCormack Office Building
One Ashburton Place, Room 1017
Boston, MA 02108
P: (617) 720-3330
F: (617) 727-4527
E: Ellen.Phillips@osd.state.ma.us

MICHIGAN
Ms. Elise Lancaster
Director, Purchasing Operations
Acquisition Services
P.O. Box 30026
DMB, Mason Building, 2nd Floor
Lansing, MI 48909
P: (517) 241-2715
F: (517) 335-0046
E: lancaster@michigan.gov

MINNESOTA
Mr. Kent Allin
Director
Materials Management Division
112 Administration Building
50 Sherburne Avenue
St. Paul, MN 55155
P: (651) 201-2400
F: (651) 297-3996
E: kent.allin@state.mn.us

MISSISSIPPI
Ms. Gina Davis
Director
Office of Purchasing, Travel & Fleet Management
Department of Finance & Administration
501 North West Street
Jackson, MS 39201
P: (601) 359-3409
F: (601) 359-3910
E: marting@dfa.state.ms.us

MISSOURI
Mr. Jim Miluski
Director
Division of Purchasing & Materials Management
P.O. Box 809
301 West High Street, HST Building #580
Jefferson City, MO 65102
P: (573) 751-3273
F: (573) 526-5985
E: jim.miluski@oa.mo.gov

MONTANA
Mr. Marvin Eicholtz
Administrator
General Services Division
Department of Administration
P.O. Box 200110
Helena, MT 59620
P: (406) 444-3119
F: (406) 444-3039
E: meicholtz@mt.gov

NEBRASKA
Ms. Brenda Pape
Materials & Procurement Manager
State Purchasing Bureau
301 Centennial Mall South, 1st Floor
P.O. Box 94847
Lincoln, NE 68509
P: (402) 471-0970
F: (402) 471-2089
E: bpape@notes.state.ne.us

NEVADA
Mr. Greg Smith
Administrator
Purchasing Division
Department of Administration
515 East Musser Street, Suite #300
Carson City, NV 89701
P: (775) 684-0170
F: (775) 684-0188
E: gmsmith@purchasing.state.nv.us

NEW HAMPSHIRE
Mr. Robert Stowell
Administrator
Bureau of Purchase & Property
State House Annex, Room 102
25 Capitol Street
Concord, NH 03301
P: (603) 271-3606
F: (603) 271-2700
E: rstowel@admin.state.nh.us

NEW JERSEY
Ms. Alice K. Small
Acting Director
Division of Purchases & Property
P.O. Box 039
Trenton, NJ 08625
P: (609) 292-4886
F: (609) 984-2575
E: Alice.Small@treas.state.nj.us

NEW MEXICO
Mr. Michael C. Vinyard
State Purchasing Agent
Purchasing Division
1100 St. Francis Drive
Joseph Montoya Building
Santa Fe, NM 87501
P: (505) 827-0472
F: (505) 827-2484
E: Michael.Vinyard@state.nm.us

NEW YORK
Mr. Jerry Gerard
Acting Director
OGS Procurement Services Group
Corning Tower, 38th Floor
Empire State Plaza
Albany, NY 12242
P: (518) 474-3695
F: (518) 486-6099
E: jerry.gerard@ogs.state.ny.us

NORTH CAROLINA
Mr. Mike Mangum
State Purchasing Officer
Division of Purchase & Contract
Department of Administration
1305 Mail Service Center
Raleigh, NC 27699
P: (919) 807-4515
F: (919) 807-4508
E: mike.mangum@ncmail.net

NORTH DAKOTA
Ms. Linda Belisle
Director
Central Services
Office of Management & Budget
600 East Boulevard, Department 118
Bismarck, ND 58505
P: (701) 328-3494
F: (701) 328-1615
E: lbelisle@state.nd.us

NORTHERN MARIANA ISLANDS
Mr. Thomas A. Tebuteb
Special Assistant for Administration
Office of the Governor
Caller Box 1007
Saipan, MP 96950
P: (670) 664-1514
F: (670) 664-1515

OHIO
Mr. Stephen A. Hunter
Administrator
General Services Division
Office of Procurement Services
4200 Surface Road
Columbus, OH 43228
P: (614) 466-7066
F: (614) 466-7525
E: Stephen.hunter@das.state.oh.us

OKLAHOMA
Ms. Betty Cairns
State Purchasing Director
Central Purchasing Division
Department of Central Services
2401 North Lincoln Boulevard, Suite 116
Oklahoma City, OK 73105
P: (405) 521-2115
F: (405) 522-6266
E: Betty_Cairns@dcs.state.ok.us

Purchasing

OREGON
Ms. Dianne Lancaster
Chief Procurement Officer
State Purchasing Office
Department of Administrative Services
1225 Ferry Street, Southeast
Salem, OR 97301
P: (503) 378-3529
F: (503) 373-1626
E: Dianne.Lancaster@state.or.us

PENNSYLVANIA
Mr. Nicholas Kaczmarek
Chief Procurement Officer
Bureau of Procurement
Department of General Services
555 Walnut Street, Forum Place, Floor 6
Harrisburg, PA 17101
P: (717) 787-5862
F: (717) 346-3819
E: nkaczmarek@state.pa.us

PUERTO RICO
Ms. Maria T. Mujica
Administrator
Purchasing, Services & Supplies
P.O. Box 7428
San Juan, PR 00916
P: (787) 724-0083
F: (787) 722-0580

RHODE ISLAND
Ms. Lorraine A. Hynes
Assistant Director/Acting Purchasing Agent
Division of Purchasing
One Capitol Hill
Providence, RI 02908
P: (401) 574-8123
E: LHynes@purchasing.state.ri.us

SOUTH CAROLINA
Mr. Robert Voight Shealy
Materials Management Officer
Office of General Services
1201 Main Street, Suite 600
Columbia, SC 29201
P: (803) 737-0600
F: (803) 737-0639
E: vshealy@mmo.state.sc.us

SOUTH DAKOTA
Mr. Jeff Holden
Director
Office of Procurement Management
523 East Capitol Avenue
Pierre, SD 57501
P: (605) 773-3405
F: (605) 773-4840
E: jeff.holden@state.sd.us

TENNESSEE
Mr. John Bissell
Interim Director
Purchasing Division
3rd Floor, WRS Tennessee Tower
312 8th Avenue, North
Nashville, TN 37243
P: (615) 741-4302
F: (615) 532-8795
E: John.Bissell@state.tn.us

TEXAS
Mr. Skip Bartek
Deputy Executive Director of Procurement
Building & Procurement Commission
1711 San Jacinto Boulevard
P.O. Box 13047
Austin, TX 78701
P: (512) 463-3337
F: (512) 236-6164
E: skip.bartek@tbpc.state.tx.us

U.S. VIRGIN ISLANDS
Mr. William Daniel
Commissioner
Department of Property & Procurement
Building Number 1, Sub Base
St. Thomas, VI 00820
P: (809) 774-0828
F: (809) 774-9704

UTAH
Mr. Douglas G. Richins
Director of Purchasing
Division of Purchasing & General Services
Department of Administrative Services
3150 State Office Building, Capitol Hill
Salt Lake City, UT 84114
P: (801) 538-3143
F: (801) 538-3882
E: drichins@utah.gov

VERMONT
Ms. Robin L. Orr
Director of Internal Services
Division of Purchasing
Purchasing & Contract Administration
1078 US Route 2-Middlesex
Montpelier, VT 05633
P: (802) 828-2211
F: (802) 828-2222
E: robin.orr@state.vt.us

VIRGINIA
Mr. W. Ron Bell
Director
Division of Purchases & Supply
P.O. Box 1199, Patrick Henry Building
1111 East Broad Street, 6th Floor
Richmond, VA 23218
P: (804) 786-3846
F: (804) 371-7877
E: Ron.Bell@dgs.virginia.gov

WASHINGTON
Mr. Kennith Harden
Assistant Director
Office of State Procurement
210 11th Avenue, Southwest, Room 201
P.O. Box 41017
Olympia, WA 98504
P: (360) 902-7432
F: (360) 586-4944
E: kharden@ga.wa.gov

WEST VIRGINIA
Mr. David Tincher
Director
Purchasing Division
2019 Washington Street, East
P.O. Box 50130
Charleston, WV 25305
P: (304) 558-2538
F: (304) 558-4115
E: dtincher@wvadmin.gov

WISCONSIN
Ms. Helen McCain
Director
Bureau of Procurement
101 East Wilson Street, 6th Floor
P.O. Box 7867
Madison, WI 53707
P: (608) 267-9634
F: (608) 267-0600
E: helen.mccain@doa.state.wi.us

WYOMING
Mr. Mac Landen
Procurement Administrator
Purchasing Section
Dept of Administration & Information
Herschler Building, Second Floor
Cheyenne, WY 82002
P: (307) 777-7253
F: (307) 777-5852
E: MLANDE@state.wy.us

Recycling

Responsible for promoting and implementing state oversight of municipal solid waste recycling, source reduction and recycling within state government and industry.

ALASKA
Ms. Kim Stricklan
Program Manager
Solid Waste Management Program
Department of Environmental Conservation
555 Cordova Street
Anchorage, AK 99501
P: (907) 269-1099
F: (907) 269-7510

ARIZONA
Ms. Tammy Shreeve
Recycling Coordinator
Department of Environmental Quality
1110 West Washington
Phoenix, AZ 85007
P: (602) 771-4171
E: tas@azdeq.gov

ARKANSAS
Mr. Steve Martin
Chief
Solid Waste Division
P.O. Box 8913
Little Rock, AR 72209
P: (501) 682-0600
F: (501) 682-0611
E: martin@adeq.state.ar.us

CALIFORNIA
Mr. Jim Ferguson
Assistant Director
Division of Recycling
801 K Street, MS 19-01
Sacramento, CA 95814
P: (916) 323-3836
F: (916) 327-2144

COLORADO
Mr. Gary Baughman
Director
Hazardous Materials & Waste Management Division
4300 Cherry Creek Drive South
Denver, CO 80246
P: (303) 692-3300
F: (303) 759-5355

CONNECTICUT
Mr. Richard J. Barlow
Bureau Chief
Waste Bureau
Department of Environmental Protection
79 Elm Street
Hartford, CT 06106
P: (860) 424-3021
F: (860) 424-4060

DELAWARE
Mr. Pasquale S. Canzano
Chief Executive Officer
Solid Waste Authority
1128 South Bradford Street
P.O. Box 455
Dover, DE 19903
P: (302) 739-5361
F: (302) 577-8656

DISTRICT OF COLUMBIA
Mr. William Howland
Director
Department of Public Works
2000 14th Street, Northwest
6th Floor
Washington, DC 20009
P: (202) 673-6833
F: (202) 671-0642

FLORIDA
Mr. Charlie Goddard
Chief
Bureau of Solid & Hazardous Waste
Department of Environmental Protection
2600 Blairstone Road, MS 4550
Tallahassee, FL 32399
P: (850) 245-8797
F: (850) 245-8803

GEORGIA
Mr. Greg Mason
Interim Executive Director
Environmental Facilities Authority
233 Peachtree Street, Northeast
Harris Tower, Suite 900
Atlanta, GA 30303
P: (404) 584-1000
F: (404) 584-1069

GUAM
Mr. Lawrence Perez
Director
Department of Public Works
542 North Marine Drive
Tamuning, GU 96913
P: (671) 646-3131
F: (671) 649-6178
E: dpwdir@mail.gov.gu

ILLINOIS
Mr. Hans Detweiler
Deputy Director of Energy & Recycling
Department of Commerce & Economic Opportunity
620 East Adams
Springfield, IL 62701
P: (312) 814-2266
E: hans_detweiler
@commerce.state.il.us

INDIANA
Ms. Monica Hartke-Tarr
Branch Chief
Source Reduction & Recycling
Pollution Prevention & Tech. Assistance
100 North Senate Avenue, Room W041
Indianapolis, IN 46204
P: (317) 233-5431
E: mhartke@idem.in.gov

IOWA
Ms. Elizabeth Christiansen
Deputy Director
Dept. of Natural Resources
Wallace State Office Building
502 East 9th Street
Des Moines, IA 50319
P: (515) 281-8975

KANSAS
Mr. William Bider
Director
Bureau of Waste Management
1000 Southwest Jackson Street
Suite 320
Topeka, KS 66612
P: (785) 296-1600
F: (785) 296-8909

KENTUCKY
Mr. Bruce Scott
Director
Division of Waste Management
14 Reilly Road
Frankfort, KY 40601
P: (502) 564-7042
F: (502) 564-7091
E: bruce.scott@ky.gov

LOUISIANA
Ms. Linda Levy
Administrator
Environmental Assistance Division
Department of Environmental Quality
P.O. Box 4313
Baton Rouge, LA 70821
P: (225) 219-3241
F: (225) 219-3309
E: deqassistance@la.gov

MAINE
Mr. George MacDonald
Director
State Planning Office Recycling Program
38 State House Station
Augusta, ME 04333
P: (207) 287-6077

MARYLAND
Ms. Hilary Miller
Program Administrator
Recycling, Marketing & Operations Program
2500 Broening Highway
Baltimore, MD 21224
P: (410) 537-3314
F: (410) 537-3321

MASSACHUSETTS
Mr. Ian A. Bowles
Secretary
Executive Office of Environmental Affairs
100 Cambridge Street, 9th Floor
Boston, MA 02114
P: (617) 626-1101
F: (617) 626-1181

MICHIGAN
Ms. Amy Butler
Chief
Environmental Science & Services Division
P.O. Box 30457
Lansing, MI 48909
P: (517) 335-2419

MINNESOTA
Ms. Dana Badgerow
Commissioner
Department of Administration
200 Administration Building
50 Sherburne Avenue
St. Paul, MN 55155
P: (651) 201-2555
F: (651) 297-7909
E: dana.badgerow
@state.mn.us

MISSISSIPPI
Mr. John D. Burns
Management
Recycling & Solid Waste Reduction Program
P.O. Box 10385
Jackson, MS 39289
P: (601) 961-5005
F: (601) 961-5703
E: John_D_Burns
@deq.state.ms.us

Recycling

MISSOURI
Mr. Dennis Hansen
Chief
DEQ Solid Waste Management Program
P.O. Box 176
1738 East Elm
Jefferson City, MO 65102
P: (573) 751-3937
F: (573) 526-3902
E: dennis.hansen@dnr.mo.gov

MONTANA
Ms. Janet Kelly
Director
Department of Administration
125 North Roberts Street
P.O. Box 200101
Helena, MT 59620
P: (406) 444-3033
F: (406) 444-6194
E: jakelly@mt.gov

NEBRASKA
Mr. Michael J. Linder
Director
Department of Environmental Quality
1200 N Street, Suite 400
P.O. Box 98922
Lincoln, NE 68509
P: (402) 471-0275
F: (402) 471-2909

NEVADA
Mr. Leo Drozdoff
Administrator
Division of Environmental Protection
901 South Stewart, Suite 4001
Carson City, NV 89701
P: (775) 687-9301
F: (775) 687-5856
E: ldrozdof@ndep.nv.gov

NEW JERSEY
Mr. Guy Watson
Bureau Chief
Bureau of Recycling & Planning
Departmant of Environmental Protection
P.O. Box 402
Trenton, NJ 08625
P: (609) 984-3438
F: (609) 777-0769
E: Guy.Watson@dep.state.nj.us

NEW MEXICO
Ms. Auralie Ashley-Marx
Bureau Chief
Solid Waste Bureau
P.O. Box 26110
1190 St. Francis Drive, N4050
Santa Fe, NM 87505
P: (505) 827-2775
F: (505) 827-2902
E: auralie.ashley-marx@state.nm.us

NEW YORK
Mr. Jeffrey Schmitt
Director
Bureau of Solid Waste Reduction & Recycling
625 Broadway
Albany, NY 12207
P: (518) 402-8678

NORTH CAROLINA
Mr. Brian Haynesworth
Manager
Facility Management Division
431 North Salisbury Street
1313 Mail Service Center
Raleigh, NC 27699
P: (919) 733-3514
F: (919) 733-1430
E: brian.haynesworth@ncmail.net

NORTH DAKOTA
Mr. Scott Radig
Director
Division of Waste Management
918 East Divide Avenue, 3rd Floor
Bismark, ND 58501
P: (701) 328-5166
F: (701) 328-5200
E: sradig@nd.gov

NORTHERN MARIANA ISLANDS
Mr. Jose S. Demapan
Secretary
Department of Public Works
Caller Box 10007, Capitol Hill
Saipan, MP 96950
P: (670) 235-5827
F: (670) 235-6346

OHIO
Mr. Sean D. Logan
Director
Department of Natural Resources
1930 Belcher Drive
Columbus, OH 43224
P: (614) 265-6879

OKLAHOMA
Mr. Scott Thompson
Director
Land Protection Division
P.O. Box 1677
Oklahoma City, OK 73118
P: (405) 702-5100
F: (405) 702-5101
E: scott.thompson@deq.state.ok.us

OREGON
Ms. Elin Shepard
State Recycling Coordinator
Department of Administrative Services
1225 Ferry Street, Southeast U100
Salem, OR 97301
P: (503) 378-2865 Ext. 241
F: (503) 373-7210
E: elin.d.shepard@state.or.us

PENNSYLVANIA
Mr. Kenneth Reisinger
Director
Bureau of Waste Management
Department of Environmental Protection
P.O. Box 8471
Harrisburg, PA 17105
P: (717) 783-2388
F: (717) 787-1904

PUERTO RICO
Mr. Jose Negron
Interim Director
Solid Waste Management Authority
P.O. Box 40285
San Juan, PR 00918
P: (787) 765-7575
F: (787) 753-2220

RHODE ISLAND
Mr. A. Austin Ferland
Chair & CEO
Resource Recovery Corporation
65 Shun Pike
Johnston, RI 02919
P: (401) 942-1430
F: (401) 946-5174
E: recycle@loa.com

SOUTH CAROLINA
Mr. Patrick Walker
Chief
Bureau of Land & Waste Management
Dept. of Health & Environmental Control
2600 Bull Street
Columbia, SC 29201
P: (803) 896-4000
F: (803) 896-4001
E: walkerpt@dhec.sc.gov

SOUTH DAKOTA
Ms. Vonni Kallemeyn
Administrator
Waste Management Program
Foss Building
523 East Capitol Avenue
Pierre, SD 57501
P: (605) 773-3153
F: (605) 773-6035
E: vonni.kallemeyn@state.sd.us

TENNESSEE
Mr. Jim Fyke
Commissioner
Department of Environment & Conservation
1st Floor, L & C Annex
401 Church Street
Nashville, TN 37243
P: (615) 532-0106
F: (615) 532-0120

TEXAS
Mr. Gregg Werkenthin
Division Director
Facilities Leasing & Space Allocation Division
Building & Procurement Commission
P.O. Box 13087
Austin, TX 78711
P: (512) 239-5505
F: (512) 239-5533

U.S. VIRGIN ISLANDS
Mr. Darryl Smalls
Commissioner
Department of Public Works
6002 Estate Anna's Hope
Christiansted, VI 00820
P: (340) 773-1789
F: (340) 773-0670

UTAH
Ms. Sonja Wallace
Pollution Prevention Coordinator
Dept. of Environmental Quality - Office of Planning/Public Affairs
168 North 1950 West
P.O. Box 144810
Salt Lake City, UT 84114
P: (801) 536-4477
F: (801) 536-4457
E: swallace@utah.gov

VERMONT
Mr. Marc Roy
Chief
Recycling & Conservation Section
103 South Main Street
Waterbury, VT 05671
P: (802) 241-3874
F: (802) 241-3273
E: marc.roy@state.vt.us

VIRGINIA
Mr. David K. Paylor
Director
Department of Environmental Quality
629 East Main Street
P.O. Box 10009
Richmond, VA 23240
P: (804) 698-4390
F: (804) 698-4019
E: dkpaylor@deq.virginia.gov

WASHINGTON
Mr. Cullen Stephenson
Program Manager
Solid Waste & Financial Assistance
P.O. Box 47600
Olympia, WA 98504
P: (360) 407-6103

WEST VIRGINIA
Mr. Richard P. Cooke
Director
Solid Waste Management Board
601 57th Street, Southeast
Charleston, WV 25304
P: (304) 926-0499 Ext. 1680
F: (304) 926-0472
E: dcooke@wvswmb.org

WISCONSIN
Ms. Catherine Cooper
Coordinator
Waste Management Program
101 South Webster, 3rd Floor
P.O. Box 7921
Madison, WI 53707
P: (608) 267-3133
F: (608) 267-2768

WYOMING
Mr. John V. Corra
Director
Department of Environmental Quality
122 West 25th Street, 4W
Cheyenne, WY 82002
P: (307) 777-7937
F: (307) 777-7682
E: jcorra@state.wy.us

Revenue

Administers state tax laws and the collection and processing of state taxes.

ALABAMA
Mr. Tom Surtees
Commissioner
Department of Revenue
50 Ripley Street, 4th Floor
Montgomery, AL 36132
P: (334) 242-1170
F: (334) 242-0550

ALASKA
Mr. Patrick Galvin
Commissioner
Department of Revenue
P.O. Box 110400
Juneau, AK 99811
P: (907) 465-2300
F: (907) 465-2389

AMERICAN SAMOA
Hon. Velega Savali
Treasurer
Department of Treasury
American Samoa Government
Pago Pago, AS 96799
P: (684) 633-4155
F: (684) 633-4100

ARIZONA
Mr. Gale Garriott
Director
Department of Revenue
1600 West Monroe
Phoenix, AZ 85007
P: (602) 716-6090
F: (602) 542-2072

ARKANSAS
Mr. John H. Theis
Assistant Commissioner of Revenue
Policy & Legal Revenue Division
P.O. Box 1272
Little Rock, AR 72203
P: (501) 682-7000
F: (501) 682-1161
E: john.theis@rev.state.ar.us

CALIFORNIA
Mr. Selvi Stanislaus
Executive Officer
Franchise Tax Board
P.O. Box 115
Rancho Cordova, CA 95741
P: (916) 845-4543
F: (916) 845-3191

COLORADO
Ms. Roxy Huber
Executive Director
Department of Revenue
1375 Sherman Street
Denver, CO 80261
P: (303) 866-5610
F: (303) 866-2400

CONNECTICUT
Ms. Pamela Law
Commissioner
Department of Revenue Services
25 Sigourney Street
Hartford, CT 06106
P: (860) 297-4900
F: (860) 297-5698
E: drs@po.state.ct.us

DELAWARE
Mr. Patrick Carter
Director
Division of Revenue
State Treasury
820 North French Street, 8th Floor
Wilmington, DE 19801
P: (302) 577-8686
F: (302) 577-8656
E: patrick.carter@state.de.us

FLORIDA
Mr. Jim Zingale
Executive Director
Department of Revenue
1379 Blountstown Highway
Tallahassee, FL 32304
P: (850) 488-5050
E: zingalej@dor.state.fl.us

GEORGIA
Mr. Bart L. Graham
Revenue Commissioner
Department of Revenue
1800 Century Center Boulevard, Northeast
Atlanta, GA 30345
P: (404) 417-2100

GUAM
Mr. Artemio B. Illagan
Acting Director
Department of Revenue & Taxation
13-1 Mariner Drive, Tiyan
P.O. Box 23607
Barrigada, GU 96921
P: (671) 475-1817
F: (671) 472-2643

HAWAII
Mr. Kurt Kawafuchi
Director
Department of Taxation
830 Punchbowl Street
Honolulu, HI 96813
P: (808) 587-1540
F: (808) 587-1560
E: Tax.Directors.Office@hawaii.gov

IDAHO
Mr. Royce Chigbrow
Chair
Tax Commission
800 Park Boulevard
Boise, ID 83722
P: (208) 334-7660

ILLINOIS
Mr. Brian A. Hamer
Director of Revenue
Department of Revenue
101 West Jefferson Street, # 6-500
Springfield, IL 62794
P: (217) 785-7570
F: (217) 782-6337

INDIANA
Mr. John Eckart
Commissioner
Department of Revenue
100 North Senate Avenue, Room N248
Indianapolis, IN 46204
P: (317) 232-8039
F: (317) 232-2103

IOWA
Mr. Mark Schuling
Director
Department of Revenue
Hoover Building
1305 East Walnut Street
Des Moines, IA 50319
P: (515) 281-3204
E: mark.schuling@idrf.state.ia.us

KANSAS
Ms. Joan Wagnon
Secretary
Revenue Department
915 Southwest Harrison Street, 2nd Floor
Topeka, KS 66612
P: (785) 296-3909
F: (785) 296-7928

KENTUCKY
Ms. Marian Davis
Commissioner
Department of Revenue
200 Fair Oaks Lane
Frankfort, KY 40620
P: (502) 564-4581
F: (502) 564-3875

LOUISIANA
Ms. Cynthia Bridges
Secretary
Department of Revenue
P.O. Box 66258
Baton Rouge, LA 70896
P: (225) 219-2700
F: (225) 219-2708

MAINE
Mr. Jerome Gerard
Director
Revenue Services
24 State House Station
Augusta, ME 04333
P: (207) 287-2076

MARYLAND
Mr. James M. Arnie
Director
Revenue Administration Division
Office of the Comptroller
110 Carroll Street, Room 105
Annapolis, MD 21401
P: (410) 260-7445
F: (410) 974-3456
E: jarnie@comp.state.md.us

MASSACHUSETTS
Mr. Alan L. LeBovidge
Commissioner
Department of Revenue
100 Cambridge Street, 8th Floor
Boston, MA 02114
P: (617) 626-2201
F: (617) 626-2299

MICHIGAN
Mr. Jeff Guilfoyle
Manager
Office of Revenue & Tax Analysis
430 West Allegan Street
Lansing, MI 48922
P: (517) 373-2697

MINNESOTA
Mr. Ward Einess
Commissioner
Department of Revenue
600 North Robert Street, 4th Floor
St. Paul, MN 55146
P: (651) 556-6003
F: (651) 556-3133
E: ward.einess@state.mn.us

MISSISSIPPI
Mr. Joe Blount
Chair
State Tax Commission
P.O. Box 22828
Jackson, MS 39225
P: (601) 923-7411
F: (601) 923-7423
E: jblount@mstc.state.ms.us

MISSOURI
Ms. Trish Vincent
Director
Department of Revenue
Truman Building, Room 670
P.O. Box 311
Jefferson City, MO 65105
P: (573) 751-4450
F: (573) 751-7150
E: trish.vincent@dor.mo.gov

MONTANA
Mr. Dan Bucks
Director
Department of Revenue
P.O. Box 5805
Helena, MT 59604
P: (406) 444-3696
F: (406) 444-1505
E: dbucks@mt.gov

NEBRASKA
Mr. Doug Ewald
Tax Commissioner
Department of Revenue
P.O. Box 94818
Lincoln, NE 68509
P: (402) 471-2971
F: (402) 471-5608

NEVADA
Mr. Dino DiCianno
Executive Director
Department of Taxation
1550 East College Parkway, Suite 115
Carson City, NV 89706
P: (775) 684-2000
F: (775) 684-2020
E: dicianno@tax.state.nv.us

NEW HAMPSHIRE
Mr. George P. Blatsos
Commissioner
Department of Revenue Administration
P.O. Box 457
Concord, NH 03302
P: (603) 271-2318
F: (603) 271-6121
E: gblatsos@rev.state.nh.us

NEW JERSEY
Ms. Maureen Adams
Acting Director
Division of Taxation
P.O. Box 281
Trenton, NJ 08695
P: (609) 292-6400

Dr. Carol O'Cleireacain
Acting Director
Division of Taxation
P.O. Box 281
Trenton, NJ 08695
P: (609) 292-6400

NEW MEXICO
Ms. Jan Goodwin
Secretary
Department of Taxation & Revenue
1100 South St. Francis Drive
P.O. Box 630
Santa Fe, NM 87504
P: (505) 827-0341
F: (505) 827-0331
E: jgoodwin@state.nm.us

NEW YORK
Ms. Barbara Billett
Commissioner
Department of Taxation & Finance
State Office Campus, Building 9
Albany, NY 12227
P: (518) 457-2244
F: (518) 473-7204

NORTH CAROLINA
Mr. Norris Tolson
Secretary
Department of Revenue
501 North Wilmington Street
P.O. Box 871
Raleigh, NC 27640
P: (919) 733-7211
F: (919) 733-0023
E: norris.tolson@dornc.com

NORTH DAKOTA
Mr. Cory Fong
Commissioner
Tax Department
600 East Boulevard Avenue, 7th Floor
Bismarck, ND 58505
P: (701) 328-2770
F: (701) 328-3700

NORTHERN MARIANA ISLANDS
Ms. Estrellita S. Ada
Director of Revenue & Tax
Division of Revenue & Taxation
Caller Box 10007, Capitol Hill
Saipan, MP 96950
P: (670) 664-1000
F: (670) 664-1015
E: revtax@gtepacifica.net

OHIO
Mr. Richard A. Levin
Tax Commissioner
Department of Taxation
30 East Broad Street, 22nd Floor
Columbus, OH 43215
P: (614) 466-2166
F: (614) 644-8292

OKLAHOMA
Mr. Thomas Kemp
Chair
Tax Commission
2501 North Lincoln Boulevard
Oklahoma City, OK 73194
P: (405) 521-3160
F: (405) 522-0074

OREGON
Ms. Elizabeth S. Harchenko
Director
Department of Revenue
955 Center Street, Northeast, Room 457
Salem, OR 97301
P: (503) 945-8214
F: (503) 945-8290
E: elizabeth.s.harchenko@state.or.us

PENNSYLVANIA
Mr. Thomas Wolf
Secretary
Department of Revenue
1133 Stawberry Sqaure
Harrisburg, PA 17128
P: (717) 783-3680
F: (717) 787-3990

PUERTO RICO
Mr. Juan Carlos Mendez Torres
Secretary of the Treasury
Department of Treasury
PO Box 9024140
San Juan, PR 00902
P: (787) 721-2020

RHODE ISLAND
Mr. John J. Nugent
Associate Director
Revenue Services & Taxation
Division of Taxation
1 Capitol Hill
Providence, RI 02908
P: (401) 222-3050

SOUTH CAROLINA
Mr. Ray N. Stevens
Director
Department of Revenue
P.O. Box 125
Columbia, SC 29214
P: (803) 898-5040
E: StevensR@sctax.org

SOUTH DAKOTA
Mr. Paul Kinsman
Secretary
Department of Revenue & Regulation
Anderson Building
445 East Capitol Avenue
Pierre, SD 57501
P: (605) 773-5131
F: (605) 773-5129
E: paul.kinsman@state.sd.us

TENNESSEE
Mr. Reagan Farr
Commissioner
Department of Revenue
1200 Andrew Jackson Building
Nashville, TN 37219
P: (615) 741-2461
F: (615) 741-2883

TEXAS
Ms. Susan Combs
Comptroller of Public Accounts
Office of the Comptroller of Public Accounts
P.O. Box 13528, Capitol Station
Austin, TX 78711
P: (512) 463-4444
F: (512) 475-0450
E: scombs@cpa.state.tx.us

U.S. VIRGIN ISLANDS
Ms. Gizette Thomas
Director
Internal Revenue Bureau
9601 Estate Thomas
St. Thomas, VI 00802
P: (340) 774-5865
F: (340) 714-9345

Revenue

UTAH
Mr. Rodney G. Marrelli
Executive Director
State Tax Commission
210 North 1950 West
Salt Lake City, UT 84134
P: (801) 297-3845
F: (801) 297-3891
E: rmarrelli@utah.gov

VERMONT
Mr. Jim Reardon
Commissioner
Department of Finance & Management
109 State Street
Montpelier, VT 05602
P: (802) 828-2376
F: (802) 828-2428
E: jim.reardon@state.vt.us

VIRGINIA
Ms. Janie Bowen
Tax Commissioner
Department of Taxation
Main Street Centre
600 East Main Street, 23rd Floor
Richmond, VA 23219
P: (804) 786-3301
F: (804) 786-4208
E: janie.bowen@tax.virginia.gov

WASHINGTON
Ms. Cindi L. Holmstrom
Director
Department of Revenue
P.O. Box 47454
Olympia, WA 98504
P: (360) 586-3462
F: (360) 586-2163
E: cindih@dor.wa.gov

WEST VIRGINIA
Mr. James Alsop
Director
Department of Revenue
P.O. Box 963
Charleston, WV 25305
P: (304) 558-0211
F: (304) 558-2324
E: ralsop@tax.state.wv.us

WISCONSIN
Mr. Roger M. Ervin
Secretary of Revenue
Department of Revenue
P.O. Box 8933
#624-a
Madison, WI 53708
P: (608) 266-6466
F: (608) 266-5718

WYOMING
Mr. Edmund J. Schmidt
Director
Department of Revenue
Herschler Building
122 West 25th Street, 2nd West
Cheyenne, WY 82002
P: (307) 777-5287
F: (307) 777-7722
E: Ed.Schmidt@wyo.gov

Savings and Loan

Administers laws regulating the operation of savings and loan associations in the state.

ALABAMA
Mr. John Harrison
Director
Banking Department
401 Adams Avenue, Suite 680
Montgomery, AL 36130
P: (334) 242-3585
F: (334) 242-3500
E: john.harrison
@banking.alabama.gov

ALASKA
Mr. Mark R. Davis
Director
Department of Commerce, Community & Economic Development
Banking, Securities & Corporations
P.O. Box 110807
Juneau, AK 99811
P: (907) 465-2521
F: (907) 465-2549

ARIZONA
Mr. Tom Wood
Manager
Banks, Trust Companies & Savings and Loans
Financial Institutions Division
2910 North 44th Street, Suite 310
Phoenix, AZ 85018
P: (602) 255-4421
F: (602) 381-1225

ARKANSAS
Mr. Michael B. Johnson
Securities Commissioner
Securities Department
Heritage West Building
201 East Markham, Room 300
Little Rock, AR 72201
P: (501) 324-9260
F: (501) 324-9268

CALIFORNIA
Mr. Michael A. Kelley
Commissioner
Department of Financial Institutions
111 Pine Street, Suite 1100
San Francisco, CA 94111
P: (415) 263-8507
F: (415) 989-5310

COLORADO
Mr. Chris Myklebust
Commissioner
Division of Financial Services
Department of Regulatory Agencies
1560 Broadway, Room 1520
Denver, CO 80202
P: (303) 894-7741
F: (303) 894-7886

CONNECTICUT
Mr. Howard Pitkin
Commissioner
Department of Banking
260 Constitution Plaza
Hartford, CT 06103
P: (860) 240-8100
F: (860) 240-8178

DELAWARE
Mr. Robert A. Glen
Commissioner
Office of State Banks
555 East Lockerman Street, Suite 210
Dover, DE 19901
P: (302) 739-4235
F: (302) 739-3609

DISTRICT OF COLUMBIA
Mr. Thomas Hampton
Director
Department of Insurance, Securities & Banking
810 1st Street, Northeast
Suite 701
Washington, DC 20002
P: (202) 442-7773
F: (202) 535-1196

FLORIDA
Hon. Alex Sink (D)
Chief Financial Officer
Department of Financial Services
Fletcher Building, Suite 516
200 East Gaines Street
Tallahassee, FL 32399
P: (850) 413-2850
F: (850) 413-2950
E: alex.sink@fldfs.com

GEORGIA
Mr. Rob Braswell
Commissioner
Department of Banking & Finance
2990 Brandywine Road, Suite 200
Atlanta, GA 30341
P: (770) 986-1621
F: (770) 986-1655
E: robertb@dbf.state.ga.us

HAWAII
Mr. Dominic B. Griffin III
Commissioner
Division of Financial Institutions
335 Merchant Street
Room 221
Honolulu, HI 96813
P: (808) 586-2820
F: (808) 586-2818

IDAHO
Mr. Gavin Gee
Director
Department of Finance
700 West State Street, 2nd Floor
Boise, ID 83702
P: (208) 332-8010
F: (208) 332-8097
E: gavin.gee
@finance.idaho.gov

ILLINOIS
Mr. D. Lorenzo Padron
Director
Division of Banking
310 South Michigan Avenue, Suite 2130
Chicago, IL 60604
P: (312) 793-1418
F: (312) 793-0756
E: DLPadron@idfpr.com

INDIANA
Ms. Judith Ripley
Director
Department of Financial Institutions
30 South Meridian Street, Suite 300
Indianapolis, IN 46204
P: (317) 232-3955
F: (317) 232-7655
E: jripley@dfi.state.in.us

IOWA
Mr. Thomas B. Gronstal
Superintendent
Division of Banking
200 East Grand Avenue, Suite 300
Des Moines, IA 50309
P: (515) 281-4014
F: (515) 281-4862

KANSAS
Mr. Tom Thull
Commissioner
Office of the State Banking Commissioner
700 Southwest Jackson Street, Suite 300
Topeka, KS 66603
P: (785) 296-2266
F: (785) 296-0168

KENTUCKY
Mr. Cordell Lawrence
Executive Director
Office of Financial Institutions
1025 Capital Center Drive
Frankfort, KY 40601
P: (502) 573-3390
F: (502) 573-0086
E: cordell.lawrence@ky.gov

LOUISIANA
Mr. Sidney E. Seymour
Chief Examiner
Office of Financial Institutions
8660 United Plaza Boulevard
Second Floor
Baton Rouge, LA 70809
P: (225) 925-4660
F: (225) 925-4548
E: sseymour
@ofi.louisiana.gov

MAINE
Mr. Howard Gray
Superintendent
Bureau of Banking
36 State House Station
Augusta, ME 04333
P: (207) 624-8648

MARYLAND
Mr. Charles W. Turnbaugh
Commissioner of Financial Regulation
Department of Labor, Licensing & Regulation
500 North Calvert Street
Room 402
Baltimore, MD 21202
P: (410) 230-6100
F: (410) 333-0475
E: cturnbaugh
@dllr.state.md.us

MASSACHUSETTS
Mr. Steven Antonakes
Commissioner
Division of Banks
1 South Station, 3rd Floor
Boston, MA 02110
P: (617) 956-1500
F: (617) 956-1599

Savings and Loan

MICHIGAN
Ms. Linda A. Watters
Commissioner
Office of Financial & Insurance Services
Department of Labor & Economic Growth
611 West Ottawa Street, Third Floor
Lansing, MI 48933
P: (877) 999-6442
F: (517) 241-3953
E: ofis-sec-info@michigan.gov

MINNESOTA
Mr. Glenn Wilson
Commissioner
Department of Commerce
85 7th Place East, Suite 500
St. Paul, MN 55101
P: (651) 296-6025
F: (651) 282-2568
E: glenn.wilson@state.mn.us

MISSISSIPPI
Mr. John S. Allison
Commissioner
Department of Banking & Consumer Finance
501 North West Street
901 Woolfolk Building, Suite A
Jackson, MS 39202
P: (601) 359-1031
F: (601) 359-3557
E: jallison@dbcf.state.ms.us

MISSOURI
Mr. Eric McClure
Commissioner
Division of Finance
Truman Building, Room 630
P.O. Box 716
Jefferson City, MO 65102
P: (573) 751-2545
F: (573) 751-9192
E: eric.mcclure@ded.mo.gov

MONTANA
Ms. Annie Goodwin
Commissioner
Department of Administration
P.O. Box 200546
301 South Park, Suite 316
Helena, MT 59620
P: (406) 841-2920
F: (406) 841-2930
E: angoodwin@mt.gov

NEBRASKA
Mr. John Munn
Director
Department of Banking & Finance
P.O. Box 95006
Lincoln, NE 68509
P: (402) 471-2171
E: john.munn@bkg.state.ne.us

NEVADA
Mr. Steven Kondrup
Acting Commissioner
Financial Institutions Division
2501 East Sahara Avenue
Suite 300
Las Vegas, NV 89104
P: (702) 486-4120
F: (702) 486-4563
E: skondrup@fid.state.nv.us

NEW HAMPSHIRE
Mr. Peter C. Hildreth
Commissioner
Banking Department
64 B Old Suncook Road
Concord, NH 03301
P: (603) 271-3561
F: (603) 271-1090
E: phildreth@banking.state.nh.us

NEW JERSEY
Mr. Steven M. Goldman
Commissioner
Department of Banking & Insurance
P.O. Box 325
Trenton, NJ 08625
P: (609) 292-5360
F: (609) 663-3601
E: commissioner@dobi.state.nj.us

NEW MEXICO
Mr. William J. Verant
Director
Financial Institutions Division
Regulation & Licensing Department
2550 Cerrillos Road
Santa Fe, NM 87505
P: (505) 476-4885
F: (505) 476-4511
E: william.verant@state.nm.us

NEW YORK
Mr. Richard Neiman
Superintendent
Banking Department
1 State Street
New York, NY 10001
P: (212) 827-7099
F: (518) 473-7204

NORTH CAROLINA
Mr. Joseph A. Smith Jr.
Commissioner of Banks
Banking Commission
316 West Edenton Street
4309 Mail Service Center
Raleigh, NC 27699
P: (919) 733-3016
F: (919) 733-6918
E: jsmith@nccob.org

NORTH DAKOTA
Mr. Timothy J. Karsky
Commissioner
Department of Financial Institutions
2000 Schafer Street, Suite G
Bismarck, ND 58501
P: (701) 328-9933
F: (701) 328-9955
E: tkarsky@nd.gov

NORTHERN MARIANA ISLANDS
Mr. James A. Santos
Director
Department of Commerce
Caller Box 10007, Capital Hill
Saipan, MP 96950
P: (670) 664-3000
F: (670) 664-3070
E: commercedept@vzpacifica.net

OHIO
Mr. Michael Roark
Deputy Superintendent
Division of Financial Institutions
77 South High Street, 21st Floor
Columbus, OH 43215
P: (614) 728-8400

OKLAHOMA
Mr. Mick Thompson
Commissioner
State Banking Department
4545 North Lincoln Boulevard, Suite 164
Oklahoma City, OK 73105
P: (405) 521-2782
F: (405) 522-2993

OREGON
Mr. Floyd G. Lanter
Division Administrator
Division of Finance & Corporate Securities
350 Winter Street, Northeast
Room 410
Salem, OR 97301
P: (503) 378-4387
F: (503) 947-7862

Mr. David C. Tatman
Division Administrator
Division of Finance & Corporate Securities
350 Winter Street, Northeast, Room 410
Salem, OR 97301
P: (503) 378-4387
F: (503) 947-7862

PENNSYLVANIA
Ms. Victoria A. Reider
Acting Secretary of Banking
Department of Banking
17 North Second Street, 13th Floor
Harrisburg, PA 17101
P: (717) 214-8343
F: (717) 787-8773

RHODE ISLAND
Mr. Dennis F. Ziroli
Associate Director & Superintendent of Banking
Banking Regulations Division
233 Richmond Street
Providence, RI 02903
P: (401) 222-2405
F: (401) 222-5628
E: dziroli@dbr.state.ri.us

SOUTH CAROLINA
Hon. Thomas Ravenel (R)
State Treasurer
Office of the Treasurer
P.O. Box 11778
Columbia, SC 29211
P: (803) 734-2101
F: (803) 734-2690
E: treasurer@sto.sc.gov

TEXAS
Mr. Danny Payne
Commisssioner
Department of Savings & Mortgage Lending
2601 North Lamar Boulevard, Suite 201
Austin, TX 78705
P: (512) 475-1353
F: (512) 475-1360

U.S. VIRGIN ISLANDS
Mr. John McDonald
Director
Division of Banking & Insurance
#18 Kongens Gade
St. Thomas, VI 00802
P: (340) 774-7166
F: (340) 774-9458

UTAH
Mr. G. Edward Leary
Commissioner
Department of Financial Institutions
324 South State, Suite 201
P.O. Box 146800
Salt Lake City, UT 84114
P: (801) 538-8761
F: (801) 538-8894
E: ELEARY@utah.gov

VERMONT
Ms. Paulette J. Thabault
Commissioner
Department of Banking, Insurance, Securities & Health Care
89 Main Street
Drawer 20
Montpelier, VT 05620
P: (802) 828-3301
F: (802) 828-3306

VIRGINIA
Mr. E. Joseph Face Jr.
Director
Bureau of Financial Institutions
1300 East Main Street, Suite 800
P.O. Box 640
Richmond, VA 23218
P: (804) 371-9657
F: (804) 371-9416
E: joe.face@scc.virginia.gov

WASHINGTON
Mr. David Kroeger
Director
Banks Division
Department of Financial Institutions
P.O. Box 41200
Olympia, WA 98504
P: (360) 902-8704
F: (360) 753-6070

WEST VIRGINIA
Mr. Larry A. Stark
Commissioner
Division of Banking
Building 3, Room 311-A
1800 Washington Street, East
Charleston, WV 25305
P: (304) 558-2294
F: (304) 558-0442
E: lstark@wvdob.org

Secretary of State

Statewide official who oversees a variety of electoral, registration, publication, and legislative duties for the state.

Information provided by:

National Association of Secretaries of State
Leslie Reynolds
Executive Director
444 North Capitol Street, NW
Suite 401
Washington, DC 20001
P: (202) 624-3525
F: (202) 624-3527
reynolds@sso.org
www.nass.org

ALABAMA
Hon. Beth Chapman (R)
Secretary of State
Office of the Secretary of State
State House
600 Dexter Avenue
Montgomery, AL 36104
P: (334) 242-7205
F: (334) 242-4993
E: beth.chapman@sos.alabama.gov

ARIZONA
Hon. Jan Brewer (R)
Secretary of State
Office of the Secretary of State
7th Floor, State Capitol
1700 West Washington Street
Phoenix, AZ 85007
P: (520) 628-6583
F: (520) 628-6938
E: lglenn@azsos.gov

ARKANSAS
Hon. Charlie Daniels (D)
Secretary of State
Office of the Secretary of State
256 State Capitol Building
Little Rock, AR 72201
P: (501) 682-1010
F: (501) 682-3510
E: larowland@sosmail.state.ar.us

CALIFORNIA
Hon. Debra Bowen (D)
Secretary of State
Office of the Secretary of State
1500 11th Street
Sacramento, CA 95814
P: (916) 653-7244
F: (916) 653-1458
E: Debra.bowen@sos.ca.gov

COLORADO
Hon. Mike Coffman (R)
Secretary of State
Office of the Secretary of State
1700 Broadway, Suite 250
Denver, CO 80290
P: (303) 894-2200
F: (303) 869-4860
E: secretary@sos.state.co.us

CONNECTICUT
Hon. Susan Bysiewicz (D)
Secretary of State
Office of the Secretary of State
State Capitol, Room 104
Hartford, CT 06105
P: (860) 509-6200
F: (860) 509-6209
E: Susan.Bysiewicz@po.state.ct.us

DELAWARE
Hon. Harriet Smith Windsor (D)
Secretary of State
Office of the Secretary of State
Townsend Building
P.O. Box 898
Dover, DE 19903
P: (302) 739-4111
F: (302) 739-3811
E: hnsmith@state.de.us

DISTRICT OF COLUMBIA
Hon. Stephanie Scott (appointed)
Secretary of the District
Office of the Secretary
1350 Pennsylvania Avenue, Northwest
Suite 419
Washington, DC 20004
P: (202) 727-6306
F: (202) 727-3582
E: Stephanie.Scott@dc.gov

FLORIDA
Hon. Kurt Browning (R)
Secretary of State
Office of the Secretary of State
R. A. Gray Building
500 South Bronough Street, Suite 100
Tallahassee, FL 32399
P: (850) 245-6500
F: (850) 245-6125
E: secretaryofstate@dos.state.fl.us

GEORGIA
Hon. Karen Handel (R)
Secretary of State
Office of the Secretary of State
State Capitol, Room 214
Atlanta, GA 30334
P: (404) 656-2881
F: (404) 656-0513
E: Jayers@sos.state.ga.us

IDAHO
Hon. Ben T. Ysursa (R)
Secretary of State
Office of the Secretary of State
State Capitol, Room 203
Boise, ID 83720
P: (208) 334-2300
F: (208) 334-2282
E: bysursa@sos.idaho.gov

ILLINOIS
Hon. Jesse White (D)
Secretary of State
Office of the Secretary of State
213 State Capitol
Springfield, IL 62756
P: (217) 782-2201
F: (217) 785-0358
E: jessewhite@ilsos.net

INDIANA
Hon. Todd Rokita (R)
Secretary of State
Office of the Secretary of State
201 State House
Indianapolis, IN 46204
P: (317) 232-6532
F: (317) 233-3283
E: assistant@sos.state.in.us

IOWA
Hon. Michael A. Mauro (D)
Secretary of State
Office of the Secretary of State
State House, Room 105
Des Moines, IA 50319
P: (515) 281-8993
F: (515) 242-5952
E: sos@sos.state.ia.us

KANSAS
Hon. Ron Thornburgh (R)
Secretary of State
Office of the Secretary of State
120 Southwest 10th Avenue
Memorial Hall
Topeka, KS 66612
P: (785) 296-4575
F: (785) 368-8033
E: Ron_Thornburgh@kssos.org

KENTUCKY
Hon. Trey Grayson (R)
Secretary of State
Office of the Secretary of State
700 Capitol Avenue, Suite 152
Frankfort, KY 40601
P: (502) 564-3490
F: (502) 564-5687
E: sos.secretary@ky.gov

LOUISIANA
Hon. Jay Dardenne (R)
Secretary of State
Office of the Secretary of State
P.O. Box 94125
Baton Rouge, LA 70804
P: (225) 342-4479
F: (225) 342-5577
E: admin@sos.louisiana.gov

MAINE
Hon. Matthew Dunlap (D)
Secretary of State
Office of the Secretary of State
148 State House Station
Augusta, ME 04333
P: (207) 626-8400
F: (207) 287-8598
E: sos.office@maine.gov

MARYLAND
Hon. Dennis Schnepfe (D) (appointed)
Interim Secretary of State
Office of the Secretary of State
State House
Annapolis, MD 21401
P: (410) 974-5521
F: (410) 974-5190
E: support@sos.nv.gov

MASSACHUSETTS
Hon. William Francis Galvin (D)
Secretary of the Commonwealth
Office of the Secretary of the Commonwealth
State House, Room 337
Boston, MA 02133
P: (617) 727-9180
F: (617) 742-4722
E: cis@sec.state.ma.us

MICHIGAN
Hon. Terri Lynn Land (R)
Secretary of State
Office of the Secretary of State
430 West Allegan Street, 4th Floor
Lansing, MI 48918
P: (517) 373-2510
F: (517) 373-0727
E: secretary@michigan.gov

MINNESOTA
Hon. Mark Ritchie (DFL)
Secretary of State
Office of the Secretary of State
180 State Office Building
100 Constitution Avenue
St. Paul, MN 55155
P: (651) 296-2803
F: (651) 297-5844
E: secretary.state@state.mn.us

MISSISSIPPI
Hon. Eric Clark (D)
Secretary of State
Office of the Secretary of State
P.O. Box 136
401 Mississippi Street
Jackson, MS 39205
P: (601) 359-1350
F: (601) 359-1499
E: administrator@sos.state.ms.us

MISSOURI
Hon. Robin Carnahan (D)
Secretary of State
Office of the Secretary of State
600 West Main
P.O. Box 1767
Jefferson City, MO 65101
P: (573) 751-4936
F: (573) 552-3082
E: SOSMain@sos.mo.gov

MONTANA
Hon. Brad Johnson (R)
Secretary of State
Office of the Secretary of State
P.O. Box 202801
Helena, MT 59620
P: (406) 444-2034
F: (406) 444-3976
E: sosinfo@mt.gov

NEBRASKA
Hon. John A. Gale (R)
Secretary of State
Office of the Secretary of State
1445 K Street, Suite 2300
P.O. Box 94608
Lincoln, NE 68509
P: (402) 471-2554
F: (402) 471-3237
E: secretaryofstate@sos.ne.gov

NEVADA
Hon. Ross Miller (D)
Secretary of State
Office of the Secretary of State
101 North Carson Street, Suite 3
Carson City, NV 89701
P: (775) 684-5708
F: (775) 684-5724
E: sosmail@sos.nv.gov

NEW HAMPSHIRE
Hon. William M. Gardner (D) (elected by the Legislature)
Secretary of State
Office of the Secretary of State
State House, Room 204
Concord, NH 03301
P: (603) 271-3242
F: (603) 271-6316
E: kladd@sos.state.nh.us

NEW JERSEY
Hon. Nina Mitchell Wells (D) (appointed)
Secretary of State
Office of the Secretary of State
P.O. Box 300
Trenton, NJ 08625
P: (609) 984-1900
F: (609) 292-9897
E: feedback@sos.state.nj.us

NEW MEXICO
Hon. Mary Herrera (D)
Secretary of State
Office of the Secretary of State
325 Don Gaspar, Suite 300
State Capitol Annex, North
Santa Fe, NM 87503
P: (505) 827-3600
F: (505) 827-3634
E: MaryE.Herrera@state.nm.us

NEW YORK
Hon. Lorraine Cortes-Vazquez (D) (appointed)
Secretary of State
Office of the Secretary of State
41 State Street
Albany, NY 12231
P: (518) 474-0050
F: (518) 474-4765
E: info@dos.state.ny.us

NORTH CAROLINA
Hon. Elaine F. Marshall (D)
Secretary of State
Office of the Secretary of State
P.O. Box 29622
Raleigh, NC 27626
P: (919) 807-2005
F: (919) 807-2010
E: Secretary@sosnc.com

NORTH DAKOTA
Hon. Alvin A. Jaeger (R)
Secretary of State
Office of the Secretary of State
600 East Boulevard Avenue
Department 108
Bismark, ND 58505
P: (701) 328-2900
F: (701) 328-2992
E: sos@nd.gov

OHIO
Hon. Jennifer Brunner (D)
Secretary of State
Office of the Secretary of State
180 East Broad Street
Columbus, OH 43266
P: (614) 466-2655
F: (614) 644-0649
E: jbrunner@sos.state.oh.us

OKLAHOMA
Hon. M. Susan Savage (D) (appointed)
Secretary of State
Office of the Secretary of State
State Capitol, Room 101
Oklahoma City, OK 73105
P: (405) 521-3911
F: (405) 521-3771
E: Susan.savage@sos.state.ok.us

OREGON
Hon. Bill Bradbury (D)
Secretary of State
Office of the Secretary of State
136 State Capitol
Salem, OR 97310
P: (503) 986-1523
F: (503) 986-1616
E: oregon.sos@sos.or.us

PENNSYLVANIA
Hon. Pedro A. Cortés (D) (appointed)
Secretary of the Commonwealth
Office of the Secretary of the Commonwealth
302 North Office Building
Harrisburg, PA 17120
P: (717) 787-8727
F: (717) 787-1734
E: pcortes@state.pa.us

PUERTO RICO
Hon. Fernando J. Bonilla (appointed)
Secretary of State
Office of the Secretary of State
Department of State
P.O. Box 9023271
San Juan, PR 00902
P: (787) 723-4343
F: (787) 725-7303
E: FJbonilla@estado.gobierno.pr

RHODE ISLAND
Hon. A. Ralph Mollis (D) (elected by the Legislature)
Secretary of State
Office of the Secretary of State
218 State House
Providence, RI 02903
P: (401) 222-2357
F: (401) 222-1356
E: aralphmollis@sec.state.ri.us

SOUTH CAROLINA
Hon. Mark Hammond (R)
Secretary of State
Office of the Secretary of State
P.O. Box 11350
Columbia, SC 29211
P: (803) 734-2170
F: (803) 734-1661
E: rdaggerhart@sos.sc.gov

SOUTH DAKOTA
Hon. Chris Nelson (R)
Secretary of State
Office of the Secretary of State
State Capitol
500 East Capitol Avenue
Pierre, SD 57501
P: (605) 773-3537
F: (605) 773-6580
E: sdsos@state.sd.us

Secretary of State

TENNESSEE
Hon. Riley Darnell (D)
(elected by the Legislature)
Secretary of State
Office of the Secretary of State
First Floor, State Capitol
Nashville, TN 37243
P: (615) 741-2819
F: (615) 741-5962
E: riley.darnell
@state.tn.us

TEXAS
Hon. Roger Williams (R)
(appointed)
Secretary of State
Office of the Secretary of State
P.O. Box 12887
Austin, TX 78711
P: (512) 463-5770
F: (512) 475-2761
E: secretary
@sos.state.tx.us

VERMONT
Hon. Deborah L.
Markowitz (D)
Secretary of State
Office of the Secretary of State
26 Terrace Street
Montpelier, VT 05609
P: (802) 828-2148
F: (802) 828-2496
E: dmarkowitz
@sec.state.vt.us

VIRGINIA
Hon. Katherine K.
Hanley (D)
(appointed)
Secretary of the Commonwealth
Office of the Secretary of the
Commonwealth
1111 East Broad Street, 4th
Floor
Patrick Henry Building
Richmond, VA 23201
P: (804) 786-2441
F: (804) 371-0017
E: kate.hanley
@governor.virginia.gov

WASHINGTON
Hon. Sam Reed (R)
Secretary of State
Office of the Secretary of State
Legislative Building, 2nd Floor
P.O. Box 40220
Olympia, WA 98504
P: (360) 902-4151
F: (360) 586-5629
E: sreed@secstate.wa.gov

WEST VIRGINIA
Hon. Betty S. Ireland (R)
Secretary of State
Office of the Secretary of State
Building 1, Suite 157K
1900 Kanawha Boulevard, East
Charleston, WV 25305
P: (304) 558-6000
F: (304) 558-0900
E: wvsos@wvsos.com

WISCONSIN
Hon. Douglas J.
La Follette (D)
Secretary of State
Office of the Secretary of State
30 West Mifflin Street
9th and 10th Floors
Madison, WI 53703
P: (608) 266-8888
F: (608) 266-3159
E: doug.lafollette
@sos.state.wi.us

WYOMING
Hon. Max Maxfield (R)
Secretary of State
Office of the Secretary of State
State Capitol
Cheyenne, WY 82002
P: (307) 777-5333
F: (307) 777-6217
E: Secofstate@state.wy.us

Securities

Regulates the sale of securities and registers securities prior to public sale.

ALABAMA
Mr. Joseph P. Borg
Director
Securities Commission
770 Washington Avenue, Suite 570
Montgomery, AL 36130
P: (334) 242-2984
F: (334) 242-0240

ALASKA
Mr. Mark R. Davis
Director
Department of Commerce, Community & Economic Development
Banking, Securities & Corporations
P.O. Box 110807
Juneau, AK 99811
P: (907) 465-2521
F: (907) 465-2549

ARIZONA
Mr. Matthew J. Neubert
Director
Corporation Commission
Securities Division
1300 West Washington, 3rd Floor
Phoenix, AZ 85007
P: (602) 542-4242
F: (602) 594-7470

ARKANSAS
Mr. Michael B. Johnson
Securities Commissioner
Securities Department
Heritage West Building
201 East Markham, Room 300
Little Rock, AR 72201
P: (501) 324-9260
F: (501) 324-9268

CALIFORNIA
Mr. Timothy L. Le Bas
Assistant Commissioner & General Counsel
Department of Corporations
Office of Law & Legislation
1515 K Street, Suite 200
Sacramento, CA 95814
P: (916) 445-7205
F: (916) 445-7975

COLORADO
Mr. Fred J. Joseph
Securities Commissioner
Division of Securities
1580 Lincoln Street, Suite 420
Denver, CO 80203
P: (303) 894-2320
F: (303) 861-2126

CONNECTICUT
Mr. Ralph A. Lambiase
Director of Securities
Department of Banking
260 Constitution Plaza
Hartford, CT 06103
P: (860) 240-8230
F: (860) 240-8295

DELAWARE
Mr. James B. Ropp
Securities Commissioner
Division of Securities
Carvel State Office Building
820 North French Street, 5th Floor
Wilmington, DE 19801
P: (302) 577-8424
F: (302) 577-6987

DISTRICT OF COLUMBIA
Mr. Thomas Hampton
Director
Department of Insurance, Securities & Banking
810 1st Street, Northeast
Suite 701
Washington, DC 20002
P: (202) 442-7773
F: (202) 535-1196

FLORIDA
Mr. Don Saxon
Commissioner
Office of Financial Regulation
200 East Gaines Street
The Fletcher Building
Tallahassee, FL 32399
P: (850) 410-9805
F: (850) 410-9748

GEORGIA
Ms. Tonya Curry
Director, Division of Securities
Division of Business Services & Regulation
Two Martin Luther King Jr. Drive, SE
802 West Tower
Atlanta, GA 30334
P: (404) 656-3920
F: (404) 651-6451

HAWAII
Ms. Tung Chan
Commissioner of Securities
Department of Commerce & Consumer Affairs
Division of Business Regulation
335 Merchant Street, Room 203
Honolulu, HI 96813
P: (808) 586-2744
F: (808) 586-2733

IDAHO
Ms. Marilyn T. Chastain
Securities Bureau Chief
Department of Finance
700 West State Street, 2nd Floor
Boise, ID 83702
P: (208) 332-8004
F: (208) 332-8099
E: marilyn.chastain@finance.idaho.gov

ILLINOIS
Ms. Tanya Solov
Director of Securities
Securities Department
69 West Washington Street, Suite 1220
Chicago, IL 60602
P: (312) 785-7367

INDIANA
Mr. Wayne Davis
Securities Commissioner
Securities Division
302 West Washington, Room E-111
Indianapolis, IN 46204
P: (317) 232-6681
F: (317) 233-3675

IOWA
Mr. Craig A. Goettsch
Superintendent of Securities
Securities Bureau
340 East Maple Street
Des Moines, IA 50319
P: (515) 281-4441
F: (515) 281-3059

KANSAS
Mr. Chris Biggs
Commissioner
Office of the Securities Commissioner
618 South Kansas Avenue
Topeka, KS 66603
P: (785) 296-3307
F: (785) 296-6872

KENTUCKY
Ms. Colleen Keefe
Director
Division of Securities
1025 Capital Center Drive
Frankfort, KY 40601
P: (502) 573-3390
F: (502) 573-0086
E: colleen.keefe@ky.gov

LOUISIANA
Ms. Rhonda Reeves
Deputy Securities Commissioner
Office of Financial Institutions
8660 United Plaza Boulevard
Second Floor
Baton Rouge, LA 70809
P: (225) 925-4512
F: (225) 925-4548
E: rreeves@ofi.louisiana.gov

MAINE
Mr. Michael J. Colleran
Securities Administrator
Securities Division
State House Station 121
Augusta, ME 04333
P: (207) 624-8551
F: (207) 624-8590

MARYLAND
Ms. Melanie Senter Lubin
Securities Commissioner
Division of Securities
200 Saint Paul Place
Baltimore, MD 21202
P: (410) 576-6360
F: (410) 576-6532
E: mlubin@oag.state.md.us

MASSACHUSETTS
Mr. Bryan Lantagne
Director
Securities Division
One Ashburton Place, Room 1701
Boston, MA 02108
P: (617) 727-3548
F: (617) 248-0177

MICHIGAN
Ms. Linda A. Watters
Commissioner
Office of Financial & Insurance Services
Department of Labor & Economic Growth
611 West Ottawa Street, Third Floor
Lansing, MI 48933
P: (877) 999-6442
F: (517) 241-3953
E: ofis-sec-info@michigan.gov

Securities

MINNESOTA
Mr. Scott P. Borchert
Director, Enforcement Division
Department of Commerce
85 East 7th Place
Suite 500
St. Paul, MN 55101
P: (651) 296-4026
F: (651) 296-4328

MISSISSIPPI
Mr. James O. Nelson II
Assistant Secretary of State
Business Regulation &
Enforcement Division
700 North Street
Jackson, MS 39202
P: (601) 359-6371
F: (601) 359-2663

MISSOURI
Mr. Matthew Kitzi
Securities Commissioner
Office of the Secretary of State
600 West Main Street
Jefferson City, MO 65101
P: (573) 751-4704
F: (573) 526-3124
E: matt.kitzi@sos.mo.gov

MONTANA
Hon. John Morrison (D)
State Auditor
Office of the State Auditor
840 Helena Avenue
Helena, MT 59601
P: (406) 444-2040
F: (406) 444-3497

NEBRASKA
Mr. Jack E. Herstein
Assistant Director
Department of Banking &
Finance
1230 "O" Street, Suite 400
P.O. Box 95006
Lincoln, NE 68509
P: (402) 471-3445

NEVADA
Mr. Chris Lee
Deputy Secretary of State
Securities Division
555 East Washington Avenue,
5th Floor
Suite 5200
Las Vegas, NV 89101
P: (702) 486-2440
F: (702) 486-2452
E: nvsec@sos.nv.gov

NEW HAMPSHIRE
Mr. Mark Connolly
Deputy Secretary of
State/Director of Securities
Regulation
Bureau of Securities Regulation
State House Annex
Suite 317A, 3rd Floor
Concord, NH 03301
P: (603) 271-1464
F: (603) 271-7933
E: mconnolly
@sos.state.nh.us

NEW JERSEY
Mr. Franklin L. Widmann
Bureau Chief
Bureau of Securities
153 Halsey Street, 6th Floor
P.O. Box 47029
Newark, NJ 07101
P: (973) 504-3600
F: (973) 504-3601

NEW MEXICO
Mr. Bruce R. Kohl
Director
Securities Division
Regulation & Licensing
Department
2550 Cerrillos Road
Santa Fe, NM 87505
P: (505) 476-4580
F: (505) 476-4511
E: bruce.kohl@state.nm.us

NEW YORK
Mr. Gary Connor
First Deputy Bureau Chief
Investor Protection & Securities
Bureau
120 Broadway
23rd Floor
New York, NY 10271
P: (212) 416-8200
F: (212) 416-8816

NORTH CAROLINA
Mr. David S. Massey
Deputy Securities Administrator
Securities Division
300 North Salisbury Street
Suite 100
Raleigh, NC 27603
P: (919) 733-3924
F: (919) 821-0818
E: dmassey
@mail.secstate.state.nc.us

NORTH DAKOTA
Ms. Karen Tyler
Commissioner
Securities Department
600 East Boulevard Avenue
State Capitol, 5th Floor
Bismarck, ND 58505
P: (701) 328-2910
F: (701) 255-3113

OHIO
Mr. G. Brent Bishop
Commissioner
Division of Securities
77 South High Street, 22nd
Floor
Columbus, OH 43215
P: (614) 644-6406

OKLAHOMA
Mr. Irving L. Faught
Administrator
Department of Securities
1st National Center, Suite 860
120 North Robinson
Oklahoma City, OK 73102
P: (405) 280-7700
F: (405) 280-7742

OREGON
Mr. Floyd G. Lanter
Division Administrator
Division of Finance &
Corporate Securities
350 Winter Street, Northeast
Room 410
Salem, OR 97301
P: (503) 378-4387
F: (503) 947-7862

PENNSYLVANIA
Mr. Robert M. Lam
Commissioner
Securities Commission
1010 North 7th Street
2nd Floor
Harrisburg, PA 17102
P: (717) 787-8061
F: (717) 783-5122

PUERTO RICO
Mr. Felipe B. Cruz
Assistant Commissioner
Commission of Financial
Institutions
1492 Ponce De Leon Avenue
Suite 600
San Juan, PR 00907
P: (787) 723-3131 Ext. 2222

RHODE ISLAND
Ms. Maria D'Alessandro
Associate Director &
Superintendent of Securities
Department of Business
Regulation
233 Richmond Street
Suite 232
Providence, RI 02903
P: (401) 222-3048
F: (401) 222-5629

SOUTH CAROLINA
Mr. T. Stephen Lynch
Deputy Securities Commissioner
Securities Division
Rembert C. Dennis Office
Building
1000 Assembly Street
Columbia, SC 29201
P: (803) 734-4731
F: (803) 734-0032

SOUTH DAKOTA
Mr. Gale Sheppick
Director
Division of Securities
Anderson Building
445 East Capitol Avenue
Pierre, SD 57501
P: (605) 773-4823
F: (605) 773-5953
E: gale.sheppick
@state.sd.us

TENNESSEE
Ms. Daphne D. Smith
Assistant Commissioner for
Securities
Securities Division
500 James Robertson Parkway
Davy Crockett Tower, Suite 680
Nashville, TN 37243
P: (615) 741-2947
F: (615) 532-8375

TEXAS
Ms. Denise Voigt Crawford
Commissioner
State Securities Board
208 East 10th Street, 5th Floor
Austin, TX 78701
P: (512) 305-8300
F: (512) 305-8310

UTAH
Mr. Wayne Klein
Director
Division of Securities
Department of Commerce
160 East 300 South, 2nd Floor
Salt Lake City, UT 84111
P: (801) 530-6615
F: (801) 530-6980
E: wklein@utah.gov

VERMONT
Ms. Anna Drummond
Deputy Commissioner of Securities
Department of Banking, Insurance, Securities & Health Care Administration
89 Main Street, Drawer 20
Montpelier, VT 05620
P: (802) 828-3420
F: (802) 828-2896

VIRGINIA
Mr. Ronald W. Thomas
Director
Division of Securities & Retail Franchising
1300 East Main Street
9th Floor
Richmond, VA 23219
P: (804) 371-9051
F: (804) 371-9911

WASHINGTON
Mr. Michael E. Stevenson
Director of Securities
Department of Financial Institutions
Securities Division
150 Israel Road, Southwest
Tumwater, WA 98501
P: (360) 902-8760
F: (360) 902-0524

WEST VIRGINIA
Mr. Chester F. Thompson
Deputy Commissioner of Securities
Office of the State Auditor
Securities Division
Building 1, Room W-100
Charleston, WV 25305
P: (304) 558-2257
F: (304) 558-4211

WISCONSIN
Ms. Patricia D. Struck
Administrator
Division of Securities
345 West Washington Avenue
P.O. Box 1768
Madison, WI 53701
P: (608) 266-1064
F: (608) 264-7979

WYOMING
Mr. Thomas Cowan
Division Director
Securities Division
State Capitol, Room 109
200 West 24th Street
Cheyenne, WY 82002
P: (307) 777-7370
F: (307) 777-5339

Small and Minority Business Assistance

Provides assistance and information on financing and government procurement opportunities to small and minority business ventures.

ALABAMA
Mr. Neal Wade
Director
Development Office
401 Adams Avenue, 6th Floor
Suite 670
Montgomery, AL 36130
P: (334) 353-1717
F: (334) 242-5669
E: waden@ado.state.al.us

ALASKA
Mr. Greg Winegar
Director
Division of Investments
P.O. Box 34159
Juneau, AK 99803
P: (907) 465-2510
F: (907) 465-2103

AMERICAN SAMOA
Mr. Faleseu Eliu Paopao
Director
Department of Commerce
American Samoa Government
Executive Office Building, Utulei
Pago Pago, AS 96799
P: (684) 633-5155
F: (684) 633-4195

ARKANSAS
Mr. Sylvester Smith
Team Leader
Small & Minority Business Unit
#1 Capitol Mall, Room 4C-300
Little Rock, AR 72201
P: (501) 682-1260
F: (501) 682-7341
E: ssmith@1800ARKANSAS.cor

CALIFORNIA
Mr. Dennis Trinidad
Small Business Advocate
Governor's Office of Planning & Research
1400 Tenth Street
Sacramento, CA 95814
P: (916) 341-7336
F: (916) 445-6305

COLORADO
Ms. Kelly Manning
Director
Small Business Development Center
1625 Broadway, Suite 1710
Denver, CO 80202
P: (303) 892-3840
F: (303) 892-3848

Mr. LeRoy Romero
Division Director
Minority & Women's Business Office
1625 Broadway, Suite 1700
Denver, CO 80202
P: (303) 892-3840
F: (303) 892-3848
E: l.romero@state.co.us

CONNECTICUT
Ms. Meg Yetishefsky
Business Connections
165 Capitol Avenue
Hartford, CT 06106
P: (860) 713-5228
F: (860) 713-7484
E: meg.yetishefsky@po.state.ct.us

DELAWARE
Ms. Judy McKinney-Cherry
Director
Economic Development Office
Carvel State Office Building, 10th Floor
820 North French Street
Wilimington, DE 19801
P: (302) 577-8497
F: (302) 739-2535
E: judy.cherry@state.de.us

DISTRICT OF COLUMBIA
Mr. Gustavo F. Velasquez
Director
Office of Human Rights
441 4th Street, Northwest
Suite 570N
Washington, DC 20001
P: (202) 727-4559
F: (202) 727-9589

GEORGIA
Ms. Gilda Watters
Director
Governor's Small Business Center
200 Piedmont Avenue
Suite 1306, West Tower
Atlanta, GA 30334
P: (404) 656-6315
F: (404) 657-4681

HAWAII
Mr. Theodore E. Liu
Director
Department of Business Economic Development & Tourism
P.O. Box 2359
Honolulu, HI 96804
P: (808) 586-2355
F: (808) 586-2377

IDAHO
Mr. Karl T. Tueller
Deputy Director
Department of Commerce & Labor
P.O. Box 83720
Boise, ID 83720
P: (208) 334-3570
F: (208) 334-2631
E: karl.tueller@cl.idaho.gov

INDIANA
Ms. Claudia Cummings
Deputy Commissioner
Minority & Women's Business Enterprises
402 West Washington Street
Room W469
Indianapolis, IN 46204
P: (317) 232-3061
F: (317) 233-6921

IOWA
Mr. Jeff Rossate
Division Administrator
Business Development Division
200 East Grand Avenue
Des Moines, IA 50319
P: (515) 242-4707
E: jeff.rossate@iowalifechanging.com

KANSAS
Ms. Rhonda Harris
Director
Office of Minority & Women Business Development
1000 Southwest Jackson Street, Suite 100
Topeka, KS 66612
P: (785) 296-3425
F: (785) 296-3490

KENTUCKY
Mr. Mark Johnson
Branch Manager
Small & Minority Business Branch
500 Mero Street
Capitol Plaza Tower, 23rd Floor
Frankfort, KY 40601
P: (502) 564-2064
F: (502) 564-5932
E: markl.johnson@ky.gov

LOUISIANA
Mr. Michael Olivier
Secretary
Department of Economic Development
Capitol Annex, 1050 North Third Street
P.O. Box 94185
Baton Rouge, LA 70804
P: (225) 342-5388
F: (225) 342-5389
E: olivier@la.gov

MAINE
Mr. John Richardson
Commissioner
Department of Economic & Community Development
59 State House Station
Augusta, ME 04333
P: (207) 287-2736
F: (207) 287-3005
E: brenda.harvey@maine.gov

MARYLAND
Mr. James McLean
Executive Director
Governor's Office of Business Advocacy & Small Business Assistance
217 East Redwood Street
Baltimore, MD 21202
P: (410) 767-6541
E: jmclean@choosemaryland.org

MASSACHUSETTS
Ms. Sandra E. Borders
Director
Office of Diversity & Equal Opportunity
One Ashburton Place, Room 213
Boston, MA 02108
P: (617) 727-7441
F: (617) 727-0568

MINNESOTA
Ms. Dana Badgerow
Commissioner
Department of Administration
200 Administration Building
50 Sherburne Avenue
St. Paul, MN 55155
P: (651) 201-2555
F: (651) 297-7909
E: dana.badgerow@state.mn.us

MISSOURI
Ms. Donna M. White
Director
Office of Supplier & Workforce Diversity
Truman Building, Room 630
P.O. Box 809
Jefferson City, MO 65102
P: (573) 751-8130
F: (573) 522-8078
E: Donna.White@oa.mo.gov

MONTANA
Mr. Anthony Preite
Director
Department of Commerce
301 South Park
P.O. Box 200501
Helena, MT 59620
P: (406) 841-2704
F: (406) 841-2701
E: tpreite@mt.gov

NEBRASKA
Mr. Richard Baier
Director
Department of Economic Development
P.O. Box 94666
Lincoln, NE 68509
P: (402) 471-3111
F: (402) 471-3778

NEW HAMPSHIRE
Mr. Jack Donovan
Executive Director
Business Finance Authority
14 Dixon Avenue, 2nd Floor
Concord, NH 03301
P: (603) 271-6457
F: (603) 271-2396
E: JackD@nhbfa.com

NEW JERSEY
Ms. Virginia S. Bauer
CEO & Secretary
Commerce, Economic Growth & Tourism Commission
20 West State Street
Trenton, NJ 08625
P: (609) 292-2444
F: (609) 292-0082
E: Virginia.Bauer@commerce.state.nj.us

NEW MEXICO
Ms. Nancy Baker
Regional Representative
Economic Development Department
1100 South Saint Francis Drive
Suite 1060
Santa Fe, NM 87505
P: (505) 827-0228
F: (505) 827-0328
E: Nancy.Baker@state.nm.us

NEW YORK
Mr. Patrick Foye
Commissioner
Empire State Development
633 Third Avenue
New York, NY 10017
P: (212) 803-3700
F: (518) 474-2474

Mr. Jorge I. Vidro
Director
Minority & Women's Business Services
633 Third Avenue
New York, NY 10017
P: (212) 803-2200

NORTH CAROLINA
Mr. Scott Daugherty
Executive Director
Small Business & Technology Development Center
5 West Hargett Street, Suite 600
Raleigh, NC 27601
P: (919) 715-7272
F: (919) 715-7777
E: sdaugherty@sbtdc.org

NORTH DAKOTA
Mr. Shane Goettle
Director
Commerce Department
1600 East Century Avenue, Suite 2
P.O. Box 2057
Bismarck, ND 58502
P: (701) 328-5300
F: (701) 328-5320

NORTHERN MARIANA ISLANDS
Mr. Oscar C. Camacho
Director
Economic Development Division
P.O. Box 502149
Saipan, MP 96950
P: (670) 234-6245
F: (670) 234-7144
E: administration@cda.gov.mp

OHIO
Ms. Karen Conrad
Manager
Office of Small Business
77 South High Street, 28th Floor
Columbus, OH 43215
P: (614) 466-2718
F: (614) 466-0829

OKLAHOMA
Mr. Ken Talley
Economic Development Specialist
Office for Minority & Disadvantaged Business Enterprises
900 North Stiles Avenue
P.O. Box 26980
Oklahoma City, OK 73126
P: (405) 815-5218
F: (405) 815-5109

OREGON
Mr. Raleigh Lewis
Certification Manager
Office of Minority, Women, & Emerging Small Business
350 Winter Street, Northeast, Room 300
Salem, OR 97301
P: (503) 947-7921
F: (503) 373-7041
E: omwesb.web@state.or.us

PENNSYLVANIA
Ms. Isabelle W. Smith
Director
Center for Entrepreneurial Assistance
Commonwealth Keystone Building
4th Floor
Harrisburg, PA 17120
P: (717) 720-7423
F: (717) 787-4088

RHODE ISLAND
Mr. Louis Soares
Associate Director
Small Business Services
One West Exchange Street
Providence, RI 02903
P: (888) 284-9704

SOUTH CAROLINA
Ms. Margaret A. Woodson
Director
Office of Small & Minority Business Assistance
1205 Pendleton Street, Room 329
Columbia, SC 29201
P: (803) 734-0657
F: (803) 734-2498
E: mwoodson@oepp.sc.gov

SOUTH DAKOTA
Mr. Richard Benda
Secretary
Department of Tourism & Economic Development
Capitol Lake Plaza
711 East Wells Avenue
Pierre, SD 57501
P: (605) 773-3301
F: (605) 773-3256
E: richard.benda@state.sd.us

TENNESSEE
Mr. Rick Meredith
Assistant Commissioner
Business Services Division
William R. Snodgrass Tennessee Tower
11th Floor, 312 8th Avenue, North
Nashville, TN 37243
P: (615) 741-2626
F: (615) 532-8715

Ms. Lorie Shauntee
Diversity Business Liaison
Business Services Division
William R. Snodgrass Tennessee Tower
11th Floor, 312 8th Avenue, North
Nashville, TN 37243
P: (615) 741-2626
F: (615) 532-8715
E: lorie.shauntee@state.tn.us

TEXAS
Mr. Edward Johnson
Executive Director
Building & Procurement Commission
1711 San Jacinto
Austin, TX 78701
P: (512) 463-6363
E: edward.johnson@tbpc.state.tx.us

U.S. VIRGIN ISLANDS
Mr. Frank Schulterbrandt
Chief Executive Officer
Economic Development Authority
1050 Norre Gade
P.O. Box 305038
St. Thomas, VI 00803
P: (340) 774-0100
F: (340) 779-7153

Small and Minority Business Assistance

VERMONT
Mr. David Tucker
Director
State Economic Opportunity
Office
103 South Main Street
Waterbury, VT 05671
P: (802) 241-2450
F: (802) 241-1225

VIRGINIA
Mr. Stacy L. Burrs
Director
Department of Minority
Business Enterprise
1100 East Main Street, Suite
300
Richmond, VA 23219
P: (804) 786-6585
F: (804) 371-7359
E: stacy.burrs
@dmbe.virginia.gov

WISCONSIN
Ms. Ruby Brooks
Director
Bureau of Minority Business
Development
101 West Pleasant Street, Suite
205
Miwaukee, WI 53212
P: (414) 220-5365

Ms. Pam Christenson
Acting Administrator
Business Development Division
201 West Washington Avenue,
5th Floor
Madison, WI 53703
P: (608) 267-9384

Social Services

Responsible for the delivery of services to children, disabled, and elderly.

ALABAMA
Dr. Page Walley
Commissioner
Department of Human Resources
Gordon Persons Building, Suite 2104
50 North Ripley Street
Montgomery, AL 36130
P: (334) 242-1310
F: (334) 242-1086

ALASKA
Ms. Karleen K. Jackson
Commissioner
Health & Social Services
P.O. Box 110601
Juneau, AK 99811
P: (907) 465-3030
F: (907) 465-3068

AMERICAN SAMOA
Mr. Talia Fa'afetai I'aulualo
Director
Department of Human & Social Services
American Samoa Government
Pago Pago, AS 96799
P: (684) 633-1187
F: (684) 633-7449

ARIZONA
Ms. Tracy L. Wareing
Director
Department of Economic Security
1717 West Jefferson
Phoenix, AZ 85007
P: (602) 542-5678

ARKANSAS
Ms. Joni Jones
Director
Division of County Operations
P.O. Box 1437, Slot S301
Little Rock, AR 72203
P: (501) 682-8375
F: (501) 682-8367
E: joni.jones@arkansas.gov

CALIFORNIA
Mr. Cliff Allenby
Interim Director
Department of Social Services
744 P Street
Sacramento, CA 95814
P: (916) 657-2598
F: (916) 654-6012
E: cliff.allenby@dss.ca.gov

COLORADO
Ms. Karen Legault Beye
Executive Director
Department of Human Services
1575 Sherman Street
Denver, CO 80203
P: (303) 866-5700
F: (303) 866-4740

CONNECTICUT
Mr. Michael Starkowski
Commissioner
Department of Social Services
25 Sigourney Street
Hartford, CT 06106
P: (860) 424-5008

DELAWARE
Mr. Vincent P. Meconi
Secretary
Department of Health & Social Services
Herman M. Holloway, Sr. Campus
1901 North DuPont Highway, Main Building
New Castle, DE 19720
P: (302) 255-9040
E: Vincent.Meconi@state.de.us

DISTRICT OF COLUMBIA
Ms. Kate Jesberg
Interim Director
Department of Human Services
64 New York Avenue, NE
6th Floor
Washington, DC 20001
P: (202) 671-4200
F: (202) 671-4381

FLORIDA
Mr. Bob Butterworth
Secretary
Department of Children & Families
1317 Winewood Boulevard
Building 1, Room 202
Tallahassee, FL 32399
P: (850) 487-1111
F: (850) 922-2993

GEORGIA
Ms. B. J. Walker
Commissioner
Department of Human Resources
2 Peachtree Street, Northwest
Room 29-250
Atlanta, GA 30303
P: (404) 463-3390
F: (404) 651-8669

GUAM
Mr. Arthur U. San Agustin
Director
Department of Health & Social Services
123 Chalan Kareta, Route 10
Mangilao, GU 96923
P: (671) 735-7102
F: (671) 734-5910
E: chiefdsc@dphss.govguam.net

HAWAII
Ms. Lillian B. Koller
Director
Department of Human Services
P.O. Box 339
Honolulu, HI 96809
P: (808) 586-4997
F: (808) 586-4890

IDAHO
Ms. Michelle Britton
Administrator
Division of Family & Community Services
450 West State Street
5th Floor, Pete T. Cenarrusa Building
Boise, ID 83720
P: (208) 334-0461
F: (208) 334-6699

ILLINOIS
Mr. Erwin McEwen
Acting Director
Department of Children & Family Services
406 East Monroe Street
Springfield, IL 62701
P: (217) 785-2509
F: (217) 785-1052

INDIANA
Mr. E. Mitch Roob Jr.
Cabinet Secretary
Family & Social Services Administration
402 West Washington Street, Room W461
Indianapolis, IN 46206
P: (317) 233-4454
F: (317) 233-4693

IOWA
Ms. Sally Titus Cunningham
Deputy Director
Department of Human Services
Hoover State Office Building
1305 E. Walnut St.
Des Moines, IA 50319
P: (515) 281-5758
F: (515) 281-4597

KANSAS
Mr. Don Jordan
Secretary
Department of Social & Rehabilitation Services
915 Southwest Harrison Street
Topeka, KS 66612
P: (785) 296-3274
F: (785) 296-4685

KENTUCKY
Mr. Mark Birdwhistell
Secretary
Cabinet for Health & Family Services
275 East Main Street, 5W-A
Frankfort, KY 40601
P: (502) 564-7042
F: (502) 564-7091

LOUISIANA
Ms. Ann Williamson
Secretary
Department of Social Services
755 Third Street
P.O. Box 3776
Baton Rouge, LA 70821
P: (225) 342-0286
F: (225) 342-8636
E: Ann.Williamson@dss.state.la.us

MAINE
Ms. Brenda M. Harvey
Acting Commissioner
Department of Human Services
11 State House Station
Augusta, ME 04333
P: (207) 287-2736
F: (207) 287-3005
E: brenda.harvey@maine.gov

MARYLAND
Ms. Brenda Donald
Secretary
Department of Human Resources
311 West Saratoga Street
Baltimore, MD 21201
P: (410) 767-7109
E: bdonald@dhr.state.md.us

MASSACHUSETTS
Mr. Harry Spence
Commissioner
Department of Social Services
24 Farnsworth Street
Boston, MA 02210
P: (617) 748-2000

Social Services

MICHIGAN
Ms. Marianne Udow
Director
Department of Human Services
P.O. Box 30037
Lansing, MI 48909
P: (517) 373-1121
F: (517) 335-6101
E: udowm@michigan.gov

MINNESOTA
Mr. Cal Ludeman
Commissioner
Department of Human Services
Human Services Building
540 Cedar Street
St. Paul, MN 55155
P: (651) 431-2907
F: (651) 431-7443
E: cal.ludeman@state.mn.us

MISSISSIPPI
Mr. Derra Dukes
Director
Office of Social Services Block Grant
Department of Human Services
750 North State Street
Jackson, MS 39202
P: (601) 359-4500

MISSOURI
Ms. Brenda Campbell
Division Director
Division of Senior & Disability Services
Department of Health & Senior Services
P.O. Box 570
Jefferson City, MO 65102
P: (573) 526-3626
F: (573) 751-8687
E: Brenda.Campbell@dhss.mo.gov

Ms. Deborah E. Scott
Director
Department of Social Services
221 West High, Room 240
P.O. Box 1527
Jefferson City, MO 65102
P: (573) 751-4815
F: (573) 751-3203

MONTANA
Ms. Joan Miles
Director
Department of Public Health & Human Services
111 North Sanders, Room 301/308
P.O. Box 4210
Helena, MT 59604
P: (406) 444-5622
F: (406) 444-1970

NEBRASKA
Mr. Scott Adams
Director
Department of Health & Human Services
P.O. Box 95044
Lincoln, NE 68509
P: (402) 471-3121
E: roger.lempke@ne.ngb.army.mil

NEVADA
Mr. Michael Willden
Director
Department of Health & Human Services
505 East King Street, Room 600
Carson City, NV 89706
P: (775) 684-4000
F: (775) 684-4010
E: mwillden@dhhs.nv.gov

NEW HAMPSHIRE
Mr. John A. Stephen
Commissioner
Department of Health & Human Services
129 Pleasant Street
Concord, NH 03301
P: (603) 271-4331
F: (603) 271-4912
E: jstephen@dhhs.state.nh.us

NEW JERSEY
Mr. Kevin M. Ryan
Commissioner
Department of Human Services
222 South Warren Street
P.O. Box 700
Trenton, NJ 08625
P: (609) 292-3717

Ms. Jennifer Velez
Acting Commissioner
Department of Human Services
P.O. Box 726
Trenton, NJ 08625
P: (609) 292-0901

NEW MEXICO
Mr. Stuart A. Ashman
Cabinet Secretary
Department of Cultural Affairs
Bataan Memorial Building
407 Galisteo Street, Suite 250
Santa Fe, NM 87503
P: (505) 827-6364

Ms. Pamela S. Hyde
Cabinet Secretary
Department of Human Services
2009 South Pacheco, Pollon Plaza
P.O. Box 2348
Santa Fe, NM 87504
P: (505) 827-7750
F: (505) 827-3185

NEW YORK
Mr. David Hansell
Commissioner
Office of Temporary & Disability Assistance
40 North Pearl Street
Albany, NY 12243
P: (518) 408-3847
F: (518) 486-9179

NORTH CAROLINA
Ms. Sherry Bradsher
Director
Division of Social Services
325 North Salisbury Street
2401 Mail Service Center
Raleigh, NC 27699
P: (919) 733-3055
F: (919) 733-9366
E: sherry.bradsher@ncmail.net

NORTH DAKOTA
Ms. Carol K. Olson
Executive Director
Department of Human Services
600 East Boulevard Avenue
3rd Floor - Judicial Wing
Bismarck, ND 58505
P: (701) 328-2310
F: (701) 328-2359
E: socols@nd.gov

NORTHERN MARIANA ISLANDS
Mr. Joseph P. Villagomez
Secretary of Public Health
Department Public Health
P.O. Box 500409
Saipan, MP 96950
P: (670) 236-8201
F: (670) 234-8930
E: jkvsaipan@aol.com

OHIO
Ms. Helen Jones-Kelley
Director
Department of Job & Family Services
30 East Broad Street, 31st Floor
Columbus, OH 43215
P: (614) 466-6282
F: (614) 466-2815
E: jonesh@odjfs.state.oh.us

OKLAHOMA
Mr. Howard Hendrick
Secretary
Department of Human Services
P.O. Box 25352
Oklahoma City, OK 73125
P: (405) 521-3646
F: (405) 521-6684

OREGON
Dr. Bruce Goldberg
Director
Department of Human Services
500 Summer Street, Northeast
4th Floor, E-15
Salem, OR 97301
P: (503) 945-5944
F: (503) 378-2897
E: dhs.info@state.or.us

PENNSYLVANIA
Ms. Estelle B. Richman
Secretary
Department of Public Welfare
Health & Welfare Building, Room 333
Harrisburg, PA 17105
P: (717) 787-2600
F: (717) 772-2062

PUERTO RICO
Mr. Felix Matos Rodriguez
Secretary
Department of the Family
P.O. Box 11398
San Juan, PR 00910
P: (787) 294-4900
F: (787) 294-0732

RHODE ISLAND
Mr. Gary Alexander
Acting Director
Department of Human Services
Louis Pasteur Building
600 New London Avenue
Craston, RI 02920
P: (401) 462-2121
F: (401) 462-3677

SOUTH CAROLINA
Ms. Kathleen M. Hayes
Director
Department of Social Services
P.O. Box 1520
Columbia, SC 29202
P: (803) 898-7360
F: (803) 898-7277

SOUTH DAKOTA
Ms. Deb Bowman
Secretary
Department of Social Services
Kneip Building
700 Governors Drive
Pierre, SD 57501
P: (605) 773-3165
F: (605) 773-4855
E: deb.bowman@state.sd.us

TENNESSEE
Mr. Ed Lake
Assistant Commissioner
Community & Field Services
400 Deaderick Street
15th Floor
Nashville, TN 37248
P: (615) 313-4703
F: (615) 741-4165

TEXAS
Ms. Anne Heiligenstein
Deputy Executive Director for Program Services
Health & Human Services Commission
P.O. Box 13247
Austin, TX 78711
P: (512) 424-6620
F: (512) 424-6587

U.S. VIRGIN ISLANDS
Ms. Sedonie Halbert
Commissioner
Department of Human Services
Knud Hansen Complex, Building A
1303 Hospital Grounds
St. Thomas, VI 00802
P: (340) 774-0930
F: (340) 774-3466

UTAH
Ms. Lisa-Michele Church
Executive Director
Department of Human Services
120 North 200 West, Room 319
P.O. Box 45500
Salt Lake City, UT 84103
P: (801) 538-4002
F: (801) 538-4016
E: lmchurch@utah.gov

VERMONT
Mr. James Morse
Commissioner
Department for Children & Families
103 South Main Street
Waterbury, VT 05671
P: (802) 241-2100
F: (802) 241-2979

VIRGINIA
Mr. Anthony Conyers Jr.
Commissioner
Department of Social Services
7 North 8th Street
Richmond, VA 23219
P: (804) 692-1903
F: (804) 692-1949
E: anthony.conyers@dss.virginia.gov

WASHINGTON
Ms. Robin Arnold-Williams
Secretary
Department of Social & Health Services
P.O. Box 45010
Olympia, WA 98504
P: (360) 902-7800

WEST VIRGINIA
Ms. Martha Yeager Walker
Cabinet Secretary
Department of Health & Human Resources
Capitol Complex Building 3, Room 206
1900 Kanawha Boulevard, East
Charleston, WV 25305
P: (304) 558-0684
F: (304) 558-1130
E: marthaywalker@wvdhrr.org

WISCONSIN
Mr. Kevin Hayden
Secretary
Department of Health & Family Services
1 West Wilson Street, Room 650
Madison, WI 53702
P: (608) 266-9622
E: haydekr@dhfs.state.wi.us

WYOMING
Mr. Tony Lewis
Interim Director of Family Services
Department of Family Services
Hathaway Building, 3rd Floor
2300 Capitol Avenue
Cheyenne, WY 82002
P: (307) 777-7561
F: (307) 777-7747

State Data Center

Center that acts as an information clearinghouse for the Census Bureau and other data sources within the state.

ALABAMA
Ms. Annette Watters
Manager
State Data Center
University of Alabama
P.O. Box 870221
Tuscaloosa, AL 35487
P: (205) 348-6191
F: (205) 348-2951
E: awatters@cba.ua.edu

AMERICAN SAMOA
Mr. Vai Filiga
Statistician
Department of Commerce
American Samoa Government
Pago Pago, AS 96799
P: (684) 633-5155
F: (684) 633-4195
E: JRScanlan@samoatelco.com

ARIZONA
Mr. Samuel Colon
State Demographer, Estimates
Department of Economic Security
1789 West Jefferson, First Floor
Phoenix, AZ 85007
P: (602) 542-5984
F: (602) 542-7425
E: SColon@azdes.gov

ARKANSAS
Ms. Sarah Breshears
Division Chief
Census State Data Center
2801 South University
Little Rock, AR 72204
P: (501) 569-8530
F: (501) 569-8538
E: sgbreshears@ualr.edu

CALIFORNIA
Mr. Mark Hill
Program Budget Manager
Department of Finance
915 L Street
Sacramento, CA 95814
P: (916) 322-2263

COLORADO
Ms. Elizabeth Garner
State Demographer
Demography Office
Department of Local Affairs
1313 Sherman Street, Room 521
Denver, CO 80203
P: (303) 866-4147
F: (303) 866-2660

CONNECTICUT
Mr. Bill Kraynak
State Census Liaison
State Data Center
Office of Policy & Management
450 Capitol Avenue
Hartford, CT 06106
P: (860) 418-6230
E: william.kraynak@po.state.ct.us

DELAWARE
Mr. Michael Mahaffie
GIS Coordinator
Office of State Planning Coordinator
540 South DuPont Highway, Suite 7
Dover, DE 19901
P: (302) 739-3090
F: (302) 831-3579
E: mike.mahaffie@state.de.us

DISTRICT OF COLUMBIA
Ms. Joy Phillips
Director
State Data Center
801 North Capitol Street, Northeast
Suite 4000
Washington, DC 20002
P: (202) 442-7600
F: (202) 442-7637

FLORIDA
Mr. Terry Kester
Deputy Secretary
Enterprise Information Technology Services
Department of Management Services
4050 Esplanade Way, Suite 235
Tallahassee, FL 32399
P: (850) 922-2680
F: (850) 922-6149

GEORGIA
Mr. Robert Giacomini
Director of Research
Office of Planning & Budget
270 Washington Street, SW
Suite 8100
Atlanta, GA 30334
P: (404) 656-6505
E: robert.giacomini@opb.state.ga.us

GUAM
Mr. Anthony Lamorena
Director
Bureau of Statistics & Plans
P.O. Box 2950
Barrigada, GU 96932
P: (671) 472-4201
F: (671) 646-8861

IDAHO
Mr. Karl T. Tueller
Deputy Director
Department of Commerce
P.O. Box 83720
Boise, ID 83720
P: (208) 334-3570
F: (208) 334-2631
E: karl.tueller@cl.idaho.gov

ILLINOIS
Ms. Suzanne Ebetsch
Coordinator
Division of Policy Development, Planning & Research
620 East Adams
Springfield, IL 62701
P: (217) 782-1381
F: (217) 524-4876

INDIANA
Ms. Roberta Brooker
Interim Director
State Data Center
140 North Senate Avenue
Indianapolis, IN 46204
P: (317) 232-3693
E: rbrooker@statelib.lib.in.us

IOWA
Ms. Beth Henning
Management Analyst
State Data Center
State Library of Iowa
1112 East Grand Avenue
Des Moines, IA 50319
P: (515) 281-4350
F: (515) 242-6543
E: beth.henning@lib.state.ia.us

KANSAS
Mr. Marc Galbraith
Director
Research & Information Services
State Capitol, Room 345-N
Topeka, KS 66612
P: (785) 296-3296
F: (785) 296-6650
E: marcg@kslib.info

KENTUCKY
Mr. Ron Crouch
Director
State Data Center
Urban Studies Institute
426 West Bloom Street
Louisville, KY 40208
P: (502) 852-7990
F: (502) 852-7386

LOUISIANA
Mr. Neal Underwood
Director
Office of Electronic Services
P.O. Box 94095
Baton Rouge, LA 70804
P: (225) 219-4025
F: (225) 219-4027
E: neal.underwood@la.gov

MAINE
Mr. Eric Von Magnus
Manager
Census Data Center
38 State House Station
Augusta, ME 04333
P: (207) 287-2989

MARYLAND
Ms. Jane Traynham
Manager
State Data Center
301 West Preston Street
Room 702
Baltimore, MD 21201
P: (410) 767-4450
F: (410) 767-4480
E: jtraynham@mdp.state.md.us

MASSACHUSETTS
Mr. John Gaviglio
Data Manager
State Data Center
UMASS Donahue Institute
220 Middlesex House, Box 35520
Amherst, MA 01003
P: (413) 545-0176
F: (413) 545-3420

MICHIGAN
Ms. Lisa Webb Sharpe
Director
Department of Management & Budget
320 South Walnut
Lansing, MI 48909
P: 517-373-1004
E: webbsharpel@michigan.gov

MINNESOTA
Ms. Dana Badgerow
Commissioner
Department of Administration
200 Administration Building
50 Sherburne Avenue
St. Paul, MN 55155
P: (651) 201-2555
F: (651) 297-7909
E: dana.badgerow@state.mn.us

MISSISSIPPI
Mr. David Swanson
Director
Center for Population Studies
Leavel Hall, Room 101
University, MS 38677
P: (662) 232-7288
F: (662) 915-7736
E: dswanson@olemiss.edu

MONTANA
Mr. Dick Clark
Chief Information Officer
Information Technology Services Division
Department of Administration
P.O. Box 200113
Helena, MT 59620
P: (406) 444-2700
F: (406) 444-2701
E: dclark@mt.gov

NEBRASKA
Mr. Jerome Deichart
Director
Center for Public Affairs Research
University of Nebraska Omaha
Omaha, NE 68182
P: (402) 554-2134
F: (402) 554-4946

NEVADA
Mr. Robert Murdock
Administrator
Research & Analysis Bureau
500 East Third Street
Carson City, NV 89713
P: (775) 684-0387
F: (775) 684-3955
E: ramurdock@nvdetr.org

NEW HAMPSHIRE
Mr. Thomas J. Duffy
Senior Planner
State Data Center
Office of Energy & Planning
57 Regional Drive, Suite 3
Concord, NH 03301
P: (603) 271-1768
F: (603) 271-1728
E: tom.duffy@nh.gov

NEW JERSEY
Mr. Len Preston
Director
State Data Center
P.O. Box 388
Trenton, NJ 08625
P: (609) 984-2216
F: (609) 984-6833
E: lpreston@dol.state.nj.us

NEW MEXICO
Ms. Elizabeth Davis
Research Program Officer
Economic Development Department
1100 St. Francis Drive
P.O. Box 20003
Santa Fe, NM 87504
P: (505) 827-0264
F: (505) 827-0211
E: Elizabeth.Davis@state.nm.us

NEW YORK
Mr. Robert Scardamalia
Chief Demographer
State Data Center
30 South Pearl Street
Albany, NY 12245
P: (518) 292-5300
E: rscardamalia@empire.state.ny.us

NORTH CAROLINA
Ms. Francine Stephenson
Manager
State Data Center
116 West Jones Street
20320 Mail Service Center
Raleigh, NC 27699
P: (919) 733-7061
F: (919) 715-3562
E: Francine.Stephenson@ncmail.net

NORTH DAKOTA
Ms. Lisa Feldner
Chief Information Officer
Information Technology Department
600 East Boulevard Avenue, Room 103
Bismarck, ND 58505
P: (701) 328-1000
F: (701) 328-0301
E: lfeldner@nd.gov

NORTHERN MARIANA ISLANDS
Mr. James A. Santos
Director
Department of Commerce
Caller Box 10007, Capital Hill
Saipan, MP 96950
P: (670) 664-3000
F: (670) 664-3070
E: commercedept@vzpacifica.net

OHIO
Mr. Steve Kelley
Director
Office of Strategic Research
Department of Development
77 South High Street, 27th Floor
Columbus, OH 43215
P: (614) 466-2116
E: skelley@odod.state.oh.us

OKLAHOMA
Mr. Jeff Wallace
Assistant Director of Research
State Data Center
900 North Stiles
P.O. Box 26980
Oklahoma City, OK 73126
P: (405) 815-5184
F: (405) 815-5163

OREGON
Mr. Mark Reyer
State Economist
DAS - State Data Center
1225 Ferry Street, Southeast, U20
Salem, OR 97301
P: (503) 378-6430
E: mark.reyer@state.or.us

PENNSYLVANIA
Ms. Sue Copella
Director
State Data Center
777 West Harrisburg Pike
Middletown, PA 17057
P: (717) 948-6336
F: (717) 948-6754
E: sdc3@psu.edu

PUERTO RICO
Mr. Jose Guillermo Davila
Director
Office of Budget & Management
254 Cruz Street
P.O. Box 9023228
San Juan, PR 00902
P: (787) 725-9420
F: (787) 721-8329

RHODE ISLAND
Mr. Mark Brown
Principal Research Technician
Department of Administration
1 Capitol Hill
Providence, RI 02908
P: (401) 222-6183
F: (401) 222-2083

SOUTH CAROLINA
Mr. Bobby Bowers
Director
Office of Research & Statistics, Budget & Control Board
Rembert C. Dennis Building, Room 425
1000 Assembly Street
Columbia, SC 29201
P: (803) 734-3793
E: bobby@drss.state.sc.us

SOUTH DAKOTA
Ms. Nancy Nelson
Director
State Data Center
University of South Dakota
School of Business, 414 East Clark
Vermillion, SD 57069
P: (605) 677-5287
F: (605) 677-5427
E: nnelson@exchange.usd.edu

TENNESSEE
Mr. Bill Ezell
Chief Information Officer
Office for Information Resources
William R. Snodgrass Tennessee Towers
16th Floor, 312 8th Avenue, North
Nashville, TN 37243
P: (615) 741-3700
F: (615) 532-0471
E: bill.ezell@state.tn.us

State Data Center

TEXAS
Mr. Brian Rawson
Director
Department of Information Resources
300 West 15th Street, Suite 1300
P.O. Box 13564
Austin, TX 78701
P: (512) 463-9909
F: (512) 475-4759
E: brian.rawson@dir.state.tx.us

U.S. VIRGIN ISLANDS
Mr. Dayle Barry
Coordinator
Conservation Data Center
Eastern Caribbean Center, UVI
#2 John Brewer Bay
St. Thomas, VI 00802
P: (340) 693-1030
F: (340) 693-1025

UTAH
Mr. Richard Ellis
Director
Governor's Office of Planning & Budget
State Capitol Complex, Suite E210
P.O. Box 142210
Salt Lake City, UT 84114
P: (801) 538-1562
F: (801) 538-1547
E: RELLIS@utah.gov

Mr. John Nixon
Director
Governor's Office of Planning & Budget
State Capitol Complex, Suite E210
P.O. Box 142210
Salt Lake City, UT 84114
P: (801) 538-1562
F: (801) 538-1547
E: jnixon@utah.gov

VERMONT
Mr. Will Sawyer
Lead Coordinator
State Data Center
Center for Rural Studies
207 Morrill Hall, University of Vermont
Burlington, VT 05405
P: (802) 656-0892
E: william.sawyer@uvm.edu

VIRGINIA
Ms. Dolores A. Esser
Commissioner
Employment Commission
703 East Main Street
Richmond, VA 23219
P: (804) 786-3001
F: (804) 225-3923
E: dee.esser@vec.virginia.gov

WASHINGTON
Mr. Irv Lefberg
Chief of Forecasting
Forecasting Unit
P.O. Box 43113
Olympia, WA 98504
P: (360) 902-0590

WISCONSIN
Mr. Phil Wells
Census Data Consultant
Demographic Services Center
101 East Wilson, 10th Floor
Madison, WI 53708
P: (608) 266-1927
F: (608) 267-6931

WYOMING
Mr. Buck McVeigh
Administrator
Economic Analysis Division
Dept. of Administration & Information
1807 Capitol Avenue, Suite 206
Cheyenne, WY 82002
P: (307) 777-7504
F: (307) 632-1819
E: bmcvei@state.wy.us

State and Public Libraries

Serves the information and research needs of state executive and legislative branch officials. Also oversees the development of public libraries in the state and federal programs related to such libraries.

ALABAMA
Ms. Rebecca Mitchell
Director
Public Library Service
6030 Monticello Drive
Montgomery, AL 36130
P: (334) 213-3901
F: (334) 213-3993
E: rmitchell@apls.state.al.us

ALASKA
Ms. Kay Shelton
Director
Division of Libraries, Archives & Museums
Department of Education
P.O. Box 110571
Juneau, AK 99811
P: (907) 465-2912
F: (907) 465-2151
E: kay_shelton@eed.state.ak.us

AMERICAN SAMOA
Ms. Cheryl Morales Polataivao
Territorial Librarian
Feleti Barstow Public Library
P.O. Box 997687
Pago Pago, AS 96799
P: (684) 633-5816
F: (684) 633-5816
E: feletibarstow@yahoo.com

ARIZONA
Ms. Gladys Ann Wells
Director
State Library Archives & Public Records
Archives & Public Records
State Capitol, Room 200
Phoenix, AZ 85007
P: (602) 542-4035
F: (602) 542-4972
E: gawells@lib.az.us

ARKANSAS
Ms. Carolyn Ashcraft
State Librarian
State Library
One Capitol Mall, 5th Floor
Little Rock, AR 72201
P: (501) 682-2848
F: (501) 682-1899
E: cashcraf@asl.lib.ar.us

CALIFORNIA
Ms. Susan Hildreth
State Librarian
State Library
P.O. Box 942837
Sacramento, CA 94237
P: (916) 654-0174
E: shildreth@library.ca.gov

COLORADO
Mr. Gene Hainer
State Librarian & Assistant Commissioner
State Library
201 East Colfax Avenue, Room 309
Denver, CO 80203
P: (303) 866-6730
F: (303) 866-6940
E: hainer_g@cde.state.co.us

CONNECTICUT
Mr. Kendall F. Wiggin
State Librarian
State Library
231 Capitol Avenue
Hartford, CT 06106
P: (860) 757-6510
F: (860) 757-6503
E: kwiggin@cslib.org

DELAWARE
Ms. Annie Norman
Director & State Librarian
Division of Libraries
43 South DuPont Highway
Dover, DE 19901
P: (302) 739-4748 Ext. 126
F: (302) 739-6787
E: annie.norman@state.de.us

DISTRICT OF COLUMBIA
Ms. Ginnie Cooper
Executive Director
Public Libraries
901 G Street, Northwest
Suite 400
Washington, DC 20001
P: (202) 727-1101
F: (202) 727-1129

FLORIDA
Ms. Judith Ring
Director
Division of Library & Information Services
R. A. Gray Building
Tallahassee, FL 32399
P: (850) 245-6600
F: (850) 245-6735
E: jring@dos.state.fl.us

GEORGIA
Dr. Lamar Veatch
State Librarian
Public Library Services
1800 Century Place, Suite 150
Atlanta, GA 30345
P: (404) 982-3560
F: (404) 982-3563
E: lveatch@georgialibraries.org

GUAM
Ms. Connie Mendiola
Territorial Librarian
Guam Public Library
254 Martyr Street
Hagatna, GU 96910
P: (671) 475-4751
F: (671) 477-9777

HAWAII
Ms. Jo Ann Schindler
State Librarian
State Public Library System
44 Merchant St.
Honolulu, HI 96813
P: (808) 586-3704
F: (808) 586-3715
E: joann@librarieshawaii.org

IDAHO
Ms. Ann Joslin
State Librarian
State Library
325 West State Street
Boise, ID 83702
P: (208) 334-2150
F: (208) 334-4016
E: ann.joslin@libraries.idaho.gov

ILLINOIS
Ms. Anne Craig
Director
State Library
300 South Second Street
Gwendolyn Brooks Building
Springfield, IL 62701
P: (217) 785-2994
E: acraig@ilsos.net

INDIANA
Ms. Roberta Brooker
Interim Director
State Library
140 North Senate Avenue
Indianapolis, IN 46204
P: (317) 232-3693
E: rbrooker@statelib.lib.in.us

IOWA
Ms. Mary Wegner
State Librarian
State Library
Ola Babcock Miller Building
Des Moines, IA 50319
P: (515) 281-4105
F: (515) 281-6191
E: mary.wegner@lib.state.ia.us

KANSAS
Ms. Christie Pearson Brandau
State Librarian
State Library
300 Southwest 10th Avenue
Topeka, KS 66612
P: (785) 296-3296
F: (785) 296-6650
E: christieb@kslib.info

KENTUCKY
Mr. Wayne Onkst
State Librarian & Commissioner
Department for Libraries & Archives
300 Coffeetree Road
Frankfort, KY 40602
P: (502) 564-8300, Ext. 312
F: (502) 564-5773
E: wayne.onkst@ky.gov

LOUISIANA
Ms. Rebecca Hamilton
State Librarian
State Library
P.O. Box 131
Baton Rouge, LA 70821
P: (225) 342-4923
F: (225) 219-4804
E: rhamilton@crt.state.la.us

MAINE
Mr. J. Gary Nichols
State Librarian
State Library
64 State House Station
Autusta, ME 04333
P: (207) 287-5600
F: (207) 287-5615
E: gary.nichols@maine.gov

State and Public Libraries

MARYLAND
Ms. Irene M. Padilla
Assistant Superintendent for Library Development and Services
Department of Education
200 West Baltimore Street
Baltimore, MD 21201
P: (410) 767-0435
F: (410) 333-2507
E: ipadilla@msde.state.md.us

MASSACHUSETTS
Mr. Robert C. Maier
Director
Board of Library Commissioners
98 North Washington Street, Suite 401
Boston, MA 02114
P: (617) 725-1860
F: (617) 725-0140
E: robert.maier@state.ma.us

MICHIGAN
Ms. Nancy Robertson
State Librarian
State Library
P.O. Box 30007
Lansing, MI 48909
P: (517) 373-5504
F: (517) 373-4480
E: nrobertson@michigan.gov

MINNESOTA
Ms. Suzanne Miller
Director
Library Services & School Technology
1500 Highway 36 West
Roseville, MN 55113
P: (651) 582-8791
F: (651) 582-8752
E: suzanne.miller@state.mn.us

MISSISSIPPI
Ms. Sharman B. Smith
Executive Director
Library Commission
3881 Eastwood Drive
Jackson, MS 39211
P: (601) 961-4039
F: (601) 354-6713
E: sharman@mlc.lib.ms.us

MISSOURI
Ms. Margaret Conroy
State Librarian
Office of the Secretary of State
P.O. Box 387
Jefferson City, MO 65102
P: (573) 751-2751
F: (573) 751-3612

MONTANA
Ms. Darlene Staffeldt
State Librarian
State Library
P.O. Box 201800
1515 East 6th Avenue
Helena, MT 59620
P: (406) 444-3115
F: (406) 444-0266
E: dstaffeldt@mt.gov

NEBRASKA
Mr. Rod Wagner
Director
Library Commission
The Atrium
1200 North Street, Suite 120
Lincoln, NE 68508
P: (402) 471-4001
F: (402) 471-2083
E: rwagner@nlc.state.ne.us

NEVADA
Mr. Guy Rocha
Interim Administrator & State Librarian
State Library & Archives
100 North Stewart Street
Carson City, NV 89701
P: (775) 684-3317
F: (775) 684-3311
E: glrocha@clan.lib.nv.us

NEW HAMPSHIRE
Mr. Michael York
State Librarian
State Library
20 Park Street
Concord, NH 03301
P: (603) 271-2397
F: (603) 271-6826
E: myork@library.state.nh.us

NEW JERSEY
Ms. Norma E. Blake
State Librarian
State Library
P.O. Box 520
Trenton, NJ 08625
P: (609) 292-6200
F: (609) 292-2746
E: nblake@njstatelib.org

NEW MEXICO
Mr. Richard Akeroyd
State Librarian/Division Director
Office of the State Librarian
1209 Camino Carlos Rey
Santa Fe, NM 87507
P: (505) 476-9762
F: (505) 476-9761
E: richard.akeroyd@state.nm.us

NEW YORK
Ms. Janet M. Welch
State Librarian & Assistant Commissioner for Libraries
State Library
Cultural Education Center
Albany, NY 12230
P: (518) 474-5930
F: (518) 486-6880
E: jwelch2@mail.nysed.gov

NORTH CAROLINA
Ms. Mary Boone
State Librarian
State Library
109 East Jones Street
4640 Mail Service Center
Raleigh, NC 27699
P: (919) 807-7405
F: (919) 733-8748
E: mary.boone@ncmail.net

NORTH DAKOTA
Ms. Doris Ott
State Librarian
State Library
604 East Boulevard Avenue
Department 250
Bismarck, ND 58505
P: (701) 328-2492
F: (701) 328-2040
E: dott@nd.gov

OHIO
Ms. Joanne Budler
State Librarian
State Library
274 East 1st Street
Columbus, OH 43201
P: (614) 644-7061
F: (614) 466-3584
E: jbudler@sloma.state.oh.us

OKLAHOMA
Ms. Susan McVey
Director
Department of Libraries
200 Northeast 18th Street
Oklahoma City, OK 73105
P: (405) 521-2502
F: (405) 525-7804
E: smcvey@oltn.odl.state.ok.us

OREGON
Mr. Jim Scheppke
State Librarian
State Library
250 Winter Street, Northeast
Salem, OR 97301
P: (503) 378-4367
F: (503) 585-8059
E: jim.b.scheppke@state.or.us

PENNSYLVANIA
Ms. Mary Clare Zales
Commissioner for Libraries
Office of Commonwealth Libraries
333 Market Street
Harrisburg, PA 17126
P: (717) 787-2646
F: (717) 772-3265
E: mzales@state.pa.us

RHODE ISLAND
Mr. Howard Boksenbaum
Chief Library Officer
Office of Library & Information Services
One Capitol Hill, Suite 4
Providence, RI 02908
P: (401) 222-3153
E: howardbm@olis.ri.gov

SOUTH CAROLINA
Mr. David Goble
Director
State Library
1500 Senate Street
Columbia, SC 29211
P: (803) 734-8656
F: (803) 734-8676

SOUTH DAKOTA
Ms. Dorothy M. Liegl
State Librarian
State Library
800 Governors Drive
Pierre, SD 57501
P: (605) 773-3131
F: (605) 773-4950
E: dorothy.liegl@state.sd.us

TENNESSEE
Ms. Jeanne D. Sugg
State Librarian & Archivist
Library & Archives
403 7th Avenue, North
Nashville, TN 37243
P: (615) 741-7996
F: (615) 532-9293
E: jeanne.sugg@state.tn.us

TEXAS
Ms. Peggy D. Rudd
Director & Librarian
Library & Archives
Commission
1201 Brazos Street
Austin, TX 78711
P: (512) 463-5460
F: (512) 463-5436
E: prudd@tsl.state.tx.us

U.S. VIRGIN ISLANDS
Mr. Wallace Williams
Territorial Librarian
Division of Libraries, Archives
& Museums
1122 Kings Street
St. Croix, VI 00820
P: (304) 773-5715
E: wallacewilliams@msn.com

UTAH
Ms. Donna Jones Morris
State Librarian
State Library
Department of Community &
Culture
250 North 1950 West, Suite A
Salt Lake City, UT 84116
P: (801) 715-6770
F: (801) 715-6767
E: dmorris@utah.gov

VERMONT
Ms. Sybil Brigham McShane
State Librarian
Department of Libraries
Pavillion Office Building
Montpelier, VT 05609
P: (802) 828-3265
F: (802) 828-2199
E: sybil.mcshane
@dol.state.vt.us

VIRGINIA
Mr. Nolan T. Yelich
State Librarian
The Library of Virginia
800 East Broad Street
Richmond, VA 23219
P: (804) 692-3535
F: (804) 692-3594
E: nyelich@lva.lib.va.us

WASHINGTON
Ms. Jan Walsh
State Librarian
State Library Division
6880 Capitol Boulevard
Tumwater, WA 98501
P: (360) 704-5253
F: (360) 586-7575
E: jwalsh@secstate.wa.gov

WEST VIRGINIA
Mr. James D. Waggoner
Secretary
Library Commission
State of West Virginia Cultural
Center
Charleston, WV 25305
P: (304) 558-2041 Ext. 2084
F: (304) 558-2044
E: waggoner@wvlc.lib.wv.us

WISCONSIN
Mr. Richard Grobschmidt
Division Administrator
Division for Libraries,
Technology & Community
Learning
125 South Webster Street
Madison, WI 53707
P: (608) 266-2205
F: (608) 267-1052
E: richard.grobschmidt
@dpi.state.wi.us

WYOMING
Ms. Lesley D. Boughton
State Librarian
State Library, Department of
Administration & Information
2301 Capitol Avenue
Cheyenne, WY 82002
P: (307) 777-5911
F: (307) 777-6289
E: lbough@state.wy.us

State Police

Patrols the state's highways and enforces the motor vehicle laws of the state.

ALABAMA
Maj. Cary Sutton
Division Chief
Service Division
500 Dexter Avenue
Montgomery, AL 36130
P: (334) 242-1799
F: (334) 242-4385

AMERICAN SAMOA
Mr. Sotoa Savali
Commissioner
Department of Public Safety
American Samoa Government
P.O. Box 3699
Pago Pago, AS 96799
P: (684) 633-1111
F: (684) 633-7296

ARIZONA
Mr. Roger Vanderpool
Director
Department of Public Safety
2102 West Encanto Boulevard
P.O. Box 6638
Phoenix, AZ 85005
P: (602) 223-2359
F: (602) 223-2917

ARKANSAS
Col. Steve Dozier
Director
State Police
#1 State Police Plaza Drive
Little Rock, AR 72209
P: (501) 618-8200
F: (501) 618-8222
E: steve.dozier
@asp.arkansas.gov

CALIFORNIA
Mr. Mike Brown
Commissioner
Highway Patrol
Business, Trans. & Housing Agency
2555 First Avenue
Sacramento, CA 95818
P: (916) 657-7152
F: (916) 657-7324

COLORADO
Col. Mark V. Trostel
Chief
State Police
Department of Public Safety
700 Kipling Street, Suite 3000
Lakewood, CO 80215
P: (303) 239-4403
F: (303) 239-4481
E: mark.trostel
@cdps.state.co.us

CONNECTICUT
Mr. John Danaher
Commissioner
Department of Public Safety
1111 Country Club ROad
Middletown, CT 06457
P: (860) 685-8000
F: (860) 685-8354

DELAWARE
Col. Thomas F. Macleish
Superintendent
State Police
P.O. Box 430
Dover, DE 19901
P: (302) 739-5901
F: (302) 739-5966
E: Thomas.Macleish
@state.de.us

DISTRICT OF COLUMBIA
Ms. Cathy L. Lanier
Chief of Police
Metropolitan Police Department
300 Indiana Avenue, NW
Room 5080
Washington, DC 20001
P: (202) 727-4218
F: (202) 727-9524

FLORIDA
Mr. Gerald Bailey
Commissioner
Department of Law Enforcement
P.O. Box 1489
Tallahassee, FL 32302
P: (850) 410-7001

GEORGIA
Col. Bill Hitchens
Commissioner
Department of Public Safety
P.O. Box 1456
Atlanta, GA 30371
P: (404) 624-7477
F: (404) 624-6706

IDAHO
Col. Jerry Russell
Director
State Police
P.O. Box 700
Meridian, ID 83680
P: (208) 884-7003
F: (208) 884-7090

ILLINOIS
Mr. Larry Trent
Director
State Police
125 East Monroe Street, Room 107
Springfield, IL 62794
P: (217) 782-7263
F: (217) 785-2821
E: larry_trent
@isp.state.il.us

INDIANA
Dr. Paul Whitesell
Superintendent
State Police
100 North Senate Avenue, Room N340
Indianapolis, IN 46204
P: (317) 232-8241

IOWA
Col. Robert O. Garrison
Chief
State Patrol
Wallace State Office Building
502 East 9th Street
Des Moines, IA 50319
P: (515) 281-5824

KANSAS
Col. William Seck
Superintendent
Highway Patrol
122 Southwest 7th Street
Topeka, KS 66603
P: (785) 296-6800
F: (785) 296-3049
E: wseck
@mail.khp.state.ks.us

KENTUCKY
Mr. John Adams
Commissioner
Department of State Police
919 Versailles Road
Frankfort, KY 40601
P: (502) 695-6303
F: (502) 573-1479

LOUISIANA
Col. Henry Whitehorn
Superintendent of State Police
Department of Public Safety
7919 Independence Boulevard
P.O. Box 66614
Baton Rouge, LA 70896
P: (225) 925-6118
F: (225) 925-3742
E: hwhitehorn
@dps.state.la.us

MAINE
Col. Craig A. Poulin
Chief
State Police
36 Hospital Street
Augusta, ME 04333
P: (207) 624-7200
F: (207) 624-7042
E: craig.a.poulin@maine.gov

MARYLAND
Col. Thomas E. Hutchins
Superintendent
Department of Maryland State Police
1201 Reisterstown Road
Pikesville, MD 21208
P: (410) 653-4219
F: (410) 653-4269
E: superintendent@mdsp.org

MASSACHUSETTS
Col. Mark F. Delaney
Superintendent
State Police
470 Worcester Road
Framingham, MA 01702
P: (508) 820-2300
F: (617) 727-6874

MICHIGAN
Col. Peter C. Munoz
Director
State Police
714 South Harrison Road
East Lansing, MI 48823
P: (517) 336-6158
F: (517) 336-6551

MINNESOTA
Col. Mark A. Dunaski
Chief
State Patrol
444 Cedar Street
Suite 130, Town Square
St. Paul, MN 55101
P: (651) 201-7117
E: mark.dunaski@state.mn.us

MISSISSIPPI
Lt. Col. David Shaw
Commissioner
Bureau of Investigation
P.O. Box 958
Jackson, MS 39205
P: (601) 987-1212
F: (601) 987-1488

MISSOURI
Col. James F. Keathley
Superintendent
State Highway Patrol
1510 East Elm
P.O. Box 568
Jefferson City, MO 65102
P: (573) 526-6120
F: (573) 526-1111
E: james.keathley
@mshp.dps.mo.gov

MONTANA
Hon. Mike McGrath (D)
Attorney General
Office of the Attorney General
Department of Justice
P.O. Box 201401
Helena, MT 59620
P: (406) 444-2026
F: (404) 444-3549
E: contactdoj@mt.gov

NEBRASKA
Maj. Bryan Tuma
State Patrol
P.O. Box 94907
Lincoln, NE 68509
P: (402) 471-4545
F: (402) 479-4002

NEVADA
Col. Chris Perry
Chief
Highway Patrol
555 Wright Way
Carson City, NV 89711
P: (775) 687-5300
E: cperry@dps.state.nv.us

NEW HAMPSHIRE
Col. Frederick H. Booth
Director
Division of State Police
33 Hazen Drive
Concord, NH 03305
P: (603) 271-2450
F: (603) 271-2527
E: fbooth
@safety.state.nh.us

NEW JERSEY
Col. Rick Fuentes
Superintendent
State Police
P.O. Box 7068
West Trenton, NJ 08628
P: (609) 882-2000
F: (609) 530-4383

NEW MEXICO
Mr. Farron W. Segotta
State Police Chief/Deputy
Secretary of Operations
Department of Public Safety
4491 Cerrillos Road
P.O. Box 1628
Santa Fe, NM 87501
P: (505) 827-9219
F: (505) 827-3395
E: faron.segotta
@state.nm.us

NEW YORK
Mr. Preston Felton
Interim Superintendent
State Police
1220 Washington Avenue,
Building 22
Albany, NY 12226
P: (518) 457-6721

NORTH CAROLINA
Col. Fletcher Clay
Commander
State Highway Patrol
P.O. Box 29590
4702 Mail Service Center
Raleigh, NC 27699
P: (919) 733-7952
F: (919) 733-1189

NORTH DAKOTA
Col. Bryan Klipfel
Superintendent
Highway Patrol
600 East Boulevard Avenue
Department 504
Bismarck, ND 58505
P: (701) 328-2455
F: (701) 328-1717
E: bklipfel@nd.gov

NORTHERN MARIANA ISLANDS
Ms. Rebecca Warfield
Commissioner
Department of Public Safety
Caller Box 10007, Capital Hill
Saipan, MP 96950
P: (670) 664-9022
F: (670) 664-9027
E: doris@cjpa.gov.mp

OHIO
Col. Richard H. Collins
Superintendent
State Highway Patrol
1970 West Broad Street
PO Box 182074
Columbus, OH 43223
P: (614) 466-9144

OKLAHOMA
Mr. Kevin Ward
Secretary of Safety & Security
Department of Public Safety
P.O. Box 11415
Oklahoma City, OK 73136
P: (405) 425-2424
F: (405) 425-2324

OREGON
Mr. Tim McClain
Superintendent
Department of State Police
400 Public Service Building
255 Capitol Street, Northeast,
4th Floor
Salem, OR 97310
P: (503) 378-3720
F: (503) 378-8282
E: osp.ghq@state.or.us

PENNSYLVANIA
Col. Jeffrey B. Miller
Commissioner
State Police
1800 Elmerton Avenue
Harrisburg, PA 17110
P: (717) 783-5558
F: (717) 787-2948

PUERTO RICO
Mr. Pedro A. Toledo Davila
Superintendent
Puerto Rico Police
P.O. Box 70166
San Juan, PR 00936
P: (787) 793-1234
F: (787) 781-0080

RHODE ISLAND
Col. Brendan P. Doherty
Superintendent
State Police
311 Danielson Pike
North Scituate, RI 02857
P: (401) 444-1000
F: (401) 444-1105

Maj. Steven M. O'Donnell
Acting Superintendent
State Police
311 Danielson Pike
North Scituate, RI 02857
P: (401) 444-1000
F: (401) 444-1105
E: sodonnell
@risp.state.ri.us

SOUTH CAROLINA
Col. Russell F. Roark III
Commander
Highway Patrol
5400 Broad River Road
Columbia, SC 29212
P: (803) 896-7888
F: (803) 896-7922

SOUTH DAKOTA
Col. Daniel C. Mosteller
Superintendent
Highway Patrol
Department of Public Safety
118 West Capitol Avenue
Pierre, SD 57501
P: (605) 773-3105
F: (605) 773-6046
E: dan.mosteller
@state.sd.us

TENNESSEE
Mr. David Mitchell
Commissioner
Department of Safety
1150 Foster Avenue
Nashville, TN 37243
P: (615) 741-3063
E: dave.mitchell
@state.tn.us

TEXAS
Col. Thomas A. Davis Jr.
Director
Department of Public Safety
P.O. Box 4087
Austin, TX 78773
P: (512) 424-2000
E: thomas.davis
@txdps.state.tx.us

U.S. VIRGIN ISLANDS
Mr. Elton Lewis
Commissioner
Police Department
Alexander Farrelly Criminal
Justice Ctr.
Charlotte Amalie
St. Thomas, VI 00802
P: (340) 774-2211
F: (340) 715-5517
E: elton.lewis@us.army.mil

State Police

UTAH
Col. Lance Davenport
Colonel
Department of Public Safety
Utah Highway Patrol
4501 South 2700 West
Salt Lake City, UT 84119
P: (801) 965-4379
F: (801) 965-4716
E: ldavenport@utah.gov

VERMONT
Col. James W. Baker
Director
State Police
103 South Main Street
Waterbury, VT 05671
P: (802) 244-7345

VIRGINIA
Col. W. Steven Flaherty
Superintendent
Department of State Police
7700 Midlothian Turnpike
P.O. Box 27472
Richmond, VA 23235
P: (804) 674-2087
F: (804) 674-2132
E: supt@vsp.virginia.gov

WASHINGTON
Mr. John R. Batiste
Chief
State Patrol
General Administration Building
P.O. Box 42600
Olympia, WA 98504
P: (360) 753-6540

WEST VIRGINIA
Col. David Lemmon
Superintendent
State Police
725 Jefferson Road
South Charleston, WV 25309
P: (304) 746-2111
F: (304) 746-2230
E: dlemmon@wvsp.state.wv.us

WISCONSIN
Mr. David L. Collins
Superintendent
Division of State Patrol
4802 Sheboygan Avenue, Room 551
P.O. Box 7912
Madison, WI 53707
P: (608) 266-0454
F: (608) 267-4495
E: david.collins@dot.state.wi.us

WYOMING
Col. Sam Powell
Administrator
Highway Patrol
5300 Bishop Boulevard
Cheyenne, WY 82009
P: (307) 777-4301
F: (307) 777-4288

State Security

Develops and oversees operations to insure the safety of state citizens from threats of violence and terrorism.

ALABAMA
Mr. James Walker
Director
Homeland Security
2 North Jackson
Montgomery, AL 36104
P: (334) 956-7250
F: (334) 223-1120
E: jim.walker@dhs.alabama.gov

ALASKA
Maj. Gen. Craig Campbell
Adjutant General
Department of Military & Veterans Affairs
P.O. Box 5800
Fort Richardson, AK 99505
P: (907) 428-6003
F: (907) 428-6019
E: craig.campbell2@us.army.mil

AMERICAN SAMOA
Mr. Sotoa Savali
Commissioner
Department of Public Safety
American Samoa Government
P.O. Box 3699
Pago Pago, AS 96799
P: (684) 633-1111
F: (684) 633-7296

ARIZONA
Mr. Roger Vanderpool
Director
Department of Public Safety
2102 West Encanto Boulevard
P.O. Box 6638
Phoenix, AZ 85005
P: (602) 223-2359
F: (602) 223-2917

ARKANSAS
Mr. David Maxwell
Director & Homeland Security Adviser
Department of Emergency Management
P.O. Box 758
Conway, AR 72033
P: (501) 730-9750
F: (501) 730-9778
E: david.maxwell@adem.state.ar.us

CALIFORNIA
Mr. Mike Brown
Commissioner
Highway Patrol
Business, Trans. & Housing Agency
2555 First Avenue
Sacramento, CA 95818
P: (916) 657-7152
F: (916) 657-7324

Mr. Henry R. Renteria
Director
Governor's Office of Emergency Services
3650 Schriever Avenue
Mather, CA 95655
P: (916) 845-8510
F: (916) 845-8511
E: henry_renteria@oes.ca.gov

COLORADO
Mr. Peter Weir
Executive Director
Department of Public Safety
700 Kipling Street, Suite 3000
Lakewood, CO 80215
P: (303) 239-4398
F: (303) 239-4670
E: Public.Safety@cdps.state.co.us

CONNECTICUT
Mr. James M. Thomas
Director
Division of Homeland Security
55 West Main Street
Waterbury, CT 06702
P: (860) 418-6394
E: james.thomas@po.state.ct.us

DELAWARE
Mr. David B. Mitchell
Director of Homeland Security
Department of Safety and Homeland Security
330 Transportation Circle
P.O. Box 818
Dover, DE 19901
P: (302) 744-2680
F: (302) 739-4874

DISTRICT OF COLUMBIA
Ms. Cathy L. Lanier
Chief of Police
Metropolitan Police Department
300 Indiana Avenue, NW
Room 5080
Washington, DC 20001
P: (202) 727-4218
F: (202) 727-9524

FLORIDA
Mr. Gerald Bailey
Commissioner
Department of Law Enforcement
P.O. Box 1489
Tallahassee, FL 32302
P: (850) 410-7001

GEORGIA
Col. Bill Hitchens
Commissioner
Department of Public Safety
P.O. Box 1456
Atlanta, GA 30371
P: (404) 624-7477
F: (404) 624-6706

GUAM
Brig. Gen. Donald Goldhorn
Adjutant General
Homeland Security
430 Route 16, Building 300, Room 113
Barrigada, GU 96913
P: (671) 735-0406
F: (671) 735-0836

HAWAII
Maj. Gen. Robert G.F. Lee
Adjutant General
Department of Defense
3949 Diamond Head Road
Honolulu, HI 96816
P: (808) 733-4258
F: (808) 733-4236

IDAHO
Maj. Gen. Lawrence LaFrenz
Adjutant General
Military Division
4040 West Guard Building 600
Boise, ID 83705
P: (208) 422-5242
F: (208) 422-6179

ILLINOIS
Mr. Larry Trent
Director
State Police
125 East Monroe Street, Room 107
Springfield, IL 62794
P: (217) 782-7263
F: (217) 785-2821
E: larry_trent@isp.state.il.us

Mr. Andrew Velasquez
Director
Emergency Management Agency
2200 South Dirksen Parkway
Springfield, IL 62701
P: (217) 782-2800
F: (217) 524-7967
E: andrew.velasquez@illinois.gov

INDIANA
Mr. J. Eric Dietz
Executive Director
Department of Homeland Security
302 West Washington Street, Room E-208
Indianapolis, IN 46235
P: (317) 232-3986
F: (317) 232-3895
E: jedietz@dhs.in.gov

IOWA
Mr. David Miller
Administrator
Iowa Homeland Security & Emergency Management Division
7105 Northwest 70th Avenue
Camp Dodge - W4
Johnston, IA 50131
P: (515) 281-3231
F: (515) 725-3290
E: David.Miller@Iowa.gov

KANSAS
Maj. Gen. Tod M. Bunting
Adjutant General
Adjutant General's Department
2800 Southwest Topeka Boulevard
Topeka, KS 66611
P: (913) 274-1001
F: (913) 274-1682

KENTUCKY
Maj. Gen. Donald C. Storm
Adjutant General
Department of Military Affairs
Boone National Guard Center
100 Minuteman Parkway
Frankfort, KY 40601
P: (502) 607-1558
F: (502) 607-1240

LOUISIANA
Col. Jeff Smith
Acting Director
Homeland Security & Emergency Preparedness
7667 Independence Boulevard
Baton Rouge, LA 70806
P: (225) 925-7345
F: (225) 925-7348
E: jsmith@ohsep.louisiana.gov

State Security

MAINE
Mr. Mark Gilbert
Director of Security & Intelligence
Adjutant General's Office
33 State House Station
Augusta, ME 04333
P: (207) 626-4440
F: (207) 626-4430
E: mark.gilbert@me.ngb.army.mil

MARYLAND
Mr. Dennis Schrader
Director
Homeland Security Office
Jeffrey Building
Annapolis, MD 21401
P: (410) 974-2389

MASSACHUSETTS
Mr. Kevin Burke
Secretary
Executive Office of Public Safety
One Ashburton Place, Suite 2133
Boston, MA 02108
P: (617) 727-7775
F: (617) 727-4764

MICHIGAN
Col. Peter C. Munoz
Director
State Police
714 South Harrison Road
East Lansing, MI 48823
P: (517) 336-6158
F: (517) 336-6551

MINNESOTA
Mr. Michael Campion
Commissioner
Department of Public Safety
Bremer Tower, Suite 1000
445 Minnesota Street
St. Paul, MN 55101
P: (651) 201-7000
F: (651) 297-5728
E: michael.campion@state.mn.us

MISSISSIPPI
Mr. J.W. Ledbetter
Director
State Emergency Management Agency
P.O. Box 4501
1410 Riverside Drive
Jackson, MS 39296
P: (601) 352-9100

Mr. Mike Womack
Executive Director
State Emergency Management Agency
#1 MEMA Drive
P.O. Box 5644
Pearl, MS 39288
P: (601) 933-6362
F: (601) 933-6800
E: mwomack@mema.ms.gov

MISSOURI
Mr. Mark S. James
Director
Department of Public Safety
301 West High Street
Truman Building, Room 870
Jefferson City, MO 65102
P: (573) 751-4905
F: (573) 751-5399
E: Mark.James@dps.mo.gov

MONTANA
Mr. Dan McGowan
Administrator
Disaster & Emergency Services
Department of Military Affairs
P.O. Box 4789
Ft. Harrison, MT 59636
P: (406) 841-3911
F: (406) 841-3965
E: dmcgowan@mt.gov

NEBRASKA
Hon. Rick Sheehy (R)
Lieutenant Governor
Office of the Lieutenant Governor
State Capitol, Room 2315
P.O.Box 94863
Lincoln, NE 68509
P: (402) 471-2256
F: (402) 471-6031

NEVADA
Mr. Frank Siracusa
Director
Emergency Management
2525 South Carson Street
Capitol Complex
Carson City, NV 89711
P: (775) 687-4240
F: (775) 687-6788
E: fsiracusa@dps.state.nv.us

NEW HAMPSHIRE
Mr. Bruce Cheney
Executive Director
Bureau of Emergency Management
10 Hazen Drive
Concord, NH 03305
P: (603) 271-6911
F: (603) 225-7341
E: bcheney@nh911.state.nh.us

NEW JERSEY
Mr. Richard L. Canas
Director
Office of Homeland Security & Preparedness
P.O. Box 091
Trenton, NJ 08625
P: (609) 584-4000
F: (609) 631-4916

NEW MEXICO
Mr. Tim Manning
Director
Office of Homeland Security
Department of Public Safety
130 South Capitol
Santa Fe, NM 85504
P: (505) 476-1050
F: (505) 476-1057
E: Tim.Manning@state.nm.us

NEW YORK
Mr. F. David Sheppard
Director
Office of Homeland Security
Executive Chamber
633 Third Avenue, 38th Floor
New York, NY 10017
P: (518) 402-2227
F: (212) 803-3715

NORTH CAROLINA
Mr. Bryan E. Beatty
Secretary
Department of Crime Control & Public Safety
512 North Salisbury Street
4701 Mail Service Center
Raleigh, NC 27699
P: (919) 733-2126
F: (919) 715-8477
E: bbeatty@nccrimecontrol.org

NORTH DAKOTA
Col. Bryan Klipfel
Superintendent
Highway Patrol
600 East Boulevard Avenue
Department 504
Bismarck, ND 58505
P: (701) 328-2455
F: (701) 328-1717
E: bklipfel@nd.gov

Mr. Greg Wilz
Director
Department of Homeland Security
P.O. Box 5511
Bismarck, ND 58506
P: (701) 328-8100
F: (701) 328-8181
E: gwilz@nd.gov

NORTHERN MARIANA ISLANDS
Mr. Patrick P. Tenorio
Governor's Special Assistant
Office of Homeland Security
Caller Box 10007, Capitol Hill
Saipan, MP 96950
P: (670) 664-2208
F: (670) 664-2211
E: ten04@hotmail.com

OHIO
Mr. Henry Guzman
Director
Department of Public Safety
1970 West Broad Street
P.O. Box 182081
Columbus, OH 43218
P: (614) 466-3383
F: (614) 466-0433

OKLAHOMA
Mr. Kevin Ward
Secretary of Safety & Security
Department of Public Safety
P.O. Box 11415
Oklahoma City, OK 73136
P: (405) 425-2424
F: (405) 425-2324

OREGON
Mr. Tim McClain
Superintendent
Department of State Police
400 Public Service Building
255 Capitol Street, Northeast, 4th Floor
Salem, OR 97310
P: (503) 378-3720
F: (503) 378-8282
E: osp.ghq@state.or.us

PENNSYLVANIA
Mr. James F. Powers Jr.
Director
Office of Homeland Security
2605 Interstate Drive
Harrisburg, PA 17110
P: (717) 651-2715

PUERTO RICO
Mr. Pedro A. Toledo Davila
Superintendent
Puerto Rico Police
P.O. Box 70166
San Juan, PR 00936
P: (787) 793-1234
F: (787) 781-0080

RHODE ISLAND
Maj. Gen. Robert T. Bray
Adjutant General
National Guard Headquarters
Command Readiness Center
645 New London Avenue
Cranston, RI 02920
P: (401) 275-4102
F: (401) 275-4338

SOUTH CAROLINA
Mr. Robert M. Stewart
Chief
State Law Enforcement Division
P.O. Box 21398
Columbia, SC 29221
P: (803) 896-7001

SOUTH DAKOTA
Mr. John Berheim
Coordinator of Homeland Security
Office of Homeland Security
Department of Public Safety
118 West Capitol Avenue
Pierre, SD 57501
P: (605) 773-3231
F: (605) 773-3580
E: john.berheim@state.sd.us

Mr. Tom Dravland
Secretary
Department of Public Safety
118 West Capitol Avenue
Pierre, SD 57501
P: (605) 773-3178
F: (605) 773-3018
E: tom.dravland@state.sd.us

TENNESSEE
Mr. David Mitchell
Commissioner
Department of Safety
1150 Foster Avenue
Nashville, TN 37243
P: (615) 741-3063
E: dave.mitchell@state.tn.us

TEXAS
Mr. Steve McCraw
Director
Office of Homeland Security
Office of the Governor
P.O. Box 12428
Austin, TX 78711
P: (512) 463-1953
F: (512) 475-0876

U.S. VIRGIN ISLANDS
Mr. Renaldo Rivera
Adjutant General
National Guard
4031 LaGrande Princess, Lot 1B
Christiansted, VI 00820
P: (340) 712-7710
F: (340) 712-7711
E: renaldo.rivera@vi.ngb.army.mil

UTAH
Mr. Michael Kuehn
Director
Division of Homeland Security
4501 South 2700 West
P.O. Box 141775
Salt Lake City, UT 84114
P: (801) 965-4498
F: (801) 965-4608
E: mkuehn@utah.gov

VERMONT
Ms. Kiersten Bourgeois
Secretary of Civil & Military Affairs
Office of the Governor
109 State Street
Montpelier, VT 05609
P: (802) 828-3333
F: (802) 828-3339

VIRGINIA
Mr. Robert P. Crouch Jr.
Assistant To the Governor for Commonwealth Preparedness
Office of Commonwealth Preparedness
1111 East Broad Street
Patrick Henry Building
Richmond, VA 23219
P: (804) 225-3826
F: (804) 225-3882
E: robert.crouch@governor.virginia.gov

WASHINGTON
Maj. Gen. Timothy J. Lowenberg
Adjutant General
National Guard
Camp Murray, Building 1
Tacoma, WA 98430
P: (253) 512-8201
F: (253) 512-8497

WEST VIRGINIA
Mr. James Spears
Secretary
Department of Military Affairs & Public Safety
State Capitol Complex
Building 6, Room 122
Charleston, WV 25305
P: (304) 558-2930
F: (304) 558-6221
E: jspears@wvdmaps.gov

WISCONSIN
Mr. Johnnie Smith
Administrator
State Emergency Management Agency
P.O. Box 7865
Madison, WI 53707
P: (608) 242-3251
F: (608) 242-3247
E: johnnie.smith@dma.state.wi.us

WYOMING
Mr. Joe Moore
Director
Office of Homeland Security
Herschler Building, 1E
122 West 25th Street
Cheyenne, WY 82002
P: (307) 777-4663
F: (307) 777-8515

Telecommunications

Responsible for communications planning and organizing a statewide plan for total communications, especially with local government emergency matters.

Information provided by:

National Association of State Telecommunications Directors
Karen Britton
Director
P.O. Box 11910
Lexington, KY 40578
P: (859) 244-8187
F: (859) 244-8001
kbritton@csg.org
www.nastd.org

ALABAMA
Mr. Andy Cannon
Assistant Director, Office of Operations
Information Services Division
Department of Finance
64 North Union Street, Suite 200
Montgomery, AL 36130
P: (334) 242-3045
F: (334) 242-7002
E: andy.cannon@isd.alabama.gov

ALASKA
Mr. Stanley G. Herrera
Director & Chief Technology Officer
Division of Enterprise Technology Services
Department of Administration
P.O. Box 110206
Juneau, AK 99811
P: (907) 465-5735
F: (907) 465-3450
E: stan_herrera@admin.state.ak.us

ARIZONA
Mr. Michael Totherow
Director
Telecommunications Program Office
Department of Administration
100 North 15th Avenue, Suite 481
Phoenix, AZ 85007
P: (602) 542-2888
E: michael.totherow@azdoa.gov

ARKANSAS
Mr. Don McDaniel
Administrator, Enterprise Network Services
Department of Information Services
P.O. Box 3155
Little Rock, AR 72203
P: (501) 682-5027
F: (501) 682-4316
E: don.mcdaniel@arkansas.gov

CALIFORNIA
Ms. Sandra Bierer
Deputy Director, Statewide Telecommunications & Network Division
Department of Technology Services
P.O. Box 1810
Rancho Cordova, CA 95741
P: (916) 657-9380
F: (916) 657-9129
E: sandra.bierer@dts.ca.gov

COLORADO
Mr. Paul Nelson
Network Manager
Division of Information Technologies
Department of Personnel & Administration
2452 West 2nd Avenue, #19
Denver, CO 80223
P: (303) 866-2872
F: (303) 922-1811
E: paul.nelson@state.co.us

CONNECTICUT
Mr. Bernard O'Donnell
Director
Communication Services
Department of Information Technology
101 East River Drive
East Hartford, CT 06108
P: (860) 622-2444
F: (860) 622-4900
E: bernard.odonnell@ct.gov

DELAWARE
Ms. Kay Buck
Senior Telecommunication Specialist
Department of Technology & Information
William Penn Building
801 Silver Lake Boulevard
Dover, DE 19904
P: (302) 739-9649
F: (302) 677-7002
E: kay.buck@state.de.us

FLORIDA
Mr. John Ford
Director, Telecommunications & Wireless Services
Enterprise Information Technology Services
Department of Management Services
4030 Esplanade Way, Suite 115J
Tallahassee, FL 32399
P: (850) 921-2334
F: (850) 922-5162
E: john.ford@dms.myflorida.com

GEORGIA
Mr. Charlie Sasser
Director of Support Services
Operations Division
Georgia Technology Authority
254 Washington Street, Ground Floor
Atlanta, GA 30334
P: (404) 463-2350
F: (404) 656-0421
E: csasser@gta.ga.gov

HAWAII
Mr. Lester Nakamura
Administrator
Information & Communications Services Division
DAGS
P.O. Box 119
Honolulu, HI 96810
F: (808) 586-1922
E: lnakamura@state.hi.us

IDAHO
Mr. Joe Roche
Administrator
Division of Information Technology & Communication Services
Department of Administration
650 West State Street, Room 100
Boise, ID 83720
P: (208) 332-1841
F: (208) 334-2307
E: joe.roche@adm.idaho.gov

ILLINOIS
Mr. Steve Hayden
Special Projects
Division of Telecommunications
Central Management Services
120 West Jefferson Street
Springfield, IL 62702
P: (217) 782-9492
E: steve_hayden@cms.state.il.us

INDIANA
Mr. William Pierce
Systems Consultant
Office of Technology
100 North Senate Avenue, Room N-551
Indianapolis, IN 46204
P: (317) 233-2009
F: (317) 232-0748
E: bpierce@iot.in.gov

IOWA
Ms. Victoria Wallis
Telecommunications Administrator
Engineering Division
Communications Network
400 East 14th Street
Des Moines, IA 50131
P: (515) 725-4630
F: (515) 725-4765
E: victoria.wallis@iowa.gov

KANSAS
Mr. David Timpany
Manager of Quality Assurance
Division of Information Systems & Communications
Department of Administration
900 Southwest Jackson, Room 751-S
Topeka, KS 66612
P: (785) 296-6150
F: (785) 296-1168
E: dave.timpany@da.ks.us

KENTUCKY
Mr. Brad Watkins
Director
Communication Services
Commonwealth Office for Technology
101 Cold Harbor Drive
Frankfort, KY 40601
P: (502) 564-8703
E: brad.watkins@ky.gov

LOUISIANA
Mr. Derald Kirkland
Director-IT Telecommunications Administrator
Office of Telecommunications Management
150 3rd Street
State Office Building, 12th Floor
Baton Rouge, LA 70801
P: (225) 342-7701
F: (225) 342-6867
E: derald.kirkland@la.gov

MAINE
Ms. Ellen Lee
Director, Performance Management & Administration
Department of Administrative & Financial Services
Office of Information Technology
26 Edison Drive, 145 State House Station
Augusta, ME 04333
P: (207) 624-8866
F: (207) 287-4563
E: ellen.lee@maine.gov

MARYLAND
Ms. Sandra Smith
Director, Voice Systems
Department of Budget & Management
301 West Preston Street, Suite 1304
Baltimore, MD 21201
P: (410) 767-4649
F: (410) 333-5163
E: ssmith@dbm.state.md.us

MASSACHUSETTS
Ms. April May
Telecommunications Manager
Information Technology Division
One Ashburton Place, Room 801
Boston, MA 02108
P: (617) 626-4645
F: (617) 626-4685
E: april.may@state.ma.us

MICHIGAN
Mr. Jack Harris
Director
Telecommunications & Network Management
Department of Information Technology
608 West Allegan Street, 1st Floor
Lansing, MI 48913
P: (517) 241-7567
F: (517) 241-1633
E: harrisjl@michigan.gov

MINNESOTA
Mr. Dan Oehmke
Director, Account Management & Consulting
Office of Enterprise Technology
658 Cedar Street, Room 510
St. Paul, MN 55155
P: (651) 201-1037
F: (651) 297-5368

MISSISSIPPI
Mr. Jimmy Webster
Data Network Manager
Information Technology Services
Telecommunications Division
301 North Lamar Street, Suite 508
Jackson, MS 39201
P: (601) 359-2690
F: (601) 354-6016
E: jimmy.webster@its.state.ms.us

MISSOURI
Ms. Nancy Bochat
Telecommunications Manager
Information Technology Services Division
Truman Building, Room 280
P.O. Box 809
Jefferson City, MO 65102
P: (573) 751-5067
F: (573) 526-3299
E: nancy.bochat@oa.mo.gov

MONTANA
Mr. Carl Hotvedt
Chief, Network Technology Services Bureau
Information Technology Services Division
Department of Administration
Mitchell Building, Room 22
Helena, MT 59620
P: (406) 444-1780
F: (406) 444-5545
E: chotvedt@mt.gov

NEBRASKA
Ms. Jayne Scofield
IT Administrator
Network Services
Office of the CIO
501 South 14th Street
Lincoln, NE 68509
P: (402) 471-2761
F: (402) 471-3339
E: jayne.scofield@cio.ne.gov

NEVADA
Mr. David Richards
Director, Telecommunications
Department of Information Technology
505 East King Street, Room 403
Carson City, NV 89701
P: (775) 684-7340
F: (775) 684-7345

NEW JERSEY
Mr. David Blackwell
Telecommunications Manager
Office of Information Technology
200 Riverview Plaza
P.O. Box 212
Trenton, NJ 08625
P: (609) 633-0195
F: (609) 777-3938
E: david.blackwell@oit.state.nj.us

NEW MEXICO
Ms. Jacqueline Miller
Deputy Director
Communications Division
Department of General Services
715 Alta Vista, P.O. Box 26110
Santa Fe, NM 87505
P: (505) 476-1849
F: (505) 827-2998
E: jacque.miller@state.nm.us

NEW YORK
Mr. Peter J. Arment
First Deputy Director
Division of Telecommunications
Empire State Building
Corning Tower Building, 27th Floor
Albany, NY 12242
P: (518) 402-2324
F: (518) 473-7145
E: peter.arment@oft.state.ny.us

NORTH CAROLINA
Mr. Steve Stoneman
Executive Director
Telecommunications Services
4110 Mail Service Center
P.O. Box 17209
Raleigh, NC 26719
P: (919) 981-5261
F: (919) 850-2827
E: steve.stoneman@ncmail.net

NORTH DAKOTA
Mr. Mike J. Ressler
Deputy Chief Information Officer
Information Technology Department
, Room 103
600 East Boulevard Avenue
Bismarck, ND 58505
P: (701) 328-3190
F: (701) 328-1075
E: mressler@state.nd.us

OHIO
Mr. Dan Orr
Network Services Program Administrator
IT Service Delivery, Network Services
Department of Administrative Services
1320 Arthur E. Adams Drive, Suite 310
Columbus, OH 43221
P: (614) 728-4701
E: dan.orr@ohio.gov

OKLAHOMA
Mr. Joe Airington
Information Systems Network Administrator
Communications Operations-ISD
Office of State Finance
State Capitol Building, B-7
Oklahoma City, OK 73105
P: (405) 521-4170
F: (405) 521-3089
E: joe.airington@osf.ok.gov

OREGON
Mr. Darin Rand
Voice Services Manager
State Data Center
Department of Administrative Services
955 Center Street, Northeast U510
Salem, OR 97383
P: (503) 378-3366
F: (503) 378-8333
E: darin.rand@state.or.us

PENNSYLVANIA
Mr. Charles Strubel
Director of Commonwealth Telecommunications
Governor's Office of Administration
Bureau of Infrastructure & Operations
1 Technology Park
Harrisburg, PA 17110
P: (717) 705-3681
E: cstrubel@state.pa.us

PUERTO RICO
Ms. Melba Acosta
Director
Office of Budget & Management
254 Cruz Street
P.O. Box 9023228
San Juan, PR 00902
P: (787) 725-9420
F: (787) 724-1374

Telecommunications

RHODE ISLAND
Mr. Clarence Bussius
Enterprise Telecommunications Manager
Division of Information Technology
6 Harrington Road
Cranston, RI 02920
P: (401) 462-1432
E: clarence.bussius@doit.ri.gov

SOUTH CAROLINA
Mr. Tom Fletcher
Deputy CIO, Operations
State Budget & Control Board
Office of Chief Information Officer
4430 Broad River Road
Columbia, SC 29210
P: (803) 896-0404
F: (803) 896-0099
E: fletcher@cio.sc.gov

SOUTH DAKOTA
Mr. Dennis Nincehelser
Director
Division of Telecommunications
Sammons Building
910 East Sioux
Pierre, SD 57501
P: (605) 773-4264
F: (605) 773-3741
E: dennis.nincehelser@state.sd.us

TENNESSEE
Mr. Jack McFadden
Planning Consultant
Office of Information Resources
Department of Finance & Administration
312 8th Avenue, North, 17th Floor
Nashville, TN 37243
P: (615) 741-5080
E: jack.mcfadden@state.tn.us

TEXAS
Mr. Brian Kelly
Director
Telecommunications Division
Department of Innovation Resources
300 West 15th Street, Suite 1300
Austin, TX 78701
P: (512) 463-9672
F: (512) 463-3304
E: brian.kelly@dir.state.tx.us

UTAH
Mr. Scott Peterson
Network Planning Group Manager
Department of Technology Services
6000 State Office Building
Salt Lake City, UT 84114
P: (801) 538-3149
F: (801) 538-3622
E: speters@utah.gov

VERMONT
Ms. Susan Davis
Manager of Network Services
Network Engineering (GOVnet)
Department of Information & Innovation
133 State Street, 5th Floor
Montpelier, VT 05633
P: (802) 828-4665
F: (802) 828-2221
E: sdavis@govnet.state.vt.us

VIRGINIA
Ms. Anne Hardwick
Associate Director
Telecommunications & Network Services
Information Technologies Agency
110 South 7th Street
Richmond, VA 23219
P: (804) 371-5525
F: (804) 371-5556
E: anne.hardwick@vita.virginia.gov

WASHINGTON
Mr. Roland Rivera
Assistant Director
Telecommunication Services Division
512 12th Street, Southeast
P.O. Box 42445
Olympia, WA 98504
P: (360) 902-3335
F: (360) 902-3453
E: denisee@dis.wa.gov

WEST VIRGINIA
Mr. Carlos Neccuzi
Information Systems Specialist
Office of Technology
One Davis Square
P.O. Box 50110
Charleston, WV 25305
P: (304) 558-8122
F: (304) 558-8887
E: cneccuzi@wvadmin.gov

WISCONSIN
Ms. Jan Schneider
Section Chief - LAN/WAN/Video
Division of Enterprise Technology
Department of Administration
5830 Femrite Drive
Madison, WI 53717
P: (608) 224-4050
E: janet.schneider@wisconsin.gov

WYOMING
Mr. Earl Atwood
Administrator
Information Technology Division
Department of A & I
2001 Capitol Avenue
Cheyenne, WY 82002
P: (307) 777-5600
F: (307) 777-6725
E: earl.atwood@wy.gov

Tourism

Coordinates promotional and advertising programs for the tourism industry in the state.

ALABAMA
Mr. Lee Sentell
Director
Bureau of Tourism & Travel
401 Adams Avenue, Suite 126
Montgomery, AL 36104
P: (334) 242-4169
F: (334) 242-1478

ALASKA
Ms. Caryl McConkie
Development Manager
Department of Commerce, Community & Economic Development
Office of Economic Development
P.O. Box 110801
Juneau, AK 99811
P: (907) 465-5478
F: (907) 465-3767
E: caryl_mcconkie@commerce.state.ak.us

AMERICAN SAMOA
Ms. Virginia Samuelu
Deputy Director
Office of Tourism, Department of Commerce
American Samoa Government
PO Box 1147
Pago Pago, AS 96799
P: (684) 699-9411
F: (684) 699-9414
E: amsamoa@amerikasamoa.info

ARIZONA
Ms. Margie Emmerman
Director
Office of Tourism
1110 West Washington Street, Suite 155
Phoenix, AZ 85007
P: (602) 364-3717

ARKANSAS
Mr. Richard Davies
Director
Parks & Tourism
#1 Capitol Mall
Little Rock, AR 72201
P: (501) 682-7777
F: (501) 682-1364
E: richard.davies@mail.state.ar.us

CALIFORNIA
Ms. Caroline Beteta
Deputy Secretary
Division of Tourism
1102 Q Street, Suite 6000
Sacramento, CA 95814
P: (916) 444-4429
F: (916) 444-0410

COLORADO
Ms. Kim McNulty
Director
Tourism Office
1625 Broadway, Suite 1700
Denver, CO 80202
P: (303) 892-3840
F: (303) 892-3725
E: kim.mcnulty@state.co.us

CONNECTICUT
Ms. Jennifer Aniskovich
Executive Director
Commission on Arts, Tourism, Culture, History & Film
755 Main Street
One Financial Plaza
Hartford, CT 06103
P: (860) 566-4770
F: (860) 566-5078
E: janiskovich@ctarts.org

DELAWARE
Ms. Judy McKinney-Cherry
Director
Economic Development Office
Carvel State Office Building, 10th Floor
820 North French Street
Wilimington, DE 19801
P: (302) 577-8497
F: (302) 739-2535
E: judy.cherry@state.de.us

DISTRICT OF COLUMBIA
Mr. William A. Hanbury
President & CEO
DC Convention & Tourism Corporation
901 7th Street, Northwest
4th Floor
Washington, DC 20001
P: (202) 789-7017
F: (202) 789-7037
E: bill@washington.org

FLORIDA
Ms. Keisha Rice
Deputy Director
Office of Tourism, Trade & Economic Development
The Capitol, Room 2001
Tallahassee, FL 32399
P: (850) 487-2568
F: (850) 487-3014

GEORGIA
Mr. Dan Rowe
Deputy Commissioner of Tourism
Department of Industry, Trade & Tourism
75 Fifth Street, Northwest, Suite 1200
Atlanta, GA 30303
P: (404) 962-4082
F: (404) 962-4093
E: georgiatourism@georgia.org

GUAM
Mr. Gerald Perez
General Manager
Visitor's Bureau
401 Pale San Vitores Road
Tumon, GU 96913
P: (671) 646-5278
F: (671) 646-8861

HAWAII
Mr. Rex D. Johnson
President & CEO
Tourism Authority
1801 Kalakaua Avenue
Honolulu, HI 96815
P: (808) 973-2255
F: (808) 973-2253

IDAHO
Mr. Carl G. Wilgus
Administrator, Tourism Development
Department of Commerce & Labor
700 West State Street
Boise, ID 83720
P: (208) 334-3570
F: (208) 334-2631
E: carl.wilgus@visit.idaho.gov

ILLINOIS
Mr. Jan Kostner
Deputy Director of Tourism
Tourism Bureau
620 East Adams Street
Springfield, IL 62701
P: (217) 557-5790

INDIANA
Hon. Becky Skillman (R)
Lieutenant Governor
Office of Tourism Development
State Capitol, Room 333
Indianapolis, IN 46204
P: (317) 232-4545
F: (317) 232-4788

IOWA
Ms. Nancy Landess
Office Manager
Tourism Office
200 East Grand Avenue
Des Moines, IA 50309
P: (515) 242-4702
F: (515) 242-4718
E: nancy.landess@iowalifechanging.com

KANSAS
Ms. Becky Blake
Director
Travel & Tourism
1000 Southwest Jackson Street, Suite 100
Topeka, KS 66612
P: (785) 296-8478
F: (785) 296-6793

KENTUCKY
Mr. Randell L. Fiveash
Commissioner
Department of Tourism
500 Mero Street
Capital Plaza Tower, 22nd Floor
Frankfort, KY 40601
P: (502) 564-4930
F: (502) 564-5695
E: randy.fiveash@ky.gov

LOUISIANA
Ms. Angele Davis
Secretary
Department of Culture, Recreation & Tourism
P.O. Box 94361
Baton Rouge, LA 70802
P: (225) 342-8115
F: (225) 342-3207
E: adavis@crt.state.la.us

MAINE
Ms. Patricia Eltman
Director
Office of Tourism
59 State House Station
Augusta, ME 04333
P: (207) 287-4400
E: judith.a.deangelis@maine.gov

MARYLAND
Mr. Dennis Castleman
Assistant Secretary
Division of Tourism, Film & the Arts
217 East Redwood Street, 9th Floor
Baltimore, MD 21202
P: (410) 767-6266
F: (410) 333-2065
E: dcastleman@choosemaryland.org

Tourism

MASSACHUSETTS
Ms. Betsy Wall
Executive Director
Office of Travel & Tourism
10 Park Plaza, Suite 4510
Boston, MA 02116
P: (617) 973-8500
F: (617) 973-8525

MICHIGAN
Mr. George Zimmerman
Vice President
Travel Michigan
300 North Washington Square
Lansing, MI 48913
P: (517) 335-1879
E: zimmermanng@michigan.org

MINNESOTA
Mr. John Edman
Director
Explore Minnesota Tourism
121 7th Place East, #100
St. Paul, MN 55101
P: (651) 296-2755
F: (651) 296-7095
E: john.edman@state.mn.us

MISSISSIPPI
Mr. Craig Ray
Director
Division of Tourism
P.O. Box 849
Jackson, MS 39205
P: (601) 359-3297
F: (601) 359-5757
E: cray@mississippi.org

MISSOURI
Mr. Blaine Luetkemeyer
Director
Division of Tourism
Truman Building, Room 290
P.O. Box 1055
Jefferson City, MO 65102
P: (573) 751-3051
F: (573) 751-5160

MONTANA
Mr. Anthony Preite
Director
Department of Commerce
301 South Park
P.O. Box 200501
Helena, MT 59620
P: (406) 841-2704
F: (406) 841-2701
E: tpreite@mt.gov

NEBRASKA
Mr. Richard Baier
Director
Department of Economic Development
P.O. Box 94666
Lincoln, NE 68509
P: (402) 471-3111
F: (402) 471-3778

NEVADA
Mr. Tim Maland
Executive Director
Commission on Tourism
301 North Carson Street
Carson City, NV 89701
P: (775) 687-4322
F: (775) 687-6779

NEW HAMPSHIRE
Ms. Alice L. DeSouza
Director
Division of Travel & Tourism
P.O. Box 1856
Concord, NH 03302
P: (603) 271-2665
F: (603) 271-6870
E: adesouza@dred.state.nh.us

NEW JERSEY
Ms. Nancy Byrne
Executive Director of Tourism
Office of Travel & Tourism
P.O. Box 820
Trenton, NJ 08625
P: (609) 292-6963
F: (609) 633-7418

NEW MEXICO
Mr. Michael Cerletti
Cabinet Secretary
Tourism Department
491 Old Santa Fe Trail
Santa Fe, NM 87503
P: (505) 827-7400
F: (505) 827-7402
E: Mike.Cerletti@state.nm.us

NEW YORK
Mr. Patrick Foye
Commissioner
Empire State Development
633 Third Avenue
New York, NY 10017
P: (212) 803-3700
F: (518) 474-2474

NORTH CAROLINA
Ms. Lynn Minges
Executive Director
Division of Tourism, Film & Sports Development
301 North Wilmington Street
4324 Mail Service Center
Raleigh, NC 27699
P: (919) 733-7472
F: (919) 733-8582
E: lminges@nccommerce.com

NORTH DAKOTA
Ms. Sarah Otte-Coleman
Director
Department of Tourism
1600 East Century Avenue, Suite 2
Bismarck, ND 58501
P: (701) 328-2525
F: (701) 328-4878
E: socoleman@nd.gov

NORTHERN MARIANA ISLANDS
Mr. Perry J.P. Tenorio
Managing Director
Visitor's Authority
P.O. Box 500861
Saipan, MP 96950
P: (670) 664-3200
F: (670) 664-3237
E: gov.wia1@gtepacifica.net

OHIO
Ms. Alicia Reece
Assistant Director
Division of Travel & Tourism
Department of Development
77 South High Street, 29th Floor
Columbus, OH 43215
P: (614) 466-8844
F: (614) 644-8151

OKLAHOMA
Mr. Hardy Watkins
Executive Director
Tourism & Recreation Department
120 North Robinson, 6th Floor
Oklahoma City, OK 73102
P: (405) 230-8301

OREGON
Mr. Todd Davidson
Executive Director
Tourism Commission
775 Summer Street, Northeast
Salem, OR 97301
P: (503) 986-0007
F: (503) 986-0001

PENNSYLVANIA
Mr. Mickey Rowley
Deputy Secretary
Tourism, Film and Economic Development Marketing
Commonwealth Keystone Building
4th Floor
Harrisburg, PA 17120
P: (717) 787-3003
F: (717) 787-6825

PUERTO RICO
Ms. Terestela Gonzalez-Denton
Director
Puerto Rico Tourism Company
P.O. Box 9023960
San Juan, PR 00901
P: (787) 721-2400
F: (787) 722-6238

RHODE ISLAND
Mr. David C. DePetrillo
Director of Tourism
Tourism Division
1 West Exchange Street
Providence, RI 02903
P: (401) 222-2601
F: (401) 273-8270
E: Ddepetri@riedc.com

SOUTH CAROLINA
Mr. Chad Prosser
Director
Department of Parks, Recreation & Tourism
Edgar A. Brown Building
1205 Pendleton Street, Suite 248
Columbia, SC 29201
P: (803) 734-0166
F: (803) 734-1409
E: cprosser@scprt.com

SOUTH DAKOTA
Ms. Billie Jo Waara
Director
Office of Tourism
Capitol Lake Plaza
C/o 500 East Capitol Avenue
Pierre, SD 57501
P: (605) 773-3301
F: (605) 773-3256
E: billiejo.waara@state.sd.us

TENNESSEE
Ms. Susan Whitaker
Commissioner
Department of Tourist Development
320 6th Avenue, North
Nashville, TN 37243
P: (615) 741-9001
F: (615) 532-0477

TEXAS
Ms. Julie Chase
Director
Market Texas Tourism
Office of the Governor
P.O. Box 12428
Austin, TX 78711
P: (512) 936-0091
F: (512) 936-0303

U.S. VIRGIN ISLANDS
Ms. Beverly Nicholson Doty
Commissioner
Department of Tourism
Elainco Building
78 Contant 1-2-3
St. Thomas, VI 00802
P: (340) 774-8784
F: (340) 774-4390

UTAH
Ms. Leigh Von Der Esch
Managing Director
Governor's Office of Economic Development
Tourism
324 South State Street, Suite 500
Salt Lake City, UT 84111
P: (801) 538-1370
F: (801) 538-1399
E: lvondere@utah.gov

VERMONT
Mr. Bruce Hyde
Commissioner
Department of Tourism & Marketing
6 Baldwin Street
Montpelier, VT 05602
P: (802) 828-3649
F: (802) 828-3233
E: bruce.hyde@state.vt.us

VIRGINIA
Ms. Alisa L. Bailey
President & CEO
Tourism Authority
901 East Byrd Street
19th Floor
Richmond, VA 23219
P: (804) 371-8174
F: (804) 786-1919
E: abailey@virginia.org

WASHINGTON
Mr. Peter McMillin
Managing Director
Tourism & Business Development
P.O. Box 42525
Olympia, WA 98504
P: (360) 725-4172
F: (360) 753-4470
E: peterm@cted.wa.gov

WEST VIRGINIA
Ms. Betty Carver
Commissioner
Tourism Division
90 MacCorkle Avenue, Southwest
Charleston, WV 25303
P: (304) 558-2200
F: (304) 558-2956
E: bcarver@wvtourism.com

WISCONSIN
Ms. Kelli Trumble
Secretary
Department of Tourism
P.O. Box 8690
Madison, WI 53707
P: (608) 266-2345
F: (608) 266-3403

WYOMING
Ms. Diane Shober
Director of Travel & Tourism Business Council
214 West 15th Street
Cheyenne, WY 82002
P: (307) 777-2800
F: (307) 777-2837
E: Diane.Shober@Visitwyo.Gov

Training and Development

Responsible for the training and development of state employees.

ALABAMA
Ms. Sharleen Smith
Manager of Training
State Personnel Department
64 North Union Street, Suite 300
Montgomery, AL 36130
P: (334) 242-3494
F: (334) 242-1110

ALASKA
Ms. Dianne Kiessel
Director
Division of Personnel
P.O. Box 110201
333 Willoughby Avenue, 10th Floor
Juneau, AK 99911
P: (907) 465-4429
F: (907) 465-3415
E: dianne_kiesel@admin.state.ak.us

AMERICAN SAMOA
Mr. Puni Penei Sewell
Director
Department of Human Resources
American Samoa Government
Pago Pago, AS 96799
P: (683) 644-4485
F: (684) 633-1139
E: sewells_l@hotmail.com

ARIZONA
Ms. Joellyn Pollock
Director
Arizona Government University
100 North 15th Avenue, #470
Phoenix, AZ 85007
P: (602) 771-2948
F: (602) 542-7544
E: JPollock@azgu.gov

ARKANSAS
Mr. Steve Keeton
Manager
Department of Finance & Administration
1509 West 7th Street
Room 101, DFA Building
Little Rock, AR 72201
P: (501) 682-5351
F: (501) 682-5335
E: steve.keeton@dfa.state.ar.us

CALIFORNIA
Mr. Michael N. Saragosa
Executive Director
Employment Training Panel
1100 J Street, Suite 400
Sacramento, CA 95814
P: (916) 327-5262
F: (916) 327-5280

COLORADO
Mr. David Kaye
Director
Division of Human Resources
Department of Personnel & Administration
1313 Sherman Street, # 122
Denver, CO 80203
P: (303) 866-2393
F: (303) 866-2021
E: david.kaye@state.co.us

CONNECTICUT
Ms. Anna Ficeto
Deputy Commissioner
Department of Administrative Services
165 Capitol Avenue
Hartford, CT 06106
P: (860) 713-5105
F: (860) 713-7480
E: anna.ficeto@po.state.ct.us

DELAWARE
Mr. Robert Strong
Director
Division of Employment & Training
Department of Labor
4425 North Market Street, Room 328
Wilmington, DE 19802
P: (302) 761-8129
F: (302) 577-3996
E: robert.strong@state.de.us

FLORIDA
Ms. Monesia Brown
Director
Agency for Workforce Innovation
107 East Madison Street
Suite 100, Caldwell Building
Tallahassee, FL 32399
P: (850) 245-7298
F: (850) 921-3223
E: monesia.brown@awi.state.fl.us

GEORGIA
Ms. Diane M. Frazier
Director
Training & Organizational Development Division
529A Church Street
Decatur, GA 30030
P: (404) 371-7371
F: (404) 371-7388

GUAM
Ms. Pat A. Florig
Administrator
Training & Development Division/DOA
P.O. Box 884
Hagatna, GU 96932
P: (671) 475-1249
F: (671) 477-3671

HAWAII
Ms. Marie C. Laderta
Director
Department of Human Resources Development
235 South Beretania Street, 14th Floor
State Office Tower
Honolulu, HI 96813
P: (808) 587-1100
F: (808) 587-1106
E: marie.c.laderta@hawaii.gov

IDAHO
Ms. Connie Pratt
Training Manager
Workforce Development & Training
700 West State Street
Boise, ID 83720
P: (208) 429-5508
F: (208) 334-3182
E: cpratt@dhr.idaho.gov

ILLINOIS
Mr. Larry Plummer
Manager
Agency Training & Development Division
Stratton Office Building, Room 500
401 South Spring
Springfield, IL 62706
P: (217) 557-0225

INDIANA
Ms. Lisa Tabor
Training Director
State Personnel Department
402 West Washington Street
Room W161
Indianapolis, IN 46206
P: (317) 234-3111
E: ltabor@spd.in.gov

IOWA
Ms. Mollie K. Anderson
Director
Department of Administrative Services
Hoover Building, 3rd Floor
1305 East Walnut
Des Moines, IA 50319
P: (515) 281-5360
F: (515) 281-6140
E: mollie.anderson@iowa.gov

KANSAS
Mr. David Kerr
Secretary
Department of Commerce
1000 Southwest Jackson Street, Suite 100
Topeka, KS 66612
P: (785) 296-2741
F: (785) 296-3665

Mr. George Vega
Director
Division of Personnel Services
Division of Personnel Services
900 Southwest Jackson, Room 951-S
Topeka, KS 66612
P: (785) 296-2541
F: (785) 296-3655
E: george.vega@da.state.ks.us

KENTUCKY
Mr. Brian Crall
Secretary
Personnel Cabinet
200 Fair Oaks Lane, Suite 516
Frankfort, KY 40601
P: (502) 564-7430
E: brian.crall@ky.gov

LOUISIANA
Mr. Sam Breen
Administrator
Comprehensive Public Training Program
P.O. Box 94095
1201 North 3rd Street, Suite 1-170
Baton Rouge, LA 70804
P: (225) 342-4739
F: (225) 219-4191

MAINE
Mr. Denis Normandin
Director
Office of State Training
4 State House Station
Augusta, ME 04333
P: (207) 287-2551
F: (207) 287-2896

MARYLAND
Ms. Andrea Fulton
Executive Director
Office of Personnel Services & Benefits
Department of Budget & Management
301 West Preston Street, Room 609
Baltimore, MD 21201
P: (410) 767-4715
F: (411) 333-5262
E: afulton@dbm.state.md.us

MASSACHUSETTS
Mr. Paul Dietl
Interim Director
Human Resources Division
1 Ashburton Palce, Room 301
Boston, MA 02108
P: (617) 878-9705
F: (617) 727-1175
E: paul.d.dietl@massmail.state.ma.us

Mr. John O'Leary
Chief Human Resources Officer
Human Resource Division
One Ashburton Place, Room 301
Boston, MA 02108
P: (617) 878-9703
F: (617) 727-1175

MINNESOTA
Ms. Patricia Anderson
Commissioner
Department of Employee Relations
200 Centennial Building
658 Cedar Street
St. Paul, MN 55155
P: (651) 296-3095
F: (651) 296-1990
E: patricia.anderson@state.mn.us

MISSISSIPPI
Ms. Lesly Lloyd
Assistant State Personnel Director
Office of Training
301 North Lamar Street, Suite 100
Jackson, MS 39201
P: (601) 359-2722
F: (601) 576-5028
E: llloyd@spb.state.ms.us

MISSOURI
Mr. Chester White
Director
Office of Administration
Division of Personnel
P.O. Box 388
Jefferson City, MO 65102
P: (573) 751-3053
F: (573) 751-8641
E: chester.white@oa.mo.gov

MONTANA
Ms. Janet Kelly
Director
Department of Administration
125 North Roberts Street
P.O. Box 200101
Helena, MT 59620
P: (406) 444-3033
F: (406) 444-6194
E: jakelly@mt.gov

NEVADA
Ms. Patricia Hoppe
Training Manager
Department of Personnel
555 East Washington Avenue
Suite 1400
Las Vegas, NV 89101
P: (702) 486-2928
F: (702) 486-2661
E: phoppe@dop.nv.gov

NEW JERSEY
Mr. John J. Heldrich
Chair
State Employment & Training Commission
P.O. Box 940
Trenton, NJ 08625
P: (609) 633-0605
F: (609) 633-1359

NEW MEXICO
Dr. Eli Fresquez
Bureau Chief
Training & Organizational Development Bureau
State Personnel Office
2600 Cerrillos Road
Santa Fe, NM 87505
P: (505) 476-7765
F: (505) 476-7764
E: eli.j.fresquez@state.nm.us

NEW YORK
Ms. Nancy Groenwegen
Commissioner
Department of Civil Service
State Office Campus, Building 1
Albany, NY 12239
P: (518) 457-6212
F: (518) 457-7547

Mr. George Sinnott
Commissioner
Department of Civil Service
State Office Campus, Building 1
Albany, NY 12239
P: (518) 457-3701
F: (518) 457-7547
E: gcs1@cs.state.ny.us

NORTH CAROLINA
Ms. Ann Cobb
Director
Office of State Personnel
101 West Peace Street
Raleigh, NC 27603
P: (919) 733-8343
F: (919) 733-8359

NORTH DAKOTA
Ms. Linda Jensen
Director of Training
Central Personnel Division
600 East Boulevard Avenue, 14th Floor
Bismarck, ND 58505
P: (701) 328-3290
F: (701) 328-1475
E: ljensen@nd.gov

NORTHERN MARIANA ISLANDS
Ms. Edith DeLeon Guerrero
Director
Workforce Investment Agency
Caller Box 10007, Capitol Hill
Saipan, MP 96950
P: (670) 664-1700
F: (670) 322-7333
E: gov.wia1@gtepacifica.net

OHIO
Mr. Hugh Quill
Director
Department of Administrative Services
30 East Broad Street, Suite 4040
Columbus, OH 43215
P: (614) 466-6511
F: (614) 644-8151
E: hugh.quill@das.state.oh.us

OKLAHOMA
Ms. Carrie Rohr
Assistant Administrator
Human Resource Development Services Division
2101 North Lincoln Boulevard
Oklahoma City, OK 73105
P: (405) 521-2177
F: (405) 524-6942

OREGON
Mr. Twyla Lawson
Manager
Training Development & Recruitment Services
155 Cottage Street, Northeast
Salem, OR 97301
P: (503) 378-2744
F: (503) 986-3432
E: Twyla.lawson@state.or.us

PUERTO RICO
Ms. Marta Beltran
Administrator
Human Resources Administrative Office
Ponce De Leon Avenue, 1507
P.O. Box 8476
San Juan, PR 00910
P: (787) 706-5967
F: (787) 706-5697

RHODE ISLAND
Ms. Adelita Orefice
Director
Department of Labor & Training
1511 Pontiac Avenue
Cranston, RI 02920
P: (401) 462-8870
F: (401) 462-8872
E: aorefice@dlt.state.ri.us

SOUTH CAROLINA
Mr. Samuel Wilkins
Director
Office of Human Resources
Budget & Control Board
1201 Main Street, Suite 1000
Columbia, SC 29201
P: (803) 737-0904
F: (803) 737-3529
E: swilkins@ohr.sc.gov

SOUTH DAKOTA
Ms. Ellen Zeller
Director
Classification & Training
State Capitol
500 East Capitol Avenue
Pierre, SD 57501
P: (605) 773-3148
F: (605) 773-4344
E: ellen.zeller@state.sd.us

TENNESSEE
Dr. Lynn Goodman
Director
Employee Development & Equal Employment Opportunity
James K. Polk Building, 2nd Floor
Nashville, TN 37243
P: (615) 741-5546
F: (615) 532-0728

Training and Development

U.S. VIRGIN ISLANDS
Mr. Kenneth Hermon
Director
Division of Personnel
GERS Complex, 3rd Floor
48B-50C Kronprindsens Gade
St. Thomas, VI 00802
P: (340) 744-8588
F: (340) 714-5040

UTAH
Mr. James N. West
Director
Policy Division
State Office Building, Room 2120
P.O. Box 141531
Salt Lake City, UT 84114
P: (801) 538-3075
F: (801) 538-3081
E: jameswest@utah.gov

VERMONT
Ms. Nancy Simoes
Director
Workforce Planning
Osgood Building
103 South Main Street
Waterbury, VT 05671
P: (802) 241-1114
F: (802) 241-1119
E: nsimoes@per.state.vt.us

VIRGINIA
Mrs. Sara Redding Wilson
Director
Department of Human Resource Management
101 North 14th Street, 12th Floor
Richmond, VA 23219
P: (804) 225-2237
F: (804) 371-7401
E: sara.wilson@dhrm.virginia.gov

WASHINGTON
Ms. Christina Valadez
Assistant Director
Division of Human Resources Development
P.O. Box 47530
Olympia, WA 98504
P: (360) 664-6340
F: (360) 586-6695
E: chrisv@dop.wa.gov

WEST VIRGINIA
Ms. Billie Jo Stryle-Anderson
Director
Division of Personnel
1900 Kanawha Boulevard, East
Building 6, Room 416
Charleston, WV 25305
P: (304) 558-3950
F: (304) 558-1399
E: bstreyleanderson@wvadmin.gov

WISCONSIN
Mr. Robert Toomey
Administrator
Office of State Employment Relations
345 West Washington, 2nd Floor
Madison, WI 53702
P: (608) 266-0664
F: (608) 267-1020

WYOMING
Ms. Joan Evans
Director
Department of Workforce Services
122 West 25th Street
Herschler Building, 2 East
Cheyenne, WY 82002
P: (307) 777-8650
F: (307) 777-5857
E: jevans1@state.wy.us

Transportation and Highways

Umbrella agency responsible for planning, designing, constructing and maintaining public transportation services, highways and facilities throughout the state.

ALABAMA
Mr. Joe McInnes
Transportaiton Director
Department of Transportation
1409 Coliseum Boulevard
Montgomery, AL 36130
P: (334) 242-6311
F: (334) 262-8041

ALASKA
Mr. Leo Von Scheben
Commissioner
Department of Transportation & Public Facilities
3132 Channel Drive
Juneau, AK 99801
P: (907) 465-3900
F: (907) 586-8365

ARIZONA
Mr. Victor Mendez
Director
Department of Transportation
206 South 17th Avenue
Phoenix, AZ 85007
P: (602) 712-7227

ARKANSAS
Mr. Dan Flowers
Director of Highways & Transportaiton
State Highway & Transportation Department
P.O. Box 2261
10324 Interstate 30
Little Rock, AR 72203
P: (501) 569-2211
F: (501) 569-2400

CALIFORNIA
Mr. Will Kempton
Director
Department of Transportation
1120 N Street
P.O. Box 942673
Sacramento, CA 94273
P: (916) 654-5267
F: (916) 654-6608
E: will_kempton@dot.ca.gov

COLORADO
Mr. Russell George
Executive Director
Department of Transportation
4201 East Arkansas Avenue, Suite 262
Denver, CO 80222
P: (303) 757-9208
F: (303) 757-9656

CONNECTICUT
Mr. Ralph J. Carpenter
Commissioner
Department of Transportation
P.O. Box 317546
2800 Berlin Turnpike
Newington, CT 06131
P: (860) 594-3000
F: (860) 594-3008

DELAWARE
Ms. Carolann Wicks
Secretary
Department of Transportation
P.O. Box 778
Bay Road, Route 113
Dover, DE 19903
P: (302) 760-2303
F: (302) 739-5736

DISTRICT OF COLUMBIA
Mr. Emeka Moneme
Director
Division of Transportation
2000 14th Street, Northwest
6th Floor
Washington, DC 20009
P: (202) 673-6813
F: (202) 671-0642

FLORIDA
Ms. Stephanie Kopelousos
Secretary of Transportation
Department of Transportation
605 Suwannee Street
Tallahassee, FL 32399
P: (850) 414-4100

GEORGIA
Mr. Harold Linnenkohl
Commissioner
Department of Transportation
2 Capitol Square, Southwest
Atlanta, GA 30334
P: (404) 656-5206
F: (404) 463-6336
E: harold.linnenkohl@dot.state.ga.us

HAWAII
Mr. Barry Fukunaga
Interim Director of Transportation
Department of Transportation
869 Punchbowl Street, Room 509
Honolulu, HI 96813
P: (808) 587-2150
F: (808) 587-2167

IDAHO
Ms. Pamela Lowe
Executive Director
Transportation Department
P.O. Box 7129
Boise, ID 83707
P: (208) 334-8807
F: (208) 334-3858
E: Pamela.Lowe@itd.idaho.gov

ILLINOIS
Mr. Milton R. Sees
Acting Secretary
Department of Transportation
3215 Executive Park Drive
Springfield, IL 62764
P: (217) 782-5597
F: (217) 782-6828

INDIANA
Mr. Karl B. Browning
Commissioner
Department of Transportation
100 North Senate Avenue
IGCN Room N755
Indianapolis, IN 46204
P: (317) 232-5533
F: (317) 233-1481

IOWA
Ms. Nancy J. Richardson
Director
Department of Transportation
800 Lincoln Way
Ames, IA 50010
P: (515) 239-1111
F: (515) 239-1120

KANSAS
Ms. Debra L. Miller
Secretary of Transportation
Department of Transportation
700 Southwest Harrison Street
Topeka, KS 66612
P: (785) 296-3461
F: (785) 296-1095

KENTUCKY
Mr. Bill Nighbert
Secretary
Transportation Cabinet
200 Mero Street
Frankfort, KY 40622
P: (502) 564-4890
F: (502) 564-9540

LOUISIANA
Mr. John Bradberry
Secretary
Department of Transportation & Development
P.O. Box 94245
1201 Capitol Access Road
Baton Rouge, LA 70804
P: (225) 379-1200
F: (225) 379-1851

MAINE
Mr. David Cole
Commissioner
Department of Transportation
Transportation Building
State House Station 16
Augusta, ME 04333
P: (207) 287-2551
F: (207) 287-2896

MARYLAND
Mr. Robert Flanagan
Secretary of Transportation
Department of Transportation
7201 Corporate Center Drive
P.O. Box 548
Hanover, MD 21076
P: (410) 865-1000
F: (410) 865-1334
E: rflanagan@mdot.state.md.us

MASSACHUSETTS
Mr. Bernard Cohen
Secretary
Executive Office of Transportation & Construction
10 Park Plaza, Suite 3510
Boston, MA 02116
P: (617) 973-7000
F: (617) 523-6454

MICHIGAN
Mr. Kirk T. Steudle
Director
Department of Transportation
425 West Ottawa Street
P.O. Box 30050
Lansing, MI 48909
P: (517) 373-0718
F: (517) 373-6457

Transportation and Highways

MINNESOTA
Hon. Carol L. Molnau (R)
Lieutenant Governor &
Commissioner, Department of Transportation
Department of Transportation
395 John Ireland Blvd.
Room 423
St. Paul, MN 55155
P: (651) 207-2930
F: (651) 296-3587

MISSISSIPPI
Mr. Larry L. Brown
Interim Executive Director
Department of Transportation
401 North West Street, 10th Floor
P.O. Box 1850
Jackson, MS 39215
P: (601) 359-7001
F: (601) 359-7050
E: lbrown@mdot.state.ms.us

MISSOURI
Mr. Pete Rahn
Director
Department of Transportation
P.O. Box 270
105 West Capitol Avenue
Jefferson City, MO 65102
P: (573) 751-4622
F: (573) 526-5419

MONTANA
Mr. Jim Lynch
Director
Department of Transportation
2701 Prospect Avenue
P.O. Box 201001
Helena, MT 59620
P: (406) 444-6204
F: (406) 444-7643
E: jilynch@mt.gov

NEBRASKA
Mr. John Craig
Director & State Engineer
Department of Roads
1500 Nebraska Highway 2
P.O. Box 94759
Lincoln, NE 65809
P: (402) 479-4615
F: (402) 479-4325

NEVADA
Ms. Susan Martinovich
Director
Department of Transportation
1263 South Stewart Street
Carson City, NV 89712
P: (775) 888-7440
F: (775) 888-7201
E: info@dot.state.nv.us

NEW HAMPSHIRE
Mr. Charles O'Leary
Commissioner
Department of Transportation
7 Hazen Drive
P.O. Box 483
Concord, NH 03301
P: (603) 271-3734
F: (603) 271-3914
E: coleary@dot.state.nh.us

NEW JERSEY
Mr. Kris Kolluri
Commissioner
Department of Transportation
P.O. Box 601
Trenton, NJ 08625
P: (609) 530-3536
F: (609) 530-3894

NEW MEXICO
Ms. Rhonda G. Faught
Cabinet Secretary
Department of Transportation
1120 Cerrilos Road
P.O. Box 1149
Santa Fe, NM 87504
P: (505) 827-5110
F: (505) 827-5469

NEW YORK
Ms. Astrid Glynn
Commissioner
Department of Transportation
Building 5, State Office Campus
Albany, NY 12232
P: (518) 457-4422

NORTH CAROLINA
Mr. W. Lyndo Tippett
Secretary
Department of Transportation
1 South Wilmington Street
Raleigh, NC 27611
P: (919) 733-2520
F: (919) 715-4088
E: ltippett@dot.state.nc.us

NORTH DAKOTA
Mr. Francis G. Ziegler
Director
Department of Transportation
608 East Boulevard Avenue
Bismarck, ND 58505
P: (701) 328-2581
F: (701) 328-1420

NORTHERN MARIANA ISLANDS
Mr. Jose S. Demapan
Secretary
Department of Public Works
Caller Box 10007, Capitol Hill
Saipan, MP 96950
P: (670) 235-5827
F: (670) 235-6346

OHIO
Mr. James G. Beasley
Director
Department of Transportation
1980 West Broad Street
Columbus, OH 43223
P: (614) 466-8990

OKLAHOMA
Mr. Gary Ridley
Director
Department of Transportation
200 Northeast 21st Street
Oklahoma City, OK 73105
P: (405) 522-1800
F: (405) 521-2093

Mr. Phil Tomlinson
Secretary
Department of Transportation
200 Northeast 21st Street
Oklahoma City, OK 73105
P: (405) 521-2631
F: (405) 521-2093

OREGON
Mr. Matthew Garrett
Director
Department of Transportation
355 Capitol Street, Northeast, Room 135
Salem, OR 97301
P: (503) 986-3289
F: (503) 986-3432
E: Matthew.l.garrett@odot.state.or.us

PENNSYLVANIA
Mr. Allen Biehler
Secretary of Transportation
Department of Transportation
400 North Street
Commonwealth Keystone Building
Harrisburg, PA 17120
P: (717) 787-2838
F: (717) 787-5491

PUERTO RICO
Mr. Carlos Gonzalez Miranda
Secretary
Department of Transportation & Public Works
P.O. Box 41269
Minillas Station
Santurce, PR 00940
P: (787) 722-2929
F: (787) 725-1620

RHODE ISLAND
Mr. Jerome F. Williams
Director
Department of Transportation
2 Capitol Hill
Providence, RI 02903
P: (401) 222-2450

SOUTH CAROLINA
Mr. H.B. Buck Limehouse
Director
Department of Transportation
955 Park Street
Columbia, SC 29201
P: (803) 737-1302

SOUTH DAKOTA
Ms. Judy Payne
Secretary
Department of Transportation
Becker-Hansen Building
700 East Broadway Avenue
Pierre, SD 57501
P: (605) 773-3265
F: (605) 773-3921
E: judy.payne@state.sd.us

TENNESSEE
Mr. Gerald Nicely
Commissioner
Department of Transportation
James K. Polk Building
505 Deaderick Street, Suite 700
Nashville, TN 37243
P: (615) 741-2848
F: (615) 741-2508

TEXAS
Mr. Randall L. James
Director
Transportation Planning & Programming
Department of Transportation
125 East 11th Street
Austin, TX 78701
P: (512) 305-9501

UTAH
Mr. John Njord
Executive Director
Department of Transportation
4501 South 2700 West
P.O. Box 141245
Salt Lake City, UT 84119
P: (801) 965-4027
F: (801) 965-4338
E: jnjord@utah.gov

VERMONT
Ms. Dawn Terrill
Secretary of Transportation
Agency of Transportation
National Life Building
Drawer 33
Montpelier, VT 05633
P: (802) 828-2657
F: (802) 828-3522
E: dawn.terrill@state.vt.us

VIRGINIA
Mr. David S. Ekern
Commissioner
Department of Transportation
1401 East Broad Street, Suite 311
Richmond, VA 23219
P: (804) 786-2701
F: (804) 786-2940
E: david.ekern@vdot.virginia.gov

WASHINGTON
Mr. Douglas B. MacDonald
Secretary of Transportation
Department of Transportation
310 Maple Park Avenue, Southeast
P.O. Box 47300
Olympia, WA 98504
P: (360) 705-7054
F: (360) 705-6888
E: MacDonD@wsdot.wa.gov

WEST VIRGINIA
Mr. Paul A. Mattox Jr.
Secretary
Department of Transportation
Building 5
1900 Kanawha Boulevard East
Charleston, WV 25305
P: (304) 558-0444
F: (304) 558-1004

WISCONSIN
Mr. Frank Busalacchi
Secretary
Department of Transportation
4802 Sheboygan Avenue
P.O. Box 7910
Madison, WI 53707
P: (608) 266-1114
F: (608) 266-9912

WYOMING
Col. John Cox
Director
Department of Transportation
5300 Bishop Boulevard
Cheyenne, WY 82009
P: (307) 777-4484
F: (307) 777-4163

Treasurer

The custodian of all state funds and securities belonging to and held in trust by the state.

Information provided by:

National Association of State Treasurers
Pam Taylor
Director
P.O. Box 11910
Lexington, KY 40578
P: (859) 244-8175
F: (859) 244-8053
ptaylor@csg.org
www.nast.net

ALABAMA
Hon. Kay Ivey (R)
State Treasurer
Office of the State Treasurer
P.O. Box 302510
Montgomery, AL 36130
P: (334) 242-7500
F: (334) 242-7592
E: alatreas
@treasury.alabama.gov

ALASKA
Hon. Brian Andrews
(appointed)
Deputy Commissioner of Revenue
Department of Revenue
Treasury Division
P.O. Box 110400
Juneau, AK 99811
P: (907) 465-4880
F: (907) 465-2389
E: brian_andrews
@revenue.state.ak.us

AMERICAN SAMOA
Hon. Velega Savali
Treasurer
Department of Treasury
American Samoa Government
Pago Pago, AS 96799
P: (684) 633-4155
F: (684) 633-4100

ARIZONA
Hon. Dean Martin (R)
State Treasurer
Office of the State Treasurer
1700 West Washington Street
1st Floor
Phoenix, AZ 85007
P: (602) 604-7800
F: (602) 542-7176
E: info@aztreasury.gov

ARKANSAS
Hon. Martha A. Shoffner (D)
State Treasurer
State Treasury
220 State Capitol
Little Rock, AR 72201
P: (501) 682-5888
F: (501) 682-3820

CALIFORNIA
Hon. Bill Lockyer (D)
State Treasurer
Office of the State Treasurer
P.O. Box 942809
915 Capitol Mall, C-15
Sacramento, CA 94209
P: (916) 653-2995

COLORADO
Hon. Cary Kennedy (D)
State Treasurer
Department of the Treasury
140 State Capitol
Denver, CO 80203
P: (303) 866-2441
F: (303) 866-2123
E: treasurer.kennnedy
@state.co.us

CONNECTICUT
Hon. Denise L. Nappier (D)
State Treasurer
Office of State Treasurer
55 Elm Street
Hartford, CT 06106
P: (860) 702-3010
F: (860) 702-3043
E: denise.nappier
@po.state.ct.us

DELAWARE
Hon. Jack Markell (D)
State Treasurer
State Treasurer's Office
540 South DuPont Highway, Suite 4
Dover, DE 19901
P: (302) 744-1000
F: (302) 739-5635
E: statetreasurer
@state.de.us

DISTRICT OF COLUMBIA
Hon. Lasana K. Mack
(appointed)
Deputy CFO and Treasurer
Office of the Chief Financial Officer
1275 K Street Northwest, Suite 600
Washington, DC 20005
P: (202) 727-6055
F: (202) 727-6049
E: lasana.mack@dc.gov

FLORIDA
Hon. Alex Sink (D)
Chief Financial Officer
Department of Financial Services
Fletcher Building, Suite 516
200 East Gaines Street
Tallahassee, FL 32399
P: (850) 413-2850
F: (850) 413-2950
E: alex.sink@fldfs.com

GEORGIA
Hon. W. Daniel Ebersole
(appointed)
Director, Office of Treasury & Fiscal Services
Office of Treasury & Fiscal Services
200 Piedmont Avenue
Suite 1202, West Tower
Atlanta, GA 30334
P: (404) 656-2168
F: (404) 656-9048
E: OTFSweb@otfs.ga.gov

GUAM
Hon. Y'Asela A. Pereira
Treasurer
Financial Management Division
P.O. Box 884
Hagatna, GU 96932
P: (671) 475-1205
F: (671) 475-1243

HAWAII
Hon. Georgina K. Kawamura
(appointed)
Director of Finance
Department of Budget & Finance
P.O. Box 150
Honolulu, HI 96810
P: (808) 586-1518
F: (808) 586-1976
E: Hi.BudgetandFinance
@hawaii.gov

IDAHO
Hon. Ron G. Crane (R)
State Treasurer
State Treasurer's Office
P.O. Box 83720
Boise, ID 83720
P: (208) 334-3200
F: (208) 332-2960

ILLINOIS
Hon. Alexi Giannoulias (D)
State Treasurer
Office of the State Treasurer
Room 219, State Capitol
Springfield, IL 62706
P: (217) 782-2211
F: (217) 558-0292
E: Agiannoulias
@treasurer.state.il.us

INDIANA
Hon. Richard E.
Mourdock (R)
State Treasurer
Office of the State Treasurer
242 State House
Indianapolis, IN 46204
P: (317) 232-6386
F: (317) 233-1780

IOWA
Hon. Michael L.
Fitzgerald (D)
State Treasurer
State Treasurer's Office
Room 114, Capitol Building
State Capitol
Des Moines, IA 50319
P: (515) 281-5368
F: (515) 281-7562
E: mike.fitzgerald@iowa.gov

KANSAS
Hon. Lynn Jenkins (R)
State Treasurer
Office of the Treasurer
900 Southwest Jackson, Suite 201
Topeka, KS 66612
P: (785) 296-0628
F: (785) 296-7950
E: lynn
@treasurer.state.ks.us

KENTUCKY
Hon. Jonathan Miller (D)
State Treasurer
State Treasurer's Office
1050 U.S. Highway
Suite 100
Frankfort, KY 40601
P: (502) 564-4722
F: (502) 564-6545
E: jonathan.miller@ky.gov

LOUISIANA
Hon. John N. Kennedy (D)
State Treasurer
Department of the Treasury
P.O. Box 44154
Baton Rouge, LA 70804
P: (225) 342-0010
F: (225) 342-0046
E: jkennedy
@treasury.state.la.us

MAINE
Hon. David G. Lemoine (D)
State Treasurer
State Treasurer's Office
39 State House Station
Augusta, ME 04333
P: (207) 624-7477
F: (207) 287-2367
E: david.lemoine@maine.gov

MARYLAND
Hon. Nancy K. Kopp (D)
(elected by the Legislature)
State Treasurer
State Treasurer's Office
Goldstein Treasury Building
80 Calvert Street
Annapolis, MD 21404
P: (410) 260-7533

MASSACHUSETTS
Hon. Timothy P. Cahill (D)
State Treasurer
Department of State Treasurer
State House, Room 227
Boston, MA 02133
P: (617) 367-6900
F: (617) 248-0372
E: tcahill@tre.state.ma.us

MICHIGAN
Hon. Robert J. Kleine
(appointed)
State Treasurer
Department of Treasury
P.O. Box 15128
Lansing, MI 48901
P: (517) 373-3223
F: (517) 335-1785
E: kleiner@michigan.gov

MINNESOTA
Mr. Tom J. Hanson
Commissioner
Department of Finance
Centennial Office Building,
Suite 400
658 Cedar Street
St. Paul, MN 55155
P: (651) 201-8010
F: (651) 296-7714
E: Tom.J.Hanson@state.mn.us

MISSISSIPPI
Hon. Tate Reeves (R)
State Treasurer
State Treasurer's Office
P.O. Box 138
Jackson, MS 39205
P: (601) 359-3600
F: (601) 576-4495
E: treeves
@treasury.state.ms.us

MISSOURI
Hon. Sarah Steelman (R)
State Treasurer
Office of the State Treasurer
P.O. Box 210
Jefferson City, MO 65102
P: (573) 751-4123
F: (573) 751-9443
E: sarah.steelman
@treasurer.mo.gov

MONTANA
Ms. Janet Kelly
(appointed)
Director
Department of Administration
125 North Roberts Street
P.O. Box 200101
Helena, MT 59620
P: (406) 444-3033
F: (406) 444-6194
E: jakelly@mt.gov

NEBRASKA
Hon. Shane Osborn (R)
State Treasurer
Office of the State Treasurer
State Capitol, Room 2003
Lincoln, NE 68509
P: (402) 471-2455
F: (402) 471-4390
E: shaneosborn
@treasurer.org

NEVADA
Hon. Kate Marshall (D)
State Treasurer
Office of the State Treasurer
Capitol Building
101 North Carson Street, #4
Carson City, NV 89701
P: (775) 684-5600
F: (775) 684-5623
E: statetreasurer
@nevadatreasurer.gov

NEW HAMPSHIRE
Hon. Catherine Provencher
(elected by the Legislature)
State Treasurer
State Treasury
25 Capitol Street, Room 121
Concord, NH 03301
P: (603) 271-2621
F: (603) 271-3922
E: cprovencher
@treasury.state.nh.us

NEW JERSEY
Hon. Bradley I. Abelow
(appointed)
State Treasurer
Office of the State Treasurer
State House
P.O. Box 002
Trenton, NJ 08625
P: (609) 292-6748
F: (609) 984-3888
E: bradley.abelow
@treas.state.nj.us

NEW YORK
Hon. Aida M. Brewer
(appointed)
Deputy Commissioner and
Treasurer
Department of Taxation &
Finance
P.O. Box 22119
Albany, NY 12201
P: (518) 474-4250
E: aida_brewer
@tax.state.ny.us

NORTH CAROLINA
Hon. Richard H. Moore (D)
State Treasurer
Department of State Treasurer
325 North Salisbury Street
Raleigh, NC 27603
P: (919) 508-5176
F: (919) 508-5167
E: richard.moore
@nctreasurer.com

NORTH DAKOTA
Hon. Kelly Schmidt (R)
State Treasurer
Office of State Treasurer
State Capitol
600 East Boulevard Avenue,
Dept. 120
Bismarck, ND 58505
P: (701) 328-2643
F: (701) 328-3002
E: treasurer@nd.gov

NORTHERN MARIANA ISLANDS
Hon. Antoinette S. Calvo
CMNI Treasurer
Department of Finance
P.O. Box 5234, CHRB
Saipan, MP 96950
P: (670) 664-1300
F: (670) 322-4643

OHIO
Hon. Richard Cordray (D)
Treasurer of State
Office of the State Treasurer
30 East Broad Street
9th Floor
Columbus, OH 43215
P: (614) 466-2160
F: (614) 644-7313

OKLAHOMA
Hon. Scott Meacham
State Treasurer
State Treasurer's Office
Room 217, State Capitol
2300 North Lincoln Boulevard
Oklahoma City, OK 73105
P: (405) 521-3191
F: (405) 521-4994
E: scott.meacham
@treasurer.ok.gov

OREGON
Hon. Randall Edwards (D)
State Treasurer
State Treasury
350 Winter Street, Northeast
Suite 100
Salem, OR 97301
P: (503) 378-4329
E: oregon.treasury
@state.or.us

PENNSYLVANIA
Hon. Robin Wiessmann
State Treasurer
Treasury Department
129 Finance Building
Harrisburg, PA 17120
P: (717) 787-2465
F: (717) 783-9760

PUERTO RICO
Mr. Juan Carlos
Mendez Torres
Secretary of the Treasury
Department of the Treasury
PO Box 9024140
San Juan, PR 00902
P: (787) 721-2020

RHODE ISLAND
Hon. Frank T. Caprio (D)
General Treasurer
Office of the General Treasurer
State House, Room 102
Providence, RI 02903
P: (401) 222-2397
F: (401) 222-6140
E: treasurer
@treasury.state.ri.us

Treasurer

SOUTH CAROLINA
Hon. Thomas Ravenel (R)
State Treasurer
Office of the Treasurer
P.O. Box 11778
Columbia, SC 29211
P: (803) 734-2101
F: (803) 734-2690
E: treasurer@sto.sc.gov

SOUTH DAKOTA
Hon. Vernon L. Larson (R)
State Treasurer
Office of the State Treasurer
State Capitol
500 East Capitol Avenue
Pierre, SD 57501
P: (605) 773-3378
F: (605) 773-3115
E: vern.larson@state.sd.us

TENNESSEE
Hon. Dale Sims
(elected by the Legislature)
State Treasurer
Treasury Department
State Capitol, First Floor
Nashville, TN 37243
P: (615) 741-2956
F: (615) 253-1591
E: dale.sims@state.tn.us

TEXAS
Ms. Susan Combs
Comptroller of Public Accounts
Office of the Comptroller of Public Accounts
P.O. Box 13528, Capitol Station
Austin, TX 78711
P: (512) 463-4444
F: (512) 475-0450
E: scombs@cpa.state.tx.us

U.S. VIRGIN ISLANDS
Hon. Maureen Rabsatt-Cullar
(appointed)
Directory of Treasury
Department of Finance
2314 Kronprindsens Gade
Charlotte Amalie, VI 00802
P: (340) 774-4750
F: (340) 776-4028

UTAH
Hon. Edward T. Alter (R)
State Treasurer
State Treasurer's Office
215 State Capitol
Salt Lake City, UT 84114
P: (801) 538-1042
F: (801) 538-1465
E: ealter@utah.gov

VERMONT
Hon. Jeb Spaulding (D)
State Treasurer
State Treasurer's Office
109 State Street, 4th Floor
Montpelier, VT 05609
P: (802) 828-1452
F: (802) 828-2772
E: jeb.spaulding@state.vt.us

VIRGINIA
Hon. J. Braxton Powell
(appointed)
State Treasurer
Department of the Treasury
P.O. Box 1879
Richmond, VA 23218
P: (804) 225-3131
F: (804) 225-3187
E: braxton.powell@trs.virginia.gov

WASHINGTON
Hon. Michael J. Murphy (D)
State Treasurer
State Treasurer's Office
Legislative Building
P.O. Box 40200
Olympia, WA 98504
P: (360) 902-9000
F: (360) 902-9044
E: michaelj@tre.wa.gov

WEST VIRGINIA
Hon. John D. Perdue (D)
State Treasurer
State Treasurer's Office
Capitol Complex Building 1, Room E-145
1900 Kanawha Boulevard
Charleston, WV 25305
P: (304) 558-5000
F: (304) 558-4097
E: john.perdue@wvsto.com

WISCONSIN
Hon. Dawn Marie Sass (D)
State Treasurer
Office of the State Treasurer
1 South Pinckney Street, Suite 550
Madison, WI 53703
P: (608) 266-1714
F: (608) 266-2647
E: dawn.sass@ost.state.wi.us

WYOMING
Hon. Joe Meyer (R)
State Treasurer
Office of the State Treasurer
200 West 24th Street
Cheyenne, WY 82002
P: (307) 777-7408
F: (307) 777-5411
E: jmeyer3@state.wy.us

Tribal Affairs

Acts as a liaison between state and tribal officials and advances the concerns of Native Americans.

ALABAMA
Ms. Eloise P. Josey
Executive Director
Indian Affairs Commission
770 South McDonough
Montgomery, AL 36104
P: (334) 232-2831
F: (334) 240-3408

ARIZONA
Mr. Kenneth Poocha
Executive Director
Commission of Indian Affairs
1400 West Washington, Suite 300
Phoenix, AZ 85007
P: (602) 542-3123
F: (602) 542-3223

CALIFORNIA
Mr. William Mungary
Chair
Native American Heritage Commission
915 Capitol Mall, Room 364
Sacramento, CA 95814
P: (916) 653-4082
F: (916) 657-5390

COLORADO
Mr. Ernest D. House Jr.
Interim Executive Secretary
Commission on Indian Affairs
130 State Capitol
Denver, CO 80203
P: (303) 866-3027
F: (303) 866-5469

CONNECTICUT
Mr. David K. Leff
Deputy Commissioner
Office of Indian Affairs
79 Elm Street
Hartford, CT 06106
P: (860) 424-3066
F: (860) 424-4070
E: david.leff@po.state.ct.us

FLORIDA
Mr. Joe Quetone
Executive Director
Governor's Council on Indian Affairs
1341 Cross Creek Way, Suite A
Tallahassee, FL 32301
P: (850) 488-0730
E: quetonej@fgcia.com

GEORGIA
Mr. David Crass
Unit Manager & State Archaeologist
Archaeological Services Unit
47 Trinity Avenue, Southwest
Suite 414H
Atlanta, GA 30334
P: (404) 656-9344
F: (404) 651-8739
E: david_crass@dnr.state.ga.us

KANSAS
Ms. Sally Howard
Chief Legal Counsel
Office of the Governor
State Capitol, 2nd Floor
Topeka, KS 66612
P: (785) 296-3232
F: (785) 368-8901

LOUISIANA
Ms. Paige Ashby
Executive Director
Office of Indian Affairs
P.O. Box 94095
Baton Rouge, LA 70804
P: (225) 219-8715
F: (225) 342-1609
E: paige.ashby@la.gov

MAINE
Ms. Diana Scully
Director
Tribal-State Commission
442 Civic Center Drive
11 State House Station
Augusta, ME 04333
P: (207) 287-9200
F: (207) 287-9229
E: diana.scully@maine.gov

MASSACHUSETTS
Mr. Maurice Foxx
Chairman
Commission on Indian Affairs
100 Cambridge Street, Suite 300
Boston, MA 02114
P: (617) 573-1291
F: (617) 573-1515

MICHIGAN
Ms. Donna Budnick
American Indian Specialist
Department of Civil Rights
110 West Michigan Avenue
Suite 800
Lansing, MI 48913
P: (517) 241-7748
F: (517) 241-7520

MINNESOTA
Mr. Joseph B. Day
Executive Director
Indian Affairs Council
1819 Bemidji Avenue
Bemidji, MN 56601
P: (218) 755-3825
F: (218) 755-3739
E: Joseph.B.Day@state.mn.us

MONTANA
Ms. Reno Charette
Coordinator of Indian Affairs
Office of the Governor
P.O. Box 200801
Helena, MT 59620
P: (406) 444-3713
F: (406) 444-1350
E: rcharette@mt.gov

NEBRASKA
Hon. Rick Sheehy (R)
Lieutenant Governor
Office of the Lieutenant Governor
State Capitol, Room 2315
P.O.Box 94863
Lincoln, NE 68509
P: (402) 471-2256
F: (402) 471-6031

NEVADA
Ms. Sherry Rupert
Executive Director
Indian Commission
5366 Snyder Avenue
Carson City, NV 89701
P: (775) 687-8333
F: (775) 687-8330
E: srupert@govmail.state.nv.us

NEW MEXICO
Mr. Benny Shendo Jr.
Cabinet Secretary
Indian Affairs Department
Wendell Chino Building, 2nd Floor
1220 South St. Francies Drive
Santa Fe, NM 87505
P: (505) 476-1600
F: (505) 476-1601

NEW YORK
Mr. David Rose
Assistant Counsel To the Governor
Office of the Governor
Executive Chamber
State Capitol
Albany, NY 12224
P: (518) 486-4808

NORTH CAROLINA
Mr. Gregory A. Richardson
Director
Indian Affairs Commission
217 West Jones Street
1317 Mail Service Center
Raleigh, NC 27699
P: (919) 733-5998
F: (919) 733-2834
E: greg.richardson@ncmail.net

NORTH DAKOTA
Ms. Cheryl M. Kulas
Executive Director
Indian Affairs Commission
600 East Boulevard Avenue, 1st Floor
Judicial Wing
Bismarck, ND 58505
P: (701) 328-2428
F: (701) 328-1537
E: ckulas@nd.gov

OKLAHOMA
Ms. Barbara Warner
Executive Director
Indian Affairs Commission
4545 North Lincoln Boulevard, Suite 282
Oklahoma City, OK 73105
P: (405) 521-3828
F: (405) 522-4427

OREGON
Ms. Karen Quigley
Executive Officer
Legislative Commission on Indian Services
167 State Capitol
900 Court Street, Northeast
Salem, OR 97301
P: (503) 986-1067
F: (503) 986-1071
E: karen.m.quigley@state.or.us

SOUTH CAROLINA
Mr. Jesse Washington Jr.
Commissioner
Human Affairs Commission
P.O. Box 4490
Columbia, SC 29204
P: (803) 737-7800
E: jesse@schac.state.sc.us

Tribal Affairs

SOUTH DAKOTA
Mr. Roger Campbell
Director
Tribal Governmental Relations
Capitol Lake Plaza
711 East Wells Avenue
Pierre, SD 57501
P: (605) 773-3415
F: (605) 773-6592
E: roger.campbell@state.sd.us

UTAH
Mr. Forrest Cuch
Director
Division of Indian Affairs
Department of Community & Culture
324 South State Street, Suite 103
Salt Lake City, UT 84111
P: (801) 538-8757
F: (801) 538-8803
E: fscuch@utah.gov

VERMONT
Mr. Jeff Benay
Chair
Governor's Advisory Commission on Native American Affairs
49 Church Street
Swanton, VT 05488
P: (802) 868-4033
F: (802) 868-4265

VIRGINIA
Mr. Frank Adams
Chair
Council on Indians
P.O. Box 1475
Richmond, VA 23218
P: (703) 225-2084
F: (703) 225-2585
E: vci@governor.virginia.gov

WASHINGTON
Mr. Craig Bill
Executive Director
Office of Indian Affairs
P.O. Box 40909
Olympia, WA 98504
P: (360) 902-8825
E: cbill@goia.wa.gov

WISCONSIN
Ms. Laura Arbuckle
Administrator
Division of Intergovernmental Relations
Department of Administration
101 East Wilson Street, 10th Floor
Madison, WI 53703
P: (608) 266-1741
F: (608) 267-3842

WYOMING
Mr. Ed Wadda
Tribal Liaison
Governor's Office
124 Capitol Building
Cheyenne, WY 82002
P: (307) 777-7434
F: (307) 632-3909

Unclaimed Property

Responsible for the marshaling, administration and disposition of unclaimed or abandoned property.

Information provided by:

National Association of Unclaimed Property Administrators
David D. Milby
Association Manager
P.O. Box 11910
Lexington, KY 40578
P: (859) 244-8150
F: (859) 244-8053
naupa@csg.org
www.unclaimed.org

ALABAMA
Hon. Kay Ivey (R)
State Treasurer
State Treasury
P.O. Box 302510
Montgomery, AL 36130
P: (334) 242-7500
F: (334) 242-7592
E: alatreas@treasury.alabama.gov

Ms. Daria Story
Assistant Treasurer
State Treasury
Room SB-07 State Capitol
Montgomery, AL 36130
P: (334) 242-7506
F: (334) 353-4080
E: daria.story@treasury.alabama.gov

ALASKA
Hon. Brian Andrews
Deputy Commissioner of Revenue
Department of Revenue
Treasury Division
P.O. Box 110400
Juneau, AK 99811
P: (907) 465-4880
F: (907) 465-2389
E: brian_andrews@revenue.state.ak.us

Ms. Rachel Lewis
Administrator
Department of Revenue - Tax Division
Unclaimed Property Section
P.O. Box 110420
Juneau, AK 99811
P: (907) 465-5885
F: (907) 465-2394
E: rachel_lewis@revenue.state.ak.us

ARIZONA
Mr. Daniel Corcoran
Unclaimed Property Administrator
Department of Revenue
1600 West Monroe
Phoenix, AZ 85007
P: (602) 716-6033
F: (602) 542-2072
E: dcorcoran@azdor.gov

Mr. Gale Garriott
Director
Department of Revenue
1600 West Monroe
Phoenix, AZ 85007
P: (602) 716-6090
F: (602) 542-2072

ARKANSAS
Mr. Steve Kelly
Deputy Auditor
State Auditor's Office
P.O. Box 251906
Little Rock, AR 72225
P: (501) 371-2114
F: (501) 683-4285
E: stevek@auditorjimwood.org

Hon. Jim Wood
State Auditor
State Auditor's Office
230 State Capitol
Little Rock, AR 72225
P: (501) 682-6030
F: (501) 682-6005
E: auditorstateofar@comcast.net

CALIFORNIA
Hon. John Chiang
State Controller
State Controller's Office
300 Capitol Mall, Suite 1850
P.O. Box 942850
Sacramento, CA 94250
P: (916) 445-2636
E: jchiang@sco.ca.gov

Mr. Rob Huarte
Chief
Division of Collections
State Controller's Office
3301 C Street, Suite 700
Sacramento, CA 95816
P: (916) 323-1824
F: (916) 323-2851
E: rhuarte@sco.ca.gov

COLORADO
Hon. Cary Kennedy (D)
State Treasurer
Department of the Treasury
140 State Capitol
Denver, CO 80203
P: (303) 866-2441
F: (303) 866-2123
E: treasurer.kennnedy@state.co.us

Ms. Patty White
Program Director
State Treasury
Unclaimed Property Division
1580 Logan Street, Suite 500
Denver, CO 80202
P: (303) 866-6070
F: (303) 866-6154
E: patty.white@state.co.us

CONNECTICUT
Ms. Madelyn Colon
Assistant Treasurer
State Treasury
Unclaimed Property Division
55 Elm Street
Hartford, CT 06106
P: (860) 702-3291
E: madelyn.colon@po.state.ct.us

Hon. Denise L. Nappier (D)
State Treasurer
Office of State Treasurer
55 Elm Street
Hartford, CT 06106
P: (860) 702-3010
F: (860) 702-3043
E: denise.nappier@po.state.ct.us

DELAWARE
Ms. Diane C. Breighner
Administrator
Bureau of Unclaimed Property
820 North French Street
Wilmington, DE 19899
P: (302) 577-8221
F: (302) 577-7179
E: diane.breighner@state.de.us

Mr. Patrick Carter
Director
Division of Revenue
State Treasury
820 North French Street, 8th Floor
Wilmington, DE 19801
P: (302) 577-8686
F: (302) 577-8656
E: patrick.carter@state.de.us

DISTRICT OF COLUMBIA
Mr. Elliott Kindred
Director, Unclaimed Property
Office of Finance & Treasury
1275 K Street Northwest, Suite 500B
Washington, DC 20005
P: (202) 442-8181
F: (202) 442-8180
E: elliott.kindred@dc.gov

Hon. Lasana K. Mack
Deputy CFO and Treasurer
Office of Finance & Treasury
1275 K Street Northwest, Suite 600
Washington, DC 20005
P: (202) 727-6055
F: (202) 727-6049
E: lasana.mack@dc.gov

FLORIDA
Mr. Walter Graham
Bureau Chief
Bureau of Unclaimed Property
Department of Financial Services
200 E. Gaines Street, 353 Fletcher Bldg.
Tallahassee, FL 32399
P: (850) 413-5522
F: (850) 413-3017
E: walter.graham@fldfs.com

Hon. Alex Sink (D)
Chief Financial Officer
Department of Financial Services
Fletcher Building, Suite 516
200 East Gaines Street
Tallahassee, FL 32399
P: (850) 413-2850
F: (850) 413-2950
E: alex.sink@fldfs.com

GEORGIA
Mr. Bart L. Graham
Revenue Commissioner
Department of Revenue
1800 Century Center Boulevard, Northeast
Atlanta, GA 30345
P: (404) 417-2100

Unclaimed Property

Ms. Kelli Womack
Program Manager
Department of Revenue
Unclaimed Property Program
4245 International Parkway, Suite A
Hapeville, GA 30354
P: (404) 968-0490
F: (404) 968-0772
E: kelli.womack@dor.ga.gov

HAWAII

Mr. Scott Kami
Administrator
Financial Administration Division
Department of Budget & Finance
P.O. Box 150
Honolulu, HI 96810
P: (808) 586-1612
F: (808) 586-1644
E: scott.a.kami@hawaii.gov

Hon. Georgina K. Kawamura
Director of Finance
Department of Budget & Finance
P.O. Box 150
Honolulu, HI 96810
P: (808) 586-1518
F: (808) 586-1976
E: Hi.BudgetandFinance@hawaii.gov

IDAHO

Mr. Ron Crouch
Unclaimed Property Administrator
Tax Commission
P.O. Box 70012
Boise, ID 83707
P: (208) 334-7598
F: (208) 334-7392
E: rcrouch@tax.idaho.gov

Mr. Sam Haws
Commissioner
Tax Commission
P.O. Box 70012
Boise, ID 83707
P: (208) 334-7500
E: shaws@tax.idaho.gov

ILLINOIS

Hon. Alexi Giannoulias (D)
State Treasurer
State Treasurer's Office
Room 219, State Capitol
Springfield, IL 62706
P: (217) 782-2211
F: (217) 558-0292
E: Agiannoulias@treasurer.state.il.us

Mr. Joshua Joyce
Director of Unclaimed Property
State Treasury
1 West Old State Capital Plaza
4th Floor
Springfield, IL 62701
P: (217) 785-4185
F: (217) 557-9365
E: jjoyce@treasurer.state.il.us

INDIANA

Hon. Steve Carter (R)
Attorney General
Office of the Attorney General
302 West Washington Street
Indianapolis, IN 46204
P: (317) 232-6201
F: (317) 232-7979

Ms. Becky Yuan
Director
Office of the Attorney General
Unclaimed Property Division
P.O. Box 2504
Greenwood, IN 46142
P: (317) 883-4537
F: (317) 883-4522
E: byuan@atg.in.gov

IOWA

Hon. Michael L. Fitzgerald (D)
State Treasurer
State Treasurer's Office
Room 114, Capitol Building
State Capitol
Des Moines, IA 50319
P: (515) 281-5368
F: (515) 281-7562
E: mike.fitzgerald@iowa.gov

Mr. Stephen Larson
Deputy Treasurer
State Treasury
Office of the State Treasurer
State Capitol Building
Des Moines, IA 50319
P: (515) 281-5644
F: (515) 281-7562
E: steve.larson@iowa.gov

KANSAS

Ms. Peggy Hanna
Deputy Assistant State Treasurer
State Treasury
900 Southwest Jackson, Suite 201
Topeka, KS 66612
P: (785) 296-5464
F: (785) 296-7950
E: peggy@treasurer.state.ks.us

Hon. Lynn Jenkins (R)
State Treasurer
Office of the State Treasurer
900 Southwest Jackson, Suite 201
Topeka, KS 66612
P: (785) 296-0628
F: (785) 296-7950
E: lynn@treasurer.state.ks.us

KENTUCKY

Hon. Jonathan Miller (D)
State Treasurer
State Treasury
1050 U.S. Highway
Suite 100
Frankfort, KY 40601
P: (502) 564-4722
F: (502) 564-6545
E: jonathan.miller@ky.gov

Ms. Brenda L. Sweatt
Director
State Treasury
Unclaimed Property Division
1050 U.S. Highway 127 South, Suite 100
Frankfort, KY 40601
P: (502) 564-4722 Ext. 447
F: (502) 564-4200
E: brenda.sweatt@ky.gov

LOUISIANA

Hon. John N. Kennedy (D)
State Treasurer
Department of the Treasury
P.O. Box 44154
Baton Rouge, LA 70804
P: (225) 342-0010
F: (225) 342-0046
E: jkennedy@treasury.state.la.us

Mr. Benny Spann
Director
State Treasury
626 Main Street
Baton Rouge, LA 70801
P: (225) 219-9400
F: (225) 219-9381
E: bspann@treasury.state.la.us

MAINE

Hon. David G. Lemoine (D)
State Treasurer
Office of the State Treasurer
39 State House Station
Augusta, ME 04333
P: (207) 624-7477
F: (207) 287-2367
E: david.lemoine@maine.gov

Ms. Barbara Raths
Deputy Treasurer
State Treasury
39 State House Station
Augusta, ME 04333
P: (207) 624-7477
F: (207) 287-2367
E: barbara.raths@maine.gov

MARYLAND

Mr. Peter Franchot
Comptroller of the Treasury
Comptroller's Office
P.O. Box 466
Goldstein Treasury Building
Annapolis, MD 21404
P: (410) 260-4801
E: pfrachot@comp.state.md.us

Ms. Lynn E. Hall
Manager
Comptroller of Maryland Office
301 West Preston Street, Room 310
Baltimore, MD 21201
P: (410) 767-1705
F: (410) 333-7150
E: lhall@comp.state.md.us

MASSACHUSETTS

Hon. Timothy P. Cahill (D)
State Treasurer
Office of State Treasurer
State House, Room 227
Boston, MA 02133
P: (617) 367-6900
F: (617) 248-0372
E: tcahill@tre.state.ma.us

Mr. Thomas P. McAnespie
Assistant Treasurer of Abandoned Property
State Treasury
One Ashburton Place, 12th Floor
Boston, MA 02108
P: (617) 367-9333
F: (617) 367-3645
E: tmcanespie@tre.state.ma.us

MICHIGAN

Hon. Robert J. Kleine
State Treasurer
Department of Treasury
P.O. Box 15128
Lansing, MI 48901
P: (517) 373-3223
F: (517) 335-1785
E: kleiner@michigan.gov

Mr. Gonzalo Llano
Administrator
Unclaimed Property Division
P.O. Box 30756
Lansing, MI 48909
P: (517) 636-5307
F: (517) 332-5986
E: llanog@michigan.gov

MINNESOTA
Mr. Dennis Munkwitz
Financial Services Director
Department of Commerce
85 7th Place East, Suite 500
St. Paul, MN 55101
P: (651) 297-1335
F: (651) 282-2568
E: dennis.munkwitz
@state.mn.us

MISSISSIPPI
Hon. Tate Reeves (R)
State Treasurer
Office of the State Treasurer
P.O. Box 138
Jackson, MS 39205
P: (601) 359-3600
F: (601) 576-4495
E: treeves
@treasury.state.ms.us

Mr. John Younger
Assistant State Treasurer
Unclaimed Property Division
State Treasury
P.O. Box 138
Jackson, MS 39205
P: (601) 359-5223
F: (601) 359-4495
E: jyounger
@treasury.state.ms.us

MISSOURI
Mr. Scott Harper
Assistant Deputy Treasurer
State Treasury
Division of Unclaimed Property
P.O. Box 1272
Jefferson City, MO 65102
P: (573) 526-6024
F: (573) 526-6027
E: scott.harper
@treasurer.mo.gov

Hon. Sarah Steelman (R)
State Treasurer
State Treasurer's Office
P.O. Box 210
Jefferson City, MO 65102
P: (573) 751-4123
F: (573) 751-9443
E: sarah.steelman
@treasurer.mo.gov

MONTANA
Mr. Lee Baerlocher
Bureau Chief
Department of Revenue
P.O. Box 5805
Helena, MT 59604
P: (406) 444-0761
F: (406) 444-1505
E: lbaerlocher@mt.gov

Mr. Dan Bucks
Director
Department of Revenue
P.O. Box 5805
Helena, MT 59604
P: (406) 444-3696
F: (406) 444-1505
E: dbucks@mt.gov

NEBRASKA
Mr. Alex Kauffman
Director of Unclaimed Property
Office of the State Treasurer
5800 Cornhusker Highway
Building 2, Suite 4
Lincoln, NE 68507
P: (402) 471-2456
E: akauffman@treasurer.org

Hon. Shane Osborn (R)
State Treasurer
State Treasurer's Office
State Capitol, Room 2003
Lincoln, NE 68509
P: (402) 471-2455
F: (402) 471-4390
E: shaneosborn
@treasurer.org

NEVADA
Mr. Jim Burke
Deputy State Treasurer
State Treasury
Unclaimed Property
555 East Washington Avenue,
Suite 4200
Las Vegas, NV 89101
P: (702) 486-4354
E: jburke
@nevadatreasurer.gov

Hon. Kate Marshall (D)
State Treasurer
Office of State Treasurer
Capitol Building
101 North Carson Street, #4
Carson City, NV 89701
P: (775) 684-5600
F: (775) 684-5623
E: statetreasurer
@nevadatreasurer.gov

NEW HAMPSHIRE
Hon. Catherine Provencher
State Treasurer
Treasury Department
25 Capitol Street, Room 121
Concord, NH 03301
P: (603) 271-2621
F: (603) 271-3922
E: cprovencher
@treasury.state.nh.us

Mr. Brian Regan
Director
Abandoned Property Division
State Treasury
25 Capitol Street, Room 205
Concord, NH 03301
P: (603) 271-1499
F: (603) 271-2730
E: bregan
@treasury.state.nh.us

NEW JERSEY
Hon. Bradley I. Abelow
State Treasurer
Office of the State Treasurer
State House
P.O. Box 002
Trenton, NJ 08625
P: (609) 292-6748
F: (609) 984-3888
E: bradley.abelow
@treas.state.nj.us

Mr. Stephen Sylvester
Assistant Director
Division of Taxation
P.O. Box 219
50 Barrack Street, 6th Floor
Trenton, NJ 08646
P: (609) 292-8822
F: (609) 292-0411
E: steve.sylvester
@treas.state.nj.us

NEW MEXICO
Ms. Stephanie Dennis
Tax Compliance Specialist
Supervisor
Taxation & Revenue
Department
P.O. Box 25123
Santa Fe, NM 87504
P: (505) 827-0762
F: (505) 827-1759
E: sdennis@state.nm.us

NEW YORK
Hon. Thomas P. DiNapoli (D)
State Comptroller
Office of the State Comptroller
110 State Street
Albany, NY 12236
P: (518) 474-5598
E: tdinapoli
@osc.state.ny.us

Mr. Lawrence Schantz
Director
Office of Unclaimed Funds
State Comptroller's Office
110 State Street, 8th Floor
Albany, NY 12236
P: (518) 473-6318
F: (518) 474-7016
E: lschantz@osc.state.ny.us

NORTH CAROLINA
Ms. Shirley Fowler
Administrator
Escheat & Unclaimed Property
State Treasury
325 North Salisbury Street
Raleigh, NC 27603
P: (919) 508-5929
F: (919) 715-0229
E: shirley.fowler
@nctreasurer.com

NORTH DAKOTA
Ms. Linda Fisher
Administrator
State Land Department
P.O. Box 5523
Bismarck, ND 58506
P: (701) 328-2800
F: (701) 328-3650
E: llfisher@state.nd.us

Mr. Gary D. Preszler
Land Commissioner
State Land Department
P.O. Box 5523
Bismarck, ND 58506
E: gpreszle@nd.gov

OHIO
Mr. Yaw O'beng
Superintendent
Division of Unclaimed Funds
Department of Commerce
77 South High Street, 20th Floor
Columbus, OH 43266
P: (614) 466-4433
F: (614) 752-5078
E: yobeng@com.state.oh.us

Unclaimed Property

Ms. Kimberly A. Zurz
Director of Commerce
Division of Administration
77 South High Street, 23rd Floor
Columbus, OH 43215
P: (614) 466-3636
F: (614) 752-5078
E: kim.zurz@com.state.oh.us

OKLAHOMA
Ms. Kathy Janes
Unclaimed Property Director
State Treasury
4545 North Lincoln Boulevard
Suite 106
Oklahoma City, OK 73105
P: (405) 522-6743
F: (405) 521-4993
E: Kathy.Janes
@treasurer.ok.gov

Hon. Scott Meacham
State Treasurer
State Treasury
Room 217, State Capitol
2300 North Lincoln Boulevard
Oklahoma City, OK 73105
P: (405) 521-3191
F: (405) 521-4994
E: scott.meacham
@treasurer.ok.gov

OREGON
Ms. Louise Solliday
Acting Director
Department of State Lands
775 Summer Street, Northeast
Suite 100
Salem, OR 97301
P: (503) 378-3805 Ext. 224
F: (503) 378-4844
E: louise.solliday
@dsl.state.or.us

Ms. Cynthia Wickham
Trust Property Manager
Department of State Lands
775 Summer Street, Northeast
Suite 100
Salem, OR 97301
P: (503) 378-3805
F: (503) 378-4844
E: cyndi.wickham
@dsl.state.or.us

PENNSYLVANIA
Ms. Mary Beth Stringent
Director of Unclaimed Property
State Treasury
Bureau of Unclaimed Property
P.O. Box 1837
Harrisburg, PA 17105
P: (717) 783-3632
F: (717) 787-9079
E: mbstringent
@patreasury.org

PUERTO RICO
Mr. Jose A. Saade
Executive Assistant
Commonwealth of Puerto Rico
Commissioner of Financial Institutions
P.O. Box 11855
San Juan, PR 00910
P: (787) 723-8734
F: (787) 723-4042
E: joses@ocif.gobierno.pr

RHODE ISLAND
Hon. Frank T. Caprio (D)
General Treasurer
Office of the General Treasurer
State House, Room 102
Providence, RI 02903
P: (401) 222-2397
F: (401) 222-6140
E: treasurer
@treasury.state.ri.us

Mr. Richard N. Coffey
Unclaimed Property Manager
State Treasury
P.O. Box 1435
Providence, RI 02901
P: (401) 222-8558
F: (401) 222-2129
E: richardc
@treasury.state.ri.us

SOUTH CAROLINA
Hon. Thomas Ravenel (R)
State Treasurer
Office of State Treasurer
P.O. Box 11778
Columbia, SC 29211
P: (803) 734-2101
F: (803) 734-2690
E: treasurer@sto.sc.gov

Ms. Barbara Rice
Assistant State Treasurer
State Treasury
P.O. Box 11778
Columbia, SC 29211
P: (803) 734-2682
F: (803) 734-2668
E: riceb@sto.sc.gov

SOUTH DAKOTA
Mr. Lloyd Johnson
Unclaimed Property Administrator
State Treasury
State Capitol Building, Suite 212
500 East Capitol Avenue
Pierre, SD 57501
P: (605) 773-3379
F: (605) 773-3115
E: lloyd.johnson
@state.sd.us

Hon. Vernon L. Larson (R)
State Treasurer
Office of the State Treasurer
State Capitol
500 East Capitol Avenue
Pierre, SD 57501
P: (605) 773-3378
F: (605) 773-3115
E: vern.larson@state.sd.us

TENNESSEE
Mr. John Gabriel
Administrator
State Treasury
Andrew Jackson Building, 10th Floor
500 Deaderick Street
Nashville, TN 37243
P: (615) 253-5354
F: (615) 734-6458
E: john.gabriel@state.tn.us

Hon. Dale Sims
State Treasurer
Treasury Department
State Capitol, First Floor
Nashville, TN 37243
P: (615) 741-2956
F: (615) 253-1591
E: dale.sims@state.tn.us

TEXAS
Ms. Susan Combs
Comptroller of Public Accounts
Office of Comptroller of Public Accounts
P.O. Box 13528, Capitol Station
Austin, TX 78711
P: (512) 463-4444
F: (512) 475-0450
E: scombs@cpa.state.tx.us

Mr. George Tamayo
Division Manager
Office of Comptroller of Public Accounts
Unclaimed Property Division
111 East 17th Street, Room 613
Austin, TX 78711
P: (512) 463-4595
F: (512) 936-6224
E: george.tamayo
@cpa.state.tx.us

UTAH
Hon. Edward T. Alter (R)
State Treasurer
State Treasurer's Office
215 State Capitol
Salt Lake City, UT 84114
P: (801) 538-1042
F: (801) 538-1465
E: ealter@utah.gov

Ms. Kim Oliver
Unclaimed Property Administrator
Division of Unclaimed Property
341 South Main Street, 5th Floor
Salt Lake City, UT 84111
P: (801) 320-5363
F: (801) 366-8886
E: kimoliver@utah.gov

VERMONT
Mr. Al LaPerle
Director of Unclaimed Property
State Treasury
109 State Street, 4th Floor
Montpelier, VT 05609
P: (802) 828-1452
F: (802) 828-2772
E: al.laperle@state.vt.us

Hon. Jeb Spaulding (D)
State Treasurer
Office of the State Treasurer
109 State Street, 4th Floor
Montpelier, VT 05609
P: (802) 828-1452
F: (802) 828-2772
E: jeb.spaulding
@state.vt.us

VIRGINIA
Ms. Vicki Bridgeman
Director of Unclaimed Property
State Treasury
P.O. Box 2478
Richmond, VA 23218
P: (804) 225-2393
F: (804) 786-4653
E: vicki.bridgeman
@trs.virgina.gov

Hon. J. Braxton Powell
State Treasurer
Department of the Treasury
P.O. Box 1879
Richmond, VA 23218
P: (804) 225-3131
F: (804) 225-3187
E: braxton.powell
@trs.virginia.gov

WASHINGTON
Ms. Cindi L. Holmstrom
Director
Department of Revenue
P.O. Box 47454
Olympia, WA 98504
P: (360) 586-3462
F: (360) 586-2163
E: cindih@dor.wa.gov

Ms. Celeste Monahan
Program Manager
Department of Revenue
P.O. Box 47472
Olympia, WA 98504
P: (360) 570-3201
F: (360) 664-8438
E: CelesteM@DOR.WA.GOV

WEST VIRGINIA
Ms. Carolyn Atkinson
Assistant General Counsel
State Treasury
One Player's Club Drive
Charleston, WV 25305
P: (304) 341-0703
F: (304) 558-5063
E: carolyn.atkinson
@wvsto.com

Hon. John D. Perdue (D)
State Treasurer
State Treasurer's Office
Capitol Complex Building 1,
Room E-145
1900 Kanawha Boulevard
Charleston, WV 25305
P: (304) 558-5000
F: (304) 558-4097
E: john.perdue@wvsto.com

WISCONSIN
Ms. Mary Celentani
Administrator
Unclaimed Property Division
State Treasury
P.O. Box 2114
Madison, WI 53701
P: (608) 267-2208
F: (608) 261-6799
E: mary.celentani
@ost.state.wi.us

Hon. Dawn Marie Sass (D)
State Treasurer
Office of the State Treasurer
1 South Pinckney Street, Suite
550
Madison, WI 53703
P: (608) 266-1714
F: (608) 266-2647
E: dawn.sass
@ost.state.wi.us

WYOMING
Hon. Joe Meyer (R)
State Treasurer
State Treasurer's Office
200 West 24th Street
Cheyenne, WY 82002
P: (307) 777-7408
F: (307) 777-5411
E: jmeyer3@state.wy.us

Ms. Nancy Russell
Director
Unclaimed Property Division
State Treasury
2515 Warren Avenue, Suite 502
Cheyenne, WY 82002
P: (307) 777-5590
F: (307) 777-5430
E: NRUSSE@state.wy.us

Veterans Affairs

Provides services and information to the state's veterans, their dependents and survivors.

ALABAMA
Mr. W. Clyde Marsh
Commissioner
Department of Veterans Affairs
770 Washington Avenue, Suite 530
Montgomery, AL 36130
P: (334) 242-5077
F: (334) 242-5102
E: clyde.marsh@va.alabama.gov

ALASKA
Mr. Jerry Beale
State Veterans Administrator
Office of Veteran Affairs
Dept. of Military & Veterans Affairs
P.O .Box 5800
Ft. Richardson, AK 99505
P: (907) 428-6016
F: (907) 428-6019

AMERICAN SAMOA
Mr. Paogofie Fiaigoa
Veterans Affairs Officer
Office of Veterans' Affairs
American Samoa Government
Pago Pago, AS 96799
P: (684) 633-4206
F: (684) 633-2269

ARIZONA
Mr. Gregg Maxon
Interim Director
Department of Veteran Services
3839 North Third Street, Suite 200
Phoenix, AZ 85012
P: (602) 255-3373
E: director@azvet.com

ARKANSAS
Mr. James L. Miller
Director
Department of Veterans' Affairs
2200 Fort Roots Drive
Building 65, Room 119
North Little Rock, AR 72114
P: (501) 370-3820
F: (501) 370-3829

CALIFORNIA
Mr. Thomas Johnson
Secretary
Department of Veterans Affairs
1227 O Street, Suite 300
Sacramento, CA 95814
P: (916) 653-2158
F: (916) 653-2456

COLORADO
Brig. Gen. H. Michael Edwards
Adjutant General
Department of Military Affairs
6848 South Revere Parkway
Englewood, CO 80112
P: (720) 250-1500

CONNECTICUT
Ms. Linda Schwartz
Commissioner
Department of Veterans' Affairs
287 West Street
Rocky Hill, CT 06067
P: (860) 721-5891
F: (860) 721-5904
E: Linda.Schwartz@po.state.ct.us

DELAWARE
Mr. Antonio Davila
Administrator
Commission of Veterans Affairs
802 Silver Lake Boulevard, Suite 100
Dover, DE 19904
P: (302) 739-2792
F: (302) 739-2794

DISTRICT OF COLUMBIA
Mr. Kerwin E. Miller
Director
Office of Veterans Affairs
441 4th Street, Northwest
Suite 570, South
Washington, DC 20001
P: (202) 724-5454
F: (202) 724-7117

FLORIDA
Mr. Leroy Collins
Executive Director
Department of Veterans' Affairs
Mary Grizzle Building, Room 311-K
11351 Ulmerton Road
Largo, FL 33778
P: (850) 487-1533
F: (727) 518-3216

GEORGIA
Mr. Pete Wheeler
Commissioner
Department of Veterans Service
Veterans Memorial Building
Suite E-970
Atlanta, GA 30334
P: (404) 656-2300
F: (404) 657-9738

GUAM
Mr. Fred A. Gofigan
Administrator
Department of Military Affairs
107 M Street, Tiyan
P.O. Box 2950
Hagatna, GU 96932
P: (617) 475-4222
F: (617) 477-8858

HAWAII
Col. Edward R. Cruickshank
Director
Office of Veterans Services
459 Patterson Road
E-Wing, Room 1-A103
Honolulu, HI 96819
P: (808) 433-0420
F: (808) 433-0385

ILLINOIS
Ms. L. Tammy Duckworth
Director
Department of Veterans' Affairs
833 South Spring Street
P.O. Box 19432
Springfield, IL 62794
P: (217) 785-4114
F: (217) 524-0344

INDIANA
Mr. Tom Applegate
Director
Department of Veterans' Affairs
302 West Washington Street
Room E120
Indianapolis, IN 46204
P: (317) 232-3922
F: (317) 232-7721

IOWA
Mr. Patrick Palmersheim
Executive Director
Department of Veteran's Affairs
Camp Dodge, Building A6A
7105 Northwest 70th Avenue
Johnston, IA 50131
P: (515) 242-5331
F: (515) 242-5659

KANSAS
Col. George S. Webb
Executive Director
Commission on Veterans Affairs
700 Southwest Jackson Street
Suite 701
Topeka, KS 66603
P: (785) 296-3976
F: (785) 296-1462

KENTUCKY
Mr. Les Beavers
Commissioner
Department of Veterans Affairs
1111 Louisville Road
Frankfort, KY 40601
P: (502) 564-9203
F: (502) 564-9240
E: les.beavers@ky.gov

LOUISIANA
Maj. Gen. Hunt Downer (D)
Legislative Director
Department of Veterans Affairs
Office of the Governor
P.O. Box 94004
Baton Rouge, LA 70804
P: (225) 342-7015
F: (225) 342-7099

MAINE
Maj. Gen. John W. Libby
Adjutant General
Military Bureau
Camp Keyes
Augusta, ME 04333
P: (207) 626-4205
F: (207) 476-4341

MARYLAND
Mr. George W. Owings III
Secretary
Department of Veterans Affairs
The Jeffrey Building
16 Francis Street
Baltimore, MD 21401
P: (410) 260-3838
E: gowings@mdva.state.md.us

MASSACHUSETTS
Mr. Thomas G. Kelley
Secretary
Executive Office of Veterans Services
239 Causeway Street, Suite 100
Boston, MA 02114
P: (617) 727-3570
F: (617) 727-5903

MICHIGAN
Brig. Gen. Carol Ann Fausone
Assistant Adjutant General - Veterans Affairs
Department of Military & Veterans Affairs
2500 South Washington Avenue
Lansing, MI 48913
P: (517) 335-6523
F: (517) 241-0674

MINNESOTA
Mr. Clark Dyrud
Commissioner
Department of Veterans Affairs
20 West 12th Street
St. Paul, MN 55155
P: (651) 296-2345
F: (612) 970-5796
E: clark.dyrud@state.mn.us

MISSISSIPPI
Mr. Adrian Grice
Executive Director
Veterans Affairs Board
P.O. Box 5947
Pearl, MS 39288
P: (601) 576-4850
F: (601) 576-4868
E: grice@vab.state.ms.us

MISSOURI
Mr. Hal Dulle
Executive Director
Veterans Commission
205 Jefferson Street, 12th Floor
P.O. Box 147
Jefferson City, MO 65102
P: (573) 751-3779
E: hal.dulle@mvc.dps.mo.gov

MONTANA
Mr. Joseph S. Foster
Administrator
Veteran's Affairs Division
1900 Williams Street
P.O. Box 5715
Helena, MT 59604
P: (406) 324-3741
F: (406) 324-3335

NEBRASKA
Mr. John Hilgert
Director
Department of Veterans Affairs
P.O. Box 95083
Lincoln, NE 68509
P: (402) 471-2458
F: (402) 471-2491

NEVADA
Mr. Tim Tetz
Office of Veterans Services
5460 Reno Corporate Drive
Reno, NV 89511
P: (775) 688-1653
F: (775) 688-1656
E: tim.tetz@veterans.nv.gov

NEW HAMPSHIRE
Ms. Mary E. Morin
Director
Veterans Council
275 Chestnut Street, Room 517
Manchester, NH 03101
P: (603) 624-9230
F: (603) 624-9236
E: mary.morin@vba.va.gov

NEW JERSEY
Maj. Gen. Glenn K. Rieth
Adjutant General
Department of Military & Veterans Affairs
P.O. Box 340
Trenton, NJ 08625
P: (609) 530-6957
F: (609) 530-7191
E: glenn.rieth@njdmava.state.nj.us

NEW MEXICO
Mr. John Garcia
Cabinet Secretary
Department of Veteran Services
Bataan Memorial Building
Santa Fe, NM 87503
P: (505) 827-6300

NEW YORK
Mr. George Basher
Director
Division of Veterans' Affairs
Corning Tower
Empire State Plaza
Albany, NY 12223
P: (518) 474-6114

NORTH CAROLINA
Mr. Charles F. Smith
Assistant Secretary
Division of Veterans Affairs
325 North Salisbury Street, #1065
1315 Mail Service Center
Raleigh, NC 27699
P: (919) 733-3851
F: (919) 733-2834
E: charlie.smith@ncmail.net

NORTH DAKOTA
Mr. Bob Hanson
Commissioner
Department of Veterans Affairs
P.O. Box 9003
Fargo, ND 58106
P: (701) 239-7165
F: (701) 239-7166

NORTHERN MARIANA ISLANDS
Ms. Ruth Coleman
Executive Officer
Military Liaison & Veterans Affairs
Caller Box 10007, Capitol Hill
Saipan, MP 96950
P: (670) 664-2650
F: (670) 664-2660
E: veterans@vzpacifica.net

OHIO
Mr. Tim Espich
Director
Governor's Office of Veterans Affairs
77 South High Street, 7th Floor
Columbus, OH 43215
P: (614) 644-0898

OKLAHOMA
Mr. Phillip Driskill
Executive Director
Department of Veterans Affairs
2311 North Central
P.O. Box 53067
Oklahoma City, OK 73152
P: (405) 521-3684
F: (405) 521-6533
E: pdriskill@odva.state.ok.us

OREGON
Mr. Jim Willis
Director
Department of Veterans' Affairs
Oregon Veterans' Building
700 Summer Street, Northeast
Salem, OR 97301
P: (503) 373-2388
F: (503) 373-2362
E: willisj@odva.state.or.us

PENNSYLVANIA
Maj. Gen. Jessica L. Wright
Adjutant General
Department of Military Affairs
Building P-0 47 200
Fort Indiantown Gap
Annville, PA 17003
P: (717) 861-8500

PUERTO RICO
Mr. Luis Ramos-Gonzales
Advocate
Office of Veterans Affairs
P.O. Box 11737
San Juan, PR 00910
P: (787) 758-5760
F: (787) 758-5788
E: luisramos@opv.gobierno.pr

RHODE ISLAND
Mr. Daniel J. Evangelista
Associate Director
Division of Veterans Affairs
480 Metacom Avenue
Bristol, RI 02809
P: (401) 462-0350
F: (401) 462-6339

SOUTH CAROLINA
Mr. Phil Butler
Director
Office of Veterans Affairs
1205 Pendleton Street, Suite 369
Columbia, SC 29201
P: (803) 734-0200
F: (803) 734-0197

TENNESSEE
Mr. John Keys
Commissioner
Department of Veterans Affairs
American Legion Building, 3rd Floor
215 Eighth Avenue, North
Nashville, TN 37243
P: (615) 741-2931
F: (615) 741-4785
E: john.keys@state.tn.us

TEXAS
Mr. James E. Nier
Executive Director
Veterans Commission
P.O. Box 12277
Austin, TX 78711
P: (512) 463-6564
F: (512) 475-2395
E: info@tvc.state.tx.us

U.S. VIRGIN ISLANDS
Mr. Justin Harrigan
Director
Office of Veterans Affairs
1013 Estate Richmond
Christiansted
St. Croix, VI 00820
P: (340) 773-6663
F: (340) 692-9563
E: justinova46@yahoo.com

Veterans Affairs

UTAH
Mr. Terry Schow
Director
Veteran's Affairs Division
Utah National Guard
550 Foothill Boulevard, #206
Salt Lake City, UT 84108
P: (801) 326-2373
F: (801) 236-2369
E: tschow@utah.gov

VERMONT
Mr. Clayton Clark
Director
Veterans Affairs
120 State Street
Montpelier, VT 05620
P: (802) 828-3379
E: clayton.clark
@state.vt.us

VIRGINIA
Mr. Vincent M. Burgess
Commissioner
Department of Veterans Services
Pocahontas Building, Ground Floor
900 East Main Street
Richmond, VA 23219
P: (804) 786-0286
F: (804) 786-0302
E: vince.burgess
@dvs.virginia.gov

WASHINGTON
Mr. John Lee
Director
Department of Veterans Affairs
505 East Union
P.O. Box 41150
Olympia, WA 98504
P: (360) 725-2151

WEST VIRGINIA
Mr. Larry Linch
Director
Division of Veterans Affairs
1321 Plaza East, Suite 109
Charleston, WV 25301
P: (304) 558-3661
F: (304) 558-3662

WISCONSIN
Mr. John Scocos
Secretary
Department of Veterans Affairs
30 West Mifflin
P.O. Box 7843
Madison, WI 53707
P: (608) 266-1311
F: (608) 267-0403

WYOMING
Maj. Gen. Edward L. Wright
Adjutant General
Military Department
5500 Bishop Boulevard
Cheyenne, WY 82009
P: (307) 772-5234
F: (307) 772-5010
E: ed.boenisch
@wy.ngb.army.mil

Vital Statistics

Maintains a statewide file of birth, death, marriage and divorce records, and issues certified copies of those records.

ALABAMA
Ms. Dorothy Harshbarger
State Registrar
Department of Public Health
201 Monroe, Suite 1150
Montgomery, AL 36104
P: (334) 206-5426
F: (334) 206-2659

ALASKA
Mr. Phillip Mitchell
Section Chief
Bureau of Vital Statistics
Department of Health & Social Services
5441 Commercial Boulevard
Juneau, AK 99801
P: (907) 465-3391
F: (907) 465-3618

ARIZONA
Ms. Susan Gerard
Director
Department of Health Services
150 North 18th Avenue
Phoenix, AZ 85007
P: (602) 542-1001
F: (602) 543-0883

ARKANSAS
Mr. Michael Adams
Director
Division of Vital Records
4815 West Markham Street
Little Rock, AR 72205
P: (501) 661-2371
F: (501) 661-2717
E: maadams@healthyarkansas.com

CALIFORNIA
Ms. Kristina Smith
Chief
Office of Vital Records
1501 Capitol Avenue, Suite 1101
P.O. Box 997413
Sacramento, CA 95899
P: (916) 552-8107

COLORADO
Mr. Bob O'Doherty
Director and Chief Information Officer
Center for Health and Environmental Information & Statistics
4300 Cherry Creek Drive South
Denver, CO 80246
P: (303) 692-2160
F: (303) 691-7704

CONNECTICUT
Mr. Daniel J. Savino
Registrar
Vital Statistics Office
410 Capitol Avenue
Hartford, CT 06106
P: (860) 509-7163
F: (860) 509-7160
E: angela.kasek@po.state.ct.us

DELAWARE
Ms. Judy Chaconas
Director
Bureau of Health Planning & Resources Management
Jesse Cooper Building
Federal & Water Streets
Dover, DE 19901
P: (302) 741-2960
F: (302) 741-2970

DISTRICT OF COLUMBIA
Ms. Kate Jesberg
Interim Director
Department of Human Services
64 New York Avenue, NE
6th Floor
Washington, DC 20001
P: (202) 671-4200
F: (202) 671-4381

FLORIDA
Mr. Meade Grigg
Director
Office of Vital Statistics
P.O. Box 210
Jacksonville, FL 32231
P: (904) 359-6900
F: (904) 359-6931

GEORGIA
Dr. Stuart T. Brown
Director
Division of Public Health
Two Peachtree Street, Northwest
Atlanta, GA 30303
P: (404) 657-2700

GUAM
Mr. Arthur U. San Agustin
Director
Department of Health & Social Services
123 Chalan Kareta, Route 10
Mangilao, GU 96923
P: (671) 735-7102
F: (671) 734-5910
E: chiefdsc@dphss.govguam.net

HAWAII
Dr. Alvin R. Onaka
Chief & State Registrar
Office of Health Status Monitoring
P.O. Box 3378
Honolulu, HI 96801
P: (808) 586-4600
F: (808) 586-4606

IDAHO
Ms. Jane Smith
State Registrar & Chief
Bureau of Health Policy & Vital Statistics
450 West State Street
1st Floor, Pete T. Cenarrusa Building
Boise, ID 83720
P: (208) 334-5932
F: (208) 334-6581

ILLINOIS
Mr. George Rudis
Director
Division of Vital Records
605 West Jefferson
Springfield, IL 62761
P: (217) 782-6554

INDIANA
Ms. Barbara Stultz
Director
Vital Records Department
2 North Meridian Street
Indianapolis, IN 46204
P: (317) 233-7523
F: (317) 233-5956
E: bstultz@isdh.state.in.us

IOWA
Ms. Jill France
Bureau Chief
Bureau of Health Statistics
Lucas Building
321 East 12th Street
Des Moines, IA 50319
P: (515) 281-4944

KANSAS
Dr. Lorne Phillips
Director
Office of Vital Statistics
1000 Southwest Jackson Street, Suite 130
Topeka, KS 66612
P: (785) 296-1417
F: (785) 296-8075

KENTUCKY
Dr. Bill Hacker
Commissioner
Department for Public Health
275 East Main Street
Frankfort, KY 40621
P: (502) 564-4212

LOUISIANA
Ms. Darlene Smith
State Registrar & Director
Office of Records & Statistics
P.O. Box 60630
New Orleans, LA 70160
P: (504) 219-4500
F: (504) 219-4478
E: vitalweb@dhh.la.gov

MAINE
Ms. Lorraine Wilson
Director
Office of Vital Records
11 State House Station
Augusta, ME 04333
P: (207) 287-3181
E: lorraine.wilson@maine.gov

MARYLAND
Dr. Isabelle L. Horon
Director
Vital Statistics Administration
201 West Preston Street, 5th Floor
Baltimore, MD 21201
P: (410) 767-5950
F: (410) 767-6840
E: horoni@dhmh.state.md.us

MASSACHUSETTS
Mr. John Auerbach
Commissioner
Department of Public Health
250 Washington Street
Boston, MA 02108
P: (617) 624-6000

MICHIGAN
Mr. Glenn Copeland
State Registrar
Division of Vital Records & Health Statistics
P.O. Box 30195
Lansing, MI 48909
P: (517) 335-9975
F: (517) 335-9264

Vital Statistics

MINNESOTA
Ms. Dianne Mandernach
Commissioner
Department of Health
625 Robert Street, North
Box 64975
St. Paul, MN 55164
P: (651) 201-5810
F: (651) 201-4986
E: dianne.mandernach@state.mn.us

MISSISSIPPI
Ms. Judy Moulder
State Registrar
Public Health Statistics
571 Stadium Drive
P.O. Box 1700
Jackson, MS 39216
P: (601) 576-7960
F: (601) 576-7505
E: jmoulder@msdh.state.ms.us

MISSOURI
Ms. Ivra Cross
State Registrar
Bureau of Vital Records
930 Wildwood
P.O. Box 570
Jefferson City, MO 65102
P: (573) 751-6381
F: (573) 526-3846
E: ivra.cross@dhss.mo.gov

MONTANA
Ms. Joyce Zahn
Chief
Support & Vital Records Services Bureau
111 North Sanders, Room 205
Helena, MT 59604
P: (406) 444-0112
F: (406) 444-7358
E: jzahn@state.mt.us

NEBRASKA
Ms. Joann Schaefer
Director
Department of Health & Human Services
Regulation & Licensure
P.O. Box 95007
Lincoln, NE 68509
P: (402) 471-8566
F: (402) 471-9449
E: roxie.anderson@hhss.ne.us

NEVADA
Ms. Luana J. Ritch
Bureau Chief
Bureau of Health Planning & Statistics
4150 Technology Way, Suite 104
Carson City, NV 89706
P: (775) 684-4242
F: (775) 684-4156
E: lritch@nvhd.state.nv.us

NEW HAMPSHIRE
Mr. Steven Wurtz
Director
Division of Vital Records
71 South Fruit Street
Concord, NH 03301
P: (603) 271-4650
F: (603) 271-3447
E: swurtz@sos.state.nh.us

NEW JERSEY
Dr. Fred M. Jacobs
Commissioner
Department of Health & Senior Services
P.O. Box 360
Trenton, NJ 08625
P: (609) 292-7837
F: (609) 292-0053
E: Fred.Jacobs@doh.state.nj.us

NEW YORK
Mr. Peter Carucci
Acting Director
Bureau of Production Systems Management
800 North Pearl Street
Albany, NY 12204
P: (518) 474-5245

NORTH CAROLINA
Mr. Glenn Cutler
Director
Vital Records Unit
225 South McDowell Street
1903 Mail Service Center
Raleigh, NC 27699
P: (919) 733-9374
F: (919) 733-1551
E: glenn.cutler@ncmail.net

NORTH DAKOTA
Mr. Darin J. Meschke
State Registrar
Division of Vital Records
600 East Boulevard Avenue
Department 301
Bismarck, ND 58505
P: (701) 328-2360
F: (701) 328-1850
E: dmeschke@nd.gov

NORTHERN MARIANA ISLANDS
Mr. John G. Moore
Commonwealth Recorder
Vital Records Section
P.O. Box 500307
Saipan, MP 96950
P: (670) 236-9830
F: (670) 236-9831

OHIO
Ms. Kelly Friar
Chief
Vital & Health Statistics
Department of Health
246 North High Street
Columbus, OH 43216
P: (614) 466-2533

OKLAHOMA
Mr. John Burks
Director
Division of Vital Records
1000 North East 10th Street
Oklahoma City, OK 73152
P: (405) 271-4040
F: (405) 271-2930

OREGON
Ms. Jennifer Woodward
DHS - Center for Health Statistics
800 Oregon Street, Suite 205-225
Portland, OR 97293
P: (971) 673-1180
F: (971) 673-1201
E: dhs.info@state.or.us

PENNSYLVANIA
Mr. Charles L. Hardester
Director
Division of Vital Records
P.O. Box 1528
New Castle, PA 16103
P: (724) 656-3286
F: (724) 656-3079

PUERTO RICO
Mr. Nicolas Fernandez-Cornier
Executive Director
Demographic Registry
P.O. Box 11854
San Juan, PR 00910
P: (787) 281-8867
F: (787) 751-5003

RHODE ISLAND
Mr. Leonard Green
Chief
Office of Vital Records
3 Capitol Hill
Providence, RI 02908
P: (401) 222-2812

SOUTH CAROLINA
Dr. Guang Zhao
Director
Public Health Statistics & Information Services
2600 Bull Street
Columbia, SC 29201
P: (803) 898-3653

SOUTH DAKOTA
Ms. Doneen Hollingsworth
Secretary
Department of Health
Hayes Building
600 East Capitol Avenue
Pierre, SD 57501
P: (605) 773-3361
F: (605) 773-5683
E: doh.info@state.sd.us

Ms. Kathi Mueller
State Registrar
Vital Records
Hayes Building
600 East Capitol Avenue
Pierre, SD 57501
P: (605) 773-4961
F: (605) 773-5683
E: kathi.mueller@state.sd.us

TENNESSEE
Ms. Sharon Leinbach
State Registrar & Director
Vital Records
Cordell Hull Building
Nashville, TN 37247
P: (615) 532-2600

U.S. VIRGIN ISLANDS
Ms. Darlene Carty
Commissioner
Department of Health
48 Sugar Estate
Charlotte Amalie
St. Thomas, VI 00802
P: (340) 774-0117
F: (340) 774-4001
E: darlene.carty@usvi-doh.org

UTAH
Mr. Jeffrey Duncan
Director
Bureau of Vital Records
Department of Health
288 North 1460 West
Salt Lake City, UT 84116
P: (801) 538-6186
F: (801) 538-7012
E: jduncan@utah.gov

VERMONT
Dr. William K. Apao
Director
Health Surveillance Division
P.O. Box 70
Burlington, VT 05402
P: (802) 863-7300

VIRGINIA
Dr. Robert B. Stroube
Commissioner
Department of Health
109 Governor Street, 13th Floor
Richmond, VA 23219
P: (804) 864-7009
F: (804) 864-7022
E: robert.stroube@vdh.virginia.gov

WASHINGTON
Ms. Teresa Jennings
Director
Center for Health Statistics
P.O. Box 47814
Olympia, WA 98504
P: (360) 236-4307
F: (360) 753-4135
E: teresa.jennings@doh.wa.gov

WEST VIRGINIA
Mr. Gary Thompson
State Registrar
Vital Registration Office
350 Capitol Street, Room 165
Charleston, WV 25301
P: (304) 558-0155
F: (304) 558-8001
E: gary.thompson@wvdhhr.org

WISCONSIN
Mr. Jason Helgerson
Administrator
Division of Health Care Financing
1 West Wilson Street, Room 350
Madison, WI 53701
P: (608) 266-8922
F: (608) 266-1096

WYOMING
Ms. Lucinda McCaffrey
Deputy State Registrar
Vital Records Services
Preventative Health & Safety Division
Hathaway Building
Cheyenne, WY 82002
P: (307) 777-7264
F: (307) 777-7439

Vocational Rehabilitation

Assists and encourages disabled persons to find suitable employment through training programs.

ALABAMA
Mr. Steve Shivers
Director
Department of Rehabilitation Services
2129 East South Boulevard
P.O. Box 11586
Montgomery, AL 36116
P: (334) 281-8780
F: (334) 281-1973
E: alanet@rehabnetwork.org

ALASKA
Ms. Gale Sinnott
Director
Division of Vocational Rehabilitation
Dept. of Labor & Workforce Development
801 West 10th Street, Suite A
Juneau, AK 99801
P: (907) 465-2814
F: (907) 465-2856

AMERICAN SAMOA
Mr. Pete Galea'i
Director
Vocational Rehabilitation
American Samoa Government
ASG Mail 3492
Pago Pago, AS 96799
P: (684) 699-1371
F: (684) 633-2393

ARIZONA
Ms. Kathy Levandowsky
Administrator
Rehabilitation Services Administration
1789 West Jefferson, 2nd Floor Northwest
Phoenix, AZ 85007
P: (602) 542-2266
F: (602) 542-3778

ARKANSAS
Mr. James C. Hudson
Director
Division of Services for the Blind
P.O. Box 1437, Slot S101
Little Rock, AR 72203
P: (501) 682-5463
F: (501) 682-0366
E: Jim.Hudson@arkansas.gov

Mr. Robert P. Trevino
Commissioner
Rehabilitation Services
1616 Brookwood Drive
P.O. Box 3781
Little Rock, AR 72203
P: (501) 296-1600
F: (501) 296-1655

COLORADO
Ms. Nancy Smith
Director
Division of Vocational Rehabilitation
1575 Sherman Street
4th Floor
Denver, CO 80023
P: (303) 866-4150
F: (303) 866-4905

CONNECTICUT
Ms. Brenda Moore
Director
Bureau of Rehabilitation Services
Department of Social Services
25 Sigourney Street, 11th Floor
Hartford, CT 06100
P: (860) 424-4846
F: (860) 424-4850

Mr. Brian Sigman
Director
Vocational Rehabilitation Division
184 Windsor Avenue
Windsor, CT 06095
P: (860) 602-4008
F: (860) 602-4030

DELAWARE
Ms. Andrea Guest
Director
Division of Vocational Rehabilitation
4425 North Market Street
P.O. Box 9969
Wilmington, DE 19809
P: (302) 761-8275
F: (302) 761-6611
E: delgen@rehabnetwork.org

Ms. Cynthia Lowell
Director
Division for the Visually Impaired
Department of Health & Social Services
1901 North DuPont Highway
New Castle, DE 19720
P: (302) 255-9810

DISTRICT OF COLUMBIA
Ms. Summer Spencer
Acting Director
Department of Employment Services
609 H Street, NE
Washington, DC 20002
P: (202) 724-7000

FLORIDA
Mr. Craig Kiser
Director
Division of Blind Services
1320 Executive Center Drive
Room 100, Atkins Building
Tallahassee, FL 32399
P: (850) 245-0300
F: (850) 245-0363

Mr. Bill Palmer
Director
Division of Vocational Rehabilitation
2002 Old St. Augustine Road, Building A
Tallahassee, FL 32301
P: (850) 245-3399

GEORGIA
Mr. Larry Beck
Assistant Commissioner for Rehabilitation Services
Department of Labor
Suite 510, Sussex Place
148 Andrew Young International Blvd NE
Atlanta, GA 30303
P: (404) 657-3000
F: (404) 657-3079
E: gard@rehabnetwork.org

GUAM
Mr. Albert San Agustin
Director
Department of Vocational Rehabilitation
1313 Central Avenue
Tiyan, GU 96910
P: (671) 475-4637
F: (671) 642-0033

HAWAII
Mr. Joe Cordova
Administrator
Vocational Rehabilitation & Services for the Blind
601 Kamokila Boulevard, Room 515
Kapolei, HI 96707
P: (808) 692-7720
F: (808) 692-7727

IDAHO
Mr. Michael J. Graham
Administrator
Division of Vocational Rehabilitation
650 West State Street, Room 150
P.O. Box 83720-0096
Boise, ID 82720
P: (208) 287-6477
F: (208) 334-5305
E: mgraham@vr.idaho.gov

Ms. Angela Roan
Administrator
Commission for the Blind & Visually Impaired
341 West Washington Street
P.O. Box 83720
Boise, ID 83720
P: (208) 334-3220
F: (208) 334-2963

ILLINOIS
Mr. Robert Kilbury
Associate Director
Office of Rehabilitation Services
100 South Grand Avenue East
Springfield, IL 62762
P: (217) 557-7084
F: (217) 558-4270

INDIANA
Mr. Michael Hedden
Deputy Director
Vocational Rehabilitation Services
402 West Washington Street
P.O. Box 7083
Indianapolis, IN 46207
P: (317) 232-1319

IOWA
Mr. Steve Wooderson
Administrator
Division of Vocational Rehabilitation Services
510 East 12th Street
Des Moines, IA 50319
P: (515) 281-4211
F: (515) 281-7645
E: swooderson@dvrs.state.ia.us

KANSAS
Mr. Dale Barnum
Director
Rehabilitation Services
3640 Southwest Topeka Boulevard
Suite 150
Topeka, KS 66611
P: (785) 267-5301
F: (785) 267-0263
E: ksnet@rehabnetwork.org

KENTUCKY
Mr. Ralph Clark
Director
Office of Vocational Rehabilitation
209 St. Clair Street
Frankfort, KY 40601
P: (502) 564-4440
F: (502) 564-6745

Mr. Steve Johnson
Commissioner
Office for the Blind
209 St. Clair Street
P.O. Box 757
Frankfort, KY 40602
P: (502) 564-4754
F: (502) 564-2951

LOUISIANA
Mr. James Wallace
Director
Rehabilitation Services
Department of Social Services
8225 Florida Boulevard
Baton Rouge, LA 70806
P: (225) 925-4131
F: (225) 925-4184
E: jwallace@dss.state.la.us

MAINE
Mr. Art Jacobson
Director
Division of Vocational Rehabilitation
Department of Labor
150 State House Station
Augusta, ME 04333
P: (207) 624-5950
F: (207) 624-5980

Mr. Harold Lewis
Director
Division for the Blind & Visually Impaired
2 Anthony Avenue, Station 150
Autusta, ME 04333
P: (207) 624-5959
F: (207) 624-5980

MARYLAND
Mr. Robert A. Burns
Assistant State Superintendent
Division of Rehabilitation Services
State Department of Education
2301 Argonne Drive
Baltimore, MD 21218
P: (410) 554-9385
F: (410) 554-9384
E: crabcake@rehabnetwork.org

MASSACHUSETTS
Mr. Elmer C. Bartels
Commissioner
Rehabilitation Commission
Fort Point Place
27-43 Wormwood Street
Boston, MA 02210
P: (617) 204-3600
F: (617) 727-1354

Mr. David Govostes
Commissioner
Commission for the Blind
88 Kingston Street
Boston, MA 02111
P: (617) 727-5550
F: (617) 727-5960

MICHIGAN
Mr. Jaye Balthazar
Director
Rehabilitation Services
201 North Washington Square
P.O. Box 30010
Lansing, MI 48909
P: (517) 373-4026
F: (517) 335-7277
E: balthazarj@michigan.gov

MINNESOTA
Ms. Kimberley T. Peck
Director
Rehabilitation Services Branch
First National Bank Building
332 Minnesota Street, Suite E200
St. Paul, MN 55101
P: (651) 296-7510
F: (651) 297-5159
E: kim.peck@state.mn.us

MISSISSIPPI
Mr. H. S. Butch McMillan
Executive Director
Department of Rehabilitation Services
1281 Highway 51
P.O. Box 1698
Jackson, MS 39215
P: (601) 853-5203
F: (601) 853-5205
E: msvrnet@rehabnetwork.org

MISSOURI
Dr. Jeanne Loyd
Assistant Commissioner
Division of Vocational Rehabilitation
3024 Dupont Circle
Jefferson City, MO 65109
P: (573) 751-3901
F: (573) 751-1441
E: jeanne.loyd@vr.dese.mo.gov

Ms. Janel Luck
Interim Division Director
Family Support Division
P.O. Box 2320
615 Howerton Court
Jefferson City, MO 65102
P: (573) 751-4247
F: (573) 751-0507

MONTANA
Mr. Joe A. Mathews
Administrator
Disabilities Service Division
111 North Sanders
P.O. Box 4210
Helena, MT 59604
P: (406) 444-2590
F: (406) 444-3632
E: mtvr@rehabnetwork.org

NEBRASKA
Mr. Frank Lloyd
Associate Commissioner & Director
Division of Rehabilitation Services
6th Floor, 301 Centennial Mall
P.O. Box 94987
Lincoln, NE 68509
P: (402) 471-3649
F: (402) 471-0788
E: nebgen@rehabnetwork.org

Ms. Pearl VanZandt
Director
Rehabilitation Services for the Visually Impaired
4600 Valley Road, Suite 100
Lincoln, NE 68510
P: (402) 471-2891
F: (402) 471-3009

NEVADA
Ms. Cecelia Collings
Administrator
Department of Employment, Training & Rehabilitation
Rehabilitation Division
505 East King Street, Room 501
Carson City, NV 89701
P: (775) 687-2589
F: (775) 684-4184
E: cgcolling@nvdetr.org

NEW HAMPSHIRE
Mr. Paul Leather
Director
Division of Vocational Rehabilitation
21 South Fruit Street, Suite 20
Concord, NH 03301
P: (603) 271-3801
F: (603) 271-7095
E: PLeather@ed.state.nh.us

NEW JERSEY
Mr. Vito J. De Santis
Director
Commission for the Blind & Visually Impaired
153 Halsey Street, 6th Floor
P.O. Box 47017
Newark, NJ 07101
P: (973) 648-3333
F: (973) 648-7364

Mr. Thomas G. Jennings
Director
Division of Vocational Rehabilitation Services
135 East State Street, 3rd Floor
P.O. Box 398
Trenton, NJ 08625
P: (609) 292-5987
F: (609) 292-8347
E: dvradmin@dol.state.nj.us

NEW MEXICO
Mr. Gary Beene
Assistant Secretary
Division of Vocational Rehabilitation
435 St. Michael's Drive, Building D
Santa Fe, NM 87505
P: (505) 954-8511
F: (505) 954-8562

NEW YORK
Dr. Rebecca Cort
Interim Deputy Commissioner
Vocational & Educational Services for People with Disabilities
State Education Department
One Commerce Plaza, Room 1606
Albany, NY 12234
P: (518) 474-2714
F: (518) 474-8802

NORTH CAROLINA
Ms. Linda Harrington
Director
Division of Vocational Rehabilitation Services
Department of Health & Human Services
2801 Mail Service Center
Raleigh, NC 27699
P: (919) 855-3500
F: (919) 733-7968

Vocational Rehabilitation

Ms. Debbie Jackson
Director
Division of Services for the Blind
309 Ashe Avenue - Fisher Building
2601 Mail Service Center
Raleigh, NC 27699
P: (919) 733-9822
F: (919) 733-9769
E: sbnc@rehabnetwork.org

NORTH DAKOTA
Mr. Wayne L. Kutzer
Director
Department of Career & Technical Education
State Capitol, 15th Floor
600 East Boulevard Avenue
Bismarck, ND
P: (701) 328-2259
F: (701) 328-1255

NORTHERN MARIANA ISLANDS
Ms. Margarita O. Taitano
Director
Vocational Rehabilitation Service
P.O. Box 1521
Commonwealth of the Northern Marianas
Saipan, MP 96950
P: (670) 664-6448
F: (670) 322-6536

OHIO
Mr. John Connelly
Administrator
Rehabilitation Services Commission
400 East Campus View Boulevard
Columbus, OH 43235
P: (614) 438-1214
F: (614) 785-5010
E: john.connelly@rsc.state.oh.us

OKLAHOMA
Ms. Linda S. Parker
Director
Department of Rehabilitation Services
3535 Northwest 58th Street, Suite 500
Oklahoma City, OK 73112
P: (405) 951-3400
F: (405) 951-3529
E: oknet@rehabnetwork.org

OREGON
Ms. Linda Mock
Administrator
State Commission for the Blind
535 Southeast 12th Avenue
Portland, OR 97214
P: (503) 731-3221
F: (503) 731-3230

Ms. Stephanie Parrish-Taylor
Administrator
Office of Vocational Rehabilitation Services
Department of Human Services
500 Summer Street, Northeast
Salem, OR 97310
P: (503) 945-5949
F: (503) 947-5025

PENNSYLVANIA
Mr. William A. Gannon
Executive Director
Office of Vocational Rehabilitation
Department of Labor & Industry
1521 North 6th Street
Harrisburg, PA 17102
P: (717) 787-7312
F: (717) 787-8826

PUERTO RICO
Mr. Jose Rolon
Interim Administrator
Division of Vocational Rehabilitation
P.O. Box 191118
Santurce, PR 00915
P: (787) 729-0160
F: (787) 728-8070

RHODE ISLAND
Mr. Raymond A. Carroll
Administrator
Office of Rehabilitation Services
Department of Human Services
40 Fountain Street
Providence, RI 02903
P: (401) 421-7005, Ext. 301
F: (401) 222-3574
E: rcarroll@ors.ri.gov

SOUTH CAROLINA
Mr. Larry C. Bryant
Commissioner
Vocational Rehabilitation Department
1410 Boston Avenue
P.O. Box 15
West Columbia, SC 29171
P: (803) 896-6500
E: lbryant@scvrd.state.sc.us

SOUTH DAKOTA
Mr. Grady Kickul
Director
Division of Rehabilitation Services
Hillsview Plaza
C/o 500 East Capitol
Pierre, SD 57501
P: (605) 773-3195
F: (605) 773-5483
E: grady.kickul@state.sd.us

Ms. Gaye Mattke
Director
Services for the Blind
Hillsview Plaza
C/o 500 East Capitol
Pierre, SD 57501
P: (605) 773-5114
F: (605) 773-5483
E: gaye.mattke@state.sd.us

TENNESSEE
Ms. Andrea L. Cooper
Assistant Commissioner
Division of Vocational Rehabilitation
Department of Human Services
15th Floor, 400 Deadrick Street
Nashville, TN 37248
P: (615) 313-4714
F: (615) 741-4165
E: tndrs@rehabnetwork.org

TEXAS
Mr. Terry Smith
Assistant Commissioner
Department of Assistive & Rehabilitative Services
4800 North Lamar, Suite 320
Austin, TX 78756
P: (512) 377-0600
F: (512) 377-0682

U.S. VIRGIN ISLANDS
Ms. Beverly Plaskett
Director
Division of Disabilities & Rehabilitation Services
Knud Hansen Complex, Building A
1303 Hospital Ground
St. Thomas, VI 00802
P: (340) 774-0930
F: (340) 774-7773
E: PlaskettB@islands.VI

UTAH
Mr. Donald R. Uchida
Director
Division of Rehabilitation Services
250 East 500 South
P.O. Box 144200
Salt Lake City, UT 84114
P: (801) 538-7540
F: (801) 538-7522
E: duchida@utah.gov

VERMONT
Ms. Diane Dalmasse
Director
Vocational Rehabilitation Division
103 South Main Street
Waterbury, VT 05676
P: (802) 241-2186
F: (802) 241-3359
E: verve@rehabnetwork.org

VIRGINIA
Mr. Joseph A. Bowman
Commissioner
Department for the Blind & Vision Impaired
397 Azalea Avenue
Richmond, VA 23227
P: (804) 371-3145
F: (804) 371-3157
E: bowmanja@dbvi.virginia.gov

Mr. James Rothrock
Commissioner
Department of Rehabilitation Services
8004 Franklin Farms Drive
P.O. Box K300
Richmond, VA 23288
P: (804) 662-7010
F: (804) 662-7644
E: jim.rothrock@drs.virginia.gov

WASHINGTON
Ms. Lou Oma Durand
Director
Services for the Blind
402 Legion Way, Suite 100
P.O. Box 40933
Olympia, WA 98504
P: (360) 725-3835
E: loudurand@dsb.wa.gov

Mr. Michael O'Brien
Director
Division of Vocational Rehabilitation
Department of Social & Health Services
Post Office Box 45340
Olympia, WA 98504
P: (360) 438-8008
F: (360) 438-8007

WEST VIRGINIA
Ms. Deborah Lovely
Director
Division of Rehabilitation Services
State Capitol
P.O. Box 50890
Charleston, WV 25305
P: (304) 766-4601
F: (304) 766-4905
E: debbiel@mail.drs.state.wv.us

WISCONSIN
Ms. Charlene Dwyer
Administrator
Division of Vocational Rehabilitation
201 East Washington Avenue, Room A100
P.O. Box 7852
Madison, WI 53707
P: (608) 261-2126
F: (608) 266-1133

WYOMING
Mr. Jim McIntosh
Administrator
Division of Vocational Rehabilitation
Department of Employment
1100 Herschler Building
Cheyenne, WY 82002
P: (307) 777-7389
F: (307) 777-5939

Waste Management

Develops and maintains a comprehensive waste management program in the state.

ALASKA
Ms. Kim Stricklan
Program Manager
Solid Waste Management Program
Department of Environmental Conservation
555 Cordova Street
Anchorage, AK 99501
P: (907) 269-1099
F: (907) 269-7510

ARIZONA
Ms. Amanda Stone
Waste Programs Division Director
Department of Environmental Quality
1110 West Washington
Phoenix, AZ 85007
P: (602) 771-4208
F: (602) 771-2302
E: stone.amanda@azdeq.gov

ARKANSAS
Mr. Steve Martin
Chief
Solid Waste Division
P.O. Box 8913
Little Rock, AR 72209
P: (501) 682-0600
F: (501) 682-0611
E: martin@adeq.state.ar.us

CALIFORNIA
Mr. Mark Leary
Executive Director
Integrated Waste Management Board
1001 I Street
Sacramento, CA 95814
P: (916) 341-6544
F: (916) 319-7319
E: mleary@ciwmb.ca.gov

COLORADO
Mr. Gary Baughman
Director
Hazardous Materials & Waste Management Division
4300 Cherry Creek Drive South
Denver, CO 80246
P: (303) 692-3300
F: (303) 759-5355

CONNECTICUT
Mr. Michael Harder
Interim Bureau Chief
Bureau of Waste Management
79 Elm Street
Hartford, CT 06106
P: (860) 424-3021
F: (860) 424-4060
E: michael.harder@po.state.ct.us

DELAWARE
Ms. Nancy C. Marker
Program Manager II
Solid Waste & Hazardous Management Branch
89 Kings Highway
Dover, DE 19901
P: (302) 739-9403
F: (302) 739-3491

FLORIDA
Ms. Mary Jean Yon
Director
Division of Waste Management
MS #4500
2600 Blair Stone Road
Tallahassee, FL 32399
P: (850) 245-8705

GEORGIA
Mr. Mark Smith
Branch Chief
Hazardous Waste Management Branch
2 Martin Luther King, Jr. Drive, SE
Suite 1154 East
Atlanta, GA 30334
P: (404) 656-7802
F: (404) 651-9425

GUAM
Ms. Lorilee Crisostomo
Administrator
Environmental Protection Agency
17-3304/15-6101 Mariner Avenue, Tiyan
P.O. Box 22439
Barrigada, GU 96921
P: (671) 475-1658
F: (671) 734-5910
E: lorilee@guamcell.net

HAWAII
Mr. Steven Chang
Branch Chief
Solid & Hazardous Waste Branch
919 Ala Moana Boulevard
Room 212
Honolulu, HI 96814
P: (808) 586-4226
E: schang@eha.health.state.hi.us

IDAHO
Mr. Orville Green
Administrator
Waste & Remediation Division
1410 North Hilton
Boise, ID 83706
P: (208) 373-0148
F: (208) 373-0154
E: orville.green@deq.idaho.gov

ILLINOIS
Mr. Doug P. Scott
Director
Environmental Protection Agency
1021 North Grand Avenue, East
P.O. Box 19276
Springfield, IL 62794
P: (217) 782-9540
F: (217) 782-9039

INDIANA
Mr. Bruce Palin
Assistant Commissioner
Department of Environmental Management
100 North Senate Avenue
Room N1154
Indianapolis, IN 46204
P: (317) 233-6591
F: (317) 232-3403
E: bpalin@dem.state.in.us

KANSAS
Mr. William Bider
Director
Bureau of Waste Management
1000 Southwest Jackson Street
Suite 320
Topeka, KS 66612
P: (785) 296-1600
F: (785) 296-8909

KENTUCKY
Mr. Bruce Scott
Director
Division of Waste Management
14 Reilly Road
Frankfort, KY 40601
P: (502) 564-7042
F: (502) 564-7091
E: bruce.scott@ky.gov

LOUISIANA
Ms. Linda Levy
Administrator
Environmental Assistance Division
Department of Environmental Quality
P.O. Box 4313
Baton Rouge, LA 70821
P: (225) 219-3241
F: (225) 219-3309
E: deqassistance@la.gov

MAINE
Mr. Mark Hyland
Director
Bureau of Remediation & Waste Management
Department of Environmental Protection
17 State House Station
Augusta, ME 04333
P: (207) 287-2651
F: (207) 287-7826
E: Mark.Hyland@maine.gov

MARYLAND
Mr. Horacio Tablada
Director
Waste Management Division
Department of Environment
1800 Washington Boulevard
Baltimore, MD 21230
P: (410) 631-3304
F: (410) 631-3321
E: htablada@mde.state.md.us

MASSACHUSETTS
Ms. Arleen O'Donnell
Acting Commissioner
Department of Environmental Protection
One Winter Street, 2nd Floor
Boston, MA 02108
P: (617) 292-5975
F: (617) 574-6880

MINNESOTA
Mr. Brad Moore
Commissioner
Pollution Control Agency
520 Lafayette Road
St. Paul, MN 55155
P: (651) 296-7301
F: (651) 296-6334
E: Brad.Moore@pca.state.mn.us

MISSOURI
Mr. Jim Hull
Director
Solid Waste Management Program
Division of Environmental Quality
P.O. Box 176
Jefferson City, MO 65102
P: (573) 526-3900

MONTANA
Mr. Richard Opper
Director
Department of Environmental Quality
1520 East Sixth Avenue
P.O. Box 200901
Helena, MT 59620
P: (406) 444-6701
F: (406) 444-4386
E: ropper@mt.gov

NEBRASKA
Mr. Michael J. Linder
Director
Department of Environmental Quality
1200 N Street, Suite 400
P.O. Box 98922
Lincoln, NE 68509
P: (402) 471-0275
F: (402) 471-2909

NEVADA
Mr. Allen Biaggi
Director
Division of Environmental Protection
901 South Stewart, Suite 5001
Carson City, NV 89701
P: (775) 684-2700
F: (775) 684-2715
E: abiaggi@dcnr.nv.gov

Mr. Eric Noack
Bureau Chief
Bureau of Waste Management
901 South Stewart Street, Suite 4001
Carson City, NV 89701
P: (775) 687-9366
E: enoack@ndep.nv.gov

NEW HAMPSHIRE
Mr. Anthony P. Giunta
Director
Department of Environmental Services
29 Hazen Drive
P.O. Box 95
Concord, NH 03301
P: (603) 271-2905
F: (603) 271-2456
E: aguinta@des.state.nh.us

NEW JERSEY
Mr. Frank Coolick
Administrator
Solid & Hazardous Waste Program
401 East State Street
P.O. Box 414
Trenton, NJ 08625
P: (609) 984-1418
F: (609) 777-0769

NEW MEXICO
Mr. John Goldstein
Director
Water & Waste Management Division
P.O. Box 26110
1190 St. Francis Drive, N4050
Santa Fe, NM 87505
P: (505) 827-1758

NEW YORK
Mr. Alexander "Pete" Grannis (D)
Commissioner
Department of Environmental Conservation
625 Broadway
Albany, NY 12207
P: (518) 402-8540
F: (518) 474-5450

NORTH CAROLINA
Mr. Dexter Matthews
Director
Division of Waste Management
401 Oberlin Road, Suite 150
Raleigh, NC 27605
P: (919) 508-5400
F: (919) 733-4061
E: dexter.matthews@ncmail.net

NORTH DAKOTA
Mr. Scott Radig
Director
Division of Waste Management
918 East Divide Avenue, 3rd Floor
Bismark, ND 58501
P: (701) 328-5166
F: (701) 328-5200
E: sradig@nd.gov

NORTHERN MARIANA ISLANDS
Mr. Jose S. Demapan
Secretary
Department of Public Works
Caller Box 10007, Capitol Hill
Saipan, MP 96950
P: (670) 235-5827
F: (670) 235-6346

OHIO
Mr. Michael Savage
Division Chief
Division of Hazardous Waste Management
50 West Town Street, Suite 700
Columbus, OH 43215
P: (614) 644-2917
E: mike.savage@epa.state.oh.us

OKLAHOMA
Mr. Scott Thompson
Director
Land Protection Division
P.O. Box 1677
Oklahoma City, OK 73118
P: (405) 702-5100
F: (405) 702-5101
E: scott.thompson@deq.state.ok.us

OREGON
Mr. Alan Kiphut
Acting Division Administrator
Department of Environmental Quality
811 South West 6th Avenue
Portland, OR 97204
P: (503) 229-5918
F: (503) 229-6124
E: hw@deq.state.or.us

PENNSYLVANIA
Mr. Kenneth Reisinger
Director
Bureau of Waste Management
Department of Environmental Protection
P.O. Box 8471
Harrisburg, PA 17105
P: (717) 783-2388
F: (717) 787-1904

PUERTO RICO
Mr. Jose Negron
Interim Director
Solid Waste Management Authority
P.O. Box 40285
San Juan, PR 00918
P: (787) 765-7575
F: (787) 753-2220

RHODE ISLAND
Mr. Leo Hellested
Chief
Office of Waste Management
235 Promenade Street
Providence, RI 02908
P: (401) 222-2797
F: (401) 222-3812
E: hellested@dem.ri.gov

SOUTH CAROLINA
Mr. Patrick Walker
Chief
Bureau of Land & Waste Management
Dept. of Health & Environmental Control
2600 Bull Street
Columbia, SC 29201
P: (803) 896-4000
F: (803) 896-4001
E: walkerpt@dhec.sc.gov

SOUTH DAKOTA
Mr. Steve M. Pirner
Secretary
Department of Environment & Natural Resources
Foss Building
523 East Capitol Avenue
Pierre, SD 57501
P: (605) 773-5559
F: (605) 773-6035
E: steve.pirner@state.sd.us

TENNESSEE
Mr. Mike Apple
Director
Division of Solid & Hazardous Waste Management
401 Church Street, 5th Floor
Nashville, TN 37243
P: (615) 532-0780
F: (615) 532-0886

TEXAS
Ms. Jacqueline S. Hardee
Director
Waste Permits Division
P.O. Box 13087
Austin, TX 78711
P: (512) 239-4150
F: (512) 239-5533

U.S. VIRGIN ISLANDS
Mr. Darryl Smalls
Commissioner
Department of Public Works
6002 Estate Anna's Hope
Christiansted, VI 00820
P: (340) 773-1789
F: (340) 773-0670

UTAH
Mr. Dennis R. Downs
Director
Division of Solid & Hazardous Waste
288 North 1460 West
P.O. Box 144880
Salt Lake City, UT 84114
P: (801) 538-6785
F: (801) 538-6715
E: ddowns@utah.gov

VERMONT
Mr. P. Howard Flanders
Director
Waste Management Division
103 South Main Street
Waterbury, VT 05671
P: (802) 241-3888
F: (802) 241-3296
E: p.howard.flanders@anr.state.vt.us

Waste Management

VIRGINIA
Mr. David K. Paylor
Director
Department of Environmental Quality
629 East Main Street
P.O. Box 10009
Richmond, VA 23240
P: (804) 698-4390
F: (804) 698-4019
E: dkpaylor@deq.virginia.gov

WASHINGTON
Mr. Bill Backous
Program Manager
Environmental Assessment Programs
Department of Ecology
P.O. Box 47600
Olympia, WA 98504
P: (360) 407-6699
E: bbac461@ecy.wa.gov

WEST VIRGINIA
Ms. Lisa McClung
Director
Division of Water & Waste Management
601 57th Street, Southeast
Charleston, WV 25304
P: (304) 926-0495
E: lmcclung@wvdep.org

WISCONSIN
Ms. Suzanne Bangert
Director
Waste Management Bureau
101 South Webster, 3rd Floor
Madison, WI 53707
P: (608) 266-0014
F: (608) 267-2768

WYOMING
Mr. John V. Corra
Director
Department of Environmental Quality
122 West 25th Street, 4W
Cheyenne, WY 82002
P: (307) 777-7937
F: (307) 777-7682
E: jcorra@state.wy.us

Water Resources

Responsible for water conservation, development, use and planning in the state.

ALABAMA
Mr. Edward Davis
Acting Division Director
Office of Water Resources
401 Adams Avenue, Suite 434
Montgomery, AL 36104
P: (334) 232-5499

ALASKA
Mr. Gary Prokosch
Director
Division of Mining, Land & Water
Department of Natural Resources
550 West 7th Avenue, Suite 1070
Anchorage, AK 99501
P: (907) 269-8645
F: (907) 269-8947

AMERICAN SAMOA
Mr. John Marsh
Interim Chief Executive Officer
American Samoa Power Authority
American Samoa Government
Pago Pago, AS 96799
P: (684) 644-2772
F: (684) 644-5005

ARIZONA
Mr. Herb Guenther
Director
Department of Water Resources
500 North 3rd Street
Phoenix, AZ 85004
P: (602) 417-2410
F: (602) 417-2401

ARKANSAS
Mr. Randy Young
Executive Director
Soil & Water Conservation Commission
101 East Capitol, Suite 350
Little Rock, AR 72201
P: (501) 682-1611
F: (501) 682-3991
E: randy.young@arkansas.gov

CALIFORNIA
Mr. Lester Snow
Director
Department of Water Resources
1416 Ninth Street
Sacramento, CA 95814
P: (916) 653-7007
F: (916) 653-5028
E: ddeanda@water.ca.gov

COLORADO
Mr. Hal D. Simpson
State Engineer
Division of Water Resources
1313 Sherman Street
Room 818
Denver, CO 80203
P: (303) 866-3581
F: (303) 866-3589
E: hal.simpson@exchdwr.state.co.us

CONNECTICUT
Mr. Robert Smith
Chief
Inland Water Resources Division
79 Elm Street
Hartford, CT 06106
P: (860) 424-3706
F: (860) 424-4075
E: Robert.smith@po.state.ct.us

DELAWARE
Mr. Kevin Donnelly
Director
Division of Water Resources
89 Kings Highway
Dover, DE 19901
P: (302) 739-4860
F: (302) 739-3491

DISTRICT OF COLUMBIA
Mr. Jerry Johnson
General Manager
DC Water & Sewer Authority
5000 Overlook Avenue, Southwest
Washington, DC 20032
P: (202) 787-2000
F: (202) 787-2333

FLORIDA
Ms. Janet Llewellyn
Director
Division of Water Resource Management
2600 Blairstone Road, MS 3500
Tallahassee, FL 32399
P: (850) 245-8336
F: (850) 245-8356

GEORGIA
Mr. Nolton G. Johnson
Chief
Water Resources Branch
2 Martin Luther King Jr., Drive SE
Suite 1058 East Tower
Atlanta, GA 30334
P: (404) 656-6328
F: (404) 463-6432

GUAM
Mr. David Craddick
General Manager
Guam Waterworks Authority
126 Lower East Sunset Boulevard, Tiyan
P.O. Box 1020
Hagatna, GU 96932
P: (671) 479-7823
F: (671) 479-7879

HAWAII
Mr. Dean A. Nakano
Acting Deputy Director
Commission on Water Resource Management
1151 Punchbowl Street
Room 227
Honolulu, HI 96813
P: (808) 587-0214
F: (808) 587-0219

IDAHO
Mr. David R. Tuthill Jr.
Director
Department of Water Resources
322 East Front Street
P.O. Box 83720
Boise, ID 83720
P: (208) 287-4800
F: (208) 287-6700

ILLINOIS
Mr. Gary Clark
Acting Director
Office of Water Resources
1 Natural Resources Way
Springfield, IL 62702
P: (217) 785-3334

INDIANA
Mr. Mike Neyer
Director
Division of Water
402 West Washington Street, Room W264
Indianapolis, IN 46204
P: (317) 232-4160
E: mneyer@dnr.state.in.us

IOWA
Mr. Charles Corell
Bureau Chief
Water Quality Bureau
Wallace Building
502 East 8th Street
Des Moines, IA 50319
P: (515) 281-4582
F: (515) 281-8895

KANSAS
Mr. Karl Mueldener
Director
Division of Water Resources
109 Southwest 9th Street, 2nd Floor
Topeka, KS 66612
P: (785) 296-5500
F: (785) 296-5509

Mr. Tracy D. Streeter
Director
Kansas Water Office
901 South Kansas Avenue
Topeka, KS 66612
P: (785) 296-3185
F: (785) 296-0878

KENTUCKY
Mr. Jeffrey Pratt
Director
Division of Water
14 Reilly Road
Frankfort, KY 40601
P: (502) 564-3410
F: (502) 564-4245
E: jeff.pratt@ky.gov

LOUISIANA
Mr. Jim Welsh
Assistant Secretary
Office of Conservation
Department of Natural Resources
P.O. Box 94275
Baton Rouge, LA 70804
P: (225) 342-5540

MAINE
Mr. David P. Littell
Commissioner
Department of Environmental Protection
State House Station 17
Augusta, ME 04333
P: (207) 287-2812
F: (207) 287-2814
E: david.p.littell@maine.gov

Water Resources

MARYLAND
Ms. Pamela Lunsford
Director
Capital Grants & Loans Administration
580 Taylor Avenue
Annapolis, MD 21401
P: (410) 260-8447
F: (410) 260-8404
E: plunsford@dnr.state.md.us

MASSACHUSETTS
Mr. Frederick A. Laskey
Executive Director
Water Resources Authority
100 First Avenue
Boston, MA 02129
P: (617) 242-6000
F: (617) 788-4893

MICHIGAN
Mr. Richard Powers
Chief
Water Bureau
P.O. Box 30273
Lansing, MI 48909
P: (517) 335-4176
F: (517) 335-0889

MINNESOTA
Mr. Brad Moore
Commissioner
Pollution Control Agency
520 Lafayette Road
St. Paul, MN 55155
P: (651) 296-7301
F: (651) 296-6334
E: Brad.Moore@pca.state.mn.us

MISSISSIPPI
Mr. Sam Mabry
Director
Office of Land & Water Resources
P.O. Box 10631
Jackson, MS 39289
P: (601) 961-5200
F: (601) 354-6965

MISSOURI
Mr. Mike Wells
Director
Water Resources Program
P.O. Box 176
1101 Riverside Drive
Jefferson City, MO 65102
P: (573) 751-4732
F: (573) 751-7627
E: Mike.Wells@dnr.mo.gov

MONTANA
Ms. Mary Sexton
Director
Department of Natural Resources & Conservation
1625 11th Avenue
Helena, MT 59620
P: (406) 444-2074
F: (406) 444-2684
E: msexton@mt.gov

NEBRASKA
Ms. Ann Bleed
Acting Director
Department of Natural Resources
P.O. Box 94676
Lincoln, NE 68509
P: (402) 471-2363
F: (402) 471-2900

NEVADA
Ms. Tracy Taylor
State Engineer
Division of Water Resources
901 South Stewart, Suite 2002
Carson City, NV 89701
P: (775) 684-2800
F: (775) 684-2811
E: ttaylor@water.nv.gov

NEW HAMPSHIRE
Mr. Harry Stewart
Director
Water Division
P.O. Box 95
Concord, NH 03302
P: (603) 271-3308
F: (603) 271-2867
E: hstewart@des.state.nh.us

NEW JERSEY
Ms. Michele Putnam
Director
Division of Water Supply
P.O. Box 402
Trenton, NJ 08625
P: (609) 292-7219
F: (609) 292-1654

NEW MEXICO
Mr. John R. D'Antonio
State Engineer/Secretary, Interstate Stream Commission
Office of the State Engineer
130 South Capitol Street, NEA Building
P.O. Box 25102
Santa Fe, NM 87504
P: (505) 827-6166
F: (505) 827-3806

NEW YORK
Ms. Sandra Allen
Director
Division of Water
625 Broadway
Albany, NY 12207
P: (518) 402-8233

NORTH CAROLINA
Mr. John Morris
Director
Division of Water Resources
1611 Mail Service Center
Raleigh, NC 27699
P: (919) 715-5422
F: (919) 733-3558
E: john.morris@ncmail.net

NORTH DAKOTA
Mr. Dale L. Frink
State Engineer
Water Commission
State Office Building
900 East Boulevard Avenue
Bismarck, ND 58505
P: (701) 328-2750
F: (701) 328-3696
E: dfrink@swc.nd.gov

NORTHERN MARIANA ISLANDS
Mr. Jesus B. Castro
Division Manager
Water Division
P.O. Box 501220
Saipan, MP 96950
P: (670) 235-7025
F: (670) 235-7053

OHIO
Mr. Steven J. Grossman
Executive Director
Water Development Authority
88 East Broad Street, Suite 1300
Columbus, OH 43215
P: (614) 466-0152
F: (614) 644-9964

OKLAHOMA
Mr. Duane Smith
Executive Director
Water Resources Board
3800 North Classen
Oklahoma City, OK 73118
P: (405) 702-5100
F: (405) 702-5101

OREGON
Mr. Phil Ward
Director
Water Resources Department
725 Summer Street, Northeast, Suite A
Salem, OR 97301
P: (503) 986-0900
F: (503) 986-0903
E: Director@wrd.state.or.us

PENNSYLVANIA
Mr. Michael DiBerardinis
Secretary
Department of Conservation & Natural Resources
Rachel Carson State Office Building
P.O. Box 8767
Harrisburg, PA 17105
P: (717) 772-9084
F: (717) 772-9106

PUERTO RICO
Mr. Javier Velez-Arocho
Secretary
Department of Natural & Environmental Resources
P.O. Box 366147
San Juan, PR 00936
P: (787) 767-8056
F: (787) 767-8122

RHODE ISLAND
Ms. Alicia M. Good
Assistant Director
Office of Water Resources
235 Promenade Street
Providence, RI 02908
P: (401) 222-3961, Ext. 7214
F: (401) 222-3564
E: alicia.good@dem.ri.gov

SOUTH CAROLINA
Mr. Bud Badr
Chief
Hydrology Section
Land, Water & Conservation Division
1000 Assembly Street
Columbia, SC 29201
P: (803) 734-6362
F: (803) 734-9200
E: badrb@dnr.sc.gov

SOUTH DAKOTA
Mr. Jim Feeney
Administrator
Water Resources Assistance Program
Foss Building
523 East Capitol Avenue
Pierre, SD 57501
P: (605) 773-4216
F: (605) 773-4068
E: jim.finney@state.sd.us

TENNESSEE
Mr. W. David Draughon Jr.
Senior Director
Water Resources
401 Church Street
Nashville, TN 37247
P: (615) 532-0152
F: (615) 532-0503

TEXAS
Ms. Carolyn Brittin
Director
Water Resources Planning
1700 North Congress Avenue
P.O. Box 13231
Austin, TX 78711
P: (512) 463-7850
F: (512) 475-2053

U.S. VIRGIN ISLANDS
Mr. Aaron Hutchins
Director
Division of Environmental Protection
Cyril E. King Airport
Terminal Building, 2nd Floor
St. Thomas, VI 00802
P: (340) 774-3320
F: (340) 714-9549

UTAH
Mr. Dennis J. Strong
Director
Division of Water Resources
1594 West North Temple, Suite 310
P.O. Box 146201
Salt Lake City, UT 84114
P: (801) 538-7230
F: (801) 538-7279
E: dennisstrong@utah.gov

VERMONT
Mr. Wallace McLean
Director
Division of Water Quality
103 South Main Street
Waterbury, VT 05671
P: (802) 241-3770
F: (802) 241-3287

VIRGINIA
Mr. David K. Paylor
Director
Department of Environmental Quality
629 East Main Street
P.O. Box 10009
Richmond, VA 23240
P: (804) 698-4390
F: (804) 698-4019
E: dkpaylor@deq.virginia.gov

WASHINGTON
Mr. Joe Stohr
Program Manager
Water Resources Program
P.O. Box 47600
Olympia, WA 98504
P: (360) 407-6144
F: (360) 407-6574
E: jost461@ecy.wa.gov

WEST VIRGINIA
Ms. Lisa McClung
Director
Division of Water & Waste Management
601 57th Street, Southeast
Charleston, WV 25304
P: (304) 926-0495
E: lmcclung@wvdep.org

WISCONSIN
Mr. Todd Ambs
Administrator
Division of Water
101 South Webster
P.O. Box 7921
Madison, WI 53703
P: (608) 264-6278
F: (608) 267-2800

WYOMING
Mr. Michael Purcell
Director
Water Development Commission
Herschler Building 4W
122 West 25th Street
Cheyenne, WY 82002
P: (307) 777-7626
F: (307) 777-6819

Welfare

Administers the delivery of financial and medical benefits to low-income families and individuals.

ALABAMA
Dr. Page Walley
Commissioner
Department of Human Resources
Gordon Persons Building, Suite 2104
50 North Ripley Street
Montgomery, AL 36130
P: (334) 242-1310
F: (334) 242-1086

ALASKA
Ms. Ellie Fitzjarrald
Director
Division of Public Assistance
Department of Health & Social Services
P.O. Box 110640
Juneau, AK 99811
P: (907) 465-2680
F: (907) 465-5154

AMERICAN SAMOA
Mr. Talia Fa'afetai I'aulualo
Director
Department of Human & Social Services
American Samoa Government
Pago Pago, AS 96799
P: (684) 633-1187
F: (684) 633-7449

ARIZONA
Ms. Veronica Bossack
Assistant Director
Division of Benefits & Medicial Eligibilty
1717 West Jefferson
Phoenix, AZ 85007
P: (602) 542-3596

ARKANSAS
Ms. Joni Jones
Director
Division of County Operations
P.O. Box 1437, Slot S301
Little Rock, AR 72203
P: (501) 682-8375
F: (501) 682-8367
E: joni.jones@arkansas.gov

CALIFORNIA
Mr. Cliff Allenby
Interim Director
Department of Social Services
744 P Street
Sacramento, CA 95814
P: (916) 657-2598
F: (916) 654-6012
E: cliff.allenby@dss.ca.gov

COLORADO
Ms. Karen Legault Beye
Executive Director
Department of Human Services
1575 Sherman Street
Denver, CO 80203
P: (303) 866-5700
F: (303) 866-4740

CONNECTICUT
Mr. Michael Starkowski
Commissioner
Department of Social Services
25 Sigourney Street
Hartford, CT 06106
P: (860) 424-5008

DELAWARE
Ms. Elaine Archangelo
Director
Division of Social Services
Herman M. Holloway, Sr. Campus
1901 North Dupont Highway-Lewis Building
New Castle, DE 19720
P: (302) 255-9668

DISTRICT OF COLUMBIA
Ms. Kate Jesberg
Interim Director
Department of Human Services
64 New York Avenue, NE
6th Floor
Washington, DC 20001
P: (202) 671-4200
F: (202) 671-4381

FLORIDA
Mr. Bob Butterworth
Secretary
Department of Children & Families
1317 Winewood Boulevard
Building 1, Room 202
Tallahassee, FL 32399
P: (850) 487-1111
F: (850) 922-2993

GEORGIA
Ms. Mary Dean Harvey
Director
Division of Family & Children Services
Two Peachtree Street, Suite 18-486
Atlanta, GA 30303
P: (404) 657-7660
F: (404) 508-7289

GUAM
Mr. Arthur U. San Agustin
Director
Department of Health & Social Services
123 Chalan Kareta, Route 10
Mangilao, GU 96923
P: (671) 735-7102
F: (671) 734-5910
E: chiefdsc@dphss.govguam.net

HAWAII
Ms. Patricia Murakami
Administrator
Benefit, Employment & Support Services Division
820 Mililani Street
Suite 606
Honolulu, HI 96813
P: (808) 586-5230
F: (808) 586-5229

IDAHO
Mr. Russ Barron
Administrator
Division of Welfare
2nd & 6th Floors, Pete T. Cenarrusa Bldg
450 West State Street
Boise, ID 83720
P: (208) 334-5696

ILLINOIS
Mr. Barry S. Maram
Director
Department of Healthcare & Family Services
201 South Grand Avenue, East
Springfield, IL 62763
P: (217) 782-1200

INDIANA
Mr. Jeff Wells
Director
Office of Medicaid Policy & Planning
402 West Washington Street, Room W461
Indianapolis, IN 46204
P: (317) 234-2407

IOWA
Ms. Ann Wiebers
Administrator
Division of Financial, Health & Work Supports
FHWS-5th Floor
1305 East Walnut
Des Moines, IA 50319
P: (515) 281-3131
F: (515) 281-7791

KANSAS
Ms. Bobbi Mariani
Director
Economic & Employment Support
915 Southwest Harrison Street, 6th Floor
Topeka, KS 66612
P: (785) 296-3349
F: (785) 296-6960

KENTUCKY
Mr. Mark Washington
Commissioner
Department for Community Based Services
275 East Main Street, 3W-A
Frankfort, KY 40621
P: (502) 564-3703
F: (502) 564-6907

LOUISIANA
Mr. Adren O. Wilson
Assistant Secretary
Office of Family Support
627 North 4th Street
P.O. Box 94065
Baton Rouge, LA 70804
P: (225) 342-3950
F: (225) 219-9399
E: Adren.Wilson@dss.state.la.us

MAINE
Ms. Judy Williams
Director
Bureau of Family Independence
11 State House Station
Augusta, ME 04333
P: (207) 287-3106

MARYLAND
Ms. Brenda Donald
Secretary
Department of Human Resources
311 West Saratoga Street
Baltimore, MD 21201
P: (410) 767-7109
E: bdonald@dhr.state.md.us

MASSACHUSETTS
Ms. Julia E. Kehoe
Commissioner
Department of Transitional Assistance
600 Washington Street
Boston, MA 02111
P: (617) 348-8500
F: (617) 348-8575

MICHIGAN
Ms. Marianne Udow
Director
Department of Human Services
P.O. Box 30037
Lansing, MI 48909
P: (517) 373-1121
F: (517) 335-6101
E: udowm@michigan.gov

MINNESOTA
Mr. Cal Ludeman
Commissioner
Department of Human Services
Human Services Building
540 Cedar Street
St. Paul, MN 55155
P: (651) 431-2907
F: (651) 431-7443
E: cal.ludeman@state.mn.us

MISSISSIPPI
Mr. Donald Taylor
Executive Director
Department of Human Services
750 North State Street
Jackson, MS 39202
P: (601) 359-4500

MISSOURI
Ms. Janel Luck
Interim Division Director
Family Support Division
P.O. Box 2320
615 Howerton Court
Jefferson City, MO 65102
P: (573) 751-4247
F: (573) 751-0507

MONTANA
Ms. Joan Miles
Director
Department of Public Health & Human Services
111 North Sanders, Room 301/308
P.O. Box 4210
Helena, MT 59604
P: (406) 444-5622
F: (406) 444-1970

NEBRASKA
Ms. Chris Peterson
CEO
Department of Health & Human Services, Finance & Support
P.O. Box 95044
Lincoln, NE 68509
P: (402) 471-3121

NEVADA
Ms. Nancy Kathryn Ford
Administrator
Division of Welfare & Supportive Services
1470 East College Parkway
Carson City, NV 89706
P: (775) 684-0504
F: (775) 684-0646
E: nkford@welfare.state.nv.us

NEW HAMPSHIRE
Mr. John A. Stephen
Commissioner
Department of Health & Human Services
129 Pleasant Street
Concord, NH 03301
P: (603) 271-4331
F: (603) 271-4912
E: jstephen@dhhs.state.nh.us

NEW JERSEY
Ms. Jeanette Page-Hawkins
Director
Division of Family Development
P.O. Box 716
Trenton, NJ 08625
P: (609) 588-2400
F: (609) 584-4404

NEW MEXICO
Mr. Fred Sandoval
Director
Income Support Division
Human Services Department
2009 South Pacheco, Pollon Plaza
Santa Fe, NM 87504
P: (505) 827-7250

NEW YORK
Mr. David Hansell
Commissioner
Office of Temporary & Disability Assistance
40 North Pearl Street
Albany, NY 12243
P: (518) 408-3847
F: (518) 486-9179

NORTH CAROLINA
Ms. Pheon Beal
Director
Division of Social Services
325 North Salisbury Street
2401 Mail Service Center
Raleigh, NC 27699
P: (919) 733-4534
F: (919) 733-9386
E: pheon.beal@ncmail.net

NORTH DAKOTA
Ms. Carol K. Olson
Executive Director
Department of Human Services
600 East Boulevard Avenue
3rd Floor - Judicial Wing
Bismarck, ND 58505
P: (701) 328-2310
F: (701) 328-2359
E: socols@nd.gov

NORTHERN MARIANA ISLANDS
Ms. Eleanor S. Dela Cruz
Administrator
Nutrition Assistance Program
Caller Box 10007, Capital Hill
Saipan, MP 96950
P: (670) 235-9889
F: (670) 235-9250

OHIO
Ms. Helen Jones-Kelley
Director
Department of Job & Family Services
30 East Broad Street, 31st Floor
Columbus, OH 43215
P: (614) 466-6282
F: (614) 466-2815
E: jonesh@odjfs.state.oh.us

OKLAHOMA
Ms. Mary Stalnaker
Director
Family Support Services Division
P.O. Box 25352
Oklahoma City, OK 73125
P: (405) 521-3076
F: (405) 521-4158

OREGON
Ms. Ramona L. Foley
Assistant Director
DHS - Children, Adults & Families
500 Summer Street, Northeast
2nd Floor, E-62
Salem, OR 97301
P: (503) 945-5600
F: (503) 581-6198
E: dhs.info@state.or.us

PENNSYLVANIA
Ms. Estelle B. Richman
Secretary
Department of Public Welfare
Health & Welfare Building, Room 333
Harrisburg, PA 17105
P: (717) 787-2600
F: (717) 772-2062

PUERTO RICO
Mr. Felix Matos Rodriguez
Secretary
Department of the Family
P.O. Box 11398
San Juan, PR 00910
P: (787) 294-4900
F: (787) 294-0732

RHODE ISLAND
Mr. John Young
Associate Director
Department of Human Services
Furand Building
600 New London Avenue
Cranston, RI 02920
P: (401) 462-3575

SOUTH CAROLINA
Ms. Kathleen M. Hayes
Director
Department of Social Services
P.O. Box 1520
Columbia, SC 29202
P: (803) 898-7360
F: (803) 898-7277

SOUTH DAKOTA
Ms. Deb Bowman
Secretary
Department of Social Services
Kneip Building
700 Governors Drive
Pierre, SD 57501
P: (605) 773-3165
F: (605) 773-4855
E: deb.bowman@state.sd.us

TENNESSEE
Ms. Virginia T. Lodge
Commissioner
Department of Human Services
Citizens Plaza, 15th Floor
400 Deaderick Street
Nashville, TN 37248
P: (615) 313-4700
F: (615) 741-4165

Welfare

TEXAS
Mr. Albert Hawkins
Executive Commissioner
Health & Human Services Commission
P.O. Box 13247
Austin, TX 78711
P: (512) 424-6603
F: (512) 424-6587

Ms. Adelaide Horn
Commissioner
Department of Aging & Disability Services
P.O. Box 149030
Austin, TX 78714
P: (512) 438-3030
F: (512) 438-4220

U.S. VIRGIN ISLANDS
Mrs. Ermine Boschulte
Administrator
Division of Financial Programs
Knud Hansen Complex, Building A
1303 Hospital Grounds
St. Thomas, VI 00802
P: (340) 774-2399
F: (340) 774-3466

UTAH
Ms. Kristen Cox
Executive Director
Department of Workforce Services
140 East 300 South
Salt Lake City, UT 84145
P: (801) 526-9210
F: (801) 526-9211
E: kristencox@utah.gov

VERMONT
Ms. Betsy Forrest
Deputy Commissioner
Economic Services Division
Department for Children & Families
103 South Main Street
Waterbury, VT 05671
P: (802) 241-2853
F: (802) 241-2830
E: betsyf@ahs.state.vt.us

VIRGINIA
Mr. Anthony Conyers Jr.
Commissioner
Department of Social Services
7 North 8th Street
Richmond, VA 23219
P: (804) 692-1903
F: (804) 692-1949
E: anthony.conyers@dss.virginia.gov

WASHINGTON
Ms. Robin Arnold-Williams
Secretary
Department of Social & Health Services
P.O. Box 45010
Olympia, WA 98504
P: (360) 902-7800

WEST VIRGINIA
Ms. Martha Yeager Walker
Cabinet Secretary
Department of Human Services
Capitol Complex Building 3, Room 206
1900 Kanawha Boulevard, East
Charleston, WV 25305
P: (304) 558-0684
F: (304) 558-1130
E: marthaywalker@wvdhrr.org

WISCONSIN
Mr. Bill Clingan
Administrator
Division of Workforce Solutions
201 East Washington Avenue
Madison, WI 53707
P: (608) 266-6824

WYOMING
Mr. Tony Lewis
Interim Director of Family Services
Department of Family Services
Hathaway Building, 3rd Floor
2300 Capitol Avenue
Cheyenne, WY 82002
P: (307) 777-7561
F: (307) 777-7747

Workers Compensation

Administers laws providing insurance and compensation for workers for job-related illnesses, injury or death.

ALABAMA
Mr. Scotty Spates
Director
Workers' Compensation Division
649 Monroe Street
Montgomery, AL 36131
P: (334) 242-2868
F: (334) 353-8262

ARIZONA
Mr. Larry J. Etchechury
Director
Industrial Commission
800 West Washington Street
P.O. Box 19070
Phoenix, AZ 85007
P: (602) 542-4411
F: (602) 542-7889
E: letchechury@ica.state.az.us

ARKANSAS
Mr. Alan McClain
CEO
Workers' Compensation Commission
324 Spring Street
P.O. Box 950
Little Rock, AR 72203
P: (501) 682-3930
F: (501) 682-2777
E: amcclain@awcc.state.ar.us

CALIFORNIA
Ms. Carrie Nevans
Acting Administrative Director
Division of Workers' Compensation
1515 Clay Street, 17th Floor
Oakland, CA 94612
P: (510) 286-7100

COLORADO
Mr. Bob Summers
Director
Division of Workers Compensation
633 17th Street, Suite 400
Denver, CO 80202
P: (303) 318-8700
F: (303) 318-8710

CONNECTICUT
Mr. John A. Mastropietro
Chair
Workers' Compensation Commission
Capitol Place
21 Oak Street, 4th Floor
Hartford, CT 06106
P: (860) 493-1500
F: (860) 247-1361
E: john.mastropietro@po.state.ct.us

DELAWARE
Mr. John F. Kirk III
Administrator
Office of Workers' Compensation
P.O. Box 9954
Wilmington, DE 19802
P: (302) 761-8200
F: (302) 761-6601
E: jkirk@state.de.us

DISTRICT OF COLUMBIA
Mr. Charles L. Green
Associate Director
Office of Workers' Compensation
64 New York Avenue, Northeast
Washington, DC 20002
P: (202) 671-1048
F: (202) 671-1929
E: charles.green@dc.gov

FLORIDA
Mr. Tanner Holloman
Director
Division of Workers' Compensation
200 East Gaines Street
Tallahassee, FL 32399
P: (850) 413-1600
E: tanner.holloman@fldfs.com

GEORGIA
Mr. Stan Carter
Executive Director
State Board of Workers' Compensation
270 Peachtree Street, Northwest
Atlanta, GA 30303
P: (404) 656-2048

HAWAII
Mr. Gary S. Hamada
Administrator
Disability Compensation Division
830 Punchbowl Street, Room 211
Honolulu, HI 96813
P: (808) 586-9161
F: (808) 586-9219
E: Gary.S.Hamada@hawaii.gov

IDAHO
Mr. R.D. Maynard
Commissioner
Industrial Commission
317 Main Street
P.O. Box 83720
Boise, ID 83720
P: (208) 334-6017
F: (208) 334-2321
E: rmaynard@iic.state.id.us

ILLINOIS
Mr. Dennis R. Ruth
Chair
Workers' Compensation Commission
100 West Randolph #8-200
Chicago, IL 60601
P: (312) 814-6560

INDIANA
Ms. Linda Hamilton
Chair
Worker's Compensation Board
402 West Washington Street, Room W-196
Indianapolis, IN 46204
P: (317) 232-3809
E: lhamilton@wcb.in.gov

IOWA
Mr. Chris Godfrey
Commissioner
Division of Workers' Compensation
1000 East Grand Avenue
Des Moines, IA 50319
P: (515) 281-8335
F: (515) 281-6501

KANSAS
Ms. Paula Greathouse
Director
Division of Workers Compensation
800 Southwest Jackson Street, 7th Floor
Topeka, KS 66612
P: (785) 296-2996
F: (785) 296-0839
E: Paula.Greathouse@hr.state.ks.us

KENTUCKY
Mr. William P. Emrick
Executive Director
Office of Workers' Claims
657 Chamberline Avenue
Frankfort, KY 40601
P: (502) 564-5550, Ext. 4439
F: (502) 564-5934
E: william.emrick@ky.gov

LOUISIANA
Ms. Karen Winfrey
Assistant Secretary of Labor
Office of Workers' Compensation
P.O. Box 94094
Baton Rouge, LA 70804
P: (225) 342-3111
F: (225) 342-5665
E: os@ldol.state.la.us

MAINE
Mr. Paul R. Dionne
Executive Director/Chair
Workers' Compensation Board
27 State House Station
Augusta, ME 04333
P: (207) 287-7086
F: (207) 287-7198
E: paul.dionne@maine.gov

MARYLAND
Ms. Mary K. Ahearn
Executive Director of Administration
Workers' Compensation Commission
10 East Baltimore Street
Baltimore, MD 21202
P: (410) 864-5308
F: (410) 333-8122
E: Mahearn@Wcc.state.md.us

MASSACHUSETTS
Mr. Paul V. Buckley
Commissioner
Department of Industrial Accidents
600 Washington Street, 7th Floor
Boston, MA
P: (617) 727-4900
F: (617) 727-6477

MICHIGAN
Mr. Jack A. Nolish
Director
Workers' Compensation Agency
Department of Labor & Economic Growth
7150 Harris Drive, P.O. Box 30016
Lansing, MI 48909
P: (517) 322-1106
F: (517) 322-6689
E: nolishj@michigan.gov

MINNESOTA
Mr. Scott Brener
Commissioner
Department of Labor & Industry
443 Lafayette Road, North
St. Paul, MN 55155
P: (651) 284-5010
F: (651) 284-5721
E: scott.brener@state.mn.us

Workers Compensation

MISSISSIPPI
Mr. Liles Williams
Chair
Workers' Compensation Commission
1428 Lakeland Drive
P.O. Box 5300
Jackson, MS 39296
P: (601) 987-4200

MISSOURI
Ms. Pat Secrest
Director
Division of Workers' Compensation
3315 West Truman Boulevard
P.O. Box 58
Jefferson City, MO 65102
P: (573) 751-4231
F: (573) 751-2012
E: pat.secrest@dolir.mo.gov

MONTANA
Mr. Keith Messmer
Bureau Chief
Workers' Compensation Regulation Bureau
Department of Labor & Industry
P.O. Box 8011
Helena, MT 59604
P: (406) 444-6541
F: (406) 444-3465

NEBRASKA
Mr. Glenn Morton
Administrator
Workers' Compensation Court
P.O. Box 98908
Lincoln, NE 68509
P: (402) 471-3602
F: (402) 471-2700
E: gmorton@wcc.state.ne.us

NEVADA
Mr. Charles Verre
Chief Administrative Officer
Workers' Compensation Section
788 Fairview Drive, Suite 300
400 West King Street, Suite 400
Carson City, NV 89703
P: (775) 486-9087

NEW HAMPSHIRE
Ms. Kathryn J. Barger
Director
Workers' Compensation Division
Department of Labor
95 Pleasant Street
Concord, NH 03301
P: (603) 271-3176

NEW JERSEY
Mr. Christopher Leavey
Administrator
Division of Workers' Compensation
P.O. Box 381
Trenton, NJ 08625
P: (609) 292-8802
F: (609) 984-3924
E: cleavey@dol.state.nj.us

NEW MEXICO
Mr. Glenn R. Smith
Director
Workers' Compensation Administration
2410 Centre Avenue, Southeast
P.O. Box 27198
Albuquerque, NM 87125
P: (505) 841-6007
F: (505) 841-6009

NEW YORK
Mr. Donna Ferrara
Chair
Workers' Compensation Board
20 Park Street
Albany, NY 12241
P: (518) 473-8900

NORTH CAROLINA
Mr. Buck Lattimore
Chair
Industrial Commission
4336 Mail Service Center
Raleigh, NC 27699
P: (919) 807-2525

NORTH DAKOTA
Ms. Sandy Blunt
Director
Workforce Safety & Insurance
1600 East Century Avenue, Suite 1
Bismarck, ND 58503
P: (701) 328-3762
F: (701) 328-3820

NORTHERN MARIANA ISLANDS
Mr. Frank Cabrera
Workers' Compensation Commission
P.O. Box 501247
Capitol Hill
Saipan, MP 96950
P: (670) 664-8024
E: cabreraF@NMIretirement.com

OHIO
Ms. Marsha P. Ryan
Administrator
Bureau of Workers' Compensation
30 West Spring Street
Columbus, OH 43215
P: (800) 644-6292
F: (877) 520-6446

OKLAHOMA
Ms. Marsha Davis
Administrator
Workers' Compensation Court
1915 North Stiles
Oklahoma City, OK 73105
P: (405) 522-8776

OREGON
Mr. John L. Shilts
Administrator
Workers' Compensation Division
350 Winter Street, Northeast
Salem, OR 97310
P: (503) 947-7500
F: (503) 947-7514
E: John.L.Shilts@state.or.us

PENNSYLVANIA
Ms. Elizabeth Crum
Deputy Secretary for Compensation & Insurance
Bureau of Workers' Compensation
7th & Forrester Streets, Room 1700
Harrisburg, PA 17120
P: (717) 787-5082
E: ecrum@state.pa.us

RHODE ISLAND
Mr. Matthew P. Carey III
Assistant Director
Division of Worker's Compensation
1511 Pontiac Avenue, Bldg. 69, 2nd Floor
P.O. Box 20190
Cranston, RI 02920
P: (401) 462-8127
F: (401) 462-8105
E: mcarey@dlt.state.ri.us

SOUTH CAROLINA
Mr. Gary R. Thibault
Executive Director
Workers' Compensation Commission
1612 Marion Street
P.O. Box 1715
Columbia, SC 29201
P: (803) 737-5744
F: (803) 737-5768

SOUTH DAKOTA
Mr. James E. Marsh
Director
Division of Labor & Management
Kneip Building
700 Governors Drive
Pierre, SD 57501
P: (605) 773-3681
F: (605) 773-4211
E: james.marsh@state.sd.us

TENNESSEE
Ms. Sue Ann Head
Administrator
Workers' Compensation Division
710 James Robertson Parkway, 2nd Floor
Nashville, TN 37243
P: (615) 741-2395
F: (615) 532-1468
E: wc.info@state.tn.us

TEXAS
Mr. Albert Betts Jr.
Commissioner
Division of Workers' Compensation
Division of Workers' Compensation
7551 Metro Center Drive, Suite 100
Austin, TX 78744
P: (512) 804-4431

UTAH
Ms. Joyce A. Sewell
Director
Division of Industrial Accidents
160 East 300 South, 3rd Floor
P.O. Box 146610
Salt Lake City, UT 84114
P: (801) 530-6988
E: jsewell@utah.gov

VERMONT
Mr. J. Stephen Monahan
Director
Workers' Compensation & Safety Division
Department of Labor
National Life Building, Drawer 20
Montpelier, VT 05620
P: (802) 828-2286
F: (802) 828-2195

VIRGINIA
Ms. Virginia R. Diamond
Chair
Workers' Compensation
Commission
1000 DMV Drive
Richmond, VA 23220
P: (804) 367-8657
F: (804) 367-9740

WASHINGTON
Mr. Frank Fennerty
Labor Member
Board of Industrial Insurance
Appeals
2430 Chandler Court, Southwest
P.O. Box 42401
Olympia, WA 98504
P: (360) 753-6824
F: (360) 586-5611
E: fennerty@biia.wa.gov

WEST VIRGINIA
Mr. Bill Kenny
Deputy Commissioner
Insurance Commission
1124 Smith Street, Room 413
Charleston, WV 25301
P: (304) 558-3354
E: bill.kenny
@wvinsurance.gov

WISCONSIN
Ms. Frances Huntley-Cooper
Division Administrator
Workers Compensation
Division
201 East Washington Avenue
P.O. Box 7901
Madison, WI 53707
P: (608) 266-6841
F: (608) 267-0394
E: Frances.Huntley-Cooper
@dwd.state.wi.us

WYOMING
Mr. Gary W. Child
Administrator
Workers' Safety &
Compensation Division
Cheyenne Business Center
1510 East Pershing Boulevard
Cheyenne, WY 82002
P: (307) 777-7441
F: (307) 777-6552

Workforce Development

Administers job training and services for the unemployed, underemployed and economically disadvantaged in the state.

Information provided by:

National Association of State Workforce Agencies
Richard A. Hobbie
Executive Director
444 North Capitol Street
Suite 142
Washington, DC 20001
P: (202) 434-8020
F: (202) 434-8033
rhobbie@naswa.org
www.naswa.org

ALABAMA
Ms. Phyllis Kennedy
Director
Department of Industrial Relations
649 Monroe Street
Room 2204
Montgomery, AL 36131
P: (334) 242-8990
F: (334) 242-3960
E: Phyllis.Kennedy@dir.alabama.gov

ALASKA
Mr. Guy Bell
Assistant Commissioner
Department of Labor & Workforce Development
P.O. Box 21149
Juneau, AK 99802
P: (907) 465-2700
F: (907) 465-2784
E: guy_bell@labor.state.ak.us

Mr. Clark "Click" Bishop
Commissioner
Department of Labor & Workforce Development
P.O. Box 21149
Juneau, AK 99802
P: (907) 465-2700
F: (907) 465-2784
E: commissioner_labor@labor.state.ak.us

Mr. Thomas W. Nelson
Director
Employment Security Division
Dept. of Labor & Workforce Development
P.O. Box 25509
Juneau, AK 99802
P: (907) 465-5933
F: (907) 269-4738
E: thomas_nelson@labor.state.ak.us

ARIZONA
Mr. Patrick F. Harrington
Assistant Director
Division of Employment & Rehabilitation Services
Department of Economic Security
1789 West Jefferson, Site Code 901A
Phoenix, AZ 85007
P: (602) 542-4910
F: (602) 542-2273
E: PHarrington@azdes.gov

Ms. Rochelle L. Webb
Acting Program Administrator
Employment Administration
1789 West Jefferson, SC 901A
P.O. Box 6123
Phoenix, AZ 85007
P: (602) 542-3667
F: (602) 542-3690
E: RochelleWebb@azdes.gov

ARKANSAS
Mr. Artee Williams
Director
Department of Workforce Services
P.O. Box 2981
Little Rock, AR 72203
P: (501) 682-2121
F: (501) 682-2273
E: artee.williams@arkansas.gov

CALIFORNIA
Ms. Victoria L. Bradshaw
Secretary
Labor & Workforce Development Agency
801 K Street, Suite 2101
Sacramento, CA 95814
P: (916) 327-9064
F: (916) 327-9158
E: victoria.bradshaw@labor.ca.gov

Mr. Jaime Fall
Deputy Secretary of Employment & Workforce
Labor & Workforce Development Agency
Labor & Workforce Development Agency
801 K Street, Suite 2101
Sacramento, CA 95814
P: (916) 327-9064
F: (916) 327-9158
E: jaime.fall@labor.ca.gov

Ms. Pam Harris
Acting Chief Deputy Director
Director's Office
Employment Development Department
800 Capitol Mall, MIC 37
Sacramento, CA 95814
P: (916) 654-8210
F: (916) 657-9753
E: pharris@edd.ca.gov

Mr. Patrick Henning
Director
Employment Development Department
800 Capitol Mall, Room 5000
Sacramento, CA 95814
P: (916) 654-8210
F: (916) 657-5294
E: PHenning@edd.ca.gov

COLORADO
Mr. Don J. Mares
Executive Director
Department of Labor & Employment
1515 Arapahoe Street, Suite 375
Denver, CO 80202
P: (303) 318-8000
F: (303) 318-8048
E: don.mares@state.co.us

Mr. Don Peitersen
Director
Division of Employment & Training
Department of Labor & Employment
633 17th Street, Suite 1200
Denver, CO 80202
P: (303) 318-8002
F: (303) 318-8048
E: don.peitersen@state.co.us

CONNECTICUT
Ms. Patricia Mayfield
Commissioner
Department of Labor
200 Folly Brook Boulevard
Wethersfield, CT 06109
P: (860) 263-6505
F: (860) 263-6529
E: patricia.mayfield@po.state.ct.us

DELAWARE
Mr. Thomas B. Sharp
Secretary of Labor
Department of Labor
4425 North Market Street, 4th Floor
Wilmington, DE 19802
P: (302) 761-8000
F: (302) 761-6621
E: tom.sharp@state.de.us

Mr. Robert Strong
Director
Employment & Training
Department of Labor
4425 North Market Street, Room 328
Wilmington, DE 19802
P: (302) 761-8129
F: (302) 577-3996
E: robert.strong@state.de.us

DISTRICT OF COLUMBIA
Ms. Susan O. Gilbert
Interim Director
Department of Employment Services
Employment Security Building
500 H Street, Northeast
Washington, DC 20210
P: (202) 724-7100
F: (202) 724-6111
E: susan.gilbert@dc.gov

FLORIDA
Ms. Monesia Brown
Director
Agency for Workforce Innovation
107 East Madison Street
Suite 100, Caldwell Building
Tallahassee, FL 32399
P: (850) 245-7298
F: (850) 921-3223
E: monesia.brown@awi.state.fl.us

Ms. Barbara Griffin
Deputy Director
Workforce Services, Early Learning & External Affairs
Agency for Workforce Innovation
107 East Madison Street
Tallahassee, FL 32399
P: (850) 245-7137
F: (850) 921-3226
E: Barbara.Griffin@awi.state.fl.us

Ms. Cynthia Lorenzo
Deputy Director
Agency for Workforce Innovation
107 East Madison Street
Tallahassee, FL 32399
P: (850) 245-7153
F: (850) 921-3226
E: Cynthia.Lorenzo@awi.state.fl.us

GEORGIA
Mr. Michael L. Thurmond
Commissioner
Department of Labor
Sussex Place, Room 600
148 International Boulevard, Northeast
Atlanta, GA 30303
P: (404) 232-3001
F: (404) 232-3017
E: commissioner@dol.state.ga.us

HAWAII
Mr. Nelson B. Befitel
Director
Department of Labor & Industrial Relations
Princess Keelikolani Building
830 Punchbowl Street, Room 321
Honolulu, HI 96813
P: (808) 586-8844
F: (808) 586-9099
E: dlir.director@hawaii.gov

IDAHO
Mr. Roger B. Madsen
Director
Commerce & Labor
317 West Main Street
Boise, ID 83735
P: (208) 332-3579
F: (208) 334-6430
E: rmadsen@cl.idaho.gov

ILLINOIS
Mr. Jack Lavin
Director
Department of Commerce & Economic Opportunity
100 West Randolph, Suite 32-400
Chicago, IL 60601
P: (312) 814-7179
F: (312) 814-1843
E: jlavin@ildceo.net

Mr. James P. Sledge
Director
Department of Employment Security
33 South State Street
Chicago, IL 60602
P: (312) 793-5700
F: (312) 793-9834
E: james.sledge@illinois.gov

INDIANA
Mr. Andrew Penca
Commissioner
Department of Workforce Development
Indiana Government Center, South
10 North Senate Avenue, Room SE 302
Indianapolis, IN 46204
P: (317) 232-7676
F: (317) 233-1670

IOWA
Mr. David Neil
Interim Director
Workforce Development
1000 East Grand Avenue
Des Moines, IA 50319
P: (515) 281-8067
F: (515) 281-4698
E: dave.neil@iwd.iowa.gov

KANSAS
Ms. Rae Anne Davis
Deputy Secretary
Workforce Development
Department of Commerce
1000 Southwest Jackson, Suite 100
Topeka, KS 66612
P: (785) 296-6043
F: (785) 296-1404
E: rdavis@kansascommerce.com

Mr. Jim Garner
Secretary
Department of Labor
401 Southwest Topeka Boulevard
Topeka, KS 66603
P: (785) 296-7474
F: (785) 368-6294
E: jim.garner@dol.ks.gov

Mr. Davis Kerr
Secretary
Department of Commerce
1000 Southwest Jackson Street
Suite 100
Topeka, KS 66612
P: (785) 296-2741
F: (785) 296-3655
E: dkerr@kansascommerce.com

KENTUCKY
Ms. Susan Craft
Division Director
Division of Workforce & Employment Services
Office of Employment & Training
275 East Main Street, 2WA
Frankfort, KY 40621
P: (502) 564-3906
F: (502) 564-7459
E: Susan.Craft@ky.gov

Mr. Andrew Frauenhoffer
Executive Director
Office of Employment & Training
275 East Main Street
Frankfort, KY 40621
P: (502) 564-5331
F: (502) 564-7452
E: andrew.frauenhoffer@ky.gov

Ms. Beth Smith
Commissioner
Department for Workforce Investment
500 Mero Street
3rd Floor, Capitol Tower Plaza
Frankfort, KY 40601
P: (502) 564-0372
F: (502) 564-5959
E: Beth.Smith@ky.gov

LOUISIANA
Mr. John Warner Smith
Secretary of Labor
Department of Labor
P.O. Box 94094
1001 North 23rd Street
Baton Rouge, LA 70804
P: (225) 342-3011
F: (225) 342-3778
E: jwsmith@ldol.state.la.us

MAINE
Ms. Jill Duson
Director
Bureau of Rehabilitation Services
Department of Labor
150 State House Station
Augusta, ME 04333
P: (270) 624-5954
F: (270) 624-5980
E: jill.c.duson@maine.gov

Ms. Laura Fortman
Commissioner of Labor
Department of Labor
P.O. Box 259
Augusta, ME 04332
P: (207) 287-3787
F: (207) 287-5292
E: laura.fortman@maine.gov

MARYLAND
Ms. Catherine Leapheart
Director of Field Operations
Department of Labor, Licensing & Regulation
Division of Workforce Development
1100 North Eutaw Street, Room 209
Baltimore, MD 21201
P: (410) 767-2831
F: (410) 333-5162
E: cleapheart@dllr.state.md.us

Mr. Thomas E. Perez
Secretary
Department of Labor, Licensing & Regulation
500 North Calvert Street, Room 401
Baltimore, MD 21202
P: (410) 230-6020
F: (410) 333-0853
E: tperez@dllr.state.md.us

MASSACHUSETTS
Ms. Suzanne M. Bump
Director
Department of Workforce Development
1 Ashburton Place, Room 2112
Boston, MA 02108
P: (617) 727-6573
F: (617) 727-1090
E: suzanne.m.bump@state.ma.us

Workforce Development

Ms. Jennifer James
Deputy Director
Department of Workforce Development
One Ashburton Place, Room 2112
Boston, MA 02108
P: (617) 626-7122
F: (617) 727-1090
E: jennifer.james@state.ma.us

Ms. Susan Lawler
Director
Division of Career Services
Department of Workforce Development
19 Staniford Street, 1st Floor
Boston, MA 02114
P: (617) 626-5680
F: (617) 727-8671
E: slawler@detma.org

Mr. Edward T. Malmborg
Director
Division of Unemployment Insurance
19 Staniford Street, 3rd Floor
Boston, MA 02114
P: (617) 626-6593
F: (617) 727-0315
E: emalmborg@detma.org

Ms. Bernadette O'Malley
Chief of Staff
Department of Workforce Development
One Ashburton Place, Suite 2112
Boston, MA 02108
P: (617) 626-7103
F: (617) 727-1090
E: bernadette.omalley@state.ma.us

MICHIGAN

Ms. Sharon M. Bommarito
Deputy Director
Department of Labor & Economic Growth
Cadillac Place, Suite 13-650
3024 West Grand Boulevard
Detroit, MI 48202
P: (313) 456-2403
F: (313) 456-2424
E: BommaritoSharon@michigan.gov

Mr. Andy S. Levin
Deputy Director
Department of Labor & Economic Growth
611 West Ottawa Street
P.O. Box 30004
Lansing, MI 48909
P: (517) 373-3034
F: (517) 373-2129
E: levina@michigan.gov

Ms. Brenda Njiwaji
Director
Bureau of Workforce Programs
Victor Office Center, 5th Floor
201 North Washington Square
Lansing, MI 48913
P: (517) 335-5858
F: (517) 241-8217
E: njiwajib@michigan.gov

MINNESOTA

Ms. Bonnie Elsey
Director
Department of Employment & Economic Development
Workforce Development
332 Minnesota Street, Suite E200
St. Paul, MN 55101
P: (651) 296-1822
F: (651) 284-3307
E: bonnie.elsey@state.mn.us

MISSISSIPPI

Ms. Tommye Dale Favre
Executive Director
Department of Employment Security
P.O. Box 1699
Jackson, MS 39215
P: (601) 321-6100
F: (601) 321-6104
E: tdfavre@mdes.ms.gov

Mr. Les Range
Chief Operating Officer & Deputy Executive Director
Department of Employment Security
P.O. Box 1699
Jackson, MS 39215
E: lrange@mdes.ms.gov

MISSOURI

Ms. Katharine Barondeau
Director
Department of Labor & Industrial Relations
Division of Employment Security
P.O. Box 59
Jefferson City, MO 65102
P: (573) 751-8086
F: (573) 751-4945
E: Katharine.Barondeau@dolir.mo.gov

Mr. Nimrod T. Chapel Jr.
Director
Department of Labor & Industrial Relations
421 East Dunklin
P.O. Box 504
Jefferson City, MO 65104
P: (573) 751-9691
F: (573) 751-4135
E: rod.chapel@dolir.mo.gov

Mr. Roderick Nunn
Director
Division of Workforce Development
P.O. Box 1087
Jefferson City, MO 65102
P: (573) 751-3349
F: (573) 751-8162
E: rod.nunn@ded.mo.gov

MONTANA

Mr. Keith Kelly
Commissioner
Department of Labor & Industry
P.O. Box 1728
Helena, MT 59624
P: (406) 444-2840
F: (406) 444-1394
E: kkelly@mt.gov

NEBRASKA

Mr. Fernando "Butch" Lecuona III
Commissioner of Labor
Department of Labor
Department of Labor
P.O. Box 94600
Lincoln, NE 68509
P: (402) 471-2600
F: (402) 471-9867
E: flecuona@dol.state.ne.us

NEVADA

Mr. Terry Johnson
Director
Department of Employment, Training & Rehabilitation
500 East Third Street, Suite 200
Carson City, NV 89713
P: (775) 684-3911
F: (775) 684-3908
E: tljohnson@nvdetr.org

Ms. Cynthia A. Jones
Administrator
Department of Employment, Training & Rehabilitation
Employment Security Division
500 East Third Street, Suite 260
Carson City, NV 89713
P: (775) 684-3909
F: (775) 684-3910
E: cajones@nvdetr.org

NEW HAMPSHIRE

Mr. Richard S. Brothers
Commissioner
Department of Employment Security
32 South Main Street
Concord, NH 03301
P: (603) 228-4000
F: (603) 228-4145
E: richard.s.brothers@nhes.nh.gov

Mr. Darrell Gates
Deputy Commissioner
Department of Employment Security
32 South Main Street
Concord, NH 03301
P: (603) 228-4064
F: (603) 228-4145
E: darrell.l.gates@nhes.nh.gov

NEW JERSEY

Ms. Marilyn D. Davis
Deputy Commissioner
Department of Labor & Workforce Development
P.O. Box 110
13th Floor, Suite E
Trenton, NJ 08625
P: (609) 292-1070
F: (609) 633-9271
E: marilyn.davis@dol.state.nj.us

Ms. JoAnn Hammill
Assistant Commissioner
Department of Labor & Workforce Development
P.O. Box 055, 10th Floor
Trenton, NJ 08625
P: (609) 292-2000
F: (609) 777-0483
E: joann.hammill@dol.state.nj.us

Mr. David J. Socolow
Commissioner
Department of Labor & Workforce Development
P.O. Box 110
Trenton, NJ 08625
P: (609) 292-2975
F: (609) 633-9271
E: janet.sliwinkski@dol.state.nj.us

NEW MEXICO
Ms. Betty Sparrow Davis
Cabinet Secretary
Department of Labor
401 Broadway, Northeast
P.O. Box 1928
Albuquerque, NM 87103
P: (505) 841-8405
F: (505) 841-8491
E: bdoris@state.nm.us

NEW YORK
Mr. Mario J. Musolino
Executive Deputy Commissioner
Department of Labor
State Campus, Building 12
Room 592
Albany, NY 12240
P: (518) 457-4318
F: (518) 457-6296
E: mario.musolino@labor.state.ny.us

Ms. M. Patricia Smith
Commissioner
Department of Labor
State Campus, Building 12
Room 592
Albany, NY 12240
P: (518) 457-9000
F: (518) 457-6297
E: patricia.smith@labor.state.ny.us

NORTH CAROLINA
Mr. Harry E. Payne Jr.
Chair
Employment Security Commission
P.O. Box 25903
Raleigh, NC 27611
P: (919) 733-7546
F: (919) 733-1129
E: harry.payne@ncmail.net

Mr. Thomas S. Whitaker
Chief Deputy Commissioner
Employment Security Commission
P.O. Box 25903
Raleigh, NC 27611
P: (919) 733-4636
F: (919) 733-1129
E: tom.whitaker@ncmail.net

NORTH DAKOTA
Ms. Maren L. Daley
Executive Director
Job Service North Dakota
1000 East Divide Avenue
P.O. Box 5507
Bismarck, ND 58506
P: (701) 328-2836
F: (701) 328-1612
E: mdaley@nd.gov

OHIO
Ms. Helen Jones-Kelley
Director
Department of Job & Family Services
30 East Broad Street, 31st Floor
Columbus, OH 43215
P: (614) 466-6282
F: (614) 466-2815
E: jonesh@odjfs.state.oh.us

Mr. Bruce Madson
Labor Policy Coordinator
Department of Job & Family Services
30 East Broad Street, 32nd Floor
Columbus, OH 43215
P: (614) 466-6283
F: (614) 466-2815
E: madsob@odjfs.state.oh.us

Terry Thomas
Assistant Director
Department of Job & Familiy Services
30 East Broad Street, 32nd Floor
Columbus, OH 43215
P: (614) 466-6283
F: (614) 466-2815
E: thomat@odjfs.state.oh.us

OKLAHOMA
Mr. Jon Brock
Executive Director
Employment Security Commission
2401 North Lincoln Boulevard
Will Rogers Memorial Office Building
Oklahoma City, OK 73105
P: (405) 557-7201
F: (405) 557-7174
E: jon.brock@oesc.state.ok.us

OREGON
Ms. Camille Preus-Braly
Director/Commissioner
Community College & Workforce Development
255 Capitol Street, Northeast, Suite 300
Salem, OR 97310
P: (503) 378-8648 Ext. 357
F: (503) 378-8434
E: cam.preus-braly@state.or.us

Ms. Laurie A. Warner
Director
Employment Department
155 Cottage Street, Northeast, U20
Salem, OR 97301
P: (503) 378-3106
F: (503) 373-7643

PENNSYLVANIA
Mr. Stephen Schmerin
Secretary
Department of Labor & Industry
Labor and Industry Building, Room 1700
Harrisburg, PA 17121
P: (717) 787-5279
F: (717) 787-8826
E: sschmerin@state.pa.us

Ms. Sandi Vito
Deputy Secretary
Department of Labor & Industry
Workforce Development
7th & Forster Streets
Harrisburg, PA 17120
P: (717) 705-2630
F: (717) 787-8826
E: svito@state.pa.us

Mr. John Vogel
Director
Bureau of Workforce Development Partnership
Labor & Industry Building
7th and Forster Streets, 12th Floor
Harrisburg, PA 17120
P: (717) 787-3354
F: (717) 783-7115
E: johvogel@state.pa.us

PUERTO RICO
Ms. Maria Del Carmen Fuentes
Administrator
Right to Employment Administration
Department of Labor & Human Resources
505 Munoz Rivera Avenue, P.O. Box 364452
Hato Rey, PR 00936
P: (787) 754-5151 Ext. 2000
F: (787) 758-0690
E: mfuentes@adt.govierno.pr

RHODE ISLAND
Ms. Adelita Orefice
Director
Department of Labor & Training
1511 Pontiac Avenue
Cranston, RI 02920
P: (401) 462-8870
F: (401) 462-8872
E: aorefice@dlt.state.ri.us

SOUTH CAROLINA
Mr. Roosevelt Ted Halley
Executive Director
Employment Security Commission
P.O. Box 995
Columbia, SC 29202
P: (803) 737-2617
F: (803) 737-2629
E: thalley@sces.org

SOUTH DAKOTA
Ms. Pamela Roberts
Secretary of Labor
Department of Labor
700 Governors Drive
Pierre, SD 57501
P: (605) 773-3101
F: (605) 773-4211
E: pamela.roberts@state.sd.us

Workforce Development

TENNESSEE
Mr. Robert C. Henningsen
Deputy Commissioner
Department of Labor &
Workforce Development
710 James Robertson Parkway
8th Floor, Andrew Johnson
Tower
Nashville, TN 37243
P: (615) 741-6642
F: (615) 741-5078
E: Bob.Henningsen
@state.tn.us

Mr. Don Ingram
Employment Service
Administrator
Division of Employment
Security
500 James Robertson Parkway
12th Floor, Davy Crockett
Tower
Nashville, TN 37245
P: (615) 253-4809
F: (615) 253-5091
E: Donald.Ingram
@state.tn.us

Mr. James G. Neeley
Commissioner
Department of Labor &
Workforce Development
Andrew Johnson Tower, 8th
Floor
Nashville, TN 37243
P: (615) 741-6642
F: (615) 741-5078
E: james.neeley@state.tn.us

TEXAS
Mr. Larry Temple
Executive Director
Workforce Commission
TWC Building
101 East 15th Street, Room 618
Austin, TX 78778
P: (512) 463-0735
F: (512) 475-2321
E: larry.temple
@twc.state.tx.us

UTAH
Ms. Kristen Cox
Executive Director
Department of Workforce
Services
140 East 300 South
Salt Lake City, UT 84145
P: (801) 526-9210
F: (801) 526-9211
E: kristencox@utah.gov

VERMONT
Mr. Tom Douse
Deputy Commissioner
Department of Labor
P.O. Box 488
Montpelier, VT 05601
P: (802) 828-4301
F: (802) 828-4022
E: tdouse@labor.state.vt.us

Ms. Pat Moulton Powden
Commissioner
Department of Labor
5 Green Mountain Drive
P.O. Box 488
Montpelier, VT 05601
P: (802) 828-4301
F: (802) 828-4181
E: pat.moulton.powden
@state.vt.us

VIRGINIA
Ms. Dolores A. Esser
Commissioner
Employment Commission
703 East Main Street
Richmond, VA 23219
P: (804) 786-3001
F: (804) 225-3923
E: dee.esser
@vec.virginia.gov

Mr. Nicholas "Nick" Kessler
Deputy Commissioner
Employment Commission
703 East Main Street
Richmond, VA 12119
P: (804) 786-1697
F: (804) 225-3923
E: nicholas.kessler
@vec.virginia.gov

WASHINGTON
Ms. Karen Turner Lee
Commissioner
Employment Security
Department
P.O. Box 9046
Olympia, WA 98507
P: (360) 902-9301
F: (360) 902-9383
E: klee@esd.wa.gov

WISCONSIN
Ms. Roberta Gassman
Secretary
Department of Workforce
Development
P.O. Box 7946
Madison, WI 53707
P: (608) 267-9692
F: (608) 266-1784
E: roberta.gassman
@dwd.state.wi.us

WYOMING
Ms. Joan Evans
Director
Department of Workforce
Services
122 West 25th Street
Herschler Building, 2 East
Cheyenne, WY 82002
P: (307) 777-8650
F: (307) 777-5857
E: jevans1@state.wy.us

Ms. Cindy Pomeroy
Director
Department of Employment
1510 East Pershing Boulevard
Cheyenne, WY 82002
P: (307) 777-7672
F: (307) 777-5805
E: cpomer@state.wy.us